THE SPORT A...

PRICE GUIDE

TO THE

Non-Sports Cards
1930-1960

By

CHRISTOPHER BENJAMIN

AND

DENNIS W. ECKES

ISBN 0-937424-53-6

Second Printing

ABOUT THE AUTHORS

It was not by chance that Chris Benjamin became a gum card collector: on his first day in kindergarten, he discovered a small candy store strategically located beside the school. With ten cents cold cash in his pocket every day —milk money provided by an unsuspecting parent— he soon amassed a treasured collection of Hopalong Cassidy, Wild Man, and Wild West cards. Since that time each new set issued by the gum companies has found in him a willing buyer. During the past ten years, Mr. Benjamin has concentrated on cataloging for posterity all the card sets issued in the United States and Canada since 1879. To this end, he established the Hobby Card Index, a central file of card information and research, and the Card Collectors Archive, a type set of cards for study and display. Mr. Benjamin holds a B.A. in political science and an M.A. in Latin American Studies from American University, and also attended the School of Advanced International Studies of Johns Hopkins University. He is director of the United States Cartophilic Society and publishes *The Card Collectors Bulletin,* America's first and oldest card hobby magazine. Mr. Benjamin is also editor of *Non-Sport Update* magazine, and his other works include *The Illustrated Wrapper Checklist, The Garbage Patch Kid, Updates and Additions to the ACC, The Arm and Hammer Price Guide, The Tobacco Card Price Guide,* and *Most Valuable Baseball Cards.*

Denny Eckes has been an avid trading card collector since the age of eight. He interrupted that hobby long enough to acquire an education, family, and career. He returned to the hobby about 18 years ago. In 1976 he founded Den's Collectors Den, one of the largest and most reputable sports memorabilia establishments in the country. Mr. Eckes holds a B.S. in chemistry and an M.B.A. in quantitative methods, both from the University of Maryland. Before the establishment of Den's Collectors Den, he held positions as research chemist, information analyst, scheduling engineer, and program manager for a large engineering firm. Among his other published works are *The Sport Americana Baseball Card Price Guide, The Sport Americana Football, Hockey, Basketball and Boxing Card Price Guide, The Sport Americana Alphabetical Baseball Card Checklist, The Sport Americana Baseball Team Checklist,* and *The Sport Americana Baseball Address List.* Mr. Eckes was co-recipient of the first special achievement award for contributions to the hobby at the 1980 National Sports Collectors Convention.

ACKNOWLEDGEMENTS

Each successive edition of *The Sport Americana Price Guide to the Non-Sports Cards* has been acclaimed by hobbyists as "the finest card catalog ever published." We believe that the current edition, the fourth in the series, surpasses any work we have done in the past, and that it will become an invaluable guide for established collectors and newcomers alike.

The authors of this Price Guide are responsible for collecting and developing the information and material presented herein (Benjamin) and for the layout and page-by-page construction of the book (Eckes). A project of this scope would be impossible without the contributions of other individuals. We continue to be inspired by the past efforts of the "oldtimers" who championed the cause of card-collecting in its formative days, legendary researchers like Jefferson Burdick, Buck Barker, et al. We also salute those contemporary hobbyists who have directly aided us in putting together these volumes. Roxanne Toser provided many of the cards and checklists appearing on these pages from her extensive collection of non-sports cards, and provided valuable information about values as well. John Neuner, "The Wrapper King," sent us over one-half of his collection to be photographed and answered all our questions about wrappers. Most of the display boxes illustrated in the text were provided by Robert Marks, who single-handedly took pictures of his entire collection on our behalf. We thank Marty Ballistreri for his diehard enthusiasm about non-sports cards and for "infecting" us with it; Bill Nielsen for generously supplying us with cards and information; and Sal Visalli and Jack Byrd for their past contributions to our ongoing project of card classification and evaluation.

Many other collectors have assisted the authors by sending checklists, photocopies, price information, background material, and cards for us to study and record. With gratitude we acknowledge the following people who have helped with past and present volumes: Bill Ackers, Jerry and Lyn Adamic, Mark Angert, Jimmy Austin, George Bammer, Diana Beckman, Paul Brenner, Marvin Brown, Ken Bush, Tony Cento, David Chamberlain, Lou Chericoni, Tom Church, Jim Cuthbert, Les Davis, Val DeCarlo, Bill Dodge, Robert Dubois, Shirley Eross, Ronald Evans, John Farnetti, Larry Fortuck, Robert Foster, Mike Gallela, Leon Geisler, Pete Gilleeny, Alan Gilman, Sheldon Goldberg, Steve Goldman, Jeff and "Mo" Goldstein, Mike and Howie Gordon, Clayton Grimm, Jr., Bill Hall, Linda Hardman, Orve Johansson, Buck Kane, Dotty Kaufman, Jeff Kilian, Charles Koble, Paul Koch, Ruth Kohn, Mike Kucharski, Chuck Ladoucer, Lew Lipset, Kenneth Lunn, James Macumber, Paul Marchant, Chris McCann, Todd McWilliams, Bill Mullins, John Newbraugh, Bob Nolan, Dennis Owyang, Enzo Palombit, Jack Pollard, Stephen Powers, Robert Price, Tom Reid, Frank Reighter, Tony Salamone, Jody Slates, Conrad Somerville, Mike Strauss, Paul Tenpenny, H.G. Treacher, George Wallace, Bernard Wermers, Ernie White, Stephen Woods, Maryann Wolf, and Robert Youhouse. Our sincere thanks to you all!

To our typists and clerical aides, who cheerfully dedicated themselves to producing accurate results despite the detailed requirements of the project, we owe our thanks: Sue Demma, Carol Johnson, Millie Phillips, and particularly Carollyn Roach.

We must also single out the following people: Mary Hall, who sends us cartons of new material every year; Sherryl Schmick, who proofreads our copy and is a champion card finder; Paul Schmick, who photographed many of the cards and wrappers appearing in these volumes; and the late John Wagner, Jeff Burdick's pal and our invaluable advisor. A special debt of gratitude is owed those collectors who have supported the Hobby Card Index and author Chris Benjamin over the years.

The authors, and collectors everywhere, express their appreciation to the companies past and present who have produced cards: the inventiveness and quality of your trading cards has exerted a profound influence upon our lives.

Finally, we salute the collector, for without him the cards themselves are meaningless.

THE SPORT AMERICANA PRICE GUIDE TO THE NON—SPORTS CARDS
TABLE OF CONTENTS

iv

THE SPORT AMERICANA PRICE GUIDE TO THE NON—SPORTS CARDS
TABLE OF CONTENTS

The Top of the Order

BESTSELLERS
THAT COMPLETE
BASEBALL CARD
COLLECTIONS

Share in the rewards of this
billion dollar industry. Order these
fast-selling, brand new 1992 bestsellers.
Sport Americana Guides — first reference
among collectors and dealers.

 1. The Sport Americana
Baseball Card Price Guide #14
By Dr. James Beckett $15.95
ABOUT THE AUTHOR: "If James Beckett isn't
the most powerful person in the sports card
industry, he's as close as anyone can get to
that stature."
THE SPORTING NEWS / AUGUST 5, 1991

 2. The Sport Americana
Baseball Card Alphabetical
Checklist #5
By Dr. James Beckett $14.95

 3. The Sport Americana
Team Baseball Card Checklist #6
By Jeff Fritsch $12.95

The Sport Americana
Basketball Card Price Guide
and Alphabetical Checklist

By Dr. James Beckett
ISBN: 0-937424-55-2   List Price $12.95
Specifications: 6x9, 192 pages, B & W Illustrations.

Two books in one!

This book features all basketball cards issued since 1948 and lists all the cards of a particular player consecutively and by manufacturer through 1991. Although the hobby is still young, its popularity has grown in recent years with the rise of such living legends as Kareem Abdul Jabbar and Michael Jordan and the expansion of the N.B.A.

The Sport Americana Price Guide
to the Non-Sports Cards No. 4

By Christopher Benjamin
ISBN: 0-937424-57-9   List Price $14.95
Specifications: 6x9, 512 pages, Over 2,500 B & W Illustrations.

The most comprehensive reference work ever written on non-sports cards issued from 1961-1991. This is an unusual book. Besides its pricing information, it actually is a book people will *read* from cover to cover. Full of nostalgia and fun. Includes cards featuring Desert Storm, rockstars, TV shows, comic characters, and war cards. A must for collectors; a treat for anyone over 20!

INTRODUCTION

The fourth edition of the *Sport Americana Price Guide to the Non-Sports Cards* represents a combination of two major elements. The first is the research approach of card historian Chris Benjamin, founder of the Hobby Card Index and The Card Collector's Archive. The second is the illustrated format developed by publisher Denny Eckes in his successful Sport Americana series of books. The result is an attractive and interesting format which is as useful and comprehensible to the novice collector as it is to the veteran. Every set recorded in this volume is illustrated front and back (except where the cards are blank-backed), with wrappers, display boxes, and checklists included in the presentation wherever possible.

All the cards listed in this book were issued in the United States. This is not ethnocentricism but a simple desire to identify and catalog American cards for the American collector.

The contents of Number 4 of the Non-Sports Guide are limited to trading cards and novelties issued with confections and bubble gum during the period 1930 to 1960. Certain other trading cards which follow gum and candy card formats and competed in the marketplace for the collector's dollar have also been included. Questions about the cards, wrappers and boxes appearing in this book, or about any gum or candy issues not described or pictured here, plus any comments and suggestions should be directed to Chris Benjamin, c/o Non-Sport Guide, P.O. Box 606, Laurel, MD 20725. Do not call or write Denny Eckes or Den's Collectors Den, as it will significantly hinder a rapid response. Please include a self-addressed, stamped envelope with your correspondence.

Questions or comments about any of the previous three volumes should also be directed to Mr. Benjamin at the address above. Please send photocopies of cards and related material rather than written descriptions.

To insure a prompt reply, all correspondence must be accompanied by a self-addressed, stamped envelope. Photo-copies of cards are always preferable to written descriptions.

Illustrations for the sets presented herein are almost all at 50% of original size for standard size cards and 65% of original size for small-size cards. Extra-large or extra-small items have been reduced or enlarged as required to accommodate specific displays. Precise measurements of original material are always presented in the headings or in the card summaries.

The authors thank you for purchasing this volume. We have worked diligently to provide you, the collector, with accurate information and prices. However, the following points cannot be overemphasized:

This book is a guide. It is not the "for sale" list of anyone. The prices are not thoughts or desires of the authors, publisher, distributors or advertisers. They are what the marketplace, through the law of supply and demand, has determined. Throughout the year prices on "any" card might increase or decrease. You and you alone are the final judge as to whether you should or should not buy or sell a particular card at a particular price.

1

Once upon a time in America, trading cards were considered either a novelty or a nuisance which just happened to be packed in some of the products found in the marketplace. If you liked them, you saved them; if not, you dumped them on the street or gave then away to the women and children. The great outbursts of tobacco cards produced during the 1885-1891 and 1909-1911 periods, for example, were part of gigantic promotional campaigns directed solely at adult males who smoked or chewed tobacco. Other cards, like Arm & Hammer birds and the famous Arbuckle Coffee sets, were aimed only at consumers of household goods: adult females. Children were not a primary market because they had little or no purchasing power. Only the penny candy and caramel card sets issued between 1907 and 1914 were printed to attract both juvenile and adult sales.

This early use of trading cards as an advertising medium, in an era when many manufacturers preferred to build a reputation by word-of-mouth, meant that the use of card inserts was tied closely to competition among related products. If one firm resorted to using cards as a promotion, others would follow suit. This "copycat" style of business caused long gaps of time in which virtually no cards of any sort were issued. The periods 1892-1897 and 1902-1908, for example, were "hard times" for card collectors. The onset of great social upheavals, like World War I and the Great Depression, also prevented companies from issuing cards.

The early card collectors themselves were a different breed than those from the generations that followed. For one thing, there was no radio or television to provide instant news and pictures, so people relied on images printed on paper and cardboard for information and entertainment. Many families build up scrapbooks full of clippings, cards, and other paper memorabilia which reflected the world and society of the times. Insert cards were just one of the many different items available to collectors, and they were mostly selected at random or found by chance. Our research reveals that very few of the early collectors were determined or capable of assembling complete sets of cards.

Bubble gum, and the kids it attracted, changed all that. After a lean period stretching from 1919 to 1932 (the heyday of those infamous "strip cards" so miserably conceived and designed), the Goudey Gum Company of Boston shocked the confectionary trade with its "Indian Gum" and "Big League" sets of 1933. The gum packs of both had fancy wrappers, a large slab of tasty gum, and a multi-color artwork card of giant proportions (compared to cards of former eras). This was a slap to the face of the Great Depression, a challenge to competitors to sink or swim, and possibly, just the right "tonic" for a society mired in an economic morass. Goudey posted record sales based, for the first time, on sales to kids, not adults. The confectionary trade was amazed but not dazed. Those who were able to join in the competition engaged Goudey head-on. Children were the big winners in all of this. They were now, and henceforth would be, the target market in the new "Bubble Gum Age," an epoch in which they could choose from a wellspring of glorious cards of every form and description.

These "bubble gum kids" (BGK's), now several generations strong, have elevated card collecting to a respected status in society. The words "trading card" and "bubble gum card" are understood by the general population, and cards are featured on network and cable television shows. The fact that the industry leader, Topps, has issued its last two sets ("The Simpsons" and "Operation Desert Storm") without gum really doesn't matter. The "Bubble Gum Age" might be slipping away, but the remarkable heritage of the 1930-1960 period will remain with us always. Cards will always be created in "bubble gum card" style, and kids — of yesteryear, today, and the future — will always be the "target market."

The appeal of non-sport card collecting can be summed up in one word: variety. There are thousands of sets from which to choose, and each set poses its own particular challenge. Most remarkably, the majority of cards remain within the limitations of a modest budget. The entire world — and perhaps the entire universe, if one counts the science fiction sets — lies within the grasp of the non-sport card collector.

WHAT'S IN A NAME?

Recently there has been considerable discussion among collectors as to the attractiveness of the term "non-sports." Several alternative names have been suggested for this category of cards. However, the authors confess to having no difficulty with the original term, not only because of the irrefutable Shakespearean logic, but also with respect to the very etymology of the word. The prefix "non" merely means "not" and carries no derogatory meaning by itself. (Words such as non-flammable, non-toxic, and non-smoker certainly carry no antagonizing meaning). When connected by a hyphen to the word "sports" it becomes a generic term which is more accurate than any alternative yet coined. Most "non-sports" collectors feel no real or imagined inferiority to their counterparts in the sports card hobby because of this name. Pragmatically speaking, the word "non-sports," no matter what its origin, is the term that has been and is being used, understood, and accepted.

HOW TO COLLECT

There are no set rules on how to collect non-sports cards. Card collecting is a hobby, a leisure pastime. What you collect, how much you collect, and how much time and money you spend collecting are entirely up to you. The amount of time you wish to spend, the funds you have available for collecting, and your own personal likes and dislikes determine how you collect. What will be presented here is information and ideas that might help you in your enjoyment of the hobby.

Several avenues are open to you for obtaining cards. You can purchase current issues in the traditional way at the local candy, grocery, or drug store with the bubble gum or other products included. If you live near a food or candy wholesaler, it is well worth the effort to purchase cards directly from this source. Many companies which offer cards in their products also offer complete sets in premium offers listed on the packaging. You can purchase complete sets from mail order dealers or collectors who advertise in publications like *The Wrapper, The Card Collectors Bulletin,* and the *Non-Sport Update.* Advertising in local newspapers is another way of obtaining cards and meeting other collectors. Local flea markets and antique shops often have cards on hand. Finally, the card conventions staged in various cities around the country provide an excellent opportunity for the collector to purchase cards in a price-competitive atmosphere.

VALUE

The value of a trading card is determined by many factors. Among these factors are the age of the card, the subject(s) depicted on the card, the amount of the card printed, the attractiveness and popularity of the set in which the card appears, and most importantly, the physical condition of the card.

None of these factors has an absolute influence on value except for physical condition. For example, cards from some sets issued in the 1880's are extremely durable and were printed in great quantities. They might be worth far less than cards from a 1970's set which were distributed on a limited basis or withdrawn from the market. Some cards — like those picturing Hitler in the Horrors of War series (R—69) — have a higher value due to subject matter. However, condition is an absolute determinant of value. Given two of the same card, the one in the best condition ALWAYS has the higher value.

PRICES AND DEALERS

The prices in the Sport Americana Price Guide to the Non-Sports Cards are the retail "going rates" for cards and sets listed in this book as of February, 1991. However, pricing —like grading— is subject to a number of variables, including personal opinion, regionalism, and where and from whom the cards are purchased. We've all heard stories of fabulous buys at flea markets, antique shops, etc., but in reality, most collectors obtain their cards from card dealers. Dealers are profit seekers who perform the very important service of providing collectors with cards. They have expenses —travel, advertising, postage, convention fees, sorting and handling, etc. The prices that some dealers charge may vary from those listed in this book. In some cases, this may be due to cost factors, but they may also reflect different opinions about specific sets or cards in general. Other factors, such as the discovery of large quantities of a certain set, may drastically reduce some prices overnight. The best approach to buying cards is to know exactly what you want and what you want to pay for it, give or take a little. This guide and the hobby periodicals advertised in it should enable you to keep up with all the "trends" and to make intelligent decisions.

SINGLE CARD AND SET PRICES

Unlike some of the set prices listed in the 1988 Non-Sport Guide, which covered the years 1961-1988, set prices for cards of the 1930-1960 era are virtually all "factored" with a premium to reflect the very real difficulty of assembling the entire run of any series. The amount of the extra value of any set depends upon the scarcity of the cards in general, shortage of a specific card or cards within the series, and "built in" printing defects, such as off-center cutting, out-of-focus pictures, etc., which plague many issues. In the 1930-1960 time frame, individual card values are very well established, and the premium value attached to a complete set is widely recognized and accepted in the collecting community. Buyers can expect to find "complete set" premiums or 10-35% over the sum of the individual card value for most of the sets listed in this volume in the "excellent" grade. Naturally, the premium value of sets in lesser or "mixed" grade is much lower.

The single card prices set forth in this book depend on surveys of market prices as they exist today, plus the authors' insight into the "intrinsic" worth of a specific set in relation to other sets of its era, and to sets of other eras. Please remember that it is much easier to deal with prices expressed in certain increments, and that trying to express subtle value differences, e.g., card "A" is really worth 13 cents and card "B" is really worth 17 cents, would cause more harm than good. After all, dealers and collectors shouldn't be forced to carry calculators to make simple deals. As the hobby continues to grow, there will be a greater impetus to separate cards, wrappers, and display boxes into general price groups. The prices in this book reflect that trend.

As a general rule, please note that the first card of any series is worth at least double the "regular card" price IF it is in excellent condition. The last card of most sets in this book might also command a premium which varies according to the set and the scarcity of the final print run in that set.

WRAPPER PRICES

The interest in wrapper collecting has grown at a phenomenal pace in the 1980s and we have made a special effort to illustrate and to price the wrappers for all the sets listed in this book. A word of caution: quantities of wrappers from the period from 1930 to 1960 are constantly being discovered. What was "scarce" yesterday may be all too common today, and the wrapper collector must be on his toes to keep up with the latest "finds" in this highly active part of the hobby. Prices for these items fluctuate widely, and prospective buyers are advised to proceed with caution when contemplating a major purchase.

DISPLAY BOXES

Collecting display boxes from bubblegum sets is not a new idea —some collectors have been doing it for years. There has been a dramatic increase in this field in recent times, however, and it is nothing more than a logical step in progression: first cards, then wrappers, now boxes. Perhaps the biggest boost to box collecting came from wrapper collectors. They were the first people in the hobby to point out the disproportionate relationship between wrappers and boxes. Most wrappers, no matter how scarce they are today, came packed in quantity in a single box. Even on a one-to-one basis, a wrapper has more chance of survival than a box. A crushed or crumpled wrapper can be redeemed because wax paper can be smoothed (and even ironed); a box that is smashed or "modified for display" (i.e., lid torn off) may not be salvageable even if it escapes the trash bin. The remarkable thing is that many boxes have survived these perils and have found their way into the hands of collectors. We have made a determined attempt to illustrate the boxes from various sets and price them according to market trends. Most of the boxes pictured in this volume are part of the Bob Marks Collection, and we thank "The Box King" for his efforts on our behalf.

PRICE PRESENTATIONS IN THIS BOOK

Cards in *The Sport Americana Price Guide to the Non-Sports Cards* are priced in the manner they are normally found in a buy-sell environment. Set prices are provided for each set for which the sum total of items has been established. The typical, individual card in each set listed is always priced. A wrapper and box price is also presented whenever such items are illustrated in the display. If more that one wrapper or box exists for a set or series, each is individually priced. Collateral items, such as 3-D glasses, pins, etc., are also priced, but items such as store signs and order sheets are not priced. The latter items exist for many sets, but most are one-of-a-kind items not likely to reach the marketplace.

The two columns of prices correspond to "excellent" and "average." For a description of condition grades, consult the condition guide in this book. There are no prices for hybrid conditions such as "very good to excellent" or "excellent to mint." Collectors must judge for themselves if the cards fall into such grades and should consult the price levels in this guide for possible adjustments to accommodate such cards. Because all of the cards in this volume were printed before 1961, collectors might have trouble finding cards from this era in top grade. Lesser condition cards should be avoided unless they are extremely scarce, and even then, price must match condition. The "excellent" price column is for cards of that grade only, and cards not meeting the strict requirements of that category must be priced accordingly.

Only one price is given for wrappers — excellent. Most wrappers, however, do have some imperfections which are to be expected from the nature of their use as packaging. Some defects are allowable in the excellent grade, but collectors are advised that the discussion in the "Value" summary applies to wrappers as well as cards.

Boxes are also priced in both "excellent" and "average" grades. As more and more collectors are attracted to this fascinating part of the hobby, we expect that a more definitive set of criteria for judging grades and values will ensue. The "excellent" stated in our display refers to intact items with but minor defects or damage. Boxes with lids or other parts detached cannot be placed in this category. However, boxes which have been folded flat — either by removing side staples or compacted along pre-scored joints — are acceptable for this grade.

MEASUREMENTS

Ever card in this book has been measured personally by the authors down to a scale of 1/32". Exact measurements are an important tool in identifying card sets, as many previous books contain grossly inaccurate dimensions. Although the reader should have no difficulty identifying card sets using our index and illustrated text, the measurements given with every set constitute a confirmation of the other data presented. The authors recognize the fact that the dimensions for cards from the same set may vary as much as 1/8" in either direction (simply because of cutting variances), especially in older series.

ADVERTISING IN THE PRICE GUIDE

The advertisements appearing in this Price Guide were accepted in good faith; however, neither the authors, the publisher, the distributors nor the other advertisers in this book accept any responsibility for any particular advertiser not complying with the trrms of his or her ad. Should you come into contact with any of the advertisers in this Guide as a result of their advertisement herein, please mention that you found out about them from this source.

ERRATA

In a book of this size and scope, it is inevitable that errors in typing, sequence, and spelling have occurred. If you find a mistake, if you can provide a missing checklist title, or if you wish to comment about any part of the book, please write (do not call) to Chris Benjamin, c/o Sport Americana, Den's Collectors Den, P.O. Box 606, Laurel, Maryland 20725.

HOW TO USE
THE PRICE GUIDE

NUMBER OF CARDS IN SET

TITLE OF SET

DIMENSIONS OF CARD

SUPPLEMENTAL INFORMATION ON THE SET

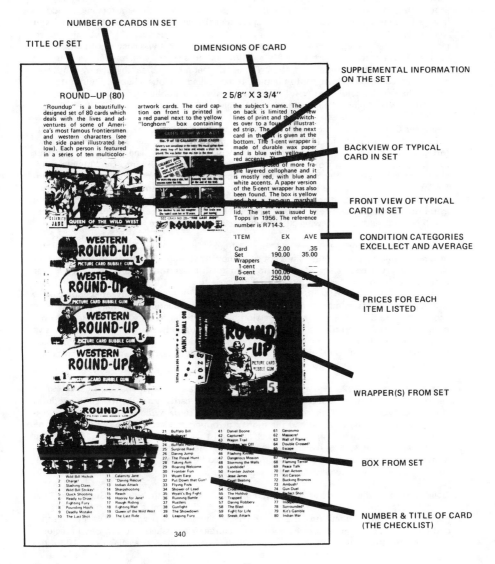

ROUND—UP (80)

2 5/8″ X 3 3/4″

"Roundup" is a beautifully-designed set of 80 cards which deals with the lives and adventures of some of America's most famous frontiersmen and western characters (see the side panel illustrated below). Each person is featured in a series of ten multicolor-

artwork cards. The card caption on front is printed in a red panel next to the yellow "longhorn" box containing

the subject's name. The on back is limited to lines of print and the switches over to a four illustrated strip. The of the next card in the is given at the bottom. The 1-cent wrapper is made of durable wax paper and is blue with yellow red accents of more fragile layered cellophane and it is mostly red, with blue and white accents. A paper version of the 5-cent wrapper has also been found. The box is yellow two-gun marshall lid. The set was issued by Topps in 1956. The reference number is R714-3.

BACKVIEW OF TYPICAL CARD IN SET

FRONT VIEW OF TYPICAL CARD IN SET

CONDITION CATEGORIES EXCELLECT AND AVERAGE

ITEM	EX	AVE
Card	2.00	.35
Set	190.00	35.00
Wrappers		
1-cent		—
5-cent	100.00	—
Box	250.00	

PRICES FOR EACH ITEM LISTED

WRAPPER(S) FROM SET

BOX FROM SET

				21	Buffalo Bill		41	Daniel Boone	61	Geronimo
1	Wild Bill Hickok	11	Calamity Jane		Bullseye!		42	Captured!	62	Massacre!
2	Charge!	12	'Daring Rescue				43	Wagon Trail	63	Wall of Flame
3	Slashing Claws	13	Indian Attack	24	Buffalo Hunt			Am Off	64	Double Crossed!
4	Wild Bill Strikes!	14	Sharpshooting	25	Surprise Raid		46	Flashing Knives	66	Escape
5	Quick Shooting	15	Reach	26	Daring Jump		47	Dangerous Mission	67	Flaming Terror
6	Ready to Draw	16	Hooray for Jane!	27	The Royal Hunt		48	Storming the Walls	68	Peace Talk
7	Fighting Fury	17	Rough Riding	28	Taking Aim		49	Landslide!	69	Fast Action
8	Pounding Hoofs	18	Fighting Mad	29	Roaring Welcome		50	Frontier Justice	70	Kit Carson
9	Deadly Mistake	19	Queen of the Wild West	30	Frontier Fun		51	Jesse James	72	Bucking Broncos
10	The Last Shot	20	The Last Ride	31	Wyatt Earp			Cruel Beating	73	Ambush!
				32	Put Down that Gun!				74	Gun Duel
				33	Flying Fists	54			Deflect Shot
				34	Shower of Lead	55	The Holdup		
				35	Wyatt's Big Fight	56	Trapped	77	Indians
				36	Running Battle	57	Daring Robbery	78	Surrounded!
				37	Hustlers	58	The Blast	79	Kit's Gamble
				38	Gunfight	59	Fight for Life	80	Indian War
				39	The Showdown	60	Sneak Attack		
				40	Leaping Fury				

NUMBER & TITLE OF CARD (THE CHECKLIST)

340

7

WHEN BUBBLE GUM WAS KING

The period from 1933 to 1941 has been characterized as "The Golden Age of Trading Cards," and rightly so. To be sure, there were other intervals when magnificent cards were produced: the 1885-1891 and 1909-1911 explosions of fabulous tobacco cards, engineered by James Buchanan Duke and his American Tobacco Company, are splendid examples, and the post-World War II era in which Bowman and Topps battled for supremacy in the gum/card marketplace also saw a brief revival of creative genius. But it is the 1933-1941 time frame, with set after set of miniature works of art and imagination captured on cardboard, that have made an indelible impression on the hearts and minds of collectors past and present. In those nine years, when "Bubble Gum Was King," a small yet important part of the American psyche was changed forever by children, gum, and cards.

Although gum seems to be a product of modern times, it has been used in a social context for centuries. The basic ingredient, chicle, was chewed by the Aztecs and any number of other indigenous groups with access to gum-producing trees. It wasn't until the Industrial Revolution, however, that gum became a fad item in society. The first machinery for producing gum was patented in 1871 by Thomas Adams, who made a fortune by adding licorice powder to the mixture and offering it under the famous "Black Jack" label (it is still sold today). The drawback of chewing gum was the same then as now: the flavor diminished rapidly, and the remaining product became harder the longer it was chewed. American gum companies searched for more than 30 years to find an element which would increase the marketability of their product. In 1906, Frank H. Fleer made a breakthrough by producing gum which could be "blown" into bubbles. It was called "Blibber-Blubber," but unfortunately it had to be sold in a "wet" condition, which the public found unacceptable. The novelty value of "bubble" gum seemed to have met with an early demise.

The Fleer Company, however, was persistent in its quest to market bubblemaking gum. Its determination paid off in 1928,, when Fleer chemist Walter Diemer perfected a "dry" formula for the product, which Fleer called "Dubble Bubble." The gum was an instant success, prompting a rush of both new and established companies into the "bubble gum" trade. The big losers in this process were the candy manufacturers who had ruled the confectionary market since the turn of the century, plus a host of smaller chewing gum firms who couldn't convert and compete. Bubble gum not only offered consumers another choice in the store, but also competed directly in the all-important price slot. It was a blow from which neither candy nor chewing gum products ever fully recovered.

Granted, the leap from "chewing" to "bubble" gum was quantum, but something was still missing in the equation. With hindsight, we know that trading cards were the unknown element, but the companies of the period had to discover this for themselves. Fleer, for example, had produced several sets of trading cards to be distributed with its chewing gum during the 1920's, but made no move in this direction with the newly-invented bubble gum. Nor did any of its competitors make the card/gum connection. No doubt, the terrible economic conditions of the Great Depression had something to do with the delay. On the other hand, the Depression also generated a voracious public appetite for inexpensive "diversion" products such as penny gum. The invention of bubble gum, the reshaped confectionary market, and the final ingredient — trading cards — were about to create an era in which "bubble gum was king."

Historians point to 1928 as the beginning of the "Bubble Gum Age," but card collecting, as we know it, started in 1933. Before that date, trading cards were distributed in products aimed mostly at adults. Children generally were given cards by adults or found them discarded in the streets, and few had the money or opportunity to collect directly from the source. The penny pack of bubble gum changed all that. Kids, not grown-ups, became the target market, and in a psychological sense, card collecting changed status from an intermittent adult diversion to one of the institutionalized "trappings" of childhood, with associations and memories often lasting a lifetime.

Goudey started the "gold rush" of trading cards in 1933 with "Indian Gum" and "Big League" baseball cards. Over the next few years, National Chicle, also based in Boston, provided the main competition for Goudey, with each company producing a variety of sport and non-sport sets. A number of independent manufacturers issued cards, mostly in regional markets, and there also a variety of lower-grade "strip" card sets available. By 1936, the early industry leaders were being challenged by a formidable newcomer based in Philadelphia — Gum Incorporated. Headed by the quixotic but undeniably brilliant J. Warren Bowman, Gum, Inc. created series after series of some of the most beautiful and imaginative cards ever made. By 1941, Goudey and National Chicle were all but gone from the market, and only the cataclysm of global war kept Gum, Inc. from absolute domination of the market.

It has been said that war was both the key to J. W. Bowman's success and also his subsequent downfall. True, America's entry into the conflict cut off Bowman's supply of raw materials and halted production, but Bowman was his own worst enemy. His sensational success in the gum trade was based on Gum, Inc.'s fabulous reputation for cards, not gum, and his dependence on paper and ink made him vulnerable to the needs of the war effort. Meanwhile, another company called Topps continued to produce its product — gum only — in the small window of opportunity left open by the war economy. Topps shrewdly coined a patriotic jingle ("Don't talk chum, chew Topps Gum") and maintained an active market operation while Bowman and Gum,Inc. were mired in inactivity. J. W. Bowman, buoyed by his past successes, and confident of future prosperity, did little to counter the threat posed by Topps. Ego, not war, destroyed the Bowman empire.

Collecting 1930's cards is a challenging and rewarding hobby. While many sets listed here are not widely popular, supplies of top grade non-sports cards of this era are becoming increasingly difficult to find. Indeed, the quantity of new, or "mint," cards from this period was never very great; that, plus the abuse which "mint" grading has suffered in collecting circles, has lead us to use price columns for "excellent" and "average" grades only (Please refer to the condition guide for descriptions of these grades). Wrappers and display boxes from most 1930's sets command premium prices, and where only one example is known to exist, we have used the word "speculative"in the price section.

As a final observation, we might well be entering a stage in the growth of the non-sport hobby where 1930's cards are becoming too expensive for most collectors to afford. It has already happened in sports cards, and the non-sport hobby is constantly receiving publicity as a still-moderate marketplace with opportunities for "investment" money. Although we believe that new collectors, not speculators will create the heaviest demands on already limited supplies, there can be no doubt that an increasing number of people seem to be competing for a decreasing supply of cards. Every collector should allow for the future when purchasing cards today, and we hope this guide will provide the accurate, detailed information so necessary to make intelligent choices.

ACTION GUM (96)   2 3/8" X 2 7/8"

Action Gum was hardly "The Greatest Card Series Ever Produced" (as Goudey Gum did claim on the back of every card), but it is popular among today's collectors. None of the 96 cards in the set refers to a wartime event, so it is believed that the date of the issue was 1938-39. The color artwork and texts of Action Gum cards are bland when compared to War Gum and Horrors of War. The action-packed center design of the wrapper is done in blue and yellow on a red background; the panels contain premium offers for service rings and a "Snappy Aviator's Hat." Sixty cards of this set were issued in Canada by World Wide Gum under the title "Action Series." They are easily identified by the title, gray-stock backs, and English/French text. The reference number for Action Gum is R1.

ITEM	EX	AVE
Card	10.00	2.50
Set	1200.00	300.00
Wrapper	150.00	––

PLANE ATTACKS CONVOY — No. 15

ACTION GUM

U.S. ISSUE

CANADIAN ISSUE

25 Leaving Aircraft Carrier	49 Armed Might Speaks	73 To a Watery Grave
26 Bombers in Formation	50 Tanks Fording River	74 Flame Throwers
27 The Marines Charge	51 To the Rescue	75 Anti-Aircraft Gun
28 Sinking in Flames	52 Loading the Bomber	76 "Tin Fish" From Skeeter
29 World's Largest Bomber	53 Tanks in Combat	77 Firing Death Bomb
30 "Commence Firing"	54 Hard-Hitting Advance	78 Camouflaged Planes
31 Freighter Torpedoed	55 Bombing Harbor Forts	79 "Range and Altitude"
32 Planes to the Rescue	56 "Peel Off"	80 "Hedgehopping"
33 Light Artillery	57 Navy Blimp	81 Fighting Pursuers
34 "Sky Birds" Take Off	58 "Listening In"	82 Mother Ship and Subs
35 Surprising Enemy Sub	59 Down in Flames	83 The Marines Advance
36 Mosquitoes in Action	60 Marines Land	84 Grenade Throwers
37 Attack on Air Field	61 Motorcycle in Action	85 Scout Crew in Action
38 Night Bombers Depart	62 Mine Sweeping	86 Protecting Docks
39 3" Anti-Aircraft Gun	63 Caught in Balloon Cables	87 Plane Launches Torpedo
40 Cruisers' Scout Planes	64 Engineers Make Crossing	88 Laying a Screen
41 Navy Bomber Dives	65 Tossing Thunderbolts	89 Full Speed Ahead
42 Planes Screen Advance	66 Infantry Advances	90 Bombers Lay "Eggs"
43 "Wasps" of the Air	67 Artillery Moves Up	91 Taking the "Short Cut"
44 16" Coast Defense Gun	68 Army "Half Track Car"	92 Pom-Pom Gun in Action
45 Convoying Freighters	69 8" Railway Gun	93 Ambulance Rushes Aid
46 Away at Dawn	70 Long Range Flying Boat	94 Knocking Out Bombers
47 Landing by "Chute"	71 Single Seater Fighter	95 Signal Listening Post
48 Dive Bombing a Fort	72 Time to Bail Out	96 A Shattering Broadside

1 Tanks Attack	13 Pursuit Planes Dogfight
2 Torpedo Bombers	14 Team Work Aloft
3 Eliminating Enemy Nests	15 Plane Attacks Convoy
4 Night Bombing Attack	16 Cruisers Make Turn
5 Offshore Air Patrol	17 Motorcycle Scout
6 Direct Hit	18 Smashing Tank Attack
7 Parachute Invasion	19 Pursuit Plane Victory
8 Supply Train Attacked	20 Sky Bird Fighter
9 Pictures Under Fire	21 Battleship Formation
10 A Withering Broadside	22 Attack on Carrier
11 The Infantry Moves In	23 Tops in Fighting Speed
12 Machine Gun and Crew	24 Spotting Night Raiders

ACTION PICTURES (24) 2 1/8" X 2 5/8"

Action Pictures, "A brand new series...crammed full of interesting and comic action," was marketed by Novelty Gum of Chicago in 1934. Each card has an orange and white drawing on a black background with orange borders. "Action," or movement, is created by moving a line screen back and forth across the picture. The wrapper is orange with black, yellow, and white accents, and it has a cut-away wax paper screen printed on the lower half. Collectors could obtain a stronger "Cellophane Screen" or a "Foil Placque of Pres. Roosevelt" by exchanging ten wrapper coupons with the retailer (the Roosevelt placque is rarely seen by collectors). The reference number is R103.

ITEM	EX	AVE
Card	15.00	5.00
Set	450.00	150.00
Wrapper	300.00	100.00

1 The Talking Polly	13 Bubble Boy
2 Drummer Boy	14 Maude
3 The Trumpeter	15 Simple Simon
4 Groona Groona	16 The Villain
5 Two Little Pigs	17 Organ Grinder
6 A Wise Old Owl	18 Cat and the Fiddle
7 The Galloping Hare	19 Scooter Boy
8 Football Hero	20 The Bad Wolf
9 Little Black Sambo	21 Weary Willie
10 The Battling Champs	22 Tony Squeeze Box
11 Pretty Butterfly	23 The Dancing Duck
12 Billy Goat	24 The Skipping Kitten

ADVENTURE PICTURES (10)   2 1/2" X 3"

Cards of the Adventure Picture series, produced by Holloway, are rarely seen by collectors. In fact, there is only a single card of this set in the famous Burdick museum collection. The card illustrated is one of three made public in 1988 by veteran hobbyist Paul Koch. Adventure Pictures come printed on either thick or thin stock. The thick cardboard variety might have been issued singly on small candy boxes; cards printed on thin stock were distributed in strips. The reference number is R2.

ITEM	EX	AVE
Card	15.00	5.00
Set	200.00	60.00

PARTIAL CHECKLIST

1 Christopher Columbus
2 Ferdinand de Soto
10 Commander Byrd

ADVENTURES OF THE ARMY, NAVY AND THE MARINES (60?)   2 3/8" X 2 7/8"

The Army, Navy and Marines series issued by Leader Novelty is a classic case of deceptive marketing. The set total of 96, then 240, then 400, as printed on card backs, were never realized. Instead we must assume, if all the numbers implied in each printing sequence actually exist, that the set total appears to be no more than sixty cards. The first print run contained 24 cards: twelve odd-numbered "Army" cards and twelve even-numbered "Navy" cards. This Army/odd and Navy/even pattern continued in the second print run of 24, which began at number 96 and ended at 119. The only Marine cards known carry "deca-numbers" — 350, 370, 380 — and probably only twelve were issued.

Each service branch has its own frame style, coloration (brown for Army, red for Navy, yellow for Marines), and package-front design. The package fronts are considered scarcer than the cards because coupons on the back could be redeemed for various premiums. Each card formed the back of a small candy box and had two perforated edges for easy removal. The reference number is R3.

ITEM	EX	AVE
Card		
Army	6.00	2.00
Navy	6.00	2.00
Marines	10.00	3.50
Package Fronts		
Army	15.00	5.00
Navy	15.00	5.00
Marines	25.00	7.50
Complete Box		
Army	75.00	20.00
Navy	75.00	20.00
Marines	100.00	30.00

11

Adventures of the Army, Navy and the Marines

N100	U.S.S. Relief Hospital Ship
A101	Walkie-Talkie
N102	Douglas TBD Torpedo Bomber
A103	Parachute Troopers Bailing Out
N104	Superstructure of Aircraft Carrier
A105	Mobile Anti-Aircraft
N106	Tank Landing Speed Boat
N108	U.S.S. Anderson
A109	B-24D Army Bomber
N110	6 in. Gun Turret
N112	U.S.S. Breckinridge
A113	Motorcycle Patrol
N114	Torpedo Launched From Destroyer
A115	Coast Defense Fortifications
N116	U.S.S. Potomac
A117	U.S. Cavalryman
A119	Army Motorcyclists
M350	Marines Attacking
M370	Anti-Tank Gun Attack
M380	Thunderbolt Pursuit P-47

A1	Army Plane B-19
N2	Submarine
A3	Heavy Army Tank
N4	Mosquito Boat
A5	Light Army Tank
N6	Navy Dive Bomber
A7	Army Ski Patrol
N10	Battleship in Action
N12	Patrol Bomber
A13	155 m.m. Howitzer
A15	Parachute Troops
N18	Aircraft Carrier
A19	YP38 Interceptor
N20	Aerial Bombs
A21	Bantam Car
N22	5 in. Gun Crew In Action
A23	Sound Detector
N24	Torpedo Attack
N96	Sub-Chaser
A97	Army P.T. 13
N98	Navy Mechanics
A99	Machine Gun Crew

AEROPLANE SERIES (25)

Wischmann's Aeroplane Series was distributed in "Picture Pack Gum" during the early 1930's. Although each card carries a line about a "contemplated series of 250," only twenty-five were ever printed. The fronts have simple color drawings of famous aircraft while the backs contain a short text and advertising. The cards are printed on heavy cardboard stock and are not numbered. Small color-artwork pins, depicting unnamed aviators, bear the Wischmann name and are probably associated with this set, but are found less frequently than the cards. The

1 3/8" X 2 1/2"

wrapper has never been seen, and the set price listed below does not include pins. The reference number is R5.

ITEM	EX	AVE
Card	8.00	2.00
Set	240.00	60.00
Pin	10.00	3.00

Across the Atlantic with Amelia Earhardt
Akron — The Largest Dirigible
A New Altitude Record
The Breiven — West Across the Atlantic
Bleriot — Crossed the Channel, France to England, 1909
Conquering The Antarctic With Byrd
World's Altitude Gliding Record — Egar Dittmar — Germany
De La Cierva
Dornier I
Winning the Dole Air Derby — Goebel and the Woolaroc
Graf Zeppelin
A French Plane Used During the World War
The Heart's Content — the First Solo Flight Westward Over the North Atlantic.

Lockheed Monoplane
Latest Army Pursuit Plane XP-936
Modern Aerial Police
To the North Pole in the Norge with Amundsen
Round the World in 8½ Days with Post and Gatty
Refueling Record — By the Hunter Brothers
Sopwith Dolphin — Used During the World War
Spad — French Plane Used During the World War
Taking Off to Australia with C. Kingford Smith in the Southern Cross
A Modern Tri-Motor Passenger Plane
Lindbergh's Spirit of St. Louis
The First Successful Flight by the Wright Brothers

AFRICAN ANIMAL JIG CARDS (24) 2 3/8" X 2 7/8"

The honor of creating one of the most unusual trading card sets in history belongs to the National Licorice Company. The 24 color-artwork cards of this set, when placed in proper order, create a beautiful (if improbable) tableau of African wildlife (9½" X 17¼"). Each card is numbered and titled on the back, and each is missing one,

No. 24—HIPPOPOTAMUS

Derives its name from two Greek words that mean "River Horse." Despite an awkward looking body they are graceful swimmers. They have long tusklike teeth which yield a good quality of ivory.

There are twenty-four cards in this series, each card a complete picture in itself, and when all from Number One to Number Twenty-Four inclusive are assembled, you will be surprised to find you have built a beautiful African Jungle Scene size 9½ x 17¼. Now that you have one of the African Animal Jig cards you will most certainly want the other twenty-three to complete this unique picture.

One-weed and made by
NATIONAL LICORICE COMPANY
Brooklyn   Philadelphia   Moline

two, or four borders, depending upon its place in the panorama. Cards with licorice stains cannot be graded excellent. No wrapper or other packaging has been seen. Note: the set price implies "reasonable" alignment, or fit, between cards in the assembled panorama. The reference number is R6.

ITEM	EX	AVE
Card	15.00	4.00
Set	525.00	125.00
Wrapper	300.00	—

1 Flamingo	7 Elephant	13 Giraffe	19 Gnu
2 Ibex	8 Python	14 Rhinoceros	20 Crocodile
3 Bird of Paradise	9 Water Buck	15 Ostrich	21 Kaffir Tribe
4 Lioness	10 Hyena	16 Cape Buffalo	22 Leopard
5 Lion	11 Zebra	17 Okapi	23 Eland
6 Monkey	12 Gorilla	18 Cheetah	24 Hippopotamus

R−6 AFRICAN JUNGLE SCENE (9 1/2" X 17 1/4") FORMED BY PROPERLY ARRANGING THE 24 CARDS IN THE SET.

AIRPLANE PICTURES (10) 2 1/2" X 3"

Alphabetically speaking, this is the second scarce card series issued by the Holloway Company of Chicago. The fronts contain color drawings of airplanes; the backs identify and describe the plane (black print on tan stock). The card number appears on the back and there are ten titles in the set. The partial checklist below was furnished by Paul Koch. Another title — "Boeing Model 100" — is present in the Burdick Collection but the number cannot be seen. Cards of this series are found printed on both heavy and thin cardboard stock. The reference number is R7.

EPISODE NO. 2

Sikorsky Amphibian

This is a very popular type of plane where travel is over land and water. The hull of the plane enables it to float and a touch of a button drops the wheels, thus providing the plane with the ability to take off and alight on water or land. It is equipped with two engines and is capable of speeds from 35 to 125 miles per hour, it derives its name from its Russian designer who has experimented with all types of planes. Colonel Lindbergh used this type of plane when he inaugurated the mail and passenger line between the United States and Cuba.

This is one of a series of Airplane pictures packed with Holloway Milk Made Candies.

M. J. HOLLOWAY & CO., CHICAGO, ILL.

ITEM	EX	AVE
Card	15.00	5.00
Set	200.00	60.00

2 Sikorsky Amphibian
3 Curtiss Seaplane
4 DO−X

AIRPLANE PICTURES (14K)

Kerr's Butter Scotch Inc. issued this airplane series in 1940. The fronts contain "official" black and white photos set against a cloudy blue-green sky and are borderless. The backs are tan with a black print text which identifies and describes the aircraft. The cards are not numbered but each carries a "Key Letter" on the back. Collectors who were able to spell out the company name with the key letters could send in the cards to receive an airplane model kit. The cards were probably not returned, thus accounting for the scarcity of the set. The length of the set is not known. The reference number is R9.

ITEM	EX	AVE
Card	10.00	4.00

A-8	Sikorsky Observation Amphibian	P-35	Seversky Pursuit Plane
A-18	Curtiss Attack Plane	P-37	
B-15	Boeing Bomber	SBC-3	Curtiss Scout Bomber
B-17	Boeing Bomber "Flying Fortress"	SB2U-2	Chance Vought Scout Bomber
FM-1	Bell Multiplace Fighter	SF-1	Grumman Scout
F3F-1	Grumman Fighter	TBD-1	Douglas Torpedo Bomber
NJ-1	North American Basic Trainer	XF2A-1	Brewster Fighter

AIRPLANES (30)

Cards of the airplane series marketed by Cameron Sales of Chicago do not carry the manufacturer's name. So often were they found in excellent condition and without product stains that for many years collectors doubted that they were associated with the confectionary trade. The discovery of a partial wrapper proves that individual cards were issued with Cameron's Penny Roll. It also shows that complete sets were available via the mail for 25 cents — hence, all those clean, excellent cards. The fronts have color-enhanced photos of flying aircraft which are identified in the white bottom border. The backs each have two color squadron insignia set on shell-white stock. Both sides have glossy surfaces and the cards are not numbered. The wrapper price stated is for a complete specimen. The reference number is R10.

46th Bombardment

48th Bombardment

ITEM	EX	AVE
Card	3.00	.75
Set	100.00	25.00
Wrapper	100.00	——

Bell P39
Boeing Flying Fortress B17E
Consolidated B24
Consolidated PBY5A
Corsair F4U
Curtiss "HellDiver"
Curtiss P40F
Douglas A20
Douglas C53
Douglas Dauntless Dive Bomber
Douglas Dauntless Scout Bomber
Douglas Devastator Torpedo
  Bomber

Grumman Amphibian Utility Plane
Grumman "Avenger" Torpedo
  Bomber
Grumman "Hellcat" F6F
Grumman Wildcat
"Kingfisher" Observation Scout
  Plane
Lockheed P38
Lockheed Twin Engined Patrol
  Bomber
Lockheed "Ventura" Bomber
Martin B26

Mars Navy Flying Boat Service and
  Cargo
Martin "Mariner" Bomber
Naval Air Transports Giant R4D
  Plane
Navy's "Coronado" Flying Boat
  PB2Y2
Navy's Martin Marauder
North American B25
North American P51
Vought Sikorsky "Vindicator"
  (Scout Bomber)
Vultee A31

CURTISS "HELLDIVER"

NON-SPORT UPDATE
P.O. BOX 5858, HARRISBURG, PA 17110

AIRPLANE SERIES (40)

2" X 3"

The Airplane Series is a set of 40 blank-backed airplane and pilot cards well known to collectors but generally ignored because of a lack of information. However, Ken

Bush recently discovered a card with a tab attached which, if nothing else, provides the name of the set. The cards come with contiguous rouletted edges, in-

dicating that they were marketed in sheets rather than in strips. The manufacturer is unknown, but card number 18, which refers to 1941, establishes the date of issue. The checklist below was furnished by Ken Bush and Tony Salamone. No reference number has been assigned.

ITEM	EX	AVE
Card	2.50	1.00
Set	125.00	45.00

1 F80 Shooting Star
2 Orville Wright
3 Wilbur Wright
4 Wright Brothers First Flight in an English-Driven Heavier-than-Air Flying Machine. December 1903
5 P-47 "Thunderbolt"
6 Route of Earhart Plane, "Friendship," from Newfoundland to Wales — 1928
7 Amelia Earhart
8 Amelia Earhart's Plane "Friendship" — A Fokker Tri-Motor Seaplane
9 Curtiss "Helldiver"
10 Early Curtiss Seaplane
11 Glen H. Curtiss
12 Red Wing Biplane
13 B-17 Flying Fortress

14 B-17 Bombing Jap Battle Ship "Haruna"
15 Colin P. Kelly
16 View of West Point from the Hudson River, Colin P. Kelly Graduated in 1937
17 P-38 "Lightning"
18 Sikorsky Heliocopter 1941
19 Igor I. Sikorsky
20 Sikorsky's Biplane, "Ilia Mourometz"
21 B24 Liberator
22 Rickenbacker Forced Down at Sea for 22 Days in World War II
23 Eddie V. Rickenbacker
24 Spad Biplane
25 B-36 "Flying Cigar"
26 Howard Huges Returning from Record
27 Howard Huges

28 no title
29 P-51 "Mustang"
30 J. H. Doolittle Won the Thompson Trophy — 1932
31 James H. Doolittle
32 "Super-Solution" Speedwing
33 Boeing "Stratacruiser"
34 Byrd's Plane "Condor"
35 Richard E. Byrd
36 Byrd's Fokker Trimotor Monoplane
37 B47 Stratojet
38 Lindbergh's Plane Spirit of St. Louis, on Display at the Smithsonian Inst. Wash. D.C.
39 Chas. A. Lindbergh
40 Lindbergh's Flight in the "Spirit of St. Louis," from New York to Paris Nonstop 1927

ALLIES IN ACTION (140)

2 7/16" X 2 3/4"

Although it appears before "Commando Ranger" in our alphabetical listing, "Allies in Action" is actually a sequel to that set. Produced by the W. H. Brady Company, the 140 strip cards of this series were issued in two distinct

parts. The first print run of cards, numbered AA71 to AA140, are much easier to find than the second run numbered AA141 to AA210. Compared to other strip card sets of the period, the first half of Allies in Action is

difficult to complete, while the second half so far has proved impossible to finish. The "pictograms," as the manufacturer calls them, come with gray or white backs and with blue or black print on the backs. The fronts contain multicolor war drawings with lateral "V" borders. Note: no set price is given as no set is known to exist. The reference number is R11.

ITEM	EX	AVE
Card (AA71-AA140)	4.00	1.50
Card (AA141-AA210)	8.00	3.00

AA-71 Flying Fortress Knocks Down Nazis
AA-72 Plane Torpedo Buckles U-Boat
AA-73 Combat Planes Punish Jap Navy
AA-74 Gun Crew at Battle Station
AA-75 Loosing Y-Gun Ash-Can
AA-76 Frontline Repair Depot
AA-77 "Havocs" Hammers Hitlers Harbors
AA-78 Another Jap Joins Davy Jones
AA-79 Swift Sea and Air Action
AA-80 Sub Bombs Axis Oil Dumps
AA-81 Axis Atrocities Will Be Avenged
AA-82 Beating Off Axis Air Attack
AA-83 Allied Airman Tear Tanks Apart
AA-84 Allied Navies Rule the Waves
AA-85 U.S. Army Air Corps Insignia
AA-86 Loading Jeeps on Carrier Plane

AA-87 Combat Troops Make Glider Landing
AA-88 Yanks Boarding Troop Transport
AA-89 Armorers Loading Bomb Bay
AA-90 Air Warfare Analysis
AA-91 Torpedo Plane Combat Procedure
AA-92 British Spitfire Dominates Dogfight
AA-93 Navy Fighters in Formation
AA-94 Big British Bombers Pound Enemy
AA-95 Russian Bombers Plaster Objectives
AA-96 Air Corps Attacks Axis Landings
AA-97 A.A. Searchlight Pins Nazi Planes
AA-98 Jeep Towing Field Gun
AA-99 Merchant Marine in Convoy
AA-100 Axis Ship Going Under

AA-101 The Sun Sets for Tojo's Nips
AA-102 Railway Gun Defends Coast
AA-103 Flying Tigers Taking Off
AA-104 Dropping Flares on Axis Targets
AA-105 Trench Mortar Blasting Axis
AA-106 Tragedy in Toulon Harbor
AA-107 Air Minesweeper Detonates Mines
AA-108 Death of a Deadly Jap Sniper
AA-109 Fast Catapult Take Off
AA-110 Sighting Jap Destroyer
AA-111
AA-112 Torpedo Away To A Hit
AA-113 Chart Of Operations
AA-114 Zooming Away Victorious
AA-115
AA-116 Into The Thick Of It
AA-117 Hot Reception In Aleutians
AA-118

15

AA-119 Side Gun Riddles Fighters
AA-120 Back To Base Alive
AA-121 Mechanical Ears in Action
AA-122 Extensive Landing Operations
AA-123
AA-124 Barrage Balloon Protection
AA-125 Half-Tracks Repel Air Assault
AA-126 PT Boat Attacks Shore Batteries
AA-127 Pushing thru Steaming Jungles

AA-128 The End of the Terrible Trail
AA-129
AA-130
AA-131 Trolling for Metal Monsters
AA-132
AA-133 Skytroops Consolidate for Combat
AA-134 Scout Plane Warns Supply Column

AA-135
AA-136
AA-137 Scratch One Flat Top
AA-138
AA-139 Hard Hitting Hudsons
AA-140 Lockheed Lighting Lashes Foe

Very Few Titles Known in AA-141/ AA-210 Series

AMERICA AT WAR (48)　　2 7/16" X 2 11/16"

One of the last sets to be produced before war time material restrictions shut down trading card production,

America at War was issued by the W.S. Company in 1942. The set title appears in the top red panel of every card; each

multi-color drawing bears a number in a white circle and is captioned at the bottom. The backs repeat the set title, card number, and caption (which may vary slightly from the front) and have a short text. Each card is marked "1942." Note: add 25% value for a set of intact strips. The reference number is R12.

ITEM	EX	AVE
Card	3.00	1.00
Set	160.00	55.00

501 Bombing Jap Planes at Lae
502 Truck Convoy on Burma Road
503 Jap Destroyer Destroyed
504 Tank Action at Mindanao
505 U.S.S. Anderson
506 Repelling Japs at Moresby
507 Routing Japs at Darwin
508 Flying Tigers in Burma
509 Bombing by Parachute
510 Operating While Being Bombed
511 Parachute Action
512 U.S. Naval Attack at Marshall Island

513 Battling at Singapore
514 Corregidor Underground H.Q.
515 General Stillwell
516 Barrage Baloon
517 The Answer to Pearl Harbor
518 Phillippine Guerilla Action
519 Coming Invasion of Europe
520 Chiang Kai-Shek
521 Burning Oil at Cavite
522 Tank Trap
523 Pulling Away from Sinking Ship
524 Boarding The Troop Ship

525 American Raid on Wotje Island
526 Observation Post
527 Bombardier's "Greenhouse"
528 Bomber Returning to Carrier
529 Navy Tunnel at Corregidor
530 Stalin
531 Submarine Conning Tower
532 Plane Protecting "Commandos"
533 Tanks in Africa
534 Sinking Japs in Coral Sea
535 Colin P. Kelly
536 Rescue Men in Asbestos

537 Victory in Coral Sea
538 Night Attack in Australia
539 Sergeant Wireless Operator
540 New Battleships Rushed
541 "Scarsdale Jack" — Ace
542 Capsized Jap at Gilbert Island
543 Machine Guns at Bataan
544 U.S. Marine Transport Plane
545 Nazi Bomber Crashes
546 U.S. Planes Bomb Tokyo
547 Defending Darwin Harbor
548 Mopping Up Jap Parachutists

AMERICAN BEAUTIES (24)　　2 1/2" X 3 3/16"

American Beauties, one of the most popular sets on the bubble gum list, was probably never sold with gum! Perhaps Warren Bowman, the flamboyant owner of Gum Inc. was aiming to avoid criticism by marketing these spicy subjects directly to a more sophisticated clientele without the gum that might attract kids. The blank-backed cards were sold in variety and tobacconists stores and in packs of 12 for five cents (see illustration), in cellophane packs, and in nine card sheets. Each card

has the line "Gum, Inc., Phila., Pa." printed inside the frame line. The color artwork was obtained from a series of larger arcade cards being sold concurrently by the Mutoscope Company.

In addition, the 24 poses used by Gum Inc. in the American Beauties set appeared in a variety of formats: ink blotters, playing cards, 8" X 11" paper enlargements, etc. The rights to these other formats were licensed by Mutoscope, not Gum Inc., and they have no connection with the American Beauties series except for a simple sharing of artwork (an implied link with Gum Inc. has been used to justify outrageous prices for common items with the 24 shared designs). To date, only one authentic Gum Inc. tie-in with American Beauties has been discovered: a series of small note pads using an actual card as the cover (see illustration). It is not known if all 24 poses occur in the note pad issue.

As to date of issue, Jefferson Burdick first mentioned American Beauties in the December 1944 issue of the "The Card Collector's Bulletin". They continued to be sold after the war ended. The reference number is R59.

ITEM	EX	AVE
Card	18.00	4.00
Set	500.00	125.00
Sheet (9 cards)	175.00	45.00
Paper Band	35.00	——

AMERICAN BEAUTIES NOTE PAD

A Good Hook-up	Miss-Placed Confidence
A Live Wire	No Stares!
Ankles Aweigh	On De-Fence
A Peek-a'-Knees	Out on a Limb
A Perfect Pair	Peek a View
Caught in the Draft	Playing Safe
Figures Don't Lie	Short on Sails
Foil Proof	Sitting Pretty
Forced Landing	Sport Model
Free Wheeling	Sure Shot
French Dressing	Thar She Blows
Just the Type	Weight Control

AMERICAN G—MEN (48)   2 5/16" X 2 3/4"

The horizontally-aligned cards of this American G-Men set are numbered 101 to 148. The set title is located in a white badge design on the front of each card and the words "City-State-Nation" are printed underneath "G-Men."

These multi-color artwork cards were originally issued in strips but are rarely found that way today. They are numbered front and back but the caption appears only on the obverse side. A panel at the top of each card carries

a slogan, such as "Crime Does Not Pay" or "Safety First." The text on the back is uncharacteristically long for a strip card issue and claims to be "actual stories of bandits and cops...from the records of the Crime Detection Department of the City, State, and Nation." The manufacturer of this set is not known. Note: intact strips increase cards values by 50%. The reference number is R13-1.

ITEM	EX	AVE
Card	6.00	2.00
Set	350.00	110.00

THE HOBBY CARD INDEX OPERATES THE MOST CONTINUOUS AND COMPREHENSIVE CROSS-REFERENCE FILE ON CARDS IN THE U.S.

101 Hijackers	113 Blackmailers	125 Street Crossing	137 Counterfeiters
102 Counterfeiters	114 Hold-Up Men	126 Saved in Fire	138 Mail Robbers
103 Fences	115 Sneak Thieves	127 First Aid	139 Burglars
104 Slot Machine Racketeers	116 Petty Crooks	128 Accident	140 Sneak Thieves
105 River Thieves	117 Lunatics	129 Too Late	141 Pickpockets
106 Dope Peddlers	118 Murderers	130 Danger	142 Stolen Cars
107 Diamond Smugglers	119 River Thieves	131 Accident	143 Crooked Gamblers
108 Kidnappers	120 Chinatown Charlie	132 Runaway	144 Hold-Up Men
109 Roof Thieves	121 Tramps	133 Bank Robbers	145 Bank Robbers
110 Deserted Shack	122 Burglars	134 Murderers	146 Murderers
111 Stolen Cars	123 Pants Thieves	135 Gunmen	147 Gunmen
112 Burglars	124 Kidnappers	136 Blackmailers	148 Hitch Hikers

AMERICAN G—MEN (48)　　2 5/16″ X 2 3/4″

701 Opium Smugglers	717 Moonlight Ghost	733 Baseball Murder	
702 Insurance Racket	718 Pueblo Phantom	734 Miami Hijackers	
703 Alarm Clock Clue	719 Knife VS Gun	735 Hot Money	
704 Lonely Shack	720 Hillbilly Killers	736 Five, Six Pick Up Stiffs	
705 Broken Bones	721 Black-Mailer Nailed	737 Coal Shute Shooting	
706 Cornered Rat	722 Dynamite Destroyer	738 Great Guy?	
707 Blowout! Crash!	723 Shanghier Captured	739 Outlaw Hideout	
708 Pineapple Bombs	724 Wire Tappers	740 Lunch Bandits	
709 Snakes Den	725 Black Legion	741 Jewelry Thief	
710 He Got His Man	726 Cafeteria Crime	742 Kidnapped and Rescued	
711 Laugh of Death	727 Baggage Battle	743 Subway Slaughter	
712 Gang War	728 Smuggling Aliens	744 Undercover Man	
713 Bank Robber	729 Escaped Convict	745 Northern Justice	
714 Desert Mystery	730 Toughie Squeals	746 Oriental Rivals	
715 Air Patrol	731 Big Shot	747 Underworld Desperados	
716 Racketeers Reward	732 Crazy Charlie	748 Foiling a Kidnapper	

The "other" American G-Men set is easily identified by its vertically-aligned cards and numbering system (701-748). The multi-color artwork of each card is set upon a shield design: the set title (minus "City-State-Nation") is print-ed in a red device at top. The cards are numbered front and back. A line on the reverse states "This is one in a series of exciting picture cards of thrilling stories of crooks and cops." The manufacturer has yet to be identified. Note: intact strips raise the value by 50%. The reference number is R13-2.

ITEM	EX	AVE
Card	6.00	2.00
Set	350.00	110.00

AMERICAN HISTORICAL CHARACTERS (30)　　2 3/8″ X 2 7/8″

1 George Washington	1 Captain John Smith
2 Washington the Surveyor	2 John Smith Condemned to Death
3 Valley Forge	3 Pocohontas Rescues John Smith
1 John Paul Jones	1 Daniel Boone
2 The Drake Runs Up the White Flag	2 Daniel Boone Escapes the Indians
3 Fight between "Richard" and "Serapes"	3 Boone Captured by Indians
1 Stephen Decatur	1 Sitting Bull
2 Decatur Fires the Philadelphia	2 Sitting Bull Ambushes Custer
3 Fight between "United States" and "Macedonian"	3 Sitting Bull and His Braves Chased into the Canadian Wilderness
1 Captain Kidd	1 Buffalo Bill
2 Captain Kidd Flees from the Ships of the Great Mogul	2 Buffalo Bill the Dead Shot
3 The Trial of Captain Kidd	3 Buffalo Bill's Wild West Show
1 Christopher Columbus	1 Jesse James
2 Columbus at the Court of Queen Isabella	2 Jesse James Holds Up a Stage
3 Columbus Discovers America	3 Jessee James is Murdered by the Ford Brothers

Outstanding color artwork is the highlight of this 30-card series issued by the American Caramel Co. of Lancaster, Pa. Ten famous Americans are spotlighted in three card sub-sets: a portrait card, always the "No. 1" card, contains bibliographical details, while the "No. 2" and "No. 3" cards portray and describe events in that person's life. Cards of this series are often found with caramel stains or trim-med to remove stained areas: these are worth 50% less than the values listed below. No wrapper or package has been discovered for this set. The reference number is R14.

ITEM	EX	AVE
Card	12.00	3.00
Set	450.00	100.00

AMERICA'S DEFENDERS (6)
VARIOUS SHAPES

Given the materials shortages caused by the war, it is difficult to see how the Milkes Company could have produced these elaborate candy

boxes in 1942. The government, no doubt, recognized the propaganda value of the project and lent support. These are not your standard

size candy boxes! The color artwork of Capt. Colin Kelly (illustrated) is 9 inches tall and 3½ inches wide and is free-standing as long as the rest of the box (2½" X 4½') behind it is intact. Details of Kelly's heroic feat are printed on one side panel. The box held approximately one ounce of "molasses kisses" and pictured a complete set of America's Defenders on the "advertising" side (opposite from the artwork). Prices are for complete boxes, and each item is priced according to subject. The reference number is R190.

ITEM	EX	AVE
Army Truck	100.00	35.00
Bomber	100.00	35.00
Colin Kelly	200.00	75.00
General McArthur	250.00	100.00
Machine Gunner	150.00	50.00
Pursuit Ship	100.00	35.00

ANIMAL QUIZ CARDS (48)
1 3/4" X 2 5/8"

A casual observer might spot an Animal Quiz Card and judge it to be part of a children's game issued by a toy manufacturer or publisher. Certainly, the "playing card"

format — rounded corners, glossy finish, and "Do You Know?" game rules printed on the back — would give that impression. Yet the mere fact that these cards were dis-

tributed in packages of York Caramels makes them trading cards as well as components of a game. The fronts are blue and red on shell-white stock; red ink only is used on the backs. Each card poses four questions about the animal pictured on front. The set was not listed in Burdick's 1939 card guide, and the date of issue is unknown. The reference number is R16.

ITEM	EX	AVE
Card	10.00	3.00
Set	500.00	150.00

ANIMALS (54)
2 1/4" X 3 1/4"

Single cards of this animal series are striking when viewed by themselves; placed together, the artwork tends to be overwhelmed by the mono-color background. There are two varieties of cards. An unnumbered issue on thin, glossy stock has printed backs with caption, text, and advertising. Another style, most often found in nine-card sheets, is blank-backed, numbered, and printed on thick board. The "thin" variety was

Animals

first mentioned in the 1946 Burdick catalog but the date of issue, almost certainly prewar, has yet to be determined. The firm name on the back, Schranz & Bieber, may have been a fireworks or novelty company which provided a prize for collectors finding a "Lucky Card." The reference numbers are R15-1 and R15-2.

ITEM	EX	AVE
Card		
Thin	6.00	2.00
Thick	3.00	1.00
Sheet		
(thick only)	30.00	10.00
Set		
Thin	375.00	120.00
Thick	175.00	60.00
In Sheets	200.00	75.00

Number in ( ) refers to thick variety

Anteater (27)	Lynx (22)
Ape (5)	Mink (42)
Armadillo (30)	Monkey (38)
Badger (26)	Moose (24)
Bear (35)	Musk-Ox (49)
Beaver (40)	Muskrat (54)
Bison (41)	Opossum (3)
Camel (19)	Otter (14)
Cat (34)	Pig (39)
Chamois (32)	Polar Bear (4)
Chipmunk (15)	Porcupine (1)
Cow (28)	Rabbit (17)
Deer (51)	Racoon (33)
Dog (45)	Rat (6)
Donkey (2)	Reindeer (47)
Elephant (23)	Rhinoceros (20)
Fox (9)	Seal (8)
Giraffe (31)	Sheep (46)
Goat (37)	Skunk (44)
Hippopotamus (53)	Sloth (16)
Horse (36)	Squirrel (29)
Hyena (50)	Tapir (21)
Ibex (12)	Tiger (52)
Jaguar (48)	Walrus (7)
Kangaroo (11)	Wolf (25)
Lion (13)	Woodchuck (18)
Llama (10)	Zebra (43)

ARMY AIR CORPS INSIGNIA (100)(100)

The 100 cards comprising the Army Air Corps Insignia series were issued in two distinct varieties. First, there are the candy box cards cut directly from the 1-cent packages of Switzer's Licorice Cigerettes. Cards of this series measure 1 1/2" X 2 7/8", are blank-backed, and are printed using a single color (blue, green, red, etc.) on tan cardboard stock. According to an offer printed on the side of the box, collectors could "Send 15 Insignia (any kind) and 15 cents and receive a full set in four colors." Not only does this explain the origin of the second variety of insignia

TWO SIZES

cards, it also indicates why type 1 cards are scarce.

The second variety of Army Air Corps Insignia cards are printed in four colors on shell-white stock. Each card measures 2" X 3" and has "Switzer's Air Battle Game" printed on the back. A copyright line bears the date 1938. Since type 2 cards were available only in sets, they tend to be found in lots rather than singly. The "Switzer's Giant Bubble Gum" advertised on the front of type 2 cards is mere advertising and has no direct relationship with this set. The checklist of titles is identical for both varieties. The reference numbers are R17-1 for type 1 and R17-2 for type 2. Note: These reference numbers were mistakenly reversed in earlier guides.

ITEM	EX	AVE
Card		
Type 1	10.00	3.00
Complete		
Box	50.00	15.00
Type 2	5.00	1.50
Sets		
Type 1	1200.00	350.00
Type 2	550.00	180.00

1 58th Service Squadron
2 11th Photo Section
3 4th Observation Squadron
4 26th Attack Squadron
5 50th Observation Squadron
6 7th Observation Squadron
7 6th Composite Group
8 12th Photo Section
9 72nd Bombardment Squadron
10 23rd Bombardment Squadron
11 Bolling Field Detachment
12 6th Photo Section
13 60th Service Squadron
14 5th Photo Section
15 75th Service Squadron
16 44th Observation Squadron
17 2nd Photo Section
18 47th School Squadron
19 46th School Squadron
20 66th Service Squadron

21 33rd Pursuit Squadron
22 1st Photo Section
23 2nd Balloon Squadron
24 68th Service Squadron
25 53rd School Squadron
26 110th Observation Squadron
27 116th Observation Squadron
28 99th Bombardment Squadron
29 23rd Photo Section
30 2nd Bombardment Group
31 20th Bombardment Squadron
32 49th Bombardment Squadron
33 9th Airship Squadron
34 35th Pursuit Squadron
35 36th Pursuit Squadron
36 80th Service Squadron
37 4th Composite Group
38 21st Airship Group
39 91st Observation Squadron
40 71st Service Squadron

41 62nd Service Squadron
42 1st Pursuit Group
43 7th Bombardment Group
44 9th Bombardment Group
45 9th Bombardment Squadron
46 28th Bombardment Squadron
47 54th Bombardment Squadron
48 11th Bombardment Squadron
49 154th Observation Squadron
50 118th Observation Squadron
51 8th Pursuit Group
52 37th Attack Squadron
53 101st Observation Squadron
54 8th Attack Squadron
55 2nd Wing
56 3rd Pursuit Squadron
57 17th Attack Group
58 43rd Pursuit Squadron
59 111th Observation Squadron
60 94th Pursuit Squadron
61 73rd Attack Squadron
62 95th Attack Squadron
63 64th Service Squadron
64 79th Pursuit Squadron
65 102nd Observation Squadron
66 3rd Attack Group
67 19th Airship Squadron
68 2nd Observation Squadron
69 20th Pursuit Group
70 12th Observation Group
71 22nd Observation Squadron
72 105th Observation Squadron
73 30th Bombardment Squadron
74 67th Service Squadron
75 15th Photo Section
76 18th Pursuit Group
77 25th Bombardment Squadron
78 38th Observation Squadron
79 19th Pursuit Squadron
80 57th Service Squadron

81 41st Observation Squadron
82 20th Photo Section
83 6th Pursuit Squadron
84 59th Service Squadron
85 112th Observation Squadron
86 107th Observation Squadron
87 17th Pursuit Squadron
88 90th Attack Squadron
89 12th Observation Squadron
90 13th Attack Squadron
91 31st Bombardment Squadron
92 27th Pursuit Squadron
93 70th Service Squadron
94 108th Observation Squadron
95 1st Wing
96 16th Observation Squadron
97 96th Bombardment Squadron
98 77th Pursuit Squadron
99 34th Attack Squadron
100 88th Observation Squadron

21

ARMY, NAVY AND AIR CORPS (48)   2 3/8" X 2 11/16"

Another war time strip card set, Army, Navy and Air Corps was issued by the W.S. Company in 1942. The fronts have multi-color drawings of war scenes, and all but the end-of-row cards have rouletted edges on two sides. The set title is printed on a patriotic panel at the top of each card. The number and caption appear on both front and back (some captions may vary between sides), and the backs carry a short explanation of the obverse scene. The number reference is R18. Cards in strips are worth 25% more than single cards.

ARMY ★ NAVY and AIR CORPS
No. 619
U.S. Bombs Japanese Convoy
Flying low, A-20 bombers, drop parachute bombs over Jap supply column, sowing a path of destruction and annihilation in its wake.
This is one of a Series of 48 Cards
©W.S. 1942, N.Y.C. Litho in U.S.A.

ITEM	EX	AVE
Card	4.00	1.50
Set	220.00	80.00

601 Sailors "Learning the Ropes"
602 Periscope Sights Enemy
603 Sentry Patrol at Miami
604 Movie Stars in Canteens
605 General Wainwright
606 "Take Battle Stations"
607 "Bombing Orders"
608 Panama Coast Artillery
609 Off to a "Landing Raid"
610 American Submarine
611 His First Meal in Ireland
612 General MacArthur at Corregidor
613 U.S. Airplanes Protecting Convoy

614 The Army Comes to Miami
615 Prime Minister of England
616 Home Safe After Bombing Japs
617 U.S. Marines "Landing Party"
618 President Roosevelt
619 U.S. Bombs Japanese Convoy
620 Japanese Freighter Afire
621 Camouflaged Filipino Artillery
622 Tokio is "Burned up"
623 U.S. Coast Artillery In Action
624 Right Through "Gas"
625 U.S. Navy In North Atlantic
626 "P.T." Mosquito Boat

627 Action at Marshall Island
628 General Douglas MacArthur
629 Japs Bombing Defenseless Natives
630 A Gift from General MacArthur
631 U.S. Torpedoes in Coral Sea
632 Bombers Over the Pacific
633 Guard Duty on a Bridge
634 Dive Bombing Tokio Airport
635 "Jeep" Jounces Japs
636 U.S. Sub Gets Jap Tanker
637 U.S.O. Service Dance
638 U.S. Army's Newest Anti-Aircraft

639 General Marshall
640 "Dough Boys" In Malaya
641 Attacking Rabaul
642 Defending Corregidor
643 Hit and Run at Cebu By U.S.
644 In the Hills at Bataan
645 Establishing a "Bridge Head"
646 Out for Submarine Patrol
647 Pacific Coast Defense
648 U.S.S. Marble Head Repels Attack

AUTO LICENSE PLATES (36)(69)(66)(30) 1 1/2" X 3 1/4"

1936 Series — the cards have rounded corners and measure 1½" X 3¼". The backs carry a statement that Goudey produced "license plates of every state and foreign country." but only 36 cards were issued in the 1936 series. The undated license plate on the wrapper is yellow with blue letters; the rest of the wrapper is white with "license plate" side panels. The reference number is R19-1.

ITEM	EX	AVE
Card	5.00	2.00
Set	215.00	80.00
Wrapper	125.00	40.00

TEXAS "Lone Star State"
Capitol: AUSTIN   Population: 5,964,477

Arkansas (35-698)
Connecticut (6980)
Florida (624-573)
Illinois (621-T94)
Indiana (5493)
Iowa (50-2496)

Kansas (23-7498)
Kentucky (216-194)
Louisiana (20-569)
Maine (601-510)
Maryland (16-709)
Massachusetts (620-785)

Michigan (A24673)
Minnesota (A39-931)
Mississippi (106-907)
Missouri (501-100)
Montana (10-356)
Nebraska (19-294)

New Hampshire (98-542)
New Jersey (H9078)
New Mexico (362)
New York (5Y62-43)
North Carolina (630-920)
North Dakota (2-369)

Ohio (GT-284)
Oklahoma (529-846)
Oregon (205-946)
South Carolina (A02-946)
South Dakota (26-5321)
Texas (502-496)

Utah (102-694)
Vermont (19-306)
Virginia (85-964)
West Virginia (203-069)
Wisconsin (6589)
Wyoming (23-8195)

1937 Series — most cards are 1½" X 3¼" and have rounded corners. Some states (see illustration of Tennessee card) have specially shaped plates. The 1937 series contains license plates for 69 states, provinces, territories and countries. Color variations have been reported: Iowa appears with black or blue backgrounds, and Wyoming has been seen in white on brown and yellow on black. Three wrappers with identical artwork but different primary colors have been discovered: orange print on dark blue; dark blue print on orange; and yellow print on dark blue. The reference number is R19-2.

ITEM	EX	AVE
Card	4.00	1.50
Set	325.00	115.00
Wrappers (3)		
Each	75.00	30.00

Alabama (300-581C)	Maine (560)	Ohio (GT-428)	British Columbia (13-150
Arizona (J521)	Maryland (16-097)	Oklahoma (259F468)	British Guiana (P.3593)
Arkansas (180-009)	Massachusetts (48-177)	Oregon (265-409)	British Honduras (B.P.2)
California (8Z-15-11)	Michigan (234)	Pennsylvania (PA23)	Canal Zone (201)
Colordao (10-1282)	Minnesota (B298-322)	Rhode Island (?)	Curacao and Aruba (1303-C)
Connecticut (6980)	Mississippi (131-114)	South Carolina (A-62-094)	District of Columbia (162-034)
Delaware (1-045)	Missouri (50-010)	South Dakota (26-3215)	Egypt (4701CEV-1)
Florida (324-657)	Montana (2-28)	Tennessee (10-800)	England (BHP-506)
Georgia (201-903)	Nebraska (23-3412)	Texas (649-205)	Guatemala (1430)
Idaho (12-280)	Nevada (16-840)	Utah (67-015)	Hawaii (41-020)
Illinois (216-419)	New Hampshire (89-524)	Vermont (50-390)	Italy (MI.1/4544)
Indiana (4539)	New Jersey (H9078)	Virginia (19-469)	
Iowa (7-5012)	New Mexico (1)	Washington (B-7286)	
Kansas (5-869)	New York (6K22-40)	West Virginia (200-169)	
Kentucky (J9084)	North Carolina (306-290)	Wisconsin (58-661)	
Louisiana (25-906)	North Dakota (12-b08)	Wyoming (0-2)	

Newfoundland (2246)	
Ontario (90-A-06)	
Palestine (M529H)	
Panama (5921)	
Peru (3407)	
Puerto Rico (10869)	
Sweden (A3453)	
Trinidad & Tobago (P124)	
Turkey (4571)	
Virgin Islands;St. Croix (02)	

1938 Series — consists of 66 cards. All have rounded corners and measure 1½" X 3¼" (unless specially shaped). No color variations have been reported for cards. but the wrappers come in red print on yellow or black print on green. The box (illustration provided by Bob Marks) is the only intact specimen known for any year of Auto License Plates. The reference number is R19-3.

ITEM	EX	AVE
Card	4.00	1.50
Set	315.00	110.00
Wrappers (2)		
Each	75.00	35.00
Box	200.00	50.00

Alabama (107-030)	Nebraska (8-5033)	Alberta (49-605)
Arizona (A5610)	Nevada (70-41)	British Columbia (63-700)
Arkansas (118-510)	New Hampshire (13-300)	British Guiana (H.5593)
California (IA-50-40)	New Jersey (10022)	British Honduras (B.H.4)
Colorado (60-6100)	New Mexico (308)	District of Columbia (5775)
Connecticut (WC980)	New York (7K62-37)	England (BWK-366)
Delaware (1-045)	North Carolina (123-200)	Guatemala (1438)
Florida (2-64-800)	North Dakota (4-400)	Italy (MI-1-5544)
Georgia (22-589)	Ohio (GT-638)	Manitoba (92-327)
Idaho (93-250)	Oklahoma (231-092)	Ontario (90A50)
Illinois (160-780)	Oregon (204-606)	Puerto Rico (15869)
Indiana (321-010)	Pennsylvania (L-727)	Quebec (20-200)
Iowa (31-1720)	Rhode Island (E5111)	Saskatchewan (16-710)
Kansas (90-570)	South Carolina (A-10-110)	Sweden (C-2681)
Kentucky (2398)	South Dakota (34-1206)	Trinidad & Tobago (T424)
Louisiana (201-310)	Tennessee (355 199)	Turkey (4571)
Maine (3270)	Texas (265-061)	Virgin Islands (b2)
Maryland (125-121)	Utah (10-733)	Yukon Ty. (420)
Massachusetts (90-242)	Vermont (54-892)	
Michigan (Z-2600)	Virginia (37-260)	
Minnesota (B548-770)	Washington (E-7039)	
Mississippi (190-144)	West Virginia (120-750)	
Missouri (14-555)	Wisconsin (121-300)	
Montana (9-810)	Wyoming (0-2)	

1939 Series — only 30 cards issued. Dimensions are 1½" X 3¼" and corners are rounded. No color variations have been reported for cards or wrappers. The reference number is R19-4.

ITEM	EX	AVE
Card	4.00	1.50
Set	140.00	50.00
Wrapper	75.00	30.00

Alabama (S226-104)	Nebraska (14-350)
California (2A 40 73)	New Jersey (ZK 919A)
Colorado (78-3119)	New Mexico (290)
Delaware (25-070)	New York (506-405)
Illinois (187-680)	North Carolina (404-002)
Indiana (401-288)	North Dakota (9-388)
Iowa (50-4160)	Ohio (A-567-A)
Kansas (20 1045)	Oklahoma (68 508)
Kentucky (3406)	South Dakota (20-7431)
Louisiana (150-061)	Tennessee (50 268)
Maryland (30-140)	Vermont (48-055)
Massachusetts (70-357)	West Virginia (50-406)
Minnesota (B8-990)	Wisconsin (60-950)
Mississippi (209-641)	British Columbia (30-157)
Missouri (67-450)	District of Columbia (30-388)

BATTLESHIP GUM (50)

2 3/8" X 2 7/8"

1 U.S.S. Pennsylvania	26 U.S.S. Sicard
2 U.S.S. California	27 U.S.S. Melville
3 U.S.S. West Virginia	28 U.S.S. Dobbin
4 U.S.S. Maryland	29 U.S.S. Barracuda (V1)
5 U.S.S. Mississippi	30 U.S.S. S-44
6 U.S.S. Nevada	31 U.S.S. Argonaut (V4)
7 U.S.S. New York	32 U.S.S. Bushnell
8 U.S.S. Texas	33 U.S.S. Holland
9 U.S.S. Arkansas	34 Eagle Boats (1-60)
10 U.S.S. Memphis	35 U.S.S. Tulsa
11 U.S.S. Raleigh	36 U.S.S. Guam
12 U.S.S. Milwaukee	37 U.S.S. Medusa
13 U.S.S. Omaha	38 U.S.S. Vestal
14 U.S.S. Portland	39 U.S.S. Bridge
15 U.S.S. Indianapolis	40 U.S.S. Brazos
16 U.S.S. Augusta	41 U.S.S. Nitro
17 U.S.S. Chicago	42 U.S.S. Sirius
18 U.S.S. Northampton	43 U.S.S. Vega
19 U.S.S. Pensacola	44 U.S.S. Chaumont
20 U.S.S. Saratoga	45 U.S.S. Henderson
21 U.S.S. Langley	46 U.S.S. Kittery
22 U.S.S. Lexington	47 U.S.S. Relief
23 Navy Planes	48 U.S.S. Sandpiper
24 Naval Bombing Plane	49 U.S.S. Bireo
25 U.S.S. Childs	50 U.S.S. Macon

Fifty different U.S. Navy warships comprise the Battleship Gum series issued by Newport Products in the late 1930's. The multi-color artwork fronts have the ship name and the card number printed in red ink. The backs are gray and contain a brief technical description of the ship (black print). The beautifully-colored 1 cent wrapper is rarely seen and the display box for this set has yet to be uncovered by collectors. The reference number is R20.

ITEM	EX	AVE
Card	10.00	3.00
Set	625.00	175.00
Wrapper	500.00	—

BEAUTIFUL SHIPS (24)

2 3/8" X 2 7/8"

Until recently, collectors believed this set of 24 ship pictures was issued by the Package Confectionary Co. with two different back styles. However, the discovery of a new wrapper carrying the United Candy Company name suggests that the series was either pirated or shared by the two Boston-based firms. It is now believed that the anonymous cards were issued exclusively by United Candy. Both types appear to be equally common. and neither company issued the second group of 24 cards which would have fulfilled the "series of 48" claim which is printed on every card.

Package Confectionary cards came in two types of wrappers. Entitled "Sailor Boy Smokes," both used the same basic design, but one is clear wax paper and the other is white. United Candy cards appeared in clear wax packages bearing the title "Ship Smokes." The Sailor Boy Smokes box pictured is the only one known and is dull pink in color. The reference numbers for Beautiful Ships are R135-1 (Package Confectionary) and R135-2 (United Cardy).

—No. 17—

GLOUCESTER FISHERMAN

These ships are very seaworthy, and must be, as the fishing grounds are miles out in the ocean. A large amount of our sea food is supplied by vessels sailing from the New England ports of Gloucester, Boston and Portland.

"This is one of the first-half (24) of a series of 48 picture cards of beautiful ships. Return 10 wrappers of Sailor Boy Smokes and 10¢ in coin or stamps to cover postage and you will receive a Beautiful Album in which to keep these pictures."

Package Confectionery Corporation
Boston, Mass.

—No. 22—

AMERICAN MODERN BATTLESHIP

Electricity runs this ship. It is a powerful instrument of war, carrying many large calibre guns, which are capable of hurling tons of steel projectiles fifteen or twenty miles. On board there are stores, hospitals, motion pictures and many other conveniences.

This is one of the first-half (24) of a series of 48 picture cards of beautiful ships.

ITEM	EX	AVE
Card (either type)	10.00	3.00
Set (either type)	300.00	85.00
Wrappers "Sailor Boy Smokes"		
1) Clear	100.00	——
2) White	150.00	——
"Ship Smokes"	300.00	——
Box	250.00	75.00

1	Egyptian Ship
2	Greek Ship
3	Roman Merchant
4	Viking Ship
5	Santa Marcia
6	Early English
7	Mayflower
8	Old Pirate Boat
9	Late English
10	Constitution (U.S.S.)
11	Clermont
12	Savannah
13	Clipper Ship
14	Old Whaler
15	Chinese Junk
16	Mississippi Steamboat
17	Gloucester Fisherman
18	Modern Liner
19	Racing Yacht
20	Submarine
21	Byrd's South Pole Ship
22	American Modern Battleship
23	Modern Destroyer
24	American Air-Plane Carrier

PACKAGE CONFECTIONARY
WHITE WAX PAPER WRAPPER

PACKAGE CONFECTIONARY CLEAR WAX PAPER WRAPPER

UNITED CANDY CO. CLEAR WAX PAPER WRAPPER

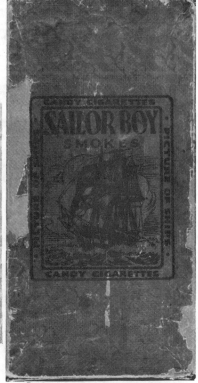

PACKAGE CONFECTIONARY
DISPLAY BOX

BELIEVE IT OR NOT (48)

2 5/16" X 2 3/4"

The Believe It Or Not series of 48 cards was produced by the Wolverine Gum Company of Detroit. Each card depicts an incredible fact from the Ripley's archives. and the primary colors of the artwork are yellow, green, and blue. The card title and number and the famous Ripley signature appear on front and back, and the backs carry descriptive text. Every card bears a copy-right date of 1937.

The set appeears to have been issued in two groups of 24 cards. The second group (25-48) seems harder to find (although some collectors believe nos. 1-24 are more difficult to obtain). The wrapper is truly scarce and the dis-play box has never been seen. The reference number is R21.

ITEM	EX	AVE
Cards		
1-24	20.00	6.00
25-48	35.00	10.00
Set	1650.00	450.00
Wrapper	650.00	––

1 The Greatest Swordsman
2 The Cruise of the Skeletons
3 A Life Saving Death Sentence
4 The Trench of Bayonets
5 The City of Mud-Eaters!
6 The Strangest Accident!
7 The Holy Scorpion Eater
8 Captain Manu's Famous Swim
9 The Marooned Man
10 Most Amazing Airplane Accident
11 A Man of Iron
12 The Greatest Cavalryman
13 The Ghost Ship
14 "Black Bart" The Stage Robber
15 The Largest Tree in the World
16 The Richest Man in the World
17 Captain Kidd Was Not a Pirate
18 Paul Revere Did Not Make the Famous Ride
19 A Record in Cannibalism
20 The Coldest Spot in the World
21 The Ship That Shot Itself
22 The Scourge of God
23 The Man Who Stubbed His Toe on $10,000,000,000...
24 Dead Man Wins a Fight
25 A Most Unbelievable Animal
26 The French Foreign Legion
27 Mighty Mites
28 Unarmed Officers of the Law
29 A Million Dollar Mistake
30 The Strangest Fishing Accident
31 The Hanging Hindu
32 The Most Abject Surrender
33 29 Horses Shot Under Him
34 The Great "John L"
35 Elephant Lights
36 The Academy of Poison
37 The Bloodless Leader
38 The Tower of Skulls
39 A Miraculous Escape
40 Airplanes Pull Harder to Go Slower
41 The Hamatcha
42 "Greater Love Hath No Man"
43 The Norseman's Jump
44 The River of Blood
45 The Royal Freak
46 The Lone Survivor
47 See Mecca and See No More
48 Faith unto Death

BIG ALARM CANDY (?)

2 5/8" X 5"

The cards of this General Candy (Chicago) set were cut from 5-cent boxes of "Big Alarm" candy. Type 1 cards — color artwork drawings of various fire trucks — comprised one side of the candy box; type 2 — "character" cards with poems — occupied the opposite side. To date, only four type 1 and two type 2 cards have been reported. However, since the set is

26

relatively unknown, the demand for it is modest and prices for available cards remain low. The reference number is R191.

ITEM	EX	AVE
Card	12.00	5.00
Complete Box	50.00	20.00

Mama Brown, in her gown,
Was sound asleep in bed,
Smelled the smoke and she awoke,
"Oh save my child" she said.

BIG CHIEF WAHOO (9)(27)

1 5/8" X 4"

Big Chief Wahoo "cards" look exactly like matchbook folders, so you are most likely to find them in matchbook collections. This clever marketing scheme — folders with tiny sticks of gum — was created by the Chicle Advertising Corporation (Toledo, OH) and sold for a penny at stores and newsstands.

Type 1 folders are numbered 1-9 and feature an illustrated lesson in "Wahoo's Injun Slango." (Chief Wahoo was a popular comic strip character created by cartoonists Saunders and Woggon.) The yellow front panel is identical on all type 1 folders, but the inside may be blank or carry advertising. Those that are blank bear the line "Another Series To Follow" on the lesson panel; those with advertising do not. The reference number is R22-1.

Type 2 folders are primarily white with red and blue accents and appear to have been a patriotic issue distributed after Pearl Harbor. The front panels bear the title "Defense Series." and the stapled "strike pad" that secured the gum reads "Save This Series of 27 Defense Pictures." The Defense Series is far scarcer than Injun Slango but is not as attractive to collectors. The reference number is R22-2.

ITEM	EX	AVE
Folder		
"Injun Slango"	20.00	8.00
"Defense Series"	20.00	8.00
Unopened Pack		
"Injun Slango"	75.00	——
"Defense Series"	100.00	——
Sets		
"Injun Slango"	225.00	90.00
"Defense Series"	675.00	250.00

1 Shower-Bath Is "Big-Rain-in-Little Room"
2 Duck Is "Chicken-Wearum-Snowshoes"
3 Hot Dog Is "Hamburger-Wearum-Tights"
4 Jalopy Is "Hoss-Power-Gottum Hiccups"
5 Ink Is "Pencil-Juice"
6 Permanent Wave Is "Hair-Gottum Cramps"
7 Percolator Is "Coffee-Pot-Go-Burp"
8 Jitterbug Is "Paleface-Do-Um-War-Dance"
9 Vacuum Cleaner Is "Growlin'-Sack-Eatum-Dirt"

TYPE 2 WRAPPER

PARTIAL CHECKLIST

Battleship	Ryan Trainer
Destroyer	Submarine
Heavy Cruiser	Torpedo Boat
Mine Trawler	Turret Guns

TYPE 1 WRAPPER

TYPE 1 AD BACK

BIG CHIEF WAHOO NEWSPAPER COMIC STRIP

BIG LITTLE BOOK SERIES (224) 2 7/16″ X 2 7/8″

Scarcity and size of set make the Big Little Book Series one of the 1930's most difficult issues to complete. The cards were issued in 1937 to promote the sales of children's books bearing the same name. Collectors have reported several interesting facts about these cards: (1) they were issued in strips; (2) some sub-sets carry multiple copyright dates (the most recent is always 1937); (3) the front and back card captions are different from one another; and (4) the sub-set sequence for G-Man ("129-161") and Buck Jones ("162-193"), as stated on the cards, is incorrect (they should read "129-160" and "161-192"). Seven char-acters are featured, each in a 32-card sub-set featuring multi-color artwork and a progressive story line. The reference number is R23.

ITEM	EX	AVE
Cards		
Flash		
Gordon	75.00	18.00
Dick Tracy	35.00	9.00
Popeye	35.00	9.00
Tom Mix	35.00	9.00
G-Man	40.00	10.00
Buck Jones	25.00	6.00
Dan Dunn	25.00	6.00
Sub-Sets		
Flash		
Gordon	3000.00	750.00
Dick		
Tracy	1350.00	315.00
Popeye	1350.00	315.00
Tom Mix	1350.00	315.00
G-Man	1550.00	350.00
Buck		
Jones	950.00	230.00
Dan Dunn	950.00	230.00
Complete		
Set	10800.00	2700.00

1 A Blast of Bugles Announced Ming's Arrival
2 With Drawn Sword Vultan Waited
3 Flash and Dales in Vultan's Box
4 They Watched the Approach of Ming's Ships
5 Bloodthirsty Monkeymen in Almost Endless File
6 King Jugrid Led the Lionmen
7 Flash Sliced Through His Armor
8 The Masked Man Leaped to His Rescue
9 Flash Was Given Instructions
10 Flash Led the Contestants
11
12 Flash Whirled His Mount
13 The Masked Man Awaited the Death Stroke
14 Flash Whirled to the Rescue

15 Flash Faced the Masked Man
16 Flash Rode Up to Salute Ming
17 Aura Stayed Her Father's Hand
18 They Lined Up in Equal Ranks
19 Closer and Closer to the Dagger Points
20 The Arena, Covered With Upstretched Dagger Points
21 Two Guards Assisted Flash
22 Aura Drew A Dagger
23 A Masked Man Grasped Aura's Wrist
24 Flash Thanked the Masked Man
25 Dale Begged Flash Not To Go
26
27
28
29 Flash Clutched the Rope as He Fell
30 Barin Clutched at Flash's Leg
31
32

FLASH GORDON
CARDS 1-32

DICK TRACY
CARDS 33-64
CHECKLIST NOT AVAILABLE

TOM MIX
CARDS 97-128
CHECKLIST NOT AVAILABLE

65 Popeye Rose Out of the Sea
66 He Gave Wimpy a Piece of His Mind
67 They Gathered About the Mysterious Box
68 Wimpy Gave His Explanation to Sally
69 Popeye Had a Job for Each of Them
70 It Was a Treasure Map!
71 Popeye Showed Salty the Treasure Map
72 How Was Popeye to Get a Boat?
73 Her Apple Pie Had Disappeared
74 Olive Insisted She Had Seen a Ghost
75 "This Ship is Haunted!" Olive Cried
76 A Moving Shadow Crept Closer
77 Popeye Reached for His Neck
78 Popeye Was Greatly Astonished
79 The "Ghost" Was Slim!
80 Slim Was A Good Lookout
81 "Yo Ho Ho an' a Can o' Spinach!"

82 A Lesson in Navigation for Salty
83 The Rescue Made Good Progress
84 A Wave Tore Salty from the Rail
85 Popeye Ordered All Hands Below
86 Wimpy's Face Was a Sickly Color
87 Wimpy Had Discovered Land
88 All Hands Rushed to the Rail
89 Popeye Inspected His Battered Boat
90 It Was a Goldpiece
91 King Boo Hoo Gave Popeye a Present
92 Slim Came In for a Rich Reward
93 The Pirates Had Come for the Treasure
94 The Air Was Filled With Flying Cocoanuts
95 Helping a Pirate to Talk
96 Popeye and His Crew Were Homeward Bound

POPEYE
CARDS 65-96

G-MAN
CARDS 129-160
CHECKLIST NOT AVAILABLE

BUCK JONES
CARDS 161-192
CHECKLIST NOT AVAILABLE

DAN DUNN
CARDS 193-224

193 Wu Fang, Notorious Chinese Criminal	209 Wu Fan's Killer Came for Dan
194 "Seek Out Dan Dunn!"	210 Dan Questioned Wu Fang
195 A Death Warrant for Dan Dunn	211 The "Truth Serum" Was Injected
196 A Secret Order Flamed Out	212 The Truth Serum Worked Perfectly
197 "I'm Going to Do It Myself!"	213 Sergeant Bannister Had Bad News
198 Wu Fang Could Wait No Longer	214 Dan Rushed Wu Fang to the Airport
199 Ace Bart Demanded Action	215 Lawyer Sharp Arrived Too Late
200 Ace Suspected a Double-Cross	216 Dan Was Warmly Congratulated
201 Dan Reported to the Chief	217 Dan Was Ready for Action
202 Good Luck Wishes from the Chief	218 A Prisoner in Ace Bart's Boat
203 Dan and Bannister Had a Tip-Off	219 Ace Scurried to His Hideout
204 The Counterfeit Bills Were Perfect	220 Dan Pointed Out the Mystery Ship
205 Wu Fang Ordered Dan's Death	221 Barnacle Got Word to His Chief
206 "Throw Up Your Hands"	222 Dan Answered the Telephone
207 Dan Discovers the Counterfeit Money	223 Babs and Wolf Became Great Friends
208 Dan Captures Wu Fang	224 Babs Struggled Through the Mire

BIG THRILL BOOKLETS (24)   2 5/16" X 2 7/8"

There are 24 booklets in the "Big Thrill Library," six each for these "fearless men": Buck Jones, Buck Rogers, Dick Tracy, and Tailspin Tommy. All are numbered one to six (on the back cover), and the story inside is accompanied by one color and two black & white illustrations. Each book- let bears a 1934 copyright date and was distributed in wax packages of Goudey's "Big Thrill" chewing gum. The paper in many booklets has become brittle so collectors are advised to consider condi- tion carefully when using the prices listed below. The ref- erence number is R24.

ITEM	EX	AVE
Booklets		
Buck Jones	30.00	7.50
Buck Rogers	75.00	18.00
Dick Tracy*	35.00	9.00
*Except Vault of Death	20.00	4.00
Tailspin Tommy	25.00	6.50
Buck Jones	215.00	50.00
Buck Rogers	540.00	130.00
Dick Tracy	235.00	60.00
Tailspin Tommy	180.00	45.00
Complete Set	1250.00	310.00
Wrapper	400.00	––

1 A Timely Arrival
2 A Murder Mystery
3 Shot from Ambush
4 Hand to Hand Struggle
5 A Den of Wolves
6 Avenging the Secret Service

1 Thwarting Ancient Demons
2 A One-Man Army
3 An Aerial Derelict
4 The Fight Beneath the Sea
5 A Handful of Trouble
6 Collecting Human Specimens

1 Saved in the Nick of Time
2 Valuable Information
3 Vault of Death
4 Cross-Country Race
5 Uncovers the Dope Ring
6 Smashes the Bombing Racket

1 The Smuggler's Last Flight
2 The Jump into Mystery
3 Trailing the Bank Bandits
4 The Woman in Black
5 The Doomed Express
6 The Battle in the Air

30

"BOX CAR" TRAINS (?)

2" X 4 1/2"

The "Box Car" series of train cut-outs appeared on candy wrappers manufactured by Curtiss, "makers of Baby Ruth and Butterfinger." Instructions on the back of each wrapper tell how to "paste them on heavy paper and cut out. They will stand up and line up like real trains." This advice, in part, accounts for the scarcity of the wrappers. The individual cars are not captioned and the length of the set has yet to be determined. The reference number is R153.

ITEM	EX	AVE
Wrappers		
Cut	15.00	5.00
Whole	75.00	20.00

BOY SCOUTS (48)   2 1/8" X 3 1/4"

1 A Scout is Courteous	18 Building an Indian Tepee	34 Sliced Meat and Potatoes on
2 A Scout is Helpful	19 The Yellow Perch	a Stick
3 A Scout is Brave	20 Homemade Moccasins	35 Boiling Corn
4 A Scout is Clean	21 A Handy Fireplace	36 The Principle of Steam
5 The North Star Compass	22 Sharks	37 Talking with Smoke
6 Cruising in a Canoe	23 A Simple Sun Dial	38 Covered Wagon Days
7 The Sailboat	24 A Broken Arm	39 The Knife
8 The Pheasant Family	25 Trail Blazing	40 The Scout Axe
9 Fire Prevention	26 Making an Eye Splice	41 Field Hockey
10 A Totem Pole for your Camp	27 The French Bowline	42 Hiking
11 Map Making	28 A Shelter for the Night	43 Bringing Him Back to Life
12 Archery	29 The Robin	44 Modern Air Travel
13 Sheep Clouds	30 Indian Sign Language	45 Pitching Horseshoes
14 Thunder Clouds	31 Testing a Ford	46 A Woodland Hut
15 The Great Ice Age	32 Dinosaurs of Long Ago	47 The Law of Gravity
16 The Hooded Cobra	33 Wig Wag Signals	48 Saving the Train
17 Below the Earth's Surface		

One of the earliest Goudey sets to be printed (a 1933 copyright date appears front and back), the Boy Scout series is admired by card collectors and scouting enthusiasts alike. The cards have red, white and blue framelines and were distributed in wax packages of "Some Boy Gum." The text on back is printed in green ink. The series of 48 color artwork cards is composed of various sub-groups with themes such as "Camp Life" and "Signs and Signals." The sub-group titles appear on front (under the centered set title) and back of every card. The reference number is R26.

ITEM	EX	AVE
Card	12.00	3.00
Set	725.00	180.00
Wrapper	300.00	––

CARD–O PLAYING CARD TYPES (MANY)   2 1/4" X 3 1/2"

No section of the Jefferson Burdick's American Card Catalog has proved so confusing over the years as the Card-O "Playing Card Types" category listed as reference number R112. The appropriateness of listing these cards with other more standarized gum and candy issues has been debated over time on the basis on both format and origin. Playing cards designed as "traders" — packaged in boxes, cardboard folders and cellophane — were sold in variety stores from the 1930's to the 1950's. No gum or candy was ever included with these "traders," and they never really attracted the gum card crowd. However, the recent discovery of a Leaf display box for Card-O Gum (see illustration) suggests that several series of "playing card types" really deserve their niche in the gum card hobby.

The other non-gum sets in the Card-O section, however, are members by association only and were included for two reasons. First, they use the same rounded-corner, playing card format as the genuine Card-O Gum issues. Secondly, all the known playing card sets, gum or non-gum, were manufactured or licensed by the Whitman Publishing Company. Burdick, who never claimed to be a gum card expert, probably had as much difficulty trying to make sense of these various sets as any other collector. That is why authentic gum issues, "traders," wartime "recognition" decks, and comic character card games all were lumped into a "catch-all" category. The format which came to characterize the term "Card-O" simply overwhelmed the issue of "proper" gum lineage.

Given the fact that variations exist for almost all of the 12 sets described below, it might appear that the Card-O classification is the cartophilic equivalent of the Bermuda Triangle. Most of the confusion, however, can be alleviated by sorting the sets into basic sub-groups and sticking to simple, accurate descriptions.

Airplanes & Warships

According to The Card Collectors Bulletin (issue No. 48, June 1, 1947), the cards of this group were all issued by Leaf Gum. Many, if not all, of the artwork drawings of airplanes and warships in all five sets appeared in Whitman's patriotic books. The Card Collectors Bulletin also reported (Dec. 1, 1948) that Leaf "dumped" its surplus Card-O gum cards on the market after the war. A partially-full Leaf display box recently purchased by Jim Nicewander was found to contain airplane cards from Series B, C, D and the unmarked, so-called "mixed" series of 46. The gum was wrapped in individual sticks, and purchasers apparently got a stick and their choice of card for a penny.

"U.S. Navy — Series A" — this title, along with the words "22 cards," is printed on

Card-O Playing Card Types

BATTLESHIP "PENNSYLVANIA"

PATROL TORPEDO BOAT

every card. Some cards also bear the sentence "Packed with Card-O Chewing Gum" on the back. but it is not known if all 22 come this way. The fronts have color drawings of various U.S. warships, and each subject is described by a short text on back. A small circle containing the letters "US" appears on front inside the picture area, and the cards are not numbered. The reference number is R112-6.

ITEM	EX	AVE
Card		
not marked		
"Gum"	2.00	.35
marked		
"Gum"	3.00	.50
Sets		
not marked		
"Gum"	60.00	10.00
marked		
"Gum"	80.00	15.00

Aircraft Carrier "Lexington"	Destroyer "Anderson"	Mine Layer "Aroostrock"
Aircraft Carrier "Ranger"	Destroyer "Farragut"	Mine Sweeper "Raven"
Battleship "Mississippi"	Destroyer "Gleaves"	Patrol Torpedo Boat
Battleship "New Mexico"	Destroyer Tender "Dixie"	Seaplane Tender "Curtiss"
Battleship "North Carolina"	Gunboat "Erie"	Submarine "O" Class
Battleship "Pennsylvania"	Heavy Cruiser "Pensacola"	Submarine "Sargo"
Battleship "Texas"	Heavy Cruiser "Portland"	Submarine "Tamber"
Boom Net Tender "Boxwood"		

"Aeroplanes — Series B" — 26 cards in set. Collector Larry Fortuck reports that there are two styles of fronts and four distinct backs:

(1) Front without numbers, back with text;

(2) Front without numbers, text back with word "JOKER" in two corners;

(3) Front without numbers, single stag outline and word "JOKER" in center;

(4) Front with numbers in bottom corners, standard playing card back.

Some cards may be found with the aeroplane flying right or left. The box pictured below, the only one discovered to date for any Card-O series, is yellow with blue and red accents. Note: all Series B cards are valued the same, regardless of variations.

ITEM	EX	AVE
Card	2.00	.35
Set	65.00	12.50
Box	400.00	100.00
Wrapper	15.00	——

CURTISS HAWK III • Turkey

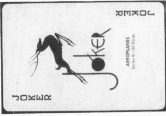

JOKER / AEROPLANES Series B—26 Cards

CURTISS HAWK III • Turkey

Airacobra	I.5
Armstrong	Koolhaven
Bell	Latecoere
Boeing	Lockheed XP-38
Bristol	Marinens
Caudron	Northrup
Curtiss Hawk III	Potez
Curtiss Hawk IVM	Renard
Curtiss XP-42	Seversky
Fairey	Supermarine
Focke	Vickers
Fokker D21	Vultee V II
Fokker T9	Vultee V XIIA

WHITMAN BOOK CONTAINING
CARD—O ARTWORK

CARD-O CHEWING GUM STICK WRAPPER
PURCHASERS GOT ONE STICK OF GUM AND
THEIR CHOICE OF CARD FOR A PENNY.
VALUE: $ 15.00

CARD-O BOX WITH LIFT OFF COVER FROM THE COLLECTION OF BOB MARKS
EACH BOX CONTAINED A STAND-UP INSERT PANEL WITH THE SAME
DESIGN AS THE COVER TOP. VALUE: $ 200.00

WHEN YOU BUY CARDS. . .
MAKE SURE THE CONDITION MATCHES THE PRICE.

34

CONSOLIDATED PB2Y2 "CORONADO"
United States

CONSOLIDATED PB2Y2 "CORONADO" • Flagship of the U.S. Naval Service, largest, fastest and with the longest range of any naval aircraft. Top speed 225 m.p.h. Range 4000 miles.

AEROPLANES—Series C—28 Cards

CONSOLIDATED PB2Y2 "CORONADO"
United States

MUNIZ M-7 • Brazil

MUNIZ M-7 • The only airplane built in South America is this Brazilian military trainer. A lowwing, two place open cockpit biplane, has dual controls and is designed for primary flight instruction. Top speed is 118 m.p.h. There is no armament equipment.

AEROPLANES—Series C—28 Cards

MUNIZ M-7 • Brazil

"Aeroplanes — Series C" — a series of 28 cards. Two types of text backs are known: with and without the word "JOKER" in two opposite corners. Like its companion sets, Series C was originally issued during 1940-41, and many of its designs appear, with slight color and text variations, in "War Planes" books published by Whitman. Back variations have no bearing on value. The reference number is R112-4.

ITEM	EX	AVE
Card	2.00	.35
Set	67.50	14.00

Blackburn Botha—England
Bloch 131—France
Boulton Paul Defiant—England
Consolidated B-24—United States
Consolidated PB2Y2 "Coronado"—United States
Curtiss O-52—United States
Curtiss P-40—United States
Curtiss-Wright C-55—United States
Curtiss XSB2C-1—United States

Douglas A20-A—United States
Douglas TBD-1 "Devastator"—United States
Grumman F4F-3—United States
Grumman Skyrocket—United States
Lockheed 12-A—United States
Martin PBM-1 "Mariner"—United States
Martin 156-C—United States
Miles Master—England
Muniz M-7—Brazil

North American "Apache"—United States
North American B-25—United States
North American 0-47A—United States
Republic P-47—United States
Ryan PT-21—United States
Short-Sunderland—England
T.B. 3—Russia
Vought-Sikorsky XF4U-1 "Corsair"—United States
Z.K.B. 26—Russia

"Aeroplanes — Series D" — a series of 27 cards. There are three different "text" backs, all showing the set title and series, but with the following variations:
(1) 22 cards found with the series total listed as "27 cards;"
(2) 5 cards found with the series total listed as "25 cards" (marked by an asterisk in the checklist below);
(3) some, perhaps all, cards may be found with the line "Packed with Card-O Chewing Gum."
The reference number is R112-5. Note: the card of "Submarine Spitfire" is worth double value when found marked "Series B."

ITEM	EX	AVE
Cards		
not marked "Gum"	2.00	.35
marked "Gum"	3.00	.50
Sets		
not marked "Gum"	67.50	14.00
marked "Gum"	95.00	16.50

GRUMMAN G-44 "WIDGEON" • United States

WESTLAND WHIRLWIND • Britain
Avoiding close-range dogfights with enemy fighters, the Whirlwind darts into bomber formations at a speed of 365 m.p.h. and blasts them with its four 20 mm. shell-firing cannon which have a range of more than 1000 yards. With a big wing span of 45 feet, this newest R.A.F. twin-engine fighter is a deadly combat plane.

AEROPLANES—Series D—27 Cards

SAVOIA MARCHETTI SM 79 • Spain
One of the few three-engine bombers in use, this plane was first built by Italy for General Franco in the Spanish Civil War which served as a proving ground for its subsequent use by the Italian Army. Fire-power is weak, consisting only of four machine guns, one firing forward, two aft of the wings, and one flexibly mounted in the rear of the fuselage. Bomb-load totals 2750 pounds, carried on internal racks. Three Piaggio engines of 1000 h.p. each give the plane a range of 1150 miles and a top speed of 255 m.p.h.

AEROPLANES—Series D—25 Cards
Packed with CARD-O CHEWING GUM

GRUMMAN G-44 "WIDGEON" • United States
A fast, deluxe amphibian designed for wealthy private fliers, the "Widgeon" are now doing yeoman service in the coastal patrol under the insignia of the Civil Air Patrol. Two 400 h.p. Ranger air cooled, inverted in-line engines give the "Widgeon" a cruising speed of 150 m.p.h. and a range of 775 miles.

AEROPLANES—Series D—27 Cards
Packed with CARD-O CHEWING GUM

Avro Lancaster—Britain
Bell P-39 "Airacobra"—United States
Boeing B-17E "Flying Fortress"—United States
Brewster F2A-3 "Buffalo"—United States
Bristol Beaufighter—Britain
Consolidated PBY—United States *
Curtiss P-40E "Kittyhawk"—United States
Curtiss 21-B—United States *

Curtiss-Wright C-46 "Commando"—United States
De Havilland Mosquito Bomber—Britain
Douglas C-54—United States
Fairey Fulmar—Britain *
Grumman G-44 "Widgeon"—United States
Grumman TBF-1 "Avenger"—United States
Handley-Page Halifax—Britain
Hawker Hurricane—Britain
I-18—Russia
IL-2 "Stormovik"—Russia
Lliushin (Sic.) DB-3F—Russia

Lockheed 144 "Constellation"—United States
PE-2—Russia
Republic P-47 "Thunderbolt"—United States
Rogojarsky SIM XIV-H—Yugoslavia *
Savoia-Marchetti SM 79—Spain
Short Stirling—Britain *
Submarine Spitfire—Britain (QJF)
Westland Whirlwind—Britain

35

Card-O Playing Card Types

MONOCOUPE 90A • *United States*

MONOCOUPE 90A • *U.S.A.*

The pioneer among two-place cabin planes the Monocoupe is still rated high in the favor of private flyers. Economical and dependable, it is powered with a Lambert 90 h.p. engine, with a maximum speed of 130 m.p.h., a cruising speed of 110 m.p.h., and a range of 600 miles. The rate of climb is 900 feet per minute and the service ceiling is 15,000 feet.

CURTISS SEAGULL • *U.S. Navy Scout Observation*

CURTISS SEAGULL • *United States Navy*

The duty of the Seagull (SO3) is to locate enemy naval forces and to direct gunfire for the battleship or cruiser on which it is based. It is powered with a 320 h.p. air-cooled in line engine, has a top speed of over 175 m.p.h. and a range of 1,000 miles. The crew consists of a pilot and gunner. In the British navy it is known as the Seamew.

Dive Bombing

START OF DIVE

DIVE BRAKES OPENED....

PULL OUT.....

DIVE BOMBING

When the signal is given by the dive bomber's leader, one plane follows another in "pushing over" from a predetermined pattern into the dive. Special wing dive brakes are opened to slow down the dive, and the pilot aims the plane with an electric sight, holding it on the target until the bomb is released. Then the "pull out" is made as the plane's guns rake the target and clear the way for the plane behind him. The illustration shows a Curtiss Helldiver in a steep dive.

PATTERN BOMBING

Pattern bombing is used at night to saturate a given area or target. The object is to smash everything within the outline of the pattern. The target is first located by pathfinder planes that fly ahead of the main group, and then marked with special flares so that it can be seen clearly by the main force of the bombers coming in at altitudes up to 20,000 feet. Avro Lancasters are here smashing a German target.

NON-RIGID AIRSHIP • *U.S.A.*

Better known as the "blimp," this type of craft is held aloft by helium gas and is powered by a gasoline motor. It is useful for in-shore patrol of submarine waters and due to its low speed, it can hover over a sighted sub and radio to land-based planes to come and finish off the enemy with bombs or depth charges. Its value from a defense and observation standpoint has been proved in World War II.

NON-RIGID AIRSHIP • *United States*

Mixed Series — 46 cards known at this time. The American Card Catalog listed it as the first Card-O plane issue, but it clearly is not since some cards are dated 1944. The mixed series may actually be parts of several different sets, yet the one common denominator is the absence of any series identification or set total. Four distinct styles, all equally common, have been reported:

(1) Full color front of single aircraft with the title and the country of origin in white border below (see "Monocoupe");

(2) Full color front of single airplane; the bottom border holds the name and type of plane, but no country. A tiny line reads "Copr. 1944, Whitman Pub. Co" (see "Curtiss Seagull");

(3) Full color fronts showing various aircraft strategies (see "Dive Bombing" and "Pattern Bombing");

(4) Fronts in shades of blue with thick blue frameline (see "Non-Rigid Airship").

All styles are equal in value, but since there is an uneven "set" total, new additions to the list may be valued higher. The reference number is R112-12.

ITEM	EX	AVE
Cards	2.00	.35
Set (46 known)	110.00	20.00

Aircraft Carrier	Curtiss Warhawk	Martin Marauder	Rubber Life Raft
Alligator Tank	Dive Bombing	Martin Mariner	Ryan SC
Beechcraft E	Douglas Dauntless	Monocoupe 90A	Ryan S-T-A
Bell Airacobra	Douglas Havoc	Naval Mines	Skip Bombing
Boeing Flying Fortress	Douglas Skymaster	Non-Rigid Airship	Stearman PT-13
Cessna C145 Airmaster	Ercoupe 415-C	North American Mitchell	Stinson 105
Consolidated Catalina	Evasive Action	North American Mustang	Taylorcraft
Consolidated Coronado	Grumman Avenger	Pattern Bombing	Torpedo Bombing
Consolidated Liberator	Grumman Hellcat	Piper Cub J-4	Vought Corsair
Culver Cadet	Grumman Wildcat	Precision Bombing	Waco N
Curtiss Helldiver	Intruder Raids	Rearwin Sportster	
Curtiss Seagull	Lockheed Lightning	Republic Thunderbolt	

Aircraft Identification & Insignia Sets

Aircraft Recognition Cards — the first variety, easily identified by the flat finish of the card surface, was issued by Whitman in game decks beginning in 1942. Two sets of cards, consisting of 16 planes (shown at three angles), three "Keep 'em Flying" cards, one "Victory" card, and two instruction cards, were marketed in boxes under the names "Squadron Scramble" and "Zoom."

SERIES 1

R112-8A

Baku Geki Ki-99
Bell P-39D
Boeing B-17E
Brewster F2A-3
Consolidated PB2Y-3
Curtiss P-40E
Douglas A-20A
Grumman F4F-4
Heinkel HE.III
Messerschmitt ME-109
Mitsubishi 99
Northrop A-17A
Sento Ki-001
Submarine Spitfire
Vickers Wellington
Vought Sikorsky OS2U-1

FANCY BACK

The first series of 16 airplanes came as follows: (1) blue color fancy back (type 1) in the "Zoom" box with the airplane climbing; (2) blue color simple back (type 2) in the "Squadron Scramble No. 1" box.

The second series of 16 airplanes were issued in this manner: (1) green color fancy back (type 1) in the "Zoom" box with the airplane diving; (2) green color simple back (type 2) in the "Squadron Scramble No. 2" box.

SIMPLE BACK

SERIES 2

R112-8B

Boulton Paul Defiant
Bristol Blenheim
Consolidated B-24D
Dornier D026
Focke Wulf FW190
Hawker Hurricane
Lockheed P-38E
Martin B-26C
Messerschmitt ME-110
Mitsubishi 96 Fighter
Mitsubishi 98
Nakajima 97
Republic P-47
Russia I-16
Savoia Marchetti SM 82
Short Stirling

The two card sets and all four boxes have been surfacing regularly now that card collectors have accepted playing card types as legitimate issues. Since these are card decks, the value for an entire deck is less than the sum of individual card values (a premium must be allowed for the purchase of single cards for type collections). The reference number is R112-8.

ITEM	EX	AVE
Cards (all)	1.00	.25
Sets (2 different)	50.00	16.00
Boxes "Squadron Scramble"	30.00	10.00
"Zoom"	35.00	12.50

INSTRUCTION CARDS FOR "SQUADRON SCRAMBLE" DECK

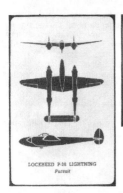

LOCKHEED P-38 LIGHTNING
Pursuit

LOCKHEED P-38 LIGHTNING • U.S.A.

A single-seat pursuit fighter with two motors. The top view shows double engine booms, wings tapered forward to narrow rounded tips, and stabilizer-elevator with parallel edges and rounded tips outside of booms. Front view shows great dihedral angle of wings extending from center of pilot nacelle, twin engines mounted low on wings, twin rudders directly behind engines. Side view shows pilot's nacelle extending ahead of engines, egg-shaped fin-rudder.

1 Boeing B17 Flying Fortress
2 Consolidated B25
3 Curtiss SBC-4 Cleveland
4 DeHaviland Mosquito
5 Douglas A20A Havoc
6 Grumman F4F-1
7 Lockheed P-38 Lightning
8 Martin PBM-I Mariner
9 Supermarine Spitfire

Aircraft Recognition Cards — variety two has a glossy surface finish and text backs like the Card-O gum types. It may have been issued as part of the "Mixed Series," but this has not been confirmed. Each card shows a specific aircraft from three perspectives; the planes are black on a blue sky/cloud background. Only nine titles have been reported to date. The reference number is R112-9.

ITEM	EX	AVE
Card	3.00	.75

Air Squadron Insignia — one of the most popular playing card sets. Created by Walt Disney Studios for various wartime squadrons, the insignia are printed two per card. The cards are not numbered and the length of the set is unknown at this time (known titles listed below). The reference number is R112-10.

ITEM	EX	AVE
Card	7.50	2.00

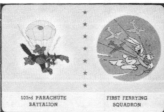

503rd PARACHUTE BATTALION

FIRST FERRYING SQUADRON

503rd PARACHUTE BATTALION

A wildcat hurtling through the air, claws outspread, ready to attack, symbolizes one of the first of our parachute troop units, activated at Fort Benning, Georgia, in 1941.

FIRST FERRYING SQUADRON

Started at the Long Beach Army Air Field in California, this first squadron ever formed for the specific purpose of ferrying planes and equipment anywhere in the world in a hurry—is trained to handle any craft from speedy P-38 Lightnings to huge Flying Fortresses.

Eagle Squadron (RAF) — 3rd Recon Troop
Submarine Base — Unites States
  Mosquito Fleet
The Flying Tiger — 57th Signal Battalion
1st Defense Battery — Jackson Air Base
13th Armored Division — 751st Tank
  Battalion

67th Bombardment Squadron — 56th
  Pursuit Squadron
445th School Squadron — Air Base
  Detachment
503rd Parachute — 1st Ferrying
774th Tank Destroyer Bat. — 21st
  Bombardment Squadron

Card-O Playing Card Types

Bombing Squadron 2
Bombing Squadron 3
Bombing Squadron 5

Fighting Squadron 2
Fighting Squadron 3
Fighting Squadron 5
Fighting Squadron 41
Fighting Squadron 71
Fighting Squadron VF72

Scouting Squadron 2
Scouting Squadron 5
Scouting Squadron 6
Scouting Squadron 41
Scouting Squadron 42

Torpedo Squadron 2
Torpedo Squadron 3
Torpedo Squadron 5

Navy Aircraft Squadron Insignia

The distinction of being the hardest Card-O style series to obtain belongs to this Navy Aircraft Squadron Insignia set. The front of each card contains a single color artwork insignia which is identified (above) and described (below). The center of the card back shows a "flying boat" in shades of blue highlighted against a white background. At top and bottom, respectively, are a white star and a white pair of Navy wings set on blue. To date, only 17 different insignia have been confirmed. The reference number is R112-7.

ITEM	EX	AVE
Card	4.00	1.50
Box	50.00	15.00

Comic Character Sets

Whitman made card games for both Popeye and Dick Tracy. These were sold directly to the public in variety stores (no gum) but were included in the Card-O category because of their playing card format.

Popeye Sectionals — the set was issued in at least 4 different boxes and consists of 24 "sectional" cards for eight different Popeye comic strip characters. Each set also includes ten "Scooner Cards" and a single instruction card. Until the summer of 1989, Popeye sectional cards were on everybody's "want" list, but then a quantity of complete, boxed sets and numerous single cards hit the market. Pre-1989 prices were high but have fallen sharply due to this new supply. The reference number is R112-11.

ITEM	EX	AVE
Card		
Sectional	3.00	1.00
Scooner &		
"Game"	2.00	.75
Set (cards		
only)	100.00	30.00
Boxes (4)		
each	50.00	20.00

39

General Subjects

Most of the information concerning this category comes from studying cards in the Burdick Collection at the Metropolitan Museum of Art in New York City. There are 124 cards known, marked either "Series A" (96) or "Series B" (28). The backs of the cards have the leaping stag/joker format (see "Aeroplanes — Series B") with the subset title and length printed underneath. The color artwork fronts may or may not have borders or captions.

"Series A" (The reference number is R112-1.)

Early American — 12 cards
Flowers — 12 cards
Horses — 12 cards
Hunting Dogs — 8 cards
Kittens — 12 cards
Latin America — 12 cards
Portraits — 12 cards
Scenic — 12 Cards
Ships — 10 cards

"Series B" (The reference number is R112-2.)

Patriotic — 12 cards
Portraits — 6 cards
Silhouette — 10 cards

Despite the fact that these two series are the hardest of the Card-O types to find, they suffer from low collector demand due to their similarity to playing card "traders" mentioned in the introduction to this section. There is no proof whatsoever that they were issued with gum.

ITEM	EX	AVE
Cards		
"A" or "B"		
(all)	3.00	.75
Sets		
"A" (96)	315.00	80.00
"B" (28)	95.00	25.00

40

Collectors have been unable to identify the manufacturer of the Cartoon Adventures set issued in 1936. Although cards 401-424 bear the name "Stephen Slesinger, Inc." and cards 425-448 are marked "John F. Dille Co.," these companies merely sold the rights to the cartoon characters depicted and probably were not directly involved in the actual production and distribution of the cards.

Cards marked "Slesinger" make up the first three subsets in the series: Tailspin Tommy (401-408), Tarzan of the Apes (409-416), and Broncho Bill (417-424). Cards bearing the "Dille" name appear on Buck Rogers cards only (425-448). In all subsets (including two sequences for "Dr. Huer" and "Wilma" in Buck Rogers), a portrait card is followed by seven action story cards. All Cartoon Adventures cards are blank-backed and have at least one rouletted edge (indicating that they were issued in strips). No relationship to a specific confectionary or gum product has been established, although it is implied by the appearance of this set on Burdick's early list of candy and gum cards. The reference number is R28. Cards found in strips are worth 25% more than the prices listed below.

ITEM	EX	AVE
Card		
Tailspin Tommy	25.00	5.00
Tarzan	40.00	10.00
Broncho Bill	25.00	5.00
Buck Rogers	60.00	15.00
Subsets		
Tailspin Tommy	250.00	50.00
Tarzan	400.00	100.00
Broncho Bill	250.00	50.00
Buck Rogers	1800.00	450.00
Set	2700.00	650.00

401 Portrait of Tailspin Tommy
402 Tommy Chases a Bandit Plane
403 "Boy, What a Shot!"
404 Tommy Has a Narrow Escape
405 Tommy, You Have Saved the President's Life! He Will Reward You!
406 Tommy, Here Are the Stolen Jewels.
407 Tommy Stops the Thieve's Take-off.
408 Tommy, Darling! I'm So Glad You Are Safe!

409 Tarzan Portrait
410 Tarzan Swings through the Trees
411 Tarzan Catches a Crocodile
412 Tarzan Slays the Great Bull-ape
413 Tarzan Aids Kala
414 Tarzan Eats High in a Tree
415 The Monkey-man Reaches for Tarzan's Knife
416 Tarzan Challenges Sheeta

417 Bronco Bill Portrait
418 "I'm Gonna Let Them Have It!"
419 "There Are Our Horses!"
420 Bill Rescues Brent
421 "I'm Wounded, Sheriff!"
422 The Spider Traps Bill
423 Bill Surprises Peg-leg
424 "Run for it, Nell!"

425 Portrait of Doctor Huer
426 Doctor Huer Tried Desperately to Radio the Earth.
427 Huer Tells Them Something Has Happened to His Machines and They Were in Danger.
428 Fear Gripped Them as the Comet Sailed through Space
429 They Were Afraid—They Couldn't Dodge Their Pursuers Much Longer.
430 The Refugees Leader Showed Them What a Strange, Mean Looking Mob He Controlled.
431 The Airscout Carried Them Westward and Landed Them in Denver.
432 Within an Hour the Gigantic Wall of Water Raced Across the Coastal Plains.

433 Portrait of Wilma
434 Buck and Wilma Saw Furious Outbreaks of Savagery from the Parapet.
435 The Patrol Officer Warns Them That the End of the World Was upon Them.
436 They Had to Protect Themselves from the Desperate Mob
437 Refugees Clung to the Doomed Buildings
438 A Speed Demon of the Air Carried Them Safely over the Sea.
439 The Viewplate Showed the Forthcoming Catastrophe
440 The Heat of Friction with Earth's Atmosphere Has Set Them Blazing.

441 Portrait of Buck Rogers
442 Their Relief Was Cut Short and Buck Pointed to a Huge Bulletin Board
443 The Hooded Figure Was Kane. Buck Was Surprised.
444 Buck and Wilma Hop Off with Their Jumping Belts.
445 The Comet Pulsed with Blinding Light.
446 Buck and Wilma Heard a Stupendous Crash. Doctor Huer Was Gone!
447 The Storm Rock Struck the Ship.
448 Buck Hid in the Shadows. Someone Was Approaching.

The Cartoon Comics set of 48 blank-backed cards appears to have been an earlier production (1935) by the same unknown manufacturer who created Cartoon Adventures. There are eight characters, each with a subset consisting of one portrait and seven action story cards. All the cards except Joe Palooka carry a "Chicago Tribune" credit line; all cards are dated 1935; and each one bears the signature of the artist. Collectors should also note that the "dialogue balloon" is used in Cartoon Comics, but not in Cartoon Adventurers. Rou-

letted edges indicate that this series was issued in strips (intact strips worth 25% more than values below). While not quite as popular as "Adventures" cards, "Comics" are nevertheless a very difficult set to complete. The reference number is R27.

ITEM	EX	AVE
Cards		
Dick Tracy	30.00	7.00
Orphan Annie	30.00	7.00
Harold Teen	20.00	5.00
Moon Mullins	20.00	5.00
Joe Palooka	30.00	7.00
Terry & the Pirates	20.00	5.00
Subsets		
Dick Tracy	300.00	70.00
Orphan Annie	300.00	70.00
Harold Teen	200.00	50.00
Moon Mullins	200.00	50.00
Joe Palooka	300.00	70.00
Terry & the Pirates	200.00	50.00
Complete Set	1500.00	425.00

101 Dick Tracy Portrait
102 Tracy! This Time You'll Stay in Jail for Good!
103 Come On Let's Get Him Junior! There He Goes Thru the Alley!
104 Your Disguise Almost Had Me Fooled Zora Arson. I'll Get You Yet!
105 Surprised to See Me? Eh? Drop That Gun!!!
106 Another Attempt on My Life! Come On After Them Chief!
107 I'm the Happiest Woman in the World Now That I Found Junior! I Am Glad to See You Together.
108 That'll Teach You to Try Your Dirty Tricks Boris Arson

109 Little Orphan Annie
110 I Am at Your Service, My Little Princess. Leapin' Lizzards.
111 Watch Over Her Punjab... She's a Very Good Child. She's a True Princess, Master.
112 She Lives Across the Tracks. Look at Her Funny Dress. Gee, the Kids at School Sure Are Stuck Up.
113 Gee But These Muffins Look Good, Annie. You'll Have to Wait Until Supper Daddy Warbucks.
114 Morgan Sure Was Swell to Let Us Live Here. We're Fixing This Old Barn into a Cozy Home.
115 She Certainly Is a Treasure Oliver. I'll Have Your Coffee in a Jiffy, Mr. Morgan.
116 We'll Be Up at the Top Annie Before You Know It. You Bet Daddy!

117 Harold Teen Portrait
118 Harold, What Time Is It by Your Nose? Mine Has Stopped Running!
119 My Manicurist Had a Scrap with her Dentist! I'll Bet They Went at It Tooth and Nail!
120 But, Mr. Lovewell, I Only Meant to Hit You Easy-Like!
121 No, I Don't Sell It No More. It Sold So Fast I Couldn't Keep It in Stock.
122 Hey! Where's Tha Fire? In Your Eyes, You Big Strong Man!
123 Now You Go Tell Mother What You Did! No—Sir! I'm No Tattle Tale.
124 Say, Pop! There's A Greasy Finger Mark on This Plate! Why Harold, That's Your Steak.

125 Moon Mullins Portrait
126 Mullins, I'm Afraid to Face Emma. This Is My Second Night Home Late. Yeah, I Know But Don't Worry, She's Too Hoarse From Last Night to Even Talk.
127 Moon, Did You Talk Lord Plushbottom into Spending $200 for a Pink Canary? Gosh No, Emmy, I'd Give Him the Bird for Nothing.

128 McJitters Your Gonna Have a Tough Time Learning the Harp at Your Age. Banjo Eyes I'm Gonna Knock Your Back Teeth Down Your Aesophagus.
129 Willie, You Shouldn't Give Mamie a Pipe for a Birthday Present. But Moon, I've Got to Stop Her From Smoking Mine.
130 Mamie, Throw the Rest of the Icewater on Lord Plushbottom.
131 Kayo, Call Me a Taxicab. Okay, Yer a Taxicab.
132 My Husband Is a Wrestler By Profession Mr. Mullins. Not By "Profession" Baby, By "Permission"—of the Other Guy.

133 Joe Palooka Portrait
134 Give It to Him Good—Knock His Ears Cauliflower. But I Ought Notter—Last Time He Didn' Get Up Fer 2 Days.
135 Now Youse Just Take This to Miss Ann. O Gee, Mom, I feel Like I'm Carryin' Lunch fer Pop.

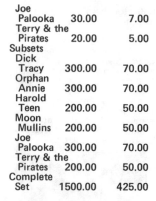

136 Mothaw Wants You for Dinner Tonight, Joe. It Will Be Full Dress Y'Know. Gee, Can I Wear My New Red Tie?
137 Oh, Joe, Please Try Not to Spill Your Tea. This Is to Be a Swell Affair. Gee, Gosh Ann, I'll Try'n Remember to—I Mean not to, Golly.
138 So, You Are Mr. Palooka, Who Is So—o Strong? Aw, Now, Lady, It's Only Me Breath.
139 Well, Guy, I'll See Ya Next Fall—Get It?
140 So You Are a Chimney Sweep, Eh? "Chimney Crickets" Heh! Heh!

141 Portrait of Terry
142 Pat, Last Night I Licked All These Pirates Myself. Well, Terry, Your Dreams Are Swell, But We've Got to Get Off This Ship or We're Lost.
143 Mr. Fang, You—You are Ungrateful—You—Have Betrayed Me—I Shall Feed You to the Dogs. Be Careful, Pat, He's Mad.

144 Go Easy with the Little Fellah—He No Hurt Us. We Get Big Fellah Too. Whew!
145 Terry, We've Just Got Word from the British Steamer Again! Find the Captain! Yep!
146 Quick, Terry, Get This Letter to your Friend Pat, It's Very Important. Okay!!

147 They'll Never Be Able to Find Out My Identity. I've Deceived Them Throughly as a Count. Gosh!
148 But, Mr. Ryan, You Are Most Unreasonable. Count Dmitri Is a Perfect Gentleman and I Dislike your Interfering.

CENTURY OF PROGRESS (?)   2 1/4" X 3"

Only nine different cards have been confirmed to date in this obscure series issued in packages of "Reedy's World Fair Gum" in 1933. The set title comes from the "Century of Progress" line printed on many (but not all) of the cards. The original pictures used to create the cards were black and white, but Reedy added a sepia tint which makes the cards look "bronzed." The backs are blank and there are no numbers. The main design and print of the wrapper are red on yellow. The reference number is R29.

ITEM	EX	AVE
Card	15.00	3.50
Set	NA	NA
Wrapper	250.00	—

Chicago - Interior View Replica of Fort Dearborn - A Century of Progress International Exposition - 1933

1833 - Chicago - A Century of Progress - 1933

Electrical Building - Chicago World's Fair - 1933

Electrical Building - "A Century of Progress" - Chicago - 1933 - World's Fair

Entrance - Electrical Building - Century of Progress - Chicago

John G. Shedd Aquarium

Replica of Fort Dearborn, 1933 Century of Progress Exposition, Chicago

Travel and Transport Building - Century of Progress - Chicago

Travel and Transportation Building - Chicago World's Fair

CHARLIE McCARTHY ADVENTURES (5)   5" X 8"

Produced by E. Rosen in 1938, this previously unknown set was discovered recently by Roxanne Toser. The "adventures" are related in five-frame comic book style on the interior side of the magnificent cover. The sixth frame contains a list of all five adventures in the set. The company name and copyright date are printed below each story. Looking at the cover illustration, you will note that the number and story title are printed on both the front of the cover and the spine. The back page of this large cardboard folder (Rosen called it a "book") was slotted to hold six lollipops. The prices given below are for "books" with front (artwork and story) and rear (lollipop holder) pages intact. No reference number has been assigned.

ITEM	EX	AVE
Book	100.00	30.00
Set	600.00	175.00

FRONT COVER

INSIDE FRONT COVER

THE GARBAGE PATCH KID — thrill to the details of the court-room battle between GPK & the Cabbage Patch Kids. Monograph includes reproductions of GPK artist John Pound's three original GPK sketches. Only $6.00 postpaid.

CHRIS BENJAMIN
9 Davis Street, St. Augustine, FL 32095

44

CHICAGO WORLD'S FAIR (32)   2 1/4" X 2 15/16"

The 32 cards of this series, produced in 1933 by Blatz Gum, actually resemble miniature chrome postcards more than trading cards. In fact, not only were they issued in gum packs by Blatz, but also in 16-card mailable cardboard packages under the title "Miniature Souvenir Views!" The latter were probably sold at newsstands and variety stores.

The gum issue is easy to recognize; the card number and title, series name, text, and producer are all printed on the back. In contrast, the "souvenir view" cards are blank-backed. In terms of value, the gum issue (The reference number is R30-1) is much harder to find than the non-gum set (The reference number is R30-2).

ITEM	EX	AVE
Cards		
Printed		
back	8.00	2.00
Blank back	2.00	.50
Sets		
Printed		
back	300.00	75.00
Blank back	75.00	18.50
Wrapper	200.00	––
Boxes		
Series 1	10.00	3.00
Series 2	10.00	3.00

1 Hall of Science
2 Clarence Buckingham Memorial Fountain, Grant Park, Chicago
3 Intra-mural Bus
4 Dairy Building
5 Agricultural Building
6 Oriental Village at the Chicago World's Fair
7 Interior of the Golden Pavilion of Jehol
8 Admiral Byrd's Polar Ship "The City of New York"
9 Electrical Group at Night
10 Hall of Science
11 Sky Ride
12 "Enchanted Island"
13 Hall of States and Federal Building, Chicago
14 Hall of Science
15 Aeroplane View of Fair Grounds
16 Court of States Building
17 Administration Building
18 Travel and Transport Building
19 The Administration Building
20 Hall of Science
21 The Interior Court of the Hall Of Science by Night
22 Golden Temple of Jehol
23 Golden Temple of Jehol
24 Three-Fluted Towers Around Dome of Federal Building
25 Hall of Science
26 Travel Building
27 The Lincoln Group
28 Panoramic View of the Century of Progress World's Fair, 1933
29 Fort Dearborn
30 Electrical Group
31 Administration Building
32 General Exhibits Group

COLLEGE PENNANTS (14)(14)   TWO SIZES

College Pennants — "a series of 14" — was apparently the first and last trading card set distributed by the Phoebe Phelps Caramel Co. (Boston). There are two sizes of cards: 2 3/8" X 2 15/16" and 1 3/8" X 2 15/16" (larger size illustrated). On the obverse of the larger card, the company name appears in a red panel at top

while the product name is printed in a yellow panel at bottom. The back is vertically-aligned and carries a short text and advertising printed in blue ink. The recently-discovered wrapper probably belongs to the larger variety of card. The reference number is R31-1.

The smaller version of College Pennants measures one inch less in height than the large size card, and it is far more difficult to find. The American Card Catalog states that the small-card set also contains 14 subjects, but it is not known if they are the same colleges represented in the large-card set. The reference number is R31-2.

College Pennants

ITEM	EX	AVE
Cards		
Large	10.00	3.00
Small	15.00	5.00
Sets		
Large	175.00	50.00
Small	260.00	80.00
Wrapper	250.00	––

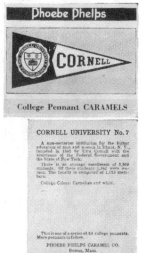

COMBAT/U.S.A. COMBAT UNITS (5)(5) 2 3/8" X 2 5/8"

This series of ten cards was listed descriptively in all previous catalogs as "War Scenes," since the cards do not have any series title printed on them and no packaging for them had ever been found. Collector Ken Bush changed all that by discovering a partial box containing two intact cards on the side panels, with titles printed overhead. Clearly, the series is divided into five-card subsets emphasizing the human and mechanical aspects of warfare. The cards have multi-colored artwork, are not numbered, and have rouletted edges on at least three sides. The text on back is printed in black ink on gray stock, and the manufacturer (Lion Specialty) and the date of issue (1942) are listed at bottom. The reference number is R166.

ITEM	EX	AVE
Card	10.00	2.50
Set	135.00	30.00
Box	75.00	25.00

46

MACHINE GUNNERS

Some of our Infantrymen command the barking muzzles of fast-firing, straight-shooting machine guns. Others are equipped with the newest, most modern long-range, rapid-fire weapons, automatic rifles, mortars, pistols, grenades, light and heavy anti-tank guns.

Lion Specialty Co. Chicago, Ill.

Copyright 1942 G.U.M

COMBAT
Air-borne Infantry
Garand Rifleman
Machine Gunners
Marines in India
Parachute Troops

U.S.A. COMBAT UNITS
Army Bomber
Jeep
Light Tank
Pursuit Planes
Tank Buster

COMIC FACES (30) | 2 13/16" X 3 5/8"

Glenn Confections of Buffalo, NY designed the Comic Faces set first to be amusing toys more than trading cards, which explains why few are found today. The secondary

No. 9
ONE OF 30 COMIC FACES
(Finger Funnies)
To have some real fun, place the card in the palm of your hand, top of picture toward your wrist, insert your finger through the center opening and it will surprise you how much it looks like a real nose.

This is one of 30 comical faces. Collect them till you get the complete set. The chewing gum you get with the card is as pure and wholesome as any you can buy.
GLENN CONFECTIONS, INC.
Buffalo, N. Y.
Copyright 1939 Printed in U.S.A.

title of the series, stated in parentheses on the back of every card, is "Finger Funnies." Each color drawing on front had a hole in the center to make a finger puppet. The cards are numbered (30 in set) but are not captioned. The reverse print is blue ink on tan stock, and the cards were issued in 1939. No wrapper or other type of packaging has been seen. The reference number is R38.

ITEM	EX	AVE
Card	25.00	7.50
Set	950.00	220.00

COMIC GUM (?)(?) | 2 3/8" X 3 15/16"

This interesting two-part set, often overlooked by mainstream collectors, dates from 1934 and may well be the first Gum, Inc. collectible ever issued. In the American Card Catalog, the components of Comic Gum — box cards and individual gum wrappers — were listed separately (see R32 and R33). This was a distinction made not only on the basis of form, but also because of a slight variation in the presentation of otherwise identical subject matter.

We have illustrated a fascinating photo, obtained from the estate of Woody Gelman, that shows a complete 150-count box of Comic Gum. The box is posed on one-inch engineering graph paper, allowing us to measure the "cards" and determine that they are identical in size to a single panel of an untwisted gum wrapper: 2 3/8" X 3 15/16". To date, this photo is the only proof that Comic Gum cards existed, because there are none in the Burdick Collection and no present-day collectors have reported finding any.

Whether or not the riddle-style joke panels printed on the box actually qualify as cards is a subjective matter. We do know that they vary from the gum wrappers in that the "answer" or "punch line" to the riddle is not given. It was replaced by the statement "Answer on Gum Wrapper." Clearly, the box illustrations were designed to prompt gum sales. Burdick's catalog listing, which cites 18 known card captions, indicates that some early card collectors couldn't resist cutting "cards" from the boxes. However, we cannot give a market value for box cards because none have resurfaced.

Comic Gum wrappers, on the other hand, have survived into modern times in limited numbers (despite the premium offer illustrated below). Each wrapper panel has at least one complete riddle and parts of one or two others. The sketches are done in red, blue and yellow, and the "set-up" and "punch lines" are printed in black ink on uncolored parts of the wax wrapper. The

riddles are a dialogue between two "pickaninnies" named "Exit" and "Aspirina." The length of the wrapper series is unknown; our partial checklist is done alphabetically by set-up lines. NOTE: all known wrappers have creases from being twisted around gum so the "excellent" grade does not apply.

Checklist Key: (C) = box card; (W) = wrapper; (C/W) = both.

ITEM	EX	AVE
Wrapper	NA	35.00

47

Aspirina, What Can Yo' Take All De Letters From and It Remains the Same? (C)
Aspirina, What Kind of Vegetables Does Yo' Uncle Tom Walk On? (C)
Aspirina, What's a Cat Got Dat No Other Animal Has? (C)
Aspirina, When Can Yo' Carry Water in a Sieve? (C/W)
Aspirina, When is a Fish Like a Bird? (W)
Aspirina, Why is a Farmer Scairt to Plant Peas Durin' War? (C)
Aspirina, Why is a Thief Called a Jail Bird? (C/W)
Cow, Does Yo' Know What Kind of Dog Lives in De Dog Star? (W)
Exit, A Duck — A Frog and a Skunk Went to De Circus — Dey Needed Money — Who Got In? (C)
Exit, How Many Bugs Make a Landlord? (C)
Exit, If Yo' Dawg Lost His Tail Where Would Yo' Get Him Another? (C)
Exit, What Canal is in Yo' Ear? (C)

Exit, What Can Go Up a Chimney Down But Can't Go Down the Chimney Up? (W)
Exit, What Happened When De Train Ran Over De Peanut? (C)
Exit, What's De Difference Between a Cat and a Match? (C)
Exit, Why Does Yo' Laugh Up Yo' Sleave? (C)
Frum What Word of Six Letters Can Yo' Take One and Have Twelve Left? (C/W)
If a Goat Swallered a Rabbit, What Would Happen, Aspirina? (C)
What Five Letter Word Can Yo' Take Away Two Letters And One Remains? (W)
What Has Eyes An' Can't See? (W)
What One Letter in De Alphabet Will Spell "Potatos"? (C/W)
What State is Round at Both Ends An' High in De Middle? (W)
When De Clock Strikes 13, What Time is It, Aspirina? (C)
Why is De Number 9 Like a Peacock, Aspirina? (C/W)

RETAIL STORE DISPLAY SIGN

COMIC PICTURES (10)

2 1/2" X 3"

PARTIAL CHECKLIST

2 Laws A. Massie
3 M.I. Allhere
4 I. Smella Ratt

Holloway's Comic Pictures series is one of four of that company's trading card issues which were virtually unknown until now. The card illustrated came from a strip and is printed on thin cardboard. The satirical nature of the set is evidenced by the names on our partial checklist. Unlike the first Holloway set revised in this book — Adventure Pictures — no thick cardboard Comic Pictures have been found. There are ten numbered, multi-colored, artwork cards in the set. The ence number is R35.

ITEM	EX	AVE
Card	15.00	5.00
Set	200.00	60.00

COMMANDO–RANGER (70)

2 1/2" X 2 3/4"

Commando-Ranger was the first part of a 210-card patriotic issue by W.H. Brady; the second part, Allies in Action, has already been reviewed in our alphabetical listing. Although the producer probably intended the sets to be regarded as a single series, collectors have come to consider them as separate entities because of the differences in names and numbering prefixes.

The "Commando-Ranger "pictograms" use the same red and

blue "V" side panels and rough color artwork as Allies in Action. The cards numbers, CR-1 to CR-70, are located on the back along with the text. Gray stock backs with either green or blue print are commonly found; cards with black print on off-white stock are less common. Every card has at least one rouletted edge, indicating that they were issued in strips (add 25% premium for intact strips). The reference number is R34.

ITEM	EX	AVE
Card	5.00	1.50
Set	425.00	125.00

CR-1	Landing at Dieppe	CR-18	Tank-Flanked Jeeps Forge Forward	CR-37	Carnage and Havoc in the Harbor
CR-2	Tank—Plane Teamwork				
CR-3	Blasting Rail Lines	CR-19	Blasting Ports and Harbors	CR-38	Paratroops Support Ground Troops
CR-4	Terror Stalks thru Tropics	CR-20	Axis Tank in Tank Trap		
CR-5	Air Umbrella Over Channel	CR-21	Building Timber-Base Tank Trap	CR-39	Carrier Based Plane Support
CR-6	Anti-Tank Gun Gets Enemy Tank	CR-22	Detecting Enemy Soft Spots	CR-40	Blue Bursts from Battleships
CR-7	Snow Suited Snipers	CR-23	Courageous Lieut. Col. Raft	CR-41	Fierce Fire from Fox-Holes
CR-8	Face Black-out Before Raid	CR-24	Capturing Enemy General	CR-42	Flame Throwers Searing Enemy
CR-9	Strangling Enemy Sentry	CR-25	The Spill of Death		
CR-10	Tank Leaves Landing Barge	CR-26	Daring Daylight Dogfighter	CR-43	Mile-a-Minute Mosquito Boat
CR-11	Accurate Anti-Aircraft Duel	CR-27	Silent Secret Signals	CR-44	Overpowering Jap Sub Crew
CR-12	Walkie-Talkie Communications	CR-28	Support Under, On and Above	CR-45	Heavy Tank Support
CR-13	Blasting Bridge to Bits	CR-29	Tank-Destroyer Scores Direct Hit	CR-46	AA Guns Guard Invasion Fleet
CR-14	Tank and Cycle-Mounted Units	CR-30	Camouflaged Advance	CR-47	Double Quick Cable Crossing
CR-15	Capturing Enemy Defender	CR-31	Armored-Car Annihilates Nazis	CR-48	Helpless Hitlerite in Head-Hold
CR-16	Laying Down Smoke Screen	CR-32	Marksman Picks Off Sniper	CR-49	Cycle Corp Courier Command
CR-17	Dropping Down on Rifleman	CR-33	AA Gunners Bagging Bombers	CR-50	Hand Grenade Explosions
		CR-34	Amphibian Invasion Tank	CR-51	Paratrooper Plunges thru Space
		CR-35	Hand-to-Hand Combat		
		CR-36	Gas-Coats Guard Grenadiers		

CR-52	We Wield Weapons Well
CR-53	Vital Dive Bomber Support
CR-54	Camouflaged Gun Emplacement
CR-55	Machine Gunning Enemy
CR-56	Torpedo Plane Plasters Port
CR-57	Dive Bombing Nazi Navy
CR-58	Tin-Boat Slips Torpedo
CR-59	Mobile Cannon Dealing Death
CR-60	Invasion Barge Fleet
CR-61	Hitler the Hater
CR-62	Rope Bridge Over Stream
CR-63	Beating-Up Axis Bullies
CR-64	Cargoliner Rendezvous
CR-65	Bitter Bayonet Struggle
CR-66	Turret-Tank Shielding Sappers
CR-67	Greenhouse—Gun Peppers Pursuers
CR-68	Cutting Hidden Barb-Wire
CR-69	Invaders Board Troop Transport
CR-70	Dog Heroes in Action

COPS AND ROBBERS (35)   2 3/8" X 2 15/16"

Thirty-five characters are pictured in Fleer's Cops and Robbers series: of this total, 30 are robbers and five are cops. Each picture can be found in five different tints: brown, green, orange, purple, and red. The hoodlums and detectives are all fictional, as the witty names and satirical desciptions (on back) would suggest.

The cards were apparently issued without a wrapper. Three sticks of Dubble Bubble gum accompanied each card, packaged in small paper sleeves glued to the back of the 1 9/16" X 2 3/8" "evidence tab" attached to every card. These evidence tabs could be redeemed via the mail for a Fleer-issued detective commission and badge.

Almost all of the Cops and Robbers cards which have survived are missing evidence tabs, and cards with tabs intact command a premium price. Most collectors do not try to assemble their sets in a particular color because the combination of the various colors is more pleasing to the eye. The reference number is R36.

ITEM	EX	AVE
Cards		
Without tab	10.00	2.50
With tab	40.00	10.00
With tab & gum sleeves	50.00	15.00
Sets		
Without tabs	425.00	100.00
With tabs	1750.00	425.00
All one color	add 25%	add 15%

1 Ranger Colt
2 Rough House Hogan
3 Pinto Pete
4 Slow Motion Smith
5 Bunco Bertie
6 Shifty Sam
7 Benny Gray
8 Chief Inspector Kennedy
9 Bruiser Bill
10 Terry the Terror
11 Rudolph Razzberry
12 Dapper Dan Dugan
13 Cuthbert Dimwit
14 Bertie Bohunk
15 Constable Corntassel
16 Hijack Herbie
17 Stove Pipe Steve
18 Rube Riley
19 Beau-zo
20 HiHat Hector
21 Schemer Snitch
22 Marshal Dangerfield
23 Dixie Dan
24 Gaston the Gorilla
25 Dead Eye Dick
26 Nosey Nertz
27 Nick the Necker
28 Big Shot Connolley
29 Inspector Smart
30 Black Hand Tony
31 Admiral Bilgewater
32 Mustapha Bath
33 Hong Kong Wow
34 Wolf Masterson
35 Ivan Awfulbush

CRIME DID NOT PAY (?)

2 1/2" SQUARE

This unusual set of black and white portraits of gansters is easily dated to mid-1934 by the events cited in several of the biographical sketches and

the "REWARD For the Capture of Dillinger" line printed on the back of each card. The center pictures are actual photos of hoodlums and are

surrounded by partial artwork faces of other "criminal types." When placed together correctly, these cards make a striking visual display. They are not numbered and the length of the set and the company which issued them are unknown. The wrapper, which is specifically mentioned on the back of each card, has never been seen. The reference number is R37.

ITEM	EX	AVE
Card	100.00	30.00

Clyde Barrow
Tommy Carroll
Raymond Hamilton
Alvin Karpis

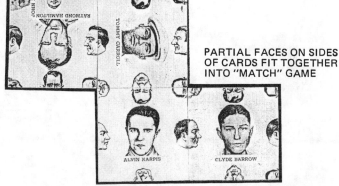

PARTIAL FACES ON SIDES OF CARDS FIT TOGETHER INTO "MATCH" GAME

DARBY'S PICTURE PUZZLES (50)

1 1/2" X 2 1/2"

These small puzzle cards were distributed by the Darby Company of Baltimore in packages of "Buyone Candy." The

drawings are black and white with either red or green accents (one color per card). The card number is printed on

the front only. Anyone solving all the riddles depicted on the cards could send the set to the factory and receive a free box of candy (cards were returned). Only 19 of the 50 titles are known, but despite its apparent scarcity, the set is not widely collected. The reference number is R181.

ITEM	EX	AVE
Card	10.00	3.00
Set	600.00	185.00

DARE DEVILS (24)

2 3/8" X 2 7/8"

The National Chicle Company copyrighted the artwork and stories of the Dare Devils set in 1933, but the 24-card series was not marketed until a few years later. According to the wrapper, the cards tell of "Death Defying Deeds in the Air," "Daring Deeds of Firemen and Policemen," "Famous Gangsters on the Spot," "Official G-Men Cap-

tures," "Wild West Dare Devils," and "Do-Or-Die Heroes." The artwork contains brilliant colors and sharp details, with the set title and the card caption appearing at the bottom below the picture. The cards are numbered both front and back, and the reverses have "official and true" stories. The center

design of the wrapper is green with orange print and an orange "Official Stories" seal. The reference number is R39.

ITEM	EX	AVE
Card		
1-12	15.00	4.00
13-24	12.00	3.00
Set	400.00	100.00
Wrapper	250.00	—

Dare Devils

ORIGINAL ARTWORK FOR DARE DEVILS CARD No. 20

DEFENDING AMERICA (48) 2 3/8" X 2 11/16"

One of the final sets issued before World War II, "Defending America" was produced by the W.S.Corporation of New York City. Since the series was printed in strips, each card has "nubs" on the horizontal edges. The card numbers run from 201 to 248, and the artwork is simple and rendered in basic tones of red, blue, brown, green and yellow. The text backs are printed in black ink on gray stock. The reference number is R40. NOTE: cards in strips command a 50% premium over the prices listed below.

ITEM	EX	AVE
Card	3.50	1.00
Set	200.00	50.00

201 Big Battle Ship Guns	213 Torpedoes in Tubes	225 "Dog Fight" Training	237 Anti-Aircraft Night Firing
202 Torpedo Plane	214 "Mosquito" Boat	226 Parachute Troops	238 Machine Gun
203 Patrol Bombers	215 U.S.S. Mississippi	227 Modern Parachute Release	239 Railroad Gun
204 Catapult Planes	216 "Cruiser" Battle Manoeuvres	228 Navy Dive Bomber	240 Anti-Aircraft Traces Fire
205 U.S. Navy Submarine	217 Medium Tank	229 Navy Dirigible	241 Army Truck Rides Cable
206 Wheeling into Position	218 Truck Convoy	230 Long Range Bomber	242 Erecting New "Tank" Bridge
207 Convoy Protection	219 Scout Car	231 Observation Squadron	243 Army Builds Bridge
208 Fire Control Station	220 Armored Gun Car	232 Loading Torpedo	244 Repelling "Gas" Attack
209 Destroyer	221 "Treat 'em Rough" Tank	233 Twelve Inch Gun	245 "Chemical" Warfare
210 Periscope Sight	222 Tank Combat Practice	234 Anti-Aircraft Training	246 Aerial Photographer
211 Gun Fire	223 Track Laying "Tank"	235 Coast Defense Gun	247 Searchlight "Spots" Planes
212 Scouting Patrol	224 Heavy Tank	236 Mobile Anti-Aircraft	248 Electric Ear "Hears" Planes

DICK TRACY (144) 2 3/8" X 2 7/8"

The Dick Tracy set of 144 color "picture story" cards was issued by the Walter Johnson Candy Co. (Chicago) in 1 cent packages of "Dick Tracy Caramels." The series is a running account of the adventures of Chester Gould's famous detective as he battles various criminals and villains. Each card has a captioned picture on front and an extensive story episode on back. Cards 1-96 bear a "series of 96" statement while cards 97-144 proclaim a "series of 144." The wrapper is a red and blue design centered on clear wax paper. In the early 1980's, a horde of cards numbered 121-144 surfaced in the marketplace, raising questions about their authenticity, and continued doubts keep prices low for cards of this sequence. The reference number is R41.

ITEM	EX	AVE
Card		
1-96	10.00	3.00
97-120	15.00	4.00
121-144	4.00	1.00
Set	1700.00	400.00
Wrapper	200.00	—

1 Tracy Spots Ribs Mocco		
2 Big Boy Awaits Tracy		
3 Texie Takes Command		
4 Big Boy Packs Up		
5 Tracy Overhears a Conversation		
6 Texie on the Spot		
7 Tracy Questions the Gardner		
8 Pat Shadows a Suspect		
9 Tracy Aboard the Alonia		
10 Big Boy Eliminates Becky		
11 Big Boy Caught in the Act	32 The Doors Were Locked	53 Steve Gets Good News
12 Tracy Hands Out a Beating	33 Junior Runs into Tracy	54 Junior Disappears
13 Mucelli and His Gang	34 The Gang Gets Nervous	55 A Cold Trap
14 Junior Stumbles on a Clue	35 Tracy Takes a Fall	56 Stowaways Caught
15 Junior Refuses to Talk	36 Through a Secret Tunnel	57 A Cold Brakeman
16 Junior Is Chloroformed	37 He Raised His Gun to Fire	58 Dick Tracy's Surprise
17 Preparing for Torture	38 Buggs Gets Instructions	59 An Important Post Card
18 Tracy Covers Mucelli	39 Tracy Turns Cab Driver	60 Watching the Mail
19 Gangland Bullets Get Tracy	40 Buggs Hailed the Cab	61 Under the Wheels
20 Suspected of Shooting Tracy	41 A Sudden Departure	62 Steve Commits Assault
21 Junior Goes to Jail	42 Still Hanging On	63 The Intercepted Message
22 Dick Tracy Comes Back	43 A Welcome Surprise	64 Tracy in the Air
23 To Prove Junior's Innocence	44 Buggs Had Them Covered	65 The Dead Mailman
24 Tracy Suddenly Vanishes	45 The Reflection in the Mirror	66 Tracy on the Trail
25 Mucelli Is Fooled	46 The Trapdoor in the Floor	67 A Queer Hiding Place
26 Junior Still in Jail	47 The Lie Detectograph	68 Off the Scent
27 Junior Dashed to Safety	48 The Hero of the Hour	69 Steve Meets a Friend
28 Junior Goes Hungry	49 Steve and Old Hank Steele	70 The Stolen Hand Car
29 A Surprise Awakening	50 Hank Steele's Story	71 The Section Hands' Story
30 Two Men and a Woman	51 Steve Gets Good News	72 Trapped on the Trestle
31 Junior Held His Breath	52 Tracy Leaves Town	73 The High Dive

74 A Miraculous Escape	93 Della an Innocent Victim	112 Steve's Treachery	131 Safe from the Avengers
75 Tracy Takes a Fall	94 A Murderous Death Weapon	113 Two Criminal Minds	132 Stooge and Steve
76 Tracy Is Rescued	95 Face to Face with Steve	114 Stooge Reveals His Plot	Disappointed
77 Tracy Lies in Wait	96 Over the Cliff	115 Criminals Under Cover	133 The Intruders Are Discovered
78 A Highway Hold-Up	97 In the Killer's Cell	116 A Dark, Desperate Deed	134 Hank Steele's Caretaker
79 A Gun Battle	98 Steve Hires a Crafty Lawyer	117 A Bolt for Freedom	Surprised
80 The Flaming Wreck	99 Tracy Prepares for Trial	118 The Explosion	135 Steve and Stooge Resort to
81 Still on the Trail	100 The State Versus Steve	119 Convicts at Large	Torture
82 A Key to the Mystery	101 The Plea for the Defense	120 Dick Tracy Again on the Trail	136 A Woman Takes a Hand
83 Steve Reveals His Plans	102 Sentenced for Life	121 Hunted by the Law	137 The Tables are Turned
84 Tracy Demands Speed	103 At the Penitentiary	122 The Convicts Hit the Hay	138 Steve Makes a Desperate Move
85 Good News for Hank Steele	104 Convict No. 2017	123 Chased into the Open	139 Steve Uses a Weighty
86 Junior and Steve Arrive	105 "Take That," Snarled Steve	124 Steve and Stooge at Bay	Argument
87 An Amazing Discovery	106 Birds of a Feather	125 Stooge Viller Takes a Chance	140 Stooge Discloses His Plan
88 Bad News for Steve	107 Steve in a Rage	126 Stooge Offers Farm Relief	141 Dick Tracy Makes a
89 Della Gets Instructions	108 Stooge Viller's Trickery	127 Preparing for a Long Trip	Suggestion
90 A Bold Front	109 A Letter from Tracy	128 The Convicts Plot Revenge	142 Steve Gets Ladylike
91 Quick on the Draw	110 Junior Dreams of Dick Tracy	129 Junior Thinks of Tracy	143 On the High Seas
92 The Mysterious Shot	111 Steve Lays His Plans	130 A Mysterious Visitor	144 Junior Foresees Grave Danger

DICK TRACY (24)

PARTIAL CHECKLIST

1 Tracy and the Health Farm
2 Tracy and the Auto Thieves
3 Tracy Against the Maroon Mask Leader
4
5
6
7 Tracy Against Steve and Stooge
8
9 Tracy Saves Junior From the Kidnappers
10 Tracy Solves the Mystery Death
11 Tracy Avenges the Bellhop
12
13 Tracy Traps Lips Manton
14 Tracy Gets a Valet
15
16 Tracy Tricks a Trickster
17 Junior Tracy's Mother and Larceny Lu
18 Tracy and the Perfume Thieves
19
20 Tracy Finds Junior's Mother
21 Pat Helps Catch Larceny Lu
22 Tracy in the Country
23 Dick Tracy and Boyle
24

2" X 3 1/8"

The cards of this Dick Tracy series were cut directly from the backs of candy boxes manufactured by the Novel Package Corporation (Brooklyn, NY). Although the card backs advertise a "series of 48," no card above No. 23 has been reported to date, and it is believed that the series was curtailed at 24 titles. The colorful "Dick Tracy Detective" front box panel has a coupon on the reverse which advertises mail-in offers for four different Dick Tracy items. The date of issue is unknown. The reference number is R42.

ITEM	EX	AVE
Card	15.00	5.00
Coupon/		
Front	20.00	7.50
Set (24)	475.00	150.00
Complete box	85.00	30.00

DON'T LET IT HAPPEN OVER HERE (24)

The International Chewing Gum Company of Cambridge, Mass., produced the "Don't Let It Happen Over Here" series in 1938. Sensationalism was the keynote of this set. Advertising on the wrapper states that "The card packed with this piece of gum is one of a large series showing MURDER, DEATH and DESTRUCTION taking place in the world today. BE GLAD YOU LIVE IN THE GOOD

2 1/2" X 3 1/8"

OLD U.S.A." The artwork and text on the cards were "pictures of real happenings as reported in the press and were drawn for us by artists who are ex-soldiers." While the style of Don't Let It Happen Over Here cards is attractive to many modern collectors, it appears to have been "stomped" in the 1938 marketplace by Gum, Inc.'s "Horrors of War" series. The reference number is R44.

ITEM	EX	AVE
Card	40.00	10.00
Set	1300.00	325.00
Wrapper	500.00	325.00

1 Communists Shot Like Beasts
2 Bombs Rain from Air—400
   Killed
3 Death Rides in the Skies
4 Terror Stalks Streets of Paris
5 World War Averted
6 Bandits Hung on Telegraph Poles
7 Prefers Death to Disgrace
8 Palestine—An Armed Camp
9 Ruler of the Sea Defied
10 21 Shot at Sunrise
11 Poison Gas the Unseen Killer
12 Brutal Nazi Lash
13 One Million Fighting Men
14 Assassins Shoot at Midnight
15 Killing Has Become Fun!
16 Whipped until Dead
17 Horror Camps in Naziland
18 750 Killed—1350 Wounded
19 The Four Hundred Million Dollar
   Grab
20 What Country Next?
21 A Living Death
22 War against Women and Children
23 Uncle Sam's Flying Fortress
24 They Are Gone Forever

DOPEY'S DOMINOES (7)   15/16" X 11 1/4"

"Dopey Makes Big Bubbles with Dopey Bubble Gum. There's not a bit of trouble, And Gee, It's Lots of Fun." The "Dopey" wrapper which contains this ditty (as well as another) is far more interesting than the card set, which is merely seven blank-backed, numbered cards containing four dominoes each. The colorful wrapper, on the other hand, contains mail-in premium offers for a magazine, a lariat, invisible ink and G-Man paper, and a live turtle with a Snow White or dwarf decal on the shell!

Dopey Bubble Gum was manufactured by the Yankee Doodle Gum. Co. of Chicago. The reference number is R45.

ITEM	EX	AVE
Card	25.00	8.00
Set	225.00	75.00
Wrapper	75.00	——

DOUGHBOYS, MINUTE MEN,   2 9/16" X 3 3/16"
NURSES & TROOPERS (?)

The original catalog listing for this unique series of American Mint Corporation candy containers — formerly only "Doughboys" — has now been expanded to include three more types: "Minute Men," "Nurses," and "Troopers." The "Doughboys" are far more plentiful than any other variety — 20 titles appear in our checklist below — and most are found with the wrapper (or label) still intact on the cardboard cylinder. (The "Doughboy" wrappers in the Burdick museum collection have been removed and flattened.) Six countries have been confirmed so far for "Minute Men," and of these, "China" is the identical soldier which appears in the "Doughboy" series as "Japan." Only one title has been seen to date for "Nurse" ("Yanks") two for "Troopers" ("Russia" &

Doughboys, Minute Men,
Nurses & Troopers

"Ethiopia"). The reference number is R43. NOTE: for wrappers removed from cylinders, deduct 35% of the value listed below.

ITEM	EX	AVE
Cylinders		
"Dough-boy"	100.00	30.00
"Minute Men"	125.00	40.00
"Nurse"	150.00	45.00
"Trooper"	150.00	45.00

FLATTENED DOUGHBOY LABEL AFTER REMOVAL FROM CYLINDER

DOUGHBOYS	MINUTE MEN
Afghanistan	China
Arabia	England
Austria	Ethiopia
England	Scotland
Ethiopia	Turkey
France	United States
French Foreign Legion	
Greece	TROOPERS
India	
Italy	Ethiopia
Japan	Russia
Poland	
Russia	NURSES
Scotland	
Spain	Yanks
Sweeden	
Switzerland	
Turkey	
United States	

MAIL US 20 OF THESE
DOUGHBOY COUPONS
and we will send you FREE one of
these toys: ☐ MOUTH-ORGAN
☐ POP-GUN ☐ GLOBE-BANK
AMERICAN MINT CORP.
114 East 13th St., New York, N.Y,

MAIL PREMIUM COUPON PACKED INSIDE DOUGHBOY CONTAINER

DO YOU KNOW (44K)

DO
YOU KNOW
The LEMUR has a howl like a dog
and appears only at night; for
this reaso it is called
the ghost.

1 3/8" DIAMETER

"Do You Know" is a series of discs brought to light by Paul Koch. Although their origin is unknown, and the discs do not bear any identifying marks, they have been included here since they share a similar format with the Leader Discs and Sealcraft issues covered elsewhere in this volume. Each disc has an uncaptioned artwork picture on the front and a simple identification of the subject on the back. The basic colors are red, yellow, blue and green. No reference number has been assigned. Forty-five titles have been confirmed to date.

ITEM	EX	AVE
Disc	1.50	.50

Alpaca	Hippopotamus	Raccoon
Ant Eater	Jackal	Reindeers
Arctic Fox	Kangaroo	Rhinoceros
Badger	Lemur	Rocky Mountain Goat
Barbery Ape	Leopard	Seal
Bison	Llama	Skunk
Camel	Lynx	Snow Leopard
Cheetah	Moose	Squirrels
Coyote	Musk Ox	Tapir
Elephant	Ocelot	Wart Hog
Fat Tailed Sheep	Opposums	Weasel
Fox	Orang-outan	Wolf
Giraffe	Porcupine	Wolverine
Gorilla	Prong Horn Antelope	Zebra
Grizzly Bear	Puma	

FIGHTING PLANES (24)   2 1/2" X 3"

Coast Patrol Plane

One of the more renowned sets from Shelby Gum (Shelby, OH) is this series of 24 warplanes issued in packages of "Fighting Plane Chewing Gum." The soft color artwork is basically shades of blue with red and yellow accents. Card numbers are located within a wing design on back, with a short text and advertising below. The cardboard stock is thinner than most 1930's issues and captions are printed in the picture area below each aircraft. Collectors rate the exciting wrapper, which is dark blue with red and yellow highlights, a very difficult catch. The reference number if R47.

ITEM	EX	AVE
Card	8.00	2.00
Set	225.00	55.00
Wrapper	350.00	––

1	Coast Patrol Plane	9	Bell P-39 Airacobra
2	Grumman F4F-3	10	Curtiss P-40
3	Douglas TBD-1	11	North American BT-9
4	Vultee V-12A	12	Douglas SBD-3
5	Seversky P-35	13	Consolidated PB2Y
6	Curtiss X5B2C-1	14	Spartan FBW-1 Zeuss
7	Bell's Airabonita	15	Grumman XF4F-1
8	Lockheed P-38	16	Curtiss Hawk 75

17	Bell YSM-1
18	Grumman F2F-1
19	Yought Sikorsky OS2U-1
20	Martin PBM-1
21	Curtiss SBC-4
22	Consolidated PBY-3
23	Douglas 8A-5
24	Curtiss P-36

FILM FUNNIES (24)(24)   2 7/16" X 3 1/8"

It appears that Gum, Inc. may have anticipated trouble when it marketed the 24-card set entitled "Film Funnies," perhaps over the issues of copyright or royalties. Neither the cards nor the wrapper bear any information about the manufacturer except for a post office box in Philadelphia. The regular issue of colorful artwork cards features caricatures of unnamed movie stars. On each card, one of the characters asks a question for which five possible answers are provided on the other side. Twenty-four correct answers sent into the company made the sender eligible for a prize. The reference number for this regular series is R48-1.

Several years ago, a second "variation" series was discovered. The obverse artwork of each card is identical to its corresponding number in the "regular" set, but the movie star is named. Text on the card backs was also modified to include each star's name. Opinion about the value of these Film Funnies variation cards is divided because they were probably never issued to the public and the quantity available is conjectural. The reference number is R48-2.

REGULAR ISSUE

VARIATION ISSUE

ITEM	EX	AVE
Card		
Regular	25.00	6.00
Variation	50.00	15.00
Set		
Regular	800.00	175.00
Variation	1600.00	400.00
Wrapper	250.00	––

57

Film Funnies

1. I just swallowed a dime and three pennies—can't you tell?
2. Is it true you're working for the government?
3. Is your nose the biggest thing in pictures? He's doing alright!
4. Hey cowboy! What's going on here?
5. Stop reaching! Haven't you got a tongue?
6. You should count up to one hundred before hitting the other fellow!
7. Quiet, or I'll make you eat every word you say!
8. Bob, will you call me a taxi?
9. What's the matter Joe? Why can't you see?
10. Your majesty, if you eat any more chicken you'll burst!
11. Don't you think sheep are the dumbest animals?
12. What can I do for you my dear?
13. Looks like a trick door Mae!
14. If I buy you a drum you'll disturb me!
15. I'm starved and we have no food!
16. Quiet! You shouldn't say I look like that monkey!
17. Look out! Or you'll get all black!
18. Why are you late?
19. What did Juliet say to Romeo when she met him on the balcony?
20. Didn't I tell you to notice when the soup boiled over?
21. Why are you using two suits?
22. Let's eat up the street!
23. How can I keep fish from smelling?
24. You don't know me do you?

VARIATION ISSUE

CHECKLIST

1. W.C. Fields
2. Oliver Hardy
3. Jimmy Durante
4. Jackie Cooper
5. Chico Marx
6. Jimmy Cagney
7. Polly Moran
8. Bob Woolsey
9. Joe E. Brown
10. Charles Laughton
11. Myrna Loy
12. Greta Garbo
13. Mae West
14. Farina
15. Jack Oakie
16. Edmund Lowe
17. Maurice Chevalier
18. Slim Summerville
19. Frederic March
20. Jimmy Dunn
21. Clark Gable
22. Bing Crosby
23. Eddie Cantor
24. George Arliss

FIREMAN PICTURES (10)   2 1/2" X 3"

Cards of this Holloway series have only been found on three multi-set strips discovered by Paul Koch (each strip had a single card from six different sets). The color artwork is captioned beneath the picture and the cardboard stock is thinner than most traditional 1930's cards. Ten different episodes of "The Story of Andy Blue" make up the set. Low demand has kept the price of this scarce but obscure series at moderate levels. The reference number is R202.

EPISODE NO. 9

The Story of Andy Blue

Andy Blue had performed the most thrilling rescue in the history of the fire department, when he had saved a mother and her child. The whole city acclaimed him and he was honored at a civic reception. His superiors attended and expressed their pride at his performance. The mayor of the city pinned a medal on Andy's chest and it was the proudest day of the young fireman's life. Andy's mother was so happy that she actually cried. Andy Blue was promoted to more important posts and was fast realizing his ambition to be an outstanding figure in the fire-fighting world.

This is one of a series of Fireman pictures packed with Holloway Milk Made Candies.

M. J. HOLLOWAY & CO., CHICAGO, ILL.

Inspecting the Force

ITEM	EX	AVE
Card	15.00	5.00
Set	200.00	60.00

FIRST COLUMN DEFENDERS (24)   2 1/2" X 3 1/8"

In 1940, many Americans were preoccupied with our country's defenses, which, according to Goudey Gum's "First Column Defenders," were pretty darned strong. Each card front contains a multi-color drawing surrounded by red, white and framelines. The back text, which can be found printed in either blue or black ink, is intensely patriotic and often includes quotes from famous American soldiers and writers.

• No. 7 •
OUR FLAG PASSES BY

"The Salute to the Flag is the outward expression of our love for our Country and the respect we have for its ideals and institutions."

"As the Cross is the symbol of the Christian's faith, and the Star of David is the emblem of the Jew's religion, so is the Flag of the United States the badge of the American's political faith. And as the Sign of the Cross is the symbol of religious sacramental, so is the salute to the Flag the American's national sacramental. It is a privilege to pay reverential tribute to such an emblem."

James A. Moss, Colonel, U.S.A., Retired President General, The U.S. Flag Assn.

This card is one of a NEW SERIES!
START YOUR COLLECTION NOW

FIRST COLUMN DEFENDERS

Chewing Gum

THE GOUDEY GUM CO., Boston, Mass., U.S.A.
Makers of OH BOY Gum
Copr. 1940 The Goudey Gum Co.

The wrapper is an example of pre-war hysteria, stating that "The purpose of this Card Series is to kindle a deeper sense of Patriotism by portraying the Ideals and Principles on which our Country is founded. FIRST COLUMN is the OPPOSITE of Fifth Column!!" The reference number for First Column Defenders is R50.

ITEM	EX	AVE
Card	15.00	4.00
Set	500.00	130.00
Wrapper	350.00	—

1 Raising the Flag	9 One Nation Indivisible	17 Changing the Guard
2 Man Without a Country	10 Coast Guard Patrol	18 Coastal Forts Prepare
3 The Call for Courage	11 Fighters in Echelon	19 Anti-Aircraft Defense
4 Our Mechanized Army	12 Future Admirals on Parade	20 Bringing Hospital Aid
5 First Line of Defense	13 Generals in the Making	21 Offshore Scouting Patrol
6 The American Eagle	14 The Light of Liberty	22 Protecting Panama Canal
7 Our Flag Passes By	15 The Eyes of the Fleet	23 Combat Intelligence
8 The Color Guard	16 Soldiers of the Sea	24 Combat Car Move Up

FLAGS (72)

1 5/8" X 2 1/8"

The 72 flags issued by Interstate Gum were printed on the inside of single-stick, chewing gum wrappers. It is not known at this time if the sticks were sold separately or were packaged in a larger wrapper or box. An album to house the flag pictures was available via the mail in exchange for a three-cent stamp. Each flag picture had dotted line borders for cutting to fit the appropriate album space.

An album full of flags could be redeemed for various prizes. The dimensions in the heading refer to a trimmed flag; a complete wrapper measures 2½" X 2¾". The set was first listed in Burdick's 1939 catalog and the current reference number is R49.

ITEM	EX	AVE
Wrapper		
Complete	10.00	3.00
Trimmed	2.00	.50
Set		
Untrimmed	800.00	250.00
Trimmed	160.00	40.00

FLAGS (29/36)

1 1/2" X 2 7/16"

The Wilbur-Suchard Chocolate Company distributed these flag cards in their chocolate products. There are two different series: cards marked series of "29" also appear in the "series of 36". Neither set could be completed without sending in a list of the set titles to the company: the

U.S. card and an album were then sent back. The color flag designs are set upon simple white backgrounds and are captioned underneath. The cards are not numbered and are inexpensive because of plentiful supply and low demand. The set was first listed in Burdick's 1939 catalog and the current reference number is R51. NOTE: the United States flag is genuinely scarce (it is not in the Burdick museum collection) but as part of a low profile series, it does not attract much attention. Set price does not include the U.S. card.

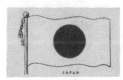

"36" BACK

"29" BACK

ITEM	EX	AVE
Card	1.00	.25
"United States"	100.00	35.00
Set (35)	45.00	10.00

Flags

Argentina
Austria
Belgium
Bolivia
Brazil
Chile
China
Colombia
Costa Rica
Cuba
Czecho-slovakia
Denmark

France
Germany
Great Britain
Greece
Hawaiian Islands
Honduras
Hungary
Ireland
Italy
Japan
Mexico
Netherlands

Nicaragua
Norway
Peru
Porto Rico
Rumania
Russia
Spain
Sweden
Switzerland
Turkey
United States
Venezuela

"UNITES STATES" CARD
COULD ONLY BE OBTAINED
FROM THE COMPANY
VIA THE MAIL

ZOWIE ~ ANOTHER STRIKE! PLENTY OF **WILBUR'S CHOCOLATE** GIVES ME EXTRA ENERGY TO **KEEP WINNIN'!**

WHEN A FELLAH'S FEELIN' TIRED THE BEST THING TO DO IS EAT SOME **SUCHARD SWISS CHOCOLATE** TO STEADY HIS NERVES!

FLAGS OF THE NATIONS (50)   2 5/16" X 2 7/8"

No. 47
United States. Capital—Washington, D. C.
Noted for its great manufacturing industries
such as steel, textile, automobiles and farming
implements. Great producers of wheat, cotton,
corn, rice, sugar and fruits.

FLAGS OF THE NATIONS
This is one of fifty cards in the

FLAG GUM

BALTIMORE CHEWING GUM CO.
Baltimore, Md.

Argentina
Austria
Belgium
Bolivia
Brazil
Bulgaria
Chile
China
Colombia
Costa Rica
Cuba
Czechoslovakia
Denmark
Dominican Republic
Ecuador
Egypt
England
Finland
France
Germany
Greece
Greenland
Holland
Ireland
Italy

Japan
Lithuania
Mexico
Nicaragua (Holding Flag)
Nicaragua (Holding Bowl)
Norway
Panama
Paraguay
Peru
Poland
Portugal
Rumania
Salvador
Scotland
Siam
Spain
Sweden
Switzerland
Turkey
Ukrania
Union of Socialist Soviet Republics
United States
Uruguay
Venezuela
Yugoslavia

Flags of the Nations is a series of 50 cards depicting national types and flags. It was produced by the Baltimore Chewing Gum Company and distributed in "Flag Gum." The cards have distinctive blue borders and are numbered on the back, which also contains a short description of the country. Some cards have also been seen without numbers and the checklist below is arranged alphabetically should the collector encounter some of this variety. There are two poses for Nicaragua. The reference number is R52; no wrapper has been seen to date. NOTE: cards with identical fronts, but without numbers, were also issued by Kenny's Coffee and Weber Baking.

ITEM	EX	AVE
Card	7.00	2.00
Set	400.00	110.00

61

FLEER FUNNIES (368K)   2 3/4" X 4 1/2"

Unlike the Comic Gum wrappers reviewed earlier in this book, the wax paper "Fleer Funnies" comic strips do not appear to have been twist-wrapped around gum. Instead, the creases indicate that they were folded, perhaps inside a small outer wrapper. There are two distinct series. The first 130 numbered, monocolor wrappers portray stick characters; on these, the "fortune" appears above the comic strip and the "fact" is printed below. Funnies numbered 131 and above are multi-colored and feature the antics of Pudge, Bud, Tim, and Pep (the dog). All multi-color comics have both the fact and fortune at bottom. The Fleer Funnies series appears to date from the early or mid-1930's, and the reference number is R53. The highest numbered comic seen to date is No. 368.

ITEM	EX	AVE
Comics		
1-130	6.00	3.00
131 & up	10.00	5.00
Box	250.00	85.00

ENLARGEMENT OF PROMOTIONAL SHEET GLUED TO BOX

THE CARD COLLECTORS BULLETIN....
.... SERVING THE HOBBY SINCE 1938.

Fleer Funnies

ILLUSTRATED: THREE DIFFERENT
VIEWS OF A "FLEER FUNNIES"
DISPLAY BOX

FLEER MASKS (?)

4 5/8" X 5 3/8"

How this series of multi-color paper masks remained unknown to collectors until just recently is a mystery. What is certain, however, is that the masks do not belong to the R180 category listed in the American Card Catalog (those masks are printed on 3¾" X 4½" wrappers marked "Fleer Heads Up Gum"). Each mask has the words "Frank H. Fleer Corporation, Philadelphia, Penn." printed on the right side flap. The left side flap bears instructions for using rubber bands or string to make the mask functional. It is believed that these masks were handed out over the counter as purchase incentives or prizes because they are generally found in excellent condition without creases or folds. No reference number has been assigned.

ITEM	EX	AVE
Mask	20.00	7.00

FRANK BUCK (48)

1 The tapir that turned
2 A leopard on the loose
3 The peril in the pit
4 Crushing coils
5 Giant jungle man
6 Caging a king cobra
7 The spitting horror
8 Terrible tusks
9 The leopard's last leap
10 Pinning a python
11 The killer of the shallows
12 Claws vs. coils
13 Monkey milks tree
14 The leopard on the limb
15 The striped threat
16 Looping a lizard
17 Green water aboard
18 The pig in the python
19 The prodigal bear
20 Bringing him down
21 The battling bull
22 Dawn at the water hole
23 When devils duel
24 The killer of Kuali
25 Monkey mischief
26 Little tough guy
27 Courage and claws
28 The scaly threat
29 First aid to a jungle killer
30 The lure of bloody bait
31 Held by a half-hitch
32 Elephant rage
33 Learning to loop a lariat
34 Savagery breaks through
35 The gall of a tiger
36 Tail-hair magic
37 Swamp peril
38 A flare for a tiger
39 Hurled by an elephant
40 The trap in the tree
41 Trapping a tiger
42 Desperate knife-work
43 Socking a simian
44 Sinister serpent worship
45 Black hate and slashing claws
46 The kink in Kinkley
47 Caging a cassowary
48 The bogged bullock

2 1/2" X 3"

Gumakers of America, based in Clifton Heights, PA, hit the jackpot with the Frank Buck "Bring 'Em Back Alive" series of 1938. Everything associated with the set — from the beautiful green wrapper (emblazoned with Buck's portrait and a fearsome orange tiger) to the snappy adventures related on the cards — was done in high style. There was but one minor problem: most of the cards were cut slightly off center (either axis), so dimensions may vary slightly among individual cards. This is especially important to note since the excellent card and set prices listed below apply only to cards which are reasonably well centered. In addition, the cardboard used for this set tends to flake apart at the edges, another factor which affects grade and value. There is no perceptible difference in scarcity between cards marked "A" and "B" (although the size of the card numbers is different). The reference number is R55.

ITEM	EX	AVE
Card	15.00	4.00
Set	900.00	230.00
Wrapper	500.00	––

FUNNIES (24)

General Gum of Chicago is responsible for producing the Funnies set of 24 novelty cards, which hit the market in 1934. The red, white and blue cards were designed to be used in conjunction with a

paper "screen" — provided as part of the wrapper — which made the pictures "move" in simulated action. Without the screen, they are a dizzying sight. The collector could

PERRY WINKLE goes Wham-Tam-Bam on his big bass drum. Of course, it isn't really a bass drum—just his Ma's wash tub. The Rinky-Dinks are cheering as Perry marches by.

Next time you get "Funnies" Gum, watch for Andy and Chester.

FREE! Cut ten 10 Andy Gump Heads from 10 gum wrappers—Paste to your picture and to will GET YOUR rigid permanent CELLULOID SCREEN for working your "FUNNIES"

● In order to make "FUNNIES" move—lay screen over picture on card—then move screen slowly back and forth. Be sure to hold screen closely against card, keeping it smooth and straight ●

GENERAL GUM, INC. ● CHICAGO

2 7/16" X 2 7/8"

obtain a rigid celluloid screen by cutting 10 Andy Gump heads from wrapper corners and sending them in to the company. The cards are not numbered and the backs contain a short text, instructions to create "action," and a promotional line about another card in the set. The reference number is R56.

ITEM	EX	AVE
Card	15.00	5.00
Set	475.00	150.00
Rigid Screen	20.00	8.00
Wrapper	350.00	––

RIGID CELLULOID SCREEN AVAILABLE VIA MAIL

Although Uncle "Bim" Gump, the well known Australian billioniare, has more bags of gold than the mint, he hasn't much more hair than his nephew "Andy." Bam – bam – look at him pound the table! – he's serious but he sure looks funny.

Andy Gump, that lovable old bald-headed, big-nosed, chinless chap is always getting into some sore of scrape. As usual, he is wildly shouting "Oh Min!" – and look at him yell!

Aunt Mame goes "SOCK" and Uncle Willie's very urgent engagement at the pool parlor will have to wait until some future date. Look – Uncle Willie lost his cigar in the crash!

Harold Teen and Lillums are just on the verge of going "SMACK" when Tuffy sticks his head up from behind the sofa and reminds Harold that he owes him a nickel – Boy, are they surprised!

Here's Kayo Mullins with a big seegar in his mouth and from the way he's huffing and puffing, looks as though he can't make up his mind whether to get sick or get a kick out of it.

Here's Tiny Tim and it sure looks as though his sister Dotty is playing another prank on him. Maybe this is her idea of spooning – What do you think?

Here's Winnie Winkle lovelier than ever, dancing with Prince Charming – but what on earth is wrong – did she make a social error or has the bold bad Prince asked her to marry him? At any rate, is her face red!

Here we have Orphan Annie giving Sandy a lecture on chasing cats. Watch her shake her finger at him. She'll make a gentleman dog out of him or know the reason why.

Hot Dog! – Look at Dick Tracy and Junior blazing away at Spaldoni, Big Boy or one of the gang. Nice shooting, fellows – a great piece of detective work.

Kayo Mullins swings his trusty baseball bat and WHAM – looks as though Emmy Schmaltz got it right on the breezer. What do you think?

Little Orphan Annie is telling Daddy Warbucks how she would like to buy a great big basket of groceries for an awfully nice poor family she and Sandy discovered when they were out walking.

Look at Shadow Smart inhale that soda – Slup, Slup and it disappears like magic – and by the worried look on Poppa Jenk's face, Shadow hasn't paid for it yet! Wonder who Shadow is haunting today?

"Look pleasant please," says Harold Teen to his pal Shadow Smart – and about that time he sprays water all over poor Shadow – Hot Dawg! – everybody's getting a big kick out of it.

Looks as though Perry just told his Dad – "Rip" Winkle – a funny story of some kind – the old boy's rocking so hard he's about to go Plop! Some fun!

"Now listen, Mister Moonshine Mullins, is that the gentlemanly way to treat Lord Plushbottom? First you use him for an ash tray and then a leaning post. Tsk-Tsk-Tsk!"

"Oh Ma! Ma! Smitty's in the doughnuts again – Hurry, hurry or you won't have any left for dinner. Gee, he's eating them so fast it makes your head swim!

Oh–Oh!! Looks like Clarence, Gasoline Alley's bad boy, is up to his old tricks again – turned the hose right smack on Skeezix and zowie – is he all wet!

Perry Winkle goes Wham-Tam-Bam on his big bass drum. Of course, it isn't really a bass drum – just his Ma's wash tub. The Rinky-Dinks are cheering as Perry marches by.

Pompous "Bimbo" takes a bow – Looks as though Millie De Stross and her Mama have him eating out of their hands. But just you wait, Bim will get wise some day that all they want is a slice of his billions Then, look out!

Sandy and Annie have been through thick and thin together. Annie is seen congratulating Sandy for chasing away that mean old tramp. Look at Sandy puff out his chest – he sure is proud to be of service to Annie.

Uncle Avery thinks no more of spending a dime than he does of jumping out of a twenty-story window. Here we have him trying to put over a deal with Uncle Walt and Doc, but all they do is give him the Ha, Ha!

Uncle Walt should be old enough to know when grownups play kid games they're bound to get hurt. Here he's helping Skeezix blow up a balloon and BANG!! – Right smack in the eye!

Watch little Herbie go for the jam! He'll probably get it all over his face and hands – then try to blame it on his faithful dog, "Scwaps."

"When I was your age, Chester, I held the school record for the high jump, broad jump, hundred yard dash and I was the marble champion of Bloomington etc. etc., boasts Andy, waving his arms. "Soups on!" shouts Tilda!

FUNNY CAPERS CARDS (?)   2 1/4" X 3 1/8"

"Funny Capers Cards" appear to have been a gum issue distributed solely to promote sales of two standard card deck games, "Razzle" and "Pit." All the obverses reported have identical artwork backgrounds with centerpieces containing large numbers at top and game instructions or advertising at bottom. All the backs seen thus far bear a mail premium offer for a "beautiful scarf pin" in exchange for 25 wrappers of Chase's "Funny Capers Chewing Gum." None of these wrappers have been uncovered to date, and no reference number has been assigned to the set.. The set total is unknown.

ITEM	EX	AVE
Card	6.00	2.00

GAMES AND PUZZLES (9)   15/16" X 11 1/4"

Although it was originally listed in the early catalogs under "Jiminy Cricket," there is no mention of that gum brand on the cards. The words "games and puzzles" do appear on every card, so listing this set under that heading makes it easier for collectors to find. The "card" is really a narrow but very long cardboard package stiffener/gum tray with a printed design on one side. Each card is numbered and captioned on front (backs are blank). The 2¾" X 13" one-cent wrapper has seven different poses of Jiminy Cricket on the bottom fold and advertises three mail premiums on the top side. The set was produced by Dietz Gum (Chicago) in 1940. The reference number is R77.

ITEM	EX	AVE
Card	25.00	8.00
Set	270.00	85.00
Wrapper	200.00	—

GAMES AND PUZZLES (?)   VARIOUS SIZES

An obscure set of cards of which little is known, "Games and Puzzles" (an assigned title) fascinates specialized collectors because it is the only non strip-card series issued by W.S. The cards themselves come in a variety of sizes, formats, and artwork and consist of illusions, tricks, miniature jigsaws, and games. Every card carries instructions and a 1941 copyright date on the reverse. The length of set and method of distribution are not known. The reference number is R188.

ITEM	EX	AVE
Card	10.00	4.00

GENERALS & THEIR FLAGS (24)   2 5/16" X 2 3/4"

W.S. Corporation produced the "Generals & Their Flags" set in 1939. It consists of 24 artwork strip cards (numbered 425-448) which picture famous generals of the world along with their respective flags. The set title, card caption, and number are printed on both sides (captions may vary slightly in wording between front and back). The vertically-aligned backs carry a short text printed in black ink. Every card has rouletted edges on two sides, except for "end" cards, which have but one. The reference number is R58. NOTE: cards intact in strips are worth 50% more than the prices listed below.

ITEM	EX	AVE
Card	4.00	1.00
Set	115.00	27.50

425 Gen. Pershing - United States	437 Gen. Diaz - Mexico
426 Gen. Bolivar - Venezuela	438 Gen. McKenzie - Canada
427 Gen. Batista - Cuba	439 Com'dr. Essad Pasha - Albania
428 Gen. De Rivera - Spain	440 Gen. Haller - Poland
429 Gen. Joffre - France	441 Gen. Kitchener - England
430 Gen. Moltke - Rumania	442 Ali Pasha - Egypt
431 Gen. Rhodes - Greece	443 Gen. Horvath - Czechoslavakia
432 Gen. Savoff - Bulgaria	444 Gen. Guyon - Hungary
433 Gen. Balbo - Italy	445 Gen. Letchitsky - Russia
434 Gen. Von Pasha - Turkey	446 Gen. Goltz - Lithuania
435 Gen. Mannerheim - Finland	447 Gen. J. De Meza - Denmark
436 Gen. Chiang Kai Shek - China	448 Gen. O'Duffy - Ireland

G—MEN & Heroes of the Law — The Ultimate Con

by Larry Fortuck

At a show in 1988, a man who has become a collector friend brought me a list of G—Men cards he was missing from when he was a boy. Looking at his list, I saw that he did't know that the G—Men set contained only 168 skip-numbered cards. When I explained about the missing numbers and the misleading "240 thrilling action pictures" line which appears on some of the cards, he was flabbergasted. "I can't believe this," he exclaimed! "One reason I stopped collecting G—Men was because I couldn't finish the set." This man had been conned by GUM, INC., a con that continued for 51 years.

G—MEN & HEROES OF THE LAW (Reference number R60) was issued by Gum, Inc. in 1936 and 1937. The cards were designed in bright colors with comic strip artwork typical of the period. Each card tells an "official story" about ""G—Men and Famous Police Organizations and Heroes of the Law" as they battled a formidable array of gangsters and hoodlums. It seems paradoxical that a card set with such a strong moral theme would be marketed in such a devious manner!

Why was the G—Men set skip-numbered? It could have been a simple market strategy to keep kids buying cards or a complex move to protect against copyright infringement (Group 1, Type 3 cards below may be counterfeit). Either way, there's solid evidence that even the skip-numbered cards were not issued consecutively. At some point, Gum, Inc. went back and started to fill in the missing numbers. This was never completed, possibly because the outbreak of World War II shifted public interest, and Gum, Inc. responded by printing the Horrors of War set starting in early 1938.

The fact that Gum, Inc. printed cards in sheets of 24 is confirmed by collectors who obtained uncut sheets from the estate of George Moll (art director of Gum, Inc. and Bowman Gum). Since there are 168 cards in the G—Men set, a division by 24 indicates seven sheets were printed, with all cards on each sheet printed only once. With this in mind, the set can be divided into specific groups:

Group 1 — "The first 24," which are found three ways: 1) no "Gum, Inc." or copyright date on the card; 2) "Gum, Inc." and "1936" on card; 3) no "Gum, Inc." or date, thinner stock, and one or two rouletted edges (issued in strips, not gum packs). Cards 1-24 in numerical sequence; all three show "series of 240" on reverse.

Group 2 — "The common low numbers," are 48 cards found two ways: 1) with "collection of 240 thrilling action pictures" on back; 2) with the same statement but minus the "240" set total. Cards 25, 26, 29, 32, 33, 36, 39, 40, 42, 44, 46, 47, 50, 51, 53, 55, 58, 59, 62, 65, 66, 69, 72, 74, 77, 80, 81, 84, 86, 87, 89, 92, 93, 96, 97, 103, 111, 119, 125, 129, 131, 137, 147, 151, 155, 158, 162, 166.

Group 3 — "The red ampersands," are 24 cards with a red ampersand (the "&" symbol) in the obverse set title (the "&" is yellow in Groups 1 and 2). These come with and without the "240" back statement as in Group 2. Cards 56, 60, 63, 67, 75, 79, 82, 91, 98, 101, 104, 106, 109, 112, 114, 117, 120, 123, 126, 128, 132, 135, 139, 142.

Group 4 — "The 1936 high numbers," are 24 cards dated "1936" which have front left numbers and the word "Trademark" added to the obverse set title. No "240" statement is on the cards. Cards 201, 203, 206, 208, 210, 212, 214, 219, 227, 233, 239, 242, 248, 253, 257, 262, 266, 269, 271, 275, 277, 279, 281, 283.

Group 5 — "The 1937 high numbers," are 24 cards with the same details as Group 4 but are marked "1937." Cards 307, 311, 319, 326, 335, 343, 349, 355, 362, 371, 381, 389, 397, 401, 405, 411, 415, 419, 424, 427, 431, 437, 445, 451.

Group 6 — "The left hand low numbers," are 24 cards with front left numbers, "Trademark" in the obverse set title, and a "1936" copyright date. Cards 28, 38, 45, 49, 57, 64, 76, 83, 88, 94, 100, 107, 115, 121, 127, 136, 149, 156, 169, 177, 181, 185, 191, 196.

Group 1, 2 and 3 cards are the easiest to collect. Group 4 is tough and Group 5 is even tougher. Group 6 may seem inpossible to find. Why is this? We know that Group 1 cards (1-24) were released at least three times and Group 2 and Group 3 cards at least twice. In contrast, Group 4, 5 and 6 cards were issued only once.

Since Group 4 and 5 cards are high numbers, we might expect them to be scarce. But Group 6 is special because they appear to have been part of a short-lived effort to fill in "skipped" low numbers. It is these 24 cards which stop collectors from finishing off their sets.

My thanks to Bob Lutton and to all the other collectors who supplied information. As a bonus, we discovered a new variation in Group 2: a card with a red ampersand (instead of the normal yellow one).

This article first appeared in *Non-Sport Update* (October 1990). Comments or information may be sent to Larry Fortuck, 2501 Alabama, Joplin, MO 64804.

G—MEN & HEROES OF THE LAW (168) 2 1/2" X 3 1/16"

"G-Men & Heroes of the Law" differs from the other most sought after sets of bubble gum's Golden Age in one important respect: it is extremely difficult to complete because there are five cards which are almost impossible to find. Other classic sets, such as "Horrors of War," have cards which are demand-scarce. These can be obtained IF you choose to pay the price. The "hard" cards in G-G-Men, however, are rarely offered for sale because they are supply-scarce. That is why completing a G-Men set is considered a benchmark accomplishment within the collecting community.

The 48 high numbers comprising the 201-451 sequence are in themselves a formidable challenge. Most often, they are found in "average" rather than "excellent" condition, so "upgrading" is a familiar term to G-Men collectors. All in all, Gum, Inc.'s G-Men series is probably the "Mt. Everest"

SEE FEATURE STORY FOR SPECIFIC DETAILS.

of non-sports collecting, but it is a climb well worth making.

Two completely different wrappers have been reported for the G-Men set. One is a plain white wrapper with the words "G-Men Bubble Gum" on front (some collectors believe this was manufactured by Pressner, a Gum, Inc. competitor — see next listing). The other wrapper has a colorful artwork design with government men gunning down a mobster. The white G-Men wrapper is by far the scarcest of the two. The reference number for G-Men is R60. See the checklist for individual card prices.

ITEM	EX	AVE
Wrappers		
White	450.00	——
Green	200.00	——
Set (168)	6500.00	2150.00
Box		Speculative

GREEN G-MEN WRAPPER

WHITE G-MEN WRAPPER

NOTE: STRIP CARD VARIETY NUMBERED 1-24 ARE
VALUED AT 20% LESS THAN LISTED PRICES

1	G-Men Riddle the Killer "Who Couldn't Be Caught" — Pretty Boy Floyd	30.00	7.50
2	G-Men Wipe Out Leaders of "Secret 10" — Bobby Mais	15.00	3.50
3	Capturing a Killer & His Gang! — Sergt. Reilly	15.00	3.50
4	A Gamble with Death! — Corp. Quinn	15.00	3.50
5	A Midnight Graveyard Battle! — Private Steward	15.00	3.50
6	A Shot from the Hip That Saved a Trooper's Life — Trooper Taylor	15.00	3.50
7	A Trooper's Race with Death! — Trooper McCormick	15.00	3.50
8	A Trooper's Fight with Flame! — Trooper O'Brien	15.00	3.50
9	Daring Bandits Get Their Just Deserts! — Trooper Dickerson	15.00	3.50
10	G-Men Track Down Notorious Public Enemy! — John Dillinger	25.00	7.00
11	G-Men Track Wily Fugitives Across United States — Machine Gun Kelly	18.00	5.00
12	A Treacherous Shot in the Dark! — Corp. Maynard	15.00	3.50
13	A Duel to the Death! — Trooper Poppe	15.00	3.50
14	Foiling Four Wanted Killers — Trooper Herbold	15.00	3.50
15	A Mountain Cabin Gun-Fight! — Trooper Wilson	15.00	3.50
16	A Murderous Madman's Battle! — Sergt. McCarthy	15.00	3.50
17	Sure Death Defied! — Trooper Perry	15.00	3.50
18	Shooting It Out with a Desperate Fugitive! — Corporal Simpson	15.00	3.50
19	Two G-Men Meet a Heroic Death! — Baby Face Nelson	20.00	6.00
20	G-Men Run Down a Daring Kidnapper — Harvey Bailey	15.00	3.50
21	A Desperate Running Fight! — Lieut. Gorenflo	15.00	3.50
22	A Trooper's Sacrifice to Duty! — Trooper Haley	15.00	3.50
23	Blasting Out a Gang of Killers! — Trooper Chambers	15.00	3.50
24	A Knife Thrust in the Dark! — Trooper Kelleher	15.00	3.50
25	A Campfire's Ghastly Ashes	12.00	3.00
26	Trapping a Human Vulture	12.00	3.00
28	G-Men Deliver Death	125.00	35.00
29	A Death Duel with Escaping Convicts	12.00	3.00
32	Unrelenting Justice Overtakes a Swampland Killer	12.00	3.00
33	A Murder on an Arizona Trail	12.00	3.00
36	The Filling Station Massacre	12.00	3.00
38	Grapple with Bloody Death	50.00	12.00
39	Kidnapped Courage	12.00	3.00
40	Unearthing a Deadly Arsenal	12.00	3.00
42	Murder from Ambush	12.00	3.00
44	Trapping the Jewel Conspirators	12.00	3.00
45	Satan's Disciple	50.00	12.00
46	Luggage Packed with Death	12.00	3.00
47	The Death of "Dutch Anderson" — Dutch Anderson	12.00	3.00
49	Far Flung Fingers of the Law	50.00	12.00
50	The Trail of the Mystery Bonds	12.00	3.00
51	Chinese Death	12.00	3.00

53	Blasting Crime from the Canadian Rockies	12.00	3.00
55	Talking Blood that Told a Madman's Secret	12.00	3.00
56	Following the Blood Tracks of the "Lucky Lone Wolf"	12.00	3.00
57	Mining for Murder	125.00	35.00
58	Disguises of the Law!	12.00	3.00
59	A G-Man Flirts with Secret Death	12.00	3.00
60	The Gold Train Murder!	12.00	3.00
62	Ending the Rule of a Man Killing Mob	12.00	3.00
63	The Chinese Symbol of Death!	12.00	3.00
64	The Killers in Tunnel 13	50.00	12.00
65	A City Lived in Terror Until...	12.00	3.00
66	G-Men Clear Up a Famous "Snatch Case"	12.00	3.00
67	Murder in Unaka Mountains	12.00	3.00
69	A Dying Hero's Winning Fight!	12.00	3.00
72	Justice within the Arctic Circle	12.00	3.00
74	A Death Defying Pursuit	12.00	3.00
75	The Phantom Bandits of the Pacific Coast	12.00	3.00
76	The Trail of the Secret Symbols	50.00	12.00
77	Capturing the "Stinger" of the Underworld — Tony the Stinger	12.00	3.00
79	Caging a Blond Tigress!	12.00	3.00
80	The Clue that Couldn't Be Drowned	12.00	3.00
81	"Rubbing Out" the Sunday Gang	12.00	3.00
82	Sleeping Evidence Awakes!	12.00	3.00
83	A Bullet-Collected Debt	50.00	12.00
84	Checkmating a Desperate Bank Robbing Gang	12.00	3.00
86	A Murdered Trooper Is Avenged	12.00	3.00
87	G-Men "Mop Up" the Barker-Karpis Gang	12.00	3.00
88	Target of Death! — Tommy Carroll	125.00	35.00
89	The Flight of the Black Duck	12.00	3.00
91	Grilling a Lying Gunman	12.00	3.00
92	Murder Committed by the Victim's Hands	12.00	3.00
93	A Telltale Bullet Lands an Unsuspected Bandit Gang!	12.00	3.00
94	G-Men Strike in the Dark	125.00	35.00
96	The End of a Killer's Trail	12.00	3.00
97	G-Men Complete Their Record Catch	12.00	3.00
98	Vengeance follows an Outlaw Gang	12.00	3.00
100	The Dragnet Snares Its Prey	125.00	35.00
101	The Capture of "The Crank"	12.00	3.00
103	G-Men Answer Public Enemy Number 1 — Alvin Karpis	12.00	3.00
104	The Fingerprint's Confession	12.00	3.00
106	Murder without Motive	12.00	3.00
107	Trapping a "Cop Killer"	50.00	12.00
109	Fog Phantoms that Could Not Elude the Law	12.00	3.00
111	Justice Patrols the Arizona Border	12.00	3.00
112	The Mad Killer's Frozen Trail	12.00	3.00
114	Swift Pursuit!	12.00	3.00
115	Binding the Beast	50.00	12.00
117	Torn Dollars	12.00	3.00
119	Machine Guns Foil a Get-Away at Alcatraz	12.00	3.00
120	Death Rides the Waves	12.00	3.00
121	G-Men Blot Out a Crime Career	50.00	12.00
123	Radio Eavesdrops on Crime!	12.00	3.00
125	Capturing the Killers of the Hatchet-Gang	12.00	3.00
126	The Ape-Man Burglar	12.00	3.00
127	The Gallows Prey	50.00	3.00
128	The Terror of the Mails! — Gardner	12.00	3.00
129	Eyes That Betrayed a Human Spider	12.00	3.00
131	Smuggling on the Rio Grande	12.00	3.00
132	The Crime Teacher	12.00	3.00
135	A Murder Leaves Its Roadmap	12.00	3.00
136	A Bullet Finds & Frees	50.00	3.00
137	The Crime in the Mirror	12.00	3.00
139	A Killer's Last Stand!	12.00	3.00
142	A Mountain Moonshine Murder	12.00	3.00
147	Duty Defies Death	12.00	3.00
149	A Desperate Crime at Sea	50.00	12.00
151	Death Among the Gravestones	12.00	3.00
155	A Rancher's Camera Eye	12.00	3.00
156	The Mask of Death	50.00	12.00
158	Crime Telegraphs Its Loot	12.00	3.00
162	Heroism on the High Seas	12.00	3.00
166	Death Blast in the Mountains	12.00	3.00
169	Death Rewards an Extortionist	50.00	12.00
177	A Boat Betrays Its Killer Crew	50.00	12.00
181	Death Ends a Crimson Trail	50.00	12.00
185	G-Men Discover a Dead Hand's Secret	50.00	12.00
191	Death in a Poison Cup	50.00	12.00
196	Gun Butts & Bullets	50.00	12.00
201	Crime's Crimson Target	35.00	8.00
203	A G-Man Finds a Murderer's Mark	35.00	8.00
206	Blood on the Moon	35.00	8.00
208	Knife Thrust in the Dark	35.00	8.00
210	Tracking a Living Dead Man	35.00	8.00
212	Death Defies the Sky	35.00	8.00
214	G-Men Play the Final Ace	35.00	8.00
219	Bloodstained Desert Gold	35.00	8.00
227	The "Law Hater"	35.00	8.00
233	Machine Gun Vengeance	35.00	8.00
239	Decoy of Death	35.00	8.00
242	In the Grip of the Jinx	35.00	8.00
248	The "Little Giant of the Law"	35.00	8.00
253	Snake of the Underworld	35.00	8.00
257	Death Streaks the Night	35.00	8.00
262	A Murder Blast Defied	35.00	8.00
266	The Stroke of Fate	35.00	8.00
269	A Red Trail's Blazing End	35.00	8.00
271	Grip of Steel	35.00	8.00
275	Capture in the Forest Shadows	35.00	8.00
277	The Clue of the Chiming Clock	35.00	8.00
279	The Fire Ring	35.00	8.00
281	Smuggled Cargo	35.00	8.00
283	G-Men Ride the Air Lanes	50.00	12.00
307	G-Men and the Phantom	50.00	12.00
311	The "Tri-State Terrors"	50.00	12.00
319	Pursuit in the Wilderness	50.00	12.00
326	Doom of the Mad Marksman	50.00	12.00
335	Hail of Death	50.00	12.00
343	Swampland Vengeance	50.00	12.00
349	Crushing the "Cry Baby Bandits"	50.00	12.00
355	The Cry in the Night	50.00	12.00
362	Death Dealt at Dawn	50.00	12.00
371	G-Men and the Electric Eye	50.00	12.00
381	The Crimson Thread	50.00	12.00
389	Payment in Blood and Fire	50.00	12.00
397	Midnight Sharpshooters	50.00	12.00
401	The Deadly Draw	50.00	12.00
405	Courage Backed to the Wall	50.00	12.00
411	Capture at the Cattle Ford	50.00	12.00
415	River Pirate Loot	50.00	12.00
419	Silencing Gangland's Guns	50.00	12.00
424	The Death Call	50.00	12.00
427	Race in the Little Red Car	50.00	12.00
431	Moonlight Man Hunt	50.00	12.00
437	Loop of the Law	50.00	12.00
445	The Whispered Clue	50.00	12.00
451	The Voice from the Ether Cone	75.00	18.00

71

GOLDEN WEST (18)   2" X 3"

Although the cards of the "Golden West" series are devoid of identifying marks or

1 The Tenderfoot.
2 Billy Meets the Cowboys.
3 Billy's Pony.
4 A New Friend.
5 Learning the Ropes.
6 Trouble in Camp.
7 The Cattle Rustlers.
8
9 Captured.
10 A Messenger of Trouble.
11 Kidnapped.
12 Captive.
13 Bill Gets a Break.
14 Saved by a Shot.
15 The Outlaws Flee.
16 The Rescue.
17 More Trouble?
18 Reward.

manufacturer credits, the format suggests that the set was produced by Holloway. The cards relate the adventures of Kit, a noble lawman, and Billy, his (inevitable) boy companion, in 18 sequenced episodes. The fronts bear soft

> 17. More Trouble?
>
> Kits stared at the dead men. "Holy Smoke!" he exclaimed, "if it ain't Stage Coach Pete! He's wanted in every county from Powder River to Rio Grande!" Billy drew closer to listen to a noise. "Kits!" he whispered, "I hear horses coming!" Who was riding up the lonely trail to the cabin? Kits put his hand on his six-gun and waited tensely.
>
> SAVE AN ENTIRE SET OF 18 PICTURES AND GET A LARGE "GOLDEN WEST" PICTURE SUITABLE FOR FRAMING.

color drawings only. The card title, text, and number are printed on the back (blue ink on cream stock). An offer for a large Golden West picture ("suitable for framing") appears on every card, but no address or details are provided. Golden West was not listed in the early catalogs and has not yet been assigned a reference number.

ITEM	EX	AVE
Card	6.00	1.50
Set	130.00	30.00

"GOOFY" GAMES AND PUZZLES (9)   15/16" X 11 1/4"

At first glance, the cards of this set appear to be identical to those of the "Games and Puzzles" series already reviewed. However, there is one major difference: these have the words "Goofy Bubble Gum" printed on every card. Other than that, the "Goofy" Games and Puzzles cards

served the same dual-purpose function — prize plus package stiffener/gum tray — as did Jiminy Cricket cards. "Goofy" cards are all numbered and captioned, and there are nine in the set. No reference number has been assigned. The series was produced by Dietz, and the color-

ful wrapper has advertising offers for several mail premiums.

ITEM	EX	AVE
Card	30.00	10.00
Set	300.00	100.00
Wrapper	250.00	——

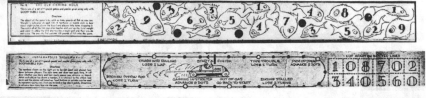

GOVERNMENT AGENTS VS PUBLIC ENEMIES (24)   2 3/8" X 3"

The "Government Agents vs Public Enemies" series, produced by M. Pressner & Co., was once thought to have been issued exclusively in strips (based upon the rouletted side edges of the cards). Now a smooth-edged variety, printed on gray (rather than cream colored) stock has been found. This discovery has led some collectors to suggest that

smooth-edge Pressner cards were distributed in gum packs (perhaps the white wrapper listed in the G-Men presentation), but no proof is available to substantiate that contention. Both types of Pressner cards bear a 1936 copyright line on front and back, although the obverse line is often lost in the artwork. The "tall" and "wide" dimen-

sions vary slightly between types, but the significance of this has yet to be established. The reference number is R61. NOTE: cards intact in strips are valued at a 50% premium over single cards.

ITEM	EX	AVE
Card	8.00	2.00
Set	230.00	55.00

A-201	Blazing Guns	A-206	A Desperate Fight and	A-211	Trailing the Criminal	A-215 Chase with Death	A-220 The Indian Murders
A-202	Trapped		Capture	A-212	"Hands Up—All of You"	A-216 Guns of Vengeance	A-221 The Wounded Gangster
A-203	Convict's Reward	A-207	Face to Face with Death	A-213	The Clue That Led to	A-217 Signature of Death	A-222 A Mad Killer Surrenders
A-204	A Wise Guy	A-208	The Slave Murders		Capture	A-218 The Christmas Day Capture	A-223 Traveling with Death
A-205	A Fight to the Finish	A-209	"Shoot to Kill"	A-214	Capture Without Guns	A-219 Straight to the Wanted Man	A-224 The Fighting Family
		A-210	Two Hour Capture				

GUESS WHAT? (20K)   5" X 5 1/4"

Until quite recently, the only known type of Williamson's "Guess What?" candy wrappers was the "Be A Comic Artist" variety featuring heads of famous cartoon characters.

However, John Neuner ("The Wrapper King") has since uncovered four more types. One is a "plain bottom" connect-the-dots specimen; the others are "Shadow Pictures," "Illusions," and "Be A Comic Artist" (animals) with fancy "Oh Henry" ads at bottom. Of the new types, the "Oh Henry" wrappers give Chicago and San Francisco as company locations; the connect-the-dots type lists only Chicago. The original cartoon character style has Chicago and Brooklyn as business sites. All the Williamson wrappers in this category are dull finish, plain paper items with little appeal to the general collecting public. The reference number is R62.

ITEM	EX	AVE
Wrapper	75.00	40.00

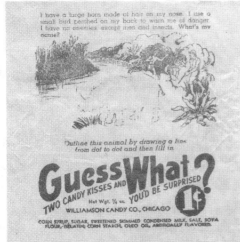

CARDBOARD ADVERTISING
INSERT FROM A
"GUESS WHAT?" BOX

GUESS WHAT? (?)

2 1/4" X 3 5/8"

Williamson Candy must have really thought the "Guess What?" theme was special: this series of candy box cards also bears that name. Research indicates that the first round of "Guess What?" boxes were issued just prior to the outbreak of World War II, and they were probably curtailed by it. The company re-entered the candy market in the early 1950's and the "Guess What?" candy box line was revived, possibly using the same designs as the original set. In practical terms, collectors have been unable to distinguish between pre- and post-war boxes, except where a two-number zone code was added to the company addresss. Since the set is neither attractive nor widely collected, the question of value between the older and newer varieties is really immaterial. The original reference number is R187; the "new" variety reference number is R776 (see post-war card section of this book). NOTE: complete boxes in excellent condition are not difficult to find.

ITEM	EX	AVE
Card	2.00	.50
Box	20.00	5.00

GUESS WHO (100?)

2 3/8" X 3"

The candy and gum companies of the thirties were big on running contests and offering prizes, but they were stingy devils when it came to paying off! Consider, for example, the premise behind the "Guess Who?" series. It was issued by an anonymous company with nothing but a post office box address in Philadelphia. This unknown firm offered one of 14 exciting prizes to any boy or girl who could correctly name all the movie stars on a "complete set" of 10 puzzle cards. Doesn't seem difficult, does it? Except that there were at least six (and probably 10) completely different cards printed for each number! This enabled the issuer to juggle the list of correct answers indefinitely and to avoid awarding prizes. The card drawings are printed in one ink color on cream stock: green, blue, brown, olive, black, and red have been reported for various cards, and some cards have been seen in two colors. The set is so complex and apparently devious that few modern collectors care to deal with it. The reference number is R63.

ITEM	EX	AVE
Card	10.00	3.00

HEROES OF PEARL HARBOR (6K)

1 7/8" X 3"

The "Remember Pearl Harbor"/"Heroes of Pearl Harbor" box illustrated on page 115 of the 1983 Non-Sport Guide turned out to be a fabrication put together by a well-intentioned collector. The box shown here — from the collection of John Neuner — proves that two "Heroes" cards were printed on the front and back panels of a single candy box. Judging from the theme, this series was probably issued by the Candyland Company (Brooklyn) in early 1942. The blank-backed cards are red and blue with some white accents, and they are not numbered. Since the sides were "scored" by machine to allow easy removal, the left and right card edges have "nubs." Only six servicemen have been listed as of this time. The reference number is R66.

Lieutenant Hans C. Christianson
Capt. Colin Kelly Jr., Who Sank the Haruna
2nd Lieutenant Louis G. Meslener
Private William M. Northway
Private Ralph S. Smith
Private Elmer W. South

ITEM	EX	AVE
Card	20.00	6.00
Complete Box	125.00	35.00

HEROES OF THE SEA (24)

2 5/16" X 2 3/4"

"Heroes of the Sea," another strip card series produced by the W.S. Corporation, was marketed in 1939. The 24 cards in the set are numbered 449-472, and the copyright date is printed on both sides of every card. The rough color artwork and lack of details are characteristic of most W.S. card sets. Captions on some cards differ slightly in wording front to back. The text backs use olive-blue print on gray stock. The reference number is R67. NOTE: cards or sets intact in strips are worth 25% more than the prices listed below.

449 Admiral Sturdee	457 Ponce de Leon	465 Capt. Cook
450 Columbus	458 Comm. Perry	466 Capt. Ericson
451 Balboa	459 Sir Francis Drake	467 Cartier
452 Admiral Sims	460 Magellan	468 Capt. Moses Rogers
453 John Paul Jones	461 Henry Hudson	469 William Beebe
454 Admiral Dewey	462 Admiral Cradock	470 Admiral Nelson
455 Capt. Diehl	463 Capt. Rostrom	471 Capt. Chris Jones
456 Capt. Bligh	464 Capt. W. T. Turner	472 Capt. Basil Roberts

ITEM	EX	AVE
Card	4.00	1.00
Set	115.00	27.50

HISTORY OF AVIATION (10)

5 1/2" SQUARE

Five daring American aviators and their famous airplanes are the subjects of this "1936 History of Aviation Series" created by Goudey Gum. The color artwork pictures are actually paper album pages; directions for punching ring holes are printed on the back. According to the advertising, the series came only with "Air Service Gum." This wrapper has not been seen, and it is likely that the album pictures were handed out with the purchase of a Goudey product. The backs of pilot pages carry extensive biographical text; the backs of aircraft pages give interesting technical details about each plane. The reference number is R65. NOTE: pages with holes punched cannot be graded "excellent."

ITEM	EX	AVE
Album page	20.00	5.00
Set	250.00	60.00

Nº 1. HOWARD HUGHES — "Aviation Speed King"

No. 1 . . . 1936 HISTORY OF AVIATION SERIES

HOWARD HUGHES

"Aviation Speed King"

ON January 14, 1936 this modest young man, only 33 years old, established a new cross country flight record. This youthful daredevil from California crowned his thrilling air achievements by making the fastest cross country flight ever made by man. He became America's newest speed king of aviation.

Without stop Hughes flew from Burbank, California, to Newark, New Jersey in 9 hours, 27 minutes and 10 seconds—smashing the best previous time record by more than half an hour.

He took off on the afternoon of January 13, at 3:15 P.M., E.S.T., without fanfare or public notice of any sort. Just a capable young man who set out to do a job in an earnest, businesslike fashion. He hadn't tried to make the flight in secrecy. But at Newark no one was expecting his arrival until his plane swooped down out of the night sky at 12:42—10 A.M., E.S.T. Officials of the National Association promptly confirmed Hughes' record breaking performance.

Except for a little hunger he found no discomfort during the flight. He was too busy to take time out to eat. Instead of taking personal credit for the great feat, Hughes was proud of the performance of his speedy plane and motor. Otherwise to him it was all a matter of course. He had been planning to come to New York on business anyway. The record smashing monoplane is a single seated Northrop Gamma mail plane with a new-type super-charged, radial motor (Wright G Cyclone) built to army specifications.

This tall, dark-haired American flyer also holds the speed record for land planes. September 1935 he averaged 352.46 miles an hour over a closed course near Santa Ana, Calif.

Previously Hughes was best known to the public as a motion picture producer. One of his productions being "Hell's Angels", an aviation story.

This is one of the 1936 History of Aviation Series of famous pilots and planes offered to create greater interest in aviation, and for the purpose of instruction and education in aviation. The complete series will make a beautiful and valuable collection. Each subject added to the collection suitable for enclosing in a loose leaf book. See instructions at the side for punching holes.

GOUDEY GUM COMPANY • Boston, Mass.

To Punch Holes

Nº 7. HUGHES' RECORD SMASHER — Northrop Gamma Mail Plane

No. 7 . . . 1936 HISTORY OF AVIATION SERIES

HUGHES' RECORD SMASHER

Northrop Gamma Mail Plane

IN this great, powerful, stream-lined monoplane Howard Hughes made the newest non-stop cross country flight record. The flight covered about 2450 miles. The time was 9 hours, 27 minutes and 10 seconds. The average speed was close to 260 miles an hour for the entire distance. Over one long stretch a speed of 295 miles an hour was made.

To lessen resistance and cut fuel use most of the distance was flown at 18,000 feet. At times Hughes used oxygen tanks for breathing. But there was no discomfort. The cabin was well heated. The flight proved certain advantages of high altitude flying.

A new-type super-charged, radial motor (Wright G Cyclone) built to army specifications was used. At 15,000 feet it develops 700 horsepower. And gives 925 h.p. for take off at sea level. It is equipped with a two speed blower or super-charger. This makes it possible to use very high power near the ground. The second gear shift is the Hamilton constant speed propeller which gives maximum bite on the air at take off and automatically adjusts the pitch of the blade through steady climbing till they are at high pitch at the ceiling where they remain for altitude flying.

It is a single seat monoplane. Wing spread is 47 ft. 9½ inches. The length is 31 ft. 2 inches. Weight fully loaded about 10,000 lbs. The Northrop Corp., Inglewood, Calif., are the manufacturers.

This is one of the 1936 History of Aviation Series of famous planes and pilots offered to create greater interest in aviation, and for the purpose of instruction and education in aviation. The complete series makes a beautiful and valuable collection. Each subject added to the collection suitable for enclosing in a loose leaf book. See instructions at the side for punching holes.

THESE PICTURES COME ONLY WITH AIR SERVICE GUM

GOUDEY GUM COMPANY • Boston, Mass.

To Punch Holes

1 Howard Hughes—"Aviation Speed King"
2 Captain Edward V. Rickerbacker—"Ace of Aces"
3 Wiley Post—"Great 'Round the World Flyer"
4 Colonel Charles A. Lindbergh—the "Lone Eagle"
5 Rear Admiral Richard E. Byrd
6 Wiley Post's "Winnie Mae"—Lockheed Vega Craft
7 Hughes' Record Smasher—Northrop Gamma Mail Plane
8 Lindbergh's "Spirit of St. Louis"—a Ryan Monoplane
9 "Over the North Pole with Byrd"—in a Fokker
10 Wings Over the Pacific—"China Clipper"

Nº 3. CAPT. EDWARD V. RICKENBACKER — "Ace of Aces"

Nº 10. WINGS OVER THE PACIFIC — "China Clipper"

Nº 3. WILEY POST — "Great 'round the World Flyer"

Nº 6. WILEY POST'S "WINNIE MAE" — Lockheed Vega Craft

HOLLYWOOD SCREEN STARS (40)   2 3/8" X 3"

The Shelby Gum Company of Shelby, Ohio, boasted that its one-cent package of "Hollywood Picture Star Gum" was "The greatest penny's worth on earth." Who could deny that claim? Not only did you get a big chunk of swell tasting gum, but also a color picture of your favorite "Hollywood Screen Star," a "Your Fortune" feature on every card, and two pieces of nifty "stage money" to cut from the wrapper. In addition, a "beautiful album" to house 20 cards was awarded randomly to purchasers who found a "prize" slip in their gum pack. Information about obtaining the album via the mail (for one piece of stage money and 6 cents in stamps) was also printed on one of the two different back layouts that exist for these cards. The "album" back has red print on gray stock, and the fronts list a movie credit for the star. Cards without the album offer do not list movies for the stars and are printed in brown ink on tan stock on back. In addition, some cards with blank backs have been reported. [The series was also issued in Canada (English/French fortune) by Hamilton Chewing Gum Co.] The wrapper has a red and green center on clear wax paper and two "stage money" panels. The reference number is R68. (The reference number for the Canadian version is V289.)

ITEM	EX	AVE
Set	1000.00	250.00
Wrapper	150.00	––
Flyer	75.00	25.00
Album	125.00	45.00
Box	600.00	200.00

CANADIAN VERSION PRODUCED BY HAMILTON CHEWING GUM LTD.

RETAIL STORE ADVERTISING SHEET

Hollywood Screen Stars

CARD		EX	AVE
1	Andy Devine	25.00	6.00
2	Ramon Novarro	15.00	3.50
3	George Brent	15.00	3.50
4	Ben Blue	15.00	3.50
5	Dick Powell	15.00	3.50
6	Ken Maynard	18.00	4.00
7	Tom Tyler	18.00	4.00
8	Andy Clyde	15.00	3.50
9	Tom Mix	18.00	4.00
10	William Desmond	15.00	3.50
11	Slim Summerville	15.00	3.50
12	Jackie Cooper	18.00	4.00
13	Stan Laurel	30.00	7.00
14	Charlie Chase	15.00	3.50
15	Clark Gable	50.00	10.00
16	Harry Langdon	12.00	3.00
17	Lew Ayres	15.00	3.50
18	Robert Montgomery	15.00	3.50
19	Oliver Hardy	30.00	7.00
20	Wallace Berry	18.00	4.00
21	Patricia Ellis	12.00	3.00
22	Helen Vinson	12.00	3.00
23	Marion Schockley	12.00	3.00
24	Helen Hayes	15.00	3.50
25	Joan Blondell	18.00	4.00
26	Zasu Pitts	15.00	3.50
27	Marie Dressler	15.00	3.50
28	Betty Compson	12.00	3.00
29	Rosalie Roy	12.00	3.00
30	Sheila Terry	12.00	3.00
31	Shirley Temple	50.00	10.00
32	Bebe Daniels	15.00	3.50
33	Joan Crawford	20.00	5.00
34	Gloria Stuart	12.00	3.00
35	Polly Moran	12.00	3.00
36	Thelma Todd	12.00	3.00
37	Tala Birell	12.00	3.00
38	Loretta Young	18.00	4.00
39	Jean Harlow	35.00	8.00
40	Ruby Keeler	20.00	5.00

ROSALIE ROY
appearing in Universal pictures

1938 BLOTTER FROM SHELBY GUM

THE J. WARREN BOWMAN STORY

from an article in *The Philadelphia Record*, May 15, 1938, by W. Penn, Jr.

J. Warren Bowman at his desk

J. Warren Bowman started in the penny chewing-gum business eight years ago in a corner of the five-story loft building at 3249 Woodland Ave. (Philadelphia, PA) with a total capital of $25, a barrel of sugar, a barrel of glucose and large strong arms.

His 300 employees now occupy the entire building. For the last few months he has been taking in $44,000 a week on only one of his three chewing gum products, and since he has already grossed about $1,000,000 since the start of the year, he sees no reason why he won't gross $2,500,000 by the end of the year — even though the normal penny chewing-gum business of the entire United States is only $3,500,000 a year.

1929 Success Story.

Bowman's career composes one of those amazing success stories that were typical of American life before 1929, but which stopped with some abruptness then. "Married, divorced and bankrupt before he was 21," as he expresses it, he married his third wife at Elkton (MD) last week — he's 42 now — wealthy, and is on his way to becoming a national figure with his latest product, a bubble gum called by children "war gum."

Bowman last year engaged in considerable litigation with former associates in his business, which started by making "By Gum," then branched out into "Blony," and next "Lone Ranger" gum. (The only difference between Blony and Lone Ranger is the name.) In the court settlement Bowman agreed to make a down payment of $60,000 to his former associates and $4000 a month for a considerable period to pay off the remainder of the price that gave him entire control of the plant.

Bowman went to his friends, including State Senator Harry Shapiro, who was his attorney in the case, obtained the money for the down payment (Senator Shapiro was given 12½ percent of the shares) and then looked around for ways of boosting the sale of his gum to make sure he'd have that $4000 every month.

Big Idea Bursts.

One night last December Bowman was reading an account of the Chinese-Japanese undeclared war and listening to the radio commentator talking about it at the same time. The big idea was born right there: Because children love thrills and excitement and love to collect things, he would give them with their penny bubble gum a series of pictures of the Chinese-Japanese war, the war in Spain and the Ethiopian campaign. He called in George Moll, advertising executive, who toned down Bowman's ideas somewhat so as not to stir up the anti-war feelings of American parents.

In a short time millions of sticks of penny bubble gum were rolling from Bowman's machines, each of them containing a terrifying scene from some modern battle, notifying the young purchaser: "This package of Bubble Gum contains one of a series of 240 picture cards showing the HORRORS OF WAR and teaching the importance of peace." The wrapper reads: "Horrors of WAR" — with the first two words very small, and the last very large, in red ink. The wrapper also shows bombs bursting and men dying.

W. Penn Jr., asked Bowman if he had no twinges of conscience about the violence of the message conveyed to children through bubble gum, but Moll, replying for him, said the firm is doing a great deal to aid the cause of peace "by exposing the horrors of war."

Bowman, who is ingenious enough to devise his own gum-wrapping machinery, is constantly thinking of new advertising exploits. Now he is experimenting with toy balloons, which he frees from the roof of his factory.

Editors note: The article above was written less than six months after J. Warren Bowman conceived the idea for Horrors of War. Although the Horrors of War card set was to prove his most famous brainchild, the career of J. Warren Bowman was in its infancy in 1938. Certainly the most inventive, bravest, and most dynamic of all bubble gum card executives (the mitigating effects of colleague George Moll notwithstanding), Bowman's work is described throughout the pre-war section of this book under the auspices of Gum, Incorporated. In the post-war section of the book, which follows, after Bowman changed the name of the company, cards of the Bowman Gum Company are all attributable to the J. Warren Bowman genius. For 28 years Bowman's offerings to the card field were some of the most artistic and imaginative ever produced — American Beauties, G—Men, Horrors of War, Lone Ranger, Mickey Mouse, Superman, Uncle Sam and Home Defense, War Gum, Wild Man, Wild West, to name but a few.

Nor were Bowman's exploits limited to the non-sports field — his Play Ball baseball cards of 1939-41 and his baseball, football and basketball card sets of the late 1940's and early to mid-1950's were, in their way, classics. The constant battles with competitors (initially Leaf and later Topps) for rights to produce card sets (particularly for athletes) culminated in the sale of the Bowman Gum Company to Topps in early 1956. (The litigation and in-fighting between gum companies during Bowman's last eight years of existence would make excellent topics for future articles.)

The description and pricing of the Horrors of War card set which follows is formatted in a slightly different manner than other sets in this book. Because of the importance of this set in the non-sport field, the authors feel that the format used allows for a clearer understanding of the subject matter and a better correlation between text and visual display. Now, for your enjoyment, without further ado, we present . . . .

HORRORS OF WAR (288) 2 1/2" X 3 1/8"

"Horrors of War," perhaps the most famous non-sport card set of all time, was marketed in 1938 by Gum, Inc. of Philadelphia. The sensational graphic artwork and propaganda-laden text turned the series into an overnight success, and it was even featured in LIFE magazine. The first 48 cards have small size numbers prefaced with the abbreviation "No." Of these, 1-24 are considered slightly more difficult to obtain than 25-48. Card No. 1 is especially hard to find in top condition (most copies are out of focus). Cards 25-192 are the most common in the series, and a switch from small to larger numbers (minus the "No.") was made with card 49. Cards in the 193-240 sequence finish off the "traditional" or "first" series of Horrors of War (HOW), and they are much tougher to find than the first 192. In a sense, these last 48 cards were the original "high" numbers of HOW because evidence exists that Gum, Inc. planned the set to total only 240 cards. The nightmarish artwork of card No. 240, "The Frightful Cost of War," and the fact that it was the original "last" card in the set are factors which have made it the "key" card in the set. All of the first 240 cards advertise a set total of 240 although the wording varies within specific print runs. They were issued in gum pack wrappers with four different sets of war designs (see illustrations) and in six different colors: blue, green, orange, rose, white, and yellow. Of these, green and white are the colors most commonly encountered.

CARD FROM 1-24 SERIES; SMALL NUMERAL WITH "No." IN FRONT

CARD FROM 49-96 SERIES; LARGE NUMERAL WITHOUT THE "No."

CARD FROM HIGHER SERIES; LARGE NUMERAL WITHOUT "No."

CARD FROM THE 193-240 SERIES. NOTE LINE AT THE BOTTOM ADVERTISING ADDITIONAL SERIES

CARD 240, LAST NUMBER OF ORIGINAL SERIES OF 240 CARDS:
GRUESOME ARTWORK CONTRIBUTES TO MAKING THIS CARD THE
KEY CARD IN THE ENTIRE SET

THREE FIGURE CENTER DESIGN
ALL WITH TWO-POINTED HATS

ONE FIGURE CENTER DESIGN
WITH CYLINDER HAT WITH BRIM

FOUR FIGURE CENTER DESIGN
ALL ORIENTAL-LOOKING FACIALLY

THREE FIGURE CENTER DESIGN
ALL WITH ROUND HELMETS

THE FOUR WRAPPER DESIGNS OF THE INITIAL 1-240 SERIES
EACH WRAPPER APPEARED IN SIX DIFFERENT COLORS

There are two boxes associated with the original "240" set of HOW. The first is the retail store box, pictured here for the first time in any card catalog. This box has printed side panels which read "Horrors of WAR Picture Card and Bubble Gum 1 cent." The packs were arranged in layers of nine. The multi-colored artwork on the top flap of the box depicts Japanese bombers devastating a Chinese city. This box is not known to exist in any modern collection, and it has not been priced in the values section for this reason.

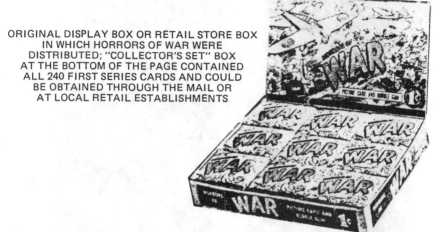

ORIGINAL DISPLAY BOX OR RETAIL STORE BOX IN WHICH HORRORS OF WAR WERE DISTRIBUTED; "COLLECTOR'S SET" BOX AT THE BOTTOM OF THE PAGE CONTAINED ALL 240 FIRST SERIES CARDS AND COULD BE OBTAINED THROUGH THE MAIL OR AT LOCAL RETAIL ESTABLISHMENTS

The remarkable marketing sense of Gum, Inc. owner J. Warren Bowman also led him to package the first 240 cards of HOW into a specially-boxed "Collector's Set" (the first true collector's set in the history of the hobby). It was available via the mail and in retail stores. The box is red and has a 24-card sheet of HOW cards pasted on the cover, with the six center cards hidden by a large label. Inside, cellophane-wrapped stacks of cards sit in the individual compartments of a cardboard insert tray. It is an awe-inspiring sight, and the whole package sold for $1.00! Unlike the retail store box described above, these special edition Collector's Set boxes appear in the card market from time to time. It was recently revealed that Gum, Inc. made their overstock of these boxes available to the public after the end of World War II (when the company changed its name to Bowman Gum). Although this fact should have a moderating influence on market value, the Collector's Set box is still a very costly, high-demand item.

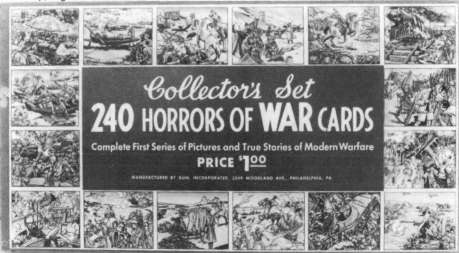

Handsome Collector's Set of 240 Cards
at a Special Price . . . $1⁰⁰

JUST the thing thousands have been waiting for! A complete set of the first 240 cards giving the only picture history of the wars in China, Spain and Ethiopia! Packed in a beautiful gift box telling interesting facts about the manufacture of the cards and how to collect them as a hobby.

You will learn how and when the cards were first introduced; the men responsible for them; the amount of cardboard used; the area they would cover if spread out, and many other things.

There are suggestions for Card Collectors; ways to have fun with the cards by arranging them in displays; projecting them on a screen; playing games with them and other uses too numerous to mention. Get this amazing set and see for yourself!

Complete Collectors' Sets of HORRORS OF WAR Picture Cards, Series 1 to 240, are sold in stores where War Gum is sold. If your neighborhood store does not yet have these sets you may obtain one by sending direct to GUM, INC., DEPT. 5, 3249 Woodland Avenue, Philadelphia, Pennsylvania. Box with 240 different cards will be mailed to you C.O.D.

← USE THIS COUPON

GUM, INCORPORATED, Dept. 5
3249 Woodland Avenue, Philadelphia, Pa.
Gentlemen. Please send me one Collector's Set of 240 HORRORS OF WAR Picture Cards, First Series. On receipt of package I will pay the mailman $1.00, plus a few cents for postage.

NAME
STREET
CITY   STATE

GUM, INCORPORATED
3249 Woodland Avenue, Philadelphia, Pa.

NOTE TO PARENTS:
If you know a boy or girl who is having a birthday soon, this Set will make a gift that is sure to please! Entertaining! Instructive! Valuable! — A! a Bargain Price!

On the backs of the cards in the 193-240 group, we find the statement "Additional Series Coming! Look For Them!" and sure enough, Gum, Inc. printed another run of 48 cards. These cards were sold in a brand new red and yellow wrapper entitled "MORE Horrors of WAR" (Bowman always tried to print the word "war" in the largest type feasible). These were actually bonus packs containing "Bubble Gum and TWO Picture Cards" for a penny. As explained on the bottom flap: "This package contains one of the SECOND SERIES of Horrors of War picture cards and true stories of modern warfare —— also one of the First Series of 240 cards as an EXTRA GIFT. Save to complete the entire collection." All of these "second series" cards are difficult to find in top condition, especially the three cards picturing Adolph Hitler (277, 283 & 286), the most sought-after numbers in the entire series of 288.

THE THREE "HITLER" CARDS IN THE HIGH NUMBER SERIES OF HORRORS OF WAR. ALL ARE TOP VALUE, HIGH DEMAND CARDS

THE "MORE HORRORS OF WAR" WRAPPER IN WHICH THE HIGH NUMBERS (241-288) OF THE SERIES WERE PACKED. THE WORDS "HORRORS OF" ARE BETWEEN THE LARGE WORD "MORE" AND THE VERY LARGE WORD "WAR," BUT ARE NOT VISIBLE ON OUR ILLUSTRATION BECAUSE OF THE LIMITATIONS OF BLACK AND WHITE PHOTOGRAPHIC TECHNIQUES TO DISTINGUISH A RED ON BLACK (OR BLACK ON RED) PATTERN. THE WRAPPER IS BRIGHT RED WITH YELLOW DRAWINGS AND LETTERING. IT IS THE MOST VALUABLE OF ALL HORRORS OF WAR WRAPPERS

As you might imagine, the appearance of Horrors of War cards created a massive public disturbance across the nation. Some groups labeled Bowman a warmonger because of the decidedly anti-Japanese tone of the first series cards. Other people thought he was a visionary patriot. The poor souls who simply objected to the gruesome artwork were drowned out by a wave of "gee, look what we've got here" newspaper articles and the howling banshees debating the pros and cons of "bubble gum diplomacy." Through it all, Bowman comported himself on the basis of two fundamental truths: (1) any publicity is better than no publicity — just spell the name right — and (2) kids, not adults, bought bubble gum cards. At the same time he was publicizing the fact that his art director, George Moll, was a peaceful Sunday school teacher, he was also arranging for some errant cases of HOW cards to turn up in Japan, where they nearly caused anti-American riots (Bowman blamed the "find of cards" on Chinese merchants in the Philippines)! Say what you will about Bowman's methods, the unprecedented success of HOW practically eliminated his competitors from the marketplace and made him into a millionaire.

On a final note, there are some card variations of interest. For one thing, the backs of HOW cards are occasionally found with overprinted messages. The most common of these is a rubber-stamped "prize" announcement: "You're LUCKY! You get a package of cards FREE." Less frequently encountered are cards with machine-printed message boxes in the middle of the text backs. These were given away in gum packs of other Gum, Inc. sets and were meant to attract buyers to HOW. They were also sent to schools for distribution to students and were the "cargo" in Bowman's famous "balloon barrage" of Philadelphia. These overprinted cards are valued at a minimum of 100% over the value of the card on which they appear. The reference number for the American issue of Horrors of War is R69. The first series of 240 cards was also printed for distribution in Canada. These Canadian cards have gray backs, and the line "Printed in Canada" is found in the bottom right corner of the reverse. It is not known if there is a "Canadian" HOW wrapper(s) or box (the reference number for the Canadian issue is V278). Canadian HOW cards are far scarcer than their American counterparts, but are not widely collected, especially in the United States. NOTE: Individual card prices are listed in the checklist.

ITEM	EX	AVE
Set (1-288)	7000.00	1750.00
Collector's Set (1-240) (includes box)	5000.00	—
Wrappers		
White	125.00	—
Green	125.00	—
Yellow	175.00	—
Orange	175.00	—
Rose	175.00	—
Blue	225.00	—
"More" (2nd series)	500.00	—

RUBBER STAMP OVERPRINTED CARD; FREE PACK PRIZE

MACHINE—PRINTED OVERPRINT CARD; FOUND IN OTHER GUM, INC. PRODUCTS AND GIVEN AWAY THROUGH PROMOTIONS

FIRST SERIES CANADIAN CARD NOTE "PRINTED IN CANADA" LINE

LATER SERIES CANADIAN CARD NOTE "PRINTED IN CANADA" LINE AND CHANGE TO LARGE NUMERALS WITHOUT "No."

Horrors of War

		EX	AVE
1	Marco Polo Bridge Is Scene of First Fighting	60.00	15.00
2	Chinese "Big Sword" Corps Resists Jap Forces	15.00	3.00
3	U.S. Marine Shot While Aiding Americans	15.00	3.00
4	War Planes Over Tientsin	15.00	3.00
5	Chinese Pursuers Shoot Down Jap Planes	15.00	3.00
6	Suicide Squad of Japs Is Blasted at Woosung	15.00	3.00
7	Blowing Down the Ancient Walls of Paoshan	15.00	3.00
8	Tokio Tank Fires on British Troops and Refugees	15.00	3.00
9	U.S.S. Panay Is Attacked by the Japanese	15.00	3.00
10	Twenty Naked Chinese Nationalists Charge Foe	15.00	3.00
11	Japanese Flagship Assailed in Whangpoo	15.00	3.00
12	Chinese Bombs Rain Death in Shanghai	15.00	3.00
13	Trapping the Japanese at Nankow Pass	15.00	3.00
14	Bomb Kills Passengers on Shanghai Trolley	15.00	3.00
15	U.S.S. Augusta Is Hit by Shell as Shanghai Burns	15.00	3.00
16	Japanese Attack Train at Wusih	15.00	3.00
17	Girl Scout Carries Flag to Doomed Men	15.00	3.00
18	Japanese Bomb Orphanage at Kashing	15.00	3.00
19	Murder at a Monarchist's Funeral	15.00	3.00
20	Spanish Insurgents Bomb Government Territory	15.00	3.00
21	The Siege of Toledo	15.00	3.00
22	Big Shells Kill Madrid Children at Play	15.00	3.00
23	Early Campaign Tactics of Italy in Ethiopia	15.00	3.00
24	Italian Squadrons Flying Low Slaughter Ethiopians	15.00	3.00
25	Chinese Fight Japs Inside Their Own Lines	12.00	2.50
26	Shells Splinter Deck of Tender with U.S. Refugees	12.00	2.50
27	Mobs Add Terror to Shanghai Shambles	12.00	2.50
28	Shanghai Shoppers Blown Up by Bombs	12.00	2.50
29	Tokio Airman Attacks British Envoy	12.00	2.50
30	Street Fighting Tactics in Shanghai	12.00	2.50
31	Japanese Bombers Raid South Station	12.00	2.50
32	Shelling the "Lost Battalion" at Close Range	12.00	2.50
33	Japanese Slain in Ambush Near Peiping	12.00	2.50
34	Tokio Bombers Invade the Dead	12.00	2.50
35	Anti-Aircraft Guns Blaze as Japs Bomb Power Plant	12.00	2.50
36	Sanitarium Evacuates Its Patients Under Fire	12.00	2.50
37	Japanese Seize Vessel and Destroy U.S. Flag	12.00	2.50
38	Scaling the Gates of Nanking	12.00	2.50
39	Foe's Planes Trail the Chiangs	12.00	2.50
40	Panay Machine Gunners Fight Back	12.00	2.50
41	Chinese Victims of War	12.00	2.50
42	Mob Burns a Madrid Cathedral	12.00	2.50
43	A Loyalist Submarine Goes to a Watery Grave	12.00	2.50
44	The Bombardment of Almercia	12.00	2.50
45	Surrender of Rebels at Teruel	12.00	2.50
46	Haile Selassie Mans a Machine Gun	12.00	2.50
47	Fierce Wallega Tribesmen Attack Italian Aces	12.00	2.50
48	Bombing an American School Building	12.00	2.50
49	Fugitives from the War Zones	8.00	1.50
50	Japanese Bomb Chinese Troops in Junks	8.00	1.50
51	Tokio Tanks in Action at Nanking	8.00	1.50
52	Chinese Use Gas in Counteroffensive	8.00	1.50
53	Bomb Wounds the Panay Commander	8.00	1.50
54	U.S.S. Panay Sinks as Crew Abandons Ship	8.00	1.50
55	Nanking's Week of Horror	8.00	1.50
56	Nanking Retreat Turned into a Rout	8.00	1.50
57	Japanese Soldiers Burn Their Dead	8.00	1.50
58	The Dynamiting of Tsingtao	8.00	1.50
59	Chinese Granadiers Bomb Japanese Launch	8.00	1.50
60	American Homes Looted at Hangchow	8.00	1.50
61	Blowing Up the Wen River Railway Bridge	8.00	1.50
62	Bombers Raid Jap Airdrome in New Defensive	8.00	1.50
63	The Chiangs Decorate Their Crack Fliers	8.00	1.50
64	Japanese Engineers Build a Pontoon Bridge	8.00	1.50
65	Chinese Women's Battalion on the March	8.00	1.50
66	"Hedge-Hoppers" Strafe Chinese Positions	8.00	1.50
67	Women Fighters in Action in Spain	8.00	1.50
68	Rebel Howitzers Attack in Snowstorm	8.00	1.50
69	Gun Shells Daring War Reporters in Spain	8.00	1.50
70	Subway Blast Kills Madrid Civilians.	8.00	1.50
71	The Emperor Leaves Ethiopia	8.00	1.50
72	Attack on American Legation at Addis Ababa	8.00	1.50
73	British Commander Breaks Up a Blockade	8.00	1.50
74	The Starving Children of China	8.00	1.50
75	Hsia Ching-yuan Saves His Doomed Men	8.00	1.50
76	Warning of an Air Raid in China	8.00	1.50
77	The Attack on the Gallant Ladybird	8.00	1.50
78	River Gate Is Death Trap for Chinese in Rout	8.00	1.50
79	Japans Triumphal Entry into Nanking	8.00	1.50
80	Chiang's Son Leads Red Army Against Japs	8.00	1.50
81	Japanese Airmen Bombard Schools in Canton	8.00	1.50
82	U.S. Airman Shot Down Flying for China	8.00	1.50
83	Tokio Flotilla Runs Machine Gun Gauntlet	8.00	1.50
84	Tokio Marines Take Tsingtao without a Fight	8.00	1.50
85	Jap Planes Bomb Yellow River Bridge	8.00	1.50
86	Chinese Schoolgirls Enlist for War Service	8.00	1.50
87	Chinese Bombers Raid Japanese Territory	8.00	1.50
88	"Human Hands" Warn Newspaper Publishers	8.00	1.50
89	Woman Photographer Crushed by Loyalist Tank	8.00	1.50
90	Depth Bomb Sinking Pirate Submarine	8.00	1.50
91	Floods Wash Out Fighting in Spain	8.00	1.50
92	Pirate Sub Torpedoes Dutch Freighter	8.00	1.50
93	Crack Rebel Cavalry Attacks Loyalists	8.00	1.50
94	Torpedoing the Rebel Cruiser Baleares	8.00	1.50
95	Ras Seyum's Bodyguard Defends Palace	8.00	1.50

		EX	AVE
96	Native Uprisings Harass Italian Rule	8.00	1.50
97	Chinese Army Hides Beneath Umbrellas	8.00	1.50
98	Dummy Chinese War Planes Are "Bait" for Japs	8.00	1.50
99	Ghoulish Dogs Haunt the Ruins of China	8.00	1.50
100	Blizzard Halts Military Operations	8.00	1.50
101	Japanese General Killed in Ambush	8.00	1.50
102	Chinese Guerillas Wreck a Supply Train	8.00	1.50
103	Chinese Reds Flee Across Ice-filled River	8.00	1.50
104	The Music of Death	8.00	1.50
105	U.S. Marines Halt Japanese Troops	8.00	1.50
106	Man-Made Floods Drown Japanese Troops	8.00	1.50
107	Japanese Machine-gun Enemy Air Pilot	8.00	1.50
108	Gibraltar Gives Refuge to Spaniards	8.00	1.50
109	Loyalist Flame-thrower in Action	8.00	1.50
110	Rebel Bomb Floods Air Raid Shelter	8.00	1.50
111	Loyalist and Rebels Meet in Sea Battle	8.00	1.50
112	Hand-to-Hand Fighting in Aragon	8.00	1.50
113	Franco's Planes Strafe Barcelona by Night	8.00	1.50
114	Bomb Blows Penthouse from Roof of Building	8.00	1.50
115	Barcelona Intersection Turned into Shambles	8.00	1.50
116	"Surrender or Perish"	8.00	1.50
117	Loyalists Surrender Arms and War Machines	8.00	1.50
118	Dynamite-slingers Contest Rebel's Drive	8.00	1.50
119	Ethiopians Catch Italian Tank in Lion Trap	8.00	1.50
120	Italian Artillery Attacks Amba Aradam	8.00	1.50
121	Japanese Apply Torch to Dead Farmer	8.00	1.50
122	Hongkong Builds New Fortifications	8.00	1.50
123	Wine-sotted Soldier Kills Villagers	8.00	1.50
124	Japanese Bomb Railhead at Suchow	8.00	1.50
125	Seeking Life in the Face of Death	8.00	1.50
126	Chinese Cavalry Surrounds Garrison of Japs	8.00	1.50
127	Spear-Armed Farmers Assault Japanese	8.00	1.50
128	Chinese Universities Flee from War	8.00	1.50
129	Swimming Jap Cavalry Repulsed by Chinese	8.00	1.50
130	Japanese Tunnel Under Wall to their Doom	8.00	1.50
131	Chiang Kai-shek Commanding His Troops	8.00	1.50
132	Chinese Motorized Unit with Amphibious Tanks	8.00	1.50
133	Loyalists Take Rebels Prisoners in Barcelona	8.00	1.50
134	Loyalist Air Raid at Majorca	8.00	1.50
135	A Battle from a Rooftop in Barcelona	8.00	1.50
136	Loyalists Bombard Algeciras with Big Guns	8.00	1.50
137	Movie Crowds Are Caught by Rebel Shells	8.00	1.50
138	Bombed Church Dome Crushes War Orphans	8.00	1.50
139	Franco Retakes Teruel in Bloody Night Battle	8.00	1.50
140	Rebels Clean Up Teruel After Recapture	8.00	1.50
141	Populace Streams Underground to Avoid Bombs	8.00	1.50
142	Fleeing Loyalists Freeze in Mountains	8.00	1.50
143	Italians Bomb Red Cross Unit at Kworam	8.00	1.50
144	Meat "on-the-Hoof," Dropped from the Sky	8.00	1.50
145	Lake Dwellers "Sell Out" to Japs	8.00	1.50
146	Chinese Terrorists Meet Death in Nanking	8.00	1.50
147	Airmen Destroy Pontoon Bridge to Trap Japs	8.00	1.50
148	Clearing the Battlefield for Action in China	8.00	1.50
149	"Delousing Party" Behind the Japanese Lines	8.00	1.50
150	Chinese Airmen Score Spectacular Triumph	8.00	1.50
151	Swords and Bayonets Clash in Bloody Fight	8.00	1.50
152	Shanghai University Head Slain by Gunmen	8.00	1.50
153	Death Among the Water Lilies	8.00	1.50
154	Jap Planes Bomb Uniform Factory at Canton	8.00	1.50
155	Cantonese Parade through Coffin-lined Streets	8.00	1.50
156	Japs Burn Villages to Smoke Out Guerilas	8.00	1.50
157	The Scourge of War in Spain	8.00	1.50
158	Planes Dump Explosives in Lerida School	8.00	1.50
159	Mistake in Identity Causes Loyalist Slaughter	8.00	1.50
160	Setting Off Propaganda Rockets in Spain	8.00	1.50
161	Franco Assumes Personal Command Near Lerida	8.00	1.50
162	Spanish Volunteers Swim Icy River	8.00	1.50
163	Loyalist President Leaves Barcelona	8.00	1.50
164	Catalan Women Build New Fortifications	8.00	1.50
165	Pontoon Bridges Aid Rebels to Cross Segre River	8.00	1.50
166	Liquid-Fire-Throwers Burn Their Way Through Loyalists	8.00	1.50
167	Askari Cavalrymen Advance on Adowa	8.00	1.50
168	Ethiopian Defenses at Tembien	8.00	1.50
169	Peiping State Procession	8.00	1.50
170	Tokio Bombers Drone Over Sacred Mountain	8.00	1.50
171	"Little Devil" Learns Jap Military Secrets	8.00	1.50
172	Japs Drive Against Chinese "Pill Boxes"	8.00	1.50
173	Disguised Guerilla Troops Prey on Japs	8.00	1.50
174	Women Propagandists Urge Chinese Patriotism	8.00	1.50
175	Japanese Women Learn How to Shoot	8.00	1.50
176	Trapped Japs Fed by Plane	8.00	1.50
177	Mute Signs of a Resounding Battle	8.00	1.50
178	Jap Officers Commit Hara-Kiri	8.00	1.50
179	Wrecked Highway Brings Diaster to Foe	8.00	1.50
180	Jap Airplane Carriers Launch Mass Attacks	8.00	1.50
181	Men Against Machines	8.00	1.50
182	Franco Advances in Smoke Screen	8.00	1.50
183	Loyalists Open Flood Gates to Check Rebels	8.00	1.50
184	Rebels Trapped in Lerida by Ruse	8.00	1.50
185	Moors Attack City to Avenge Ancient Defeat	8.00	1.50
186	Rebels Brave Machine Guns at Lerida	8.00	1.50
187	Rebels Halted with Flares and Grenades	8.00	1.50
188	Rebels Cut Off Barcelona Power	8.00	1.50

	EX	AVE			EX	AVE
189 Rebel Plane Bombs Loyalist Hospital Train	8.00	1.50		240 The Frightful Cost of War	250.00	35.00
190 The Homeless Children of Spain	8.00	1.50		241 Russian Troops Invade Jap-Claimed Territory	30.00	6.00
191 Italian Conquest Proclaimed	8.00	1.50		242 New Soviet Planes Conceal Troops in Wings	30.00	6.00
192 Machine Guns Protect Italians from Bandits	8.00	1.00		243 Soviet Cutter Lands on Island in Jap Clash	30.00	6.00
193 Chinese Prisoners Foiled in Camp Escape	35.00	7.50		244 Russians Burn Village in Manchukuo	30.00	6.00
194 A Battle Among the Graves	35.00	7.50		245 Japs Wrest Hilltop from Soviets in Fight	30.00	6.00
195 Capture of Soviet Pilot Causes Jap Protest	35.00	7.50		246 Soviet Planes Bomb Area Japs Claim	30.00	6.00
196 Chinese Guerillas Slaughter Jap Scouts	35.00	7.50		247 Soviets Repulsed in Dawn Attack	30.00	6.00
197 Ancestors Pay Price of Treason in China	35.00	7.50		248 Jap Flares Disperse Fog and Expose Foe	30.00	6.00
198 Chinese Recapture Birth Place of Confucius	35.00	7.50		249 Japs' German-type Guns Reply to Soviet	30.00	6.00
199 Japanese Are Blasted at Yihsien	35.00	7.50		250 Russian Bombers Raid Korean Villages	30.00	6.00
200 Japs Recapture Lini in Revenge Drive	35.00	7.50		251 Devil-Worshiping Koreans View "Dog Fights"	30.00	6.00
201 Farmers of Famine	35.00	7.50		252 Russian Tank Commander Is "Purged"	30.00	6.00
202 Japs Retaliate by Bombing Passenger Ships	35.00	7.50		253 Jap Machine-Gunners Attack Reds in New Clash	30.00	6.00
203 Jap Launches Halt British Ship Whangpoo	35.00	7.50		254 Armistice Suspends Fighting on Border	30.00	6.00
204 Emperor Hirohito's Birthday Raid	35.00	7.50		255 The Last Bowl of Rice	30.00	6.00
205 The Changing Tides of Battle	35.00	7.50		256 Daring Jap Unit Takes Susung in Hankow Drive	30.00	6.00
206 The Deserted Village	35.00	7.50		257 Crowds Cheer Execution of Traitors	30.00	6.00
207 Loyalists Cross Garonne to Safety	35.00	7.50		258 Chinese Unleash Yangtze Flood to Halt Japs	30.00	6.00
208 Insurgents Plant Their Banner at the Sea	35.00	7.50		259 Chinese Pilot Makes Death Dive in Yangtze	30.00	6.00
209 Rebel Cavalry Commander Killed in Action	35.00	7.50		260 Child of the Death Rain	30.00	6.00
210 Rebels Dump Bombs on Pass into France	35.00	7.50		261 Chinese Flee as Bombs Rake Hankow	30.00	6.00
211 Rebels Capture Loyalist Gold	35.00	7.50		262 Rebels Drop Curtain of Fire in Ebro	30.00	6.00
212 Franco Pushes on Through Violent Rains	35.00	7.50		263 Lone Raider Bombs Neutral Ships	30.00	6.00
213 "Living Wall" at Alcala	35.00	7.50		264 "Don't Shoot Your Brothers"	30.00	6.00
214 "Over the Top" with Hand Grenades	35.00	7.50		265 Japs Torture Reds After Armistice	40.00	9.00
215 Loyalists Abandon Armored Train Under Fire	35.00	7.50		266 Red Police and Chinese Fight Over Flag	40.00	9.00
216 Wartime "Castel in Spain"	35.00	7.50		267 Jap Bombers Ignite U.S. Oil Tanks	40.00	9.00
217 Chinese Rout the Japs at Matowchen	35.00	7.50		268 Gun Boat Oahu Sails in Defiance of Japs	40.00	9.00
218 An Assault on an Ancient Military Citadel	35.00	7.50		269 Tokio Planes Wreck U.S. Pilot's Transport	40.00	9.00
219 Yintak...The Most Bombed Spot on Earth	35.00	7.50		270 Jap Machine-Gunners Pursue Swimming Airman	40.00	9.00
220 Japanese Attack Amoy Fortifications	35.00	7.50		271 U.S. Monacacy Threatened by Mines	40.00	9.00
221 British Scientist Bayoneted by Sentry	35.00	7.50		272 Chinese Protest Jap Use of Poison Gas	40.00	9.00
222 Chinese "Lifeline" Cut by Tokio Troops	35.00	7.50		273 Nanking Under Japanese Rule	40.00	9.00
223 Chinese Bombers Drop Leaflets on Japan	35.00	7.50		274 Rebels Bomb Barcelona's Flower Promenade	40.00	9.00
224 Suchow Falls to the Invaders	35.00	7.50		275 Loyalists Adopt Submarine Mail Service	40.00	9.00
225 Infuriated Chiang Orders Dawn Attacks	35.00	7.50		276 Spanish Raid Refugees Bury Their Dead	40.00	9.00
226 Cholera Breaks Out in Pootung	35.00	7.50		277 Hitler's Border Tour Raises War Scare	150.00	30.00
227 Chinese Trap "Lawrence of Manchuria," in Vain	35.00	7.50		278 Italians Evict French Farmers in War Move	40.00	9.00
228 Japs Rain Death in Canton Ignoring Protests	35.00	7.50		279 France Moves Troops to Frontier	40.00	9.00
229 Japanese "Human Bridges" Aid Advance	35.00	7.50		280 Italians Evict French Farmers in War Move	40.00	9.00
230 "No Man's Land" on Aliaga Slope	35.00	7.50		281 Inside the Maginot Line	40.00	9.00
231 Home-Going Madrilenos Killed by Shells	35.00	7.50		282 "Horse Whipping" of Deputy Inflames Sudetens	40.00	9.00
232 Loyalists Attach Hillside Trenches in Rain	35.00	7.50		283 Hitler Threatens Force to Free Sudetens	300.00	60.00
233 Clear Weather Leads to Loyalist Trap	35.00	7.50		284 Germany's Amazing Mobile Big Gun	40.00	9.00
234 Spanish Rebel Planes Bomb French Border	35.00	7.50		285 Sudetens and Czechs Engage in Civil War	40.00	9.00
235 Fierce Fight Marks New	35.00	7.50		286 Chamberlain Meets Hitler in Peace Effort	200.00	40.00
236 Rebels and Allies "Celebrate"	35.00	7.50		287 Premier Hodza Confers with Army Heads Over War	40.00	9.00
237 Marketing Throngs Killed in Rebel Air Attack	35.00	7.50		288 Czech President Surrenders as Mobs Cry "Fight"	60.00	15.00
238 "Miaja's Nephews" Fortify Heights	35.00	7.50				
239 Rebels Bomb Alicante, Firing British Ship	35.00	7.50				

... THIS IS BUBBLE GUM'S WAR IN CHINA

The course of the war in China may be very confusing to adult Americans but it is becoming very clear and familiar to myriad American youngsters who are bubble-gum chewers. The reasons appear in the illustrations on these pages, printed in vivid color, are given away by Gum, Inc. of Philadelphia with every slab of its "Blony" bubble gum. The buyer collects or swaps the cards. He blows the gum out of his mouth into huge balloon-like bubbles (*see opposite*).

Giving war-picture cards away is old candy-trade practice but cards have usually related old-hat history like the massacre of Custer's men. Gum, Inc. gets its wars hot off the battlefield, is satisfied with nothing older than a slaughter in Nanking. The cards are executed by Gum, Inc.'s advertising counsel, George Maull, a Sunday-school teacher, who lends a peaceful tone to the otherwise martial cards by printing on each the motto: "To know the HORRORS OF WAR is to want PEACE." It is no fault of Mr. Maull's that children now ask for the product as "War Gum."

On the back of each card are detailed captions, quoted here, which are very specific about destruction and are anti-Japanese because Mr. Maull feels America is anti-Japanese. But some future historian may trace a cause for a U.S.-Japanese war to the fact that the generation which was pre-adolescent in America in 1938 had received severe anti-Japanese prejudices through its curious liking for blowing bubbles with Blony gum.

"Sir Hughe Knatchbull-Hugessen, British Ambassador to China, was hurrying to a conference in Shanghai on Aug. 26, 1937. His car flew a Union Jack as plain notification of British status. All of a sudden a Japanese bomber swept over, dived toward the British car. There was a burst of machine-gun bullets and the Ambassador slumped in his seat, shot through the liver. Japan apologized for a 'mistake in identity' . . . but had additional explaining to do when Japanese planes also destroyed an American dairy nearby!"

"Early morning, Oct. 29, 1937, the Chinese 'doomed battalion' was defending its warehouse-fortress in Shanghai. A Girl Scout appeared in 'No Man's Land,' in her arms a big Chinese flag. Her purpose was to get it to the fort to take the place of the battle-scarred ensign flying! Shells burst all around as she made her way along an unused trench. She reached her destination, and in a few minutes the new flag was waving proudly. Then the brave girl crawled back. She had done her 'good deed' for that day."

"Generalissimo and Madame Chiang decided to flee from danger on Dec. 7, 1937. Taking off from Nanking in a speedy Boeing, they were sighted by six Japanese pursuit planes! The Jap flyers gave chase, little suspecting what distinguished quarry they were after. They followed the Chiangs in a mad chase for over 175 miles! Several times it looked like certain death for the noted Chinese General and his wife. However, their trusty pilot finally lost the pursuers in vicinity of Anking, up-river from Nanking."

"Horrors beyond human imagination took place in Nanking between Dec. 10 and 18, 1937. Generalissimo Chiang Kai-shek, despite expert advices, had left some of his best troops to make a last stand inside the city. When the walls were breached, Chinese soldiers stripped to their underclothes and ran around looking for civilian clothes to disguise themselves. Japanese shot down everyone seen running or caught in a dark alley. Soldiers and civilians were tied in groups of 50 and executed in cold blood!"

"Japan's biggest investment in China was the 100-million-dollar textile industry at Tsingtao. Rather than allow the Japanese advance to occupy this rich seaport to advantage, Chinese devastation squads spent nearly two weeks prior to Dec. 31, 1937, in systematic dynamiting of Jap factories and homes! Hundreds of fires were set. Meanwhile Chinese legions in the west were fighting desperately to stem the Japanese advance upon Tsingtao as an important continuation of the Chinese Armies' 'scorched earth policy.'"

"U. S. S. Panay, on Dec. 12, 1937, was anchored in the Yangtze River about 28 miles above Nanking. American flags, prominently displayed, gave warning of its status. Imagine the bitter surprise of its crew when at 1:38 p.m. Japanese planes began dropping bombs on its decks! The first group dive-bombed from a considerable altitude. Later, when the *Panay* was visibly smashed, they let go bombs nearer the ship. Just before the vessel sank, Japanese machine gunners approached on a boat and fired on the ship."

"War has always been a cruel butcher of men, a relentless destroyer of civilization. Japan's undeclared war against China is even more horrible because it has caused the wholesale destruction of innocent families. Cities have been laid waste, peaceful farms bombed and villagers slaughtered. Without a place to live, without food, without hope, pitiable survivors wander about the chaotic countryside, dazed and dejected. What is to become of China? What is to become of the World . . . if War is not outlawed!"

LIFE MAGAZINE ARTICLE PRINTED AFTER THE RELEASE OF "HORRORS OF WAR"

"HOW TO DO" CARDS (10)

The "How To Do" series is the fifth of six Holloway Candy Company strip card sets to be reviewed at this point in our alphabetical list. The set was unknown to any of the early card researchers; it has been assigned the reference number R203 by the Hobby Card Index. The color drawings depict puzzles, tricks, and novelties with short explanations and directions on front. The backs carry only a brief advertising statement and the company name and location. At least one Holloway strip card series comes in both thick and thin cardboard stock, but the "How To Do" set has only been found on thin board. There are probably ten cards in the set but only three titles are known at this time.

This is one of a series of "How to Do" Cards Packed with Holloway Milk Made Candies

M. J. HOLLOWAY & CO., CHICAGO, ILL.

2 1/2" X 3"

ITEM	EX	AVE
Card	15.00	5.00

PARTIAL CHECKLIST
A Whirligig
Form A Perfect Square
The Disappearing Coin

HUMPTY DUMPTY UP—TO—DATE (24)

The idea behind Humpty Dumpty Up-To-Date, a Shelby Gum Co. series, was to modernize classic nursery rhymes in humorous style. Each card front bears a color drawing of a nursery rhyme character set upon a white background. The back contains the card number, a funny rhyme, and a statement describing Shelby as "The Originators of Bubble Gum." The "Pho-To Gum" wrapper says nothing about Humpty Dumpty cards, but it is advertised on the backs of the cards. The reference number is R70.

No. 17
HUMPTY DUMPTY
UP-TO-DATE

PETER WHITE
Peter White's not very bright
And he will never smile,
Wherever he goes his monstrous nose
Precedes him by a mile.

There are 24 up-to-date Humpty Dumpty cards, one being packed with every piece PHOTO GUM.

THE SHELBY GUM CO.
SHELBY, OHIO
The Originators of Bubble Gum

2 3/8" X 3"

ITEM	EX	AVE
Card	12.00	3.00
Set	360.00	90.00
Wrapper	300.00	——

1 Margery Mutton Pie
2 Simple Simon
3 Peter Pumpkin Eater
4 Tommy Tucker
5 Little Boy Blue
6 Little Bo-Peep
7 Old Woman In A Shoe
8 Goosey Gander
9 Three Men In A Tub
10 Humpty Dumpty
11 Black Sheep
12 Jack Horner
13 The Beggars
14 Thomas A. Tattamus
15 Old King Cole
16 Jack-Be-Nimble
17 Peter White
18 Solomon Grundy
19 Old Mother Hubbard
20 Miss Muffett
21 Jack Sprat
22
23 Mother Goose
24 Three Little Kittens

HUNTED ANIMALS (25)

Hunted Animals was marketed by the Planters Nut & Chocolate Company in a product called "Big Game Peanut Blocks." The color artwork cards depict various animals and have an unusual purple tint, which on certain subjects appears unnatural. The backs contain descriptions and are numbered in large block print in the upper left corner. A sequel set advertised on the cards, "Trapped Animals," apparently was never issued. Judging by the number of sets that have been found in England, it is probable that Planters also distributed the set over there. In contrast to the cards, the wrapper is seldom encountered. The reference number is R71. NOTE: cards with candy stains cannot be graded excellent.

BIG GAME Peanut Blocks
PLANTERS NUT & CHOCOLATE COMPANY
Wilkes-Barre, Pa., Suffolk, Va., San Francisco, Cal.

1	Zebra	14	Lion
2	Grizzly Bear	15	Puma
3	American Buffalo or Bison	16	Giraffe
4	Wapiti Deer	17	Tiger
5	Orang-utan	18	African Elephant
6	Wild Bear	19	Elk
7	Polar Bear	20	Moose
8	Alligator	21	Mountain Sheep
9	Hippopotamus	22	Reindeer
10	Musk Ox	23	Cape or Black African Buffalo
11	Kangaroo	24	Leopard
12	Hyaena	25	Rhinoceros
13	Gorilla		

ITEM	EX	AVE
Card	3.00	.50
Set	85.00	15.00
Wrapper	400.00	––

I'M GOING TO BE (25)

The "I'm Going To Be" series of 25 cards was a Schutter-Johnson product issued in a one-cent wax paper candy pack. The color artwork cards depict people of different vocations in the foreground, with background scenes related to each specific job. A blue frameline and white borders surround the picture. The back has a snappy description of the subject and also bears the card number. Backs also carry advertising for various premiums offered to anyone completing a set. This was made virtually impossible since card No. 4 was distributed on an extremely limited basis. Winners had their sets returned to them with the scarce card hole-punched and stamped "VOID." The reference number is R72. NOTE: set price does not include card No. 4.

ITEM	EX	AVE
Cards		
1-3 & 5-25	7.50	2.00
Set (24)	225.00	55.00
Wrapper	250.00	––
Card No. 4		
canceled	600.00	200.00
uncanc.	1200.00	400.00

1 Clown	9 Jockey	17 Magician
2 Wrestler	10 Athlete	18 Detective
3 Animal Trainer	11 Movie Star	19 Baseball Player
4 Strongman	12 Cowboy	20 Locomotive Engineer
5 Swimmer	13 Fireman	21 Boxer
6 Radio Announcer	14 Policeman	22 Speed Cop
7 Pirate	15 Gold Miner	23 Sailor
8 Auto Racer	16 Aviator	24 Drum Major
		25 Hunter

INDIAN CHIEFS (24)   2 1/4" X 2 5/8"

The themes (and, often, the artwork) of many popular 1930's gum sets were imitated in cheaper versions by strip card companies. The Indian Chiefs set pictured here, most likely a take-off on "Indian Gum," was produced in two distinct types. Type 1 has horizontal pictures on front with the chief's name printed in a fancy panel. The color scheme is blue and red in several graduations. The text on back is found printed in black or blue-green ink. The pictures on Type 2 cards are vertical, and the chiefs are not named on front. The pictures have been "antiqued" by giving them a rust color aspect; the only color of back print reported is black. Although the two types are dissimilar in design, they have identical subjects and numbers. The reference number is R184. NOTE: cards intact in strips are worth 25% more than the prices listed below.

101 Little Crow
102 Red Cloud
103 Little Wolf
104 Magpie
105 White Bear
106 Ten Bears
107 Black Beaver
108 Lone Wolf
109 Big Tree
110 Sitting Bear
111 Kicking Bird
112 White Horse
113 Quanah Parker
114 Old Bull
115 Little Big-Man
116 Young-Man-Afraid-of-His-Horses
117 Two Moons
118 Sitting Bull
119 Chief Gall
120 Low Dog
121 Crow King
122 White-Man-Runs-Him
123 American Horse
124 High Bear

ITEM	EX	AVE
Card	2.50	.60
Set	70.00	18.00

INDIAN GUM (216)   2 3/8" X 2 7/8"

Goudey's "Indian Gum" is, undoubtedly, the most complicated of the classic gum card sets of the 1930's. One reason is that it was issued and re-issued in groups over a span of years from 1933 to 1940, and the backs advertise set totals of 24, 48, 96, 192, 216, 264, 288 and 312 cards. Adding to the confusion was the reprinting of two groups of cards with obverse detail changes: the "blue panel" and the "white background" varieties. Finally, it is evident that Goudey initially distributed part of Indian Gum using skipped numbers to promote sales. As collector Bernard Wermers reports, "Numbers 1-24 were repeated as fill-ins of skipped numbers in the 110-152 sequence. Thus No. 1 was reprinted as No. 110, No. 2 as No. 115, and so on. Accordingly, there are 216 different numbered cards in the set, but only 192 different pictures."

Indian Gum has been the subject of intense research over the years by a number of dedicated collectors. The theories that have evolved from these studies are many and varied and involve the sequence and content of print runs, the occurence of single, double, and triple-printed cards, specific card scarcities, etc. As Win Knowles has observed, "I think the cards should be broken down into about 12 scarcity ranges and priced accordingly." However, because most collectors don't want to become that involved in their sets, we shall leave a more comprehensive analysis of Indian Gum for another time and place.

Simply stated, the Indian Gum series contains 216 numbered, multi-colored artwork cards. Cards 1-216 come with the words "Indian Chewing Gum" printed in a red panel directly under the picture. Cards 1-48 are also found with this "product panel" colored blue. In addition, another 24 cards, all bearing the "series of 312" line on back, contain identical artwork and numbers of previously issued cards but have pure white (rather than colored) backgrounds behind the portrait. All cards in the 1930's Indian Gum series have green-print backs; black-print Indian Gum cards belong to a post-war re-issue. Many of the In-dian portraits in the set were copied from a group of classic Indian studies once housed in the Smithsonian Institute in Washington, D.C. (see illustration of original art with superimposed card). The reference number for the 1930's Indian Gum series is R73.

Two types of "Indian Gum" wrappers exist, each with minor variations. The most common wrapper has numbered Indian "heads" on the sides and a mounted Indian chief posed beside a teepee. Three of these wrappers with variations in "head" design and premium lists have been reported to date. Type 2 wrappers each have six identical Indian scenes on the flaps but differ in the center artwork. The display box illustrated belongs to collector Robert Marks.

The premium pictures advertised on Type 1 wrappers were described as follows: "Each fine art print vividly portrays the natural and picturesque beauty of the warlike Indians in full costumes. These prints have a decor-

ORIGINAL COLOR ARTWORK
FROM WHICH THE GOUDEY INDIAN
GUM CARD WAS COPIED, PLUS
THE CARD COPIED FROM IT

ative border design and are produced from the original paintings by the famous Indian painter Winold Reiss." Pictures painted by Cyrus E. Dallin were added to the premium list on a third Type 1 wrapper. These premiums must have been popular because the last wrapper also added a "right to substitute" warning. However, no modern collector has found a confirmed Goudey-issued Indian premium as of this writing. All of the Indian pictures seen offered as Goudey items appear to be cut from Sante Fe Railroad calendars. Collectors buying any Indian prints advertised as Goudey issues should demand a written guarantee as a condition of sale. Only three Goudey Indian premiums exist in the Burdick museum collection; they measure approximately 7" X 9" and bear no iden-

tifying marks. The reference number for these premiums is R74.

NOTE: the card prices listed below are intended as a general guide and might not reflect specific scarcities or variations currently being researched. The set price is for 216 red panel cards.

ITEM	EX	AVE
Cards		
Red panel		
1-24	10.00	2.50
25-96	7.50	2.00
97-216	12.00	3.00
Blue panel		
1-48	20.00	4.00
White background	40.00	10.00
Set (red panel)	2750.00	675.00
Wrappers		
Type 1	35.00	——
Type 2	100.00	——
Box	750.00	250.00

WHITE BACKGROUND NUMBERS:
154—156—158—160—162—165
167—168—170—179—183—185
187—193—196—100—200—201
202—204—206—207—208—209

1	Shienne Tribe
2	Warrior of the Ioway Tribe
3	Chief of the Konzas Tribe
4	Chief of the Pawnee Tribe
5	Chief of the Delaware Tribe
6	Warrior of the Sioux Tribe
7	Warrior of the Ojibway Tribe
8	Chief of the Ute Tribe
9	Chief of the Flathead Tribe
10	Chief of the Pot-o-wat-o-mies Tribe

SAME CARD WITH COLOR (L)
AND WHITE (R) BACKGROUND

Indian Gum

11 Chief of the Pawnee Tribe
12 Chief of the Sioux Tribe
13 Chief of the Pawnee Tribe
14 Chief of the Ottoes Tribe
15 Chief of the Ogallala Tribe
16 Chief of the Omaha Tribe
17 Chief of the Osages Tribe
18 Warrior of the Osages Tribe
19 Warrior of the Camanche Tribe
20 Warrior of the Kioway Tribe
21 Squaw and Child (Papoose)
22 Chief of the Sioux Tribe
23 Chief of the Manden Tribe
24 Chief of the Blackfoot Tribe
25 Geronimo
26 Red Jacket
27 Joseph Brant
28 Pontiac
29 Osceola
30 King Philip
31 Powhatan
32 Massasoit
33 Pocahantas
34 The Prophet
35 Ah-No-Je-Nahge
36 The Buffalo Bull
37 Black Hawk
38 Sitting Bull
39 Conquering Bear
40 Dutchy
41 Captain Jack
42 Tecumseh
43 American Horse
44 Billy Bowlegs
45 Santana
46 Spotted Tail
47 White-Man-Runs-Him
48 Red Tomahawk
49 Gen. Ben McCulloch
50 Daniel Boone
51 California Joe
52 Davy Crockett
53 Col. Bowie
54 Jim Bridger
55 Gen. Custer
56 William Penn
57 Myles Standish
58 "Mad Anthony" Wayne
59 "Wild Bill"
60 Buffalo Bill
61 Sam Houston
62 Gen. George Crook

63 Simon Kenton
64 La Salle
65 Mrs. Merrill
66 Joe Logston
67 Simon Girty
68 Kit Carson
69 Col. William Crawford
70 Captain John Smith
71 General Sturgis
72 Peter Minuit
73 Chief Washakie
74 Lewis Wetzel
75 The Bear
76 Pony Express
77 Attacked
78 Billy-The-Kid
79 Signaling
80 The Pony War Dance
81 Ezra Meeker
82 Huichol Tribe
83 Nascapee Tribe
84 Hopi Maiden
85 Eagle Dance
86 Acoma Tribe
87 Kichai
88 Victory Cry
89 Traveling
90 Yellowstone Kelly
91 Vapor Bath
92 Chief White Cloud
93 Wolf Collar
94 Minnevana
95 White Cap
96 Praying to the Great Spirit
97 Push-Ma-Ta-Ha
98 Graining the Buffalo Skin
99 Old Bear
100 Red Bear
101 Andy Poe
102 Sassacus
103 Steel
104 Nootka
105 Yellow Tepee
106 Medicine Man
107 Sounding Sky
108 Many Shots
109 Little White Cloud
110 Chief of the Shienne Tribe
111 General Wm. S. Harney
112 Captain Fremont
113 He Who Travels Everywhere
114 In Consultation
115 Warrior of the Ioway Tribe

116 Chief of the Konzas Tribe
117 Caught in the Circle
118 Chief of the Pawnee Tribe
119 Chief of the Delaware Tribe
120 Warrior of the Sioux Tribe
121 The Pigeon's Egg Head
122 Four Bears
123 Tobacco
124 Warrior of the Ojibway Tribe
125 Chief of the Ute Tribe
126 Chief of the Flathead Tribe
127 Chief of Pot-o-wat-o-mies Tribe
128 Chief of the Pawnee Tribe
129 Weasel Calf
130 Chief of the Sioux Tribe
131 Chief of the Pawnee Tribe
132 Chief of the Ottoes Tribe
133 Flying in a Circle
134 Wolf
135 Buffalo Hunt
136 Chief of the Ogallala Tribe
137 Chief of the Omaha Tribe
138 Chief of the Osages Tribe
139 Samoset
140 Warrior of the Osages
141 Two Crows
142 Warrior of the Camanchee Tribe
143 Rain-in-the Face
144 Warrior of the Kioway Tribe
145 Zy-You-Wah
146 Squaw and Child (Papoose)
147 Ko-pe-ley
148 Chief of the Sioux Tribe
149 Hong-Ee
150 Chief of the Mandan Tribe
151 Painting
152 Chief of the Blackfoot Tribe
153 Pottery Making
154 Luqaiot
155 Weaving
156 Genitoa
157 Rushing Bear
158 Hee-ohks-te-kin
159 Fire Dance
160 Chief Bread
161 Fishing
162 Ahyouwaighs
163 Charge on the Sun Pole
164 Trailing a Prairie Schooner
165 Tishcohan

166 The Great King
167 Kishkalwa
168 Pah-me-cow-e-tah
169 Osage Oil Wells
170 Wapella
171 Setting Fire to the Fort
172 The Battering Ram
173 Saving General Putnam
174 Caught in the Attempt
175 Custer's Last Stand
176 Throwing the Putch-Kohu
177 Struggle to Death
178 Primitive Fire Making
179 In-ne-o-cose
180 Fight on the Precipice
181 Defense of the Stockade
182 A Surprise Attack
183 Toh-ki-ee-to
184 Vengeance
185 Ee-A-Chin-Chea-A
186 Fight at the Army Post
187 Shoo-De-Ga-Cha
188 Pipe of Peace
189 Another Redskin Bites the Dust
190 Unhorsed
191 Arrow Making
192 Chief Red Cloud
193 Yo-ho-lo-micco
194 Indian Naval Warfare
195 Wampam
196 Tshi-zun-hau-kau
197 Puritan Days
198 Perils of the Plains
199 Nesjaja Hatali
200 Shar-I-Tar-Ish
201 Wa-pon-je-a
202 Wat-Che-Mon-Ne
203 Running Fox
204 Stee-Cha-Co-Me-Co
205 The Thinker
206 Alchise
207 White Deer Skin Dancer
208 Taiomah
209 Wabaunsee
210 Wood
211 Tracking Game
212 Making a Canoe
213 Marauders
214 Foiled
215 Trapped in Their Ambush
216 Torturing Their Victims

TYPE 1 WRAPPERS

97

TYPE 1 WRAPPER

Indian Gum Premiums

Alex Eagle Plume
Appeal to the Great Spirit
Arrow Top
Big Face Chief
Big Wolf
Buffalo Body
Clears Up
Home Gun
Jim Blood
Lazy Boy Medicine Man
Only Child
The Scout
Tough Bread
Yellow Head

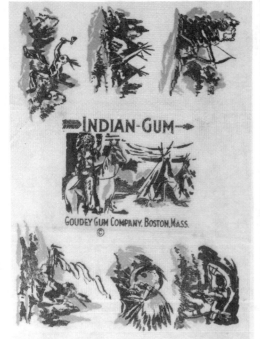

TYPE 2 WRAPPERS

INDIANS, COWBOYS, WESTERN (48?)   2 1/2" X 2 7/8"

The title of this set is a simple descriptive one assigned by Jefferson Burdick because of lack of information on the cards. The format is primitive: one-color pictures on one-color backgrounds. There are 47 titles known, and it appears likely that there are 48 to the set. The series was issued in strips, so each card has at least two "rough" edges (except for end cards, which have one). The backs are blank and the reference number is R75. The color of the photo and background for each subject were changed several times, making it possible to assemble the set in any one of four colors. For example, the "Chief Coyote" card illustrated has either brown or blue cast pictures set upon green, orange, red or yellow backdrops. NOTE: cards in strips are worth 25% more than individual cards.

ITEM	EX	AVE
Cards		
Indians	3.50	1.00
Scenes	3.00	.75
Cowboys	3.50	1.00
Movie Stars		
Buck Jones	8.00	2.00
Ken Maynard	8.00	2.00
Wallace		
McDonald	3.50	1.00
Tom Mix	10.00	3.00
George		
O'Brien	5.00	1.50
Ted Wells	3.50	1.00
Set (48)	200.00	60.00

An Indian Trial
Broncho Buster
Buck Jones
Buffalo Bill
Chief American Horse
Chief Arrow
Chief Bear Claw
Chief Black Fox
Chief Black Hawk
Chief Coyote
Chief Fish Carrier
Chief Great Bear
Chief Hollow Horn Bear
Chief John Grass
Chief Joseph
Chief Little Shell

Chief No Shirt
Chief Peta-La-Sha-Ra
Chief Red Jacket
Chief Running Elk
Chief Runs-The-Enemy
Chief Sage
Chief Sentele
Chief Spotted Tail
Chief Thunderbird
Chief Thunder Cloud
Chief Watchful Fox
Chief Wolf
Cowboy Outlaws
Cowboy Round-Up
George O'Brien
Indian Adventure

Indian Parade
Indians Awaiting Signal
Indians Declaring War
Indian Sign of Peace
Indians Ready for War
Jesse James
Jesse James Hold-Up
Ken Maynard
Montana Indians
Pony Express
Rough Rider
Stage Coach Robbery
Ted Wells
Tom Mix
Wallace McDonald

IN HISTORY'S SPOTLIGHT (24)   2 1/4" X 2 3/4"

"In History's Spotlight" was a 24-card set manufactured by the Sperry Candy Company of Milwaukee. The fronts are borderless, color artwork pictures of famous events in American history. The backs contain the card title, number and text — all printed in black ink on tan cardboard stock. In addition, the backs have puzzle piece outlines printed on them so the cards could be cut up and used as jigsaw puzzles. No wrapper or packaging has been seen. The reference number is R76.

ITEM	EX	AVE
Card	18.00	6.00
Set	600.00	200.00

1 The Fleet of Columbus	10 Retreat of the British from Concord	17 Washington Crossing the Delaware
2 DeSoto Discovers the Mississippi	11 Battle of Bunker Hill	18 Valley Forge
3 Landing of the Pilgrims	12 Washington Takes Command of the Army	19 Escape of Benedict Arnold
4 Purchase of Manhattan	13 John Paul Jones	20 Battle of Camden
5 Pocahontas and Captain John Smith	14 Declaration of Independence	21 Cornwallis Surrenders
6 Braddock's Defeat	15 "The Spirit of '76"	22 Daniel Boone
7 Boston Massacre	16 Liberty Bell	23 Constitution and the Guerriere
8 Boston Tea Party		24 Andrew Jackson at New Orleans
9 Paul Revere's Ride		

**IN DOUBT ABOUT MAKING A PURCHASE?
GET A SECOND OPINION.**

JITTERBUG CARDS (5K)

2 3/16" X 3 3/16"

It is quite likely that this series of "Jitterbug Dance Step Cards" was never distributed anywhere but in New England. The couple on the card illustrated are drawn in red and black ink on a yellow background, and the card borders are white. The card number appears in a white circle, and the specific dance step is named in large black letters. The backs carry advertising for "Jitterbug" candy and explanations of the dance step illustrated on the front. The set was issued by the F.B. Washburn Co. (Brockton, MA), and the reference number is R193. No wrapper or box has been found.

ITEM	EX	AVE
Card	10.00	3.00

JUNGLE GUM (48)

2 3/8" X 2 7/8"

"Start A Zoo — As You Chew" reads the clever advertising copy on the reverse of cards in the "Jungle Gum" series. World Wide Gum's original projection of a 192-card set never came to pass — only 48 titles were ever printed. Cards 1-24 were issued in numerical sequence, but the company resorted to skip-numbering the final 24 cards to promote sales. The card number, a descriptive text, and advertising are located on the green print backs. The animal studies used in Jungle Gum were copied directly from the Hassan Cigarette "Animal Series" of 1910. Two wrappers have been discovered: both bear the same design, but one is wax paper and the other is plain paper. The reference number is R78.

ITEM	EX	AVE
Cards		
1-24	6.50	1.50
25-71	9.00	2.00
Set	450.00	115.00
Wrappers		
Wax paper	175.00	——
Plain paper	225.00	——
Box	400.00	200.00

Jungle Gum

1 Giraffe
2 Eland
3 South African Fox
4 Chimpanzee
5 Wildebeest
6 Tiger
7 Civet-cat
8 Gorilla
9 Water Buck
10 Leopard
11 Adjutant
12 Common Kudu

13 Hooded Cobra
14 Dorcas Gazelle
15 Orang Utan
16 Bushbuck
17 Rhinoceros
18 Cape Buffalo
19 Magot
20 African Bush Pig
21 Striped Hyena
22 Lechwe
23 Mandrill
24 Secretary Vulture

25 Flying Fox
27 Baby Chimpanzee
29 Mantled Guerza
31 Lion
33 Ant-eater
35 Walrus
37 The Bald Eagle
39 Zebra
41 Toucan
43 Meerkat
45 Polar Bear
47 Okapi

49 Ostrich
51 Tapir
53 Elephant
55 King Crane
57 Kangaroo
59 Screech Owl
61 Sea Elephant
63 The Brush Tail Porcupine
65 American Bison
67 Jerboa
69 Hippopotamus
71 Ring-tailed Lemur

UNCUT SHEET OF CARDS 25-72

101

LEADER DISCS (?) 2 3/16" DIAMETER

It's logical to assume from the series name — which comes down to us from the early catalogs — that these novelty discs were produced by the Leader Novelty Candy Co. (Brooklyn, NY). Each disc is a thick piece of cardboard with a multi-color design on the front; the surface seems to be laquered. The backs have two small black & white drawings, the card number, and a very brief text. The reverse side is not laquered, and there are no marks or advertising to reveal the maker's identity. Each disc has notches at the primary compass points, which allow them to be stacked and held together with rubber bands. The diameter is the same as the Sealcraft cards listed elsewhere in this volume. The length of the set is unknown, and No. 107 is the highest disc number reported to date. The reference number is R79.

ITEM	EX	AVE
Disc	4.00	1.00

LEADER NOVELTY CANDY BOXES (?) MANY SIZES

Illustrated is one of a group of colorful three-dimensional candy boxes marketed by the Leader Novelty Candy Co. of Brooklyn, NY. The fire truck shown here is 3 1/2" long and 1 1/8" high. Coupons printed under the front flap could be redeemed for prizes. A special piece on the top of each box — in this case, a section of ladder — was designed to add a special look to each container (Leader boxes were engineered to be used as toys after the candy was gone). Each box also contained a miniature novelty or toy made of wood or metal. No reference number has been assigned to this category, and the prices listed below apply only to complete boxes.

ITEM	EX	AVE
Box	25.00	10.00

102

LEAGUE OF NATIONS (50)

2 1/2" X 3"

From all appearances, this "League of Nations" card set was probably more of a success than the international organization after which it was named. Actually, the set title is a bit misleading; several countries represented in the set were never in the League, and some — Antarctica, Bavaria, Palestine, Polynesia, and Sardinia were never even countries! But no matter, the idea was to sell gum by depicting a variety of exotic native types, and that's exactly what Novelty Gum of Chicago accomplished. There are 50 cards in the set; each is captioned front and back, but the card number is only on the back. Two wrappers, one showing natives and the other showing flags, exist. A beautiful storage box, with the set checklist printed on the flaps, was given to purchasers by the retailers. The reference number is R80.

ITEM	EX	AVE
Card	12.00	3.00
Set	750.00	185.00
Wrappers (2)		
each	200.00	——
Storage box	100.00	40.00
Advertising		
sign	100.00	35.00

RETAIL STORE ADVERTISING POSTER

103

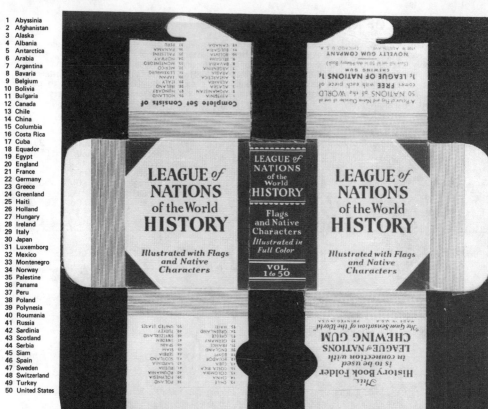

LIMERICKS (11)

2 1/2" X 3"

The method of distribution of Pulver's 11-card Limerick set is a mystery; so is its numbering sequence, 55-65. The purpose of the set, however, is perfectly clear: card owners were supposed to memorize as many limericks as possible and challenge each other to recite them. It's a clever idea which must have had them rolling in the aisles (imagine the ad-libbing which must have occurred), but the content of the Limericks makes one suspect that these gum cards were not made for children. The drawing and print on the illustrated card are green. The back has a plaid border, with the limerick and card number printed in blue. The reference number is R81.

ITEM	EX	AVE
Card	15.00	4.00
Set	200.00	55.00

LITTLE HENRY (130?)

Switzer's Licorice had a genuine talent for producing sets of candy box cards which were impossible to complete (the "Army Air Corps Insignia" set listed earlier in this book, for example). Of course, this might have been a "keep-'em-buying" tactic practiced by the company. If the "Little Henry" series is actually 130 cards in length, as the early catalogs reported,

then it would be a miracle if anyone finished it off. The card in the illustration was cut from the back of a licorice cigarette box. It is red and white in color and is not numbered. The back is blank. The reference number is R82.

ITEM	EX	AVE
Card	15.00	5.00
Set	2300.00	750.00

LONE RANGER (48)

2 1/2" X 3 1/8"

The outstanding color and detail of the artwork fronts and the exciting adventures related on the backs make Gum, Inc.'s "Lone Ranger" series one of the most popular non-sport sets ever issued.

Each card is copyrighted front and back by The Lone Ranger Inc., with 1940 given as the date. There are 48 cards in the set, of which the final 12 are the hardest to find. Lone Ranger wrappers were

once considered rare, but enough have been found to bring prices down to more reasonable levels. The reference number is R83.

ITEM	EX	AVE
Cards		
No. 1	40.00	10.00
2-36	25.00	6.00
37-47	40.00	10.00
No. 48	60.00	15.00
Wrapper	500.00	—

1 A Silver Bullet Stops a Hanging
2 Tonto and the Secret Mine
3 Tonto's Race with Death
4 The Giant Ghost
5 The Wrecked Stagecoach
6 Ghouls at Work
7 Poisoned Waters
8 Hawk's Prey
9 The Fight Over the Water Hole
10 The Substitute Dispatch Bearer
11 The Run-Away Herd
12 The Lasso Duel
13 The Counter Attack
14 The Underground River
15 The Tree Trap
16 Silver Charges the Horse Thieves
17 The Interrupted Coach Robbery
18 Barrier of Fire
19 The Burning Shack
20 Thirsty Burros
21 Saving Tonto's Scalp
22 Firebrands on the Ledge
23 Threatening Hoofs
24 Smoke Signals
25 A Double Hold-up
26 The Vicious Circle
27 Midnight Branding Party
28 Trial of the Killer
29 Blasted Canyon
30 Tonto in War Paint
31 Dead Man's Leap
32 The Phantom Rider
33 Paradise Regained
34 Fire Trap
35 The Haunted House
36 The Cattle Rush
37 His Father's Son
38 Broken Windows
39 Smugglers' Love Letters
40 A Piece of Gingham
41 The Price of Sealed Lips
42 Storming the Indian Camp by Night
43 The Bank Bandits
44 Round-up Time in Prairie Gulch
45 Horseshoes for Bad Luck
46 Gun Girl
47 The Rescue of the Wagon Train
48 Silver's Vigil

LONE RANGER PREMIUMS (5)

8" X 10"

The brilliant color and detail of these 8" X 10" Lone Ranger pictures makes them the most desirable of all 1930's premiums. Each picture was available from Gum, Inc. in exchange for "Lone Ranger Bubble Gum" wrappers and coin. The backs are marked "series A," but no more series were produced. The advertising sheet which mentions Horrors of

War is evidence that these premiums were actually produced in 1938, the same year as the Republic Pictures matinee serial on which they were based. The fabulous color montage of all five premium pictures is the front side of a promotion sheet sent to candy and gum stores. We know, from advertising pictures, what the gum roll wrappers look like, but none

have been located to date. Premium No. 1 is by far the hardest to obtain. The reference number is R83A.

ITEM	EX	AVE
Premuim		
No. 1	500.00	150.00
Premiums		
Nos. 2-5	250.00	65.00
Set	1850.00	475.00
Box		Speculative

1 Tonto Saves the Lone Ranger
2 The Lone Ranger Licks Kester
3 The Lone Ranger Rescues Joan
   at the Pit
4 Tonto Fights Off the Troopers
5 The Lone Ranger Foils a
   Murderer

Series A, Number 2. The Lone Ranger Licks Kester

The Lone Ranger has been led by Tonto's horse, White Feller, to where "Captain" Kester and his gang had tied Tonto to a tree and were giving him a cruel whipping. He arrives in time to surprise the group and to release Tonto, and is here seen landing a swift knockout blow to Kester's chin while Tonto covers the gang with the Lone Ranger's guns.

This picture is one of a series in which the Lone Ranger and his Indian friend, Tonto, are shown living bravely for the good of others and the defense of justice. The pictures were sketched as incidents during the filming of the Republic serial, "The Lone Ranger."

Titles of Available Pictures — Series A

No. 1   TONTO SAVES THE LONE RANGER
No. 2   THE LONE RANGER LICKS KESTER
No. 3   THE LONE RANGER RESCUES JOAN AT THE PIT
No. 4   TONTO FIGHTS OFF THE TROOPERS
No. 5   THE LONE RANGER FOILS A MURDERER

Additional series of five pictures each will be released later.

How to Get the Lone Ranger Pictures

This Lone Ranger pictures may be ordered by mail from the manufacturers of Lone Ranger Bubble Gum by sending wrappers from Lone Ranger Gum and coins according to the following guide:

For 1 Picture send 5 wrappers and 2 cents
For 2 Pictures send 10 wrappers and 5 cents
For 4 Pictures send 20 wrappers and 10 cents
For 5 Pictures send 25 wrappers and 15 cents

Send coins (not stamps) wrapped well in paper, with the right number of wrappers, the numbers and titles of the pictures desired, and your name and address in a sealed envelope bearing the right amount of postage (at least a three cent stamp) addressed to

GUM, INCORPORATED
3249 Woodland Avenue, Philadelphia, Pa., U.S.A.

How to Save the Pictures

Lone Ranger pictures are inspiring subjects for boys and girls to display in their homes or their own rooms.

Stand or Hang them up—a gummed hanger on the back or a tack may be used.

Frame them—a neat frame costs only 10 cents.

Glaz them—between a piece of cardboard and an 8 x 10 inch glass, worth about five cents, taping the edges with good gummed binding, form non-stickiness, or ordinary gummed tape, painted afterward.

File them—in a loose-leaf note book, inserting two or three holes in the picture, or pasting the posters on a page of a ring-binder.

Exhibit them—invite your friends to view your collection.

Save to Get the Entire Series

Picture and Text Copyright 1938, The Lone Ranger, Inc.

PROMOTION SHEET AIMED AT RETAILERS WHICH SHOWED ALL FIVE PREMIUMS

THE five pieces of LONE RANGER Bubble Gum packed in this box of HORRORS OF WAR are FREE—

EXTRA PROFIT FOR YOU!

LONE RANGER is the newest of our penny gum successes. It is riding in on a wave of nation-wide enthusiasm for the heroic Lone Ranger, whose daring exploits are followed by millions of radio listeners, movie-goers, and newspaper comic-section readers. Lone Ranger Bubble Gum is a "natural" winner. Give it a show and see it go! For regular stock, 'phone your jobber.

Bubbleman Bowman,
President, Gum, Inc.,
Philadelphia, Pa.

FREE to acquaint you with

LONE RANGER BUBBLE GUM

MEANWHILE, HORRORS OF WAR BUBBLE GUM IS BREAKING ALL SALES RECORDS!

GUM, INC. FLYER PACKED IN BOXES OF "HORRORS OF WAR"

MAGIC CANDY (48)

2 3/4" X 3 1/4"

"This is a series of Forty-eight Cards illustrating and explaining Magic Tricks. Collect all Forty-eight of these Tricks and be a real Magician." Such was the advertising lure printed on every "Magic Candy" card issued by the J.N. Collins Co. of Philadelphia. The cards are slightly larger and thicker than most 1930's issues. The fronts have illusions, tricks, and puzzles, all introduced in black and orange or blue and orange color combinations. The tie-wearing dog appears on all known cards and is not identified. The backs have the confection brand printed at top in a black panel and a "Secret Explanation" for the "magic" introduced on front. Not all of the backs have the "rabbit magician" design seen in our illustration; some cards bear a copyright date and others do not. No packaging or wrapper has been found. The reference number is R84.

ITEM	EX	AVE
Card	20.00	7.00
Set	1200.00	400.00

MAGIC CIRCUS WAGON (24?)

4 1/4" X 7 3/8"

"Magic Circus Wagon" is the name of this newly-discovered wrapper series produced by the Schutter-Johnson Candy Co. (Chicago/Brooklyn). Each brown paper wrapper is numbered in the lower right corner, and it is believed that there are 24 wrappers in the set. A poem at top center gives to the identity of a circus animal, the outline of which is revealed by wetting the blank space on the circus wagon with water. The type of candy packaged inside the wrapper is not known, and no reference number has been assigned.

ITEM	EX	AVE
Wrapper	40.00	20.00

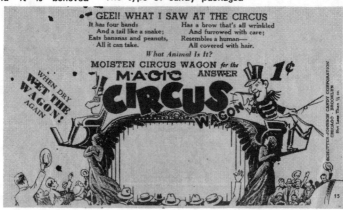

MAGIC FORTUNE CARDS (80)   1 5/8" X 2 1/2"

The "Magic Fortune Card" series by Dietz Gum of Chicago contains a total of 80 small, thick-paper cards with water-activated designs. The 1921 and 1923 patent dates printed on every card refer to this process, which was developed by the Invisible Color Print Co. of New York. After wetting, each card revealed either a horoscope, a dream message, or a birthstone. Advertising on the cards and the beautiful blue wrapper offers "a large magic color book" in exchange for 50 wrapper flaps. This exchange policy, which required removal of one-third of each wrapper, plus the water-soaking aspect of the cards has severely restricted the supply of both items to modern-day collectors. The cards are not numbered, and the only colors seen so far for the "invisible paint" are blue and brown. The reference number is R182.

ITEM	EX	AVE
Card	15.00	5.00
Set	1200.00	400.00
Wrapper	225.00	——

MAGIC TRICKS (40)   2 7/16" X 2 11/16"

Everything on the front and back of each "Magic Tricks" card — the drawing, product name, card number, caption, text, and company information — is printed in blue ink. The obverses contain illustrated tricks, and the words "Magic Chewing Gum" appear in a solid blue panel at the bottom. Everything else is printed on the backs, including lengthy explanations of each feat of prestidigitation. The series was distributed by Glenn Confections of Buffalo, NY and carries the reference number R85. No wrapper has been discovered to date.

ITEM	EX	AVE
Card	15.00	5.00
Set	750.00	250.00

MAGIC TRICKS BOOKLETS (4)   1 1/2" X 2 1/2"

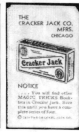

The Cracker Jack set of four "Magic Tricks Booklets" is really a set of folders. Each folder is printed in red and blue and has ten numbered pages, plus the covers. The "Tricks of Magic" folder illustrated contains instructions for performing five different tricks. A copyright date of 1931 is located on the back cover as is a picture of a Cracker Jack package. The reference number is R86.

ITEM	EX	AVE
Folder	20.00	7.00
Set	100.00	35.00

MAJIK FOLD PICTURES (9?)   5 1/2" X 10 1/4"

One of the most unusual gum premiums of the 1930's, "Majik Fold Pictures" are really an Americanized version of origami. These large black & white sectional pictures

C.E. Dallin, The Great American Sculptor, Loved the American Indians. His "Appeal to the Great Spirit" is Nationally Known. Find It Here.
Find Joan D'Arc as "Maid of Orleans," Who was Burned at the Stake.
Find Paul Revere, Who Warned "The Redcoats are Coming."
1492 Means Who? The Santa Maria.
Indians and Wild West. Recalls Buffalo?
Strength — Uncle Sam — Liberty. Who is Responsible for these Symbols?
Waterloo. Where is Napoleon?
Where is the Famous Pirate? Captain Kid's Cave.

had an "Instructions for Folding" panel at the bottom which must have mystified youngsters and tested the patience of their parents! A line on one of the pictures reads "38300 — 9 subjects", and this has been accepted as the length of the set. Majik Fold Pictures were the brainstorm of Goudey Gum and were distributed as over-the-counter premiums in 1935. One of the designs used, C.E. Dallin's "Appeal to the Great Spirit," was also used (in color) by Goudey as an Indian Gum premium. No reference number has been assigned to this set. NOTE: excellent grade (or better) is reserved for unfolded pictures.

ITEM	EX	AVE
Picture	15.00	5.00
Set	160.00	50.00

MAKE FACES (?)   1" X 2"

This wonderful series of sectional cards was created by the George Milkes Company. Each multi-color card has partial faces which line up with partial faces on other cards. There are individual numbers ("66" is the highest reported) plus "set" numbers ("11" is the highest seen) on every card. Even when a complete face is formed (see illus-tration), there are still other partial faces on the edges. Exactly how extensive is the montage is has yet to be determined because of the scarcity of the set. When the cards are arranged properly, the viewer can identify each primary character (the one facing front) by reading the name printed on his or her hat. The backs of the cards are blank, and the reference number is R87. The Milkes Company specialized in box candy, but no one has been able to establish a link between these cards and any known box.

ITEM	EX	AVE
Card	15.00	5.00

MATCHEM (10K)

"Matchem" is another Milkes Company series produced in the sectional format like the "Make Faces" set above. An important difference is that the Matchem cards have printed backs containing two or three numbered questions about objects and characters appearing on other cards. On the cards with two questions on the back, two small diagrams show the card numbers and layout required to provide answers. Cards with three questions on the back have two diagrams plus a clue printed in script. The manufacturer's name is listed on the card backs as a "game

  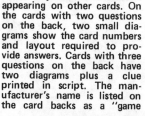  

1 1/4" X 2 1/2"

and toy" company, which makes sense because both "Matchem" and "Make Faces" (and the "Mul-T-Jokes set listed later) are really game pieces issued with candy. No packaging has been discovered for "Matchem," and the reference number is R88.

ITEM	EX	AVE
Card	15.00	5.00

MICKEY MOUSE (96)

2 1/2" X 3 1/8"

Collectors looking for the manufacturer's name on Mickey Mouse cards will find only the words "Mickey Mouse Bubble Gum, Philadelphia, Pa." The brilliant color artwork and overall quality of the series, however, points to the handiwork of Gum, Inc., and that is the name we find printed on the wrappers. The so-called "regular" series of Mickey Mouse cards are numbered 1-96 and carry the reference designation R89.

On the initial print run of 24 cards, the picture and dialogue on the front of each card answered the question posed on the back. These cards, hereafter referred to as Type 1, have the phrase "This Picture Answers Question On Other Side" printed on front. Then, in a clever marketing maneuver, cards 1-24 were reissued in a restyled format in which the artwork and dialogue on any card answered the question asked on the preceding card. Thus, collectors were forced to buy more and more cards simply to answer the questions on the ones they already owned! All subsequent print runs involving numbers 25-96 were printed in this format which we call Type 2 (see illustration of card No. 90 with phrase "Here's the Answer to Question on Card No. 89). To sum up, cards 1-24 come in Type 1 or Type 2 format; cards 25-96 are found in Type 2 format only. NOTE: cards 1-96 were also issued in Canada by the O—Pee—Chee company.

Two wrappers were used for the 1-96 series. The one with five Disney characters on the flap also has the advice "Save The Wrappers" printed to the left of the center design. The wrapper with three Disney characters on the flap is slightly smaller. Both wrappers varieties feature a "Mickey Mouse Album" offer on the bottom fold.

Two albums with different covers were available to house each group of 48 cards (see illustrations). They were obtained from the local retailer in exchange for "5 wrappers and 5 cents." The wrapper advertising promises a "Cover beautifully illustrated, all questions printed and a place for the picture card that answers each question." NOTE: the prices for albums listed below are for empty albums in "excellent" condition. Cards pasted in the albums reduce the album values, and pasted cards are valued at one-half of the "average" price.

Mickey Mouse

ITEM	EX	AVE
Cards		
Type 1		
(1-24)	30.00	8.00
Type 2		
(1-96)	20.00	5.00
Set		
(Type 2)	2400.00	600.00
Wrappers		
5 character	150.00	——
3 character	175.00	——
Albums		
Vol. 1		
(1-48)	250.00	75.00
Vol. 2		
(49-96)	350.00	125.00

TYPE 1

TYPE 2

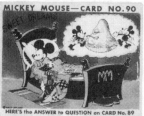

1 Let's Make Hoop-ee!
2 It's Raining Cats and Dogs!
3 Fleas, Go 'Way and Let Me Sleep!
4 Watch! It's a Snap!
5 Looks Funny When She Knits, Doesn't She? Suppose She's a Knit-Wit?
6 Let It Bee, Pluto! Let It Bee!!
7 Bad Stew Mickey! Stew Bad Minnie!
8 Just Ironing Out Some of Mickey's Difficulties!
9 Uncle Walt Told Me Take a Walk and I'm Doing It!
10 That Horse-Shoe Is Certainly a Ringer for Mickey!
11 Likes That Target, Doesn't He! Mickey's Just Stuck on That Target!
12 What Are They Reading? It's All Foreign to Me!
13 Am I Lucky! Look!!—a Four-Leaf Clover!
14 Mickey Is Sure Making a Name for Himself!
15 A Letter on a Fan? Certainly! Mickey Loves to Get Fan Mail!
16 Look! He's All Wrapped Up in His Work!
17 Look! Free Wheeling!
18 That's A Lot of Oil, Mickey! Take It! You'll Feel Better!
19 The Line Is Busy!
20 A Boy Scout? Sure! I Do a Good Turn Daily!
21 He's Sure a Handy Man Around the Mouse!
22 My! What Pig Eyes You Have!
23 That's an Awful Blow to Me, Mickey!
24 You Sure Turned the Tables on Me That Time, Pluto!
25 You Hit the Nail Right on the Head Mickey! Pon My Sole It Needs Fixing!
26 Just Pup-Posing
27 That Camel Walks a Mile for Mickey!
28 I Blow Such Nice Sounds into It! But Such Awful Sounds Come Out.
29 Here's a Dandelion I Pulled For You! You Always Pull a Dandy Line for Me!
30 You Sound Like a Pig Mickey!
31 Feeling Dippy, Mickey? Let's Go in for a Dip!
32 Can Mickey Play? No, But He Can Carry a Tune!
33 Do You Belong to Any Mickey Mouse Clubs? No, But These Mickey Mouse Clubs Belong to Me!!!
34 Pluto Smells a Trap!
35 You Can't Make a Monkey Out of Me!
36 Whoooo You. Ooo
37 Soda Pup?
38 Look! Mickey's in a Row with Minnie!
39 Are You the Engineer? No, This Is the Engine 'ere!
40 That Face Sure Looks Familiar to Me!
41 I'll Give You a Licking for This Kitty! I'm Taking My Licking Now!
42 Oh! So You're Egging Me On!
43 Dynamite Explodes! Pluto Might Too!
44 Food Comes Pretty High Nowadays! That's Over My Head Minnie!
45 You're a Great Shot, Mickey! You Hold Your End Up too, Pluto!
46 Please Help the Poor! Poor Little Skunk! He Hasn't a Scent to His Name!
47 Bee Gone!
48 Service A La Carte!
49 Crazy Trip Isn't It? Of Course! It's a Buggy Ride.
50 Here Comes Minnie! Beat It, Mickey! Drum for Your Life!
51 This Little Pig Went to Mark It.
52 Playing 'Kitten on the Keys'? Just Kiddin' on the Keys.
53 This Is the End of Me!
54 'Lo Mickey. High Minnie.
55 Look, He's All Keyed Up.

56 Pluto Has Left, What Do You Say to That? Dog-Gone.
57 They've Got Toot-Aches.
58 Look, Mickey Foots the Bill.
59 You're the Underdog Pluto. Sure But You Get Over Mickey.
60 Look, They're Coming to Blows.
61 Dishes the Life.
62 Like It Pluto? Yeh, But Don't Rub Me the Wrong Way.
63 The Mail Must Go Through.
64 I'm So Hungry I Could Eat Like a Horse. Quick, Bring Her a Bucket of Oats.
65 Guess I'll 'Knuckle' Down to Work.
66 Sure There's Fish in Here.
67 Is Minnie Taking a Screen Test? No, She's Taking a Scream Test!
68 He's Sure the Cat's Me-ouse!
69 Who Did This? I Cannot Tell a Lie I Did It with My Little Hatch-it!

70 Mickey's Getting Something Hot off His Chest!
71 Is That a Nickel? No! That's a Mickel!
72 Mickey, the Bear-Back Rider
73 I'm Alive with Fleas. Don't Worry! Where There's Life There's Soap!
74 Striking Fellow, Isn't He?
75 Ah! Something's Stirring!
76 He's Playing Them for Minnie! Certainly! They're Love Notes!
77 You Can't Make It, Mickey! That Ice Is Cracked. That's an Ice Crack to Make, Minnie!
78 How Do You Do It? What Do You Use? Look! It's a Pipe!
79 Who's Afraid of the Big Bad Woof!
80 Good Day, Juliet! Good Knight, Romeo!
81 Isn't He a Nice Skater? You Mean an Ice Skater!
82 Let Me Run for the Doctor. Don't Make It a Quack Doctor, Minnie!

83 I Churn Some Butter Every Day. Don't You Think I'm a Good Scout? Sure! You Do a Good Churn Daily!
84 We're the Fife and Brum Corps!
85 I Saw That Wood Yesterday. I Saw That Wood Now!
86 Getting Purse-nal Horace?
87 That Cat's Going to the Dogs! You Mean That Dog's Going to the Cat's!
88 That's No Man! You're Right! That's Snow-Man!
89 He Bought that Fife at the Store for Ten Cents. Ah! The Fife-and-Ten Cent Store!
90 Sweet Cards
91 Birds in the Spring!
92 People Like Uncle Walt, Don't They, Mickey? Sure, He Naturally Draws People!
93 Is That What You Do When You Get Angry? Sure, I Stamp My Foot!

94 Get Up! It's Dawn. Ah! Dawn on the Farm.
95 Do You Get Paid for Doing That? Sure! I'm Drawing 'My Salary' Now!
96 Look! Uncle Tom's Crabbin. Everythings Dark and Dreary!

Can you answer this question?

One day Mickey climbed on a bear's back when the bear wasn't looking. The bear started to run very, very fast with Mickey standing up and holding his balance like a circus rider. Minnie was looking on in great glee and while he was riding around she gave him a title.

What did Minnie call Mickey?

For the answer to this question see Card No. 73.

GET A MICKEY MOUSE ALBUM

from the store where you buy your Mickey Mouse Bubble Gum, for 5 wrappers and 5 cents. All questions printed and a place for the picture card answers.

Printed in Canada by

O-Pee-Chee Company, Limited   London, Canada

MICKEY MOUSE WITH THE MOVIE STARS (24)   2 1/2″ X 3 1/8″

Although these 24 cards of Mickey Mouse meeting and greeting movie stars (and his creator, Walt Disney) are a continuation of the 1-96 "regular" series, we have listed them separately for a number of reasons. First of all, Gum, Inc. created an entirely new wrapper based upon the celebrity theme. Secondly, the format was returned to the "answer on back of card" style of Type 1 low series cards. Finally, the 97-120 group is so much more difficult to complete (despite its smaller size) than the 1-96 low series that, in practical terms, it should be regarded as a separate entity. "Mickey Mouse with the Movie Stars," which was listed by itself in early catalogs, carries the reference number R90. NOTE: card No. 100, Walt Disney, is no scarcer than any other card but is in high demand.

113

Mickey Mouse with the Movie Stars

ITEM	EX	AVE
Cards		
97-99 &		
101-120	75.00	20.00
No. 100	150.00	40.00
Set	2400.00	640.00
Wrapper	750.00	---

Mickey Mouse with the Movie Stars—No. 9

SAVE WRAPPERS FOR COUPONS

SAVE WRAPPERS FOR COUPONS

MICKEY MOUSE BUBBLE GUM

with the MOVIE STARS

FOLLOW INSTRUCTIONS CAREFULLY

1. Save 24 wrappers and cut off this coupon on dotted line or make 24 very good copies.
2. Write on a sheet of paper the names of the movie stars on the 24 cards, Nos. 97 to 120 inclusive. Write your story not more than 100 words about your favorite movie star or about a picture in which you saw your favorite star.
3. Then place in an envelope 24 of these coupons from 24 wrappers or facsimiles with your list giving the names of the movie stars on the 24 cards Nos. 97 to 120 inclusive and your story. Print your name and address plainly in the upper left hand corner of envelope and mail to:

MICKEY MOUSE BUBBLE GUM, P. O. Box 4028, Philadelphia, Pa.

Mickey Mouse with the Movie Stars—No. 112

Number 99

MICKEY MOUSE with the MOVIE STARS

Mickey dressed like a certain movie star and then went over to see him. When the star took a look at Mickey he roared right out loud and said, "Lo, Mickey MARX!" Mickey laughed and came right back with an answer that made the star laugh harder.

WHO WAS THE STAR?
For a clue to the answer, see other side.

THE NAME OF THE MOVIE STAR IS:

MICKEY MOUSE BUBBLE GUM—The Best BUBBLE GUM in the World—Makes the BIGGEST BUBBLES

Number 112

MICKEY MOUSE with the MOVIE STARS

A great star was teaching Mickey how to be a detective! "You PHILO everything I tell you and you'll VANCE rapidly," he said. "I know I'll be great if I can get more lessons from you," said Mickey. And then the star said something that made Mickey laugh.

WHO WAS THE STAR?
For a clue to the answer, see other side.

THE NAME OF THE MOVIE STAR IS:

MICKEY MOUSE BUBBLE GUM—The Best BUBBLE GUM in the World—Makes the BIGGEST BUBBLES

97 S-o-o! You're a Wynndow Cleaner!
98 It's an Honor to Have You Play in My Spectacle!
99 'Lo Mickey Marx! 'Hi, Groucho Mouse!
100 How Do You Manage to Draw So Well, Mickey? Where There's a Will There's a Way.
101 Am I Right on the Left Page, Mickey? Of Course But I'm Left on the Right Page.
102 You Sure Made an Impression on Me.
103 Life Is Just a Bowl of Chariots
104 The Little Seizer
105 That's the Biggest Opening I've Ever Seen in Hollywood.
106 My Next Picture Will Be Silent, Mickey... So—You Won't Talk Eh!
107 I Can't Get Mickey off My Mind
108 Blondells Prefer Gentlemen.
109 I'm Getting Off Something Big.
110 Lip and Let Lip.
111 A Dime for This? Yes, Ten Cents a Trance
112 O.K. Mickey More Powell to You
113 So You're Leaving Me Flat? Yes, I'm Leaving Your Flat!
114 Doug Gone! He's Off Again
115 You Can Be Had!
116 So You're Putting on the High Hat, Eh? That's Over My Head, Mr. Menjou
117 Look Out I'm Going to Strike You! Ah! At Last I've Met My Match!
118 Le'slee How Shall We Take This? Howard This Pose Do, Mickey?
119 Sworda Mad, Eh?
120 Mickey You're Certainly Handy for a Laugh!

MINUTE BIOGRAPHIES (40)   1 3/16" X 3 7/16"

The Federal Sweets & Wafer Company of Brooklyn, NY packed its series of "Minute Biographies" in a candy product which has yet to be identified by modern collectors. The color artwork cards have a portrait of a famous person and a scene from his or her life on the front. The backs carry a short biographical summary of the subject and the company name, all printed in black ink on gray cardboard stock. Both the drawings and the text on these cards were taken from two books entitled "Minute Biographies" and "More Minute Biographies" (see the George Bernard Shaw illustrations). The cards are not numbered, and the reference number is R91.

ITEM	EX	AVE
Card	12.00	3.00
Set	600.00	145.00

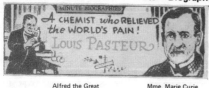

A CHEMIST who RELIEVED the WORLD'S PAIN!
LOUIS PASTEUR

LOUIS PASTEUR
Born 1822   Died 1895 in France

Pasteur studied microbes, little germs that can only be seen through a microscope. In 1885 came Pasteur's greatest triumph. Little Joseph Meister was brought to him, bitten by a mad dog. Pasteur vaccinated and cured him. Pasteur discovered a way to kill harmful microbes in milk. This process is called "Pasteurization" and is used today.

FEDERAL SWEETS & WAFER CO., Inc., Brooklyn, N.Y.
Mnfs. of "Dutch Maid Marshmallows"

Alfred the Great	Mme. Marie Curie	Gughelmo Marconi	Franklin Delano Roosevelt
P.T. Barnum	Thomas Edison	Benito Mussolini	Theodore Roosevelt
Ludwig Von Beethoven	Ferdinand Foch	Napoleon	Salome
Alexander Graham Bell	Henry Ford	Florence Nightingale	George Bernard Shaw
Daniel Boone	Stephen Foster	Louis Pasteur	Alfred E. Smith
John Burroughs	Benjamin Franklin	Adelina Patti	John Smith
Julius Caesar	Robert Fulton	William Penn	Solomon the Wise
William F. Cody (Buffalo Bill)	Henry Hudson	John J. Pershing	Joseph Stalin
Christopher Columbus	Abraham Lincoln	Pocahontas	George Washington
Calvin Coolidge	Jennie Lind	Paul Revere	Daniel Webster

THE
IRISH DIOGENES

GEORGE BERNARD SHAW CAME FROM AN IMPOVERISHED IRISH FAMILY AND RECEIVED HIS EDUCATION AT THE HANDS OF HIS MOTHER WHO WAS A GIFTED SINGER··· AT 15, HE WENT TO WORK IN A LAND AGENT'S OFFICE AT A SALARY OF 85 DOLLARS PER YEAR, BUT AFTER FIVE YEARS LEFT THE BUSINESS AND MOVED TO LONDON TO ENGAGE IN LITERARY PURSUITS···THE NEXT NINE YEARS WERE A STORY OF POVERTY AND FAILURE···FINALLY, HE TURNED TO THE STAGE··· HIS BRILLIANCE AND WIT AS A DEBATER AND LITERARY CRITIC STARTED HIM ON HIS SWIFT RISE TO WORLD FAME···

GEORGE BERNARD
·SHAW···

CENSORED AT FIRST, SHAW'S SERIES OF GREAT PLAYS ON POLITICAL, SOCIAL, RELIGIOUS AND BIOLOGICAL QUESTIONS ARE NOW ACCEPTED AS THE WORK OF ONE OF THE MASTER DRAMATISTS AND THINKERS OF THE AGE··· ALTHOUGH APPROACHING 80, SHAW IS STILL WRITING AND THE WHOLE WORLD LISTENS WITH INTEREST WHEN THIS COLORFUL AND PARADOXICAL GENIUS HANDS DOWN AN OPINION···

··· BORN JULY 26, 1856 IN DUBLIN, IRELAND ···

MOVIE STARS (19K)   2 1/2" X 3 1/4"

Because there are no clues to the manufacturer's identity printed on these cards, we shall have to accept Jefferson Burdick's catalog listing of

DON AMECHE
"Story of Alexander G. Bell – 20th Century-Fox"

them as a Gum, Inc. product. The card fronts have black & white photos of movie stars; their names, the title of one of their movies, and their studio

Gracie Allen
Don Ameche
Jack Benny
Eddie Cantor
Joan Crawford
Bette Davis
Deanna Durbin
Dorothy Lamour
Priscilla Lane
Myrna Loy
Charlie McCarthy & Edgar Bergen
Dick Powell
Tyrone Power
Edward G. Robinson
Ginger Rodgers
Mickey Rooney
Norma Shearer
Robert Taylor
Loretta Young

are listed underneath. The words "printed in U.S.A." are located to one side under the picture in tiny print. The backs are blank and the cards are not numbered. Burdick lists 24 in the series, but we have only 19 confirmed titles as of now. One movie title, "Follies of 1939," would indicate an issue date in the 1939-1942 time span. The reference number is R92.

ITEM	EX	AVE
Card	10.00	3.00
Set	300.00	85.00

MOVIE STARS (34K)   2" X 3"

This series of movie star photos in stylish frames was listed in the "recent candy and gum" sections of the early catalogs, but no manufacturer has been identified to date. There are two types

ROSALIND RUSSELL

CONSTANCE BENNETT

of cards: one style is rectangular and has a solid center section (Type a), while the other variety has a shaped top portion and a scored center section (Type b). The format of the latter allowed

Lionel Barrymore	Barbara Kent
Wallace Beery	June Knight
Constance Bennett	William Lundigan
Charles Butterworth	Robert Montgomery
Mary Carlisle	Ramon Navarro
Jackie Cooper	Maureen O'Sullivan
Joan Crawford	William Powell
Richard Cromwell	Ginger Rogers
Richard Dix	Shirley Ross
Jimmy Durante	Rosalind Russell
Madge Evans	Randolph Scott
Clark Gable	Ann Shirley
John Gilbert	Robert Taylor
Ann Harding	Thelma Todd
Jean Harlow	Franchot Tone
Helen Hayes	Lee Tracy
Katherine Hepburn	Robert Young

the photo to be made self-standing by bending back the top portion of the card along the score lines. It is believed that every movie star in the set was printed in both varieties. Neither type is numbered and both are blank-backed. Although the early catalogs speak of 55 titles, only 34 have been confirmed. The reference number is R93.

ITEM	EX	AVE
Cards		
Type a	10.00	3.00
Type b	10.00	3.00

MOVIE STARS (31K)   5" X 7"

DEAD END KIDS
in "DEAD END" – A Samuel Goldwyn Picture
AQUATONED IN U. S. A.

Another anonymous set listed in the early card catalogs, this series of large black & white movie star pictures was obviously a candy store hand-out or a mail premium. We have no clue to the identity of the company associated with these cards because they are devoid of advertising or manufacturer's marks. Each card bears the words "Aqua-toned in U.S.A." under the two lines listing the star's name, one of their movies, and their studio. The fact that some of the pictures are found with numbers (see Carole Lombard picture) suggests that they were issued at least two times OR by at least two different companies. The backs are blank, and the movie titles indicate that the series was released to the public early in 1939. The reference number is R96-1.

CAROLE LOMBARD
in "TRUE CONFESSION" — A Paramount Picture
AQUATONED IN U. S. A. NO. 6

FRED MacMURRAY
in "MEN WITH WINGS" — A Paramount Picture
AQUATONED IN U. S. A.

Gene Autry in "Western Jamboree" - A Republic Picture

Freddie Bartholomew in "Listen, Darling" An M-G-M Picture

Wallace Beery in "Stablemates" - A Metro-Goldwyn-Mayer Picture

Jack Benny in "Artists and Models Abroad" - A Paramount Picture

Bobby Breen in "Breaking The Ice" - An R.K.O. Picture

Bob Burns in "Arkansas Traveler" - A Paramount Picture

Jackie Cooper in "Gangster's Boy" - A Monogram Picture

Bing Crosby in "Sing You Sinners" - A Paramount Picture

Dead End Kids in "Dead End" - A Samuel Goldwyn Picture

Andy Devine in "Men With Wings" - A Paramount Picture

Alice Faye in "Alexander's Ragtime Band" - A 20th Century-Fox Picture

Henry Fonda in "Mad Miss Manton" - A Paramount Picture

Greta Garbo in "Conquest" - A Metro-Goldwyn-Mayer Picture

Jack Holt in "Making The Headlines" - A Columbia Picture

Buck Jones In "California Frontier" - A Columbia Picture

Buck Jones in "The Stranger From Arizona" - A Columbia Picture

Lew Lehr in "Fox Movietone News" - A 20th Century-Fox Picture

Roger Livesey in "Drums" - A United Artists Picture

Carole Lombard in "True Confession" - A Paramount Picture

Jeanette MacDonald in "Sweethearts" - A Metro-Goldwyn-Mayer Picture

Fred MacMurray in "Men With Wings" - A Paramount Picture

Joe Penner in "I'm From The City" - An R.K.O. Picture

Tyrone Power in "Jesse James" - A 20th Century-Fox Picture

Martha Raye in "Give Me A Sailor" - A Paramount Picture

Roy Rogers in "Shine On, Harvest Moon" A Republic Picture

Mickey Rooney in "Out West With The Hardys" - A Metro-Goldwyn-Mayer Picture

Randolph Scott in "The Texans" - A Paramount Picture

James Stewart in "You Can't Take It With You" - A Columbia Picture

Spencer Tracy in "Boy's Town" - A Metro-Goldwyn-Mayer Picture

"Tuffy" in "Phantom Gold" - A Columbia Picture

Jane Withers in "Rascals" - A 20th Century-Fox Picture

CARD	EX	AVE
Autry	12.00	3.00
Bartholomew	8.00	2.00
Beery	8.00	2.00
Benny	12.00	3.00
Breen	8.00	2.00
Burns	8.00	2.00
Cooper	10.00	2.50
Crosby	12.00	3.00
Dead End Kids	10.00	2.50
Devine	8.00	2.00
Faye	8.00	2.00
Fonda	12.00	3.00
Garbo	15.00	3.50
Holt	8.00	2.00
Buck Jones	8.00	2.00
Lehr	8.00	2.00
Livesey	8.00	2.00
Lombard	10.00	2.50
MacDonald	10.00	2.50
MacMurray	10.00	2.50
Penner	8.00	2.00
Power	10.00	2.50
Raye	10.00	2.50
Roy Rogers	12.00	3.00
Rooney	10.00	2.50
Randolph Scott	10.00	2.50
James Stewart	15.00	3.50
Tracy	12.00	3.00
Tuffy	8.00	2.00
Withers	8.00	2.00

WHEN YOU BUY CARDS. . .
MAKE SURE THE CONDITION MATCHES THE PRICE.

The early catalogs list Dietz Gum as the manufacturer of these tinted movie star prem-

iums, but the company name is not printed on them (it is also missing from the World War II tinted photo premiums also attributed to Dietz). The pictures were originally black & white; the company jazzed them up by tinting them (rose, blue or green) and printed them on vellum paper stock. The star's name is written in black or white ink script; some appear to be actual signatures, others do not. In most cases, the studio of the celebrity is identified in hand or machine print under their name. Approximately 25% of the photos also carry a "Printed in U.S.A." line. Only 26 names appear in our checklist, but there are probably many more yet to be reported. The reference number is R96-2.

CARD	EX	AVE
Edward Arnold		
United Artists	8.00	2.00
Fred Astaire		
RKO Radio Pictures	12.00	3.00
Humphrey Bogart		
Warner Bros. Pictures	12.00	3.00
James Cagney		
No studio listed	12.00	3.00
Chas. Chaplin		
No studio listed	15.00	4.00
Joan Crawford		
Metro-Goldwyn-Mayer	10.00	2.50
Bette Davis		
Warner Bros.	10.00	2.50
Robert Donat		
No studio listed	8.00	2.00
Douglas Fairbanks Jr.		
United Artists	10.00	2.50
Clark Gable		
Metro-Goldwyn-Mayer	15.00	4.00
Sonja Henie		
20th Century Fox	10.00	2.50
Edward Everett Hotton		
No studio listed	8.00	2.00
Al Jolson		
First National Pictures	12.00	3.00
Edmund Lowe		
No studio listed	8.00	2.00
Fred MacMurray		
Paramount Pictures	10.00	2.50
Ken Maynard		
No studio listed	10.00	2.50
Ray Milland		
Paramount Pictures	10.00	2.50
Gail Patrick		
Paramount Pictures	8.00	2.00
Dick Powell		
Warner Bros./		
Vitagraph	10.00	2.50
George Raft		
Paramount Pictures	12.00	3.00
Louise Rainer		
Metro-Goldwyn-Mayer	8.00	2.00
Martha Raye		
Paramount Pictures	10.00	2.50
Bill Robinson		
No studio listed	8.00	2.00
Evelyn Venable		
No studio listed	8.00	2.00
Fay Wray		
No studio listed	10.00	2.50
Robert Young		
M.G.M. Pictures	10.00	2.50

MOVIE STARS (9K)　　　　　　　　6" X 8"

More anonymous premiums associated with candy or gum because of early catalog listings — this time in 6-picture sheets. Each sheet is tinted in a single color (blue, brown or green) and is printed on medium weight vellum stock. It appears that some of these smaller pictures are identical to those used in the large premium series immediately preceding this listing. General salutations and motion picture titles are printed on some pictures; others simply list the star and movie studio. Prices for individual sheets vary depending on who is pictured. The reference number is R96-3.

Jack Perrin	Tim McCoy	Noah Berry
Smith Ballew	Nell O'Day	Leo Carrillo
Dorothy Page	Dean Jagger	Dick Foran
Geo. O'Brien	William Boyd	Betty Miles
Hooper Atchley	Geo. Hayes	Max Terhune
Smiley Burnette	Grant Withers	Bob Allen
Ralph Boyd	Russell Hayden	Hoot Gibson
Buck Jones	Sally Payne	Jack Randall
Tom Keene	Lon Chaney Jr.	Tom Tyler
Rufe Davis	Roy Rogers	John Wayne
Tex Ritter	Bob Steele	Fred Scott
Chester Starrett	Bob Baker	Ken Maynard
Quinn "Big Boy" Williams	Jack Hoxie	George ?
Iris Meredith	Fay McKenzie	Robert Livingston
James Ellison	Bill Radio Boyd	Roy Corrigan
Alan Bridges	Duncan Renaldo	Red Barry
John Mac Brown	Gene Autry	Lane Chandler
Jack Luden	Jeanne Kelly	Monte Blue

PRICES: Base prices per sheet are $ 10.00 for excellent grade and $ 2.50 for average grade. Add reasonable value up to 100% per sheet for more famous stars.

MOVIE STARS (24K)　　　　　　2 5/16" X 2 1/2"

Through the research efforts of Larry Fortuck, John Neuner, and the late Dick Reuss, we have been able to put together some solid information about this mysterious set of movie star cards. Other than the star's name, there is no other printing front or back. The pictures have either a light brown, chocolate brown, or gray coloration.

Twenty-four names have been checklisted to date.

How do we know that the cards under discussion came in this General Gum Co. wrapper? ...because we opened up an original pack. Two varieties of "Movie Gum" wrappers are known. There is no "contest" offered on the first; the second has the contest rules and closing date (Jan. 1st, 1934) printed under the center. The "large-sized picture of your favorite movie star" offered in the contest has not yet been identified, but might very well be one of the anonymous large premiums covered previously in this book. The reference number is R97-2. NOTE: "contest wrappers have numbers from 1 to 24 printed next to the "Save the Wrappers" line.

CARD	EX	AVE
Richard Arlen	4.00	1.00
Warner Baxter	4.00	1.00
Constance Bennett	4.00	1.00
Joan Bennett	4.00	1.00
Claudette Colbert	6.00	1.50
Jackie Cooper	6.00	1.50
Joan Crawford	6.00	1.60
Marion Davies	4.00	1.00
Marlene Dietrich	8.00	2.00
Marie Dressler	4.00	1.00
Sally Eilers	4.00	1.00
Charles Farrell	4.00	1.00
Clark Gable	10.00	2.50
Greta Garbo	10.00	2.50
Janet Gaynor	4.00	1.00
Helen Hayes	6.00	1.50
Walter Huston	6.00	1.50
Buster Keaton	8.00	2.00
Robert Montgomery	6.00	1.50
Frederic March	6.00	1.50
Conrad Nagel	4.00	1.00
Ramon Novarro	6.00	1.50
Will Rogers	8.00	2.00
Norma Shearer	4.00	1.00

ITEM	EX	AVE
Wrappers		
No contest	125.00	— —
Contest	100.00	— —

MOVIE STARS & SCENES (?/?)

This category contains two varieties of blank-backed movie-related cards printed in a variety of color tints. Type 1 cards measure 2 3/8" X 2 15/16" and appear to have been machine cut (not issued in strips). The series, as we

TWO SIZES

currently know it, contains 12 single portrait cards of movie actors and actresses plus 65 movie scenes from 12 different films. Most, if not all, of the motion pictures were made in the 1920's, so this set was probably issued right about 1930. The manufacturer and distributor(s) remain unknown. Some cards have been found in more than one color. The reference number is R94-1. NOTE: the movie "Babe Comes Home" stars Babe Ruth.

Buzz Barton
Warner Baxter
Maria Corda
Corrine Griffith
Dorothy Mackaill
Colleen Moore
Antonio Moreno
Jack Mulhall
Carmel Myers
Milton Sills
Bob Steele
Thelma Todd

"Babe Comes Home" (stars Babe Ruth)

Girl points at distraught Babe: two policemen look on
Locker room scene: team members playing joke

"Cheyenne" (stars Ken Maynard)

Ken Maynard atop white horse
Close up of Ken Maynard and girl in front of stable (horse's head behind them)
Distant shot of same couple in front of stable (no horse's head)
Old-timer, cowgirl, & cowboy sitting on bench watching exciting event
Fight in wagon shop; six participants
Ken Maynard talking with man loading rifle
Man acosts Ken Maynard & girl in front of stable (horse's head in door)
Ken Maynard lifts girl into air; happy cowboys in background (stable)
Ken Maynard in hospital room with foot on chair
Maynard in courtroom with white hat in right hand
Maynard in courtroom with injured man in arms
Maynard lifts chair to ward off villains

CARDS TYPE 1	EX	AVE
Portraits	5.00	1.50
Scenes		
Babe Comes Home (2)	150.00	50.00
Cheyenne (12)	5.00	1.50
Code of the Scarlet (2)	4.00	1.00
Danger Street (3)	4.00	1.00
Dog Law (4)	4.00	1.00
Son of the Golden West (2)	4.00	1.00
Terror Mountain (4)	4.00	1.00
The Devil's Saddle (8)	5.00	1.50
The Lawless Legion (12)	5.00	1.50
The Phantom City (9)	5.00	1.50
The Wagon Show (2)	4.00	1.00
The Young Whirlwind (5)	4.00	1.00

Movie Stars & Scenes

"Code of the Scarlet"

Mountie & townspeople; canoe in foreground, log cabins in background
Cowboy in plaid coat & white hat talking
to man in dark suit in front of trading
post

"Danger Street" (stars Warner Baxter)

Fight scene in store: Baxter stands with
clenched fists; two bad guys sprawled on
floor
Store scene: Baxter kneels over body on
floor; man wearing hat in right foreground
Baxter stands over prone girl, cop holds
gun on ruffians

"Dog Law" (stars Jack Mulhall)

Dog on hind legs with paws on Jack
Mulhall's chest
Girl playing pump organ while Mulhall
watches; two dogs & man at left
Man with whip threatens dog inside cabin
Woods scene: man restrains distraught girl
while others watch

"Son of the Golden West" (stars Bob
Steele)

Bob Steele on sidewalk addressing crowd
Bob Steele & girl in street talking to
prospector

"Terror Mountain"

Hero, in black hat, has hand on chest of
man
Fight on snow-covered steps of cabin
Woods scene: three men & horse with
fancy yoke
Interior scene: man & small boy sitting on
bed; man talks to standing girl

The Devil's Saddle" (stars Ken Maynard)

Bar scene: Maynard (center) restrains man
with gun in right hand
Bar scene: Maynard (center) talks to
group, including 3 Indians
Interior scene: Maynard, hands tied behind
back, in front of table surrounded by
crowd
Interior scene: Maynard grabs the
drunken/crooked judge, others move in
to stop him
Interior scene: Maynard restrained by
man; Maynard's gun in belt of man behind
him
Maynard on roof top kicking at man
climbing ladder
Crooked sheriff and girl with Maynard
inside cell
Maynard, girl in arms, points gloved finger
at sheriff

"The Lawless Legion" (stars Ken
Maynard

Court scene: man talks to crowd
(portraits of Lincoln & Washington on
wall)
Ken Maynard playing violin in cell
Maynard, knife in hand, standing over
poker table (between two men)
Confrontation in front of sheriff's office
(sign on shingled roof)
Man opens door; another man behind door
holds Maynard at gunpoint
Fight scene in street: man in fancy gunbelt
has another man on ground
Maynard ropes six ruffians; covered wagon
in back
Interior scene: man in chair (at table)
turns as others talk and gesture
Maynard, white horse standing by, talks
to girl on sidewalk
Sheriff's office: Maynard, in door, points
at crooked sheriff
Street scene: crooked sheriff pulls man
from horse
Street scene: sheriff talks to man holding
bridle of Maynard's horse

"The Phantom City" (stars
Ken Maynard)

Maynard, fist clenched, restrained by older
man in suit & hat
Maynard, man hanging around his neck,
shoves another in face
Maynard speaks to couple embracing on
bench under tree
Maynard points gun & gestures to black
cowboy
Cave scene: six men looking towards left
foreground
Fight on mining millrace
Interior scene: Maynard, gun drawn, enters
room with columns in center
Maynard restrains black cowboy; at right,
man sleeps in chair
Maynard confronts mob while sitting on
bar of abandoned saloon

"The Wagon Show"

Hero & man in wheelchair confront
officials
Interior scene: circus performers watch
hero (right arm extended)

"The Young Whirlwind" (stars Buzz
Barton)

Buzz talks to old man in jail cell
Buzz standing at hitching post with his
horse
Man in pilot hat & goggles restrains Buzz,
who has gun in right hand
Woods scene: men on foot confer while
others on horseback watch
Buzz Barton in front of jail (big sign over
door)
Buzz captured by outlaws (bandana covers
his mouth)
Buzz stands with girl & two men in front
of house (picket fence)

Cards with no movie title on face:

In corner of boxing ring: Patent Leather
Kid surrounded by handlers
In boxing ring: Patent Leather Kid
knocked to canvas
Circus people & hero at entrance of tent
(The Wagon Show)
Hero decks villain at picnic table under
tent; man in wheelchair at left (The Wagon
Show)
Two men seated joking with one another;
smiling man stands right behind them

Type 2 cards of this category also come in tinted colors and are blank-backed, but
they are smaller — 1 15/16"
X 3". We have 39 of these
on record and more discoveries are anticipated. All the
cards known to us at this
time are movie scenes (no
portraits), with the name of
the star, the movie title,
and the studio printed in a
small panel inside the picture area. This series seems
to be entirely separate from
Type 1 cards in the movies
depicted, the sole exception
being "Cheyenne." The manufacturer is unknown, and the
reference number is R94-2.

CARD TYPE 2	EX	AVE
Charles Chaplin	10.00	2.50
Farina	6.00	1.50
Hoot Gibson	7.50	2.00
Ken Maynard	7.50	2.00
Tom Mix	7.50	2.00
All others	4.00	1.00

R94-2 Movie Stars & Scenes

Audrey Ferris, Carroll Nye (?)
Bert Roach (Riders of the Dark)
Betty Compson, Marceline Day & Lon
Chaney (The Big City)
Bob Steele (?)
Buck Jones (Blood Will Tell)
Bud Osborne (?)
Buzz Barton (?)
Charley Chaplin (The Circus)
Davey Lee (Sonny Boy)
Farina (Holy Terror)
Fred Humes (?)
Harry Gribbon (Honeymoon)
Harry Spear, Sean Darling (?)
Hoot Gibson (?)
House Peters, Joan Crawford & James
Murray (Modern Age)
Jack Donovan (Hoof Marks)
Jack Lloyd & Jack Miller (Shooting Wild)
John Nilsan, May McVoy, Robert Frazer(?)
Ken Maynard (Senor Americano)
Lane Chandler (Open House)

Leo Maloney (?)
Mickey Daniels (Shooting Injuns)
Mickey Daniels (The Detective)
Mickey Daniels (Olympic Games)
Norma Shearer, Ramon Navaro (The
Student Prince)
Pete Morrison (?)
Rex Lease, Joan Crawford (?)
Rudolph Schildkraut (The Country
Doctor)
Ted Wells (?)
Tex Maynard (Wild Born)
Theodore Lorch (North West)
Tom Mix (?)
Tom Mix (Outlawed - 2 dif.)
Tom Mix (New Cowboy)
Tom Tyler (?)
Tom Tyler (Hearts & Hoofs)
Tom Sanschi (Cheyenne)
William Haines (Excess Baggage)
Wm Boyd & Tom Sanschi (Shooting
Straight)

MUL—T—JOKES (?) 1 1/4" X 2 1/2"

"When is de bes' time to pick watermelons? When de farmer ain't lookin'!" That's the kind of joke found on the fronts of this third set of "match cards" produced by Milkes (the others were "Make Faces" and "Matchem"). The set-ups and punch lines on the numbered, multi-color artwork fronts are revealed by properly arranging the partial designs on four cards (the correct placement is diagrammed on back). The backs bear the set title, a "100 different jokes" line, two diagrams, and a Riddle (both question and answer). The company name at bottom is listed as "Mul-T-Toy" but the Milkes name is printed beneath the set title. The actual length of the set is not known, and no reference number has been assigned.

ITEM	EX	AVE
Card	15.00	5.00

NATIONAL CHICLE NOVELTY CARDS (24) 2 7/16" X 3 1/4"

When one considers the design of the National Chicle Novelty Cards series, it is a wonder that any have survived in decent condition. Every one of these colorful artwork cards has a "gimmick" — die cut designs, finger holes, fold-overs — created to allow the owner to play with them as toys. For this reason, cards in "excellent" grade are eagerly pursued by collectors. Please note, however, that no card can be graded excellent if it has been "popped," folded, etc. For some strange reason, National Chicle decided to -number the set from 1 to 12 and from 25 to 36 (early collectors searched in vain for the missing cards!). The reference number for the set is R102. No wrapper or packaging has been seen.

Your Old Man

Bend the card as above. Pull it up and down. . . . Ain't he a Beaut?

No. 7

1 Monkey Business
2 The Razzberry
3 Izzy White or Izzy Black?
4 But-in-Ski-Licence
5 Kissing License
6 Shame on You, Auntie!
7 Your Old Man
8 Wrinkle Puss
9 Count the Cubes
10 Put and Take Top
11 The Changing Color Spot Trick
12 False Teeth
25 Be a Card Wizard!
26 Half-Wit Hambone
27 Boys! Get a Kick Outta Me!
28 Public Enemy No. 1
29 Hocus...Pocus
30 Revolving Color Wheel
31 Beauty Winner!
32 Champion Liar
33 Saturday Night Exercises
34 The Terrible Turk Mustache
35 The Donkey Has a Rider. Where Is He?
36 Cock-Eye

ITEM	EX	AVE
Card	15.00	3.50
Set	475.00	115.00

NOAH'S ARK (24) 2 3/8" X 2 7/8"

The "wholesome and delicious" product known as "Noah's Ark Gum," issued in 1933 by Flatbush Gum, contained a series of 24 animal pictures. The drawings demonstrate a rather fanciful use of color which gives the subjects a strange appearance (was this the artist's whim or an appeal to juvenile tastes?). The back, which is printed in black ink on off-white stock, bears a brief description of the animal and advertising. The cards are not numbered, but a "1933 F.G. Co." line appears on every card inside the frameline of the picture. The reference number is R100.

Leopard

Inhabits both Asia and Africa. The leopard has a beautiful spotted coat and is very skillful in hiding when hunted.

NOAH'S ARK GUM

is pure, wholesome and delicious, made from the finest ingredients.

Flatbush Gum Co., Brooklyn, N. Y.

ITEM	EX	AVE
Card	15.00	5.00
Set	475.00	155.00
Wrapper	300.00	—

African Elephant
African Lion
African Rhinoceros
Alaskan Brown Bear
American Mountain Goat
Bactrian Camel
Bison
Crocodile
Giraffe
Gorilla
Gray Fox
Gray Wolf
Hippopotamus
Indian Python
Kangaroo
Leopard
Moose
Musk Ox
Polar Bears
Puma
Tigers
Virginia Deer
Walrus
Zebra

"OUR GANG" GUM PUZZLES (25)   3 11/16" X 5 1/8"

This colorful set of 25 jig-saw puzzles appears to be a store handout item produced by Goudey Gum, but the company's name does not appear on the puzzles. Each jig-saw is numbered but none are titled. A line on one border reads "A complete series of 25 make a puzzle circus (look at our illustrated check-list to see how the cards fit together)". The dimensions in the heading refer to the puzzle with borders intact; no puzzle can be graded ex-cellect if it is missing any borders. "Our Gang" Gum Puzzles came to light for the first time several years ago, so they were unknown to the early catalogers. A reference number of R194 has been assigned.

ITEM	EX	AVE
Puzzle	20.00	5.00

PROPERLY-ALIGNED, "OUR GANG" PUZZLES CREATE
A GIANT 3-RING CIRCUS PANORAMA

PECO AIRPLANE PICTURES (28)   1 5/16" X 2 13/16"

1 Seversky Sev-S2 Monoplane
2 Martin 156-C33 to 53 Flying Boat
3 Boeing 314 Clipper Plane
4 Keith Ryder R-1 "Bumble Bee"
5 Clark GA-43 Transport Monoplane
6 Miles-Attwood Racing Monoplane
7 Arup Round-Wing Monoplane
8 Fairchild A-942 Amphibian
9 Chester "The Jeep" Racing Plane
10 Gee-Bee No. 11 Racing Monoplane
11 Howard "Pete" Racing Plane
12 Lockheed "Express" 3 Monoplane
13 Stinson Reliant SR-9FD
14 Lockheed Orion-Altair Special
15 Kinner K-Sport Two-Seater
16 Pasped Skylark Sport Two-Seater
17 Tilbury Flash Racing Plane
18 Fairchild JK-1 U.S. Navy Plane
19 Consolidated A-11 U.S. Army Plane
20 Curtiss Wright 19R Trainer
21 Howard "Mike" Racing Monoplane
22 Stinson "A" Tri-Motor Monoplane
23 Seversky BT-8 Army Trainer
24
25
26 Wedell Williams "92" Racing Plane
27
28 Boeing P-26A Army Pursuit Plane

The first series of 28 airplane cards issued by Peco probably appeared in the early 1930's. Each of the cards formed part of the tray holding the candy cigarettes and had machined perforations on two sides for easy removal of the advertising flaps. The color artwork aircraft drawings are simplistic, and the line "PAT No. 2179376" always appears within the picture area. The card number, title, and basic engine details are printed in a blue area at the base. The backs are blank and the dimensions above refer to cards with the top and bottom flaps removed. The reference number is R8-1.

ITEM	EX	AVE
Card		
w/o flaps	6.00	1.50
with flaps	8.00	2.00
Set		
w/o flaps	225.00	50.00
with flaps	300.00	65.00

PECO AIRPLANE PICTURES (28)   1 5/16" X 2 13/16"

A second set of 28 Peco Airplane Pictures was marketed close to America's entry into World War II. The color drawings on front depict more modern aircraft than the earlier series; the backs are blank. The card number, title, and a short description of the plane are printed in a red rectangle at the left. The patent line located within the picture reads "Package Pat. No. 2179376." The dimensions stated are for a card without the top and bottom tray flaps. The reference number is R8-2.

ITEM	EX	AVE
Card		
w/o flaps	6.00	1.50
with flaps	8.00	2.00
Set		
w/o flaps	225.00	50.00
with flaps	300.00	65.00

1 Douglas TBD-1 Navy Torpedo Plane
2 Grumman F4F-3 Navy Fighter
3 Vought F4-U Navy Fighter
4 Grumman F3F-1 Navy Fighter
5 Boeing B-17-B Heavy Army Bomber
6 Ryan PT-20A Army Primary Trainer
7 Stearman PT-13 Army Primary Trainer
8 Bell P-39 Army Airacobra
9 Curtiss P-40 Army Pursuit Fighter
10 Lockheed P-38 Army Interceptor Pursuit
11 Brewster F2A-2 Navy Fighter
12 Republic P-43 Army Pursuit Fighter
13 Vought OS2U-1 Navy Observation Scout
14 Martin B-26 Army Medium Bomber
15 Consolidated PDY-2 Navy Patrol Bomber
16 Vought SB2U-2 Navy Scout Bomber
17 Martin PBM-1 Navy Patrol Bomber
18 Consolidated PB2Y-1 Navy Patrol Bomber
19 Curtiss SBC-4 Navy Dive Bomber
20 Consolidated PBY-5A Navy Patrol Bomber
21 Curtiss SOC-1 Navy Scout Bomber
22 Consolidated P2Y-2 Navy Patrol Plane
23 Douglas P3D1 Navy Patrol Bomber
24 North American SNJ-2 Navy Scout Trainer
25 Douglas A-20 A Army Attack Bomber
26 Grumman F5F1 Navy Fighter
27 Douglas B-19 Heavy Army Bomber
28 Grumman JF1 Navy Utility Plane

PECO ANIMAL ALPHABET (26)   1 5/16" X 2 13/16"

Peco's "Animal Alphabet" cards were printed as the center portion of the tray carrying the candy cigarettes. There are two detail differences which suggest that the set might have been issued more than once. For example, one of the boxes illustrated (top) has no candy ingredients list and the other one (bottom) does. Also, the bottom box has a coupon printed on one flap (10 coupons & 10 cents for a baseball cap or girl's head kerchief) while the box at top has standard advertising flaps.

Each card bears a letter of the alphabet and a drawing of an animal whose name begins with that letter. There are no descriptions of the animals, and the card backs are blank. The reference number is R107.

ITEM	EX	AVE
Card		
w/o flaps	6.00	1.50
with flaps	8.00	2.00
Set		
w/o flaps	185.00	45.00
with flaps	250.00	60.00

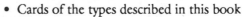

PEE WEE SAYS (24)

Red, yellow and green are the predominant colors in this cartoon-style series relating the predicaments and juvenile philosophy of Pee Wee, a cute child. The cards are not numbered, and the artist's name, Iger, is printed on each. The method of distribution and the manufacturer are not known, but it is likely that "Pee Wee Says" cards were issued in strips (the uncut sheet we have illustrated has three rows of eight cards). The reference number is R105.

ITEM	EX	AVE
Card	5.00	1.00
Set	135.00	30.00

A Telephone Sure Is Useful—Mom Cuts Biscuits with the Mouthpiece an' Baby Is Teething on the Cord

Ain't It Awful—Billy Jones' Ma Kicked Poor Fido for Bitin' Her Baby!

Ain't It Awful the Way Your Aunts and Uncles Always Kiss You When They Come Visitin'!!

Aw I Can't Do Anythin' with Music—So I Guess I'll Become an Orchestra Leader!

Aw Why Couldn't Castor 'Erl' Taste Like Lemonade!

Daddy Says Music Is a Good Aid to Digestion

Gee! I Wish I Had a Little Sister—It Gets Kind o' Tiresome Teasin' the Cat!

Gee! That's 'n Awful Lot of Weight for a Lil' Feller Like Me!

I Can't Afford a Dog So I'm Gonna Get a Moth for a Pet 'cause He Eats Nothin' But Holes!

I Didn't Catch Anythin' Today But I Will When Pa Finds Me!

I Don't See the Sense in Washin' Behind the Ears Nobody Ever Looks There!

I Know How Ya Feel, Fido—It's the Same When Mom Makes Me Take a Bath—

I'm Gonna Nickname You "Bumble Bee" 'cause When Ever I Trade Somethin' with You I Get Stung!

It Must Be Swell to Be an Elephant—It's So Easy for Him to Pick Up Things with His Vacuum Cleaner!

Just When You're Achin' for Some Candy Your Tooth Starts Achin'!!

Mom Says Heavy Meals Ain't Good for Ya and Then She Tells Me to Eat Spinach 'cause It Has Iron in It!!

Nope! I Guess I Won't Look So Good in a Suit of "Longies"—

Pa Says Exercise Will Kill All Germs—But Gee, How Do You Get 'em to Exercise?

Pa Says I Ought to Save My Pennies for a Rainy Day—What's the Use—I'm Not Allowed Out on a Rainy Day!!!

Pa Says Rabbits Multiply Faster Then (sic) Anything, But This Dumb One Can't Even Add!

Pa Says We've Come into the World to Help Others—Wonder What the Others Are Here For?

Success Sure Goes to the Heads of Some People—Stuffy Won't Show the Warts on His Hands Unless You Give Him Somethin'!

Tuffy Burns Has a Good Ear for Music But It's AWFUL Dirty!

When We Have Ice Cream for Supper I Sure Am Glad I Was Born!

127

PHYSICAL CULTURE LESSONS (?)   2 1/2" X 3"

The actual title of this set of achromatic photocards is "The Joe Bonomo Method of Physical Culture." The exercises explained on the backs of the cards have nothing to do with the publicity pictures on the front. For instance, exercise 10W

begins "Stand Erect. Grasp the back of a chair," while the "Note" which describes the obverse photo on the same card reads "Here Joe illustrates the tremendous strength of his jaw muscles ..." In previous catalogs, the set length was listed as 24

cards, but the following statement printed on the cards seems to contradict that total: "There are five to fifteen exercises to a lesson and twenty-four lessons to a complete health building course." If cards were actually printed for every exercise and lesson, then collectors have been severely underestimating the scarcity of this series for years. The cards might have been packaged in boxes of Bonomo's candy sold at Coney Island, New York. No wrapper or packaging has been found. The reference number is R106.

"THE HERCULES OF THE SCREEN" N

ITEM	EX	AVE
Card	15.00	5.00

PIRATE'S PICTURE BUBBLE GUM (72)   2 7/16" X 3 1/8"

The beautiful color artwork of Pirate's Picture Bubble Gum cards make them a favorite among collectors. The set was produced by Gum, Inc, but the company name

does not appear on the cards. They are numbered and captioned on the front only; the backs contain an imaginative story. Blank-backed paper cards have been re-

ported, and it is likely that these were cut from paper sheets given to retailers to hang in windows or showcases. The wrapper is one of the best ever designed for a card set. It contains six beautiful scenes around the center picture of a pirate swinging his cutlass. Wrapper colors are purple, orange and green on white wax paper. The reference number is R109.

68. IN THE CROW'S NEST

PIRATE'S PICTURE BUBBLE GUM

ITEM	EX	AVE
Card	15.00	4.00
Set	1350.00	350.00
Wrapper	250.00	—

1 Fighting Aloft
2 Walking the Plank
3 Slave Traders
4 Who Shall Be Captain?
5 Boarding Ship
6 Mutiny
7 Pierre Le Grand
8 Marooned
9 "I Command Surrender!"
10 Pirate Torture
11 Burning the Prize
12 Hiding Treasure
13 Blackbeard's End
14 Captain Brand's Death
15 Pirates Gambling
16 A Boarding Party
17 A Pirate Captured
18 Burning a Town

19 The Tricky Morgan
20 The Pirates Strike
21 Set Adrift
22 The Warning Shot
23 The Jolly Roger
24 Tripoli Pirates
25 Dividing Treasure
26 Killing a Traitor
27 The "Arch Pirate"
28 Four Against One
29 Dead Men Tell No Tales
30 "Double Doubloons"
31 "Man the Guns"
32 "I've Got You at Last"
33 Ghost of Captain Watson
34 Left to their Fate
35 Waiting to Attack
36 Englishmen as Slaves

37 Daring Takes a Man-of-War
38 Flogging a Captive
39 Man Who Trained Morgan
40 Dividing Gold and Silver
41 Burying the Iron Chest
42 Landing to Bury Treasure
43 A Captain Well Named
44 Sunken Ships Have No Trail
45 Two-Gun Mulrooney Wins
46 To Death Blindfolded
47 Cheng, China's Famous Pirate
48 "The Daring Act of the Age"
49 Ready to Sack Maracaibo
50 "Your Money or Your Life"
51 A Flag of Terror
52 Abandoned and Afire
53 "Board Her—No Quarter!"
54 "Join—See the World"

55 America's Famous Pirate
56 A Surprise Attack
57 Counting the Treasure
58 China's Foremost Pirate
59 Fight at Pirates Cove
60 "Fight!—or Surrender"
61 Faithfulness Rewarded
62 Paying the Ransom
63 "The Captives"
64 "Fill 'em Up"
65 El-Sid-Murad in Action
66 Trapped
67 Ending the Card Game
68 In the Crow's Nest
69 On Way to the Gallows
70 Silenced Forever!
71 Sighting a Foe
72 "Prepare for Action"

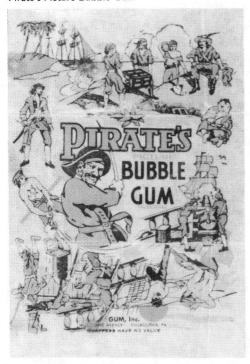

67. ENDING THE CARD GAME

"You cheated, Captain Harrington!"
Quick-tempered Jack Fenton seized his pistol from his silk sling, kicking his chair away, overturning the table, bottle of spirits, and glasses and knocking the cards from the table. Calm, self-possessed Captain Harrington, with no opportunity to draw his pistol set still on the treasure chest. Boatswain Higgins leaped for quick-tempered Jack. Will Fenton pull the trigger before Higgins reaches him? Seconds alone will tell. Pirates had a way of dealing with men who cheated in a game where money was involved. Rule III read: "If any man shall steal anything from the company, or in a game, to the value of a piece of eight, he shall be marooned or shot."

This is one of 73 cards

PIRATE'S PICTURE BUBBLE GUM
TRADE MARK

PETITE GUM (?)

1 5/8" X 4"

In the 1930's, several different companies issued gum in a unique format — matchbook covers. Gum, Inc., for example, marketed a product called "Match It," in which brand new covers from a matchbook manufacturer were packaged with a slab of bubble gum. The Chicle Advertising Distribution Corporation, of Toledo, Ohio, actually sold stick chewing gum housed in faux matchbooks, and we have already reviewed one of their sets, "Big Chief Wahoo," earlier in this book. "Petite Gum" was obviously intended for fashionable people who preferred to carry with them a few sticks of refreshing gum in a delicate and inconspicuous manner. The matchbook pictured here is lavender with silver and white accents. It contained four sticks of gum. As with Chief Wahoo, collectors are most likely to find Petite Gum folders in the occasional pile of matchbook covers at flea markets, collectibles conventions, etc. No reference number has been assigned.

ITEM	EX	AVE
Matchbook	10.00	2.00

Brand X got you behind the 8—ball?
Next time.....Insist on SPORT AMERICANA Guides

PIRATE TREASURE (48)(18)

Collector Chris McCann remembers collecting "Pirate Treasure" as a child: "A full sheet of 48 of the smaller type (1¾" X 2¾"), or a sheet of the large variety (2" X 3") was fastened to a cardboard box with compartments in it, one below each card. The collector would go to the candy store and ask to see the box. On a new box, all 48 (or 18) cards were visible, and he could pick the one he liked the best. Two edges of the cards were rouletted, and the collector would push the card down to detach it. In the compartment under the card

were a few pieces of candy and a small toy, like a whistle or a "cricket." I paid one cent each for the small card, candy and toy. The large cards were five cents, for which the buyer got a better toy and more candy."

There are three types of Pirate Treasure cards. Type 1 is small and has "Save 48 pictures for a complete story of 'Pirate Treasure'" printed on the back. Type 2 is ¼" larger on both margins than type 1, is complete at 18 titles, and has "M.J. Holloway & Co." on the back. A third type, also believed to be a Holloway issue, says "Save an entire set of 18 pictures and get a larger

TWO SIZES

pirate picture suitable for framing." This last variety has blue print on the back; the first two types have black print on the backs. In addition, type 3 is missing the "nubs" on the edges, indicating that it was machine cut and, therefore, distributed in another manner than described above. The reference number is R110.

ITEM	EX	AVE
Cards		
Type 1	6.00	2.00
Type 2	7.50	2.50
Type 3	9.00	3.00
Sets		
Type 1 (48)	360.00	110.00
Type 2 (18)	170.00	55.00
Type 3 (18)	200.00	65.00

36.—Celebrating Their Victory.

Back on their ships, the celebration of their victory lasted for days. Wine, laughter, and song were their only occupation as they sailed away to seek a hiding place for their treasure until time would dim the horror of their raid.

SAVE 48 PICTURES FOR A COMPLETE STORY OF "PIRATE TREASURE"

No. 12—Revenge.

They immediately decided to attack the other pirate ship—a galleon much larger than their own, with 53 cannons. Pretending to be tied as prisoners, they made their captives steer their little ship alongside the big one and pounced upon her deck. This cunning generalship of Quelch and Don Trinidad proved victorious and they found themselves in possession of two ships and vast riches.

M. J. HOLLOWAY & CO.
CHICAGO, ILLINOIS

No. 10—The Duel.

As one prisoner, Don Trinidad, quick of mind and mouth of tongue, taunted the first mate—called him coward—and challenged him to a duel. The mate being an expert swordsman, gladly accepted. On the island, Don Trinidad ran an exceedingly skilled point of swordsmanship beyond all imagination. In triumph he was made First Mate of the pirate ship.

SAVE AN ENTIRE SET of 18 pictures AND GET A LARGE PIRATE PICTURE SUITABLE FOR FRAMING.

"SAVE 48" CARDS — 1¾" X 2¾"   "HOLLOWAY" 2" X 3" CARD   "SET OF 18" CARD — 2" X 3

1 The Spanish Main	13 Marooned	25 A Ship for the "Taking"	37 Revenge at Last
2 Captain Quelch	14 Dividing the Loot	26 Boarding the Galleon	38 Burying the Treasure
3 Land Ho!	15 Burying the Treasure	27 The Battle	39 Attack on Crow
4 Provisions	16 The Attack on the Fort	28 Victory and Revenge	40 Against Terrific Odds
5 A Friendly Visit?	17 The Gallant Prisoner	29 Trinidad Decides Crow's Fate	41 Crow's Cunning
6 Boarding the Ship	18 Journey's End	30 The Schemer	42 Crow Barters His Life for a
7 Hand to Hand Fighting	19 Don Trinidad	31 Reinforcements	Secret
8 Cornered	20 Attacking Vultures of the Sea	32 Battling the Storm	43 Trinidad's Courage
9 Walking the Plank	21 Crow, the Pirate	33 They Capture the City	44 Treachery by Night
10 The Duel	22 Prisoners	34 Murder—Robbery—Destruction	45 Death of Gypso
11 Treachery	23 The Escape	35 Plunder	46 Trinidad's Decision
12 Revenge	24 Safe on Shore	36 Celebrating Their Victory	47 The Death of Captain Crow
			48 Trinidad's Reward

POLICEMAN PICTURES (10)

"This is one of a series of Policeman pictures packed with Holloway Milk Made Candies" — so we are advised on the back of every card.

However, this set was totally unknown until collector Paul Koch discovered several six-card strips of Holloway cards (each strip had

2 1/2" X 3"

a single card from six different sets!). The fronts contain color artwork drawings and are captioned beneath the picture. The "episodes" on the backs are numbered and have different titles than the obverse captions. The cardboard stock is thin compared to that of other Holloway sets. The reference number is R204.

ITEM	EX	AVE
Card	15.00	5.00
Set	200.00	60.00

EPISODE NO. 3
The Story of Davy Lane

Davy Lane, a fine four-year-old boy, had become lost and was taken to headquarters by Donovan, a pleasant policeman. There he was left in the squad room to await the arrival of his mother. For a moment, Davy was frightened but the policemen were so kind to him that he soon felt right at home. One of the policemen put his cap on the boy and another one handed him his club and they told him to walk up and down on the table. They said he looked like a real policeman walking his beat. When Davy's mother arrived he was having the time of his life and on the way home he told her he wanted to be a policeman. It was a big decision for so little a boy.

This is one of a series of Policeman pictures packed with Holloway Milk Made Candies.
M. J. HOLLOWAY & CO., CHICAGO, ILL.

The Hero of the Force

POPEYE COMICS (28K)

2" X 2 1/2"

The Popeye Comics four-section folders issued in "Tattoo Gum" by the Orbit Gum Co. (Chicago) open to a length of nearly eight inches. When opened, the exterior sides have four-page illustrated stories, and the interior sides contain puzzles, games, etc. Each Popeye Comic is numbered on the front cover, and the length of the set has yet to be determined

(No. 28 is the highest seen). A King Features Syndicate copyright date of 1933 is also printed on each cover. The reference number for the Popeye Comics set is R113. NOTE: brittle comics or comics with separated pages cannot be graded excellent.

ITEM	EX	AVE
Folder	30.00	6.00

1 Compass Points
2 How to Draw
3 Shadow Pictures
4 Maze Game
5 Fold-Ups
6 Fold-Ups
7 Cut-Up Puzzle
8 Sailor Knots
9
10 Shadow Pictures
11 How to Draw
12
13 Puzzle
14 How to Box
15 Crossword Puzzle
16 Puzzle
17
18 Dot Game
19
20 Cut-Up Puzzle
21 Puzzle
22
23
24 Dot Game
25 Astronomy
26 Crossword Puzzle
27 Star Making
28 Cut-Up Puzzle

PRESIDENTS (31)

2 3/8" X 2 7/8"

The United States Caramel Company produced two of the hobby's rarest cards by using a simple but devious merchandising technique. Cards from both its "Presidents" and "Famous Athletes" sets advertised a free box of candy to anyone completing either set. How difficult was this? Considering that U.S. Caramel withheld one card in each set from circulation, it proved to be impossible. A single copy of the missing card in "Famous Ath-

letes" — No. 16, Charles (Lindy) Lindstrom — was found in 1989. The missing card in the "Presidents" series — William McKinley — has never been confirmed in any collection. The discovery of Lindstrom would tend to prove that the McKinley card was actually printed. One thing is certain: U.S. Caramel didn't give away a whole lot of candy.

The 30 Presidents cards which are available are chest-up stud-

ies set upon solid color backgrounds. Each president has been found with the same photo set on three background colors: blue, orange and red. The product name, "American Heroes Caramel," is printed in a red panel beneath each picture. The cards are not numbered, and the backs carry a brief biography and the infamous candy offer. Only purists attempt to collect the series in all the background colors; most people are content to have a single card of each president. The reference number is R114. NOTE: the "excellent" price for McKinley applies ONLY to a card that has not been canceled by stamping or hole-punching.

ITEM	EX	AVE
Card	7.50	2.00
McKinley	1500.00	500.00

131

George Washington
John Adams
Thomas Jefferson
James Madison
James Monroe
John Quincy Adams
Andrew Jackson
Martin Van Buren

William Henry Harrison
John Tyler
James Knox Polk
Zachary Taylor
Millard Fillmore
Franklin Pierce
James Buchanan
Abraham Lincoln

Andrew Johnson
Ulysses S. Grant
Rutherford B. Hayes
James Abram Garfield
Chester A. Arthur
Grover Cleveland
Benjamin Harrison
William McKinley

Theodore Roosevelt
William Howard Taft
Woodrow Wilson
Warren G. Harding
Calvin Coolidge
Herbert Hoover
Franklin D. Roosevelt

PRESIDENTS (14)   2" X 3"

Here's a mystery...why did Gold Brand Confectionary start its Presidents series with No. 16, Lincoln? No one knows right now, so we'll have to take the company at its word and accept that the series consists of only 14 cards. The fronts carry portraits of the presidents set on red backgrounds. The product name, "Jig Saw Nougat," was printed below in different color combinations of print and panels. The backs, found with either black or blue print, bear a short biographical sketch plus a redemption offer for a copy of "Picture Puzzle Weekly." This required cutting off a ½" section from each of the 14 cards in the set and sending the pieces in to the company. Perhaps this accounts for the scarcity of these cards today. The "Jig Saw Nougat" wrapper has a marbled pattern with oriental style lettering. The reference number is R115.

ITEM	EX	AVE
Card	8.00	2.00
Set	150.00	37.50
Wrapper	350.00	—

Lincoln (16)
Johnson (17)
Grant (18)
Hayes (19)
Garfield (20)
Arthur (21)
Cleveland (22 & 24)
Harrison (23)
McKinley (25)
Roosevelt (26)
Taft (27)
Wilson (28)
Harding (29)
Coolidge (30)

PRESIDENTS (31)   2 1/4" X 2 3/4"

The Presidents cards created by the Independent Candy Co. (Chicago) are a good example of wasted design. The ornate frame surrounding the picture, for example, is filled with stars, crests, flags and boughs that deserve a better printing job. Likewise, the blue-tone pictures of the Presidents are indistinct and mottled, and the overall patriotic scheme of red, white and blue colors on the front are too dull to attract any attention. The card backs contain biographical data about each president and are printed in green ink on gray stock. The candy company is named at the bottom. Few collectors are attracted to a set so poorly done, but the scarcity of the cards makes them appealing to some. No wrapper or packaging has been seen. The reference number is R116.

ITEM	EX	AVE
Card	9.00	2.50
Set	350.00	95.00

George Washington — 1st President
John Adams — 2nd President
Thomas Jefferson — 3rd President
James Madison — 4th President
James Monroe — 5th President
John Quincy Adams — 6th President
Andrew Jackson — 7th President
Martin Van Buren — 8th President
William Henry Harrison — 9th President
John Tyler — 10th President
James A. Polk — 11th President
Zachary Taylor — 12th President
Millard Fillmore — 13th President
Franklin Pearce — 14th President
James Buchanan — 15th President

Abraham Lincoln — 16th President
Andrew Johnson — 17th President
Ulysses S. Grant — 18th President
Rutherford B. Hayes — 19th President
James A. Garfield — 20th President
Chester A. Arthur — 21st President
Grover Cleveland — 22nd & 24th President
Benjamin Harrison — 23rd President
William McKinley — 25th President
Theodore Roosevelt — 26th President
William H. Taft — 27th President
Woodrow Wilson — 28th President
Warren G. Harding — 29th President
Calvin Coolidge — 30th President
Herbert Hoover — 31st President

PRESIDENTS (32)

5/8" X 1 5/16"

Very few collectors have ever seen one of these red and white paper Presidents cards produced in 1938 by American Chicle. One reason is the size: things this small tend to be lost, thrown away, or ignored by everyone from the original purchaser to modern day dealers. Moreover, many were probably returned to the company because the presidential portrait was printed on a paper coupon which could be collected and redeemed for prizes (depicted on the back). It seems likely that the series was packed in a small gum box or chewing gum package, but no packaging has turned up to date. The coupons are not numbered; an "Offer Expieres 1-1-39" line is printed on the back. The reference number is R117.

ITEM	EX	AVE
Coupon	15.00	5.00

George Washington — 1st President	Andrew Johnson — 17th President
John Adams — 2nd President	Ulysses S. Grant — 18th President
Thomas Jefferson — 3rd President	Rutherford B. Hayes — 19th President
James Madison — 4th President	James A. Garfield — 20th President
James Monroe — 5th President	Chester A. Arthur — 21st President
John Quincy Adams — 6th President	Grover Cleveland — 22nd & 24th President
Andrew Jackson — 7th President	Benjamin Harrison — 23rd President
Martin Van Buren — 8th President	William McKinley — 25th President
William Henry Harrison — 9th President	Theodore Roosevelt — 26th President
John Tyler — 10th President	William H. Taft — 27th President
James A. Polk — 11th President	Woodrow Wilson — 28th President
Zachary Taylor — 12th President	Warren G. Harding — 29th President
Millard Fillmore — 13th President	Calvin Coolidge — 30th President
Franklin Pearce — 14th President	Herbert Hoover — 31st President
James Buchanan — 15th President	Franklin D. Roosevelt — 32nd President
Abraham Lincoln — 16th President	

PRESIDENTS PLAY BUCKS (36K)

2 1/4" X 5 1/4"

Money, even if it is phony, has universal appeal, and that's what Dietz Gum was banking on when it issued the Presidential Play Buck series in 1937. The picture in the center of every bill is black and white, as are the "Play Bucks" panels on the sides. The rest of the front is green and orange with black print. All the detail on the backs of the bucks is orange ink on white background. Two red, white & blue "Presidents Gum" wrappers have been found. They are identical except for the center portraits, Washington and Roosevelt, who are the first and last chief executives pictured in the set. In addition, a handsome "pocket album" was produced for storing the money.

At last count, there were 36 different banknotes confirmed for the 31 presidents in the set. Four of the presidents are depicted on bills with two denominations: the ones for Coolidge ($2/$500), Hoover ($1/$100), Franklin Roosevelt ($1/One Million), and Washington (?/$1000). Grover Cleveland, who was elected president on two separate occasions, comes marked "22nd PRESIDENT" or "24th PRESIDENT" over his picture. The official set length, stated on the pocket album, is 32 banknotes, so we can only guess why the variations were produced. Moreover, some bills have been found without a center crease, indicating that they were not distributed in gum packs. These might have been given out to students as a promotion. The reference number for President's Play Bucks is R118. NOTE: more research is necessary to determine which bills were in the original set of 32 (and which are variations) so no set price is given.

ITEM	EX	AVE
Play Buck	8.00	2.00
Wrappers		
Washington	100.00	—
Roosevelt	125.00	—
Pocket album	125.00	30.00

John Adams $10	Andrew Johnson $1
John Quincy Adams $5	Abraham Lincoln $500
Chester A. Arthur $20	James Madison $20
James Buchanan $2	William McKinley $10
Grover Cleveland (22nd) $ 10	James Monroe $5
Grover Cleveland (24th) $ 10	Franklin Pierce $2
Calvin Coolidge $2 — $500	James K. Polk $5
Millard Fillmore $2	Franklin D. Roosevelt $1 —
James A. Garfield $1	"One Million"
Ulysses S. Grant $50	Theodore Roosevelt $50
Warren G. Harding $10	William Howard Taft $10
Benjamin Harrison $5	Zachary Taylor $5
William H. Harrison $5	John Tyler $5
Rutherford B. Hayes $1	Martin Van Buren $20
Herbert Hoover $1 — $100	George Washington (?/&1000)
Andrew Jackson $20	Woodrow Wilson $100
Thomas Jefferson $20	

133

SPECIAL CARDBOARD "POCKET ALBUM" DESIGNED TO HOLD
A COMPLETE SET OF "PRESIDENTS PLAY BUCKS"

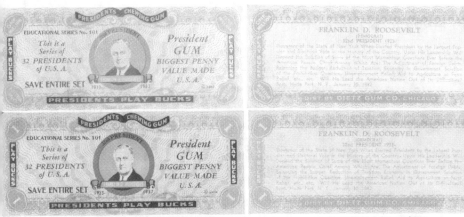

PULVER PICTURES (30)

2 1/2" X 3 1/8"

No. 100

DAVID AND GOLIATH

One of the most famous, yet most unequal battles in history is the famed battle between David and Goliath. David, a young and innocent shepherd boy, was an Israelite. The Israelites were at war with the Philistines, a very powerful enemy. Goliath, a giant of a man was the most dangerous of the Philistines. David brought some food to his brothers who were at war, and when he saw how frightened his people were, because of Goliath, he went to King Saul and offered to fight Goliath, single handed. The Israelites agreed to have David and Goliath fight, so the outcome of this duel would end the war. David was fitted out in heavy armor, but found he could not use it, so he took five smooth pebbles from the brook, tested his trusty sling shot and went forth to battle. Hitting his huge opponent in the forehead with great force, David killed Goliath, cut off his head, and returned victorious.

The greatest assortment of picture cards ever compiled.

PULVER CO., INC. (WG) ROCHESTER, N. Y.

"Oddities, Guns, Excitement, Cannons, Tortures, Spills, Wildlife, Adventure" — the Pulver Co. (Rochester, NY) promised all these neat things to buyers of their "Wham Gum." Inside each pack was a card from "The greatest assortment of picture cards ever compiled." Unfortunately, while the advertising department was running amuck, the development guys at Pulver forgot to give the series a formal name. That's why we simply call the set "Pulver Pictures."

Most of the cards deal with weapons — from harpoons to tanks — but some depict wild animals like gorillas and elephants. The cards are numbered sequentially from 100 to 129, and the artwork is unusual in its choice of colors and hues. The backs contain the card number, caption, and a lengthy text, all printed in blue ink on tan stock. The "Wham Gum" wrapper is red with blue accents and is rarely seen, perhaps because it could be collected and exchanged for three "best quality lead pencils" and a pencil pouch, all personalized with your name in gold letters. The reference number is R108. NOTE: some blank back cards have been found, and these carry an additional value of $10 per card.

100	David and Goliath	110	Short Barrel Gun on Camel	120	Toy or Salute Cannon
101	Ancient French Mortar	111	Boomerang	121	Harpooning Whales
102	Harquebus	112	Antique Cross Bows	122	Elephant Hunting
103	9mm German Luger Automatic	113	Army Tanks	123	Hand Grenade Guns
104	Anti-Aircraft Guns	114	Big Bertha	124	Tear Gas
105	Gargantua	115	Blunderbuss	125	Hand Grenade Guns
106	Machine Guns	116	Coast Artillery	126	Balloon Stockade
107	Gatling Guns	117	Torpedoes	127	Firemen's Life-Line Gun
108	Bombing Planes	118	Trebouchet	128	Elephant Hunt
109	Civil War Cannon	119	Double Barrelled Deringer	129	Broad Swords

ITEM	EX	AVE
Card	30.00	8.00
Set	1200.00	350.00
Wrapper	500.00	—

PUZZLES & TRICKS (39K)

2 3/4" X 4 3/4"

The various puzzles and tricks in this series, attributed to Cracker Jack, are printed on the "slide shells" (or trays) which fit inside a small package (the title and number flaps and the two side flaps folded up to hold the candy and toy). The simple drawings are done in red ink, and the title and "explanation" are printed in blue. The card number is printed on the detachable bottom flap, so it is often missing. There are no company marks or advertising and the backs are blank; the highest number seen so far is No. 39. The reference number is R119. NOTE: the excellent price applies only to complete, original cards.

ITEM	EX	AVE
Card	12.00	3.00

RADIO GUM (27K)

2 1/8" X 2 5/8"

United Confectioners Supply (Philadelphia) is listed as the manufacturer of these "Radio Gum" wrappers featuring pictures of male and female movie (not radio!) stars. The wrappers come in different colors — blue, green, orange, red and yellow — and each celebrity probably was issued in every color. The wrappers are chewing gum stick types and have movie film borders at top and bottom. The date of issue is reported to be 1938, and 27 movie stars have been found so far. The reference number is R196. NOTE: the prices listed are for "excellent grade only.

CARD	EX
Lew Ayres	15.00
Richard Barthelmess	12.00
Warner Baxter	12.00
Joan Blondell	15.00
John Boles	12.00
Joe E. Brown	15.00
Johnny Mack Brown	15.00
Maurice Chevalier	15.00
Gary Cooper	25.00
Richard Dixon	12.00
Douglas Fairbanks, Jr.	18.00
Kay Francis	12.00
Clark Gable	50.00
Janet Gaynor	12.00
Hoot Gibson	15.00
Mitzy Green	12.00
William Haines	12.00
Jack Holt	12.00
Harold Lloyd	15.00
Ramon Navarro	15.00
Jack Oakie	12.00
Anita Page	12.00
Will Rodgers	20.00
Norma Shearer	12.00
Laurence Tibbets	12.00
Tom Tyler	15.00
Loretta Young	15.00

RAINBOW RADIO RASCALS (6)

4 3/8" X 5 1/2"

"This is No. 5 of a series of six sketches, telling the fascinating story of chewing gum, prepared for BIG BROTHER'S RADIO RASCALS by the Rainbow Gum Co., subsidiary of the Goudey Gum Co., Boston, Mass." Basically, this is just about all you need to know about the set. The size of the cards would suggest that they were store handouts or mail premiums. The large obverse pictures are monochrome (the one illustrated is blue) and show various "Radio Rascal" players. The backs, as promised, tell how chewing gum is made, and No. 5 bears the inevitable line "never touched by human hands." The set was never listed in the early catalogs, and a reference number of R198 has been assigned to it.

ITEM	EX	AVE
Card	20.00	5.00
Set	150.00	35.00

RAY–O–PRINT OUTFITS (4K)

1 5/8" X 2"

NEGATIVE

PACKAGE

BABE RUTH

POSITIVE PRINT FROM
BABE RUTH NEGATIVE

DEVELOPING
& DISPLAY EASEL

This series of sun-exposed photo negatives would probably not qualify as a gum and candy issue except for the fact that it was produced by M.P. & Co., which has other sets listed in this book. Each "outfit" contained a negative, a piece of photo paper, and a neat metal easel to serve as both a developing and display stand. Directions were printed on the envelope: "Place glossy side of PHOTO PAPER to dull side of FILM. Slide both into holder, film side up. Place in sunlight for 2 or 3 minutes or until edges of paper turn dark." The result was a finished B&W picture like the one illustrated of Babe Ruth. The reference number is R199. NOTE: the prices listed below for the known subjects are for complete outfits consisting of envelope, negative and easel (photo paper not important).

ITEM	EX	AVE
Outfits		
Babe Ruth	200.00	75.00
Lou Gehrig	150.00	60.00
Jack		
Dempsey	100.00	35.00
Zepplin		
Hangar	10.00	3.00

REMEMBER PEARL HARBOR (?)   1 13/16" X 2 15/16"

In the 1983 Non-Sport Guide, we listed this series of candy box cards together with the

"Heroes of Pearl Harbor" set based on an "original" box which was later found to be a fabrication. We have now returned it to a separate listing. As you can see by the illustrations, the cards are part of a candy box, and once they are removed from the box, the set title is no longer apparent. The

pictures are simple multi-color drawings of military hardware and machines and all are numbered (highest seen is No. 13). The backs are blank. The cards are most often found cut from the box, so they are often ignored by collectors who don't know what they are looking at. The reference number is R120.

1	30-cal Water-cooled Machine Gun
2	
3	37mm Anti-Tank Gun
4	75mm Field Gun
5	Army Jeep
6	Medium Tank — 28 Tons
7	Motorcycle Dispatch Rider
8	Light Tank — 13 Tons

ITEM	EX	AVE
Cards		
Cut from		
panel	5.00	2.00
On panel	15.00	6.00
Intact box	100.00	35.00

SCHARLEY QUESTIONS (48)   2 3/8" X 3 1/2"

"Scharley Questions" — produced by the American Maid Confectionary Co. of Chicago, is one of the most peculiar sets of the 1930's. The series is based on the conversational interplay of two comic strip characters of the period, Charley and the Baron. The Baron has a heavy accent: thus "Charley" becomes, of course, "Scharley." He also always has the last word (or

punchline) in every one of these jokes, and when challenged on his exaggerations, inevitably replies "Vas you dere?" The cards themselves were designed in garish color combinations of black or blue on red (each card might have been printed in both combinations). The fronts carry large card numbers and an offer to exchange complete sets for "many Valuable Prem-

iums," some of which are pictured on the back. This offer, no doubt, seriously restricted the number of Scharley cards which have survived to modern times, for they are rarely seen. Luckily, the Scharley series is not much in demand. The wrapper pictured comes from the collection of John "Wrapper King" Neuner. The reference number is R121.

ITEM	EX	AVE
Card	15.00	5.00
Set	900.00	300.00
Wrapper	450.00	——

SCRAPBOOK SERIES (?)   1 1/4" X 2 1/4"

"For Your Scrapbook...One Of A Series — Save Them All." These lines, which appear on every card in the top and bottom margins, tell

the whole story about the "Scrapbook Series." The card illustrated has orange borders on three sides, and the center contains the card number and a question about the state (black print on white). The backs are blank and it is obvious that the cards were cut from some type of candy box. The manufacturer is

unknown. This series is mainly of interest to type collectors, and the card prices below are based on limited current supply. The reference number is R143.

ITEM	EX	AVE
Card	10.00	4.00

SCREEN SNAPPIES (32)　　2 3/8" X 2 7/8"

The "Screen Snappies" series was a joint production of the Loew's Theatre chain and Ridley's, a Brooklyn, NY, based novelty company. It is very likely that these cards were handed out at movie theatre snack bars because

we have no record of Ridley producing candy or gum. The cards are green and brown tone photos of contemporary film stars (each star probably comes in both colors), with card number, name, and studio credit line

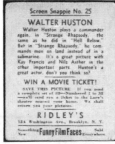

below. Each picture bears a promotional line written in script; the Walter Houston card illustrated says "See you folks at Loews." The backs are printed in black ink on off-white stock. There is a short biographical sketch of the star plus an offer to give away a free movie ticket to anyone sending in a complete set of cards (they were returned). No packaging has been seen. The reference number is R122.

ITEM	EX	AVE
Card	12.00	3.00
Set	475.00	115.00

SCREEN STARS (20)　　3 1/2" X 5 1/2"

"Ask your dealer for a photograph given Free with each package of BLATZ GUM, The Taste is Irresistible." Well, if the taste was so irresistible, why didn't anyone find out about this set until just a few years ago? One clue is the format: the ele-

gant "studio" photographs, in black & white, were printed on paper and were very fragile. The star's name is written on front in script, and a tiny photographer's credit appears in one corner. The backs contain advertising for Blatz Grape and

Mint Gum and an offer to send a complete set of 20 pictures in exchange for ten wrappers and ten cents. The numbers listed beside the names on the back do not appear on the pictures themselves. An album to house the set was also available for "ten and ten." The reference number is R197.

ITEM	EX	AVE
Card	7.00	2.00
Set	175.00	45.00

Renee Adoree
Evelyn Brent
Betty Bronson
Lew Cody
Billie Dove
William Haines
Phyllis Haver
Jean Hersholt
Gwen Lee
Edmund Lowe
Ben Lyon
Dorothy Mackaill
May McAvoy
Jack Mulhall
Charlie Murray
Conrad Nagel
Molloy O'Day
Our Gang
Vera Reynolds
Anita Stewart

SEAL CRAFT DISCS (240)　　2 3/16" DIAMETER

The Seal Craft series of 240 discs was never issued with gum or candy. It probably "rode the shirt-tails" of Leader Discs (see that listing) into the candy and gum sections of the early catalogs. Chris McCann remembers Seal Craft very well: "When I was

little, we bought Seal Craft in a local department store, in the toys and games section. Each envelope had three large cards in it (six discs per card) and a handful of rubber bands of different colors — to string the discs together. They are not bot-

tlecaps, or anything other than small, numbered, cardboard discs."

Each six-disc sheet contained five "singles" and one "trader." There were 16 different envelopes issued, amounting to a total of 240 different

Seal Craft Discs

National Issue

Local Issue

subjects and 48 duplicates. The discs were die-cut for easy removal from the sheets, and each had a series of pre-cut holes and slots for assembling into items such as bracelets, belts, etc. The patent for this "Design Forming Device" — patent number 2,076,956 — was awarded to Herman Lowenstein in 1936. As McCann further notes, "this idea was later used by Topps with Beatles Plaks and Pack-O-Fun cards."

"Seal Craft...The New Hobby" became very popular. The series was picked up as a promotion by local newspapers across the country who "personalized" the discs with their respective logos and envelopes. These newspaper Seal Craft discs bear the same subjects (see illustration of "Kangaroo") but have a different numbering system. Although the prices for them are the same as for the original issue, they carry a different reference number — M30.

The Seal Craft checklist printed here was provided by Chris McCann. Please note the various "keys" (abbreviations) for the different subsets in his variation listings. The reference number is R123.

ITEM	EX	AVE
Disc	3.00	1.00
Set	850.00	275.00
Sheet	25.00	10.00
Envelope	10.00	4.00
Flyer	15.00	6.00

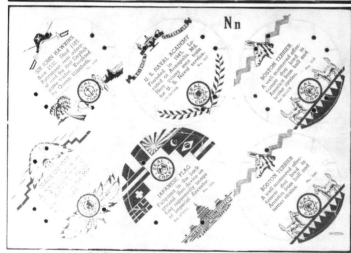

FRONT & BACK OF SEALCRAFT
SHEET — NOTE DUPLICATE CARD

140

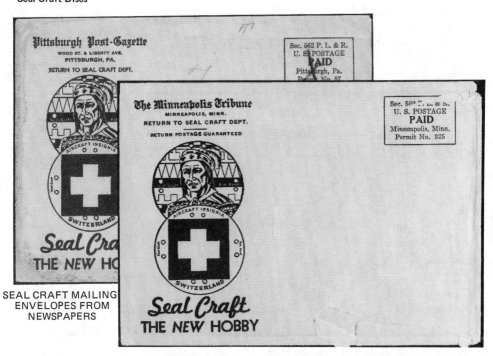

SEAL CRAFT MAILING
ENVELOPES FROM
NEWSPAPERS

The Fascinating New

Pastime and Game

for Girls and Boys

Introduced by

The Minneapolis Tribune

THE HOME NEWSPAPER—IN THE MOST HOMES

Here's How to Start
Your Tribune
Seal-Craft Collection

There will be three (3) separate sets of Seal Craft Cards available each week for 16 weeks. Each day during the period of this offer The Minneapolis Tribune will publish a Seal Craft Coupon bearing a different number.

CLIP these Seal Craft coupons from The Minneapolis Tribune. When you have three (3) consecutive coupons in numerical order from The Minneapolis Tribune (Daily Only), send them or bring them to The Tribune with 3 cents in stamps or coin, and you will receive a card containing six Seal Craft Seals. To get your Seal Craft Card offered each Sunday, you need one (1) coupon from The Minneapolis Sunday Tribune, together with 3 cents in stamps or coin. This small sum covers only postage and handling charges.

To insure getting all the necessary coupons for your complete Seal Craft Collection, we suggest you order The Minneapolis Tribune delivered to your home every day.

The Minneapolis Tribune

THE HOME NEWSPAPER—IN THE MOST HOMES

PAMPHLET FROM A NEWSPAPER EDITION OF SEAL CRAFT DISCS

SEAL-CRAFT *The New Hobby*

85	PR	William Kidd
86	PR	Edward Teach
87	CL	Pennsylvania
88	AR	20th Squadron
89	AR	28th Squadron
90	AN	Spotted Hyena
91	PR	Pierre Le Grand
92	CL	Yale
93	AN	Walrus
94	AN	Puma
95	PR	Francis Lolonois
96	AR	72nd Squadron
97	AR	30th Squadron
98	AN	Virginia Deer
99	PR	Edward Low
100	CL	Harvard
101	AN	Marmose
102	IN	Winnebago Tribe
103	AR	9th Squadron (See No. 145)
104	PR	Sir Henry Morgan
105	CL	Maryland
106	AR	96th Squadron
107	CL	Georgia
108	PR	Barth Roberts
109	IN	No-Heart
110	AN	Mink
111	AN	Antelope Jack-Rabbit
112	AR	49th Squadron
113	PR	Barbarossa
114	IN	Wolf Robe
115	CL	Dartmouth
116	AR	25th Squadron
117	PR	Jean La Fitte
118	AN	African Buffalo
119	CL	West Point
120	PR	Edward England
121	IN	Powhatan
122	AN	Wolf
123	PR	Robertson Keitt
124	AR	31st Squadron
125	CL	Indiana
126	IN	Metea
127	AR	11th Squadron
128	AN	Wart Hog
129	IN	Shingabawassin
130	PR	Stede Bonnett
131	AN	Otter
132	IN	Waneta
133	AR	23rd Squadron
134	PR	William Lewis
135	CL	California
136	AR	42nd Squadron
137	AR	Switzerland
138	IN	The Prophet
139	PR	Vincent Benavides
140	AN	Hippopotamus
141	FL	Panama
142	PR	Francis Drake
143	DG	English Setter
144	CL	Kentucky
145	AR	9th Group (See No. 103)
146	FL	Cuba
147	PR	George Lowther
148	DG	Pekingese
149	IN	Chief Wets-It
150	AR	1st Squadron
151	FL	Netherlands
152	AR	Egypt
153	DG	Dachshund
154	PR	Rahman Ben Jabir
155	AL	Alabama
156	FL	China
157	PR	Rocco Braziliano
158	DG	Bull Dog
159	AR	Estonia
160	IN	Shot-On-Both-Sides
161	IN	Spring Frog
162	AR	Finland
163	FL	France
164	PR	William Dampier
165	DG	Airdale
166	DG	Boston Terrier
167	CL	U.S. Naval Academy
168	PR	Sir John Hawkins
169	FL	Japan
170	IN	Black Coyote
171	AR	Latvia
172	CL	Columbia
173	FL	Great Britain
174	PR	Capt. John Avery
175	DG	St. Bernard
176	DG	Old Englisg Sheep Dog

177	IN	Black Hoof
178	FL	Turkey
179	CL	Washington State
180	IN	Sioux Tribe
181	IN	Chief Killer
182	IN	Micanopy
183	DG	Chesapeake Retriever
184	FL	Chile
185	CL	Virginia
186	FL	Siam
187	CL	Notre Dame
188	IN	Shawano Tribe
189	DG	Chow
190	IN	Bear Ghost
191	IN	Shabbona
192	AR	Siam
193	PR	Captain Condent
194	FL	Persia
195	DG	Bloodhound
196	DG	Belgian Shepard
197	AR	Poland
198	IN	Great Walker
199	PR	Thomas Cavendish
200	FL	Greece
201	IN	Powashek
202	FL	Italy
203	DG	Collie
204	FL	Sweden
205	CL	Oregon
206	FL	United States
207	DG	Wirehaired Fox Terrier
208	DG	Scottish Terrier
209	AR	Bolivia
210	IN	Keokuk
211	IN	Billy Bowlegs
212	FL	Uruguay
213	DG	Pointer
214	FL	Belgium
215	CL	Texas
216	FL	Syria
217	DG	Whippet
218	DG	Greyhound
219	AR	Hungary
220	IN	Sleepy Eyes
221	DG	Great Dane
222	DG	Cocker Spaniel
223	FL	Switzerland
224	IN	Red Tomahawk
225	CL	Tennessee
226	DG	Russian Wolfhound
227	AR	Greece
228	FL	Argentina
229	FL	Iceland
230	IN	Red Jacket
231	DG	Police Dog
232	DG	Eskimo Dog
233	FL	Egypt
234	IN	Wakawn
235	AR	Uruguay
236	DG	Irish Wolfhound
237	FL	Denmark
238	FL	Brazil
239	AR	Guatemala
240	IN	Cornplanter

Legend for Seal Craft Discs
Number of discs of each in ( )

AN (36)............Animals
AR (48).........Air Insignia
CL (36).......College Seals
DG (24)................Dogs
FL (24)................Flags
IN (48).............Indians
PR (24)............Pirates

1	AN	Ocelot
2	AR	Romania
3	IN	Chief Joseph
4	CL	Chicago
5	AN	Moose
5	AR	Sweeden (Error — Half of No. 51 cards are marked No. 5)
6	CL	Michigan
7	IN	Yoholo Micco
8	AR	Soviet Russia
9	AR	Brazil
10	AN	Raccoon
11	CL	Oklahoma
12	IN	Geronimo
13	AN	Rhinoceros
14	AR	Netherlands
15	CL	Nebraska
16	AR	Great Britain
17	IN	Hollow Horn Bear
18	AN	Elephant
19	AN	Skunk
20	IN	Chippeway Tribe
21	IN	King Philip
22	AR	Yugoslavia
23	CL	Missouri
24	AR	Japan
25	AN	Buffalo
26	IN	Santa Claras
27	CL	Washington (University)
28	AN	Tapir (There is no number on this card)
29	AN	Polar Bear
30	AR	Mexico
31	AN	Lion
32	IN	Tecumseh
33	AR	United States
34	IN	Joseph Brant
35	AN	Gorilla
36	AN	Jaguar
37	AR	Denmark
38	CL	Kansas State College
39	CL	Minnesota
40	IN	Sitting Bull
41	CL	Kansas

42	IN	Chinook Tribe
43	AR	Chile
44	AN	Zebra
45	AR	Norway
46	AN	Armadillo
47	CL	Wiscinsin
48	IN	Comanche Tribe
49	IN	Mohawk Tribe
50	AR	Argentina
51	AR	Sweeden (Half of No. 51 cards are marked No. 5)
52	IN	Wapello
53	AR	Belgium
54	CL	Purdue
55	AN	Giraffe
56	AN	Ant Eater
57	AR	Czechoslovakia
58	AN	Black Panther
59	CL	Ohio State
60	IN	Senace Tribe
61	AR	Turkey
62	AN	Wild Boar
63	CL	Iowa
64	IN	Osceola
65	AR	China
66	IN	Seminole Tribe
67	CL	Illinois
68	AN	Musk-Ox
69	AN	Porcupine
70	AR	France
71	IN	Black Hawk
72	AN	Kangaroo
73	AR	Portugal
74	AN	Red Fox
75	IN	Creek Tribe
76	AN	Coyote
77	AR	Persia (Iran)
78	CL	Iowa State College
79	CL	Northwestern
80	IN	Iowa Tribe
81	PR	Portugues
82	AR	99th Squadron
83	CL	Princeton
84	AN	Flying Squirrel

SEA RAIDERS (48)

A favorite among collectors, "Sea Raiders" was issued in 1933 by Goudey Gum via its affiliate company World Wide Gum. The statement "This is one of a series of 192 Sea Raiders Cards" appears on back, but the series was ter-mininated at 48 cards. The fronts have brilliant, color- artwork pirate scenes with the words "Sea Raider Chewing Gum" printed in a blue panel underneath. The backs have been found in three styles. Cards 1-24 have English text and a Boston address; cards 1-24 and 25-48 appear with English text and a Montreal address. In addition, there is a so-called "Canadian" back, with both English and French text, although one collector remembers that this variation back was also found in U.S. gum packs. Most collectors ignore these back variations because it is the fronts which are truly spectacular. The yellow wrapper has a blood-thirsty buccaneer at center surrounded by other pirate scenes. The reference number is R124.

ITEM	EX	AVE
Cards		
1-24	15.00	4.00
25-48	30.00	7.00
Set	1325.00	350.00
Wrapper	250.00	––
Box	500.00	165.00

1	Capt. Teach (Blackbeard)	25	John Halsey
2	Captain Kidd	26	John Martel
3	Pirate Galleon	27	Raveneau De Lussan
4	Avery Discussing Plot	28	John Gow
5	Fight for Supremacy	29	Richard Worley
6	The Lookout	30	Diego Grillo
7	Pirate Gold	31	Pierre Le Grand
8	Charles Gibbs	32	Thomas Tew
9	Capt. Jean Lafitte	33	John Evans
10	Hostages	34	John Bowen
11	Bartholemy Portuguez	35	Edward Low
12	Pierre Francois	36	Nathaniel North
13	Walking the Plank	37	Joseph Bradish
14	Boarding Party	38	Lord George Clifford
15	Scuttling the Ship	39	Thomas Howard
16	False Signals	40	Anne Bonny
17	Bringing Back the Loot	41	Mary Reed
18	Mutiny of the Crew	42	Alwilda
19	Captain Misson	43	Roc the Brazilian
20	Capt. Francis Lolonois	44	Major Bonnet
21	Sir Francis Drake	45	Pirate's Legacy
22	Extorting Tribute	46	"Dead Men Tell No Tales"
23	John Quelch	47	The Sport of Pirates
24	Sir Henry Morgan	48	A Difference in Weapons

SECRET SERVICE FLASHES (24)   3 3/4" X 4 3/4"

National Chicle cashed in on the "G—Man" craze of the 1930's with this series of paper "Secret Service Flashes" issued in 1935. The cartoon-style fronts follow the adventures of "Ace Hunter and

Tom Dean on the trail of the Secret Ink Gang." The number of each "Flash" is printed in a badge design in the upper front corner. The backs appear blank, but according to instructions, "mes-

sages on back will show when you wet sheet." The Flashes came folded in the orange and blue wrapper so there are actually crease lines in each. The wrapper could be collected and redeemed for bottles of "Secret Ink." The reference number for this set is R125.

1 Hello Mr. Dean! Hi Tommy!
2 Grab that kid - He's seen too much
3 Hello Editor - Milly Blake speaking
4 Hello! Washington?
5 The arrow - Now to rescue Tommy...
6 There's Tommy Dean all trussed up
7 There's Ace Hunter's plane,
8 Too late men they've got away
9 What does that mark mean Purser?
10 Put on that parachute...
11 I've gotta have this message ready...
12 Hello? Headquarters? This is Ace Hunter..
13 So - Milly Blake, Tribune reporter
14 Well, if they ain't got the chief on the spot...
15 I hope we are not too late, Milly
16 We've got 'em Ace
17 I'm leaving you here Smith...
18 Smith pinched!
19 Rats! I missed Hunter again...
20 Smith has vanished...
21 Come on, spill it, where's the jack?
22 There's 300 grand from the ship Marie in that car
23 Radio your chief to block every road to the south
24 Now Miss Smarty, I'll teach you to butt in...

ITEM	EX	AVE
Flash	20.00	5.00
Set	600.00	150.00
Wrapper	250.00	— —

SERIES OF 24 — NAVY (24)   2 1/4" X 2 3/4"

A parade of U.S. Navy history, from John Paul Jones to Richard E. Byrd, is covered in this series of 24 anonymous strip cards. The fronts bear simple color drawings of the people and events, with the caption appearing in

a yellow panel below the picture. The cards are numbered on the back above the text (black ink on gray stock). The set title is taken from the "series of 24" line printed on the back of every card. The reference

number is R127. NOTE: cards intact in strips are valued at a 25% premium.

ITEM	EX	AVE
Card	4.00	1.00
Set	115.00	27.50

U.S. NAVY AIRPLANE CARRIER SARATOGA

No. 505

This is one of a series of 24 cards

SARATOGA

The airplane carrier "Saratoga," with her sister-ship, the "Lexington," is the largest and fastest warship afloat. She can carry 94 planes and has a great cruising range. She was originally intended for a battlecruiser, but was changed after the Arms Conference at Washington.

501 U.S. Navy Dirigible Akron
502 The Oregon Steaming to Santiago
503 John Paul Jones Captures the Serapis
504 John Paul Jones
505 U.S. Navy Airplane Carrier Saratoga
506 Admiral George Dewey
507 The Kearsarge Sinking the Alabama
508 Rear Admiral William A. Moffett
509 Commander Herbert V. Wiley
510 John Ericsson
511 Dewey's Flagship, "Olympia," at Manila Bay
512 Perry at Battle of Lake Erie
513 Oliver Hazard Perry
514 Commander Richard E. Byrd
515 Old Ironsides
516 Byrd at the North Pole
517 Lindy Crossing the Atlantic
518 Colonel Charles A. Lindbergh
519 New Persuit (sic) Planes of U.S. Navy
520 Admiral David G. Farragut
521 A Modern American Battleship
522 Farragut, at Battle of Mobile Bay
523 Stephen Decatur
524 Battle Between Monitor and Merrimac

SERIES OF 48 — WESTERN (48)   2 3/8" X 2 13/16"

No. 245

This is one of a series of 48 cards

DUTCHY

Dutchy was an Apache Scout and was very friendly to the soldiers. His bosom companion was Capt. Crawford of the U.S. Army. Always ready to protect his captain, he shot down the Mexican who had killed Captain Crawford by mistake.

DUTCHY

An anonymous strip card set of 48 cards with western subjects, the cards are found two ways: 1-48 and 201-248 (see our side-by-side illustration of Nos. 13/213). The fronts are drawn in pleasant colors, and the subjects and events are named in a blue panel below the picture. The backs, which carry the card number and text, are printed in Carolina blue ink on cream

stock. The front and back card titles might vary slightly in wording. The second group of 24 cards (25-48/225/248) appear to have been "pirated" from Goudey's "Indian Gum" series. The "series of 48" line on the card backs gives this set its title. The reference number is R128. NOTE: there is a 25% premium for cards intact in strips.

ITEM	EX	AVE
Card	4.00	1.00
Set	220.00	55.00

201 Buffalo Bill			
202 "Bull Dogging"		226 Pontiac	238 Indians Attacking Stockade
203 Bill Hickok Lassoing	214 Early 49'er	227 Sioux Tribe	239 Soldiers Shooting Indians
204 Bronco Busting	215 Mad Anthony Wayne	228 Ogallala Tribe	240 Bill Cody Fighting Indians
205 Cowboy Whoopee	216 Daniel Boone	229 The Prophet	241 Red Tomahawk
206 Stampede	217 Buffalo Bill	230 Pot-O-Wat-O-Mies Tribe	242 Buffalo Bill
207 Prairie Fire	218 Joe Logston	231 American Horse	243 Massasoit
208 Stage Coach	219 William Penn	232 Pawnee Tribe	244 Spotted Tail
209 Custer's Last Stand	220 Davy Crockett	233 Chief Powhattan	245 Dutchy
210 Davy Crockett	221 Gen. George Crook	234 Indian Fighting Kit Carson	246 King Phillip
211 Deadwood Dick	222 Jim Bridger	235 Indians Attacking Train	247 Red Jacket
212 Jesse James	223 La Salle	236 Indian Captive Dance	248 Sitting Bull
213 Andy Burnett Shooting Grizzly	224 Kit Carson	237 Apaches Attacking Pioneers	
	225 Tecumseh		

SERIES OF 48 — AMERICAN HISTORY (48)   2 3/8" X 2 13/16"

An anonymous strip card set of 48 cards dealing with famous people and events in American history, from the discovery of the Mississippi River to Woodrow Wilson's first term as president. The cards are numbered 300-347, and the first 19 subjects are Indians copied, in crude fashion, from Goudey's "Indian Gum" cards. Cards 324-331 portray American presidents, and numbers 340-347 depict Civil War generals. Each picture is captioned in a panel below. The text backs are printed in Carolina blue ink on cream stock. Front and back card titles might vary in wording. The reference number is R129. NOTE: cards intact in strips are valued at a 25% premium.

ITEM	EX	AVE
Card	4.00	1.00
Set	220.00	55.00

300 Red Bear	313 Doe Wah Jack	326 Lincoln 1861
301 Ge-onimo	314 Indian Beast of Burden	327 Grant 1869
302 Satanta	315 Ogalalla	328 Cleveland 1885
303 Weasel Calf	316 General Sturgis	329 McKinley 1897
304 Pushmataha	317 Yellowstone Kelly	330 Roosevelt 1901
305 Old Bear	318 Custer Scout	331 Wilson 1913
306 Samoset	319 John Paul Jones	332 Pilgrims Landing
307 Wolf	320 Andrew Jackson	333 Paul Revere's Ride
308 Four Bears	321 John C. Fremont	334 The Monitor & Merrimac
309 The Bear	322 Commodore Bainbridge	335 Striking Gold California
310 Black Hawk	323 Commodore Decatur	336 Washington Crossing Delaware
311 Tobacco	324 Washington 1789	337 Rallying the Line
312 Tis Co Han	325 Jefferson 1801	338 Discovery of the Mississippi

339 Declaration of Independence
340 Gen. John A. Dix
341 Gen. Beauregard
342 Gen. McClellan
343 Gen. Benj. F. Butler
344 Gen. Burnside
345 Gen. Sherman
346 Stonewall Jackson
347 Gen. Robert E. Lee

SERIES OF 48 — WESTERN (48)   2 3/8" X 2 13/16"

This set is an anonymous strip card series of 48 cards featuring cowboys and Indians of the Old West. The pic-

tures, particularly those of the Indians, are better drawn than those already covered in preceding sets. The card cap-

tions are found in yellow panels beneath the pictures. The color of the ink on the text backs is black; the cardboard stock is gray. The cards are numbered on the back, and card titles might vary slightly front to back. The reference number for the set is R130. NOTE: cards intact in strips command a 25% increase in value.

ITEM	EX	AVE
Card	4.00	1.00
Set	220.00	55.00

301 Chief Gall, Sioux	313 Geronimo	325 Andy Burnett	337 General George Crook
302 Indian Hunting Buffalo	314 Crazy Horse	326 The Pioneers	338 The Old Desert Rat
303 Kit Carson	315 Chief Joseph	327 Indians Watching Immigrants	339 The Apache Kid
304 The Sheriff	316 Cowboys on Rampage	328 General George Custer	340 King Phillip
305 Defending the Wagon Train	317 Come an' Get It	329 Cowboys Swapping Stories	341 Tecumseh
306 The Overland Stage	318 Buffalo Bill	330 Blackfoot Medicine Man	342 Black Bart
307 Cowboys on the Open Range	319 Horse Rustling	331 Captain Charles King	343 The Sale of Manhattan Island
308 Sitting Bull	320 Wild Bill Hickok	332 Davy Crockett/Davey Crockett	344 Mohigan Warrior/Mohegan
309 Daniel Boone	321 Around the Chuck Wagon	333 Sioux Warrior	Warrior
310 Pontiac	322 Wagon Train	334 Red Jacket	345 Cheyene Braves
311 The Pony Express	323 Jesse James	335 Pocahontas Saving John Smith	346 The Prophet
312 Bronco Buster	324 Apaches on the Warpath	336 The Cattle Drive	347 Moqui Snake Dancer
			348 Cowboy Roping a Steer

SERIES OF 48 — WESTERN (48)   2 5/16" X 2 3/4"

This is an anonymous strip card set of 48 cards depicting western subjects. A comparison of the drawings of this series with those in

other "series of 48" strip card sets would probably uncover many shared designs. However, the cards in this group are borderless, and the

backs have the printing centered (black ink on gray stock). The numbering sequence is 801-848, and each card is numbered front and back. The card titles on the obverse and reverse might vary slightly from one another in wording. The reference number is R131. NOTE: a 25% premium is warranted for cards intact in strips.

ITEM	EX	AVE
Card	4.00	1.00
Set	220.00	55.00

801 Sitting Bull	813 Pawnee Tribe	825 Black Hawk	837 Custer Scout
802 Red Jacket	814 American Horse	826 Ogalalla	838 Kit Carson
803 Buffalo Bull	815 Pontiac	827 Tis Co Han	839 General Sturgis
804 Sioux Tribe	816 Tecumseh	828 The Bear	840 Captain Fremont
805 King Phillip	817 Geronimo	829 Indian Beast of Burden	841 Chief Powhattan
806 Ogallala Tribe	818 Red Bear	830 Four Bears	842 Indian Fighting Kit Carson
807 Dutchy	819 Satanta	831 Tobacco	843 Indians Attacking Train
808 Red Tomahawk	820 Weasel Calf	832 Doe Wah Jack	844 Indians Attacking Stockade
809 Massasoit	821 Pushmataha	833 Buffalo Bill	845 Custer's Last Stand
810 Spotted Tail	822 Old Bear	834 Joe Logston	846 Davy Crockett
811 The Prophet	823 Samoset	835 Jim Bridger	847 Deadwood Dick
812 Pot-O-Wat-Omies Tribe	824 Wolf	836 Yellowstone Kelly	848 Jesse James

SERIES OF 48 — AVIATION (48)   2 3/8" X 2 7/8"

Airplanes and only airplanes are featured in this anonymous strip card series. The cards are numbered 301-348 and carry ludicrously simple color artwork drawings of different aircraft. The planes are named in a red panel

beneath each picture. The backs are brief: the card number, "series of 48" line, name of aircraft, and a single descriptive sentence. The card titles, as they appear front and back, might vary slightly in wording. The reference

number is R132. NOTE: cards in strips are worth 25% more.

ITEM	EX	AVE
Card	4.00	1.00
Set	220.00	55.00

No. 302

This is one of a series of 48 cards

DOUGLAS
D. C. 2

Famous transport plane that daily flies the Trans-Continental Airways.

301 The D. H. Comet	313 The Avro 642	325 The Heinkel He. 71	337 The Fairey Fox
302 The Douglas D.C. 2	314 Boulton Paul O'Strand	326 The Junkers JU 52	338 The Airspeed Courier
303 The Avro Tutor	315 The Winnie Mae	327 The Boeing Bird	339 The Sikorsky S 42
304 The Miles Hawk Major	316 Short Singapore III	328 The Savoia-Marchetti S.55	340 The D. H. Dragon Six
305 The Blackburn Perth	317 D.S. Express Air Liner	329 The Dornier Wal	341 The Handley Page 42
306 The C-30 Autogiro	318 Westland Hill Pterodactyl	330 The Spirit of St. Louis	342 The China Clipper
307 The Hawker Osprey	319 The Monoplane St.11	331 The Vickers Vildebest	343 The Hawkers Nimrod
308 The Macchi-Castuldi	320 Percival Mew Gull	332 The Martin Bomber	344 The Supermarine Scapa
309 The Short R.2431	321 Armstrong Whitworth	333 The Bristol Bulldog	345 The Westland Wallace
310 The Avro Commodor	322 Handley Page Heyford	334 The Fokker F. XXXVI	346 The Spartan Cruiser
311 The Saro Cloud	323 Hawker Super-Fury	335 The Breguet 27	347 The Philipine Clipper
312 British Klemm Eagle	324 The Percival Gull	336 The Curtiss Hawk	348 The Wibault 28T

SERIES OF 48 — WESTERN (48) 2 1/16" X 2 3/8"

No. 90

This is one of a series of 48 cards

INDIAN FIGHTERS

Riding bare-back and with primitive bows and arrows the Indian fighters were dangerous enemies. Pictured are Indian warriors shooting their arrows with bull's-eye accuracy — even while at full gallop.

© W.S.

The W.S. Corporation issued this strip card series of 48 western subjects. The cards are slightly smaller in size than any of the sets previously covered, and the initials "W.S." are printed on the back. Each color artwork picture is surrounded by white borders, and the subjects are named in a panel below.

The back print is blue and the cardboard stock is gray. The reference number for the set is R185. NOTE: this set is often found in strips, which increase the value by 25%.

ITEM	EX	AVE
Card	2.00	.50
Set	105.00	27.50

49 Weasel Calf	61 Cowboy Whoopee	73 Satanta
50 Handfighting!	62 Ogalalla	74 Custer's Last Fight
51 Geronimo	63 Stage Coach	75 Red Bear
52 Chief Shon-Kaki-Hega	64 Chief Shome-Cosse	76 Mendawa—Kanton
53 Cattle Stampede	65 Tis Co Han	77 Bill Hickok Lassoing
54 Samoset	66 On the Alert!	78 Yellowstone Kelly
55 Parairie Fire	67 Pushmataha	79 Indian Canoes
56 Chief Ski-Scroka	68 Chief Te-Ton	80 Ojibway Chief
57 Black Hawk	69 "Bulldogging"	81 Four Bears
58 Saved by Stockade	70 Custer Scout	82 Indian Un-Horsed
59 Wolf	71 Mohawk Wampum	83 Old Bear
60 Chief Nonon—Dagon	72 Ambush!	84 Kanien—Gehaga

85 Bronco Busting	
86 John C. Fremont	
87 Indian Beast	
88 Chief Pa-Hatsi	
89 Tobacco	
90 Indian Fighters	
91 The Bear	
92 Chief Seattle	
93 Buffalo Bill	
94 General Sturgis	
95 Indian Fighting	
96 Doh Wah Jack	

SERIES OF 96 — MOVIE STARS (96) 2 1/4" X 2 11/16"

This set is an anonymous series of movie star strip cards with a "series of 96" line printed on back. The cards are numbered from 101-196 and are arranged in specific subgroups: Nos. 101-108 are child stars; Nos. 109-124 are female stars; Nos. 125-148 are cowboy stars; and Nos. 149-196 are male stars. The picture of each film star comes in as many as five different shades of color: blue, green, orange, red, and yellow. Cards were issued in strips of eight, with all cards on some strips printed in a common color. Collectors are advised to check for print variations and errors. The reference number is R133. NOTE: raise the value of cards in strips by 25%. The single card price below is for a "common" celebrity; values might increase up to 200% for "demand" cards of more famous stars.

No. 143

This is one of a series of 96 cards

REX BELL

Universal star. Western born, he naturally fits into the roles he portrays. Extremely good looking, he captured Clara Bow for his wife. They have one son. Spends a good deal of his time with his family on their Arizona ranch.

REX BELL

ITEM	EX	AVE
Card	4.00	1.00
Set	480.00	120.00

101 Scotty Beckett	125 Newton House	149 Charles Butterworth	173 Gary Cooper
102 Dickie Moore	126 Edmund Cobb	150 Robert Young	174 Otto Kruger
103 Baby Jane	127 Ken Maynard	151 George Brent	175 Maurice Chevalier
104 Mathew Beard	128 Lone Chandler (sic)	152 Frank Morgan	176 Joe E. Brown
105 Shirley Temple	129 Buck Jones	153 Jack Oakie	177 El Brendel
106 Jackie Cooper	130 Rex Bell	154 Stan Laurel	178 Chester Morris
107 Cora Sue Collins	131 Ted Wells	155 W.C. Fields	179 George Raft
108 Mickey Rooney	132 Yakima Canutt	156 Leo Carillo	180 Charles Chase
109 Una Merkel	133 John Wayne	157 Ted Healy	181 Andy Clyde
110 Jean Parker	134 George O'Brien	158 Cary Grant	182 William Powell
111 Mae Clark	135 Tom Mix	159 John Boles	183 Douglas Montgomery
112 Lupe Velez	136 Hoot Gibson	160 Slim Summerville	184 Nat Pendleton
113 Joan Crawford	137 Wm. Haines	161 Bing Crosby	185 Lee Tracy
114 Mary Christians	138 Bob Steele	162 Oliver Hardy	186 Warner Baxter
115 Madge Evans	139 Tom Keene	163 Nelson Eddy	187 Will Rogers
116 Jeanette McDonald	140 Wallace McDonald	164 Noah Beery, Jr.	188 Lionel Barrymore
117 Mary Carlisle	141 Art Acord	165 Wallace Beery	189 Clark Gable
118 Myrna Loy	142 Tom Keene	166 James Dunn	190 Edmund Lowe
119 Zasu Pitts	143 Rex Bell	167 Johnny Weissmuller	191 Charles Ruggles
120 Greta Garbo	144 Tom Tyler	168 Robert Taylor	192 Stuart Erwin
121 Claudette Colbert	145 Tom Mix	169 Jean Hersholt	193 Jimmy Durante
122 Norma Shearer	146 Lone Chandler (sic)	170 Franchot Tone	194 Boris Karloff
123 Jean Harlow	147 Buck Jones	171 Charles Laughton	195 Henry Armetta
124 Margaret Sullivan	148 Yakima Canutt	172 Robert Montgomery	196 Herbert Marshall

SERIES OF 96 — MOVIE STARS (96)   2 3/8" X 2 3/4"

Movie stars and movie scenes are the subjects of this anonymous "Series of 96." The cards are numbered 501-596 and have rouletted edges, a fact which confirms that they were issued in strips. The pictures are actually photos which have been tinted in various colors: blue, light and dark brown, green, and red. The biographical data printed on back might be in a single sentence or an entire paragraph. Cards Nos. 501-564 and 581-588 are film stars; cards Nos. 565-580 and 589-596 are movie scenes. The individual stars are named under their photograph, but the scenes are not captioned on the front of the card. The reference number for the set is R134. NOTE: cards in strips are valued ar 25% more than the listed prices. Cards of the more famous stars command up to 200% premium.

ITEM	EX	AVE
Card	4.00	1.00
Set	480.00	120.00

501 Carole Lombard	525 Edward Arnold	549 Lee Tracy	573 "The Cowboy and the Kid" scene
502 Dixie Dunbar	526 Allan Jones	550 Lew Ayres	574 "Under Two Flags" scene
503 Priscilla Lawson	527 Michael Whalen	551 Frank Lawton	575 "Show Boat" scene
504 Jane Wyatt	528 John King	552 Henry Hunter	576 "Sutter's Gold" scene
505 Jean Rogers	529 Thomas Beck	553 Douglas Dumbrille	577 "The Country Beyond" scene
506 Binnie Barnes	530 Don Ameche	554 Wyrley Biren	578 "Under Two Flags" scene
507 Nana Bryant	531 Victor Kilian	555 Alan Dinehart	579 "O'Malley of the Mounted" scene
508 Margaret Sullivan	532 Paul Cavanaugh	556 Melvyn Douglas	580 "O'Malley of the Mounted" scene
509 Irene Dunne	533 Jack Holt	557 Herbert Mundin	581 Martha Tibbetts
510 Helen Wood	534 Cesar Romero	558 Robert Taylor	582 Florence Rice
511 Edith Fellows	535 Don Briggs	559 Raymond Walburn	583 Joan Perry
512 Joan Perry	536 Thurston H. Hall	560 Brian Donlevay	584 Jane Darwell
513 Florence Rice	527 Henry Mollison	561 George Bancroft	585 Gloria Holden
514 Lizabeth Risdon	538 Arthur Rankin	562 Larry "Buster" Crabbe	586 Marguerite Churchill
515 Martha Tibbetts	539 Robert Allen	563 Gene Morgan	587 Edith Fellows
516 Marian Marsh	540 Noah Beery Jr.	564 Edward Everett Horton	588 Marian Marsh
517 Gloria Stuart	541 Buck Jones	565 "Crash Donovan" scene	589 "Crash Donovan" scene
518 Alice Faye	542 Karloff	566 "Sutter's Gold" scene	590 "Dracula's Daughter" scene
519 Diane Gibson	543 Lionel Stander	567 "Sutter's Gold" scene	591 "Sutter's Gold" scene
520 Sara Haden	544 J. Edward Bromberg	568 "Sutter's Gold" scene	592 "Paroled" scene
521 June Lang	545 Pinkey Tomlin	569 "Sutter's Gold" scene	593 "The Cowboy and the Kid" scene
522 Shirley Deane	546 Lloyd Nolan	570 "Dracula's Daughter" scene	594 "Dracula's Daughter" scene
523 Rita Cansino	547 Billy Borrud	571 "Crash Donovan" scene	595 "Dracula's Daughter" scene
524 Helen Morgan	548 George O'Brien	572 "Sutter's Gold" scene	596 "The Cowboy and the Kid" scene

148

SHELBY QUIZ (?)

"Collect Shelby Quiz Cards — One given with each piece of Transfer Gum." Apparently

the public didn't heed this advice, for few cards have survived and the wrapper has never been found. The card fronts are tan cardboard and contain a numbered "quiz" printed in black ink; the backs are blank and are gray. The facts revealed in the quizzes seem to be statistical data such as "railroads use about one-third of the coal" mined in the U.S. — not exactly the kind of thing that would appeal to a child, and it is children who chew bubble gum. However, "Transfer Gum" probably did contain a paper heat or water-process transfer design in each pack, and that's what attracted the kids. The reference number is R195.

ITEM	EX	AVE
Card	6.00	2.00

SHIPS & PLANES (?)

An anonymous series of unknown length, card Nos. 112-136 have been confirmed to date. The fronts have simple multi-color sketches of U.S. Naval units and various aircraft. A check in Jayne's Naval History reveals that some of the vessels were commissioned or had keels laid in 1941, and that at least one of the ships pictured was sunk in 1944.

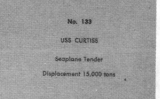

From this evidence, it seems likely that the set was issued before the attack on Pearl Harbor. The craft are named front and back; card numbers are on back only. Statistical data is ultra-brief. No reference number has been assigned as of this time. Despite their resemblance to strip cards, these cards were machine cut.

ITEM	EX	AVE
Card	2.50	.50

SKY BIRDS (108)

Although a line on each of National Chicle's "Sky Birds" cards advertises a "series of 144," there were only 108 titles issued. The subjects are famous pilots and airplanes, and there are cards for Bishop, Von Richtofen, Doolittle, and Earhart. Cards 1-24 are dated 1933 and cards 25-108 are dated 1934 (but the cards apparently were sold up until 1941). Three wrappers are known: two have plane centers with different copy on the end flaps; the other has a "pilot cap" ad in the center. Wrapper colors are blue and red on clear wax paper, and each wrapper had a "coupon" flap which could be cut off and sent in for premiums. The green-print backs carry the card number and biographical or descriptive text. The last series of cards is particularly difficult to obtain. The reference number is R136.

ITEM	EX	AVE
Cards		
1-48	12.00	3.00
49-96	18.00	4.50
97-108	75.00	18.00
Exceptions:		
No. 1	30.00	7.50
No. 20	20.00	5.00
No. 23	25.00	6.00
No. 32	20.00	5.00
No. 36	30.00	7.50
No. 48	30.00	7.50
No. 49	20.00	5.00
No. 62	25.00	6.00
No. 72	25.00	6.00
No. 108	100.00	25.00
Set	3500.00	800.00
Wrappers (3)		
Each	125.00	—

Sky Birds

1 David Putnam	28 Russell N. Boardman	55 Maj. Reed G. Landis	83 Albatross D.1
2 Rene Fonck	29 Floyd Bennett	56 The D.H.-10 Bomber	84 Sopwith Camel
3 Lieut. Thieffrey	30 Willy Coppens	57 The Bristol Fighter	85 Lt. Alan A. McLeod
4 Capt. Albert Ball	31 Maj. George A. Vaugn, Jr.	58 Captain Alcock	86 The Austin Ball
5 J.N. Hall	32 James H. Doolittle	59 Lt. John A. Macready	87 Eugene Gilbert
6 Capt. Albert Heurteaux	33 Capt. Charles E.	60 Capt. Roald Amundsen	88 C. B. (Ben) Eielson
7 Rene Dorme	Kingsford-Smith	61 Gabriel D'Annunzio	89 Nieuport Balloon Rocket Ship
8 Major Barracca	34 Frank M. Hawks	62 Wiley Post	90 "Wild Bill" Wellman
9 Roland Garros	35 Gen. Italo Balbo	63 Nieuport Triplane	91 Major de Seversky
10 Charles Nungesser	36 Colonel Charles A. Lindbergh	64 Deperdussin Monoplane	92 Capt. Francis McCubbin
11 Norman Prince	37 Clarence D. Chamberlin	65 Vickers Vampire B.R.2	93 Sopwith Tabloid
12 Frank Luke	38 Capt. James B. McCudden	66 Lt. Col. Armand Pinsard	94 Voisin 12 BN 2
13 Kiffin Rockwell	39 Edward A. Stinson	67 Sidor Malloc Singh	95 Buggatti—Spad
14 Sergt. James McConnell	40 Bernt Balchen	68 Fokker Triplane	96 A.E. 6 Bomber
15 Bert Hall	41 Spad	69 Ernst Udet	97 Capt. Thenault
16 Lt. Max Immelmann	42 Albatross-Taube, 1914	70 Capt. Frank O. D. Hunter	98 Elliot Cowdin
17 Lt. Douglass Campbell	43 Juan De La Cierva	71 Winnie Mae	99 David S. Ingalls
18 Quentin Roosevelt	44 Admiral Wm. A. Mofett	72 The Spirit of St. Louis	100 Maj. David Mck. Peterson
19 Capt. De Beauchamp	45 E. Hamilton Lee	73 Lt. Paul H. Neibling	101 Harold June
20 Edward Rickenbacker	46 Capt. Oswald Boelcke	74 Lt. Rudolf Von Eschwege	102 Lt. Alan F. Winslow
21 Capt. Georges Guynemer	47 Lieut. Edward C. Parsons	75 Elliot White Springs	103 Spad Herbemont
22 Maj. Raoul Lufberry	48 Amelia Earhart	76 Capt. Brocard	104 Halberstadt
23 Baron Manfred	49 Orville Wright	77 Capt. A. Roy Brown	105 Sopwith Torpedo Carrier
Von Richthofen	50 Ruth Nichols	78 Maj. Donald McLaren	106 Morane Parasol
24 Lieut. Frank Baylies	51 Lt. Werner Voss	79 German Gotha	107 Marchetti-Vickers (M.V.T.)
25 Joe Wehner	52 The Salamander	80 German Junkers	108 Fokker D 8
26 Col. William A. Bishop	53 Edmond Genet	81 Macchi	
27 Col. William Thaw	54 Georges Modon	82 Parnell Panther	

150

SKY BIRDS (24)

The Goudey Gum version of "Sky Birds" is a blank-backed series of 24 cards that the early catalogs say were issued in 1941. The color artwork airplanes were drawn in vivid tones of red and blue, with more attention paid to effect than detail. The card number and caption and a short description of the aircraft are all located in a red panel underneath the picture.

A small wing design bearing the words "SKY BIRDS Chewing Gum" is set into the field of each drawing, and the cards have thin white borders. There are two wrappers associated with the set: a red center type (left) with premium offers on the flaps and a blue center variety with a circle of dog-fighting airplanes. The red wrapper is marked "Goudey Gum" while the blue wrapper carries the "World Wide Gum" name (a Goudey subsidiary). The existence of the latter, plus the discovery that Sky Bird cards come with both tan and gray cardboard backs, suggest that the series may have been issued in Canada. The cards were also distributed with gum in small boxes, which also come in either red or blue colors. The reference number is R137.

2 5/16" X 2 7/8"

ITEM	EX	AVE
Card	10.00	2.50
Set	300.00	75.00
Wrappers		
Red	125.00	— —
Blue	150.00	— —
Boxes		
Red	100.00	35.00
Blue	150.00	50.00

1 U.S.A. Patrol Bomber
2 English. Gloster F 534
3 English. "Hawker Henley"
4 German. Junkers JU-86R Bomber
5 German. "Hamburger" HA-137
6 English. Hawker Hurricane
7 U.S.A. Boeing B-17
8 French. Hanriot 220
9 U.S.A. Curtis Pursuit Plane
10 German. Stuka Henschel HS-123
11 German. Dornier DO-17
12 German. Messerschmidt BT-109-R
13 Italian. Fiat Biplane
14 Italian. Breda 88
15 Russia. U.R.S.S. L-760
16 U.S.A. Curtis-Hawk 75
17 U.S.A. Brewster F-2A1
18 English. Short Sunderland
19 Swedish. Bristol Bulldog
20 U.S.A. Lockheed XP 38
21 English. Famous Spitfire
22 Japan. Mitsubishi 96 Bomber
23 U.S.A. Consolidated XPB-2Y
24 China. Northrup 8 A-1

AMERICAN WRAPPER

CANADIAN WRAPPER

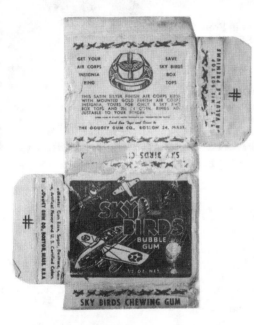

5-CENT BOX CONTAINED
CARDS AND GUM

SMILIN' JACK (128)   2 1/4" X 2 15/16"

The 128 black & white cards in the (Adventures of) Smilin' Jack set were taken from a movie matinee serial produced by Universal Pictures. The cards were originally issued in strips of eight, but minus the normal machined perforations between individual cards which are designed to make detaching easy. Seven of the eight cards on each strip are photos; the eighth card is a drawing. The card number and story line are found on the back, along with a war bonds advertisement and the name of Samuel Eppy, the manufacturer. It is believed that the set was sold with candy or, perhaps, by itself. The reference number is R4.

NOTE: complete strips are found more often than well-cut single cards, so the price for a set intact in strips amounts to less than the sum of individual card prices.

ITEM	EX	AVE
Card	2.00	.50
Set	200.00	50.00

SMILIN' JACK (12K)

2" X 3 1/8"

What a contrast between this Smilin' Jack series and the one in the preceding review! The Eppy set is composed of dull photographs and sketches, while this Novel Package Corp. version is drawn in gorgeous color. Furthermore, the Novel series is almost impossible to find, in contrast to the Eppy cards, which are common. Our illustration of a complete Novel box shows that the "card" was the detachable back panel of that box (mechanically scored for easy removal). The title side of the box contained a portrait of Smilin' Jack on the front and a mail-in coupon on the back (3 coupons & 5 cents for any one of four premiums listed). Since many of these were obviously redeemed, box fronts are even harder to find than the cards. The story-backs are printed in black ink on gray stock. A line at the bottom reads "This is one in a series of 48 exciting adventures of Smilin' Jack." Despite

Smilin' Jack

this claim, No. 12 is the highest card number seen, and veteran collectors believe that the series may have been terminated at that point. The reference number is R138.

ITEM	EX	AVE
Card Front/	15.00	5.00
Coupon	25.00	10.00
Box	150.00	50.00

SOLDIER BOYS (24)   2 1/8" X 2 7/8"

"Colorful, thrilling pictures of Soldiers and Flags of All Nations" reads the advertising on the backs of Goudey's "Soldier Boys" cards. The series consists of 24 color artwork pictures of soldiers and their national flags set upon backdrops with a martial theme. The product name, "Soldier Boys Chewing Gum," is printed in a red panel beneath each picture. The cards are numbered and titled only on the back, and the black print text is small and hard to read. A series of cloth flags could be ordered in groups of 10 by sending in 25 wrappers. The promotion advertised 70 different flags, but collectors report finding a certain batch over and over. The reference number is R142.

ITEM	EX	AVE
Card	10.00	2.50
Set	300.00	75.00
Flag	5.00	1.50
Wrapper	100.00	—
Box	350.00	125.00

1 U.S. Admiral	13 French - "Poilu"
2 Scotch	14 Irish Republic
3 Japan	15 Hungary
4 Czechoslovakia	16 Rumanian
5 Russia	17 Italian - Alpine
6 Sweden	18 French African Zouaves
7 U.S. Marines	19 Greece - The Evzone
8 Finland	20 British East Africa - An Askari
9 French - "Foreign Legion"	21 German General
10 Italian Officer	22 Austria
11 Great Britain - British Tommy	23 German
12 Poland	24 British India - "The Sikh"

SOLDIER CARDS (36)

The "Soldier Cards" issued by Rosen (Providence, RI) are color artwork drawings surrounded by heavy black frame lines and wide white borders.

The card title is printed inside the picture area on front and also on the back. Card numbers are on the back only. The size of the print used in the text varies from card to card depending on how much was written. The "series of 192" statement on each card was never fulfilled: only 36 cards were printed. The "Soldier Pop Pitching Card" wrappers have been found in yellow (lemon) and pink (cherry) colors. The reference number is R139.

ITEM	EX	AVE
Card	10.00	2.50
Set	450.00	110.00
Wrappers		
Yellow	150.00	––
Pink	175.00	––

1 France	13 China	25 Japan
2 Italy	14 Poland	26 Syria
3 Roumania	15 Switzerland	27 Greece
4 Russia	16 Australia	28 Portugal
5 Germany	17 Hungary	29 Russia
6 Spain	18 United States Army	30 West Point
7 Belgium	19 Venezuela	31 India
8 Serbia	20 Austria	32 Egypt
9 Bulgaria	21 French Colonial	33 Holland
10 English	22 Yugoslavia	34 Alpine
11 The Scots Guards	23 Senegal	35 French Foreign Legion
12 England	24 Norway	36 Sweden

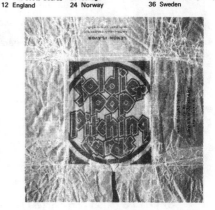

SOLDIERS (?)

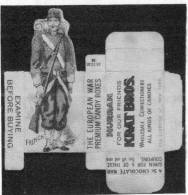

We are using a "bare-bones" title for this set simply because most collectors will never find a Krat soldier card attached to an original box. Thus, they will never know that the series was dubbed "The European War Premium Candy Boxes" by the manufacturer. [Given the title and the style of the uniforms, the early researchers probably were wrong in listing this set in the "R" (post-1930) category. It really belongs to the "E" (pre-1930) group.] Most Krat boxes were un-doubtedly dismembered, not only to have the soldier as a trading card or toy, but also because five designated end flaps could be exchanged for a five-cent candy bar. Only two color drawings have been confirmed to date: "English" and "French." The color of the box cardboard is white. The reference number is R140.

ITEM	EX	AVE
Card	50.00	20.00
Box	200.00	75.00

SOLDIERS & SAILORS (9K)

SIZES VARY

This interesting group of "stand-up" military figures were printed on the backs of candy boxes made by Lefferts Novelty Co. (Brooklyn, NY).

The cards, which come in at least two slightly different sizes, do not have machine-scored edges and had to be cut from the boxes with scissors. The color artwork is rudimentary, but the interesting design feature is that all cards are either diecut or have punch-out supports so they can be "displayed" or used as toys. Each card is captioned and the backs are blank. They

are not numbered and may come with or without an ingredients list and company name (see illustrations). The reference number R192 has been assigned by the Hobby Card Index. A complete box has yet to be found and only nine different titles are known at this time.

ITEM	EX	AVE
Card	8.00	2.00

Anti-Aircraft Gunner
Bayonet Charge
Danger Mines
Infantryman in Action
Jeep
Machine Gunner
Sailor — Ordinary Seaman
Tank Corpsman
Tommy Gunner

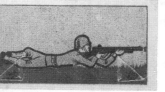

SOLDIERS OF THE WORLD (10K)

3" X 4 1/2"

It is more appropriate to call the cards of this set "stand-ups," rather than diecuts or cutouts, because they were machine-scored to pop apart easily. They were produced by General Gum (Chicago) and likely were handed out to purchasers at the store. Each shaped, color artwork card bears both the set title on the

American 1st Lieut. - 1935
Ethiopian Chieftan - 1935
French Major - 1914
German 1st Lieut. - 1914
Indian - Jacob's Horse 1st Lieut. - 1923
Italian Black Shirt 1st Lieut. - 1934
Japanese 1st Lieut. - 1935
Russian 1st Lieut. - 1934
Scot (Black Watch) 1st Lieut. - 1935
Welsh Guard 1st Lieut. - 1914

base and the subseries heading "Officer Series." Despite the implications of the latter, no other types of soldiers have been found. The cards are not numbered and the gray cardboard backs are blank. When assembled, each card becomes a double-faced (two-sided) stand-up toy or display. The reference number is R141.

ITEM	EX	AVE
Card	20.00	8.00

SPORTS PICTURES (31)

2 3/16" X 3 5/16"

From time to time we encounter a set with a general sports theme which, because it does not contain pictures of specific athletes, does not appeal to sport card collectors. The C.A. Briggs series of 31 "Sports Pictures" is just such a

set. Each artwork color front depicts a sports scene: our illustration is card No. 3, "Horse-Racing." The cards are numbered front and back, but the caption is printed on the back only. According to the offer on the back, anyone

sending in a complete set of 31 to the company could choose one of four exciting premiums: a baseball, bat, "mit," or a one pound box of chocolates (cards were returned to sender). It is assumed that Briggs made one card scarce to prevent successful redemptions, but there currently aren't enough of these cards around to determine which one it was. No reference number has been assigned, and the wrapper has yet to be seen.

ITEM	EX	AVE
Card	25.00	10.00

STORY OF WINGS (?)   6 5/16" X 6 1/2"

When John "The Wrapper King" Neuner first showed this "Story of Wings" wrapper to fellow collectors, many thought it was the elusive set referred to in the early catalogs at reference number R186. It is not, however, for that set was produced by American Chicle, and this is clearly marked Leader Novelty Candy Co. (the two wrappers are also different in size). The aircraft pictures are black and white and were probably cut from the wrappers rather than left intact. The top flap carries offers for several mail premiums, one of which was an album to house the airplane pictures. The package contained two "kisses" — probably a taffy or molasses candy chew — and a surprise — most likely a small novelty toy or trick. No copyright date is printed, but the aircraft pictured indicate a 1940 or 1941 distribution. To date, a reference number has not been assigned.

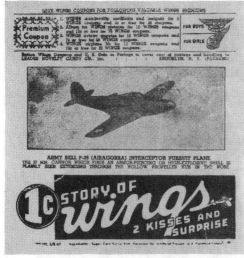

ITEM	EX	AVE
Wrapper	200.00	—

STRANGE TRUE STORIES (24)   2 1/2" X 3"

WINDOW SIGN

WRAPPER

1	The Malay Boot	13	The Mad Elephant
2	The Buffalo Charges	14	The Battle of the Ants
3	The Fight with the Shark	15	The Sausage Tree
4	The Volcano Calls	16	In the Grip of the Python
5	Capturing Rattlesnakes	17	Hunting the Giant Bear
6	The Price of a Sheep	18	Capturing an Alligator
7	China the Terrible	19	The Mongoose Attacks
8	The Fighting Rabbit	20	Hari Kiri!
9	Drowned by a Giant Clam	21	The Cobra Strikes
10	The Iron Maiden	22	Poisoned!
11	Death in the Sahara	23	The Torture of Galileo
12	Murder in the Depths	24	The Bat Man

According to Wolverine Gum, "Strange True Stories" was the "Greatest Collection of Series Cards in the History of the Confectionary Trade." The fact that they promised to produce 260 "Super Thrilling & Exciting" cards but only managed to deliver 24 has not tarnished their image one bit. Wolverine Gum had a fascination with the bizarre — their only other set was (Ripley's) "Believe It Or Not," and both sets are among the most popular of all 1930's issues. The color artwork is simple but the subject matter makes it effective. The stories related on the card backs are detailed and interesting. The cards are numbered front and back, but individual card titles are printed only on the fronts in the black panel located below the picture. The set was distributed in 1936 in one-cent packs of "Strange True Stories Gum." The reference number is R144.

ITEM	EX	AVE
Card	50.00	15.00
Set	1750.00	500.00
Wrapper	500.00	—
Window Sign	300.00	100.00

SUPERMAN (72)

2 1/2" X 3 1/8"

Thanks to the excellent artwork and text of Gum, Inc.'s "Superman" set, America's favorite comic book hero has a tremendous fan club in the trading card hobby. Copyrighted in 1941 by Superman Inc., these multi-colored adventure cards are numbered and captioned only on the reverse. In addition to the text, the backs also have a small black and white Superman design and advertising for the "Supermen of America Club." The wrapper is a brilliant yellow, red and blue design with a club "application form" to be cut off and sent in for membership. Once considered the "king" of the 1930's wrappers, "Superman, The Super Bubble Gum" has since become more plentiful and more affordable. The reference number is R145.

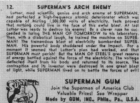

ITEM	EX	AVE
Cards		
2-48	25.00	6.00
49-71	75.00	18.00
Exceptions		
No. 1	40.00	10.00
No. 72	100.00	25.00
Wrapper	300.00	—

1 Superman
2 The Spy Trail
3 From the Jaws of Death
4 Peril in the Jungle
5 The Girl Reporter's Dream
6 Superman Vs. Bank Robbers
7 The Averted Train Wreck
8 Rescue at the Bank
9 Superman at the Circus
10 Fury of the Sea
11 Capture of the Kidnappers
12 Superman's Arch Enemy
13 Teeth of Steel
14 Maniac at Large
15 Panic in the Subway
16 Mountain Tragedy
17 Death on the Speedway
18 Prison Break
19 Wings of Mercy
20 Peril at Sea
21 The Runaway Horse
22 Wolves at Bay
23 Hurtling to Destruction
24 Attacked by Sharks
25 Trapped in the Air
26 Log Jam Peril
27 Rescue from a Rocky Reef
28 The Flames of Doom
29 Death Dive
30 Trapped in the Glacier
31 Rescue Beneath the Sea
32 Danger on High
33 The Avalanche
34 Peril in the Oil Fields
35 Hurricane Horror
36 Facing the Firing Squad
37 Distress at Sea
38 Marooned in the Clouds
39 Disaster at the Mine
40 Racing the Shells
41 Roller Coaster Rescue
42 Danger in the Jungle
43 Fight in Mid-air
44 Disaster at the Circus
45 The Runaway Ship
46 To the Rescue
47 Horror Beneath the Sea
48 Death in the Air
49 Danger at the Carnival
50 At the Bottom of the Sea
51 Superman Vs. the Spies
52 Saving the Destroyer
53 The Girl Reporter
54 Rescue from the Flames
55 Superman Wins Again
56 Superman and the Killer Whale
57 Battling the Hurricane
58 A Near-tragedy
59 The Dive of Death
60 Menace in the Mine
61 Through the Mine Field
62 Peril in the Presses
63 Terror in the Tower
64 Adventure on an Iceberg
65 The Runaway Trolley Car
66 Danger at the Dam
67 Explosion in an Oilfield
68 Saved by Superman
69 Saved from Buried Alive
70 Anger in the North Woods
71 Trapped in Quicksand
72 Superman Vs. Torpedo

SUPERMAN (48) 2 3/8" X 2 7/8"

The Superman candy-box card series manufactured by Leader Novelty and the Gum, Inc. bubble gum set, which precedes it on our list, may be worlds apart in terms of style, but they share a number of details. Both sets were produced in 1940, and both bear credit lines for "Superman, Inc." More importantly, they also share the same advertures with, in some cases, similar or identical card titles. Gum, Inc. card No. 9 and Leader's card No. 31, for example, are both entitled "Superman at the Circus." I guess when you have a hot licensing item, you can make any deal you want!

The Leader series has many interesting features. The front panel of each box has an inset picture of Superman breaking free of chains; the flip side of this panel has a coupon design with four different premium offers printed on it. The coupon redemption plan drastically reduced the supply of logo/coupon panels available to future collectors. The cards were printed on the back panels of the boxes and were machine scored at the edges for easy removal (eagerness overcame engineering in many cases because cards are often found with rips, tears, and pieces missing). Cards were numbered in two places: in a corner on the front of each card, and on one of the end flaps (see illustrations). Naturally, the end flap numbers ceased to function when the flaps were removed. Of considerable interest is the fact that some of the cards bear a Superman logo and the company name, while others do not. All cards have "Superman Inc." and "series of 48" (however, no card above No. 36 has been reported) lines. As a final point, the Leader Superman box had two compartments, one for candy and one for a toy. This served the dual purpose of increasing unit integrity and providing for sanitary inspection (you could look at the toy without touching the candy). The reference number is R146.

FRONT PANEL WITH COUPON BACK

CARD WITHOUT LOGO ON BACK

CARD WITH NUMBERED END FLAP INTACT

CARD WITH LOGO BACK

ITEM	EX	AVE
Cards		
1-24	25.00	10.00
25-36	35.00	15.00
Set	1800.00	700.00
Boxes		
1-24	100.00	35.00
25-36	135.00	50.00

1	Through the Flames	6	
2	Smashing the Gangsters	7	Saving the Workmen
3	The Race in the Sky	8	Breaking the Racket
4	The Armored Car Holdup	9	Rescue of the Major
5	A Lesson for Crooks	10	Human Tenpins

11	The Toppling Smokestack		
12	Peril in the Air		
13	The Bank Robbery		
14	The Yellow Mask		

15	The Bursting Bomb	26	Trapped in the Glacier
16	The Trap	27	Trapped in the Air
17	Millions in Gold	28	Capture of the Kidnapers
18	The Fight for Peace	29	The Averted Train Wreck
19	The Shattered Press	30	Roller Coaster Rescue
20	Through Granite Walls	31	Superman at the Circus
21	Snatched from Death	32	
22	Twisted Steel	33	Superman
23	A Shot in the Night	34	Attacked by Sharks
24	Cracked Skulls	35	The Runaway Ship
25	Fight in Mid-Air	36	Mountain Tragedy

TARZAN AND THE CRYSTAL VAULT OF ISIS (50)

One of the most popular sets of the 1930's, this Tarzan series was distributed by Schutter-Johnson in one-cent packages of "Tarzan of the Apes Candy." The color artwork is simple yet appealing, and each drawing is numbered and captioned beneath the picture. A "(C) Stephen Slesinger, N.Y." line, printed in miniature type, is located in the bottom left corner on the front of every card. The backs have the set and card titles, the card number, and a lengthy text — all printed in black ink on tan stock. The candy wrapper has a brilliant yellow and red center design, but the rest is merely clear wax paper. The reference number for this set is R147. The set was also issued in Canada by Canadian Chewing Gum; these cards have horizontal, gray cardboard backs, and the text printed in both English and French.

ITEM	EX	AVE
Card	35.00	8.00
Set	2400.00	500.00
Wrapper	500.00	—

BACK OF CANANDIAN CARD

1 The Urge of Tarzan
2 The Letter
3 The Messenger
4 The Journey
5 The Change
6 A Mystery
7 The Serpent's Gorge
8 Disaster
9 Peril Ahead!
10 The Captive
11 The Call to the Apes
12 Major Falsburg
13 The Rescue
14 The Phantom Fleet
15 The Spy's Story
16 Treachery!
17 Through the Trees
18 The Electric Menace
19 The River of Danger
20 The Cliff of Death
21 The Last of His Tribe
22 A Priceless Gift
23 Terror by Night
24 Tarzan Reconnoiters
25 The Hidden Menace Overcome
26 Alone: The Apes and the Electric Curtain
27 The Inland Empire
28 The Camp of Death
29 Saved by Inches
30 Floating to Death
31 The Plains of the Dead
32 The Fight at the Water Hole
33 Karl in Danger: The Flying Turtle
34 The Fight, Tarzan vs. Lothar
35 Danger in the Depths
36 The Elephant's Graveyard
37 The Enemy at Last
38 The Warning
39 Danger Revealed
40 The Cliff of Death: Nila Restored
41 Tarzan Approaches
42 Secrets of the Empire
43 Death of a Fiend
44 Hall of Isis: Figures of Wax
45 The Double Rescue
46 The Secret Entrance
47 The Crystal Vault
48 Priceless: The Diamond Trillion
49 Vaults of the Empire
50 The Parting

TATTOO GUM MOVIE STARS (?)

In 1932, the Orbit Gum Co. of Chicago produced a series of "sun developing" pictures of baseball players and movie stars and marketed them in packs of "Tatoo Chewing Gum." The Tattoo gum pack was smaller than the gum packages of many competitors, but was probably a better deal. Not only did you get the gum and a develop-it-yourself picture card, but also a piece of play money and a bonus game or tattoo printed on the inside of the wrapper.

Sixty baseball player pictures have been reported, and it is thought that there are an equal number of movie stars. Unfortunately, the fact the surface of each card is light-sensitive paper means that most surviving cards are faded. The play money is green on the "pirate" side and orange on the other. The single wrapper design known has been found in three different colors: blue, green, and yellow. The reference number is R308. NOTE: the "excellent" price refers ONLY to reasonably clear pictures with readable captions.

ITEM	EX	AVE
Card	12.00	5.00
Play Money	15.00	5.00
Wrappers		
Yellow	20.00	—
Blue	35.00	—
Green	35.00	—

THE FOREIGN LEGION (48)   1 5/16" X 2 3/4"

The 48-card series entitled "The Foreign Legion" is probably the most interesting of all the strip card sets. It is numbered from 325 to 372 and was produced by the New York- based W.S. Corporation in 1939. The set title appears in a panel at the top of each card in one of four colors: blue, green, red, or yellow. The front caption is printed below the picture; on some cards this differs slightly from the card title on back. All cards bear a 1939 copyright line both front and back, and most cards will have two rouletted edges (end-of-strip cards have only one). The reference number is R54. NOTE: cards intact in strips are worth 50% more than listed prices.

ITEM	EX	AVE
Card	7.00	2.00
Set	400.00	115.00

325 The Legion Marches	337 Plotting Rebellion	349 Oasis at Last	361 Native Sniper
326 The Arab Chief, El Musa	338 Routing the Enemy	350 Sighting the Enemy	362 Trouble in Tunisia
327 Desert Skirmish	339 Headsman of the Sheik	351 "Khroumers" Retreat	363 Disguised Legionnaire
328 Helping a Comrade	340 Surrender	352 Sheik ElHassan	364 Giving Orders to March
329 Desert Phantom	341 The Battle Rages	353 Inciting to Revolt	365 Algerian Uprising
330 Captain DuBois	342 Corporal LaForte	354 On the March	366 Cited for Bravery
331 Disarming Riff Sentry	343 To the Rescue	355 Hit by a Sniper	367 Sheik Mufti, Soldier's Friend
332 Attacking a Lone Legionnaire	344 Night Attack	356 Corporal Fortescu	368 Surprise Attack
333 Tribal Feud	345 Riff Conspiracy	357 Lieutenant Giroux	369 Commandant Bouton
334 The Lone Watch	346 Call to Arms	358 Egyptian Caravan	370 Abducting Rich Girl
335 Lieut. DuPree	347 Camel Caravan	359 Desert Torture	371 Surrounding the Outpost
336 Secret Dispatch	348 Legionnaires Victory	360 Catching Spy	372 Jailing Arab Spy

THE GOUDEY LINE R.R. (?)   VARIOUS SIZES

One of the jewels in the fabulous collection of Robert Marks, "The Box King," is this innovative railroad car gum container "built" by Goudey in 1935. The box was made of heavy cardboard and had a capacity of 150 pieces of gum and a total displacement of 300 cubic inches (12 X 5 X 5 inches). The chewing gum was aptly named "Chew-Choo Bubble Kiss," but the individual wrapper for this product has never been seen. It is logical to assume that Goudey created an entire train, complete with engine and caboose; however, this is the only car reported to date. No reference number has been assigned.

ITEM	EX	AVE
Box	600.00	150.00

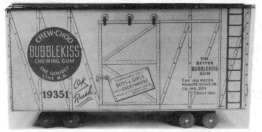

SIDE VIEW

The Goudey Line R.R.

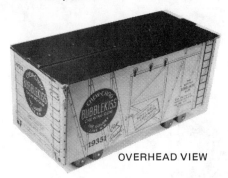

OVERHEAD VIEW

END VIEW

THE NIGHTMARE OF WARFARE (48)   2 5/16" X 2 3/4"

The anonymous strip card series entitled "The Nightmare of Warfare" was a copycat version of Gum, Inc.'s more elaborate "Horrors of War" set. The design and coloration of the cards and the intentional pirating of titles and text from a competitor all point to the W. S. Corporation as the producer. The artwork is limited to black silhouettes set against yellow backgrounds, with an occasional red accent thrown in. The vertically-aligned backs have the set title, card number, a "series of 48" line, card title, and text — all printed in black ink on gray stock. Since these are strip cards, one or two edges on all cards will be rouletted. The reference number is R99. NOTE: cards in strips are valued at a 50% premium.

The Nightmare of Warfare
No. 917
This is one of a series of 48 cards
Chinese Girl Scout
"Does Her Good Deed"
This actually occurred in the fall of 1937. A Chinese body of troops was desperately defending its position in Shanghai against the oncoming Japanese. Their flag was shot down by exploding grenades. A brave Chinese Girl Scout carried a new Chinese flag which was received with cheers by the hard-pressed patriots.

ITEM	EX	AVE
Card	4.00	1.00
Set	225.00	55.00

901 Scene of First Fighting in Present Chino-Jap War Marco Polo bridge.
902 Jap Forces Resisted by Chinese "Big Sword" Corps
903 U.S. Marine Hit by "Wild Shot"
904 Tientsin Bombed by Japanese
905 Jap Planes Shot Down by Chinese Pursuers
906 Woosung Japanese Suicide Squad
907 Ancient Walls of Paoshan Being Blown Down
908 British Troops and Refugees Fired on by Tokio Tank
909 "Famous Panay Incident"
910 20 Patriotic Nudists
911 Japanese Flagship Attacked in Whang Poo
912 Chinese City Bombed by Chinese

913 Japanese Trapped at Nankow Chinese
914 Passengers on Shanghai Trolley Killed by Bombs
915 Shell Burst on Anchored U.S.S. Augusta
916 Passenger Train Attacked
917 Chinese Girl Scout "Does her Deed"
918 Chinese Orphanage Bombed by Japanese
919 Spanish Reds Shoot Fascist Mourners
920 Government Territory Bombed by Spanish Insurgents
921 Alcazar at Toledo Besieged by Loyalists
922 Madrid Children at Play Killed by Big Shells
923 Eithiophians Terrified by Italian Bombs
924 Eithiopians Annihilated by Air Attack

925 Rebel Battleship "Espana" Sunk Off Santander by Planes
926 Japanese Advance at Shanghai, U.S. Zone Bombed
927 "Pirate" Sub Attacks British Destroyer
928 Loyalist Planes Raid Palma and Majorca
929 Insurgent Planes Bomb Guadalajara in Attempt to Sever Railroad
930 Spanish Insurgents Cannonade Madrid
931 Bombs Slaughter Spanish Civilians
932 Japs Trap Battalion of Chinese
933 Blockade of China Coast
934 Japs Bomb British Statesmen in Automobiles
935 Japs Take Nankow Pass

936 Truckful of Chinese Soldiers Murdered by Jap Machine Gun Fire
937 Death Over Barcelona
938 Women Rout Red Army During Siege of Alcazar
939 Japanese Capture Tsingtao
940 Hidden Mines Explode Killing Jap Soldiers at Whang Poo
941 British Boats Hit by Japanese Bombers
942 90 Japanese Planes Make Air Raid on American Zone
943 U.S. Marines Halt Japanese in Defense of American Zone
944 Spanish Rebels Bomb Teruel Front
945 German Army Invades Austria
946 Germany Takes Possession of Austria
947 Chinese Recapture Yulintsun
948 The Fall of Gijon to Spanish Rebels

THE SECOND WORLD WAR (48)   2 5/16" X 2 11/16"

The artwork and text of this 48-card set entitled "The Second World War" were not plagiarized from other sets, so the W.S. Corp. printed its name on the cards (unlike the preceding set). The artwork fronts are all horizontal, and the set title and card captions are printed in red panels above and below the picture. The backs are vertical (notice the similarity between these and the reverses of "The Nightmare of Warfare" series), and the print is black on gray stock. Some card captions vary slightly from front to back and a "(C) W.S. 1939, N.Y.C." line is found on every card reverse at the bottom. The cards are numbered 125 to 172 and the reference number is R126. Some machine-cut cards have been found, indicating that this series may have been marketed in another manner besides strips.

ITEM	EX	AVE
Card	5.00	1.25
Set	275.00	65.00

THE SECOND WORLD WAR

No. 130

French Mechanized Battalions

Ever alert to the swift progress made by military science the French have manufactured enormous quantities of mechanized equipment to swiftly move their brave battalions from one threatened battle front to the next.

This is one of a Series of 48 Cards
©W.S. 1939. N.Y.C.   Litho in U.S.A.

125 Germans Invade Poland
126 Warsaw Defenders Repel Nazi Invaders with Bayonets
127 Chamberlain Declares War
128 Daladier Declares War
129 Polish Civilians Flee Before Nazi Onslaught
130 French Mechanized Battalions
131 German Siege Gun Bombards Warsaw
132 Russians Invade Betrayed Poland
133 Warsaw Surrenders After Heroic Defense
134 Poles Weep as Germans Conquer
135 Guerilla Fighting Breaks out after Warsaw Falls
136 British Troops Leave for Battle Front
137 British Troops Land in France
138 Polish Civilians Hunted by Nazis
139 French Slash Salient in German Lines at Hornback
140 Submarine Sighted off Cape May, New Jersey
141 Russia Demands that Esthonian Forts be Razed
142 Nazi Submarine Sinks British Plane Carrier "Courageous"
143 Nazi U-Boat Torpedos Defenseless Athenia
144 French Attack Siegfried Line
145 Nazis Repulsed by French
146 Germans Blow Up Their Bridges on Moselle River While Retreating
147 U.S. Fleet Prepares on West Coast
148 Allied Airplanes Bomb German Zeppelin Works
149 U-Boat Bombed After Sinking Ship
150 British Planes Bombard Germany with Propaganda Leaflets.
151 Torpedoed "Kafiristan" Survivors Being Rescued
152 Naval Battle of the North Sea
153 French Air Squadron Scores Direct Hit
154 Dog Fight in the Air Over Saarbrucken
155 Canada Stands by England
156 Australia Ships her Soldiers to the Front
157 Senegolese Warriors Rush to Defence of France
158 Tank Action on the Western Front
159 French Flyer Shoots Down Nazi Pilot Over Saarlonis
160 Air Raid Alarm Makes Londoners Rush to Bomb Shelters
161 British Warships Battle Nazi Planes
162 French Hold Warndt Forest Against German Attack
163 Russian Ship Sunk by Submarine off Esthonia
164 Long Range Shelling Hits Empty Towns Behind Lines
165 British Warships Blockade Germany
166 British Depth Bomb Sinks Nazi Submarine
167 French Machine Gun Nest at Apach
168 British Plane Raid on Kiel Canal
169 Dutch Ship "Binnendijk" Sunk Near English Port
170 French Defeat Germans in Battle of Tanks
171 U.S. Destroyers Rush to Aid of American Ship "Iroquois"
172 Hitler Makes Peace Proposal to Allies Which is Turned Down

THE WORLD IN ARMS (48)

Collectors have wondered... which came first, "The World In Arms" or "War News Pictures?" The reason they ponder this question is that 24 cards of the former are also printed as a part of the latter (Nos. 49-72). Both sets were issued in 1939, and aside from the question of which came first, one thing is clear: J. Warren Bowman, the head of Gum, Inc., was out to make a buck, and printing the same cards in separate sets was just another way to do so.

"The World In Arms" cards are divided into specific subseries with their own numbering sequences: Airplanes (1-16), Field Artillery (1-4), Fortifications (1-4), Iron Cavalry (1-4), Ships (1-12), and Miscellaneous (1-8). The overstamp on the back of the "Free Sample Card" illustrated (it was given out in packs of other Gum, Inc. issues) indicates that the set was intended to be much larger: 120 cards, with 40 planes, 30 ships, 10 each of artillery, tanks, and forts, and

2 1/2" X 3 1/8"

20 miscellaneous. Instead, it became just one more of the many 1930's sets where promotion outstripped production.

The cards have beautifully drawn artwork fronts, which are even more striking since there are no captions to clutter up the pictures. The card title, subseries number, and text are printed on the back (black ink on tan stock). The artwork of 10 of the cards was also reproduced in two Rand McNally books, "America's Army" and "America's Navy," which were issued in 1942. In addition, the set was marketed in Canada under the name "Fighting Forces." These Canadian cards use the same artwork but have gray backs with a small French-language text at the bottom under the English version. The reference number for "The World In Arms" is R173. The wrapper is yellow with red, white, and blue accents.

ITEM	EX	AVE
Card	8.00	2.00
Set	450.00	110.00
Wrapper	600.00	—

SAMPLE CARD GIVEN AWAY IN ANOTHER GUM, INC. PRODUCT.

CANADIAN CARD BACK — NOTE FRENCH LANGUAGE SECTION AT BOTTOM

AIRPLANES

1. United States "Flying Fortress"
2. German Junkers Bomber
3. Italian Breda Fighters
4. British Mayo Composite "Pick-a-Back" Plane
5. Spanish Loring Reconnaissance Ship
6. Czechoslovakian Avia Fighter
7. Swedish Junkers Bombers
8. Royal Canadian Airforce Vickers "Vedette"
9. United States "DC-4"
10. Belgian Multi-seat "GR-8" Fighter
11. Irish Avro Anson Reconnaissance Plane
12. Russian Mystery Single Seat Fighter
13. French Torpedo Planes Escorting Giant Letecoere
14. Latvin Two-seat Reconnaissance Ship
15. Australian "Wirraway"
16. Dutch Fokker "D-21" Fighter

SHIPS

1. United States Battleship "Mississippi"
2. French Battleship— Dunkerque!
3. British Fifteen Ton "Hornet" Torpedo Boat
4. Japanese Detroyer "Fubuki" Sinking Junk
5. Italian Cruiser "Zara"
6. New German Submarine
7. United States Heavy Cruiser "Indianapolis"
8. Spanish Nationalist Cruiser "Canarias"
9. German Motor Torpedo Boat
10. Japanese Aircraft Carrier "Akagi"
11. British Battleship "Rodney"
12. Italian M.A.S. Boat

IRON CAVALRY

1. United States Armored Scout Car
2. United States High-speed Tank
3. Italian Flame-throwing Tank
4. Japanese Scout Motorcycle

FIELD ARTILLARY

1. United States 3-inch Anti-aircraft Gun
2. United States 77mm Field Gun
3. United States 75mm Howitzer
4. United States .30-caliber Heavy Machine Gun

FORTIFICATIONS
1. U.S. Quick-firing Rail Mounted Coast Gun
2. Guns of the Maginot Line in Action
3. Heligoland
4. The Mareth Line

MISCELLANEOUS
1. Italian Flame Throwers
2. British Death-dealing Balloon Barrage
3. Landing Russian "Air Infantry"
4. The New Garand Automatic Rifle
5. British Portable Steel Air-raid Shelter
6. Gas Raid Rescue Squad
7. Stream of Torpedoes
8. Devastating Martin-Barlow Aerial Bomb

THRILLING STORIES (60)

1 15/16" X 2 1/2"

The "Thrilling Stories" series of story booklets details the adventures of eight different characters: Corporal Blake, Crafty Keen, Flash Brown, Hal Hunter, Mirtho the Clown, Operator No. 7, Reckless Steele, and Yip Roper. When the set was last featured in this guide, it was thought that there were only 30 booklets in the set; we have since found out that there are 60. As you can see by the checklist, some characters have seven titles while others have eight. Each booklet contains an illustrated story and has eight numbered pages. The covers are designed to look like miniature books, with the name and volume number listed on the spine. If you look closely under the "volume" number, you will spot a previously unreported detail: another number, which some collectors believe will eventually tell us the sequence in which the individual booklets were issued. The booklets of Flash Brown, Mirtho the Clown, Operator No. 7, and Reckless Steele are far more difficult to find than the others. The producing company has not been identified, and no wrapper has been seen. The reference number is R25.

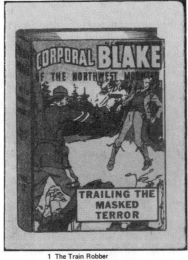

1. The Train Robber
2. Trailing the Masked Terror
3. The Telltale Mark
4. The Trail in the Snow
5. Mountie Against Giant
6. The Raging Torrent
7. The Villains Trapped
8. Once a Mountie Always a Mountie

ITEM	EX	AVE
Booklets		
Corporal Blake	20.00	6.00
Crafty Keen	20.00	6.00
Flash Brown	40.00	15.00
Hal Hunter	20.00	6.00
Mirtho the Clown	40.00	15.00
Operator No. 7	40.00	15.00
Reckless Steele	40.00	15.00
Yip Roper	20.00	6.00
Set	2400.00	750.00

1 Martin Murder Mystery
2 Accusing Fingerprints
3 The Deaf Storekeeper
4 In the Face of Death
5 The Secret Service Aide
6 The Robber's Revenge
7 Dead Man Helps

1 The Mysterious Band
2 Foiling the Kidnappers
3
4 Fight Against Death
5 The Chinese Bandits
6
7
8 The Mad Inventor

1 The Man-Eating Tiger
2 Captured by Zoodoos
3 An Envoy and a Friend
4 Saved by the Giant Bird
5 A Lady's Life in Peril
6 Hunting Human Heads
7 The Slaves in Revolt

1 A Fatal Wreck
2
3 Murder on the Flying Trapeeze
4 A Thief in the Dark
5 Kidnapped
6 A Ferocious Lion Loose
7 The Battle with the Tramp

1 Robbing the Airmail
2 Trapping the Smugglers
3 Telltale Fingerprints
4 The Carved Dagger
5 The Arsenal Explosion
6
7 Trail of the Bills

1 Over the Top
2 Death of the Serpent
3 War on Gangsters
4 The Mystery Racer
5
6 The Mad Man
7 Doomed by the Savage King
8

1 An Indian Attack
2 The Cattle Rustler
3 The Tenderfoot Springs a Surprise
4 The Sheriff's Star
5 The Runaway
6 Facing the Killer
7 The Half-Breed's Plot
8 The Shot at the Wedding

THURSTON'S MAGIC TRICKS (50)   3 1/4″ X 5 3/4″

THURSTON'S
MAGIC WAND TRICK
HOW TO DO IT

Your trick equipment consists of one black wand and one length of black thread. Before appearing to present your trick, tie one end of the black thread to one of your vest buttons . . . . then tie a knot in the other end. (Ladies must wear dark clothing . . . . tie thread to dress or coat button . . . . or buttonhole.)

Now pass your wand among your friends for inspection. While they are looking at it, grasp loose end of thread in one of your hands. When wand is returned, ask someone for his ring. While the attention is thus momentarily diverted, casually maneuver the wand about in a way that will make it easy for you to slip the knotted end of the thread into the groove in the end of the wand. (This phase of the trick must be practiced several times.) Turn this end of the wand up and take the ring, slip it over the end of the wand, let it fall to your hand at the bottom of the wand.

Now ask one of your friends to command the ring to rise up the wand. He does. The ring does rise! You accomplish this by imperceptibly moving your hand away from your body . . . . or your body away from your hand . . . . the thread will do the rest.

To complete the trick effectively, remove the ring, then return the wand for inspection. The knotted thread will slip off easily and unnoticed as you extend the lower end toward your friends.

Thurston, **THE MAGICIAN**

14117

Assigned the reference number R183 in the early catalogs, this group of leaflets explaining various magic tricks has generally eluded collectors simply because no sample has ever been adequately described or illustrated before now. The producer has been cited as "Sykes & Thompson," but that name does not appear anywhere on the paper trick. The name of Thurston, a famous magician of the 1920's and 1930's, appears in large bold letters at the top and in smaller type at the bottom. The leaflet pictured here bears the number 14117 in the lower left corner; this is probably a product identification code. The front has a substantial explanation of the trick (black print on off-white paper), and the back is blank. There is only one natural fold line running vertically about 1/2″ from the right-hand margin, so the method of distribution appears to have been something other than a standard gum package or small candy box.

ITEM	EX	AVE
Leaflet	15.00	5.00

TILO CARDS (?)

2 3/16" X 2 1/2"

Another mysterious set from the 1930's, Tilo cards are part of a two-in-one game issued in an unknown manner by Fleer. The first game involves the color artwork on one side of each card, which was covered with a special coating that hid the drawing. A clue to the picture was printed on the flip side of the card along with the statement "For answer erase coating on other side. Use pencil eraser preferably. The coating is harmless and non-injurious. Produced by the Hid-N-Picture process." Subjects seen so far include animals, ships, pirates, Indians, presidents and puzzles, and each artwork side is captioned.

The side containing the clue and instructions for erasing also explains another game, from which the set derives its name: Tilo. It is a basic form of "Scrabble" in which four of the cards — T, I, L, O — are placed in the center and players try to form other words in a radiating fashion. To quote: "Words can be spelled in three directions. The first player getting rid of all his tiles yells TILO and scores the sum of all the white numbers on the tiles of the other players." From this description, it seems logical that as many as 50 different Tilo cards may exist, but few have been reported. The company name is not printed on the cards and the packaging has not been seen. The reference number is R149.

ITEM	EX	AVE
Card	15.00	5.00

TIME MARCHES ON (48)

2 5/16" X 2 7/8"

The "Time Marches On" series of 48 cards is dedicated to "illustrating important events in the history of the United States," from the time of Columbus to the presidency of F.D.R. The cards are numbered from 601 to 648 and were originally issued in strips, although from the smoothness of the sides it does not appear that there were machined perforations between individual cards. The fronts have basic color-artwork sketches with the card number and set title above and the caption below. Backs are arranged vertically with the card number and set title repeated plus a description of the event depicted on the front (black print on gray stock). The size may vary up to 1/8" on either plane. The company which produced these cards has not yet been identified, and the reference number is R150.

ITEM	EX	AVE
Card	4.50	1.50
Set	250.00	80.00

601 Columbus Pleads with Isabella
602 Columbus Discovers America
603 Balboa Discovers Pacific
604 Ponce DeLeon at the Fountain of Youth
605 John Smith and Pocohantas
606 Indian War Dance
607 The Half Moon on the Hudson
608 Pilgrims Landing
609 First Thanksgiving Dinner
610 "Speak for Yourself John"
611 Peter Minuit Buying Manhattan Island from the Indians
612 Boston Massacre
613 Boston Tea Party
614 Patrick Henry
615 British March on to Lexington
616 Paul Revere
617 Battle of Bunker Hill
618 Franklin Reads Declaration
619 Liberty Throughout the Land
620 Washington Crossing the Delaware
621 Valley Forge
622 Lafayette Meets Washington
623 Cornwallis Surrenders

624 Washington Taking Oath
625 Paul Jones Boarding Serapis
626 First Steamboat
627 Pioneers Going West
628 Battle of Alamo
629 Transcontinental Railroad
630 Gold in California
631 Time Marches on
632 Battle of Bull Run
633 Monitor and Merrimac
634 Gettysburg Address
635 Marching Through Georgia
636 Lee Surrenders
637 Klu Klux Klan
638 Sinking of the Maine
639 Dewey at Manila
640 Sinking of the Lusitania
641 Wilson's War Massage (sic)
642 U.S. Enters World War
643 Pershing at Lafayette's Tomb
644 At the Front
645 U.S. Fleet in the World War
646 Chateau Thierry
647 Lindy Crossing the Atlantic
648 President Franklin D. Roosevelt

TINTYPE CARTOONS (18)　　　　3 1/2" X 5 1/2"

J. Warren Bowman, the flamboyant owner of Gum, Inc., became a millionaire because (1) he was willing to try anything, and (2) he wasn't afraid to ditch unsuccessful

projects. The "Tintype Cartoon" series of 18 postcards demonstrates both these qualities: it was a radical departure from the "standard" gum line, and he apparently dumped it when it didn't prove popular. The cards are typical postcard size and have divided backs and a "place stamp here" box. The fronts bear multi-color drawings with a gag line printed beneath. The artist's name — Kircheimer — is found on every picture. The cards are numbered on the back at the

end of a line which reads: "1938 by Gum, Inc., Philadelphia, Pa. Litho. in U.S.A." Collectors are more likely to find Tintype Cartoon cards at postcard shows under the "comic" section, where they are generally priced far lower than they would be in the trading card marketplace. The reference number is R189.

ITEM	EX	AVE
Card	15.00	4.00
Set	325.00	90.00

"I'M IN THE MOOD FOR MR.WATTS — THE REST OF YOU CAN GO HOME."

TOM MIX (48)　　　　2 3/8" X 2 3/4"

National Chicle's "Adventure Stories about Tom Mix and Tony at the Bar-Diamond Ranch" were issued in the form of eight-page booklets in 1934. The set is evenly divided into two series: the first printing (1-24) and the so-called "high numbers" (25-48). The numbered cover page has a single common color for each consecutive group of six titles, and their breakdown is as follows: 1st series...1-6,

blue; 7-12, yellow; 13-18, orange; 19-24, green; 2nd series...25-30, green; 31-36, yellow; 37-42, blue; 43-48, red. Each first series booklet is an episode from "Tom Mix and Tony at Bar-Diamond Ranch." The second series booklets contain episodes from "Tom Mix and Tony on the Santa Fe Trail." Two separate wrappers have been reported for the set. The one with the "booklet" center

design is orange and yellow while the other is yellow and green. All booklets bear a 1934 copyright line on the back page. In addition, every booklet numbered 25-48 has the words "second series" printed in the advertising copy. The reference number is R151.

ITEM	EX	AVE
Booklet		
1-24	20.00	5.00
25-48	30.00	7.00
Set	1500.00	350.00
Wrappers		
Orange &		
yellow	250.00	—
Green &		
yellow	350.00	—

1 Hits the Bar Diamond	14 Escapes the Poison Death		
2 Mounts Guard	15 Comes Through	26 In a Tough Spot	38 Saves Betty Brown from the
3 On the Death Riders Trail	16 His Guns Blaze in the Desert	27 Fights His Way Free	Indians
4 Shoots to Kill	17 Tony Gives Tom Mix a Big Day	28 Westward on the Santa Fe Trail	39 Conquers the Raging Buffalo
5 Downs the Sidewinder	18 Shoots It Out	29 Captures the Bandits	40 Tony Saves Two Lives
6 Thwarts Killers from the Sky	19 Rides Against Death	30 Saves the Indian Princess	41 Conquers the Unknown
7 At War on the Range	20 Too Tough to Kill	31 Gets an Indian War Bonnet	42 On the Santa Fe Trail
8 Saves the Day	21 Solves the Riddle of Thunder River	32 Tom's Pal, Sagebrush Sam	43 In Desperate Straits
9 Wins His Way	22 Deals Death to the Scorpion	33 Arrives at Santa Fe	44 Rides Through Roaring Flames
10 Draws First	23 Tom Mix and Tony Rope an	34 Rescues Betty Brown	45 Snatches a Life from the Sandstorm
11 To the Rescue	Outlaw	35 Avenges the Captain's Death	46 Unmasks Chet Charters
12 Fights Like a Man	24 Greets Unwelcomed Guests	36 In Danger	47 Gets His Man
13 Battles the Flames	25 On the Santa Fe Trail	37 Kills a Traitor	48 The End of the Marauder

TOOTSIE CIRCUS (25)   2 3/8" X 2 7/8"

The Sweets Company of America, based in New York, produced the beautiful "Tootsie Circus" series of 25 cards in 1933 (see copyright line printed under set title on front of every card). The combination of brilliant colors and sturdy cardboard stock makes this a favorite set among collectors. The subjects are named and described on the back, with the last line of every text promoting a Tootsie candy product. The back print is mid-range blue and the card stock is off-white. Because the cards are not numbered, they have been arranged alphabetically in our checklist below. No wrapper or other packaging has been reported to date. The reference number is R152.

ITEM	EX	AVE
Card	25.00	7.00
Set	800.00	210.00

THE COSSACKS

It is always thrilling to watch these dashing Russian cavalry troopers thunder around the ring, in their brightly colored uniforms. They are such splendid riders and have truly fine horses. They may pine for the wind-swept plains of Russia, but remember, Mr. Cossack, there are no tasty Chocolate Tootsie Rolls over there!

This is one of a series of Tootsie Circus Cards

Made by
THE SWEETS COMPANY OF AMERICA, INC.
New York, N.Y.

Clowns	The Dog Act
Doves and Pony	The Elephant
Freaks	The Giraffe
Indian and Pinto Pony	The Hippopotamus
Snake Charmer	The Lion
The Acrobats	The Menagerie Wagon
The Bare-back Rider	The Monkeys
The Bearded Lady	The Sword Swallower
The Bears	The Tiger
The Camel	The Trained Seals
The Clown and His Donkey	The Wild West Show
The Clowns	The Zebra
The Cossacks	

TRANSFER PICTURES & SHAPES

MANY TYPES AND SIZES

The early catalogs grouped every type of 1930's novelty transfer item — whether it was applied to cloth by heat or to skin by water — into a single classification for easy identification. We think this approach makes sense, and we will continue to use it for the time being. The reference number is R154.

The heat-to-cloth transfer picture illustrated at left was given free with the purchase of "Comic Gum," a Gum, Inc., product which we have already discussed in this volume with relation to another series. Each transfer measures about 2 1/2" X 5", and most carry a number in the 400's ("460.1," for example). From the picture of the box, we can see that the transfers show various popular subjects — Eddie Cantor and Babe Ruth, for example — but only inanimate objects or illustrated expressions have captions. In this manner, Gum, Inc. avoided paying royalties or fees to famous people. A typical transfer of this type sells for $5.00, with higher values afforded to certain pictures of sports and movie personalities. The chunks of gum in the box have "Exit and Aspirina" comics wrapped around them; the heat transfers were handed out by the retailer, and that is why they are normally found without creases or fold lines. The advertising sign we have pictured is in a current collection, but the box illustrated was part of a card company archive and modern collectors have yet to find one.

STORE ADVERTISING SIGN

We have no verified sample of the heat transfer pictures packed in "PIC Transfer Bubble Gum," but the product was manufactured by Gumakers of America, the company which marketed the famous "Frank Buck" series already reviewed in this book. We do not see this company's name on products after the U.S. entry into World War II, so it is assumed that this wrapper represents a pre-war series. The wrapper, which is blue and white, has a value of $75.00.

One look at the wrapper of the final item in this category explains everything. The "Letters, Numerals, Jitters" advertised on it were small pieces of cloth designed to be applied to clothing by heat ("jitters" refers to every shaped object other than the letters and numbers). These small decorative items were very popular among school age children of the 1930's and were issued by several companies, usually as an insert prize added to the card package. This particular issue, produced by Gum, Inc. in 1939, is the only reported instance of direct marketing of felt transfer novelies in their own gum package. The wrapper value is $150.00.

TRICK CARDS (20)

2 1/4" X 3 1/2"

The title of "Trick Cards" was assigned to this set in previous catalogs, and we will continue to use it because no wrapper or box has been discovered to tell us otherwise. The series was issued by General Gum (Chicago) and comes printed on either thin or thick cardboard stock. The obverse drawings are done in red and black, and the explanations on the reverses are printed in black ink on off-white stock. There are 20 cards in the set, and the reference number is R155. NOTE: the set was expanded to 48 cards and issued in Canada by license agreement with O-Pee-Chee Gum (reference number V305).

ITEM	EX	AVE
Card	15.00	5.00
Set	375.00	125.00

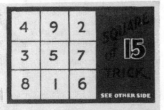

TREASURE HUNT (?)

2 1/4" X 2 9/16"

Fleer's "Treasure Hunt" was just that...purchasers of the gum could win a prize by matching four separately packed sections of a picture. An entire picture, composed of the four "labels" glued onto paper, was sent to the company for redemption. We have illustrated two different "puzzle-piece" labels along with the promotional slips which explain the "treasure hunt" and show the completed puzzle pictures. According to the advertising copy, Treasure Hunt was a combination of "Good Gum... Fine Gifts...Lots of Fun." The wrapper for this product has not yet been confirmed in any modern collection, and no reference number has been assigned.

ITEM	EX	AVE
Label	6.00	2.00

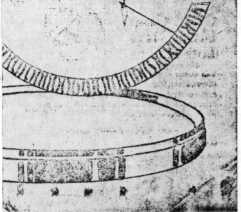

ONE OF FOUR "LABELS" REQUIRED TO MAKE THE PICTURE ILLUSTRATED ON THE PAPER SLIP AT RIGHT

Good Gum Fine Gifts Lots of Fun

This is one of four different labels necessary to make above picture. When you have complete set (all different), form picture by pasting labels on paper in proper position. Print your Name and Address PLAINLY, mail to us and we will send you above gift.

FRANK H. FLEER CORP.
2042 N. 10th Street   Philadelphia, Pa.

FLEERS TREASURE HUNT GUM 1¢

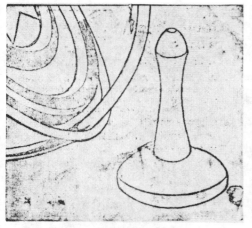

Good Gum
Fine Gifts
Lots of Fun

This is one of four different labels necessary to make above picture. When you have complete set (all different), form picture by pasting labels on paper in proper position. Print your Name and Address PLAINLY, mail to us and we will send you above gift.

FRANK H. FLEER CORP.
2042 N. 10th Street   Philadelphia, Pa.

FLEERS
TREASURE HUNT
GUM 1¢

TRUE SPY STORIES (24)   2 1/2" X 3 1/8"

"This is a True Spy Story. The names of some of the characters have been changed in order not to embarrass the government." That's what it says on the back of every "thrilling" True Spy story card issued by Gumakers of America in 1939. The set of 24 color artwork cards depict scenes from the history of espionage, from the American Civil War to World War II. Each card bears the copyright date and manufacturer's mark on both front and back. The card number appears on the back only along with an elaborate text (black print on tan stock). The fascinating store advertising poster depicts the scene from card No. 3, "The Execution of Mata Hari." Until recently, one colorful "Spy Gum" wrapper was the only packaging reported for this set (color scheme is red, yellow, and blue). It has promotional copy on the top flap which reads: "It is reported that there are over 120,000 spies in the United States. This company will give a $100,000 reward for the first information supplied to it leading to the arrest and conviction of any of these spies operating against the United States." A second wrapper recently uncovered by John "Wrapper King" Neuner has the same basic design but is done in different, less attractive tones and has advertising for a "Jeepers Creepers" felt insert on the top flap instead of the "spy" copy. No box has been found, and the reference number is R156.

ITEM	EX	AVE
Card	30.00	8.00
Set	950.00	250.00
Wrappers		
"Spy"	600.00	——
"Jeepers Creepers"	400.00	——

STORE ADVERTISING POSTER

"JEEPERS CREEPERS"
FELT EMBLEM

1 Spy Web Over Washington
2 The Vanishing Airplane
3 Execution of Mata Hari
4 Captain Katzern's Double-Bottom Trunk
5 The Bare-Footed Admiral
6 Allan Pinkerton, Lincoln's Personal Agent
7 Treachery of Lieutenant Farnsworth
8 Leon G. Turrou - Ace Spy Trapper
9 Miss "X," British Photographer Spy
10 Lawrence of Arabia, Secret Agent
11 The Senvall Confessions
12 Trebitsch Lincoln, International Spy
13 The Buzzing Corpse
14 Thompson, The Masquerading Yeoman
15 Lei La - The Chinese Mata Hari
16 The Kidnapping of Submarine C-2
17 Belle Boyd - Confederate Spy
18 Colonel Kruger's Poisoned Tea
19 The Missing Codes
20 Escape of the Manchukoan Agent
21 The Ordeal of Edith Canell
22 Taito Takahashi and His Telescope Lens
23 The Red-Bearded Fakir of Ipi
24 Spy in the Death Mask

UNCLE SAM (96) & HOME DEFENSE (48)

2 1/2" X 3 1/8"

The "Uncle Sam" series issued by Gum, Inc. in 1941 consists of two separate subsets. The first of these, numbered 1-96, depicts various scenes from the four military branches of service: Army, Navy, Air Force and Marines. Because the series was distributed before direct U.S. involvement in World War II, the focus of the set was directed to U.S. preparedness for hostilities, and it is devoid of the vivid and horrifying details of the overseas warfare which was already taking place. In this sense, "Uncle Sam" seems bland to many collectors compared to "Horrors of War" and "War Gum," and it is in far less demand than those two sets. The color artwork of cards 1-96, minus Nos. 31 and 34, were reproduced in two small-sized books entitled "America's Army" and "America's Navy" (Rand McNally 1942). Some of the cards were also illustrated in a Planter's Peanuts premium booklet (see below) distributed in the same time period. It also appears that all 96 cards were printed on two paper sheets, possibly to hang as advertising in store windows or to hand out as premiums. The wrapper for the 1-96 series has wide red and white bands with "Uncle Sam" pictured at top-center; he is flanked by five drawings of servicemen and a civilian in star designs. The reference number is R157.

27. UNCLE SAM—MARINE
Shore Rifle Practice

The second month of a marine's Recruit Depot, or base, training is devoted to target practice on the range with the service rifle. The various shooting positions are shown in this picture. Men who qualify as marksmen, sharpshooters, and expert riflemen are more valuable to the service—and increased pay goes with their increased ability. Through the years the marines have been able to capture many prizes and trophies by winning national rifle matches. The Marine Corps has won the team championship of the United States for fourteen times out of the twenty-eight times the competitions have been held. Practice makes perfect, and the marine works hard at his target practice in his eagerness to excel.

Save to get all these picture cards showing Uncle Sam's soldiers, sailors, marines, airmen and civilians in training for NATIONAL DEFENSE.

Copyright 1941, GUM, INC., Phila., Pa.   Printed in U.S.A.

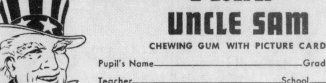

1 "You're in the Army Now"
2 Drill with Arms
3 Learning to Shoot
4 Sham Bayonet Charge
5 Gas Discipline
6 The Infantry's Supreme Duty
7 Parachute Troops
8 Field Artillery
9 Anti-Aircraft Crew
10 The Armored Force
11 Field Maneuvers
12 How to Tell an Officer's Rank
13 The Training Station
14 Semaphore Signals
15 Salute to Authority
16 "Over the Bounding Main"
17 "On Watch"
18 Navigation
19 Knots and Hitches
20 Man Overboard!
21 Fire at Sea
22 Abandon Ship!
23 Target Practice with the Turret Guns
24 War at Sea
25 What is a Marine?
26 Wall Scaling at Marine Recruit Depot
27 Shore Rifle Practice
28 Turned Over for Duty
29 Shore Duty
30 Sea Duty
31 On Foreign Soil
32 Gunners at Secondary Batteries
33 The Landing Party
34 Landing Force in Attack
35 Jungle Expedition
36 "Telling the Marines"
37 Can You Take It?
38 Flight Instruction
39 Use of the Chute
40 Take-offs and Landings
41 Gunnery in the Air Corps
42 Stunts in Combat
43 Formation Flying
44 Blind Flying
45 Learning to Dive-Bomb
46 Torpedo Bombing
47 Air Photography
48 Planes at Sea

49 "Digging In"
50 Barbed Wire Tactics
51 Parachute "Attack"
52 Ski Troops and Patrols
53 Engineers Building Bridge
54 Cavalry Charge
55 Life on a Submarine
56 Submarine Dive Drill
57 Loading a Submarine with Torpedoes
58 Submarine Torpedo Practice
59 Submarine Battle Drill
60 "Abandon Submarine" Drill
61 Keeping "Fit"
62 Motor Convoy Drivers
63 Field Radio
64 Riot Duty
65 National Disasters
66 Machine Gun Practice
67 Catapult Take-off
68 Laying a Smoke Screen
69 Safety Measures
70 The "Side Slip"
71 The Bombardier
72 Men with Wings
73 Streamlined Drill
74 Guard Duty
75 Rifle Air Defense
76 Crew of Pygmy Scout Car
77 Anti-Tank Team
78 Jujutsu for Military Police
79 Carrying the Wounded
80 Destroyer Duty
81 Inspection Aboard Destroyer
82 Destroyer Torpedo Drill
83 School for Divers
84 Blinker Signals
85 Cargo Net Landing
86 Forming an Ammunition Lane
87 Trench Construction
88 Pitching Hand Grenades
89 Marine Mountain Battery
90 Marine Sky Troops
91 The Loop
92 Prone Defense Gunner
93 High Altitude Pilots
94 Bomber Rescue Raft Tactics
95 Patrol Duty
96 Night Bomber

"EMPIRE DEFENDERS" CARDS WERE THE CANADIAN VERSION OF "UNCLE SAM"

PAGE FROM A PLANTER'S PEANUT BOOKLET

MORE PAGES FROM THE PLANTER'S PEANUT BOOK

The "Home Defense" subset, numbered 97-144, was distributed in an entirely new wrapper. Judging from the scarcity of these cards, especially the 121-144 sequence, Home Defense fell victim to the restrictions imposed by necessity after America's entry into the war. The 48 color artwork cards depicted the activities of the civilian sector as it prepared for air raids, gas attacks, and other frightening consequences of war. The possibility of such events occurring on the U.S. mainland was considered very real, and cards 97-100 were even reprinted (in black and white) in "Pic" magazine (2/3/42 edition), a popular large-format weekly of the period. Because the Home Defense subset was listed separately in the early card catalogs, it has its own reference number — R158.

ITEM	EX	AVE
Cards		
1-48	6.00	1.50
49-96	8.00	2.00
97-120	18.00	4.00
121-144	75.00	15.00
Set	3500.00	725.00
Wrappers		
Uncle Sam	150.00	—
Home Defense	750.00	—

Paper Sheets — double the value of individual cards

128. Uncle Sam's HOME DEFENSE
Fire Watcher

Similarly as Spot Wardens are assigned to fixed points during emergencies to warn of air attack, Fire Watchers are given specific points during raids to look for fires throughout a town or city and report them immediately so that protective measures can be taken. Many great conflagrations have been prevented in London through the diligence of Fire Watchers. Their work requires great courage and keen eyesight while on duty, tying in closely with the Auxiliary and Regular Fire Companies. As the enemy usually precedes the dropping of incendiary bombs with high explosive bombs the lives of Fire Watchers are in constant danger from falling shrapnel and tottering structures. The rear Fire Watcher is provided with an asbestos hood as protection from burns.

Ask for Uncle Sam Bubble Gum and complete your collection of cards Nos. 1 to 96 picturing U. S. Soldiers, Sailors, Marines and Airmen in training to Defend America.
Copyright 1941, GUM, INC., Phila., Pa.   Printed in U.S.A
Buy U. S. Defense Savings Bonds or Stamps

100. Uncle Sam's HOME DEFENSE
Air Raid Warden

The training of Air Raid Wardens for Home Defense also comes under the supervision of the Chief of Police in New York City and as a pattern for the rest of the cities of the country to follow. Sector Air Raid Wardens may be either men or women and they must be respected members of their communities. There will be one for each 500 population, distributed on the basis of police precincts. They will be the connecting link between the people and their various air protection services. They are chiefly concerned with "preventing panic that shatters morale. Their duties will include the enforcement of blackouts, directing Civilians to air raid shelters (see pictures), clearing streets, keeping traffic moving, scouting fires, bombs and enemy planes, administering first aid, etc. Each applicant is investigated and fingerprinted before being assigned to duty.

Ask for Uncle Sam Bubble Gum and complete your collection of cards Nos. 1 to 96 picturing U. S. Soldiers, Sailors, Marines and Airmen in training to Defend America.
Copyright 1941, GUM, INC., Phila., Pa.   Printed in U.S.A.
Buy U. S. Defense Savings Bonds or Stamps

120. Uncle Sam's HOME DEFENSE
"Keep 'Em Flying"

This card was prepared at the request of the United States Government. The Adjutant General's office in Washington asked for assistance from gum manufacturers in promulgating the Army's new slogan and design, and we are glad as always to cooperate with Uncle Sam. Uncle Sam Picture Cards bring our country's splendid Defense Services to the attention of millions of young Americans. They show Uncle Sam's Soldier, Sailor, Marine, and Airman in training; also Civilian Home Defense mobilization and instruction. By collecting the Uncle Sam Airman cards you can build a separate series on the training of military Air Pilots. The Air Corps is growing speedily to make the United States the greatest air power in the world. Make "Let's Go! U. S. A. Keep 'Em Flying!" your slogan too, and do your bit as a Civilian to aid the Home Defense Program.

Ask for Uncle Sam Bubble Gum and complete your collection of cards Nos. 1 to 96 picturing U. S. Soldiers, Sailors, Marines and Airmen in training to Defend America.
Copyright 1941, GUM, INC., Phila., Pa.   Printed in U.S.A.
Buy U. S. Defense Savings Bonds or Stamps

97 The Office of Civilian Defense
98 Auxiliary Fire Corps
99 Auxiliary Police
100 Air Raid Warden
101 Messengers
102 Women's Duties
103 Children's Duties
104 Enlisting Home Guard
105 Home Guard Rifle Practice
106 Spot Wardens
107 Medical Corps
108 Drivers Corps
109 Auxiliary Coast Guard
110 Amateur Radio Station Volunteers
111 Civilian Information about Bombs
112 Test Blackout
113 Protecting Windows and Doors
114 Civilian Type Gas Mask
115 Gas "Decontamination"
116 Home Shelter Room
117 Steel Shelter
118 Public Shelter
119 Civilian Pilot Reserve
120 "Keep 'Em Flying"
121 Control and Report Centers
122 The Aircraft Warning Net
123 "Hale" America
124 Family Unit
125 Individual Defense Against Incendiary Bombs
126 Lighting Supervision
127 Dispersing School Children
128 Fire Watcher
129 Bomb Squad
130 Training First Aid Instructors
131 First Aid Stations
132 Light Rescue Party
133 Heavy Rescue Party
134 Rescue Trucks
135 Factory Protection Squads

CANADIAN VERSION OF "HOME DEFENSE"

136 Use of Portable Fire Pumps
137 Mobile Food Unit
138 Road Repair Crew
139 Demolition Crew
140 Emergency Food and Housing
141 Preventing Disease
142 Guarding Water Supplies
143 Pidgeon Raising for Defense
144 Women Fliers in Defense

AGE IS NO BARRIER to active participation in our defense effort. Experienced minds are needed at home.

MIDDLE-AGED MEN who have families would be unwilling to have youth do all the work involved in the protection of our country. And young girls who will some day be American mothers want to do their bit.

WHERE DO YOU FIT IN DEFENSE?
By FIORELLO H. LA GUARDIA

THERE is a place for everyone in civilian defense. Unlike any other movement in the history of this nation, civilian defense includes all persons. Like total war, total defense is new in this world. In former times there were rules to which military leaders subscribed, but since the advent of the Nazi philosophy women and children are no longer safe in their homes, nor the aged and infirm in their hospital beds. England learned, as a consequence of incessant bombings by Hitler's aërial war machine, that the active participation of every man, woman and child is necessary for defense of her lives and property. And since Japan's attack against the United States, Americans are beginning to understand the full meaning of civilian defense.

These implications include not only the active protection of lives and property against military danger, but the protection of civilian health and welfare—the provision of adequate housing, schools, food, and recreational facilities. At all times, but especially in times of emergency, these services are the basis of a strong, secure population. The Office of Civilian Defense is recruiting volunteers to carry out both aspects of protection—protection against military danger and protection of the social structure of the community.

First let us consider the work which is achieved only through the combined efforts of the entire populace—building morale. You may be an elderly woman in a New York apartment or a high-school youth on a farm in Kansas, yet you can do just as much for the general morale as the confident young man who is out there dropping torpedoes on the Japanese ships which are trying to deprive us of our rights and our freedom. If you are near an army camp you can help our soldiers with recreational and leisure-time activities. If you don't live near a cantonment you can write to the boys in uniform, and you can tell them how we at home feel about this business of keeping America free.

Another general consideration is the health standard. We know that our nation can be strong only if its people are strong. We know that our national resources and our productive capacity are of little value unless our people are healthy in body and firm in their conviction that our community life and our community institutions are worth defending. Public health is indivisible, and we cannot protect the health of our young men in uniform or our defense industrial workers unless we protect the health of the whole community. And this means many opportunities for volunteers working under the direction of public and private agencies. Volunteers can help in hospitals, in clinics, and in visiting-nurse programs. They can learn about proper nutrition and about the foods which help keep a nation healthy. They can fight venereal diseases and correct the local conditions which help spread them. These are merely examples.

There are numerous other cases, and in each instance there is room for the individual in our defense program. A young man in Philadelphia who has always been afflicted with a nervous disease which renders him unfit for military service and for air-raid duty, spends two or three hours every night going from home to home, collecting old books. These he sends to army camps in his district. An inmate of a coast penitentiary has begun to make field hockey sticks, to be sent to the boys in uniform so that they will have still more sports equipment available. A blind man in Louisiana types letters and news releases for his local Civilian Defense office. A youngster of school age in Buffalo collects old sheets and pillow cases which may be converted into bandages by the Red Cross for emergency work. In all parts of the country, boys and girls are getting out and acting as messengers for defense groups.

As to the individual cases, let us look at that elderly woman in New York whom we mentioned a moment ago. She cannot go out on the streets and take part in Red Cross work in the event of a bombing. She cannot go from house to house assisting in our health program. But she CAN knit a sweater for a boy in camp, and she CAN make an occasional box of candy to be sent to a soldier. Then we have that high-school boy in Kansas who feels that he would like to join in the defense program. He can very handily participate in the efforts of his local Civilian Defense organization. No one will deny that the inland cities and towns may some day find themselves with the task of providing evacuees with homes and other necessities of life. We hope that evacuation will never be necessary, but 1941 warfare taught us that no point on the globe is immune to aërial bombardment. As our president warned us months ago, it is not out of the question for enemy bombers to choose Kansas City and Des Moines as their objectives. Thus the young boy may help map out available housing facilities or act as messenger at an air-warden post, control and message center, or at hospital and first-aid units.

Recently we received a letter from a young businessman, 28 years of age, living in a moderate-sized town. He is not eligible for active service, but wants to do his duty in the defense of his country. Such a person can enroll as an air-raid warden, or auxiliary fireman. He would also be a valuable asset in many of the jobs that help build his community, such as assisting the local housing authority, directing recreational work for men and boys, or participating in discussion forums.

A young woman who supports her family by holding an office job feels that she could spend a few hours a day in the cause of national defense. Any agency working for civilian defense would welcome her services, for she could be of much help by typing, filing, or operating a switchboard. As for the young girls without jobs, I would suggest that they make arrangements to participate in the Nurses Aid Training, which is operated by the Red Cross.

Then there is the housewife with several children who believes that she can manage a few hours a day away from her home duties and wants to give these hours to her country. Couldn't her services be used? Certainly they could. There is the work of tending a day nursery for children whose mothers are employed in defense industries. There is vital work in the field of diet and nutrition.

Yes, there is a place in this program for every citizen. And, with the help of every man, woman and child, we are going to see this war through and show the dictator nations just what a mistake they made when they dared attack us.

CONTINUED ON NEXT PAGE

HOME DEFENSE ARTICLE IN "PIC" MAGAZINE
INCLUDED ARTWORK FROM CARD NOS. 97-120

CONTINUED FROM PRECEDING PAGE

ONE of America's current great advantages over most other countries of the allied group is that she has had ample time to prepare for "come what may" in World War II. For years we have known that a common enemy was at large, that our active participation in hostilities was only a matter of time.

From England's courageous stand against relentless bombardment, we learned the most effective physical measures to be taken, and at the same time we discovered that neither bombs nor fire could shatter the morale of a united and determined people. Rather than wait for deadly explosives to awaken us

IN MAY, 1941, President Roosevelt appointed Mayor F. H. LaGuardia, of New York, to head the new Office of Civilian Defense. Although efforts are being concentrated on coastal areas, there is work to be done in all areas of the country.

EMERGENCY ORDER NO. 1 was issued in New York last June 3rd. In it, the Civilian Defense chief directed the immediate establishment of a Fire Department Auxiliary Corps. Members are taught the duties of firemen, to be ready to save life and property from fires, incendiary bombs in emergencies.

AUXILIARY POLICE FORCE draws its strength from special police officers, war veterans, and other physically competent men who are distributed to precincts in proportion to the need for guarding key points. Their duties also include the prevention of crime and also the protection of life and property.

AIR RAID WARDENS may be either men or women. There will be one for every 500 population, all prepared to report enemy planes, enforce blackouts, direct civilians to air raid shelter, etc. Each applicant is investigated and fingerprinted before being assigned to duty.

SALVAGE UNITS of older boys and girls are called on to save all serviceable articles. Their first chance to be of service to defense was in the aluminum drive. Young people of England have been invaluable in helping the home guardsmen.

HOME DEFENSE MESSENGERS will be charged with the responsibility of getting word through to proper authorities when wires are down and in the absence of radio operators. This work requires great daring and courage, because bombs may be falling and buildings toppling while the cyclists speed through.

WOMEN CAN PREPARE for defense jobs by taking Red Cross courses. Or, if they choose, they may help as air raid wardens, in canteen service and in community hospitals, and in the evacuation of children. Still others are operating day nurseries for children whose mothers are in defense work.

HOME GUARD RESERVES replace soldiers of the national guard during emergency periods. Preference is given to men with previous military training. Companies are housed in armories and other public buildings. Men learn, in addition to military drill, how to shoot.

TRAINING PROGRAM of Home Guard Reserve companies includes shooting balloons in anti-parachute practice. Some units use model planes which are launched at a distance and maneuvered toward riflemen in a most realistic manner.

SPOT WARDENS are stationed at fixed points to watch out for approaching enemy planes and falling bombs, and to notify report centers of developments. In some cities members of the American Legion are chosen to man the main observation posts. Most coastal cities have set their workers on 24-hour duty.

MEDICAL CORPS TRAINEES learn simple first aid, bandaging, setting of broken limbs to hold them firm en route to the hospital, and simple emergency "carries." When these preliminary courses are completed, they are taught to deal with poison gas, burns, lacerations, and more serious injuries.

MOBILE MEDICAL UNITS, for "front lines" during times of attack, are headed by car owners and taxi drivers. Space in the trunk compartment is utilized to carry first aid and fire-fighting equipment. Drivers are being trained to assist Red Cross nurses.

"PIC"

to our danger. President Roosevelt established the Office of Civilian Defense in the spring of 1941, and within six months more than a million persons had enrolled in the new organization. There are scores of ways in which civilians may assist in the defense program, as Mayor LaGuardia points out in his article on the preceding pages, and this series of drawings—distributed by Gum, Inc.—were designed to better acquaint our citizenry with the types of work in which they may take part. Further information can be acquired at your local or State Office of Civilian Defense, or at the Red Cross headquarters.

COAST GUARD AUXILIARY can be joined by respected citizens who own at least 25 percent of a boat and pass a required examination. These men promote better understanding of navigation and guard against sabotage. Boats are armed with machine guns.

VOLUNTEER "HAMS" (amateur radio station operators), of which there are some 57,000 in the United States, are invaluable as "spotters" and message relayers. Since all have already passed a Federal Communications Commission examination, there is no doubt as to their ability in these capacities.

BOMB INFORMATION is being given to civilians so that they will be ready to deal with the several types of missiles. Most commonly used bomb for cities is the 14-inch incendiary which, when set off, gives an intense flame that burns through metal and can't be put out with water or chemicals.

TO DON A MASK, the civilian must hold his breath before pulling the harness over his head, then test its air-tightness by blowing into the outlet valve. Director LaGuardia has asked for fifty million masks for cities in vulnerable districts.

CITY LIGHTS act as beacons for attacking planes, and even street lights must be hooded or extinguished during blackouts. To guide motorists and thus keep down traffic accidents, a paint which glows in the dark is applied to markers on all of the principal thoroughfares.

PROTECTING WALLS of sandbags are used around doorways of buildings. To prevent flying glass, a transparent material may be gummed on the inside of windows, or cross-sections of tape applied to the outside. Heavy wrapping paper pasted over a broken pane should make the window gas-proof.

GAS DECONTAMINATION squads mop up after air raids. Most common poison gases and their "symptoms" are: Phosgene—which smells like new-mown hay, Lewisite—geraniums, Adamsite—sickly sweet, Mustard gas—garlic, and Chloripicrin—fly paper. Decontaminators neutralize effects of gases.

BASEMENT ROOMS should have two exits to guarantee escape. The windows inside should be made gas-proof by covering with a wet blanket or rug. A large rug or blanket should similarly be placed over the door and allowed to trail.

STEEL SHELTERS like the one shown here will not withstand direct hits, but they will protect occupants from flying shrapnel and debris. Home owners in Great Britain use extensively the "Garden Variety," made of pre-cast concrete sections entirely below ground.

SOME SUBWAY STATIONS will be utilized if attacks occur in New York or Philadelphia. Air raid wardens will guide the populace to public shelters and discourage panic and hysteria. Many new factories are equipped with air raid ens—steel-doored concrete tunnels into which employees can scamper.

CIVILIAN PILOT PROGRAM has prepared thousands of young men and women on college campuses, thus providing reserve for defense. By 1944 nearly 95,000 civilian fliers will have been trained this way. Many young men who are graduates of CAB are now seeing active service in the air corps.

SYMBOL OF WORLD'S greatest forces, this design is familiar to residents in every part of the country. Americans, realizing that maximum effectiveness in the defense program can be attained only if everyone joins in, are responding gloriously.

UNIVERSAL CARDS

FOUR SETS

The Universal Toy & Novelty Mfg. Company of New York City produced these four sets of cards during the 1930's. The cards are really more closely related to smaller-sized strip cards of the 1920's in design and coloration, and they are not widely collected because they do not compare well to the general run of 1930's gum cards. At first it was thought that individual cards were cut from candy boxes; that has since been disproved by the discovery of machine-cut single cards and uncut sheets. Most likely they were handed out as incentives to buy generic penny candy.

ANIMALS

There are 16 cards in this set. Individual cards measure 2 1/4" X 3 1/4". The artwork of Universal's "Animals" series reminds one of caveman drawings. The pictures are essentially patterns which were filled in with solid colors. The lion depicted in our display, for example, is solid yellow and is standing on a red rock. Three different backs have been confirmed for these cards. Type 1 reads A "Universal" Product on back; Type 2 is the same but has a large black star and a premium offer on one side; Type 3 have either playing card designs or untitled drawings on the reverse. Types 1 and 2 are numbered front and back: the obverse numbers run from A1 to A12, while the reverse numbers are 132 to 147 (the former were probably printer or artist identifications). Type 3 cards have A1-A12 front numbers only. The reference number is R159-1.

TYPE 1

TYPE 2

TYPE 3

ITEM	EX	AVE
Card	3.00	.50
Set	55.00	10.00

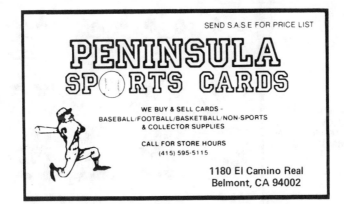
181

UNCUT SHEET OF "ANIMALS" CARDS

A1	Buffalo	A9	Rhinoceros
A2	Camel	A10	Elephant
A3	Wolf	A11	Tiger
A4	Leopard	A12	Lion
A5	Zebra	A13	Monkey
A6	Moose	A14	Musk Deer
A7	Kangaroo	A15	Bear
A8	Zebu	A16	Elephant

REVERSE SIDE OF SHEET SHOWS TYPE 3 "PLAYING CARDS" AND "DRAWING" BACKS

182

COMIC JOKES

There are 16 cards in this set. Individual cards measure 2 1/4″ X 3 1/4″. The often brutal racial and ethnic "humor" depicted in this series of illustrated jokes was alive and well in Depression America. The cards are printed on very thin cardboard and bear front numbers from C1 to C16. Although we have no illustrations, it is believed that the three varieties of backs found for the preceding Animals set are also found for Comic Jokes (in which case, back-numbered cards would be in the 132-147 run). The card featured in our presentation has the playing card/drawing back and is front-numbered only. Blank-backed Comic Jokes cards have also been found, and it is likely that they also exist for all other "Universal" sets. The reference number is R159-2.

ITEM	EX	AVE
Card	5.00	1.00
Set	95.00	18.50

C1 Fido—You Rascal, You Come Right Back Here with my False Teeth.

C2 Say Mom—You Look Just Like a Pretzel!

C3 Hey, Grandpa, Lend Me Your Beard. I Want to Play Santa Claus.

C4 I Dreamed I was a Peach, and Woke Up to Find Myself Just a Wrinkled Up Old Prune.

C5 Who Threw the Overalls in Mrs. Murphy's Chowder?

C6 When Fritz was Asked How Old He Was. He Said "Who Me? I'm Dirty und my Vife Iss Dirty Too."

C7 This Tramp Asked the Lady for a Hot Dog, But He Got a Bull Dog Instead.

C8 This Advertisement Says "Colored Woman Wants Washing. That's No Job For Me.

C9 How Much Do You Want For the Fiddle Cases Lady?

C10 Schmitz Here Says—"If You Want to Make Your Pants Last, Just Make the Coat and Vest First."

C11 Sambo Says "The Best Way to Raise Hens is to Put Them in His Elevator."

C12 Oh My Gosh! I'll Never Sit on a Bee-Hive Again. NEVER

C13 Say Pete, If a Man Had Two Fish, and One Smelt, Would He then Have Three?

C14 Say—Cohen as Long as You're Going to Drown—Pay Me Dot $5.00 You Owe Me.

C15 And Mr. Dummergonz, Send Six Holes with a Doughnut Around Each One of Them.

C16 Sure Iiza, Sure! Watermellons Is Ostrich Eggs, Cause I See an Ostrich Lay One. You Is Smart sambo! Yeah I Is Alright.

UNCUT SHEET OF COMIC JOKES

PIONEER DAYS OF EARLY AMERICA

There are 16 cards in this set. Individual cards measure 2 3/8" X 3 1/4". Cards with text backs (with or without black star and premium offer) are numbered B1-B16 on front and 100-115 on back. Cards with playing card designs or drawings on the back and and blank-backed cards are numbered B1-B16 on the front only. Once again, the cards are crudely drawn and colored and the text is sparse. Cards have been found with lines printed upside down on the back and with the title as "Animals of Early America." These do not have any extra value. The reference number is R159-3.

No. 109

This is one of a series of "Pioneer Days" of Early America

IN DANGER

The Pioneer traveled over rocky regions with a watchful eye. Here it was that they were almost sure of an Indian attack.

A "UNIVERSAL" PRODUCT

ITEM	EX	AVE
Card	4.00	.85
Set	75.00	15.00

B1 The Pioneer Often Met with Wolves
B2 The End of the Day
B3 A Pioneer Attacked by a Snake
B4 Taming Wild Horses
B5 An Indian Attack May Happen Any Time
B6 The Rocks Were Alive with Indians
B7 Hunting for Gold
B8 Hunting Buffalo
B9 Black Bear, a Bad Indian Chief
B10 Will They Get Through This Prairie Fire Alive?
B11 Indian Sets Cabin Afire with Burning Arrows
B12 A Prowling Bear at Night
B13 The Stampede
B14 Looking for Pioneers
B15 Getting Rid of a Bad Indian
B16 The Stage Coach Driver Sights Indians

UNCUT SHEET OF "PIONEER DAYS OF EARLY AMERICA"

WESTERN TRAIL

There are 16 cards in this set. Individual cards measure 2 3/8" X 2 5/8". The last of the four Universal sets of the 1930's, "Western Trail" cards are not numbered on the fronts as are the preceding series. Two types have been found : (1) with card numbers printed on the reverse (116-131), and (2) blank-backed. The card illustrated in our display bears the black star and premium offer which Universal printed on two different cards in each of its sets. To be consistent with our other Universal checklists, we have simply listed the cards alphabetically rather than by back numbers. The reference number is R159-4.

ITEM	EX	AVE
Card	4.00	.85
Set	75.00	15.00

Around the Campfire
Bronco Busting
Death Valley
Fighting the Indians
Fugitive from Law
Mexican Bandit
Pony Express Rider
Stage Coach
Stage Hold-up
The Lariat
The Pioneer Woman
The Rodeo
The Rough-riders
The Sheriff
Whooping It Up
Winning the West

U.S. NAVY WARSHIPS (8)

1 7/8" X 3"

The "U.S. Navy Warships" set of eight candy box cards was produced by the Novel Package Corporation. Because each card was cut from a box, uneven borders are common, and this should be taken into consideration when grading. The pictures are simple drawings done in three primary colors, and each ship is named in a caption below (length and displacement also given). The cards are numbered 1-8 on the front; backs are blank. Although the series is less attractive than many other 1930's series, it is a challenge to complete. The reference number is R98.

ITEM	EX	AVE
Card	10.00	3.00
Set	110.00	30.00

1 Submarine Chaser U.S.S. PC 250
2 Motor Torpedo Boat U.S.S. PT 12
3 Light Cruiser U.S.S. Brooklyn
4 Aircraft Carrier U.S.S. Ranger
5 Battleship U.S.S. Colorado
6 Coast Guard Cutter U.S.C.G.C. Comanche
7 Destroyer U.S.S. Gleaves
8 Submarine U.S.S. Tambor

U.S. WAR PLANES (8)

1 7/8" X 3"

The layout, coloration and number of cards in this set of "U.S. War Planes" is so similar to the preceding set of "U.S. Navy Warships" that it has to be another candy box set produced by Novel Package Corporation. There are, however, two design aspects which make it far more popular than the warship cards. First, one side border of each card has a panel containing four large stars. Secondly, the airplanes seem to be drawings, but they are actually blue-toned reproductions of real photographs. They are dynamically positioned on each card, and there is more discernible detail to each aircraft. Each war plane is identified in two lines of print which is located below the angle formed by the nose of the aircraft and one wing. The card number is printed in the angle between the forefront wing and the tail. The backs are blank and there are no company marks or identification. The reference number is R167.

1 SB2C-1 Curtis Dive Bomber
2 B-17 Boeing's Famous Flying Fortress
3 P-38 Lockheed Army Fighter
4 F4F-3 Grumman Fighter
5 A-17A Northrop Attack Bomber
6 P-43 Republic Stub-winged Fighter
7 PB2Y-2 Consolidated Patrol Bomber
8 A-20A Douglas Light Bomber

ITEM	EX	AVE
Card	12.00	4.00
Set	130.00	40.00

"VICTORY" CARDS (12)

1 7/8" X 3"

A set which for years was listed in the card catalogs as "Victory Gum," it seems more likely that these cards were cut from candy boxes, because the style is similar to several other candy-box card series presented in this

book. There are 12 cards in the set, each showing a serviceman of a specific rank positioned inside a large "V" (for Victory). The three dots and a dash beneath the large V stand for "V" in Morse code and are printed on every

1
2 United States General
3 United States Corporal
4 United States Midshipman
5 United States Colonel
6 United States Sailor
7 United States West Point Cadet
8 United States Buck Private
9
10 United States Navy Captain
11 United States Sergeant
12 United States Marine

card. The word "VICTORY," the large V and the dots and dash are all red; the rest of the card is yellow except for the multi-color serviceman and two small strips of blue at the top and bottom margins. Card No. 1 is missing from the Burdick Collection, and also appears on the want lists of several veteran collectors. A complete box has yet to be found. The reference number is R160.

ITEM	EX	AVE
Cards		
No. 1	35.00	10.00
2-12	15.00	5.00
Set	250.00	75.00

WALT DISNEY COMICS (32)

2 1/4" X 2 5/8"

There are 32 cards in this series of "Walt Disney Comics;" each depicts a Disney character playing a specific sport. The cards are blank-backed and were issued in strips, probably as a prize for the purchase of penny candy. The only printed ma-

terial on the card, besides the caption which appears in a red bottom border, is a credit line which reads "Walt Disney Productions." The manufacturer has yet to be identified, and the series is one of the most common strip card sets. The reference num-

ber is R161. NOTE: cards intact in strips are valued at 50% more than their single counterparts.

ITEM	EX	AVE
Card	5.00	1.50
Set	190.00	55.00

1 Dumbo Plays Push Ball
2 Goofy Hits a Homer
3 Panchito, the Bull Fighter
4 Panchito Plays Basketball
5 Minnie Mouse Plays Tennis
6 Watch It! Joe Carioca Pitching
7 Joe Carioca Tries for High Score
8 "It's a Cinch," Says Joe Carioca
9 Pluto Catches the Ball
10 Pluto Goes a Hunting
11 Panchito on the Surf Board
12 Donald Duck Bowling
13 Goofy Makes a Hole in One
14 Donald Duck Rides a Bike
15 Pluto Tries to Skate
16 Pluto Wins by a Nose
17 Donald Duck Takes a Dive
18 Minnie Mouse Enjoys her Skis
19 Goofy Does Some Fishing
20 Mickey Mouse Takes a Fall
21 Dumbo Runs a Race
22 Dumbo Plays Acrobatics
23 Dumbo Makes a Landing
24 Minnie Mouse Plays Shuffleboard
25 Mickey Mouse, King of the Sand Lot
26 Mickey Mouse, the Football Player
27 Mickey Mouse, the Champ
28 Panchito Rowing a Boat
29 Minnie Takes a Trip
30 Goofy Goes Swimming
31 Donald Duck Yachting
32 Joe Carioca Plays Polo

WALT DISNEY PICTURES (25)

5 1/8" X 7 3/16"

We have presented here — for the first time in any price guide — a picture of an Overland Candy "Walt Disney Picture." The pictures are printed on paper, have blank backs, and are approximately 5" X 7" in size. The title of each picture is printed in the bottom margin at left; a copyright line for W.D.P. (plus "Litho U.S.A.") is printed at bottom-right. Although there are 25 different Walt

Disney Pictures in the Burdick Collection, not one collector has reported having one to date. This oddity suggests that Burdick might have obtained a complete set by writing directly to the manufacturer. The Overland Candy name does not appear on any of the pictures. In his early catalogs, Burdick also reported that the pictures came in two distinct shades of color. Until some of these

multi-color artwork drawings actually find their way into the marketplace, their true value and attractiveness to collectors will never be measured. For the time being, it is safe to say that veteran "type" and Disney collectors would not hesitate to pay at least $ 50.00 for a single picture. The reference number is R162.

"Victory's Reward!" Walt Disney's "BRAVE LITTLE TAILOR."

© W. D. P. Litho U. S. A.

WAR GUM (132)

2 1/2" X 3 1/8"

"War Gum" was the last great bubble gum card series to be issued in the United States before the war effort cut off all supplies of essential materials. Produced by Gum, Inc.'s marvelous tandem, J. Warren Bowman and George Moll, the 132-card series began distribution in 1941 and continued well into 1942. This allowed the Gum, Inc. art and writing teams to cover many of the current events of the war, to report the actions of the first American heroes, and to spotlight many Allies leaders as well. Compared to "Horrors of War," the artwork and write-ups of War Gum are far less graphic and concentrate not on enemy atrocities but on the bravery of Allied servicemen and leaders. The cards are captioned both front and back (some of the titles differ slightly, mostly in the use of abbreviations) and are numbered on the back only. Collector Chris McCann reports that the artwork of 24 War Gum cards was used in the "America's Army" and the

"America's Navy" books produced by Rand McNally in 1942. The reference number is R164.

Another outstanding feature of the War Gum series is the five different wrappers in which the cards were packed. Four of these wrappers are actual miniature maps of war zones, showing Pearl Harbor, the Philippines, French Indo-China and Malaya, and Wake Island. The map wrappers all share the same color format: the land masses are white, the water is blue, and the word "War" is orange with thin blue outlines around the letters and jagged edges. The fifth wrapper comes with either a green or orange background and has a center design of a soldier rushing forward in a bayonet charge. Veteran collectors assume that the soldier wrappers were used for the so-called "second series" (85-132). The display box for War Gum has yet to be confirmed in any collection.

ITEM	EX	AVE
Cards		
No. 1	25.00	10.00
2-84	8.00	2.00
except:		
No. 11	20.00	6.00
No. 15	15.00	4.00
85-132	12.00	3.00
Set	1600.00	400.00
Wrappers		
Pearl		
Harbor	400.00	—
Wake		
Island	500.00	—
Philippines	500.00	—
Indo-China/		
Malaya	600.00	—
Soldier		
green	600.00	—
orange	750.00	—

Army Bombers Blast Japs, Off Aleutians

82. Army Bombers Blast Japs, Off Aleutians

Taking advantage of thick fogs and bad weather during the early part of June, 1942, a main Japanese task force of warships was able to approach the Aleutian Islands off the cost of Alaska. They were met by U. S. Army and Navy bombers as they attempted to set up land bases on the islands of Attu and Kiska. On June 15, it was reported that a flight of Martin B-26 Bombers had sunk one cruiser and scored direct torpedo hits on an aircraft carrier, despite bad weather. Later it was announced that at least three Jap cruisers, one destroyer, one gunboat, and one transport had been damaged. It was believed at this time that the U. S. Army's powerful medium bombers had been equipped to carry and launch torpedoes, thus greatly strengthening the hitting power of land-based planes. Good weather was expected to doom the Japs.

This is one of a series of educational cards which came wrapped in packages of War Gum. Save to complete your collection.
Copyright 1942, GUM, INC., Phila., Pa.   Printed in U. S. A.
Buy War Bonds and Stamps for VICTORY

Torpedo Boats Attack Jap Bombers

41.   Torpedo Boats Attack Jap Bombers

During General MacArthur's "birthday celebration," January 26-27, 1942, two United States motor torpedo boats, while on the open sea in a position vulnerable to attack by planes, spotted two waves of Japanese bombers approaching. Instead of fleeing for cover, the skippers of these two tiny crafts bravely placed their boats in direct line of flight and opened fire with their 50-calibre anti-aircraft guns! Their aim was good and they hit three enemy planes, bringing them down in flames. The officers and men of these two "mosquito boats" were cited by General MacArthur for bravery in action. Their action followed closely upon earlier reports of similar daring feats in Subic Bay when two U. S. torpedo boats attacked and sunk two large Japanese ships.

This is one of a series of educational cards which came wrapped in packages of War Gum. Save to complete your collection.
Copyright 1941, GUM, INC., Phila., Pa.   Printed in U. S. A.
Buy U. S. Defense Savings Bonds or Stamps.

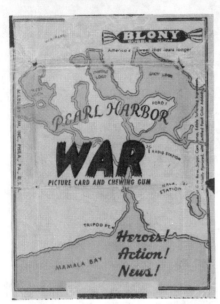

1ST SERIES WAR GUM WRAPPERS
ADVERTISE "BLONY" GUM AND
DEPICT WAR ZONES. 2ND SERIES
WRAPPERS SHOW A CHARGING
INFANTRYMAN

War Gum

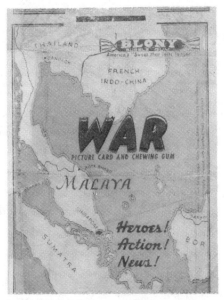

1 Franklin Delano Roosevelt
2 First American Shot Fired
3 Admiral Harold R. Stark
4 Dying Captain Carries On
5 Admiral Ernest Joseph King
6 U.S. Destroyer Sinks Enemy Sub
7 Cordell Hull
8 U.S. Sailor Mans Five-Inch Gun Alone
9 Admiral Thomas Charles Hart
10 Defense of Wake Island
11 General Douglas A. MacArthur
12 Rear Guard Holds Japs At Bay
13 Captain Colin P. Kelly, Jr.
14 Filipinos Destroy 154 Jap Boat
15 Winston Churchill
16 U.S. Flier Strafes Jap Airdrome
17 The Chiangs
18 Observer Spots Jap Battleship
19 General George Marshall
20 Filipinos Attack 54 Jap Planes
21 General Sir Archibald P. Wavell
22 Dutch Sea-Air Offensive
23 Luzon's "Sergeant York"
24 Luzon Repels New Year's Push
25 Luzon's Star Anti-Aircraft Unit
26 Malayans Check Jap Landing
27 "Heron" Fights Off Jap Planes
28 Trapping Jap Suicide Bicyclists
29 Three U.S. Pilots Faces 108 Japs
30 Commandoes "Bag" a Jap General
31 Heroic Dutch Stand at Tarakan
32 Major General H.G. Bennett
33 Sub Sinks 17,000-Ton Jap Liner
34 U.S. Torpedo Boat Attacks Jap Ship
35 Major Trapnell Wins a D.S.C.
36 MacArthur's Men Beat Off Japs
37 Japs Kill U.S. Hero Bailing Out
38 Filipino Guerrillas Raid Airdome
39 Battle of Macassar Strait
40 Survives Mine-blasted Sub
41 Torpedo Boats Attack Jap Bombers
42 U.S. "Tigers" Blast Jap Column

43 2nd Lieut. A.R. Nininger, Jr.
44 Midway Island Defies the Japs
45 Guns Blast Corregidor Invasion
46 Admiral Chester W. Nimitz
47 Mixed Battalion Smashes Japs
48 Singapore's Last Hours
49 Corregidor Speaks!
50 Ex-Football Star is Death to Japs
51 Dutch Kill Sky Troops at Sumatra
52 Filipino Wins Congressional Medal
53 Tank-Riding Igorots Wipe Out Japs
54 Third Congressional Medal Winner
55 "Ace" Lieutenant Edward H. O'Hare
56 Moro Tribesmen Slaughter Invaders
57 Dutch Hero Destroys Tanks and Self
58 MacArthur's Planes Sink Jap Ships
59 Allied Planes Raid Jap Island
60 Bombers Attack Japs in New Guinea
61 Fliers Sail 1000 Miles on Life Raft
62 MacArthur Starts Dash to Australia
63 Cruiser's Light Saves 116 Men
64 Mountbatten of the Commandos
65 Commando Raid on St. Nazaire
66 Spectacular 4000-Mile Raid on Philippines
67 Tokyo Bombed!
68 Boyd Wagner, the Jap-Killer
69 British Seize Madagascar
70 The Great Coral Sea Victory
71 Doolittle Receives Congressional Medal
72 Daring Sub Saves Corregidor's Gold
73 Hangman Heydrich Assassinated

74 Cologne Devastated by 1250 R.A.F. Warplanes
75 British Capture Rommel's Chief Aide
76 Brigadier General Chennault of the Tigers
77 Ukrainian Guerillas Blast Troop Train
78 The Battle of Midway
79 Ensign Views Midway Battle from Sea
80 MacArthur's Filipino Aid-de-Camp
81 Plane Drops Flag on Unknown Soldier's Tomb
82 Army Bombers Blast Japs, Off Aleutians
83 U.S. "Liberators" Sink Italian Cruiser
84 Stalking the Axis Submarine Raiders
85 Russian Girl Sniper Wins Coveted Medal
86 U.S. Sub Sinks Jap Ship at Launching
87 Ship Gunner Braves Torpedoes at Sinking
88 American Aces Smash Jap Airdrome in Canton
89 Yank Flier's Bombs Wreck Nazi Supply Trains
90 R.A.F. Scourges Hamburg
91 American Marines Attack Solomon Islands
92 Navy Task Force Cripples Japs in Aleutians
93 Makin Island Raid
94 Eaker Leads First All-American Bombing
95 Dieppe Raided by Commandos
96 Biggest Air Victory
97 General Charles De Gaulle
98 Wing Commander Douglas R. Bader, Legless Pilot
99 Emperor Haile Selassie
100 King George VI and Queen Elizabeth

101 Miss Lee Ya-Chiang, China's First Girl Pilot
102 Marshall Semion Budenny
103 Sergeant Pilot Gareth L. Nowell, British Ace
104 Victor Talalikhin, Russian Air Hero
105 Eve Curie, De Gaullist Worker
106 Raymond Collishaw, Britain's Greatest Aviator
107 Lieutenant General Jan Christian Smuts
108 King George II of Greece
109 "Human Bombs" Blow Up Tanks
110 Commandos Raid Tobruch
111 U.S. Bombers Attack Subs in Aleutians
112 Cutter Rams Big Italian Submarine
113 Blasting Japs on Burma Road
114 Dive-Bombers Sink Returning Japs
115 Flying Boat Captures Sub Crew
116 Captain George "Ed" Kiser
117 Willkie Visits World Battlefronts
118 MacArthur Honors Fighter Hero
119 Melnik, the Cossack
120 Marine Peppers Attackers of Hero
121 Yank High-Altitude Bombers
122 Brave Children of Malta
123 Lieutenant Paine Saves "Phyllis"
124 Alaskan "Flying Tigers"
125 Bombers Fire Lille Factories
126 Marshal Semion Timoshenko
127 Youngest Soviet Soldier
128 MT Boats Assail Jap Warships
129 Negro Swimmer Tows Survivors
130 "Marauder" Blast Jap Destroyers
131 Australia's General Rowell
132 Heroic Defense of Stalingrad

189

It almost seems that the art department at Gum, Inc. went crazy in producing the War News Pictures series since there are so many style and color variations in the set. There are seven distinct groups of cards: 1-48, 49-72, 73-84, 85-96, 97-108, 109-120, and 121-144; and the first 120 cards bear a tiny subseries code number in the bottom-right corner on the reverse. The specific details of each subseries are listed below the illustrations in the checklist. Fortunately, the words "War News" are somewhere on every card, the one common detail which makes cards of this series easy to identify.

Gum, Inc. began distributing War News Pictures in 1939 and continued into 1940. The initial wrapper was semi-clear wax with the word "WAR" set on a red center, and the advertising copy on it tried to tie in War News Pictures with the fabulously successful "Horrors of War" series which preceded it: "START IMMEDIATELY TO SAVE THIS COMPLETE SERIES. Complete sets of the first 240 Horrors of War cards, published in 1938, are now very valuable. Don't miss the opportunity to get all

of this new series of picture cards." If that was not enough, another advertising panel on the wrapper described the current set as "news pictures and illustrations of the current HORRORS OF WAR in Europe." This wrapper bears a 1939 copyright date.

The second wrapper associated with the set carries a 1940 copyright date and has a white and black newspaper design set on a yellow center. By that time, the public had already come to the conclusion that War News Pictures couldn't match Horrors of War in style and quality, so the attempt to link the two sets by advertising propaganda was abandoned in favor of passing off the cards as "valuable classroom material." J. Warren Bowman, the owner of Gum, Inc., was a man always in search of a promotional gimmick: convincing teachers to allow bubble gum cards in the schoolhouse was the kind of challenge he enjoyed!

Three additional elements of this set are fascinating to collectors. First, the subseries numbered 49-72 carries the identical color artwork of 24

cards of Gum, Inc.'s "The World In Arms" set, which was also issued in 1939. This is the only run of full color cards in War News Pictures, and only Bowman would dare to make two sets out of one! Secondly, advertising on the last run of War News Pictures cards (121-144) suggests that more cards above No. 144 were planned — but none were ever released to the public. Finally, the set contains 12 of the rarest of all 1930's cards: numbers 109-120. Over the years, collectors have constructed several theories to account for the scarcity of these cards, but no reliable information about them has been confirmed. Very few complete sets of War News Pictures are known to exist because these 12 cards are simply not available. The reference number is R165.

ITEM	EX	AVE
Cards		
1-48	10.00	2.50
49-108	8.00	2.00
109-120	150.00	35.00
121-144	20.00	5.00
Set	4400.00	1000.00
Wrappers		
1939	500.00	––
1940	750.00	––

"GAS RAID RESCUE SQUAD" WAS ONE OF 24 CARDS WHICH APPEARED, WITH DIFFERENT BACKS, IN BOTH WAR NEWS PICTURES AND "THE WORLD IN ARMS

1-48: Black and white photos and black and gray drawings; white borders; 1939 copyright; B-1-14 code.

49-72: Multi-color artwork, same pictures (but different on text) as "The World In Arms"; white borders; 1939 copyright; C-49-72 code.

73-84: Green and orange tones with orange borders; 1939 copyright; D-73-84 code.

74 British Bomb German Ships at Wilhelmshaven

On September 4, 1939, planes of the British Royal Air Force were reported to have flown over the Germans second largest naval base, at Wilhelmshaven, dropping a load of bombs on the fleet harbored there. The attack occurred at 6 p.m. in the rain. The crew of the pocket battleship shown was hanging out wash and helping load supplies at the time. According to the British account one bomb fell amidships, with serious damage. Germany declared that no damage was done, that five of the twelve British planes participating in the raid were shot down.

WAR NEWS PICTURES

Keep a permanent record of the current war in Europe. Don't miss any of these important historical pictures. Copyright 1939, GUM, INC., Phila., Pa. Printed in U.S.A.
D-73-84

73 British Flying Boats Rescue Crew of Steamer
74 British Bomb German Ships at Wilhelmshaven
75 Air Raid Sirens Send Parisians to Cellars
76 Destroyer Sinks Strangely Disguised U-Boat
77 Nazi Machine Gunners Slay Polish Cavalry
78 British Troops are Welcomed in France
79 Polish "Franctreur" Fires into Germans
80 French Use Pigs to Touch Off Mines
81 Plane Bombs U-Boat After Freighter Is Sunk
82 Aircraft Carrier "Courageous" Torpedoed
83 Russia's Red Army Moves into Poland
84 Warsaw's Last Stand

85-96: Blue and orange tones with white borders; 1939 copyright; E-85-96 code.

88 Polish Soldiers and Refugees Leave Warsaw

The exodus from the Polish capital began on September 29, 1939, for 120,000 officers and men who had laid down their arms at Warsaw. At Modlin also, 1200 officers and 30,000 men and wounded soldiers surrendered, bringing the total of Germany's prisoners to over 600,000! Meanwhile German units were occupying key points in Warsaw to prevent any sabotage by the civil population remaining, and to supervise movements of prisoners and refugees. Long processions of Polish infantrymen and cavalrymen with their supplies and carts moved slowly through villages en route to internment camps.

WAR NEWS PICTURES

Keep a permanent record of the current war in Europe. Don't miss any of these important historical pictures. Copyright 1939, GUM, INC., Phila., Pa. Printed in U.S.A.
E-85-96

85 Nazis Use Parachute—Jumpers as Spies
86 French Flyers Raid Nazi Airplane Plants
87 Poles Capture Tanks with Flaming Hand Grenades
88 Polish Soldiers and Refugees Leave Warsaw
89 Sub Crew Saved After Ocean-Bed Vigil
90 Hela Peninsula Finally Surrenders
91 U-Boat Lands Shipwrecked Crew in Ireland
92 Largest Submarine Captures Nazi Merchant Ship
93 British Flyers Down Nazis in Dog Fight at Sea
94 British Destroyer Fights Off Nazi Planes
95 Nazi U-Boat Torpedoes "Royal Oak" at Anchor
96 Nazi Bombers Raid Scotland

97-108: Black and orange tones with white borders; 1939 copyright; F-97-108 code.

107 Peasants Quit Dynamited Bridge Area

Another six-mile strip along the Rhine frontier from Strasbourg south to a point below the Swiss frontier was reported being deserted by French peasants on October 25, 1939. Some military observers associated their withdrawal with the recent destruction of three Rhine railroad bridges and the Kembs dam four bridge by the French, taken as an indication that the French command was preparing for a German attack across the river. Farmers have continued to work in the fields within the first six mile zone ordered cleared of civilians, but the last orders provided that all persons should leave. When the move is completed the area abandoned will extend 12 miles back from the Rhine.

WAR NEWS PICTURES

Keep a permanent record of the current war in Europe. Don't miss any of these important historical pictures. Copyright 1939, GUM, INC., Phila., Pa. Printed in U.S.A.
F-97-108

97 Terror in the Carpathians
98 German Cannonade Rocks Neutral Country
99 Ghost Plane Lands "with the Goods"
100 French "Suicide" Squads Hold Outposts
101 Russians Dump Propaganda in Poland
102 War on Land Is Bogged Down by Rain
103 British Freighter Fights Submarine
104 Nazi Bombers Attack Merchant Convoy
105 "City of Flint" is Seized by Nazi Raider
106 Sub Taxis Streamer's Crew to Rescue Ship
107 Peasants Quit Dynamited Bridge Area
108 Warsaw's Sorrow

109-120: Blue and orange tones with white borders; 1939 copyright; G-109-120 code.

112 Downed Nazi Flyers Use Rubber Boat to Escape

Coastal raids along Northeastern England's seaboard by German flyers in October, 1939, led to increased vigilance on the part of British airmen, resulting in Nazi casualties. In two raids, on October 17 and 22, the crews of downed planes were reported to have escaped in collapsible rubber boats. In one raid, when two German planes were sent hurtling to the sea, the crew of one was rescued by a British warship who believed that those in the second were dead. Two of the crew of four had been killed and a third was wounded in the leg. His companion was able to launch a collapsible rubber dinghy and get the wounded man into it before his bomber sank.

WAR NEWS PICTURES

Keep a permanent record of the current war in Europe. Don't miss any of these important historical pictures. Copyright 1939, GUM, INC., Phila., Pa. Printed in U.S.A.
G-109-120

109 "Independence Hall" Rescues Sub-Marine Victims
110 Undersea Horrors
111 Freighter Disables U-Boat for Warship to Capture
112 Downed Nazi Flyers Use Rubber Boat to Escape
113 Nazi Robot Pamphleteer
114 Cruiser Lands Captured Germans in Scotland
115 British Divers Take Dead Nazis from U-Boat
116 Mortars Scatter Nazis Digging Earth Works
117 Nazi U-Boat Sinks English Fishermen
118 Germans Attack French Frontier Village
119 "City of Flint" Sails Under Norwegian Escort
120 France Mobilized Pigeons at Front

121-144: Blue and orange tones with white borders; 1940 copyright; no code number; F-L-A-S-H at top center on back.

No. 142 | **F-L-A-S-H** | WAR NEWS

RUSSIANS FREEZE AT POSTS

Petsamo region January 1, 1940. Numerous Russian soldiers on that front are reported being found frozen to death at their posts. Night temperatures of 40 degrees below zero are the rule! Unused to such severe weather and dressed in partly cotton coats the Red troops consider the elements their worst enemy. Three-fourths of their losses are said to be due to cold and exposure. The picture shows a frozen detachment of Russian infantry at the mercy of a pack of wolves.

WATCH FOR NEW WAR PICTURES. KEEP A COMPLETE RECORD OF THE SECOND WORLD WAR.

Copyright 1940, GUM, INC., Phila., Pa. Printed in U.S.A.

121 Nazis Use Pocket Subs	129 Mine Blasts Indian Liner	137 Crew Scuttles Columbus
122 U-Boat Shells Mercy Ship	130 Scheer Sinks Tanker	138 Reds Make Costly Gains
123 Swimmer Captures Mine	131 Nazi Flies to London	139 Reds Shot Crossing Ice
124 French Win Big Air Fight	132 S.S. Pilsudski Is Sunk	140 Skiers Prey on Russians
125 Nazi River Patrol Is Hit	133 Reds Attack Finns by Air	141 Division Trapped on Ice
126 Dutch Flood Defense Line	134 British Defeat Graf Spee	142 Russians Freeze at Posts
127 Torpedo Cuts Ship in Two	135 Finns Lick Reds at River	143 Turku Castle Is Bombed
128 Bomb Rocks Hitler Hall	136 Graf Spee Goes to Doom	144 Ski Patrol Derails Train

WARRIORS OF THE WORLD (24) 2 1/2" X 2 7/8"

Warriors of the World, a series of 24 cards with die-cut, fold-down tops, was marketed by Bradas & Gheens of Louisville, Kentucky. Each card has a simple multi-color drawing of a soldier and the flag of his country. The middle of the card and the soldier design were scored by machine at the factory to allow the top to be pulled back as a stand. In this manner, the card became a toy or a shelf display item as the owner desired. The set title, card number, and text all appear on the front as the cards are blank-backed. There are 24 cards in the series, and the reference number is R170. Both the "excellent" and "average" prices listed below refer to intact cards; cards without tops are valued at only 20% of the listed price.

1 United States	13 Hungarian
2	14 Belgium
3 British	15
4 French	16 Switzerland
5 Italian	17 British East Indian
6 Russian	18 German
7 Chinese	19
8	20 Bulgarian
9	21 Norweigan
10 Roumanian	22 Persian
11 Swedish	23 Turkish
12 Austrian	24 Royal Highlanders

ITEM	EX	AVE
Card	15.00	3.00
Set	475.00	95.00

WAR SCENES (48) 2 1/4" X 2 11/16"

The most interesting aspect of the strip card set entitled "War Scenes" is that it has three back varieties. Type 1 backs are printed in blue ink and have the manufacturer's name (MP & Co.) and a "Made in U.S.A." line at bottom. The other two back styles are devoid of company name or origin lines and differ only in color of ink: lavender or black. All cards numbers have been found in each reverse-side ink color. The front artwork is the low grade, fast-production type characteristic of most strip card sets. The cards are numbered on the back only, and titles may vary slightly between front and back. The reference number is R168. NOTE: cards intact in strips are worth 35% above single prices.

ITEM	EX	AVE
Card	3.25	.75
Set	175.00	42.50

101 Martin Medium Bomber B-26	116 Gen. MacArthur in Australia	129 New Type Destroyers on Patrol	139 Trolley Carting Bombs to Planes
102 Curtiss Dive Bomber SB2C-1	117 Russian Cavalry	130 U.S.S. Saratoga and Bombers	140 Brig. Gen. James A. Doolittle,
103 Consolidated Heavy Bomber B-24	118 U.S. Infantry in Iceland	131 U.S. Tank Force Supported by Infantry	U.S.A,
104 Douglas Light Bomber A-20A	119 Churchill Decorating Commandos	132 Admiral Ernest J. King, U.S.N.	141 American Tanks in China
105 Boeing Flying Fortress B-17	120 U.S. Field Artillery in Bataan	133 Task Force Attacking at Talugi Harbor	142 U.S. "Tiger" Squadron in Action
106 Republic P-43	121 German Bomber Downed	134 Seaplane Catapulted from Cruiser	143 Torpedo and Dive Bombers at Midway
107 Grumman Fighter F4F-3	122 U-Boat Sunk by Plane	135 Naval Base at Pearl Harbor 1942	144 Tank Carrying Planes of the Near Future
108 Consolidated Patrol Bomber PB2Y-2	123 Before the Firing Squad	136 Ship Communication at Sea	145 Aira Cobra on Alert in Ireland
109 Russian Heavy Tanks in Action	124 Czech Riots	137 U.S. Mosquito Boat in Australia	146 Airborne Troops in Action
110 R-A-F Over France	125 Destroyers Attacking at Midway Island	138 Plane Check Up Before Take Off	147 Sinking Jap Carrier at Midway
111 Bombing an Italian Carrier	126 U.S.S. North Carolina Attacking		148 Admiral Nimitz, U.S.N. Pacific Chief
112 Battle in Libya	127 U.S. Submarines in Coral Sea		
113 Ship Building in U.S.A.	128 Heavy Cruiser and Torpedo Boat		
114 Battery at Corregidor			
115 42 St. and Broadway in Alaska			

WAR SERIES (17)

The only information available about this series comes from the early card catalogs which list the manufacturer as Federal Sales. That name, however, is not written on the cards, which are blank-backed and printed on extra thick cardboard. Instructions on the front of each multi-color artwork card advise the owner to detach the top portion and fold back another part of the bottom to make the card free-standing. A card title, but no number, appears on every card, along with the statement "Build your own complete war series." Most War Series cards found in the hobby are intact (unfolded) with detachable parts unpunched, leading us to suspect that they were handouts or mail premiums rather than packaged items. The checklist is considered complete at 17 titles, and the reference number is R163.

ITEM	EX	AVE
Card	35.00	10.00
Set	750.00	215.00

Advancing Through Gas Attack by the Enemy
Air Armada Bombing City
Anti-Aircraft Guns Firing at Bombers
Armored Car on the Move to Reinforce Position
Attack on Enemy with Sub-Machine Gun
Bayonet Squad in Hand to Hand Combat
Dreadnaught Returning Enemy's Fire
Heavy Artillery Preparing for Advance on Enemy
Machine Gunner Firing to Hold Ground Gained
Marines Landing to Take Up Positions
Pilots Bailing Out of Burning Enemy Plane
Plane Leaves for Scouting Duties
Radio Outpost Reporting Enemy's Position
Soldier Carries the Victory Flag
Tank Advancing Under Fire
Tank Officer Speeds to Headquarters for Instruction
Using Hand Grenade to Advance Over the Top

WARSHIPS (60)

According to a bold type line on the back of every card, Cameron Sales created this series of 60 Warships cards directly from official U.S. Navy photographs. The multicolor obverse pictures show a variety of naval vessels painted in unrealistic "sunset" tints; each seems to be sailing dangerously to shore. The type of ship and its name are printed in the large white margin under every picture. The craft are described briefly on the back, and details from several of the texts indicate that this series was released in 1942. The reason for its inclusion in the early card catalogs as a gum or candy set is unknown as it appears to have been marketed in multi-card packets, an unlikely form for stores selling penny candy and gum. The reference number is R169.

ITEM	EX	AVE
Card	5.00	1.00
Set	350.00	70.00

1 Battleship U.S.S. Idaho	17 Destroyer U.S.S. Anderson	29 Destroyer U.S.S. Ludlow	40 Destroyer U.S.S. Blue
2 Destroyer U.S.S. Woolsey	18 Hospital Ship U.S.S. Solace	30 Heavy Cruiser U.S.S. Salt Lake City	41 U.S.S. Destroyer (Prow View)
3 Destroyer Tender U.S.S. Prairie	19 Destroyer U.S.S. Bancroft	31 U.S.S. Destroyer (Transferring Wounded)	42 Aircraft Carrier U.S.S. Wasp
4 Destroyer U.S.S. Downes	20 Heavy Cruiser U.S.S. Tuscaloosa	32 U.S.S. Patrol Craft (Depth Charges Exploding)	43 Store Ship U.S.S. Bridge
5 Battleship U.S.S. Tennessee	21 Battleship U.S.S. Oklahoma	33 Ammunition Ship U.S.S. Nitro	44 Aircraft Carrier U.S.S. Sarotoga
6 Light Cruiser U.S.S. Atlanta	22 Destroyer U.S.S. Winslow	34 Battleship U.S.S. North Carolina	45 Aircraft Carrier U.S.S. Lexington
7 Destroyer U.S.S. Kearney	23 Destroyer U.S.S. Edison	35 Destroyer U.S.S. Buck	46 Destroyer U.S.S. Flusser
8 Heavy Cruiser U.S.S. Louisville	24 Destroyer U.S.S. Benham	36 Auxilliary U.S. S. Bowditch	47 Submarine Tender U.S.S. Fulton
9 Heavy Crusier U.S.S. Chester	25 Minesweeper U.S.S. Hovey	37 Battleship U.S.S. New Mexico	48 Destroyer U.S.S. Hambleton
10 Motor Torpedo Boat	26 Aircraft Carrier U.S.S. Enterprise	38 Aircraft Carrier U.S.S. Yorktown	49 Battleship U.S.S. Arizona
11 Submarine U.S.S. Spearfish	27 Destroyer Tender U.S.S. Dixie	39 Submarine U.S.S. Argonaut	50 Battleship U.S.S. Texas
12 Destroyer Torpedo Lang	28 Heavy Cruiser U.S.S. Minneapolis		51 Yacht Patrol Boat U.S. Navy
13 Destroyer U.S.S. Niblack			52 Aircraft Carrier U.S.S. Crew
14 Destroyer U.S.S. Case			53 Submarine U.S.S. R-19
15 Battleship U.S.S. Colorado			54 Taner U.S.S. SAGA
16 Destroyer U.S.S. Shaw			55 Battleship U.S.S. Arkansas
			56 Mine Laying Submarine U.S.S. Nautilus
			57 Light Cruiser U.S.S. Honolulu
			58 Heavy Cruiser U.S.S. New Orleans
			59 Aircraft Carrier U.S.S. Ranger
			60 Destroyer U.S.S. Worden

WAR TANK

Here is a splendid example of the type of fascinating candy box which several 1930's manufacturers —

IRREGULAR SHAPE

Milkes, Novel Package Corp., Leader Novelty — and in this case, Candyland Co. developed to tempt the children of the period. Entitled "War Tank," this red and blue box was designed to stand up like a toy and had a special top flap which added to the realistic effect. Although this is the only example of a Candyland box we have for illustration, there are probably several other designs which have yet to be identified and brought into the non-sport marketplace. No reference number has been assigned, and the current market value for a candy box card/toy from this era is $35.00 in excellent condition

WHAT'S THIS? (?)

There are two listings for sets entitled "What's This?" in the early card catalogs: in the gum section at R171 and in the miscellaneous section at W640. However, both varieties of cards, R171 and W640, can be found in the gum and candy portion of the Burdick Collection (Metropolitan Museum of Art, NYC), so we will deal with both types in this presentation.

Type 1 "What's This?" cards are blank-backed and are not numbered. They measure 2 1/2" X 3", and the color scheme observed for the six examples known to exist is blue print on white stock.

TWO SIZES

Type 2 cards are slightly larger (2 1/2" X 3 1/2"), and the obverses have black print and artwork on tan stock. The cards are numbered, by hand on the front and in type on the back. While the answer to the question posed by the illustration is answered on the front on type 1 cards, type 2 cards have the answer printed on the reverse side. Type 2 cards also have the following statement on the back in orange print: "This is a contest card. Send four such cards with your drawings also giving your age to: Universal Toy & Novelty Mfg. Co." (NYC). Under this is printed a 1936 copyright credit for Milt Gross and Simon & Schuster. No packaging for either type has been uncovered to date.

ITEM	EX	AVE
Cards		
Type 1 (6K)	15.00	4.00
Type 2 (40K)	15.00	4.00

The cards of the Wild West Series issued by Gum, Inc. are found in two different styles. One variety, known as type 1, is printed on thin cardboard stock, has red (1-24) or blue (26-49) "Picture Puzzle Bubble Gum" panels on front, and has gray backs with a red line overlay which allowed the owner to cut the card into a miniature puzzle. Type 2 cards are printed on heavier stock, have the product name in a white panel on front, have tan stock backs without the puzzle line overprint, and are only found in the 26-49 sequence. Type 1 cards in the 1-24 sequence indicate a series of 24; both type 1 and type 2 cards in the 26-49 run are marked as a series of 49. The missing link, card No. 25, was a special limited edition card which entitled the finder to a prize, and it was released in an extremely limited number by the manufacturer. It is not considered one of the regular cards in the set but is avidly sought after as one of the rarest of all non-sport cards. The wrapper incorporates red, blue and yellow designs on white waxed paper. The reference number is R172. The set was also issued in Canada by O-Pee-Chee with two different French/English language backs (see illustrations below).

ITEM	EX	AVE
Card		
Gray/ puzzle	8.00	2.00
Tan/no puzzle	10.00	2.50
No. 25	750.00	250.00
Set	500.00	120.00
Wrapper	100.00	——

1 Davy Crockett Defending the Alamo
2 Defending a Wagon Train Attack
3 A Wagon Train Attack
4 Attacking One of the First Trains
5 Pony Express Rider
6 Jesse James Holdup
7 Bronco Busting
8 A Prairie Fire
9 A Round-up
10 A Battle with a Grizzly
11 Shooting Up an Indian Village
12 Buffalo Bill Killing a Buffalo
13 Kit Carson Fighting an Indian
14 Custer's Last Stand
15 Indian Captive Dance
16 Cattle Stampede
17 Wild Bill Hickcock Gets His Man
18 Bulldogging a Steer
19 Cowboy Fun
20 Indians Attacking a Stockade
21 Roping Wild Horses
22 Prospecting for Gold
23 The Bullwhacker
24 Arrival of the Post Coach
25 PREMIUM CARD
26 The Medicine Man
27 Rangers Raid Bandits
28 The Sheriff Gets His Man
29 Fighting a Blizzard
30 Celebrating!
31 Night Visitors
32 The Dude Learns
33 Branding a Calf
34 Trading with Indians
35 Captured
36 Homesteaders' Race
37 Lost in the Desert
38 Safe at the Fort
39 A Mountain Ford
40 A Surprise Attack
41 Fighting a Buffalo
42 A Friendly Race
43 When Home Was a Fort
44 Time for Chuck
45 The Horse-thieves
46 The Hold-up
47 A Puma at Bay
48 Saving the Wounded
49 Fighting Off Indians

CARD NO. 25

CANADIAN (O-PEE-CHEE) VERSION OF "WILD WEST" SERIES WAS CALLED "FAR WEST GUM" AND CAME WITH TWO DIFFERENT COLOR BACKS (GRAY & TAN).

WORLD WAR GUM (96)   2 3/8" X 2 7/8"

The 96-card set of Goudey's "World War Gum" consists of black and white photos from World War I surrounded by buff (1-48) or orange (49-96) colored borders. Each picture is captioned front and back, but the card number appears only on the reverse. The text backs are printed in green ink on white stock. Goudey began distributing the series in early 1933, and some collectors believe it might have been the first bubble gum card set the company ever issued. The wrapper has a bright red center with four blue-tone war scenes in the corners. Packs were distributed in 100-count boxes and sold for a penny. Albums to house the set were probably given out by store owners (neither the cards nor the wrapper has any mention of them), and two were needed to hold the complete set. The reference number is R174.

ITEM	EX	AVE
Card	8.00	2.00
Set	950.00	225.00
Wrapper	150.00	——
Box	300.00	75.00
Album	100.00	35.00

65 Dead Soldier
66 German Machine Gun Crew
67 German Flag Review
68 Austrian Machine Gun
69 Italian Big Gun
70 Soldier Shot (Before He Got Out of Trench)
71 Tank Crashing Through
72 The British Attack
73 Bulgarian Soldiers
74 Bringing in German Wounded
75 British Gun in Action
76 Through Barbed Wire
77 Two Minutes "Then Over the Top"
78 A German Captured
79 Advance Under Fire
80 Cavalry and Ruined Church
81 A Retreat
82 Surrender
83 English Soldiers "Over the Top"
84 German Tanks (Land Battleships)
85 American Infantry
86 "Grenade"
87 U.S. Machine Gun
88 Building a Railroad Under Fire
89 A Rest Between Fights
90 "Snipers"
91 Front Line Trench
92 A "Mop-Up" Squad
93 Throwing Grenades
94 "Gas Attack"
95 Infantry Advance
96 French Field Guns Firing

37 Rebuilding a Bridge
38 French First Aid
39 Tuning Tank Motor
40 Camouflaged Artillery
41 Breath of Death
42 American Sniper
43 Sergeant Alvin C. York
44 Long Range Hits
45 Decorated for Bravery
46 Delousing
47 Marines Arriving Home
48 The Heroes Return
49 Going Up to the Front
50 Cavalry Advance
51 Big Gun Crew Working
52 War Tragedy
53 War Disaster
54 Marching with Masks
55 Surprise Attack
56 Thanking Yankee Soldiers
57 Prisoner Camp
58 German Machine Gun Nest
59 Throwing Hand Grenades
60 Up to the Trenches
61 Picking Off the Enemy
62 "Rolling Along"
63 Taps
64 Big Bombardment

1 War Is Declared
2 Recruiting
3 Drawing "Draft" Numbers
4 Arriving at Camp
5 Practice at Camp
6 Ocean Protection
7 Up to the Front
8 To the Front Reinforcements
9 Side Door
10 First Pay Day
11 "Over the Top"
12 A Night Attack
13 Across No Man's Land
14 Kitchen Duty
15 German Drive Begins
16 Indentifying Wounded
17 Daylight Signaling
18 A Tank Attack
19 In the Argonne Forest
20 Under Fire
21 Front Line Trenches
22 "A Cup of Cold Water"
23 Emergency Invention
24 Grenade Attack
25 Resting Between Drives
26 "Calamity Jane"
27 Bringing in Prisoners
28 Medical Corps Work
29 "One Pounder" Trench Gun
30 Doughboys March on
31 Outpost Duty
32 Clemenceau and Pershing
33 One Pound Gun in Action
34 Anti-Aircraft
35 Balloon Observation
36 "Mopping Up"

FRONT COVER OF ALBUM

BACK COVER OF ALBUM

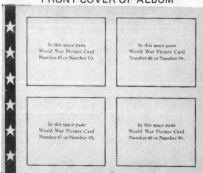

TYPICAL PAGE IN ALBUM

STATISTICAL PAGE OF ALBUM

WORLD WAR II PREMIUMS (20) 5" X 7"

There is absolutely nothing printed on these 5" X 7" tinted premium photos which connects them to a gum company. We have to rely on the early card catalogs to give us clues, and they tell us that the set was issued by Dietz Gum. Even the subject matter is a bit of a mystery because Dietz never marketed a war-related card set and premiums are generally associated with cards. There are 20 pictures in the set, and they are similar in appearance to the Dietz Movie Stars set (R96-2) already covered in this book, except that they are printed on flat-finish paper (the movie stars are glossy). The premiums seem to have been issued in 1939, and each has a small title-and-text box located inside the picture area. Most collectors are either unaware of the set or are unable to identify it; it is mostly in demand by war card and "type" collectors. The reference number is R175.

ITEM	EX	AVE
Premium	20.00	8.00
Set	500.00	175.00

A British Advance
A Badly Battered British Plane Makes For Base
A Dutch Tank Comes to Grief
A French Loud Speaker on the Western Front
A Temporary Barricade
As Nazis Advance Through Belgium
At The West Wall
British Rescue Survivors of H.M.S. Hardy
Coastal Command Planes Aid in Rescue

Doing Their Bit in Wales
Dutch Offer Stiff Resistance
Finis to a Proud German Sea Fighter
First Cruiser Admitted Lost by the British
5 Die as Nazi Bomber Explodes
German Men of Steel in Norway
Germans Replace Destroyed Bridge
HMS Ark Royal Comes to Port
Paris Sets a New Style
Street Barricade in Belgium
Victims Return to Their Bombed Homes

YELLOW KID SCRIP (?) 2 5/16" X 2 13/16"

Pulver's "Yellow Kid Scrip," issued in 1933, was sort of like a lottery for kids. It was issued in a bubble gum style package (red, orange and green), but we will have to take the word of the early catalogers that there was actually gum in the packs. The promotion was simple: scrip in seven different denominations could be purchased and then redeemed for various prizes. Those that we know about are a 100-piece jigsaw puzzle (500 Points), a "League Special" baseball (1200 points), and $1.00 in cash (6000 points). All cards are identical except for the denominations; each bears the advisement at top that "Yellow Kid Scrip Is Valuable," while a line at bottom calls it "Profit Sharing Scrip." The relationship of the "Yellow Kid" chewing gum stick wrappers illustrated below to the cards is not known, but they are an interesting addendum to this set. The reference number is R176.

ITEM	EX	AVE
Scrip		
5 to 25	20.00	7.00
50	30.00	12.00
100	50.00	18.00
Wrappers		
Large	500.00	––
Chewing gum		
each	50.00	––

ADVERTISING POSTER LISTING PRIZE VALUES FOR YELLOW KID SCRIP

"ZOOM" AIRPLANES (175)   2 1/2" X 3 1/8"

The series of airplane cards issued in "Zoom Bubble Gum" ("2 cards...1 cent") have proved confusing to collectors for several reasons. First of all, there are only 75 confirmed titles known in the 1-100 number sequence. This could have been a "Lead-'em-on" type of marketing device or, perhaps, the photos planned for the missing numbers might have been censored. To add to the confusion, all 75 cards of the first series were issued with white as well as colored borders (orange, yellow, green and blue). In contrast, the second series (101-200) has ONLY colored borders — meaning that collectors have to make hard choices about how they are going to assemble a set. The missing titles above No.

100 in our checklist were printed, they are simply unknown to us at this time. Zoom Airplanes were manufactured by Gum Products, Inc. of Cambridge, Mass., and were distributed to the public in 1940 and 1941. The numbers and text for all 175 cards are printed on the front; the backs are blank. The reference number is R177.

There are two wrappers associated with the set. The first has a red, white and blue center with six airplanes "Zooming" in the top panel. It does not have a copyright date printed on it and was probably used for the first series of 75 cards. The second wrapper has a different design in the center, which is orange with green accents. It bears a

copyright date of 1941 and has two different mail offers printed on the top and bottom panels. The top offer is for a 12-page album containing photographs of "72 of the finest and best airplanes in the world" (25 "Zoom" wrappers plus 10 cents). The promotion on the bottom panel offered a choice of any two large (9 1/2" X 12 1/2") airplane pictures, plus a surprise, also for 25 "Zoom" wrappers and 10 cents. Because this second wrapper advertises a "New Series," collectors believe it was used to market the 101-200 sequence of cards. NOTE: we have provided a checklist of the 10 large airplane pictures listed on the 1941 wrapper although we do not have one of these pictures to illustrate.

200

Zoom Airplanes

ITEM	EX	AVE
Cards		
1-100 white	6.00	1.50
1-100 color	8.00	2.00
101-200	10.00	2.50

Set — Price depends on border combinations but figure 25% above sum of single card prices.

Wrappers		
Not dated	150.00	—
Dated 1941	300.00	—
Premium		
Picture	35.00	15.00
Album	150.00	50.00

1 Curtiss P-40
2 Bell XFM-1
3 Lockheed XC-35
4 Douglas TBD-1
5 Grumman F-3F-1
6 Canadian Fairey Battle Bomber
7 not issued?
8 Republic YP-43
9 Northrop A-17A
10 not issued?
11 Bristol Bolingbroke Bomber
12 Vought-Sikorsky OS2U-2
13 not issued?
14 Seversky P-35
15 Consolidated XPB2Y-1
16 Westland Lysander II
17 not issued?
18 Lockheed P-38
19 North American SNJ-2
20 Curtiss A-18
21 not issued?
22 Douglas A-20-A
23 Grumman F4F-3
24 Grumman F2F-1
25 Republic "Guardsman" 2-PA
26 not issued?
27 Douglas Digby B-18A
28 Curtiss XSO3C-1
29 Douglas SBD-1
30 not issued?

31 Curtiss P-36A
32 Avro Anson Trainer
33 not issued?
34 North American BT-9
35 Consolidated XBP2Y-1
36 Curtiss P-36
37 Vultee YA-19
38 not issued?
39 Martin B-26
40 not issued?
41 Cessna AT-8
42 not issued?
43 Vought-Sikorsky SB2U-1
44 North American AT-6A
45 not issued?
46 Stearman N2S-1
47 Consolidated PBY-1
48 Curtiss SBC-4
49 Boeing SB-15
50 Curtiss A-12
51 Curtiss-Wright
52 Lockheed P-38
53 not issued?
54 North American B-25

55 not issued?
56 North American BT-14
57 Ryan S-T
58 British Sunderland
59 Northrop N-3PB
60 Lockheed
61 not issued?
62 Lockheed B-14
63 not issued?
64 Randolph Field
65 Douglas 8A-5
66 Grumman Goose G-21A
67 not issued?
68 Lockheed P-38
69 Bell Airacobra
70 Consolidated XB-24
71 Douglas DB-7A
72 Douglas B-18-A
73 Curtiss Falcon 22
74 not issued?
75 Stearman N3-1
76 Vought-Sikorsky XF4U-1
77 Consolidated Model 32
78 not issued?

79 Stearman PT-13B
80 Boeing Stratoliner
81 not issued?
82 Cessna Crane T-50
83 not issued?
84 Curtiss XSO3C-1
85 Grumman J2F-2
86 Grumman Skyrocket
87 Douglas B-19
88 not issued?
89 Bellanca "Flash"
90 North American Harvard II
91 not issued?
92 Brewster F2A2
93 Bellanca Cargo Aircruiser
94 Curtiss-Wright
95 not issued
96 Consolidated PBY-5
97 not issued?
98 Grumman G-36A
99 Vultee
100 Republic P-35
101 Curtiss SNC-1
102 Curtiss-Wright

Zoom Airplanes

103 Curtiss XSB2C-1
104 Consolidated B-24
105
106 Douglas B-19
107 Ryan Drangonfly
108 Vultee Vanguard 48C
109 Vickers Supermarine Stanraer
110
111 Lockheed Lodestar Model 18
112 Lockheed Model 12
113
114 Fleetwings XBT-12
115
116 North American Yale NA-64
117 Noorduyn Norseman IV
118 Grumman Goblin G23
119
120 Douglas SBD-1
121 British "Sunderland"
122
123 British "Hereford"
124 British "Blenheim"
125 Curtiss SNC-1
126 Bristol-Beaufort
127 Campbell D-96
128 Aeronca
129 Twin Beechcraft
130 Seversky-2XP
131 Abrams
132 Sikorsky S-43
133 Seversky SEV-3M
134
135 Miles Master

136 North American NA66
137 Hammond YA
138
139 Grumman OA-9
140 Duramold Model 46
141 Kinner Playboy
142 Bell "Airaboneta"
143
144 Canadian Norseman
145 Cessna Airmaster
146 Barkley-Grow
147
148 Curtiss SOC-1
149 Curtiss-Wright Condor
150 Doublas 8A-5
151 The Caribou
152
153 Percival Q-6
154 Ryan PT-20
155 Howard
156 Vultee Valiant
157 Consolidated Model 31
158 Boulton Paul Defiant
159
160
161 Hawker Hurricane
162
163
164
165 Douglas DC-5
166 Vought-Sikorsky S-42
167 Beechcraft D17R
168 Martin Clipper

169 Vickers-Armstrong's Nellington
170 Bristol Bombay
171 Hall Aluminum
172
173 Handley Page Hampden
174 Bristol Blenheim
175 Kinner Envoy
176 North American Training Plane
177 Grumman Widgeon
178 Stinson Reliant
179 Curtiss "Hawk"
180 Ryan S-T-M
181 Beechcraft 18
182 Aeronca
183 Argonaut
184 Applegate Amphibian
185 Beechcraft 18A
186 Beechcraft F17D
187 Martin Maryland
188 Short B-3
189 Fleetwing Seabird
190 Fleetwings XBT-12
191 Beechcraft E17B
192 Bell Airacuda
193 Vultee V-12
194 North American NA-25
195 Bellanca "Flash"
196
197 Waco F-7
198 Bellanca Skyrocket
199 Fairchild F-24
200 Bellanca Cruisair

Premiums

Airacobra (Fighter)
Airacuda (Fighter)
Curtiss P-40 (Fighter)
Curtiss SBC-4 (Scout Bomber)
Douglas SBD-1 (Dive Bomber)
Flying Fortress (Bomber)
Gruman F4F3 (Fighter)
Lockheed P-38 (Pursuit)
Martin B-26 (Bomber
Vought-Sikorsky XF4U-1 (Fighter)

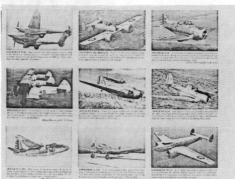

**ZOOM PREMIUM ALBUM CONTAINED PRINTED PHOTOGRAPHS
OF THE AIRPLANE CARDS ISSUED IN THE GUM PACKS**

THE BATTLE OF THE BUBBLE GUM TITANS

By the end of 1945, "The War to End All Wars, Part II" was over and the nations of the world were attempting, in their respective ways, to return to normal lifestyles. War economies, however, create sudden and massive changes in economic infrastructure, and reversing those changes is not a simple matter. The entire process of manufacturing, from securing supplies of raw materials to the re-engineering of physical plants, plus the re-development of vital service industries — all this could not take place overnight. The gum companies, like most other American firms, had to resume operations from scratch.

Only one of the industry giants of the pre-war era survived to become part of the brave new confectionary world: Gum, Incorporated, now renamed Bowman Gum. By 1941, Goudey and National Chicle had already been "stomped" into near-oblivion by Gum, Inc., and the World War finished them off (Goudey did manage to re-issue part of its "Indian Gum" series and dump overstocks of various 1930's cards, including "Sport King" after the war). As for the group of smaller, mainly regional, gum producers that operated in the 1930's, virtually none attempted a comeback. The enigmatic Frank H. Fleer company made the passage from pre- to post-war times in its chosen path of near-anonymity; who could say what their role might be. Clearly, Gum, Inc., now Bowman Gum was on top of the heap, living in a mansion, while the rest of the gum firms were confined to low-income housing. Had Bowman not been so impressed with the view at the top, so self-important, they might have discovered the termite gnawing away at their foundation. In metaphorical terms, that termite was named Topps.

From 1942 to 1945, while Bowman "slept," Topps was producing large quantities of flavored chewing gum in convenient penny packs. This gum was cheap, easy to carry, and, most importantly, "in production" and backed by an aggressive advertising campaign. Topps' promotional coups included coining the patriotic slogan "Don't talk chum, Chew Toops Gum!" and donating thousands of silver-foil "Bazooka Gum" wrappers for the Victory Parade in New York City. Meanwhile, Bowman was obsessed with developing "Warren's Gum," the "finest chewing gum ever produced," a vanity item if there ever was one!

Bowman resumed card production in 1948 with a short series of baseball cards, which was apparently done in black and white due to shortages of color ink. In 1949, the company issued a much larger baseball set, this time with colored backgrounds, and seemed to be regaining its touch in a creative sense. The year 1950 was the best of the post-war Bowman era: not only did the company distribute a gorgeous multi-color artwork baseball series, but the fantastic "Wild West" and "Wild Man" series as well. This wellspring of beautiful cards, both sport and non-sport, continued through 1953, but 1954 and 1955 were years of rapid decline. By 1956, J. Warren Bowman and his firm were bankrupt and suffered the worst, and most appropriate, fate in the "jungle" that is the confectionary trade: bought out by their chief competitor, Topps. The "termite" had become the "terminator."

Give Topps credit for their accomplishments. They started small and built a steady market for their products. When Bowman began issuing cards in 1948, Topps countered with several series of their own in 1949. As the size of Bowman's cards grew, Topps increased the dimensions of their own and actually surpassed Bowman in 1952 with "Giant Size" editions of both sport and non-sport sets. Every strategic move made by Bowman was countered and · overcome by Topps. The coup de grace to the Bowman empire was engineered when Topps began signing baseball players to exclusive contracts for the production of cards. Non-sports cards, the backbone of Bowman's success before World War II, were not enough by themselves to sustain him in the post-war marketplace. Topps recognized that baseball cards had become more important than non-sports cards and acted accordingly. That was the end of the line for Bowman and its brilliant but erratic leader.

Competition brings out the best efforts of rivals, and card collectors have certainly reaped the benefits of the cartophilic fisticuffs between Bowman and Topps. The period 1949-1955 provided card enthusiasts with a number of classic artwork sets, plus many more of lesser quality covering a variety of subjects and themes. After the defeat of Bowman, the lack of competition for Topps resulted in a switch in emphasis from artwork to photography, and the grand artwork traditions of 1930's card crafting, which enjoyed a brief revival in the 1950's, passed from view. Occasionally they resurface, in sets like "Civil War News" and "Mars Attacks," but most modern artwork in card production is satirical, and therefore, less inspiring. Luckily, the cards of this magic time have survived to remind us of the glorious past.

It is ironic that the very first set in our post-war list of non-sport issues is the worst example of "crossover" demand from sports card collectors. The set of 100 cards was issued in 1956 by Gum Products, and it contains a wide variety of subject matter. Unfortunately for non-sport collectors, it also contains many cards of athletes, of which the boxers have received the most attention in recent times. Prices of the latter have escalated far beyond the intrinsic value of the cards themselves as "investment" and "speculation" money continues to flee from traditional baseball cards into cards depicting other sports. In the case of card No. 86, Max Schmeling, propaganda based on an unconfirmed rumor (that the card was pulled from the set by public outcry) has pushed the "mar-

ket price" well beyond reasonable limits. Although this card definitely is less commonly found than other cards in the set, it can be easily found if you care to "pay the price." In other words, the card is more demand scarce than supply scarce, and demand is something that can be — and in this case, has been — manipulated.

For this reason, we are issuing a price advisory for the "Adventure" set. What this means in practical terms is that we will not address the values of the cards in the set which are subject to wild speculation. This would not serve the interests of non-sport collectors, and any price we might suggest would not deter sports card collectors from participating in the speculative trend which is occurring. Suffice it to say that the Adventure set has never been very popular among non-sport collectors. Until recently, the cards were

almost always found in sets or near-sets, and single cards were rarely bought and sold. The color artwork does not compare well with other sets of the period, and the text is far too general (non-sport collectors like specific details and events). We suggest the following values for single cards (non-athletes): $1.50 for "excellent" grade, and 35 cents for "average" condition.

The color drawings are printed on heavy cardboard and have large white borders. The backs contain the card number, card title, and a short text (blue print on gray stock). The display sign illustrated measures 5 3/8" X 6 1/2" and has a single card stapled to it at the top; it probably was packed in the dull-looking display box and was intended to be set up at one end when the box cover was removed [box value = $250.00, insert card value = $60.00]. The companies named on the box — one is American and the other is Canadian — plus the 'Printed in U.S.A." line on the cards and box indicate that the cards were also distributed in Canada. The bubble gum advertised was probably a small-wrapper "nugget" or "stick" because no standard-sized wrapper has been uncovered. The reference number is R749.

Adventure

1 At The End of Rainbow—Gold
2 The Procupine—Attack Proof?
3 Indian Rope Trick—Fake or Fact?
4 Manolete—Bullfighter Supreme
5 "One Day Man Will Fly..."
6 The Space Man of the Future
7 The Greatest Show on Earth
8 Baskets + Rebounds = Points
9 An Army of Ski Enthusiasts
10 Bobsledding—Lake Placid Style
11 Willie Pep—Hartford Wonder
12 The Thousand—Thrill Sport
13 Norkay—Conqueror of Everest
14 Shy, Beautiful and Wild···
15 Ivory Coast Snake Dance
16 Pan American Pacers Pant···
17 Devilfish and Child's Play
18 Over the Bounding Waves
19 A Tourist Paradise
20 Not for Beginners···
21 Red-Stopper in Korea
22 Post-War Battlers···
23 Audie Murphy···Real Life Hero
24 Manning the Honest John···
25 The Navy's Regulus

26 Sunburns and Floor Burns
27 Bottlenosed Dolphin
28 Mobile St. Bernards
29 As American as the Hot Dog
30 Too Close for Comfort
31 Canadian Tommy Burn's
32 Jack Johnson—Jabber
33 Jesse Willard of Kansas
34 Dempsey—Manassa Mauler
35 Gene Tunney, Undefeated Champ
36 The Muskellunge—Fighter
37 No Circus Stunt This···
38 Dirt Track Hot-Rodders
39 One Down—Zeros to Go
40 Mountain-Climbing, Monkey Style
41 Louis, the Brown Bomber
42 Charles-All-Star Athlete
43 Jersey Bouncer—Joe Walcott
44 Brockton Blockbuster···
45 Rainmaking—Scientific Magic
46 Aerial Torpedoes and Shellfire
47 The Stanley Steamer—1906
48 Marquette—Priest, Explorer
49 Skimming Over the Ice

50 Happy Hunting Grounds···
51 Boston's Skyline···
52 Racing, with a Pinch of Salt
53 The Pilot Boat Pet—
54 Not All Pilots Fly—
55 Boston's Golden Greek—
56 Into the Air and Over—
57 Wedding of the Year···1956
58 Leathernecks Courageous···
59 King of the Wild Frontier···
60 The Navy's "Flying Saucer"
61 Flying at 3000-Miles-an-Hour
62 Sitting on Top of the World
63 Hockey's Hardy Perennials
64 The Pintail Flyaway—
65 A Hunter's Dream Come True—
66 British Navy—African Style
67 Ride 'em Cowboy
68 Breaking a Horse—Cowboy Style
69 Shrine of Democracy
70 Snowshoe Thompson—Mailman
71 When a Feller Needs a Friend—
72 A Fisherman's Life is Happy—
73 The Groundhog's Northwest—
74 In the Great Northwest—
75 Famed for their Mimicry

76 The Great John L.—
77 Lightning Fast—Jim Corbett
78 Fitzsimmons—KO Specialist
79 Jeffries—California Grizzly
80 Marvin Hart—Interim Champ
81 Letting Loose on the Boards
82 A Boy's Best Friend
83 The Ageless Sport—
84 Not Flying, Just a-Jumpin'
85 Over Fence for New Record
86 The Black Uhlan of the Rhine
87 Squire of Newton and—
88 Primo Carnera—Giant Killer
89 Max Baer—Actor, Boxer
90 Braddock—Gentleman Boxer
91 Dead Heat—All the Way
92 Bob Mathias, Superman···
93 First to Clear 7-Foot Barrier
94 The Northern Light—
95 Alone with Gulls and Sea
96 Scramble, Men, Scramble
97 Cameramen—Nervy Humans
98 Sea Firefighters—Lifesavers
99 "Rusty Bacon at $10 per Pound —"
100 Conestoga—Pioneer Transport

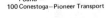

205

ADVENTURES AT THE GIANT BAR RANCH (26)(26)

1 7/8" X 4 5/8"

This title is printed on every card of two different sets produced by the Ziegler Candy Company. The first set tells the adventures of a precocious ranch brat named Zig, who wants to be treated as a full-blown cowboy by the rest of the hands on the Giant Bar Ranch. He eventually "wins his spurs" by thwarting the rustling schemes of "Dangerous Dave and his masked men." The second series of cards tells the improbable story of how Zig was kidnapped by a flying saucer full of gooney looking aliens. He escapes his predicament with the aid of kindly King Barr and Princess Candia, who belong to another friendly, "they-look-like-us" race of off-worlders. Yesterday's fascinating adventures are today's camp!

There are 26 cards in each series, and the artwork cards come in both vertical and horizontal formats. Each has the caption and number printed under the picture. As the cards also served as the candy bar tray inside the package, it is obvious that the candy rested on the blank-backed side. The set total and a "Ziegler Finest Candy" design are printed on each card. The sets belong to reference category R792. No wrappers or other packaging have been found to date.

ITEM	EX	AVE
Cards		
Rustlers	5.00	1.50
Space	5.00	1.50
Sets		
Rustlers	160.00	45.00
Space	160.00	45.00

AIRFLEET CARDS (8?)

1 5/8" X 2 3/16"

"Fly Your Own Fleet" reads the advertising copy on the "Airfleet Bubble Gum" package marketed by the Philadelphia Chewing Gum Co. in 1952. Each gum pack contained a folder and a small aluminum airplane fusilage. The thin cardboard wings and tail pieces were cut from the folder and inserted into the rigid fusilage to make a flying model airplane. A small bluetone photo of the aircraft printed in the upper-right corner of the inside-right page was designed to be cut from the folder as a trading card. The name of the airline, the card number, and the type of airplane and several paragraphs of description print on the reverse side. The wrapper is a cellophane bag; details of a contest promoting air travel are printed on the back. Because eight airlines are credited for providing the "authenic data" for this "great silver fleet," it is assumed that the set is composed of eight cards and corresponding models. The reference number is R788-1.

ITEM	EX	AVE
Folder	6.00	2.00
Card	2.50	.75
Fusilage	4.00	1.00
Wrapper	100.00	—

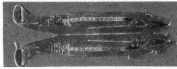

LEFT: RIGID ALUMINUM FUSILAGE

BELOW: OUTSIDE (L) AND INSIDE (R) PAGES OF FOLDER

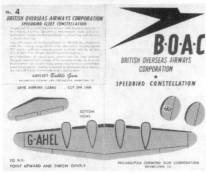
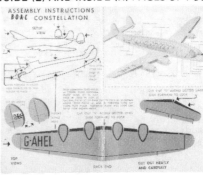

AMAZING TRICKS (28K)   2 3/16" X 3 1/2"

One of the earliest Philadelphia Chewing Gum Co. issues, "Amazing Tricks" was first listed in the February, 1953 edition of the American Card Catalog. The tricks are four-page paper folders which explain the technique involved in performing a specific trick or illusion. The folders are numbered on the front cover, which has a white-print card title on a wide black banner. The "Mystic Gum" wrappers mentioned on the back of every card have not yet been uncovered, in part because they could be sent in to the company to obtain other tricks (25 wrappers and 10 cents). The highest folder found so far is No. 28, and the reference number is R788-2.

ITEM	EX	AVE
Folder	3.50	1.00

AMERICA SALUTES THE FBI (36)   2 1/16" X 2 1/2"

The full title of this Bowman set is "America Salutes The FBI — Heroes of the Law." It consists of 36 pastel color drawings depicting famous cases and arrests, with details and text supplied by "G-Men Detective Magazine." The fronts have white borders, and the card caption is printed in the large border underneath the picture. The caption also appears on the reverse, along with the card number and text. The cards are found with both white and gray backs; blank and transposed backs (containing text from other Bowman sets) have also been found. The latter are no more valuable than normal cards and are collected mostly out of curiosity or as "types." So far, only a one-cent "FBI Bubble Gum" wrapper has been uncovered although some hobby veterans believe a five-cent variety exists. The set was issued in 1949, and the reference number is R701-6.

ITEM	EX	AVE
Card	5.00	1.50
Set	225.00	60.00
Wrapper	95.00	——

1 The Capture Came in the Lobby of a Hotel	13 Hook, Line and Sinker	26 The Four Gasoline Cans
2 A Comparison on a Speeding Train	14 Catching a Big Fish	27 Doctor, Lawyer, Killer
3 Disguised as a Returning Osage Indian	15 Rendezvous at Mitchell Field	28 A Real Crime Search
4 Jap Spies Make a Mistake	16 Madame Kasenkina Wins her Fight	29 Behind the Disguise
5 $2,000,000 of Stolen Securities	17 Tell-Tale Gun Markings	30 With Little More than "7N" of a New York Licence Number Noted
6 Trapping the Confidence Men	18 His Disguised Handwriting Actually Betrayed Swimming Pool Manager	31 Vitale Had One Foot on the Gangplank
7 Scant Feet from a Hamburger Stand	19 The Paroled Convict Problem	32 He Noticed the Tiny Thread on the Tire
8 In a Home Made Elevator	20 "Oscar" Bites the Dust	33 Checking Marine Security
9 The Matchbox Clue	21 The Killer Telephoned	34 The Suicide Was Faked
10 Twice Stopped for Speeding	22 Mary Stole a Car	35 Strapped to His Chest Was a Camera
11 FBI Sharpshooters in Chicago	23 FBI Portable Telephone	36 Exposing the Soviet Atom Plot
12 A Son of the Rising Sun	24 A Trail of Hot Money	
	25 The Man Was a Nazi Spy	

ANIMAL COLORING CARDS (3K)   2 1/2" X 3 3/8"

The illustration shows one "Animal Coloring Card" plus part of the end flap (at left) of a "Crystal Pure Pops" candy box. Despite being listed in the 1981 and 1983 editions of this guide, plus in earlier catalogs, no card except No. 3, Rhinoceros, has ever been reported to the Hobby Card Index. Although it must be considered a scarce issue, it is also a fact that virtually no one except an occasional "type" collector is searching for it; hence, the very low price. The caption and card number are printed in red, and the animal outline is blue — all on a white background. That the set predates 1960 is established by its listing in the 1960 American Card Catalog, but the exact year of issue remains a mystery. The reference number is R751.

ITEM	EX	AVE
Card	5.00	2.00

ANIMALS (24)   1 1/2" X 2 7/8"

The cards of this animal series may not be much to look at, but they are very difficult to find. The mono-color artwork has more detail than you might expect from a card printed on the interior tray of a candy cigarette package. The "name" and species of animal, plus a brief description of its diet and behavior, is printed on the retaining flaps on each side of the tray. A line on the box advises that there are "24 different animals for your scrapbook," and the cards are not numbered. So few have been seen that we do not have enough titles to provide even a partial checklist. The trays on which the animals were printed came inside the boxes of "Famous Candy Cigarettes" produced by the John Mueller Licorice Co. The reference number is R750.

ITEM	EX	AVE
Card	5.00	2.00
Set	135.00	60.00
Complete Box	20.00	8.00

ANIMALS (24)　　　　　　　　　　4 1/4" X 8 1/8"

These unusual diecut animal cards were punch-outs from the trays in Clark Bar multibar packages. A stand-up toy could be made of each by folding back the two "wings" and interlocking the slots on them (marked "A" and "B"). The animals depicted are both domestic and wild, and the artwork is the "cute" style aimed at young children (the animals are given human facial expressions). A red circle enclosing one of a string of numbers printed on the "A" flap indicates the specific card number. A sentence of "animal dialogue," printed below the subject in the base, promotes Clark Bars. The set was not listed in the early catalogs, and no reference number has been assigned.

ITEM	EX	AVE
Card	7.50	2.00
Set	215.00	55.00

ANIMALS OF THE WORLD (100)　　2 1/16" X 2 5/8"

"Animals of the World," is the correct title of this 1951 sequel to the "Bring 'Em Back Alive" series produced by Topps. The cards were marketed in brightly colored one-cent and five-cent packages of "Zoo Picture Card Gum." Advertising on the five-cent wrapper calls the series "America's Prize Animal Collection." The artwork for the series was done by artist Mary Lee Baker. We have illustrated the cover of one of her portfolios entitled "Wild Animals" and one of the large prints which it contained — "Gorilla," which is identical to the gorilla card in the "Animals of the World" set. Unopened one-cent gum packs of "Zoo Picture Card Gum" have been found in some quantity, and most of the cards in them were heavily stained on the reverse side. Such cards cannot be graded excellent. The five-cent packages contained two-card panels. Not many of these wrappers or panels have survived, and they command premium prices. Cards issued as singles have white cardboard stock on the back; cards from panels have gray cardboard on the reverse. The reference number is R714-1.

ITEM	EX	AVE
Cards		
Gray	4.00	1.00
White	4.00	1.00
Sets		
Mixed		
backs	475.00	115.00
Panels	16.00	4.00
Wrappers		
1-cent	12.00	——
5-cent	200.00	——
Box	250.00	95.00

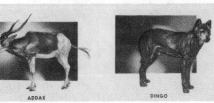

Animals of the World

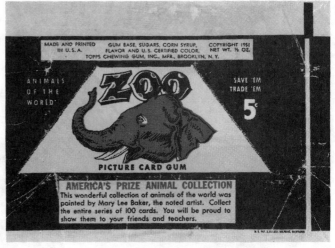

101 Red Squirrel	151 Spider Monkey
102 Alaska Brown Bear	152 Coati-mundi
103 Dugong	153 Lemur
104 Blackbuck	154 Cougar
105 Koala	155 Banting
106 Pangolin	156 Cacomistle
107 Siberian Ibex	157 Bongo
108 Brocket	158 Elephant Seal
109 Tamandua	159 Jaguar
110 Cape Hunting Dog	160 Lion
111 Gayal	161 Moose
112 Crested Procupine	162 Polar Bear
113 Chinchilla	163 Caribou
114 Hyrax	164 Nine-banded Armadillo
115 Meerkat	165 Mongoose
116 Barbary Ape	166 Pig-tailed Macaque
117 Wolverine	167 Mouflon
118 Addax	168 Uakari
119 Dingo	169 Snow Leopard
120 Chevrotain	170 African Elephant
121 Hog Deer	171 Hartebeest
122 Common Duiker	172 Beaver
123 Muskrat	173 Fossa
124 Lesser Panda	174 Pigmy Hippopotamus
125 Guanaco	175 Shrew
126 Blesbok	176 Gorilla
127 Sapajou	177 Sloth
128 Acudad	178 Vampire Bat
129 Arabian Camel	179 Yapok
130 White-tailed Deer	180 Jaguarundi
131 Reindeer	181 Gemsbok
132 Solenodon	182 Malayan Tree Shrew
133 Axis Deer	183 Kouprey
134 Tenrec	184 Whale
135 Giraffe	185 Red Fox
136 Tapir	186 Zebra
137 Mangabey	187 Wapiti
138 Lemming	188 Quagga
139 Potto	189 Walrus
140 Bandicoot	190 Marten
141 Agouti	191 Aye-aye
142 Okapi	192 Flying Phalanger
143 Cottontail Rabbit	193 Howler Monkey
144 California Sealion	194 Orang-utan
145 Hamadryas Baboon	195 Fisher
146 Onager	196 African Black Rhinocerous
147 Canada Lynx	197 Giant Anteater
148 Cuscus	198 Cheetah
149 Vicuna	199 Thylacine
150 Kiang	200 Nilghai

COVER OF THE MARY BAKER PORTFOLIO

GORILLA

ARTWORK OF GORILLA PORTFOLIO PRINT IS
IDENTICAL TO THAT ON THE
SMALLER TRADING CARD

ANTIQUE AUTOS (48)   2 1/2" X 3 3/4"

The 48-card set of "Antique Autos" was issued by Bowman Gum in 1953. The color drawings depict early car models from the Golden Age of the automobile industry, and many, if not all, of the pictures were copied from an American Tobacco Co. set issued about 1911 in "Turkey Red" cigarettes (see comparison photos below). The

backs contain a short text and a 3-D picture which could be viewed with a pair of 3-D glasses. The following statement on the display box was addressed to "Mr. Re-

tailer": "There are 6 pairs of 3-D (third dimensional) glasses in this box at no extra cost to you. Please give one pair free with each sale of 4 packages..." The yellow and blue display box held 24 packs; each pack contained five cards and a slab of gum. The automobiles are named on the front, but the title often appears in abbreviated form on the back. Card numbers are located on the back only. The reference number is R701-1.

ITEM	EX	AVE
Card	3.00	.75
Set	175.00	40.00
Wrapper	12.00	—
Box	100.00	25.00
3—D glasses	15.00	5.00

1 Pierce	13 Locomobile-Racer	25 Moline	37 Rambler
2 Corbin	14 Franklin	26 Knox	38 National
3 Pullman-Racer	15 Reo	27 Apperson	39 Stearns Racer
4 Fiat-Racer	16 Mitchell	28 Baker Electric	40 Renault
5 Cadillac	17 De Dietrich	29 Hudson	41 Mercedes Racer
6 Pope-Hartford	18 Lancia	30 Oldsmobile	42 Packard-Tourist
7 White Steamer	19 Benz-Racer	31 Ford	43 Simplex
8 Chalmers-Detroit	20 Acme Racer	32 Maxwell	44 Thomas
9 Gaeth	21 Palmer-Singer	33 Winton	45 Stoddard-Dayton Racer
10 Alco	22 Panhard	34 Isotta-Racer	46 Peerless
11 Chadwick Racer	23 Rainier	35 Lozier-Racer	47 Haynes
12 Matheson	24 Buick	36 Studebaker	48 Stevens Duryea

HISTORY REPEATS ITSELF: ARTWORK OF 1953 BOWMAN SET WAS COPIED FROM A TOBACCO SERIES ISSUED IN 1911

ARCHIE COMICS (?)   2 3/4" X 3 5/8"

According to the production codes used by Topps, this series of wax paper "Archie" comics was marketed in 1957-58. Very few comics have

survived to this day, and they appear on the want lists of even the most advanced collectors. The comic illustrated at top -- "Love and Misses" -- is No. 22 in the 1957 series and is printed in blue, red, yellow, and black colors (No. 30 is the highest comic seen for the 1958 set). The comics were packed around the rectangular gum pieces marketed in "Topps Blony Bubble Gum," a brand recently acquired by Topps when it bought out Bowman Gum. The scarcity of Archie comics has a direct connection

to the "comics for prizes" redemption offers printed on them; as little as five or as many as 125 comics could be sent in to the company for various premiums (wallets, bracelets, etc.). Although the Archie comics are considered scarce items, the plain-looking "Blony" outer wrapper is even harder to find (illustration courtesy of John Neuner). The reference number is R711-1.

ITEM	EX	AVE
Comic	10.00	3.00
Wrapper	50.00	--

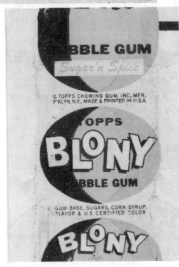

THIS ADVERTISEMENT FOR ARCHIE COMICS WAS PRINTED ON "GEE WHIZ QUIZ" (ISOLATION BOOTH) WRAPPERS

BAZOOKA COMICS (?)   SEVERAL SIZES

The original owners of Topps Gum were once involved in the tobacco industry but changed course and moved into the chicle business in 1938. Initially, the company struggled in the competitive marketplace inhabited by Fleer, Goudey, Gum, Inc., and a host of smaller manufacturers. However, a combination of shrewd marketing and good fortune brought improved prospects. When the war effort brought an abrupt halt to gum production and its, by now, irrevocably parallel business of trading card development, a window of opportunity opened for Topps. By producing four flavors of chewing gum in convenient one-cent mini-

packages, Topps gum soon became a favorite with the folks at home and the servicemen overseas. The slogan "Don't Talk Chum...Chew Topps Gum" achieved a sort of patriotic status across the country. Towards the end of the war, Topps began developing a new product called "Bazooka Gum." In a brilliant marketing stroke, Topps head Joe Shorin donated thousands of "Bazooka Gum" wrappers to be used as confetti for the Victory Parade down Wall Street. Sales of Bazooka Gum took off, and the company's climb to the forefront of the industry had begun.

The story of how "Bazooka Gum" got its name is almost

too incredible to believe. The name was concocted by a 12-year-old boy named Bob Burns, who later turned into one of America's foremost radio comedians. Burns was playing around with a group of friends when he tried to "play" a length of pipe like a musical instrument. The noise that resulted, hardly musical, evoked gales of laughter from his playmates, and Bob jokingly called his gadget a "bazooka," based on an old Arkansas expression, "blowing his bazoo," or bragging. When Burns got into show business, he "improved" the bazooka by making it even more ludicrous to the eye and ear. It became so famous that the weapon developed by the

212

Army was named after IT! Because the word "bazooka" was never trademarked or copyrighted by Burns, Topps simply adopted it for their own use.

Initially, Bazooka Gum was sold only in five-cent, foil-wrapped "rolls." Searching for a way to improve sales, Topps decided to use cartoon strips, or comics, which doubled as inner wrappers for the gum. The original comics were obtained from Fawcett and D.C. Comics — where they had been used to fill in blank spaces in the page layouts.

Examples of the multi-color strips are the "Peg," "Bubbles," and "Doc Sorebones" comics illustrated in our presentation. They come in several sizes and were packaged with Bazooka Gum in 1947 and 1948.

In 1949, Topps decided to dump the comic book strips in favor of a character that would simultaneously serve as a product symbol: "Bazooka, The Atom Bubble Boy." In a series of comic book ads aimed at young America, Bazooka performed a variety of heroic deeds while chewing gum and passing out the enclosed comics (see illustration). Not surprisingly, the latter featured the "Bubble Boy" himself and were printed on thin wax paper in an unspectacular rust monochrome. Once detached from the foil outer wrapper, Bazooka Boy comics became hard to read and were easily torn. Dull in comparison to their predecessors, they were, to their credit, a step in the final creation of the Bazooka Joe character that has since become the benchmark symbol of Topps' most famous gum.

Collecting these Bazooka Gum comics of the 1947-49 period is a true challenge. They are far enough removed from mainstream cards in form and style to discourage widespread interest, yet they are also scarce in terms of supply. The comic book strips of 1947-48 are very difficult to find and are valued in the $10.00–$15.00 range (per comic) in "excellent" grade. The rust color comics featuring "Bazooka, the Atom Boy," are much easier to find and their value depends on whether or not they are still attached to the outer foil wrapper. In general, prices are as follows: detached comic — $4.00; foil wrapper — $5.00; foil wrapper with comic attached — $10.00. The Bazooka box shown on the ordering page has not appeared in any modern collection, and the reference number for the Bazooka Comics category is R711-3.

WAX INNER WRAPPER

THE SILVER FOIL WRAPPER WAS
A BIG HIT WITH KIDS

FIRST GUM FROM TOPPS
DID NOT CONTAIN CARDS

BAZOOKA GUM WAS A
SPONSER OF THE ABBOTT &
COSTELLO RADIO SHOW

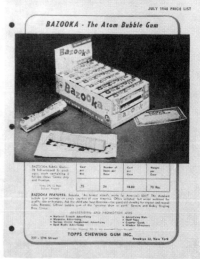

PAGE FROM CONFECTIONARY
PRICE LIST SHOWING
BAZOOKA COMICS

A 1949 ADVERTISEMENT FOR BAZOOKA GUM

COMIC BOOK AD FOR BAZOOKA GUM OFFERED 1800
DIFFERENT COLLEGE BANNERS BUT ONLY 708 WERE
LISTED ON TOPPS' FOUR-PAGE CHECKLIST

OFFICIAL BAZOOKA LIST
OF U.S. COLLEGES & UNIVERSITIES

1) Adams State College
2) Adelphi College
3) Agnes Scott College
4) Akron, University of
5) Alabama, University of
6) Alabama College for Women
7) Alabama Polytechnic Institute
8) Alabama State Teachers College
9) Albertus Magnus College
10) Albion College
11) Albright College
12) Alfred University
13) Allegheny College
14) Alma College
15) Alverno College
16) American International College
17) American University, The
18) Amherst College
19) Anderson College
20) Antioch College

21) Appalachian State Teachers College
22) Aquinas College
23) Arizona, University of
24) Arizona State College
25) Arizona State Teachers College
26) Arkansas, University of
27) Arkansas Agricultural and Mechanical College
28) Arkansas State College
29) Arkansas State Teachers College
30) Asbury College
31) Ashland College
32) Atlanta University
33) Atlantic Union College
34) Augustana College
35) Augustana College and Theological Seminary
36) Aurora College
37) Baker University
38) Baldwin-Wallace College
39) Ball State Teachers College

40) Barat College of the Sacred Heart
41) Bard College
42) Bates College
43) Baylor University
44) Beaver College
45) Belhaven College
46) Beloit College
47) Bennett College
48) Bennington College
49) Berea College
50) Bessie Tift College
51) Bethany College
52) Bethel College, The
53) Birmingham-Southern College
54) Bloomsburg State Teachers College
55) Blue Mountain College
56) Boston, Teachers College of the City of
57) Boston College
58) Boston University

59) Bowdoin College
60) Bowling Green State University
61) Bradley University
62) Briar Cliff College
63) Bridgewater College
64) Brigham Young University
65) Brooklyn College of the City of New York
66) Brooklyn Coll. of Pharmacy of Long Is. Univ
67) Brooklyn, Polytechnic Institute
68) Brown University
69) Bryn Mawr College
70) Bucknell University
71) Buffalo, University
72) Butler University
73) California, University
74) California Institute of Technology
75) Calvin College
76) Canisius College
77) Capital University
78) Carleton College
79) Carnegie Institute of Technology
80) Carroll College
81) Carson-Newman College
82) Carthage College
83) Case Institute of Technology
84) Catawba College
85) Catholic University of America
86) Cedar Crest College
87) Centenary College of Louisiana, Inc.
88) Central College
89) Central Michigan College of Education
90) Central Missouri State College
91) Central State College
92) Central State College
93) Central Washington College of Education
94) Centre College of Kentucky
95) Charleston, College
96) Chattanooga, University
97) Chestnut Hill College
98) Cheyney State Teachers College
99) Chicago, University
100) Chicago Teachers College
101) Chico State College
102) Cincinnati, University
103) Citadel, The Military College
104) Claremont Graduate School
105) Clarke College
106) Clarkson College of Technology
107) Clark University
108) Clemson Agricultural College
109) Coe College
110) Coker College
111) Colby College
112) Colgate University
113) Colorado, University
114) Colorado College
115) Colorado Agricultural and Mechanical Coll

116) Colorado School of Mines
117) Colorado State College of Education
118) Columbia College
119) Columbia University
120) Concord College
121) Concordia College
122) Connecticut, University
123) Connecticut College
124) Connecticut, Teachers College
125) Converse College
126) Cooper Union School of Engineering
127) Cornell College
128) Cornell University
129) Cortland State Teachers College
130) Creighton University, The
131) Culver-Stockton College
132) Dakota Wesleyan University
133) Danbury State Teachers College
134) Dartmouth College
135) Davidson College
136) Davis and Elkins College
137) Dayton, University
138) Delaware, University
139) Delaware State College
140) Delta State Teachers College
141) Denison University
142) Denver, University
143) De Paul University
144) DePauw University
145) Detroit, University
146) Dickinson College
147) Dillard University
148) Doane College
149) Drake University
150) Drew University
151) Drexel Institute of Technology
152) Drury College
153) Dubuque, University
154) Duchesne College
155) Duke University
156) Duluth State Teachers College
157) Dunbarton College of Holy Cross
158) Duquesne University
159) D'Youville College
160) Earlham College
161) East Carolina Teachers College
162) East Central State College
163) Eastern Illinois State Teachers College
164) Eastern Kentucky State Teachers College
165) Eastern Montana State Normal School
166) Eastern Nazarene College
167) Eastern Oregon College of Education
168) Eastern Washington College of Education
169) East Tennessee State College
170) East Texas State Teachers College
171) Eau Claire State Teachers College
172) Elmhurst College

173) Elmira College
174) Emmanuel College
175) Emmanuel Missionary College
176) Emory and Henry College
177) Emory University[1]
178) Erskine College
179) Evansville College
180) Fairmont State College
181) Fenn College
182) Findlay College
183) Fisk University
184) Fletcher School of Diplomacy
185) Florida, University
186) Florida Agricultural and Mechanical College
187) Florida Southern College
188) Florida State University
189) Fordham University
190) Fort Hays Kansas State College
191) Franklin and Marshall College
192) Franklin College of Indiana
193) Fresno State College
194) Furman University
195) Geneva College
196) George Peabody College for Teachers
197) George Pepperdine College
198) Georgetown College
199) Georgetown University
200) George Washington University, The
201) George Williams College
202) Georgia, University
203) Georgia School of Technology
204) Georgia State College for Women
205) Georgia State Womans College
206) Georgia Teachers College
207) Georgian Court College[1]
208) Gettysburg College
209) Glenville State College
210) Gonzaga University
211) Good Counsel College
212) Goshen College
213) Goucher College
214) Great Falls, College
215) Greensboro College
216) Grinnell College
217) Grove City College
218) Guilford College
219) Gustavus Adolphus College
220) Hamilton College
221) Hamline University
222) Hampden-Sydney College
223) Hampton Institute
224) Hanover College
225) Hardin-Simmons University
226) Harris Teachers College
227) Harvard University
228) Hastings College
229) Haverford College

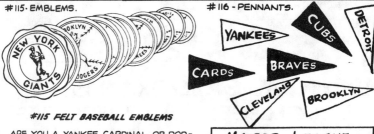

#115 - EMBLEMS.

#116 - PENNANTS.

YANKEES CUBS DETROIT

CARDS BRAVES

CLEVELAND BROOKLYN

#115 FELT BASEBALL EMBLEMS

ARE YOU A YANKEE, CARDINAL OR DODGER FAN? WEAR YOUR FAVORITE EMBLEM (APPROX. 5" DIAMETER). GET ANY ONE OF THE MAJOR LEAGUE TEAMS FOR YOUR SWEATER OR BASEBALL SUIT. MENTION THE TEAM YOU WANT.

SEND ONLY 1 BAZOOKA SILVER WRAPPER AND 10¢ FOR EACH.

#116 FELT BASEBALL PENNANTS

YOUR CHOICE OF ANY MAJOR LEAGUE TEAM AS SHOWN IN LIST. MENTION THE ONE YOU WANT.

SEND ONLY 1 BAZOOKA SILVER WRAPPER AND 10¢ FOR EACH.

MAJOR LEAGUE BASEBALL TEAMS.

AMERICAN	NATIONAL
NEW YORK	BOSTON
CLEVELAND	BROOKLYN
DETROIT	PITTSBURGH
WASHINGTON	ST. LOUIS
ST. LOUIS	NEW YORK
CHICAGO	CINCINNATI
BOSTON	PHILADELPHIA
PHILADELPHIA	CHICAGO

230) Heidelberg College
231) Henderson State Teachers College
232) Hendrix College
233) Hillsdale College
234) Hiram College
235) Hobart and William Smith Colleges
236) Hofstra College
237) Hollins College
238) Holy Cross, College
239) Holy Names College
240) Hood College
241) Hope College
242) Houghton College
243) Howard College
244) Howard University
245) Humboldt State College
246) Hunter College of the City of New York
247) Huntington College
248) Huron College
249) Idaho, College
250) Idaho, University
251) Illinois, University
252) Illinois College
253) Illinois Institute of Technology
254) Illinois State Normal University
255) Illinois Wesleyan University
256) Immaculata College
257) Immaculate Heart College
258) Incarnate Word College
259) Indiana State Teachers College
260) Indiana University
261) Iowa, State University of
262) Iowa State College
263) Iowa State Teachers College
264) Iowa Wesleyan College
265) James Millikin University
266) Jamestown College
267) John B. Stetson University
268) John Carroll University
269) Johns Hopkins University, The
270) Johnson C. Smith University
271) Judson College
272) Juilliard School of Music, The
273) Juniata College
274) Kalamazoo College
275) Kansas, University
276) Kansas City, University
277) Kansas State College of Agr. and Applied Sci.
278) Kansas State Teachers College
279) Keene Teachers College
280) Kent State University
281) Kentucky, University
282) Kentucky State College
283) Kenyon College
284) Keuka College
285) Knox College
286) Lafayette College
287) La Grange College
288) Lake Erie College
289) Lake Forest College
290) La Salle College
291) Lawrence College
292) Lebanon Valley College
293) Lehigh University
294) Le Moyne College
295) Lenoir Rhyne College
296) Lewis and Clark College
297) Limestone College
298) Lincoln Memorial University
299) Lincoln University
300) Lincoln-University of Missouri
301) Lindenwood College
302) Linfield College
303) Livingstone College
304) Loras College
305) Loretto Heights College
306) Louisiana College
307) Louisiana Polytechnic Institute
308) Louisiana State Univ. and Agr. & Mech. Col.
309) Louisville, University
310) Loyola College
311) Loyola University
312) Luther College
313) Lynchburg College
314) Macalester College
315) MacMurray College for Women
316) McPherson College
317) Madison College
318) Maine, University
319) Manchester College
320) Manhattan College
321) Manhattanville College of the Sacred Heart
322) Marietta College
323) Marquette University
324) Marshall College
325) Mary Baldwin College
326) Marygrove College
327) Mary Hardin-Baylor College

328) Maryland, University
329) Maryland State Teachers College
330) Marylhurst College
331) Mary Manse College
332) Marymount College
333) Maryville College
334) Marywood College
335) Massachusetts Institute of Technology
336) Massachusetts, University
337) Massachusetts State Teachers College
338) Mayville State Teachers College
339) Memphis State College
340) Mercer University
341) Mercyhurst College
342) Meredith College
343) Miami, University of .Coral Gables, Florida
344) Miami University... .Oxford, Ohio
345) Michigan, University
346) Michigan College of Mining and Tech
347) Michigan State College
348) Michigan State Normal College
349) Middlebury College
350) Middle Tennessee State College
351) Mills College
352) Millsaps College
353) Milwaukee-Downer College
354) Miner Teachers College
355) Minnesota, University
356) Minnesota State Teachers College
357) Misericordia, College
358) Mississippi, University
359) Mississippi College
360) Mississippi Southern College
361) Mississippi State College
362) Mississippi State College for Women
363) Missouri, University
364) Missouri Valley College
365) Monmouth College
366) Montana School of Mines
367) Montana State College
368) Montana State Normal College
369) Montana State University
370) Moorhead State Teachers College
371) Moravian College
372) Morehead State Teachers College
373) Morehouse College
374) Morgan State College
375) Morningside College
376) Morris Brown College
377) Mount Angel Seminary
378) Mount Holyoke College
379) Mount Mary College
380) Mount Mercy College
381) Mount St. Joseph-on-the-Ohio, College
382) Mount Saint Mary's College
383) Mount St. Scholastica College
384) Mount Saint Vincent, College
385) Mcunt Union College
386) Muhlenberg College
387) Mundelein College
388) Murray State Teachers College
389) Muskingum College
390) National College of Education
391) Nazareth College
392) Nebraska, University
393) Nebraska State Teachers College
394) Nebraska Wesleyan University
395) Nevada, University
396) Newark College of Engineering
397) Newberry College
398) New Hampshire, University
399) New Haven State Teachers College
400) New Jersey State Teachers College
401) New Mexico, University
402) New Mexico Coll. of Agriculture & Mech. Arts.
403) New Mexico Highlands University
404) New Mexico School of Mines
405) New Mexico State Teachers College
406) New Rochelle, College
407) New York, The College of the City
408) New York State College of Forestry
409) New York State College for Teachers
410) New York State Teachers College
411) New York University
412) Niagara University
413) North Carolina Agricultural and Tech. College
414) North Carolina, University
415) North Carolina, Women's Coll. of the Univ.
416) North Carolina College for Negroes
417) North Carolina State Coll. of Agr. and Eng.
418) North Central College
419) North Dakota, University
420) North Dakota Agricultural College
421) North Dakota State Normal and Industrial Coll.
422) North Dakota State Teachers College
423) North Georgia College
424) Northeast Missouri State Teachers College
425) Northeastern State College

426) Northeastern University
427) Northern Idaho College of Education
428) Northern Illinois State Teachers College
429) Northern Michigan College of Education
430) Northern State Teachers College
431) North Texas State Teachers College
432) Northwestern State College
433) Northwestern University
434) Northwest Missouri State Teachers College
435) Northwest Nazarene College
436) Norwich University
437) Notre Dame, University
438) Notre Dame College
439) Notre Dame of Maryland, College
440) Notre Dame College of Staten Island
441) Oberlin College
442) Occidental College
443) Ohio State University
444) Ohio University
445) Ohio Wesleyan University
446) Oklahoma, University
447) Oklahoma Agric. and Mechanical College
448) Oklahoma College for Women
449) Omaha, University
450) Oregon, University
451) Oregon College of Education
452) Oregon State College
453) Ottawa University
454) Otterbein College
455) Ouachita Baptist College
456) Our Lady of the Elms, College
457) Our Lady of the Lake College
458) Pacific, College of the
459) Pacific Lutheran College
460) Pacific Union College
461) Pacific University
462) Paine College
463) Park College
464) Parsons College
465) Pasadena College
466) Pennsylvania, University
467) Pennsylvania College for Women
468) Pennsylvania State College
469) Pennsylvania State Teachers College
470) Peru State Teachers College
471) Phillips University
472) Pittsburgh, University
473) Plymouth Teachers College
474) Pomona College
475) Portland, University
476) Prairie View Agricultural and Mechanical Coll
477) Princeton University
478) Principia College of Liberal Arts
479) Providence College
480) Puget Sound, College
481) Purdue University
482) Queens College
483) Queens College of the City of New York
484) Radcliffe College
485) Randolph-Macon College
486) Randolph-Macon Woman's College
487) Redlands, University
488) Reed College
489) Regis College
490) Rensselaer Polytechnic Institute
491) Rhode Island College of Education
492) Rhode Island State College
493) Rice Institute, The
494) Richmond, University
495) Ripon College
496) River Falls State Teachers College
497) Roanoke College
498) Rochester, University
499) Rockford College
500) Rockhurst College
501) Rollins College
502) Rocky Mountain College
503) Rosary College
504) Rosemont College
505) Rose Polytechnic Institute
506) Russell Sage College
507) Rutgers University
508) St. Ambrose College
509) St. Anselm's College
510) St. Augustine's College
511) St. Benedict, College
512) St. Benedict's College
513) St. Bernardine of Siena College
514) St. Bonaventure College
515) St. Catherine, College
516) St. Edward's Seminary
517) St. Elizabeth, College
518) St. Francis, College
519) St. Francis College
520) St. Francis Xavier College for Women
521) St. John College
522) St. John's University
523) St. Joseph College

524) St. Joseph's College
525) St. Joseph's College for Women
526) St. Lawrence University
527) St. Louis University
528) St. Martin's College
529) St. Mary College
530) St. Mary of the Springs, College of
531) St. Mary-of-the-Wasatch, College of
532) St. Mary-of-the-Woods College
533) St. Mary's College, Notre Dame
534) St. Mary's College
535) St. Michael's College
536) St. Norbert College
537) St. Olaf College
538) St. Peter's College
539) St. Rose, College of
540) St. Scholastica, College of
541) St. Teresa, College of
542) St. Thomas, College of
543) St. Vincent College
544) Salem College
545) Sam Houston State Teachers College
546) San Diego State College
547) San Francisco, University of
548) San Francisco College for Women
549) San Francisco State College
550) San Jose State College
551) Santa Clara, University
552) Sarah Lawrence College
553) Scarritt College
554) Scranton, University
555) Scripps College
556) Seattle College
557) Seattle Pacific College
558) Seton Hall College
559) Seton Hill College
560) Shaw University
561) Shepherd College
562) Shorter College
563) Sienna Heights College
564) Simmons College
565) Simpson College
566) Skidmore College
567) Smith College
568) South, The University of the
569) South Carolina, University
570) South Carolina State A and M College
571) South Dakota, University
572) South Dakota School of Mines and Technology
573) South Dakota State Coll. of A and M Arts
574) Southeastern Louisiana College
575) Southeastern State College
576) Southeast Missouri State College
577) Southern California, University
578) Southern Idaho College of Education
579) Southern Illinois University
580) Southern Methodist University
581) Southern Oregon College of Education
582) Southern State Teachers College
583) Southern Univ. and Agr. and Mech. College
584) Southwestern at Memphis
585) Southwestern College

586) Southwestern Louisiana Institute
587) Southwestern University
588) Southwest Missouri State College
589) Southwest Texas State Teachers College
590) Spelman College
591) Springfield College (International YMCA College)
592) Spring Hill College
593) Stanford University
594) Stevens Institute of Technology
595) Stephen F. Austin State Teachers College
596) Stout Institute, The
597) Stowe Teachers College
598) Sul Ross State Teachers College
599) Superior State College
600) Susquehanna University
601) Swarthmore College
602) Sweet Briar College
603) Syracuse University
604) Talladega College
605) Tarkio College
606) Temple University
607) Tennessee, University of
608) Tennessee Agr. and Industrial State College.
609) Tennessee Polytechnic Institute
610) Texas Agricultural and Mechanical College
611) Texas, University of
612) Texas Christian University
613) Texas College of Arts and Industries
614) Texas College of Mines
615) Texas State College for Women
616) Texas Technological College
617) Thiel College
618) Tillotson College
619) Toledo, University of
620) Transylvania College
621) Trinity College
622) Troy State Teachers College
623) Tufts College
624) Tulane University of Louisiana
625) Tulsa, University of
626) Tusculum College
627) Tuskegee Institute
628) Union College
629) U. S. Coast Guard Academy
630) U. S. Military Academy
631) U. S. Naval Academy
632) Upsala College
633) Ursinus College
634) Ursuline College for Women
635) Utah, University of
636) Utah State Agricultural College
637) Valparaiso University
638) Vanderbilt University
639) Vassar College
640) Vermont, Univ. of and State Agr. College
641) Villa Maria College
642) Villanova College
643) Virginia, University of
644) Virginia Military Institute
645) Virginia Polytechnic Institute
646) Virginia State College
647) Virginia State Teachers College

648) Virginia Union University
649) Wabash College
650) Wagner Memorial Lutheran College
651) Wake Forest College
652) Walla Walla College
653) Washburn Municipal University
654) Washington, State College of
655) Washington, University of
656) Washington and Jefferson College
657) Washington and Lee University
658) Washington College
659) Washington Missionary College
660) Washington University
661) Wayne University
662) Wellesley College
663) Wells College
664) Wesleyan College
665) Wesleyan University
666) Western Carolina Teachers College
667) Western College for Women
668) Western Illinois State Teachers College
669) Western Kentucky State Teachers College
670) Western Maryland College
671) Western Michigan College
672) Western Reserve University
673) Western State College
674) Western Washington College of Education
675) West Liberty State College
676) Westminster College
677) West Texas State Teachers College
678) West Virginia State College
679) West Virginia University
680) West Virginia Wesleyan College
681) Wheaton College
682) Whitman College
683) Whittier College
684) Whitworth College
685) Wichita, Municipal University of
686) Wiley College
687) Willamette University
688) William and Mary, College of
689) William Jewell College
690) Williams College
691) Willimantic State Teachers College
692) Wilmington College
693) Wilson College
694) Winston-Salem Teachers College
695) Winthrop College
696) Wisconsin, University of
697) Wisconsin State Teachers College
698) Wittenberg College
699) Wofford College
700) Woodstock College
701) Wooster, College of
702) Worcester Polytechnic Institute
703) Wyoming, University of
704) Xavier University
705) Xavier University
706) Yale University
707) Yankton College
708) Youngstown College

USE THIS HANDY COUPON

(BAZOOKA WILL SEND YOU A NEW LIST WITH EACH ORDER)
FOR EACH PENNANT SEND 10¢ AND ONE BAZOOKA
SILVER WRAPPER TO —
BAZOOKA
BOX 20
MADISON SQ. STATION
NEW YORK, 10, N.Y.

UNDERLINE EACH COLLEGE ON LIST FOR THE
PENNANTS YOU WANT. SEND IN COMPLETE
LIST. NEW ONE WILL BE RETURNED WITH
YOUR ORDER.

NAME (PRINT) —————————————————
ADDRESS ————————————————————
CITY ————————————— ZONE NO. ————
RURAL ROUTE ———————— BOX NO. ——— STATE ———
AMOUNT ENCLOSED ——————————————————

220

BAZOOKA JOE (?)

Bazooka Joe, a character named after the World War II weapon and Topps president Joe Shorin, became the company's advertising symbol after the "Bazooka, The Atom Bubble Boy" campaign was scrapped in 1951. Joe was the brainchild of Topps art director Woody Gelman, and he was drawn by former underground artist Wesley Morse. Gelman believed in "design elements," the use of eye-catching details which caught the public's attention and kept it focused. He understood that "Bazooka, The Atom Bubble Boy" failed because he was too wholesome and heroic. Gelman's new creation, Bazooka Joe, was an anti-hero in traditional terms, just your universally average kid. But he was an instant hit with other real kids, and they were the target market.

To create Bazooka Joe and His Gang, Gelman and Morse drew on both their artistic sense and a whole array of other established cartoon and movie characters of the 1920's and 1930's. Among the latter were Our Gang, Pee Wee, Skippy, "Just Kids," and "Reg'lar Fellers." Over the years, Joe's entourage has included his mom and dad, Walkie-Talkie (the dog), Tex, Jane, Herman, Percy, Toughy, Sarge, Pesty (or Orville), Pat (or L'il Pat), and Mort (or Mortimer). Gelman's "design elements" have included items such as Joe's baseball cap and Mort's improbable turtleneck sweater, but the one item that rivets our attention is Bazooka Joe's eyepatch. Joe really doesn't have any problems with his vision, but eye patches sell bubble gum (and shirts).

MANY SIZES

How famous is Bazooka Joe? He is trademarked in more than 30 countries, and his image sells some one and a half billion pieces of bubble gum every year. Bazooka Joe comics are printed in Spanish, German, French, and Hebrew, and in Nigeria, he is actually black! There are Bazooka Joe tee shirts, activity books, lollipop wrappers and View-Master reels. He has been been satirized in "Wacky Packages" and has made an appearance in "Funny L'il Joke Books." Inevitably, perhaps, a British rock band adopted the name, but it, unlike Bazooka Joe, disappeared from view. Undoubtedly, Bazooka Joe has been one of the most successful advertising symbols of all time.

Collecting Bazooka Joe comics is not as easy as it might seem. We have been unable to pinpoint an exact date when the comics first appeared, and the 1954 issue is the earliest we have to illustrate. Over the years, the comics have been continually down-sized, so that today's comics appear tiny compared to the "giants" of yesteryear. But Bazooka Joe almost never changes — literally — because the comics are simply rerun in new formats as one generation of kids grow up and another take their place. Original drawings of artist Wesley Morse were used for the first eight years, and then these were recycled until 1983, after which a new set of 40 strips drawn by Howard Cruse was utilized. So if you think that Bazooka Joe is repeating himself, you're right. While this fascinates some collectors, it also repels others.

All of the Bazooka Joe comics we've encountered have a production code printed on them somewhere. To date any comic, find the two-digit number in the code (generally in the center) which corresponds to the last two digits of any year (1-59-37 = 37th comic in 1959 run). Pricing is really a matter of common sense: value is directly proportional to age. The follow-

1954 COMIC AND SILVER WRAPPER

CELLOPHANE WRAPPER REPLACED THE SILVER
FOIL VERSION

ing chart gives the price levels as we see them; please remember that these are for comics purchased from a dealer or collector who has overhead costs figured in. It IS a bargain to pay 10-cents for a comic, of your choice, freshly pulled from a brand new two-cent pack when you consider that YOU didn't have to buy the whole box and dismantle the stubborn packages therin. The reference number is R711-2.

ITEM	EX
Wrapper	
Pre-1954	5.00 each
1954	4.00 each
1955-56	3.00 each
1957 large	3.00 each
1957 small	3.00 each
1958-1960	2.50 each
1961-1969	2.00 each
1970-1979	1.00 each
1980-1984	.35 each
1985-to-date	.10 each
1975 cards	2.00 each
Recent large boxes	1.00 each

1955 COMIC

1957 COMIC — LARGE VARIETY

1957 COMIC — SMALL VARIETY

1958 COMIC

1959 COMIC

1960 COMIC

Bazooka Joe

1980 COMIC

1983 COMIC

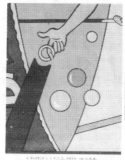

1984
COMIC
& WRAPPER

1975 CARD

BAZOOKA JOE IN ISRAEL...

AND IN GERMANY!

LARGE BOX FORMAT USED IN RECENT YEARS

BOX HAS ITS OWN COMIC ON BACK!

BECKER PRIZE PACKAGE CARDS

MANY TYPES

Like Bazooka Joe, this presentation contains items issued after 1960; we have decided to include the entire category here to insure some continuity in our discussion. All the cards presented here were manufactured by L.M. Becker Company of Brillion, Wisconsin. The only series that was issued before 1960 is the "Ring Ding" gum set of U.S. Navy Photos (listed in the American Card Catalog at R780). As far as we know,

all the others were marketed after 1964.

The "Ring Ding" wrapper is the only conventional wrapper found from this company. All the other cards, stickers, transfers, and coloring books were given away in a variety of paper "prize packages" (see illustrations). The cards also offer us a wide array of subject matter, and it has been confirmed that not all card and bag themes matched.

The U.S. Navy Photo series is the only Becker set recorded with a printed back; the backs of all other sets listed here are blank. All Becker cards are in short supply because they were issued on a regional basis, but prices are reasonable because very few collectors know about them (and others don't find them interesting). The reference number for the Becker category is R780. Note: values are for "excellent" grade.

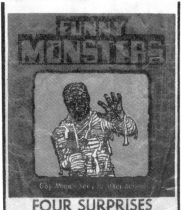

ITEM	EX
Wrappers	
All themes	35.00 each
Cards	
U.S. Navy Photos	
(1948/2" X 2 1/4")	3.00
U.S. Air Force Photos	
(1967/2 3/8" X	
3 1/2")	1.50
3-D Circus Stand-Ups	
(?/2" X 3")	3.00
Space Age	
(1970/2 5/16" X	
3 1/2")	3.00
Monsters	
(rough frame/1967/	
2 5/16" X 3 1/2")	3.00
Monsters (even frame/?/	
2 3/8" X 3 1/4")	2.00
Wild West (1967)	
Sticker	
(2 1/2" X 3 1/2")	2.00
Crayon Picture Book	
(1 3/4" X 2 1/4")	2,00
Tatto sheet	
(2 1/2" X 4 3/4")	1.00

FOUR SURPRISES
IN EVERY BAG
toys-games and a sweet treat

FOUR SURPRISES
IN EVERY BAG
toys-games and a sweet treat

AIR FORCE PHOTOS
APPEARED IN 1967

NAVY PHOTOS WERE ISSUED
IN 1948

TOP LINE OF BECKER CARDS
WERE DISTRIBUTED IN FOUR
DIFFERENT PACKAGES
ITEMS IN BOTTOM LINE ALL
CAME IN ONE "WILD WEST" BAG

1 Moisten skin 2 Cut out picture and place face down on skin 3 Press and peel off tattoo. Certified Food Colors. Safe. Harmless. Washable. © L.M.B. Co.

BLONY PAPER NOVELTIES (?)

The paper novelty items packaged inside "Blony" gum rolls come in a variety of sizes and colors, and the examples we have illustrated are numbered from a low of 31 to a high of 1001. Some of the wax paper inserts have a single complete feature plus a premium offer; others have two, three, four or five riddles and/or questions with no premium offers. Some of the items have the title written in script; most titles, however, are type face. The category was first mentioned in the June 1956 edition of The Card Collectors Bulletin, but the Blony/Bowman premium certificate bears an expiration date of 1950, and it seems likely that these paper novelties were in production

THREE SIZES

at that time (there are no production codes printed on them). The reference number for this category is R701-11.

ITEM	EX
Paper Novelties	
One-color	2.00 each
Two-color	3.00 each
Four-color	4.00 each
Wrapper	10.00

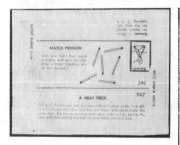

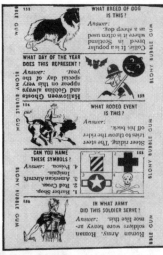

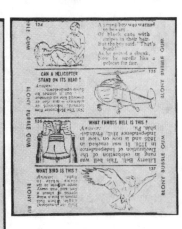

A BOWMAN "PREMIUM CERTIFICATE" WAS PACKED IN EVERY BOX OF GUM AS A REWARD TO THE RETAIL MERCHANT

BRING 'EM BACK ALIVE (100)   2 1/16" X 2 5/8"

"Frank Buck, world's greatest hunter, tells his exciting stories of trailing and capturing the ferocious beasts of the jungle to BRING 'EM BACK ALIVE." So reads the advertising on the five-cent wrapper from this 1950 Bowman Gum series of 100 cards. The set includes some stories from the original Frank Buck series issued in 1938 by Gum, Inc., the original company started by J. Warren Bowman. The cards are numbered from 1 to 100 and are the first series in a tandem of sets with a wild animal theme: "Animals of the World (al-ready covered in this book) was the sequel (101-200). The color drawings depict the adventures of master trapper Frank Buck, and the details of each episode are related on the back. The series is divided into five subsets, each with a specific symbol in which the card number is printed: "Civilization Fare-well" (5 cards); "Dangerous Living" (32 cards); "Fighting Animals" (22 cards); "Man Against Beast" (28 cards); and "Homeward Bound" (13 cards). The one-cent wrapper has alternated pictures of Frank Buck and a tiger's head and is basically white with orange and green accents. The large five-cent wrapper contained two-card panels and is mostly green except for the center design. The series was marketed in 1950, and the reference number is R714-2. NOTE: cards with gum stains cannot be graded excellent.

ITEM	EX	AVE
Card	3.00	.60
Panel	15.00	5.00
Set	375.00	90.00
Wrappers		
One-cent	75.00	--
Five-cent	200.00	--

JUNGLE EXPEDITION
No. 2 in a Series of 5 Cards of
CIVILIZATION FAREWELL
When the American hunter was planning an expedition into the jungle, he made sure he had enough native helpers. No hunter would dare go into the jungle without men to carry food and supplies and . . . most important . . . presents for the native chiefs. A good guide can be the difference between life and death!

RIVER KINGS OF THE JUNGLE
No. 17 in a Series of 32 Cards of
DANGEROUS LIVING
The members of the Wagenia Tribe were preparing for one of their traditional river games. Each team was equipped with paddles broad enough to knock its opponent into the river. When one man fell into the water, a sudden streak showed the approach of the deadly crocodile. Only the expert swimming ability of the Wagenias saved him from sudden death.

FIGHTING MEN OF AFRICA
No. 18 in a Series of 32 Cards of
DANGEROUS LIVING
A foolish enemy warrior had gone unarmed into Zulu territory and was caught unaware by a Zulu bowman. Drawing his bow to its full length, this member of the tribe of the most famed warriors of the African jungle-land sent his arrow straight into the heart of his enemy.

SNAKE WOMAN
No. 19 in a Series of 32 Cards of
DANGEROUS LIVING
In deepest Africa lives the amazing young woman known as the Pythoness. She lives alone in a native hut with a giant twenty foot python and has unbelievable powers of healing and fortune telling. She has complete control of the monstrous snake, letting it twine around her body without fear of harm.

TEST OF STRENGTH
No. 13 in a Series of 32 Cards of
DANGEROUS LIVING
The jungle opponents faced each other and shouted insults. Then they clashed together . . . bodies and arms straining. This was the "Kebuba" . . . the Wagenia version of modern wrestling. The objective in their uncivilized way was to mortally wound their opponent.

THE KING'S HELPER
No. 22 in a Series of 32 Cards of
DANGEROUS LIVING
The young boy in the Watussi tribe had been trained from the age of eight . . . taking lessons in dancing and jumping and other feats of strength. All this pointed to the big day when he would become the king's page. Now he danced round and round the fire . . . showing all he knew and praying he would be acceptable for this great job.

FRANK BUCK'S
Bring 'Em Back Alive
JUNGLE PICTURE CARD GUM

TOPPS CHEWING GUM, INC. MFR., BROOKLYN, N. Y.

Frank Buck, world's greatest hunter, tells his exciting stories of trailing and capturing the ferocious beasts of the jungle to BRING 'EM BACK alive. Many of the animals you see today in North American zoos are the prizes of Frank Buck's death-defying daring.

We are proud to help you fulfill your dreams and recapture your memories

Build A Strong Foundation for Your Collection

SCA™
Founder Member

★ **Free 26 Page Price List**
★ **Complete Line of Non Sport**
  ★ Sets   ★ Wrappers
  ★ Singles ★ Packs
★ **Full-time Mail Order (not a store)**
★ **Buying Collections**

To order send 1st class stamp. (not self-addressed envelope)
— No Stamp — No Price List —
Mastercard & VISA for orders of $25 or more. Use phone or
FAX (717) 238-3220

ROXANNE TOSER
Dept. G
4019 Green Street
Harrisburg, PA 17110
(717) 238-1936
Monday-Friday 10-9 Eastern
Saturday 10-5
No Sunday Calls

BEAUTIFULLY—COLORED DISPLAY
CARD WAS DESIGNED TO STAND UP
IN ONE END OF THE DISPLAY BOX

BUBBLE KING GUM (124K)   3 3/4" X 4 3/4"

Leaf Brands of Chicago distributed the "Bubble King"
series of comics in 1948 (date
printed on each comic). There

are four episodes per comic,
each in a two- or three-section strip. Each strip has its
own number; the one illustrated begins with number 103
(top) and ends with number
107 (bottom). The name of
the gum or candy product in
which the comics were packaged is unknown. The primary
colors are blue and red with
white and black accents. Only
two Bubble King Comics have
been reported in modern collections, and the series is so
obscure that most people
don't even know it exists. It
was not listed in any of the
early catalogs, and it has
not yet been assigned a
reference number

ITEM	EX	AVE
Comic	20.00	10.00

CARDO TRADING CARDS (66)   2 1/2" X 3 1/2"

Leaf Brands has a tradition of
confusing collectors by skip-
numbering their card sets, and
this series of "Cardo Trading
Cards" is a case in point.
It was originally thought that
the set total was 30 cards,
six in each category. We now
realize that none of the
subgroups has the same
amount of cards, and none
have a straight run of numbers. By 1983, we had as-
sembled a checklist of 66
titles, and no new ones have
been discovered since that

time. The obverses of the
cards have multi-color artwork
drawings in the center, with
four monochrome designs in
each of the wide side margins.
The size of the artwork on
the card seems to vary by subgroup, and also within some
of the subgroups; in all cases,
the card title is printed directly underneath the picture.
The blue print backs bear
the series name, subgroup
name, card number and text.
The symbols in the vertical
panel under the card number

are not explained by any-
thing written on the card,
and we can only assume that
there was additional information included with the cards.
The corners are rounded in
playing card style, and the
reference number is R754.
The manner in which these
cards were packaged is unknown at this time.

ITEM	EX	AVE
Card	2.00	.35
Set	150.00	25.00

Card-O Trading Cards

LINCOLN — 195X

Cardo Trading Cards
AUTOMOBILES

A-11 OF A SERIES

LINCOLN 195-X Cars of the future, such as this, will have the look of a glass-enclosed cockpit and will be equipped to meet the driver's almost every need. Even today as we sit at the wheel we can eat at drive-ins or plug in a hot plate, sleep on a convertible bed, listen to the radio, watch television, play records, see drive-in movies, telephone, pick up groceries and cash his check at drive-in stores and banks—all in air-conditioned comfort, lolling in a foam-rubber-cushioned easy chair.

Collect a complete set of Cardo Trading Cards. "The Original" Genuine Collectors' Cards. ©Guild Press, Inc. *©Leaf Brands, Inc. Printed in U.S.A.

OFFICIAL AUTHENTIC PLAYING CARD BACKS

AUTOMOBILES

A-1 Stutz Bearcat—1914
A-2 Chevrolet—1915
A-3 Reo—1905
A-7 Duryea—1893
A-8 First Ford—1896
A-11 Lincoln 195-X
A-13 Maxwell—1911
A-15 Stanley Steamer—1909
A-17 Mercer—1910
A-21 First Yellow Cab—1908
A-24 Woods Electric—1899
A-30 Studebaker Electric—1902

BATTLE OF THE ALAMO

Cardo Trading Cards
COWBOYS AND INDIANS

C-1 OF A SERIES

BATTLE OF THE ALAMO Texas was a part of Mexico until the Texans declared their independence. Fighting broke out and Mexico sent General Santa Anna and 6000 troops to put down the rebellion. The Texans took up their stand in the Alamo, an old mission turned into a fort, and the 187 men held out for 9 days. Santa Anna finally attacked on all four sides, killing the defenders, and so the Alamo fell. "Remember the Alamo" became the Texans' battle cry under General Sam Houston.

Collect a complete set of Cardo Trading Cards. "The Original" Genuine Collectors' Cards. ©Guild Press, Inc. *©Leaf Brands, Inc. Printed in U.S.A.

OFFICIAL AUTHENTIC PLAYING CARD BACKS

COWBOYS AND INDIANS

C-1 Battle of the Alamo
C-2 Apache Masked Dancers
C-3 Sheriff Bill Hickok
C-5 An Indian Sprang at Daniel
C-6 Argentine Gaucho Throwing Bola
C-7 Buffalo Headdress
C-9 Famous Apache Chief
C-11 Hopi Snake Dancer
C-16 Pony Express Rider
C-18 Bad Men Hold Up a Stagecoach
C-21 Rustlers in Hiding
C-22 Daniel Runs the Gauntlet
C-24 Kit Carson
C-25 Tenderfoot Dances
C-30 Chief Blackfish

PIRATES

P-1 Bartholomew Portugues' Escape
P-2 Blackbeard Threatens His Prisoners
P-4 Captain Kid Stops A Mutiny
P-5 Chinese Pirates
P-6 Pierre Le Grand Captures a Spanish Ship
P-7 Duel Between Maynard and Blackbeard
P-8 L'Olonnois Attacks a Prisoner
P-12 Lewis and the Captain
P-15 Morgan Is Sold at a Slave Market
P-19 The Jolly Roger
P-24 Mary Read, Woman Pirate
P-27 Morgan Outwits the Spanish
P-30 Prisoner Walks the Plank

CHINESE PIRATES

Cardo Trading Cards
PIRATES

P-5 OF A SERIES

CHINESE PIRATES Off the Chinese coast, on a dark night only a few years ago, a ship's bridge was swarmed by Chinese pirates armed with guns and blackjacks. They had boarded the ship at Hong Kong dressed as ordinary coolies. Imprisoning the crew, the pirates searched and robbed the passengers, took gold from the ship's safe and found a valuable shipment of opium in the hold. After smashing the ship's radio, they made their escape in a swift launch which put out from one of the islands to meet them.

Collect a complete set of Cardo Trading Cards. "The Original" Genuine Collectors' Cards. ©Guild Press, Inc. *©Leaf Brands, Inc. Printed in U.S.A.

OFFICIAL AUTHENTIC PLAYING CARD BACKS

Cardo Trading Cards
PLANES, TRAINS AND SHIPS

T-18 NUMBER OF A SERIES

THE F-94 STARFIRE is a jet interceptor which carries radar to locate enemy planes. Unlike other interceptors, it carries a pilot plus an observer to man the radar set. The radar set is in the nose with 24 rockets. When an enemy plane appears on the radar screen, the observer guides the pilot to the target and turns on the radar-controlled gunsight, which guides the F-94 into firing position. The enemy in range, the rockets are fired automatically. The pilot may never have seen the target!

Collect a complete set of Cardo Trading Cards. "The Original" Genuine Collectors' Cards. ©Guild Press, Inc. *©Leaf Brands, Inc. Printed in U.S.A.

OFFICIAL AUTHENTIC PLAYING CARD BACKS

NAUTILUS: ATOMIC-POWERED SUBMARINE

PLANES, TRAINS AND SHIPS

T-1 Bell X-5 (US)
T-2 First Wright Flyer (US)
T-3 Supersonic Jet
T-4 B-52 Stratofortress (US)
T-5 S-55 Sikorsky Helicopter (US)
T-6 Nautilus: Atomic-Powered Submarine
T-8 Navy Skyrocket (US)
T-9 Navy Cutlass Fighter (US)
T-10 Cougar Fighter, Navy (US)
T-11 DH-110 Twin-Jet Fighter (US)
T-13 Mig Fighter (USSR)
T-14 F-102 Delta Wing Fighter (US)
T-15 Navy Skyray Fighter (US)
T-16 Hawker Hunter (GB)
T-18 F-94 Starfire Interceptor (US)
T-19 Piasecki Helicopter (US)
T-20 Talgo Train
T-21 X-1A Flies 1,600 M.P.H.
T-29 F-84F Thunderstreak Fighter (US)
T-30 Military Tow Glider (US)

ABRAHAM LINCOLN

Cardo Trading Cards
PRESIDENTS

W-16 NUMBER OF A SERIES

ABRAHAM LINCOLN—President 1861-1865 People liked Abe Lincoln. They liked his great strength and his honesty. They liked the funny stories he told. And they liked his cleverness of thought and his fair approach to their problems. Abe was a peaceful sort of man, but when he saw that arms would be necessary to preserve the Union he did not hesitate to call out the army. Lincoln was in office only one month before war broke out, and he died six days after winning peace.

Collect a complete set of Cardo Trading Cards. "The Original" Genuine Collectors' Cards. ©Guild Press, Inc. *©Leaf Brands, Inc. Printed in U.S.A.

OFFICIAL AUTHENTIC PLAYING CARD BACKS

PRESIDENTS

W-3 Thomas Jefferson
W-16 Abraham Lincoln
W-18 Ulysses S. Grant
W-32 Franklin D. Roosevelt
W-33 Harry S. Truman
W-34 Dwight D. Eisenhower

CASPER (66)

Produced by Fleer in 1960, the "Casper" series is a favorite among collectors due to

the beautiful color cartoon artwork and the stunning blue and yellow wrapper. The card

fronts have a television-style frame encircling the picture, with a sentence of dialogue printed underneath. Each card is numbered on the front only, in what appears to be a wheel design. The series title and the distinctive Fleer crown are printed in the right margin. The backs contain three- or four-panel comic strips done in several colors on flat-finish stock. A 1960 copyright line for Harvey Famous Cartoons is printed inside the frameline in the last panel. Many cards of this set are found off-center; the prices listed are for reasonably well-centered cards only. The reference number for the set is R730-6.

"Golly! I feel all washed out!"

ITEM	EX	AVE
Card	3.00	.60
Set	250.00	45.00
Wrapper	175.00	——

1 "I Always Wanted to Go Overseas!"
2 "It's Better Fishing Here!"
3 "Gee! This Modern Art Is Real Crazy!"
4 "Hickory, Dickory...Sock!"
5 "There's Always Room for One More!"
6 "Whoops! I'm Being Taken to the Cleaners!"
7 "Golly! I Feel All Washed Out!"
8 "Golly! I'm Losing My Noodles!"
9 "Katnip, You're Going to the Dogs!"
10 "Shocking, Isn't It?"
11 "I See Myself Coming and Going!"
12 "I'll Bet Painters Wish They Could Do This!"
13 "Ulp!...I Hope He's a Good Skate!"
14 "Tee-Hee..Just Don't Sneeze!"
15 "I Wonder How I Look!"
16 "I Don't Carry Any Weight Around Here!"

17 "Hey! Here's Another Dumbbell!"
18 "Duh! They Don't Build Cars Like They Used to!"
19 "Now I Can See the Hole Game!"
20 "I'll Bet an Octopus Could Really Have Fun!"
21 "Who-o-o's Scaring Who-o-o?"
22 "Fan-tastic, Isn't It?"
23 "Now, Papa, Can I Feed You?"
24 "I Never Saw a Fish Like That!"
25 "Duh! Take Me to Your Leader!"
26 "Pitooey!"
27 "If Dad Wants Coffee, We're Sunk!"
28 "It May Be Cheese, But It Smells Like Trouble!"
29 "Ohhh! I Got a Code in My Node!"
30 "Okay, Boss, When Do We Eat?"
31 "Keep Pouring, He's Gaining on Us!"
32 "Gee, This Sandwich Must Weigh a Ton!"

33 "Have a Bang-Up Birthday, Katnip!"
34 "This Is a Much Batter Way!"
35 "Now If You Were Only Here in Person..."
36 "I Had to Tell You This in Person!"
37 "Duh! Who's a Bubblehead?"
38 "Papa, Are You Sure This Is the Right Train?"
39 "If You're So Smart, You Try It!"
40 "And the Weatherman Said No Showers!"
41 "After This, Let's Swing on a Star!"
42 "This Gun Is Really Loaded!"
43 "This Beats Digging Any Day!"
44 "If This Works I'll Make a Million!"
45 "Babe Ruth Never Had This Trouble!"
46 "I'm So Happy, I'm Walking on Air!"
47 "Duh! Nuts—to Everyone!"
48 "Look! No Hands!"
49 "Hot Dog! What an Idea!"

50 "I Just Hope It Doesn't Rain."
51 "Is There a Plumber in the House?"
52 "Gosh, I Thought I Had a Towel!"
53 "What a Whale of a Fishtale!"
54 "Gee, Fellas, Where Are You?"
55 "Yum Yum! Tooty-Frooty!"
56 "Let Me Introduce Myself..."
57 "Yum! Katnip, You Have Good Taste!"
58 "The Bigger They Are, The Harder They Fall!"
59 "Now I Know How It's Done!"
60 "Gee, I'd Better Get Off That Diet!"
61 "Golly! It Went Right Through Me!"
62 "A Ghost Is a Dog's Best Friend!"
63 "Boy, They're Sure Snapping Today!"
64 "Grr, Scat Cat!"
65 "Try It Again, It Doesn't Hurt!"
66 "I Told Him Not to Follow Me!"

CIRCUS CUTOUTS (4)

Collectors would be hard pressed to identify the individual characters and animals of the Campfire Marshmallow "Circus Cutouts" series once they were removed from the large, two-page cardboard folder which originally held the designs. Each cutout part has two printed

sides and is already machine scored for easy removal (no cutting necessary). According to copy on the package, "You just cut out the figures and put them together with marshmallows as the body." The dimensions in our heading refer to a single page of the two-page folder. Each

page holds three different characters/animals. There are 24 characters in the set, and these are available on four different, numbered folders. Although Campfire Marshmallows were manufactured by Cracker Jack, this set was given the reference number R755, which is apart from

Circus Cutouts

other Cracker Jack issues listed in the early catalogs. The first mention of this set was made in the June, 1959 issue of The Card Collectors Bulletin.

ITEM	EX	AVE
Folder	25.00	10.00
Set	125.00	45.00
Package wrapper	50.00	——

THE CAMPFIRE MARSHMALLOW WRAPPER ADVERTISED THE CIRCUS CUTOUTS ON BOTH FRONT AND BACK. THE LARGE FOLDER BELOW WAS PACKED INSIDE.

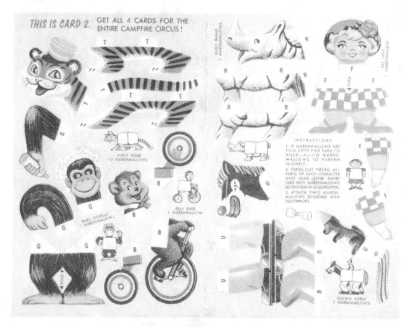

CLOVER CANDY CIGARETTE BOXES (?) 2 1/8" X 3 1/4"

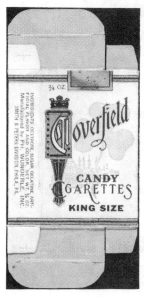

The P.H. Wunderle Company of Philadelphia sold their "Clover Brand" of candy cigarettes in boxes labelled "Pell Mell," "Cloverfield," and "Camol." The fronts of the boxes were standard "faked" brands designed to resemble the real McCoys. The backs, however, were printed with questions, riddles and magic tricks of interest to juvenile "smokers." These package-back cards were blank-backed and would be virtually unidentifiable if cut from the box. The cards are not numbered, although the numbers 46 and 16 are printed on one end flap of the sample illustrated. The dimensions in our heading refer to a "cut" card. The reference number is R795.

ITEM	EX	AVE
Card	2.00	.50
Box	15.00	5.00

COMIC CHARACTER CARDS (50)(50)   TWO SIZES

The title of this set does not appear on the cards of this category; rather, it was assigned to them by Jefferson Burdick in one of his early catalogs. There are two distinct series with different formats and proportions. The first of these is the so-called "unnamed" series in which the purchaser was invited to identify the character by filling in the letter boxes underneath each picture. Backs of the unnamed series have a "Sugar Daddy sings the silliest things!" design and lyric on the back as well as an offer to redeem 25 correctly-identified character cards for a giant lollipop. Cards of this series measure 1½" X 2¾", and some have been found with blank backs. The reference number for the unnamed series cards is R757-1.

The second type of card measures 1 1/2" X 3 3/16" and has a cut-off coupon at the bottom. The characters are named in a colored panel beneath the artwork picture. The backs are devoted to a mail-in offer for a beanie (10 coupons plus 25 cents) and a set of 12 beanie buttons (10 coupons plus 10 cents). The name "Sugar Daddy" appears on the coupon only, and collectors prefer to find these cards with the coupon intact. The reference number is R757-2. NOTE: both sets have the same checklist and were first reported in 1953.

ITEM	EX	AVE
Cards		
Unnamed	3.00	.75
Named		
With coupon	4.00	1.00
Without coupon	2.00	.50
Sets		
Unnamed	175.00	40.00
Named		
With coupon	250.00	60.00
Without coupon	115.00	30.00

1 Denny Dimwit
2 Herby
3 Pat Keen
4 Smilin' Jack
5 Harold Teen
6 Mamie
7 Nina
8 Pa Smith
9 Lord Plushbottom
10 Hilda
11 Charles C. Charles
12 Pop Jenks
13 Uncle Bim
14 Shadow
15 Moon Mullins
16 Smitty
17
18 Andy Gump
19 Ma Smith
20 The Head
21 Punjab
22 Lillums
23
24 Uncle Willie
25 Daddy Warbucks
26 Winnie Winkle
27 Chester Gump
28 Chipper
29 The Dragon Lady
30 Mr. Bibbs
31 Annie
32 Skeezix
33 Min Gump
34 Perry Winkle
35 Uncle Walt
36 Sandy
37 Kayo
38 Mr. Biggs
39
40 Downwind Jackson
41 Tiny Tim
42 Aunt Blossom
43 Lady Plushbottom
44 Pa Winkle
45 Wilmer Bobble
46 Indian Chief
47 Ma Winkle
48 Mr. AM
49 Pop Avery
50 Gramps

NAME 'EM - WIN A PRIZE !

FAMOUS COMIC CHARACTERS

NOW PACKED WITH EACH DELICIOUS

SUGAR DADDY

5¢

Collect Your Favorites -
Save 'em - Swap 'em!

POSTER – DISPLAY BOX CARD FROM THE COLLECTION OF LARRY FORTUCK

COMIC JIG—SAW PUZZLES (9K)   3 3/4″ X 5 5/8″

R.L. Albert & Son, a candy firm based in New York City, imported this collection of multi-color jigsaw puzzles from a manufacturer in Holland. Each puzzle was sold in a glassine envelope with a red frame and printing on one side, and the puzzle inside was visible to the purchaser. The candy advertised on the wrapper was a 5-inch long (but very thin) tube of tiny candy balls. The puzzles have a distinctly European flavor, and judging from the few that have survived, were probably not as popular as the company might have wished (although R.L. Albert is still in the candy business today). Only nine puzzles have been reported to the Hobby Card Index, and no reference number has been assigned.

ITEM	EX	AVE
Puzzle	5.00	1.50
Wrapper	5.00	––

EACH OF THE UNTITLED
PUZZLES HAS 15 PIECES

COMIC
JIG - SAW PUZZLE
with
CANDY

Ingred. : Sugar, Cornstarch, Artif. Flavor. Citric Acid, U. S. Cert. - Color

Made in Holland for R. L. Albert & Son, Inc., NEW YORK

THE WRAPPER IS CLEAR EXCEPT FOR THE PRINTING AND A RED FRAME LINE

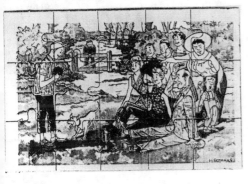

DAVY CROCKETT (80)(80)　　　　2 5/8" X 3 3/4"

When Topps issued the Davy Crockett series in 1956, Fess Parker was the hero of kids across America and they all flocked to the stores to buy the cards (it has been suggested that more empty soda bottles were redeemed at this time than at any point in recorded history!). And what beautiful cards they were, with clear color photos from the Disney movie (starring Parker as Crockett) and just enough text on the orange-colored backs to satisfy the juvenile readers. The "sort" in the boxes was so good that sets were readily put together, too easily in fact, to suit the battle-hardened trading card veterans. As the piles of orange-back duplicates grew higher and higher, with no new cards in sight, elation turned to desperation, as playmates refused to trade or flip for the "once-hot-but-now-not" Crocketts. Interest in the "King of the Wild Frontier" waned, and they moved on to other pursuits.

It was at this point that Topps decided to release its second series of green-back Crockett cards to an indifferent market. Again the cards were numbered 1-80, which made no sense to us, even with the "A" attached. Why not 81-160, Topps, was that too much to ask? And why the change of color? These changes seemed traitorous to devoted orange-back fans, and the green-backs were given the cold shoulder. Topps tinkered with something that didn't need fixing and this, plus bad timing, killed the market for their new series of Crocketts. On the other hand, it is the miscalculations of the past which create the scarcities of today — so the process, in a sense, is self-correcting.

The Davy Crockett set has reentered the limelight as a favorite of modern-day collectors. Orange-back singles and sets are readily available, but green-back sets and singles in top condition are much harder to find. Of interest to collecting purists is the fact that both color backs are found with the text area in either gray or white stock. It has also been reported that the cards were issued in Canada, which might account for some of the differences in detail between cards (all Crockett cards have a "Printed in U.S.A." line, so this line is not, in this case, a giveaway that the set was or was not issued in Canada). The 1-cent and 5-cent wrappers are very popular items, but the box is rarely seen for sale. The reference number for the set is R712-1. NOTE: add a $1.00 premium for cards with white text areas (excellent condition cards only.)

ITEM	EX	AVE
Cards		
Orange back	3.00	.75
Green back	5.00	1.00
Sets		
Orange back	290.00	65.00
Green back	500.00	110.00
Wrappers		
1-cent	200.00	——
5-cent	175.00	——
Box		speculative

DAVY SENSES TROUBLE

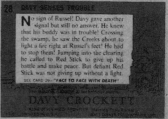

Davy Crockett

DAVY'S GAMBLE

DAVY CROCKETT CARDS & CUTOUTS (3)(1)

TWO SIZES

There are two elements to the Davy Crockett candy box series issued by the Super Novelty Candy Co. of Newark, NJ. The first and most obvious component is the set of multi-color artwork trading cards printed on the backs of the individual candy boxes. The cards measure 2 1/2" X 3 11/16" and have machine-made perforations on the edges to allow for easy removal. Once removed, the cards have no details or back print which would aid in identifying them, and they are not numbered. We have illustrated the lid from an almost full display box brought to light in Chicago several years ago; interestingly, only three different cards were observed among all the small boxes the display box contained.

The front of the small "Davy Crockett Candies and Toy" box has another interesting collectible: a 3" tall cutout-and-stand-up color photo of Fess Parker. The pose is identical to the picture on the lid of the display box, and the same stand-up is found on every box, regardless of the card which appears on the back. This stand-up is entitled "Fess Parker as Davy Crockett," and once removed from the box (there were no perforations, so it had to be cut) the manufacturer is unidentifiable. Intact boxes are valued much higher than the cards from them. The reference number is R809.

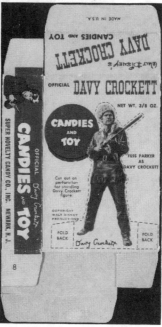

ITEM	EX	AVE
Card	5.00	1.50
Small box	30.00	7.50
Display box	150.00	50.00

At the Alamo
In Congress
Indian Fighter

DAVY CROCKETT HOT IRON PATCHES (?)

3 1/2" X 7 1/2"

Everything we need to know about this paper novelty set produced by Philadelphia Gum is printed on the large 8" X 9 3/4" display card (except the date, which was probably 1956). The tissue paper transfers measure about 3 1/2" X 7 1/2" and were stapled to the left side of the display card, which was inserted in the back end of a box of "Swell Gum." A transfer was given away free with the purchase of five pieces of gum (there were probably 20 of them stapled on each card). The transfers are one or two color sketches (brown, blue, and red colors in different combinations) and all are captioned "Davy Crockett." The gum wrappers and the display box apparently were the standard "Swell Gum" issue and did not make any specific mention of the Crockett theme. The reference number is R788-9.

ITEM	EX	AVE
Transfer	4.00	1.00
Display card (no transfers attached)	20.00	8.00

DAVY CROCKETT TATOOS (?)   1 9/16" X 3 1/2"

The "Davy Crockett Tatoo" series is a classic example of a virtually unknown collectible coming into the marketplace in substantial quantities. The tatoos are drawn using two colors and are printed on the interior side of the small outer wrapper, which is yellow with a red print title. The tatoos are not captioned, and the number in the set has yet to be established. Sharp-eyed col-

lectors have spotted a design gaffe on the exterior wrapper: a revolver, which had not been invented during Crockett's lifetime. The wrapers are marked "Bubbles Inc." and were probably issued in 1956. No reference number has been assigned.

ITEM	EX	AVE
Wrapper	20.00	––

DICK TRACY (2K)   2 3/4" X 3 7/16"

Very little is known about this Dick Tracy card issue, which was brought to our attention by collector Gordon

Burns. It appears that the cards were detached from candy boxes because they have rouletted edges. The bas-

ic colors are yellow and red, with some black, white and green accents. The characters are named in a small plaque design centered under the artwork. The cards are not numbered, however, and the backs are blank. Veteran collectors think the set might have been produced by the Super Novelty Candy Co., but this has not been confirmed. The set has yet to be assigned a reference number.

ITEM	EX	AVE
Card	7.00	2.00

DOG TRADING CARDS (36)   2 1/4" X 3 1/2"

Imagine opening a bag of candy and finding a dog inside! That's what happened in 1955 when you bought a 19-cent bag of Peter Paul "Walnettos," "Choclettos," or "Coconettos." The dogs, of course, were trading cards bearing full-color pictures of specific breeds (named underneath the photo). The backs are printed in red and black on white stock: red for the advertising copy and black for the text. The cards are not

numbered, and they have round corners (playing card style). The "header" or bag label is pictured below: it has a printed checklist of the cards on the reverse and advertises the set total as 36. It also gives us the information that three cards were inserted into every bag of candy.

In the August, 1956 issue of The Card Collectors Bulletin, card researcher and dog afficionado Buck Barker pointed

out that the Peter Paul card captioned "Scottish Terrier" was really a "Westie," or West Highland White Terrier (there is no such thing as a "White Scottie," except in a famous whiskey ad). This raises the question of how many of the other cards in the set are mis-labeled, a project for modern-day dog lovers to pursue. Barker also noted, by the way, that "most of the pictures [in this set] are the same as those shown in 'The Golden Book of Dog Stamps,' currently on sale in book & drug stores for 50 cents." The reference number is R760.

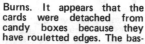

This is one of 36 Different Trading Cards featuring Dogs of every size and description from the largest Hunting Dog to the smallest Show Dog. Be first in your neighborhood to get all 36!

IRISH SETTER, with his beautiful mahogany-red coat and sleek body is one of the most handsome of all dogs. He is very intelligent, wonderfully gentle and loyal to his master. This sporting dog stands about 22 to 26 inches high, and typically the Irishman, he is happy-go-lucky in nature. He is a good worker and makes an excellent companion. Name of Irish Setter shown here is Champion Charles River Color Sergeant.

Each bag of Peter Paul Walnettos, Choclettos and Coconettos, contains 3 Different Dog Trading Cards. Collect them — trade them — and use them for games.

ITEM	EX	AVE
Card	2.00	.50
Set	85.00	20.00
Header	15.00	5.00

Airedale	Chow Chow	Eskimo Dog	Miniature Schnauzer
American Fox Hound	Cocker Spaniel	German Shepherd	Otterhound
Beagle	Collie	Golden Retriever	Pointer
Bloodhound	Dachshund	Great Dane	Pomeranian
Boston Terrier	Dalmatian	Greyhound	Saluki
Boxer	Doberman Pinscher	Irish Setter	Scottish Terrier
Brussels Griffon	English Bull Dog	Irish Wolfhound	Shetland Sheep Dog
Bull Terrier	English Foxhound	Kerry Blue Terrier	Smooth Fox Terrier
Chihuahua	English Setter	Miniature Poodle	West Highland White Terrier

ELVIS PRESLEY (66)   2 1/2" X 3 1/2"

The 1956 "Elvis Presley" series of 66 cards was distributed to the public in 1-cent and 5-cent gum packs. Most of the cards are marked "Bubbles Inc," but some are found with "Topps" printed instead (the latter might have been issued in Canada, but this has not been confirmed). The color photographs on the fronts were taken on movie lots, in recording studios, and at concerts. Captions for the movie cards are printed in a "sceneboard" while the captions for musical cards are located in a red guitar. The card backs have either a long paragraph describing some aspect of "The King's" movie career or an "Ask Elvis" feature. The 5-cent wrapper with Elvis pictured in the center is more popular and more difficult to find than the 1-cent "continuous design" wrapper. The display box (illustrated courtesy of Robert Marks) is the scarcest item associated with this set. The reference number is R710-1.

ITEM	EX	AVE
Card	5.00	1.25
Set	425.00	100.00
Wrappers		
1-cent	60.00	— —
5-cent	125.00	— —
Box		speculative

At the Keyboard

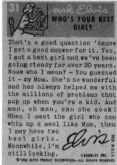

1	Go, Go, Go, Elvis.	18	Singing Session.	42	Radio Broadcast.

1 Go, Go, Go, Elvis.
2 Elvis Presley—Elvis Presley's Record Collector's Checklist.
3 Relaxing at Rehearsals.
4 Love Me Tender.
5 Soft and Mellow.
6 Elvis with His Fans.
7 Presley Press Conference.
8 Singing with the Heart.
9 Time Out between Shows.
10 America's Singing Idol.
11 Don't Be Cruel.
12 Pickin' Out a Tune.
13 Steve Allen and Elvis.
14 Down on the Farm.
15 Judging His Record.
16 Vacation Fun.
17 Studying the Script.
18 Singing Session.
19 I Want You, I Need You, I Love You.
20 A Tux for T.V.
21 Elvis Presley.
22 The Fan's Friend.
23 Ready to Ride.
24 Elvis's Movie Debut.
25 Elvis's Motorcycle.
26 Hound Dog.
27 Swinging Low.
28 Acting Outdoors.
29 Facing the Cameras.
30 Elvis the Actor.
31 At the Keyboard.
32 Tuning Up for the Show.
33 A Show for the Hometown.
34 Taking It Easy between Scenes.
35 Elvis at 17.
36 Chow Time on the Movie Set.
37 Strumming for Fun.
38 Elvis's Escort.
39 Lights, Camera, Action.
40 Serenade to a Pooch.
41 Rockin' on Stage.
42 Radio Broadcast.
43 Recording Session.
44 Elvis Special Shirt.
45 Preparing to Go on Stage.
46 America's Top Singer.
47 Clint and Cathy Reno.
48 Farm Chores.
49 New Member of the Family.
50 Hard Work.
51 Happy Homecoming.
52 Pooch Performance.
53 I Want an Honest Answer.
54 Heading for the Fair.
55 Singing Up a Storm.
56 Bad News.
57 I'm Going to Vance.
58 Rescue Ride.
59 Clint's Plane.
60 Don't Try to Stop Me.
61 Fighting Mad
62 Two Against One.
63 Setting the Trap.
64 Let Him Have It, Clint.
65 Clint Takes Aim.
66 Go Back to Vance.

FABIAN (55)

The meteoric rise to fame of "The Fabulous Fabian" is the subject of this 55-card series marketed by Topps in 1959. The fronts have gorgeous color photographs of "America's No. 1 Teenager" while the backs are occupied by a "Tell Us Fabian" feature in which the star imparts his philosophy of life. The series

encountered flat response from the public, prompting Topps to shuttle it off to the company's version of re-runs: "bricks" of 500 cards sold in generic "variety" boxes. This explains why the cards are so common but the wrapper and display box are not. The set is currently enjoying a modest revival in popularity, but it remains (along with "Menudo" and other similar sets) a testimony to the fact that self-serving, "publicity" sets don't sit well with the card collecting public. The reference number is R710-5.

ITEM	EX	AVE
Card	1.50	.35
Set	100.00	20.00
Wrapper	100.00	—
Box	200.00	60.00

1 Making a Record	19 Star of Stage and Screen	37 Warm Welcome
2 Fabian's School Friends	20 Time Out for Shopping	38 Packing for a Tour
3 Deep in Thought	21 Heading for a Trip	39 In the Driver's Seat
4 Shopping for Shirts	22 Just a Man and His Horse	40 Fabian the Favorite
5 "Hey Lump of Sugar."	23 Hound Dog Man	41 Tiger and Tiger Boy
6 The First Movie Role	24 Fabian Talks to Fans	42 The Famous Smile
7 Most Popular Boy under the Sun	25 First Aid for Fabian	43 Old-Fashioned Barn Dance
8 Thinking of the Future	26 Recording Session	44 Not Too Close, Please
9 Fabian Off to School	27 Star of Chancellor Records	45 America's No. 1 Teenager
10 Fabian Flashes a Smile	28 Time to Think	46 A Well-earned Rest
11 Fabian at Play	29 Relaxing on Long Trip	47 Quick Nap
12 Fabian in the Movies	30 Physical Check-up!	48 Lights, Action, Camera
13 Fabian Performs	31 Musical Get-together	49 Playing Back a Record
14 The Tiger Boy	32 Nature Boy	50 Terrific Teenager
15 Stretching Out on Movie Set	33 Memorizing His Lines	51 Belting Out a Song
16 A Royal Reception	34 Fabian the Swordsman	52 Fabian at School
17 Hard Worker	35 Fabian the Actor	53 A New Hit in the Making
18 The Fabulous Fabian	36 Seeing Double	54 Studying a New Song
		55 Blackboard Assignment

FACT AND FANTASY (?)

"Fact and Fantasy" is the title of a little-known feature produced by Philadelphia Gum Co. It is a rust-colored comic strip with a few red accents, and it is printed on the interior side of a "Missile Bubble Gum" wrapper. The spectacular exterior side is a foil wrapper produced for Philly Gum by Reynolds Aluminum. It is

yellow with a red and blue rocket in the center. The comic strips apparently alternated between presentations of factual and fictional material; in either case, a red emphasis balloon carries the words "It's a Fact" or "It's Fantasy" somewhere on the strip. Fact and Fantasy was first reported in the February, 1958 issue of The Card

Collectors Bulletin. This wrapper/comic must have been produced on an extremely limited basis, for very few appear in modern collections. The reference number is R788-3.

ITEM	EX	AVE
Wrapper/ Comic	25.00	—

FAMOUS AMERICAN HEROES (18)

Many of the listings in the early card catalogs during the period 1939-1960 refer to sets which have rarely, if ever, been seen by modern-day collectors. The "Famous American Heroes" series, issued in 5-cent Bazooka Gum rolls, is just such a set. As you can see by our illustration, the Heroes drawings have been made to look like stamps, but they are actually miniature cardboard cards. Our example is a two-card panel drawn in red ink on off-white stock and has the words "Collect Bazooka Stamps" printed at top-center between the two designs. The cardboard panel containing the stamps measures 1" X 4 5/8" and clearly was the package stiffener on which the gum roll rested. Given the small size of the cards, it is no wonder that so

7/8" X 1 3/8"

few have survived. There are nine different panels and 18 cards/stamps in the set. Until more are found, values for this item are likely to remain high because of the demand from specialty and type collectors. The reference number is R714-3.

ITEM	EX	AVE
Card	10.00	4.00
Panel	25.00	10.00
Set		
Cards only	215.00	50.00
Panels	500.00	125.00

FAMOUS EVENTS (60K)

This would have been the largest wrapper set on record if Topps had stayed with its original plan, which was to single out a special event in history for each and every day of the calendar year. The development team must have realized the true magnitude of the task after

dealing with the month of January (for which we have 23 confirmed comics), because there are less than 40 comics reported for the remaining eleven months. Each rust-colored comic has the date in a calendar-page box at the right, and the event is described in a panel at the top.

2" X 2 7/8"

Below the artwork is another panel which contains a brief astrological characterization of people born on that day. The comics are printed on the interior side of a Bazooka 1-cent foil wrapper. The series was issued in 1949. The series has an alternate title — "On This Day in History" — but this name only appears on old research notes, and it is not printed on the comics or wrapper. The reference number is R711-4.

ITEM	EX	AVE
Wrapper/		
Comic	5.00	2.00

Jan. 1, 1863-Lincoln Issues the Emancipation Declaration.

Jan. 2, 1647-Nathaniel Bacon is Born. He Lead the First Revolt in America Against England.

Jan. 3, 1777-Washington Won an Important Victory at Princeton.

Jan 4, 1608-Captain John Smith Returns to Virginia After Being Saved by Pocahontas.

Jan. 5, 1925-Nellie Ross Becomes the First Woman Governor in the United States.

Jan. 9, 1793-Pierre Blanchard Flies a Balloon for the First Time in America.

Jan. 10, 1738-Ethan Allen was Born. He Was to Lead the Americans to Take Fort Ticonderoga.

Jan. 11, 1910-First U.S. Aviation Meet. Many New Airplanes Shown for the First Time.

Jan 12, 1687-The French Explorer La Salle was Murdered by His Own Men.

Jan. 13, 1933-Jean Mermoz Flies from W. Africa to Brazil, Establishing a New Speed Record.

Jan. 14, 1824-The House of Representatives Chose John Quincy Adams as the 6th President of the U.S.

Jan. 15, 1942-Nehru Became the Head of the All India Congress Party.

Jan. 16, 1754-Young Major Washington was Sent to Warn the French in Ohio That They Must Withdraw.

Jan. 17, 1706-Benjamin Franklin is Born in Boston, Mass.

Jan. 18, 1911-Eugene Ely Lands a Plane on Deck of a Battleship for the First Time.

Jan. 20, 1882-Digging Begins Through Jungle and Swamp for Panama Canal.

Jan. 21, 1936-King George V Dies at Saringham House, Norfolk, England.

Jan. 22, 1943-The Eight British Army Takes Tripoli, Rommel's Last Outpost.

Jan. 24, 1848-Gold Discovered in California at a Place Called Sutter's Mill.

Jan. 25, 1881-Nelly Bly, the Star Reporter Goes Around the World in 72 days.

Jan. 26, 1911-Glenn Curtiss Makes the First Successful Take Off from the Water.

Jan. 27, 1943-American B-17s Bomb Germany for the First Time, in World War II.

Jan. 30, 1649-King Charles I Beheaded at London, England for Treason.

Feb. 11, 1847-Thomas A. Edison, Famous Inventor is Born.

March 6, 1836-Davy Crockett and Texan Defenders Were Massacred at the Alamo.

March 9, 1916-Columbus, New Mexico, Raided by Pancho Villa.

April 3, 1860-Pony Express Riders Run from Sacramento, California, to St. Joe, Missouri.

April 8, 1513-Ponce De Leon Discovers Florida While Searching for Fountain of Youth.

Famous Events

April 14, 1865-Lincoln Assassinated by Actor John Wilkes Booth in Washington Theatre.

April 18, 1775-Paul Revere's Midnight Ride from Boston to Lexington to Warn that the "British" were coming.

April 21, 1823-First Steamboat, the Virginia, Ascended the Mississippi as Far as Ft. Snelling, Minn., 729 miles.

May 7, 1915-The S.S. Lusitania Sunk by the Germans in a Submarine off Ireland.

May 8, 1902-St. Pierre, Martinique Destroyed by Volcanic Eruption of Mt. Pelee; About 30,000 Lives Lost.

May 10, 1869-Central Pacific and Union Pacific Railroads Joined with Golden Spike...First Transcontinental Railway.

May 15, 1602-Capt. Bartholomew Gosnold of Falsmouth, England, First Known White Man to Set Foot in New England.

May 23, 1701-Capt. Kidd, American Free Booter, and Nine of His Men Hanged in London for Piracy.

May 27, 1754-George Washington, Leading Virginia Militia Men Against French, Wins First Battle. (French-Indian War)

May 31, 1889-Johnstown, Pennsylvania, Flood; 2200 Lives Lost in Terrible Catastrophe.

June 17, 1775-Colonists Make Brave Stand at Bunker Hill.

June 18, 1815-Napoleon Defeated at Waterloo by Gen. Wellington.

June 25, 1876- Gen. Custer and Soldiers of 7th Cavalry Massacred at Little Big Horn by Sioux Indians.

July 4, 1776-The Bellman in the Philadelphia Town Hall is Told About the Declaration of Independence.

July 14, 1789-The Bastille, Old French Prison Captured by the Parisian Rebels.

July 22, 1933-Wiley Post Flies Around World in 7 Days, 18 Hours, 29 Minutes and 30 Seconds.

Aug. 5, 1876-Wild Bill Hickok is Shot in the Back by a Bandit Jack McCall.

Aug. 6, 1926-Getrude Ederle Swims the Difficult English Channel.

Aug. 27, 1664-Peter Stuyvesant, Director General of New Amsterdam, Without a Fight Gives Up and Listens to English Terms.

Aug. 28, 1909-Glenn Curtis Won the Gordon Bennett Cup Race, Flying an Airplane at a Speed of 46 M.P.H.

Aug. 31, 1851-The Clipper Ship, Flying Cloud Arrives in San Francisco After Record Run from N.Y.

Sept. 3, 1609-Henry Hudson Sailed Up the Hudson River Under the Dutch Flag.

Sept. 3, 1939-England and France Declare War on Germany as Poland is Blitzed by the Nazis.

Sept. 22, 1776-Nathan Hale, Patriot Spy, Is Hanged by the British in New York.

October 8, 1918-Corporal Alvin York Captured 132 German Soldiers.

Oct. 9, 1871-The Great Disastrous Fire in Chicago was Raging at its Height.

November 6, 1869-First Inter-Collegiate Football Game in the United States.

Dec. 7, 1941-Pearl Harbor was Attacked by the Japanese.

Dec. 19, 1776-During Washington's Retreat, Tom Paine Wrote Pampthlet "The Crisis."

Dec. 27, 1935-Town of Hilo Saved from Volcano by Army Planes Daming Lava Channels Thus Diverting Lava from Town

FELIX THE CAT (?)

2 7/16" X 3 11/16"

In the mid-1950's, the Phoenix Candy Company (Brooklyn) issued a series of candy box cards called "Color by the Numbers." The boxes had multi-color fronts featuring famous cartoon characters and a color-in card on the back. Since we have only identified a few of the comic personalities depicted on the boxes, we have decided to deal with them singly until more information can be found. The

Felix the Cat box illustrated has an aqua-color front with red, yellow, and black accents. The card on back is totally white except for the red and black print. The picture has a number of areas marked with numbers; these indicate which color (presumably crayon) should be used according to a number/color key printed at the bottom. The significance of the numbers 28 and 9395,

which are printed on two box flaps, has yet to be determined. The reference number is R821-2. NOTE: see "Popeye and His Pals" for another box in the "Color by the Numbers" series. Colored-in cards cannot be graded excellent.

ITEM	EX	AVE
Card	2.50	.60
Box	15.00	6.00

247

FIGHTING MARINES (96)   2 1/16" X 2 15/16"

Cards of the "Fighting Marines" series issued by Topps in 1953 have smooth edges on all sides if issued singly, or four separation "nubs" on the right or left edge if distributed in panels (the former were sold in 1-cent packs, the latter in "5-centers"). The set is a mixture of color photographs and multi-color artwork; the photos show Marines in training and their equipment, while the artwork depicts famous events in Marine Corps history and Corps' uniforms from the American Revolution to the Korean Conflict. The card fronts were given a patriotic air by the use of red and blue frame lines on the white background of the borders. Captions are printed both front and back, but the card number is located on the back only. Cards 44, 74, and 96 seem to be scarcer than any others in the set and are worth double the prices listed below. NOTE: cards with gum stains on the reverse cannot be graded excellent. The reference number is R709-1.

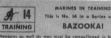

ITEM	EX	AVE
Cards		
1-48	4.00	1.00
49-96	5.00	1.25
Panel	18.00	4.00
Set	550.00	125.00
Wrappers		
1-cent	60.00	––
5-cent	90.00	––

1 Firing the Howitzer	25 Take Off!	49 The Last Moment	73 World War I
2 On the March	26 Scouting the Beach	50 In the Face of Death	74 Boxer Rebellion
3 Landing a Tank	27 Officer in Action	51 Forcing an Entrance	75 Raiding the Bahamas
4 Riding the Tank	28 Pushing Forward	52 Dangerous Landing	76 Into Korea
5 Bayonet Practice	29 "Get that Plane"	53 Riding the Tail	77 To the Shores of Tripoli
6 Firing Instructions	30 Paratrooper	54 Flying Leathernecks	78 Civil War
7 Night Combat	31 Jungle Wire	55 Raging Sea	79 First Marine Aviation
8 Obstacle Course	32 Wash Day	56 Into the Flames	80 Spanish American War
9 Flame Thrower	33 Rescue at Sea	57 Marine Engineers	81 Belleau Wood
10 Storming Ashore	34 Landing Signal	58 Staying with a Pal	82 In the Philippines
11 House to House Combat	35 "Rush for the Gun"	59 Bare-handed Attack	83 In the Caribbean
12 Clashing Steel	36 "Hit the Beach"	60 Under Fire	84 Sumatra
13 Into the Surf!	37 Gunnery Sergeant	61 Iwo Jima Hero	85 Wake Island
14 Bazooka!	38 Supplies for Battle	62 Single-handed Battle	86 Solomon Islands
15 Communications Personnel	39 "Down They Go"	63 Life Saver!	87 Iceland
16 Woman Marine	40 Battle for Tarawa	64 Dead Shot!	88 Inchon
17 Careful Aim	41 Into the Night	65 Fearless Leader!	89 Pusan
18 Mortar Sight	42 General A.A. Vandergrift	66 Exposed to Fire	90 Wonsan
19 Automatic Rifle	43 Iwo Jima	67 Dodging Bullets	91 The Revolutionary War
20 Set for Action	44 Marine Fighter	68 Grenade Attack!	92 The War in Tripoli
21 Howitzer Crew	45 Target Ahead!	69 Rear Guard	93 The Mexican War
22 Throw that Grenade	46 Attack from the Skies	70 Saving the Wounded	94 The Civil War
23 Light Machine Guns	47 Back from the Front	71 "From the Halls of Montezuma"	95 The Spanish American War
24 Final Instructions	48 Lowering a Bomb	72 Against the Indians	96 World War I

FIRE ENGINE CUTOUTS (?)

2 7/16" X 3 3/4"

A collector looking for a sample of the "Fire Engine Cutouts" series issued by the Williamson Candy Company (Chicago) is likely to find it in damaged condition. After all, these cards were designed to be cut off the boxes by pre-teens wielding dull, blunt-end scissors; probably very few have survived like the one illustrated here. The engines are not numbered and, unfortunately, the caption for each was "disengaged" from the box. The color scheme for the entire box, including the card, was red and blue on white. The reference number for the set is R763.

ITEM	EX	AVE
Cutout	3.00	1.00
Box	20.00	6.50

FIREFIGHTERS (64)

2 1/2" X 3 3/4"

According to a statement on the back of each card, Bowman's "Firefighters" series was produced with the "Cooperation of Uniformed Firemen's and Uniformed Fire Officers Associations, City of New York." The fronts bear

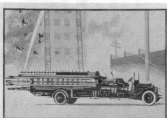

multi-color artwork pictures of fire engines, fire boats, and rescue trucks (including many fire-fighting machines from the past). The admonishments printed above the equipment descriptions actually qualify the series as the first "safety" trading card set ever produced. The set title, card caption, and card number are printed only on the reverse. To the right of the text

is an illustrated feature which identifies and describes an array of historical and modern fire-fighting paraphernalia. The reference number for the set is R701-3.

ITEM	EX	AVE
Card	5.00	1.00
Set	400.00	75.00
Wrapper	60.00	––
Box	400.00	120.00

1 Modern Fire Engine (Don't Play With Matches!)
2 Modern Hook and Ladder (Don't Start Fires!)
3 Modern Pumping Engine (Don't Play with Electric Plugs)
4 Airport Crash Truck (Don't Play with Candles!)
5 Modern Fire Department Ambulance (Don't Play with Cigarette Lighters!)
6 Modern Rescue Truck (Don't Play with Lighter Fluid!)
7 Modern Quadruple Combination (Don't Play Near Fireplace!)
8 Modern Hook and Ladder (Don't Play with Fire Alarm Boxes!)
9 Ward La France 3-stage "Booster" (Don't Burn Leaves on a Windy Day!)
10 Modern General Service Truck (Don't Leave Camp Fires Burning!)
11 Modern Pumping Engine (Don't Keep Oily Rags Around!)
12 Modern Pumping Engine (Don't PLay with Explosives!)
13 Modern Hook and Ladders (Don't Play with Firearms!)
14 Pumper-Hook and Ladder Combination (Don't Play with Fireworks!)
15 Modern Hook and Ladder (Keep Christmas Tree in Water Stand!)
16 Engine-Searchlight Combination (Keep Away From Kerosene Lamps!)
17 Engine-propelled Steam Fire Engine (Keep Furnace Doors Closed!)
18 Modern Searchlight Wagon (Obey Teachers and Authorities!)
19 Modern Quadruple (Walk–Don't Run–To Exits!)
20 Modern Quadruple Combination (Don't Mix Unknown Chemicals!)

21 1912 Knox Combination (In Case of Fire, Don't Open Windows!)
22 Knox Chief's Car—1916 (Keep Fire Escapes Clear!)
23 1901 Searchlight Unit (Keep Away from Third Rails!)
24 1912—Pumping Engine (Prevent Fires...Save Lives!)
25 1912 Pumping Engine (Don't Play with Matches!)
26 1916 Fire Patrol (Be Unfair to Fires,,,Put Them out of Business!)
27 1918 Hook and Ladder Truck (Don't Overload Electric Circuits!)
28 1914 Knox Combination (Keep Chimney in Good Repair!)
29 1911 Self-propelled Steam Engine (Don't Burn Leaves on Windy Day!)
30 WaterTower—1900 (The Match is Down—Are You Sure It's Out!)

31 1925 Hose and Chemical Combination (Fires Cost 11,000 Lives in 1951!)
32 Modern Pumping Combination (Keep Stove Free from Grease!)
33 Modern High Pressure Fog Unit (False Alarms Can Cause Much Harm!)
34 Modern Pumping Engine (A Clean Attic Is Fire Prevention!)
35 1923 Service Ladder Truck (Never Pile Rubbish Under Stairs!
36 1925 Chemical Truck (Be Fireproof—Prevent Fires!)
37 1848—Hand Operated Engine (Never Have Curtains Near Open Flame!)
38 Modern Fireboat (Porridge Hot and Porridge Cold, Play with Fire and Never Grow Old!)
39 Modern Crash Truck (If Refrigerator Leaks...Call Fire Department)
40 1926 Motorcycle Fire Engine (Don't Play Near Fireplace!)

41 1922 Triple Combination (For Any Emergency...Call Fire Department!)
42 1923—Hose Cart (Report Any Fume Odors in Street!)
43 1925 Triple Combination (Don't Play with Matches!)
44 Modern Rescue Truck (Don't Start Fires!)
45 1938—Combination (Don't Play with Candles!)
46 Modern Fire Boat (Be Unfair to Fires; Put Them Out of Business!)
47 Modern Rescue Truck and Pumper (Don't Play with Cigarette Lighters!)
48 1850 'Squirrel Tail' Engine (Be Fireproof—Prevent Fires!)
49 Smoke Ejector (Don't Play with Lighter Fluid!)
50 Modern Hook and Ladder (Don't Leave Camp Fires Burning!)
51 1935 Double Combination (Don't Keep Oily Rags Around!)
52 Horse Drawn Steam Engine (Don't Overload Electric Circuits!)

53 Modern Triple Combination (Don't Play with Firearms!)
54 Modern Special Apparatus (Don't Play with Firecrackers!)
55 Modern Triple Combination (Keep Christmas Tree in Water Stand!)
56 Modern Rescue Truck (Keep Furnace Doors Closed!)
57 Modern Fire Boat (Keep Away from Kerosene Lamps!)
58 Modern Fire Boat (Obey Teachers and Authorities!)
59 Modern Triple Combination (Walk—Don't Run—to Exits!)
60 1924 Hook and Ladder (Don't Mix Unknown Chemicals!)
61 1925 Pumping Engine (In Case of Fire, Don't Open Windows!)
62 1932 Hook and Ladder (Keep Fire Escapes Clear!)
63 Modern Pumping Engine (Keep Away from Third Rails!)
64 1939 Pumping Engine (Prevent Fire...Save Lives!)

FLAGS OF ALL NATIONS & SOLDIERS OF THE WORLD (32K)

7/8" X 1 7/16"

The first insert cards manufactured by Topps appeared in the late 1940's, and they covered a number of subjects — flags and soldiers, cars and license plates, football players, "magic" photos, and historical characters. Most of these sets shared two design elements: miniature size (7/8" X 1 7/16") and double features (meaning that the cards appeared to have two fronts, rather than a traditional front and back). Make no mistake, Topps was not merely being "cheap" in producing such downscale cards; instead, they were following the "mini" gum pack formula which had led the company to the front of the industry. When Topps realized that a switch to a larger card format was necessary to compete against Bowman, the changeover was made quite rapidly and successfully. The "double front" was simply an attempt to "pack" the miniature cards with an interest "wallop," thereby attracting customers. It was also scrapped after Topps moved into larger formats.

The set under discussion here was listed under the title "Flags" in all previous catalogs. That was confusing because the most appealing aspect of the cards are the color artwork soldiers printed on

Flags of All Nations/Soldiers Of The World

the glossy cardboard side. The flags on the other side are printed on shiny patterned cloth, but are not peelable stickers as some researchers have suggested. The series was issued in 1949, and only 32 titles have been registered so far with The Hobby Card Index. The fact that some cards appear to be more common than others suggests that a number of them were double-printed, but no conclusive list of single and double prints has been established. Based on information from the files of Topps art director Woody Gelman, John Neuner reports that this set was also distributed in 1-cent packs of Topps chewing gum, as well as in its own bubble gum wrapper. The box, rarely seen, comes from the collection of Robert Marks. The reference number is R714-7.

ITEM	EX	AVE
Card	4.00	1.00
Wrapper	75.00	––
Box	150.00	––

FLAG	SOLDIER
Admiral–Italy	Italian Naval Cadet – 1920
Admiral–Japan	Japanese Admiral – 1940
Admiral–Netherlands	Dutch Admiral – 1915
Comm. Perry's Flag	(Commodore Perry – American Naval Hero War of 1812)
Confederate States	(Gen. Robert E. Lee, Commander of the Confederate Troops)
Denmark	Royal Guardsman – Denmark
Dominican Republic	Infantryman – Dominican Republic
Ecuador	Ecuadorian Cadet
Egypt	Desert Sharpshooter Egypt
1st American Flag	U.S. Drummer 1776
General Staff–France	French Poilu – World War I
Honduras	Honduran Soldier
Hungary	Soldier of the Line Hungary – 1850
Iceland	Infantryman Iceland
India	Indian Machine Gunner
Iran	Persian Artilleryman
Iraq	Iraq Machine-Gunner
Irish Free State	Fighting Man Irish Free State
Liberia	Sergeant Liberia
Luxembourg	Major – Luxembourg – 1891
Netherlands	Dutch Sailor
Philippines	A Philippine Infantryman
Portugal	Honor Guardsman – Portuguese Legion
Pre-Revolutionary Jack	American Fighting Man 1776
Siam	Siamese Officer
Sweden	Swedish Sailor 1886
Syria	A Syrian Horseman
Turkey	Sergeant of Zeibecks Turkey – 1875
Ukranian S.S.R.	Soldier of the Red Army
USSR Airforce	First Lieutenant U.S.S.R. Air Corps
Viking Flag	Viking Warrior 12th Century

SERGEANT OF ZEIBECKS TURKEY—1875

SIAMESE OFFICER

MAJOR—LUXEMBOURG 1891

FIGHTING MAN IRISH FREE STATE

DESERT SHARPSHOOTER EGYPT

HONDURAN SOLDIER

SWEDISH SAILOR

INDIAN MACHINE GUNNER

ECUADORIAN CADET

SOLDIER OF THE LINE HUNGARY—1850

VIKING WARRIOR 12TH CENTURY

DUTCH SAILOR

251

FLAGS OF THE WORLD (80)   2 5/8" X 3 3/4"

The vividly-colored series entitled "Flags of the World" was produced by Topps in 1956. The artwork fronts depict the flags of the United States, United Nations, and 78 foreign countries all set upon gorgeous, detailed backdrops. One third of the reverse contains the card number and a list of important data about the specific country. Underneath this is an illustrated feature, "How They Say," which gives phonetic translations of common words in the language of the nation whose flag is pictured on front. Until recently, it was thought that the series was issued only in standard 1-cent and 5-cent wax packs. However, a 5-cent "test" warpper (label variety) has been discovered with a "Money of the World" advertisment on front. The currency insert idea was shelved when the set went into regular production, surfacing later in Topps' 1970 flag set of the same name. The reference number for the 1956 Flags of the World series is R714-5.

ITEM	EX	AVE
Card	1.50	.35
Set	145.00	35.00
Wrappers		
1-cent	75.00	––
5-cent regular	100.00	––
5-cent test	200.00	––

RIGHT: AUSTRALIAN VERSION
ISSUED IN 1962
BELOW: TWO CARD PANEL
WITH WRONG BACKS

ABOVE: REGULAR 1-CENT & 5-CENT WRAPPERS
BELOW: TEST WRAPPER & BANKNOTE

1 United States	21 Argentina	41 Philippines	61 Ecuador
2 Iran	22 Panama	42 Brazil	62 Indochina
3 El Salvador	23 Russia	43 Iraq	63 Yugoslavia
4 Syria	24 Austria	44 Denmark	64 Libya
5 Ceylon	25 Liberia	45 Nicaragua	65 Sweden
6 Peru	26 Great Britain	46 Afghanistan	66 Czechoslovakia
7 Turkey	27 Albania	47 Portugal	67 Mexico
8 Honduras	28 Bulgaria	48 Ethiopia	68 New Zealand
9 Union of South Africa	29 Israel	49 Poland	69 Chile
10 Bolivia	30 Saudi Arabia	50 Cuba	70 Jordon
11 Burma	31 Rumania	51 Algeria	71 Egypt
12 Venezuela	32 China People's Republic	52 Tibet	72 Pakistan
13 Greece	33 Lebanon	53 Thailand	73 Dominican Republic
14 Costa Rica	34 India	54 Spain	74 Finland
15 Ireland	35 Colombia	55 Germany West	75 Belgium
16 Haiti	36 Japan	56 Luxemburg	76 Netherlands
17 Iceland	37 South Korea	57 Paraguay	77 Norway
18 China Nationalist	38 Hungary	58 Italy	78 Guatemala
19 Canada	39 Switzerland	59 Australia	79 Monaco
20 Indonesia	40 France	60 Uruguay	80 United Nations

FLAGS OF THE WORLD - PARADE (100) 1 3/4" X 2 7/8"

This series is essentially an upsized and expanded version of the "miniature" flag & soldier set previously issued by Topps in 1949. The word "Parade" is associated with the title since it is printed on the back of every card (it is the name of the gum). The 1949 copyright printed on the 5-cent wrapper is the year of product registration for Parade Gum; this set was actually marketed in 1950 and/or 1951. The artwork cards portray the flags of

different nations as well as other entities (confederated republics, naval standards, service branches, etc.), and the set is formally classified into five subsets: Asia, Africa, Europe, Pacific, & The Americas. As a result, each card has a set number (in a black box at the top-left on the back) and a subset number (at the bottom on the back). The backs contain a short amount of data and/or text. A soldier line-drawing is located under the set number. Cards with "nubs" on the edges came in two-card panels packed in the 5-cent package (three panels per pack). In some cases, the card captions differ slightly between front and back, and cards 4 and 87 are both listed (on back) as being number 14 in the "Europe" subset. The reference number for this set is R714-6.

ITEM	EX	AVE
Card	1.50	.35
Set	180.00	40.00
Wrappers		
1-cent	35.00	—
5-cent	65.00	—
Box	175.00	50.00

1	Germany	26	Confederate States	51	Pakistan	76	Albania
2	Bolivia	27	Pre-revolutionary Jack	52	China	77	Paraguay
3	Trans Jordan	28	Byelo Russian S.S.R.	53	Norway	78	Columbus' Flag
4	Belgium	29	Netherlands	54	Nicaragua	79	Austria
5	Gold Coast	30	Burma	55	Hungary	80	Italy
6	Australia	31	Brazil	56	New Zealand	81	Tibet
7	Morocco	32	Mexico	57	Admiral—Italy	82	Alamo
8	Argentina	33	Spain	58	Latvia	83	Admiral—Norway
9	Estonia	34	Luxembourg	59	Abyssinia	84	Haiti
10	Afghanistan	35	Liberia	60	Admiral—Japan	85	Admiral—Spain
11	Iraq	36	Switzerland	61	Admiral—Great Britain	86	Guatemala
12	Uruguay	37	Lebanon	62	Armenia	87	Admiral—Netherlands
13	Iran	38	U.S. Marine Corps	63	Portugal	88	Ukranian S.S.R.
14	United States	39	Yugoslavia	64	General Staff, France	89	Turkey
15	India	40	Yemen	65	El Salvador	90	Greece
16	Iceland	41	Red Cross	66	USSR Air Force	91	France
17	United Kingdom	42	Venezuela	67	Egypt	92	Syria
18	U.S.S.R. (Russia)	43	U.S. Admiral	68	Ecuador	93	Ethiopia
19	Honduras	44	Czechoslovakia	69	Saudi Arabia	94	Bulgaria
20	1st American Flag	45	Royal Air Force	70	Dominican Republic	95	Sweden
21	Union of South Africa	46	Cuba	71	Poland	96	Irish Free State
22	Viking Flag	47	Confederate States	72	Denmark	97	Siam
23	Commodore Perry's Flag	48	Panama	73	Rumania	98	Israel
24	Chile	49	Costa Rica	74	The Philippines	99	Japan
25	Canada	50	Colombia	75	Peru	100	Finland

HONEST.....
SPORT AMERICANA GUIDES ARE TOPS!

FLEER COMIC BOOKS (?)   3 3/8" X 7 1/4"

If it weren't for the "Dubble Bubble" advertisement on the back cover, it would be impossible to associate this group of comic books with Fleer Gum. There are 24 pages, including covers, in each comic; these are broken down into a main story and several smaller features. The comic book illustrated, for example, chronicles the exploits of "Blaze Carson" in an adventure entitled "The Sheriff Shoots It Out," which is followed by two smaller 3-page stories and two 1-page items, "Target Game" and "The Unfriendly Indians." Just how the comic books were distributed — as hand-outs by retailers or through the mail — is not known. They were produced for Fleer by Vital Publications (NY) and bear a copyright date of 1950. Only one other character, "Wunder Duck," has been registered with The Hobby Card Index as of this date. The reference number for this set is R764-4.

ITEM	EX	AVE
Comic book	20.00	10.00

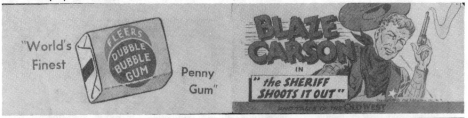

FLEER FUNNIES (?)   MANY SIZES

One thing you have to admit about Pud, the star of Fleer Funnies...he sure ages gracefully! He has been around since the mid-1930's, but as you can see (in the various comics illustrated), he never aged a bit in over 25 years. Like Bazooka Joe, the comic book symbol created by Topps, Pud was designed with two eye-catching details: his horizontally-striped shirt and vertically-striped beanie. his rotund proportions are another key element: they make him more acceptable to kids in the real world, and kids, of course, are the principal chewers of gum. The Fleer Funnies comics of the post war era were much smaller than their 1930's predecessors (about 60 percent smaller), and they have continued to be downsized over the years. They run in series, each of which has its own numbering system. Unlike Topps, Fleer didn't print production codes on the comics, so dating them can be a problem. In general, it's best to date them

255

according to style, and values are correlated to age. Fleer Funnies should be priced as Follows: 1948 to 1955...$3.00 each; 1956 to 1959...$2.00 each; the 1960's...$1.00 each; the 1970's...$ .35 each; the 1980's...$ .10 each. The reference number is R764-2.

PUD AND HIS ASSOCIATES WERE FLEER'S ANSWER TO BAZOOKA JOE (TOPPS) AND TOMMY SWELL (PHILADELPHIA GUM)

FLEER QUIZ (?)

Another wax paper penny-gum insert from Fleer, the "Fleer Quiz" was first mentioned in the August, 1961 copy of The Card Collectors Bulletin. Given the normal

"lapse time" for the reporting of new issues in CCB, the quiz inserts were probably issued in 1960 (although the series ran on into the 1970's). Each insert has a single il-

SEVERAL SIZES

lustration and asks a question; the answer is printed, upside-down, in a white panel in the lower-left corner. The bottom margin outside the frameline contains a fortune and a number (number 373 has been seen). No production codes are evident, making these paper inserts very difficult to date. In the absence of more specific details, the price per comic should not exceed $1.00. The reference number is R764-5.

FLIP—O—VISION (50)

"Flip-O-Vision, The Movie Maker Bubble Gum," was produced by Topps for sale in 1949. Each 5-cent gum pack contained a slab of gum and an unassembled, 30-page flip book folded accordian-style. Owners were directed to fold the pictures along the dotted line, separate them, and bind the end with a rubber band, thread, or string. The flip book was then ready to be used as a pocket-size movie. Although a wax paper advertising insert listed 49 subjects in the set, a 50th flip book, "The Ink Spots," is confirmed. Another confusing detail: the flip books were apparently skip-numbered because numbers 52, 53,

56 & 60 were used. We doubt that this was intentional; more likely it resulted from contractual problems with certain celebrities, causing specific numbers to be deleted from the development plan.

The October, 1949 edition of The Card Collectors Bulletin made the following report: "In order to stimulate sales of Topps Flip-O Vision, a tie-in stunt with several New York City movie houses was recently held. On specified dates, the movie theatres posted a sign outside announcing to the public that a special prize would be given to any one presenting a Flip-O-Vision card depicting the 'Mystery

1 7/8" X 4"

Star of the Week.' Candy stores in the immediate neighborhood of the theatres reported brisk sales of the Topps product." Most of the flip movies surviving into modern times have already been assembled; unassembled units are valued at a premium. The reference number is R710-2.

ITEM	EX	AVE
Flip Books		
Assembled	10.00	4.00
Unassem—		
bled	20.00	10.00
Sets		
assembled	625.00	150.00
Unassem—		
bled	1300.00	350.00
Wrapper	30.00	——

the movie maker

FLIP-O VISION

Get more fun out of your MOVIE MAKER. Use a rubber band, thread, or string around the bottom notches and collect the whole series.

Abbott & Costello
The Aldrich Family
Morey Amsterdam
Vince Barnett
William Bendix
Bomba, The Jungle Boy
Johnny Mack Brown
Burns and Allen
Cab Calloway
Rod Cameron
Harry Carey, Jr.
Jack Carson
Charlie Chan
Senator Claghorn
Lois Collier
Bing Crosby
Vic Damone

Johnny Desmond
Kirk Douglas
Jimmy Durante
Leon Errol
Billy Gilbert
Leo Gorcey
Jack Haley
Bob Hope
Ina Ray Hutton
The Ink Spots
Kay Kyser
Arthur Lake
Harpo Marx
The Marx Bros
Roddy McDowell
Victor Moore
Margaret O'Brien

Joe Palooka
Bert Parks
The Pied Pipers
Buddy Rich
Lanny Ross
Peggy Ryan
Al Schacht
Red Skelton
Jimmy Stewart
Dick Tracy
Rudy Vallee
Jimmy Wakely
Johnny Weissmuller
Tex Williams
Whip Wilson
Henny Youngman

WAX INSERT LISTED 49 OF 50 TITLES

COLLECT THE COMPLETE FLIP-O-VISION SERIES OF THE BIGGEST NAMES IN SHOW BUSINESS!!

BE THE FIRST TO HAVE YOUR OWN NAME STAMP!!

#125 – PERSONAL NAME STAMP

2 Piece rubber name stamp in shiny onyx-black plastic case. Make your own stationery. Stamp your books and papers. Print your name clearly and send only 1 FLIP-O-VISION Wrapper or 1 Wrapper from BAZOOKA, America's Finest Bubble Gum, together with 25c to: Bazooka, Box 20, Madison Square Station, New York 10, N. Y.

(Not valid where contrary to state laws.)

ANOTHER INNER WRAP OFFERED VARIOUS PREMIUMS

POST ON YOUR WINDOW

TOPPS' NEWEST WINNER!

KIDS! IT'S TERRIFIC! Make your own movies!

A different strip of 20 pictures in every package. Paste 'em, stack 'em, flip 'em and see your favorite stars in specially posed action shots.

Make Your Own Movies . . . with the biggest names in show business!

TOPPS CHEWING GUM, INC.

RETAIL STORE POSTER

IT'S TERRIFIC!! MAKE YOUR OWN MOVIES!

FLIP-O VISION BUBBLE GUM

DEALER: DISPLAY THIS CARD AND BOOST SALES!

PROMOTION SHEET

APRIL 1949 PRICE LIST

FLIP-O-VISION—Make Your Own Movies! It's Terrific!

TOPPS CHEWING GUM INC.

APRIL 1949 ORDER PAGE

FONEY ADS (72)

2 1/2" X 3 1/2"

The 1960 card set entitled "Foney Ads" was Leaf Gum's first venture into humorous trading cards. The 72-card set spoofed some of the major consumer products of the period. The fronts contain clever color drawings accompanied by satirical mottoes and advertising. The backs are mostly red in color, with the card number and a feature called "Mr. Foney's Funnies" (the gent to the left apparently is Mr. Foney). At the bottom a line reads "Foney ads are presented in a spirit of fun for your enjoyment." The wrapper is pink, with yellow, white and black accents, and bears a "C-877" production code. A parallel set was issued in Canada under the name "Mr. Baloney's Comics." The reference number is R734-1.

ITEM	EX	AVE
Card	1.50	.35
Set	120.00	27.50
Wrapper	50.00	––
Box	125.00	30.00

1 Old Mice After-Shave Lotion	19 Coward's Medal	37 Slurp Suds	55 Spill-Cream Hair Tonic
2 Leech-Nut Baby Food	20 Snoreton Salt	38 Ivoreen Soap	56 Dirty-Ex Napkins
3 Mr. Mean	21 Sick Electric Razor	39 Wormy Apples	57 Sillies Cigars
4 Chef No-Partee Pizza Dinner	22 Bad Luck Margarine	40 Witches Correspondence Course	58 Ratz Crackers
5 Mouldy Gold Cigarettes	23 Smell Gasoline	41 Scream Tooth Paste	59 Rash Dog Food
6 Nuts-Cafe	24 Pest Milk	42 Vek's Cough Drops	60 Tender-Leak Tea Bags
7 Gasoline Hair Tonic	25 Western Bunion	43 None-A-Day Vitamins	61 Cheaties
8 Hurts Rent-A-Car	26 Black Cross and Black Shield	44 Kill-Log's Chips 'N' Flakes	62 Killette Safety Blades
9 Poopsie Cola	27 Blisterene Mouth Wash	45 Ramm's Beer	63 Gritos Corn Chips
10 Robert Small	28 Keinz 5757 Varieties	46 Head-Shrinking Kit	64 Snide
11 Grandma Hag's Rotten Eggs	29 Smell-O	47 Choke-A-Cola	65 Sufferin Pain Pills
12 No-dak Film	30 Exciting Pet	48 Bad Humor Ice Cream	66 Grime-Ola Shoe Polish
13 Betty Rocker Cake Mix	31 Yellow-Dent Toothpaste	49 Rent A Ghost	67 Pills Bros. Instant Coffee
14 Time Bomb	32 Simon-Crys Auto Polish	50 Fools Cigarettes	68 Sticky Peanut Butter
15 Phony Home Permanent	33 Max Cracktor	51 Scraper-Mate	69 Fang Instant Breakfast Drink
16 Slopsicle	34 Green Runt Peas	52 Slopette	70 Botch Tape
17 Fibby's	35 Scums for the Tummy	53 Vomo-Seltzer	71 Orange Slush
18 Dr. Vest Toothbrush	36 Belch's Grape Juice	54 Mud Heiser Beer	72 7 Down

FREEDOM'S WAR (203)

2 1/16" X 2 5/8"

If you believe the advertising found on the 5-cent wrapper, "Freedom's War" was "The most complete set of military cards ever published." Perhaps not the BEST, as fans of "Horrors of War" and "War Gum" would certainly argue, but surely the most comprehensive in terms of scope. After all, the set included Korean War scenes, combat training, military insignia, weapons, medals, generals, airplanes, ships, and even a set of diecut tanks which could be made into stand-up toys. Topps used both color artwork and color photographs in making up the set. As the wrapper said, this was "A prize collection for the Sons and Daughters of Freedom."

258

Freedom's War was distributed in three printings over a two-year period that began in the summer of 1950. These three "waves" of cards were separate from each other in a number of details, yet close enough time-wise to have been confusing to collectors then and now. Initially, the entire series of 203 cards was issued in 1-cent and 5-cent gum packs, with single cards in the one-centers and three two-card panels in the "fivers." These cards have tan color backs; cards issued singly have smooth edges and cards issued in panels have "nubs" (or attachment points) on two sides. Research has indicated that every number came both as a "single" and as part of a panel. In addition, the first 103 cards of this series were printed without obverse captions, but front titles were added to the 104-203 run.

Some collectors have speculated that the captions were left off cards 1-103 of the first print run in error. It is more likely that they were added as a "design element" improvement to make succeeding cards more visually attractive and interesting. At any rate, it appears that the entire series was released another time in one- and five-cent packages, and this time ALL the cards, with the exception of the tanks (97-103), came with captions on the fronts. We must assume that there were mechanical difficulties in producing the tanks because they are the scarcest cards in the set, and they were eliminated from the third and final printing which followed.

Cards of the third "wave" of Freedom's War all have gray cardboard backs. They were issued in 1-cent, 5-cent (three 2-card panels & gum), and 10-cent (eight 2-card panels, no gum) packs. Since they were sold both as singles and in panels, grayback cards may or may not have attachment "nubs" on one edge. The tanks, cards 97-103, apparently were never printed on gray stock (at least none have ever been seen). To sum up, cards 1-96 and 104-203 can be found with either tan or gray backs; cards 97-103 are found with tan backs only; and tan backed cards 1-96 are found with or without card captions on front. In addition, tanks have been found with solid tops (non-diecut) and in color variations. Truly there are many confusing elements to this set, and collecting it according to specific print runs and formats would be a formidable and expensive task.

The red, white & blue "Freedom's War" 1-cent wrapper was the only true wax paper wrapper issued for the set (durable wax paper that resisted tears). It has been found with and without a printed price. The 5-cent wrapper, also found with and without the price, was made of layered cellophane which damaged easily. The 10-cent package consisted of very thin, red cellophane so flimsy that the card panels within often poked out through the corners. These were gumless, but on the other hand, you could see which panels were on the top and bottom, and there were 16 cards in every pack. The boxes illustrated below are for the 5-cent and 10-cent packs. The reference number is R709-2.

ITEM	EX	AVE
Cards		
1-96 Gray back	3.00	.60
1-96 Tan back	3.50	.75
104-203 Gray back	3.00	.60
104-203 Tan back	3.50	.75
Exceptions		
No. 183	10.00	2.00
No. 198	5.00	1.00
No. 199	6.00	1.25
No. 200	6.00	1.25
No. 201	10.00	2.00
No. 202	5.00	1.00
Tanks		
Diecut	60.00	15.00
Solid back	100.00	30.00
Wrappers		
1-cent	150.00	––
5-cent	250.00	––
10-cent	40.00	––
Boxes		
5-cent	350.00	100.00
10-cent	250.00	75.00

1 Surprise Attack	52 Bravery in the Field	103 M-5 Light Tank	154 Return Fire
2 Close Call	53 Concentrated Fire	104 Airborne Infantry	155 Landing
3 Trapped	54 Strange Stomach	105 Under Fire	156 Ready to Fire
4 Wounded Pilot	55 Moving into Action	106 Wiping Out Snipers	157 Time to Jump
5 Direct Hit	56 Sniper's Bullets	107 Flame Throwers in Action	158 Starry Night
6 Faced with Death	57 General of the Army	108 Under the Wire	159 Jumping a Sentry
7 "Stand or Die"	58 Fighting Armor	109 Folding a Chute	160 Suicide Attack
8 Rocket Blast	59 F-80 Jet	110 Loading the Cannon	161 On the Run
9 Flying Metal	60 Tank Destroyer	111 Team Work	162 Digging for Safety
10 Fight for Time	61 Rocket Launcher	112 Anti-Aircraft Gun	163 Dangerous Job
11 Loading Up	62 Torpedo Away!	113 "At Your Posts"	164 Stopping a Disturbance
12 Hunt for Snipers	63 Closer to Action	114 "Molotoff Cocktail"	165 Sudden Surrender
13 Dangerous Work	64 Lost	115 Fighting Man	166 Red Sniper
14 Holding the Line	65 Howitzer	116 Parachute Going Up!	167 House to House Fighting
15 Reinforcements on the Move	66 Night Attack	117 Tanks in Action	168 Ready for Action
16 First Blood	67 Alone Behind the Lines	118 P-61 "Black Widow"	169 Flaming Enemy
17 Keep Moving!	68 Fast Shooting	119 Bell X-1	170 Destroyer
18 Bombs on Target	69 Careful Aim	120 C-47 "Skytrain"	171 Aircraft Carrier
19 Into the Breech	70 Sniper Hunt	121 Bell XR-13	172 Cruiser
20 Dry Landing	71 Surprise Target	122 Snow Fighter	173 Hospital Ship
21 Death of a Pal	72 Volunteer	123 XF 92A "Interceptor"	174 Battleship
22 Point-Blank Fire	73 Flame Throwing Tank	124 Martin B-51	175 Submarine
23 Heading for Home	74 First Jump	125 B-45 "Tornado"	176 Minesweeper
24 Home-Made Bomb	75 Gas Attack	126 Army Cadets	177 Sub-Chaser
25 Bouncing Bullets	76 Getting the Range	127 V-E Day Parade	178 10th Division
26 Sights Ready!	77 "Consolidate" B-46	128 Still Flying	179 66th Division
27 Sudden Attack	78 Tank Destroyer	129 Practice Alarm	180 76th Division
28 They Won't Stop!	79 Riding on a Tank	130 "Here They Come"	181 98th Division
29 Air Attack	80 Smoke Signals	131 Machine Gun Nest	182 99th Division
30 Rushed by Reds	81 Camouflage	132 Blasted Bridge	183 General George S. Patton, Jr.
31 Jump to Safety	82 Burning a Tank	133 Get that Machine Gun	184 104th Division
32 Under Guard	83 Searchlight Checkup	134 Dangerous Spot	185 5th Air Force
33 Murderous Fire	84 Rin-Tin-Tin III	135 News for Headquarters	186 14th Air Force
34 Target Blasted!	85 Consolidated B-36	136 Change of Costume	187 2nd Infantry Division
35 Village Attack	86 F-80 "Shooting Star"	137 Brave Medics	188 8th Infantry Division
36 Strafing Fire	87 "Sabre" and "Tornado"	138 Wounded Pal	189 10th Armored Division
37 "Tanks Are Coming"	88 B-35 "Flying Wing"	139 Rocket Blast	190 U.S. Strategical and Tactical
38 Strange Weapon	89 P-47 "Thunderbolt"	140 Retreat in the Rain	Air Force
39 The Enemy Falls	90 B-47 "Stratojet"	141 Moving Tanks	191 Soldier's Medal
40 Load Fast!	91 B-17 "Flying Fortress"	142 Rescue by Helicopter	192 Purple Heart
41 Push to Pusan	92 B-29 "Superfortress"	143 Action on the Corner	193 Good Conduct Medal
42 Lucky Landing	93 A-26 "Invader"	144 Take Off	194 Air Medal
43 Exploded Mine	94 C-74 "Globemaster"	145 Submarine Duty	195 Legion of Merit
44 Sentry Line	95 P-38 "Lightning"	146 Battleship Support	196 Distinguished Flying Cross
45 Tank Retreat	96 B-24 "Liberator"	147 Running Fire	197 Victory Medal
46 Shelling of Taegu	97 M-7 Howitzer Motor Carriage	148 Dangerous Landing	198 Gen. Mark W. Clark
47 Unarmed Heroes	98 M10A1 Gun Motor Carriage	149 The Corvette	199 Gen. James H. Doolittle
48 On Guard	99 M-8 Howitzer Motor Carriage	150 Missing in Action	200 Gen. George C. Marshall
49 A Disguise Fails	100 Medium Tank M-26	151 Mortar	201 General Dwight D. Eisenhower
50 White Phosphorous	101 M-18 Gun Motor Carraige	152 Night Bombardment	202 Gen. Omar N. Bradley
51 Rattling Death	102 M-12 Gun Motor Carriage	153 Hand to Hand Struggle	203 Arctic Soldier

FRONTIER DAYS (128)

2 1/2" X 3 3/4"

Many collectors believe that Bowman's "Frontier Days," released in 1953, was a "panic" issue designed to cut costs and generate some revenue for a company in dire financial straits. That, so the theory goes, is why the artwork of a very successful former set, "Wild West," was used once again to produce this 128-card set. The fronts have color pictures with wide, white borders on the sides (various western designs are printed on the borders). The set title, card number, caption, and text are all printed on the gray cardboard backs. The initials "B.G.H.L.I." (Bowman Gum Haelan Laboratories Inc.) are printed at the bottom-right. The 1-cent wrapper is yellow and white with blue and red accents, and no price is indicated on it. The 5-cent wrapper uses the very same design but has the price clearly marked on it. The reference number is R701-5.

ITEM	EX	AVE
Card	2.50	.60
Set	375.00	90.00
Wrappers		
1-cent	90.00	––
5-cent	90.00	––

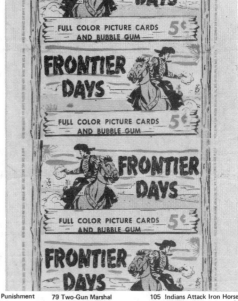

1 "Pikes's Peak or Bust"	27 Indian Lacrosse	53 Burnt-Arrow Punishment	79 Two-Gun Marshal	105 Indians Attack Iron Horse
2 Chicago Fire	28 Andrew Jackson	54 Pony in the Parlor	80 Hark! The Calliope	106 Train Robbery
3 False Face Society	29 Wagon Box Fight	55 Deputy Sheriff	81 Gun Runners	107 Torture Stake
4 White Bear	30 Night Visitor	56 River Pirate	82 James Marshall Strikes Gold	108 Geronimo
5 Perilous Work	31 Jesse James Holdup	57 Battle of New Orleans	83 Peace Pipe	109 Angry Squaw
6 Killer Bear	32 The "Mosselle" Blows Up	58 "Lone-Star" Settlers	84 Annie Oakley	110 Chuck Wagon
7 Wells Fargo Holdup	33 Indians Attack Wagon Train	59 Sign Language	85 Escaping the Comanches	111 Rangers Battle Outlaws
8 Riding Out an Earthquake	34 Praire Fire	60 "Calamity Jane"	86 Fighting a Blizzard	112 The River Rises
9 Relay	35 An Indian Never Forgets	61 Boy Captives	87 Outlaws at Bay	113 Stage Coach Robbery
10 Montana Gold	36 Daniel Boone	62 Cowboys Go to Town	88 Steamboat Burns Bridge	114 Ambush
11 Buffalo Trap	37 Battle of Tippecanoe	63 The Daltons	89 Battling a Tempest	115 Cliff Dwellers
12 Red Cloud	38 Bronco Busting	64 Villains' Cave	90 Mormons Settle Utah	116 Marcus Whitman
13 Hayfield Fight	39 Jail Break	65 Out to Stake a Claim	91 Stalking Game	117 In The Nick of Time
14 Look! The Stagecoach!	40 Wreck of the "Tennessee"	66 Virginia City Boom	92 Davy Crockett	118 Cowgirl Race
15 Citizens Rout Bandits	41 Fremont in the Rockies	67 Building Birch Bark Canoe	93 Battle of Horseshoe Bend	119 Rangers Ride
16 Heroic Captain	42 Buffalo Stampede	68 Sam Houston	94 Stampede	120 Rifles at 30 Yards
17 Hazards of Track Laying	43 The War Whoop	69 Saving the Wounded	95 Sheriff Defies Mob	121 Panning Gold
18 Snowbound Train	44 Captain Jack	70 Battle of Wild Stallions	96 Cub Pilot	122 Saddling Pony Express
19 Fishing for Salmon	45 Ransom	71 Run Out of Town	97 Buffaloes Stop Train	123 Woman's Work
20 Simon Kenton	46 Branding a Calf	72 Seeing the Show	98 Down Goes the Telegraph	124 Black Hawk
21 Death by Moonlight	47 Bill Hickok at Hays City	73 The Gold Rush is On	99 The Medicine Man	125 Battle of Bad Axe
22 Cowboy Capers	48 Stratogem	74 Dealing with Claim-Jumpers	100 Sitting Bull	126 An Easterner Learns
23 Whip Beats Pistol	49 Death at the Waterhole	75 Young Indian Learns	101 Fort Kearny Massacre	127 "Stick 'em Up"
24 Tornado	50 The Alamo	76 Chief Joseph	102 Sheep and Cattle War	128 New Orleans Bullfight
25 Peril at the Pass	51 Smoke Signals	77 Rushing a Stockade	103 Rangers Chase Apaches	
26 Bridge Disaster	52 "Buffalo Bill!!	78 Range War	104 Steamboat Race	

FRONTIER SCOUT (?)

The first mention we have of the "Frontier Scout" candy box card series came in the November, 1960 edition of the Card Collectors Bulletin. The front panel of the box provides the title for the set which, in this case, is not printed on the cards. Combined with the fact that the cards themselves are blank-backed, it would be pretty difficult to identify the issue if it were cut from the box. The artwork is simple and lacks detail, and the illustrators did their best to hide these limitations under yellow, brown, blue, orange and green "dayglow" colors. Perhaps the best feature of the cards is their red borders with white stars. The cards are not numbered. The reference number is R810.

ITEM	EX	AVE
Card	3.00	1.00
Box	20.00	6.00

FUNNY FOLDEES (66)

One of the highlights of the non-sport hobby in 1990 was watching John "Wrapper King" Neuner open up a sealed 1-cent pack of "Funny Foldees Bubble Gum." The wrapper had eluded collectors for years and, finally, we got to see it and confirm what was inside. At the same time, however, a new dilemma arose. The wrapper was marked with a 1949 copyright date, which conflicted with eyewitness accounts of when the set first appeared.

Jim Kroeger (who, along with Roxanne Toser, provided the checklist below) is absolutely sure that he bought the cards as a child in 1955. This date of issue seems to be confirmed by the "Funny Foldees" listing in the "new sets" section of the December, 1955 Card Collectors Bulletin and by the set's absence in the 1953 edition of The American Card Catalog. At this point, we have no explanation for the 1949 copyright on the wrapper except to say that many items don't make it into the marketplace immediately after they are registered. Another less-plausible theory suggests that the series was issued twice.

Altogether there are nine different faces which can be made by arranging and rearranging the various "wings" of these small metamorphic cards. The set title, which appears on the reverse of the center artwork, has the word "Funny" printed in red and the word "Foldees" printed in black. The background colors of the non-text wings and center panels change every eleven cards: 1-11 is yellow; 12-22 is blue; 23-33 is red; 34-44 is orange; 45-54 is green, but 55 is orange, the lone exception; 56-66 is yellow once again. The reference number is R708-1.

ITEM	EX	AVE
Foldee	3.00	.75
Set	250.00	55.00
Wrapper	150.00	—

Funny Foldees

1 Well, all reet! Two-gun Pete
Went down the street!
Got into quite a mix-up
With his two feet!

2 The hunter always hunts,
The clown always clowns,
As for the little lady,
Well, she just frowns!

3 Heap big Indian chief,
With a girl and a kangaroo!
Flip 'em, and find out
What they can do!

4 Here's a charming couple —
You can see it's a fact!
But how did the dog
Get into the act?

5 Just flip this card,
And you'll pull a switch,
On the cat, the imp,
And the terrible witch!

6 The girl is so sad,
And we know why —
She's got to change legs
With the bird and the guy!

7 This horse is wild,
This duck is mild —
But soon they'll get
The monkey all riled!

8 The first two aren't very pretty,
But with them is a handsome lad!
Flip 'em and change 'em about —
I ask you, is that bad?

9 Two men that fight —
A daring pair —
And a hoss that looks
Just like a nightmare!

10 Here comes the bride, there goes a bum,
But the Indian just sits tight!
If you dare to mix 'em up,
They'll make a most funny sight!

11 A cute infant, holding a rattle,
Plus two animals from the zoo!
If the baby doesn't get rattled
They will do tricks for you!

12 This is what we
Call a really funny combination!
Flip 'em, and you'll get
An entirely new creation!

13 Now here is Pop,
And his son, also his daughter
Pretty soon they ALL
Will be in hot water!

14 This trio is quite a strange one,
To find together at on time!
We'd tell you more about 'em —
But we couldn't get words to rhyme!

15 An Indian, a fast horse,
As well as the Texas Kid!
Now you flip—em card,
And then you'll flip—em lid!

16 Meet Jim, meet Jane,
And meet Jumbo too!
They will change faces,
Just to please you!

17 Three animals to do
Some tricks for you!
Flip 'em to see
A funny kind of zoo!

18 Honk honk! Honk honk!
And a hey, rub-a-dub!
Put the tub on wheels,
The house in the tub!

19 Three strange and funny characters,
And one who's held on a chain!
What's the meaning of it all?
That's really for YOU to explain!

20 These characters just can't
Believe their very own eyes!
Pretty soon, in a minute,
They'll get a NEW surprise!

21 Step up and see
The circus stars! Watch 'em mix!
You will be amazed
At their daring funny tricks!

22 Hurry up and flip the card,
And then you'll see —
There's something very fishy
About each of these three!

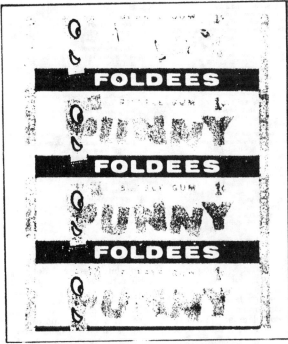

23 Here are three friends,
From three different places
Flip 'em and they
Will all change faces!

24 Meet mom and baby
With a monster between 'em!
Flip 'em — you won't believe
That you've seen 'em!

25 These men were our
Great heads of state!
Flip 'em and they
Will STILL look great!

26 The penguin, you'll agree
Is a most curious critter!
Now you Flip him —
And he'll make you titter!

27 Here's a tough egg and a poor nag,
And just a guy like me and you!
It's funny, but the horse has
More sense than the other two!

28 A studious guy, a whacky girl,
And a sad pooch, as you can see!
The poor pooch! He seems ashamed
To be found in such company!

29 Old bones, old tramp,
And a young cowhand!
The craziest trio in
All the land!

30 A fighting man, a famous writer —
But what is the big idea?
Look at who is with them!
Somebody gave us a bum steer!

31 This looks real nutty —
But we will bet
When you mix 'em
They are nuttier yet!

32 Three rare creatures
Of land and sea and air!
When they're mixed up,
They are REALLY rare!

33 Here's a man who is cleaning up,
And a girl who's a little late!
The guy who's playing hockey
Seems to be a pretty good skate!

34 Now here is a statue,
Plus a fish, and a sleepyhead,
Flip 'em, and you'll see
Who gets the bed!

35 Presenting a snake and a parrot,
Not to mention a cute baby!
Flip 'em, and you'll see,
That they are cuter — MAYBE!

36 These three peculiar characters,
As you see, are whacky!
Mix 'em up, and you'll find
They're whackier, by cracky!

37 It's raining rain on the man,
The woman thunders at her pup —
The singer weeps, wails, and moans —
We wish they'd ALL shut up!

38 Here's what we call
A real whale of a feat!
Flip 'em and you
Will surely make ends meet!

39 This is Willie the ape,
With Millie and Billy —
Change 'em all around,
And they sure look silly!

40 The guy is first,
The gal is third —
Flip 'em and see
Who gets the bird!

41 Three very strange characters,
They're all in a row!
Do they look like
Anyone that you know?

42 The clown is really
A most funny creature,
When teamed up with a senator
And also a school teacher!

43 Just flip the pictures —
If you're not too lazy —
And you'll see something
That is really crazy!

44 See the pig, see the gob,
See a lady on the run!
Change 'em all around,
And you'll have fun!

45 Introducing a lion, and a lady,
And a rootin' tootin' buckaroo!
Now switch their faces
To made laughs for you!

46 These three hail from
Far-off and distant places!
Watch 'em as they
All change their faces!

263

47 A funny man, and a sad tramp,
And with them a polar bear!
Mix the faces, and you'll have
Something that will make you stare!

48 Ha, ha, ha! And tee hee hee!
Cast a glance at these three!
Very soon you'll agree
That they are all at sea!

49 Hi, Mom! Hi, Dad!
And how is little Leo?
Did you ever see
Such a crazy, mixed-up trio?

50 A nice lady, a nice cat,
And a girl that's sweet —
Mix 'em up, all together,
And you'll get a treat!

51 Strong-arm Bill is
A man of muscle and might!
But when he's flipped,
He is quite a sight!

52 Hold that frown! Hold that tiger!
As for the girl at the side —
She shouldn't be here at all!
She just came along for the ride!

53 To tell the truth
Is our solemn duty —
These folks never won
Any prize for beauty!

54 Watch the fat turkey —
He's really making tracks!
Soon somebody is going
To get the axe!

55 Here's a pug and a lady,
With 'em is a dude!
Mix 'em up in any way,
Just according to your mood!

56 Boo, hoo, hoo! Whatever is
Whiskers going to do?
He's all mixed up
With baby, and a rooster too!

57 Take an old maid,
And a private, and a baby too —
Mix 'em up, and it means
Loads of laughs for you!

58 The lady's a chump, the guy's a champ,
The chimp's neither as you can guess!
Just flip 'em and mix 'em up
And you'll get them into a mess!

59 The cop is frowning,
The others are not!
Flip 'em — and THEN
See what you've got!

60 These three each hail
From three different nations!
Flip 'em, but look out
For international complications!

61 See the three animals
Standing in a line!
Flip 'em, and then
You'll see a REAL monkeyshine!

62 Now here is the beauty
And also the beast!
In general they're funny,
To say the least!

63 Two strange, weird critters,
Next to a little pup —
They are even stranger
When you mix 'em up!

64 Here's a horse and a pug,
With a chimp in between!
Don't they make the funniest sight
You have ever seen?

65 Three very scarey faces
For you to switch —
Then you can ask,
Which one is witch?

66 Behold the funny clown!
See the pretty miss!
Now how did an ostrich
Get mixed up with this?

FUNNY VALENTINES (66)

2 1/2" X 3 1/2"

The Topps "Funny Valentines" series is famous among collectors for its artwork, drawn by famed comic book illustrator Jack Davis. The set was originally reported to be complete at 55 cards in The American Card Catalog and The Card Collectors Bulletin, but there are definitely 66 cards, and the last eleven don't seem to be any more difficult to find than the first 55. The comic artwork fronts deliver a straight line which is answered on the back in humorous fashion. The wrappers are yellow with a red heart in the center. The monster faces left on the 1-cent wrapper and right on the 5-cent wrapper. Illustrated below are a three-card advertising panel (aimed at retailers) and two foreign sets, issued at a later date, which also used this artwork. Topps issued this first series of Funny Valentines in 1959. The reference number is R708-2.

ITEM	EX	AVE
Card	1.00	.35
Set	115.00	25.00
Wrappers		
1-cent	20.00	——
5-cent	15.00	——
Box	150.00	40.00

RIGHT: ENGLISH VERSION ISSUED
UNDER LICENSE BY A & BC GUM.
BELOW: AUSTRALIAN ISSUE BY
SCANLENS (1963).

1 I Need You
2 Don't Go Away Mad, Dear
3 You Remind Me of a Movie Star
4 I Can't Stop Chasing You
5 Stay Just as You Are!
6 Since I've Known You, Dear...
7 I Love Ya So Much...
8 You Have Everything a Man Wants
9 Your Teeth Are Like Stars
10 I've Found the Perfect Valentine Gift for You!
11 Your Name Will Be with Me Forever
12 You Ought to Be in Pictures
13 You Oughta Enter the Miss America Contest...
14 I Remember the First Time I Saw You...
15 You're Real Smooth
16 I Love Your Two Beautiful Eyes...
17 You're the Apple of My Eye
18 I Love You Because You're Different...

19 You Look Like a Millon (sic) Bucks
20 'No Wonder We Like Each Other...
21 I Love the Way Your Hair Grows Down Your Back...
22 There's a Word for You...
23 I Love Your Little Hands, Your Little Feet...
24 You're a Doll
25 I'd Like to Bring You Home to Mother...
26 You're the Girl of My Dreams...
27 There Will Never Be Another You!
28 I Don't Know What I'd Do Without You...
29 I Think of You...
30 To the Prettiest Girl in the World
31 You're the Caveman Type...
32 I've Got My Eye on You...
33 You're a Charmer...
34 Roses Are Red Violets Are Blue...
35 I Dig You...
36 You're the Strong Silent Type...
37 Say the Words That Will Make Me the Happiest Boy in the World...
38 You're Just What the Doctor Ordered...
39 There's Something About You I Like...
40 Why Can't You Love Me?
41 It Is Better to Have Loved It and Lost...

42 There's a Word for You...
43 If You Were the Only Girl in the World...
44 Some Valentine Day Advice...
45 You're So Friendly, So Gentle, So Kind...
46 You May Not Be Smart, Dear...
47 You've Got Everything
48 You've Got Something No Other Girl Has!!!
49 I Love You
50 I Think You're the Most Beautiful Girl in the World...
51 I Miss You
52 A Girl Like You Is Hard to Find...
53 I've Got a Crush on You...
54 Won't You Come Over for Dinner?
55 You Have a Wonderful Personality...
56 Mirror Mirror on the Wall Who's the Fairest One of All?
57 I'll Never Forget You, Dear
58 Looks Aren't Everything Dear
59 You Take the Prize
60 We'll Be Sweet Hearts Till the End
61 Don't Think It Hasn't Been Pleasant to Meet You...
62 You're Like a Beautiful Flower
63 You've Got Something No Other Girl Has...
64 Darling You Have Just What It Takes to Get into the Movies...
65 I Picked This Card Because It Fits You...
66 We Both Got Together to Send You This Valentine

WHEN YOU BUY CARDS. . .
MAKE SURE THE CONDITION MATCHES THE PRICE.

FUNNY VALENTINES "A" (66)

2 1/2" X 3 1/2"

Such was the success of the 1959 series of "Funny Valentines" that Topps followed it up with a second series of the cards in 1960. These are identical in style and coloration to the original set but are easily identified by the "A"

printed next to the card number. Topps went so far as to design new 1-cent and 5-cent wrappers for this second series, but used the original first series box again by updating it with the word "New." It should be noted that Topps

used to issue most of its satirical, humorous, and "monster" sets to coincide with Valentines Day and Halloween. From the wrapper artwork and the "new set" listings in the Card Collectors Bulletin (June, 1959), we know that the first series was released in February, 1959; it is logical to assume that the "A" series was marketed in February, 1960. The reference number is R708-2A.

ITEM	EX	AVE
Card	1.50	.35
Set	115.00	25.00
Wrappers		
1-cent	35.00	––
5-cent	20.00	––
Box	150.00	40.00

1A You're in a Class by Yourself
2A I Love Your Eyes
3A You're So Much Fun at Masquerade Parties!
4A Fly Away with Me!

5A You're as Strong As an Ox
6A Did I Ever Tell You, You Were Beautiful?
7A I'd Love to Hold Hands with You

8A You Remind Me of Something Grand
9A You Could Win the Miss Universe Contest!
10A It Was Love at First Sight
11A You're So Sweet!!!
12A When I'm with You It's Like Being on a Cruise...
13A You Were Made for Me
14A You've Got Something Every Girl Wants...
15A At Last I Found My Ideal
16A There's Nothing Wrong with You
17A You're One in a Million!!!
18A I'd Climb the Highest Mountain
19A Take My Heart
20A We'd Make a Lovely Couple, If It Wasn't for One Thing...
21A You've Got What It Takes
22A I'd Like to Give You Something to Remember Me By.
23A My Funny Valentine You're Sweet
24A If We Combined Your Looks and My Brains...
25A I'm Sorry I Spoke in Anger...
26A I'd Love to Take You Home
27A You Could Be a Movie Star
28A I Used to Feel Inferior

29A You Send Me
30A I Love the Way Your Nose Turns Up
31A When I'm with You I Get a Strange Feeling
32A I Didn't Forget You
33A When I Grow Up I'll Be Like You
34A Your Eyes Are Fascinating
35A Some Are Born Beautiful,— Some Are Born Smart
36A I Love Your Beautiful Teeth
37A I Could Write a Book About You
38A You Ought to Be on the Stage
39A If I Told Them How Beautiful You Are, They Wouldn't Believe Me
40A You're Like a Beautiful Greek Statue...
41A Darling I Long to Be in Your Arms...
42A I'd Love to Marry You
43A Your Voice Is Like a Canary's
44A I'm a Man Who Thinks for Himself
45A If You Really Knew How I Felt About You.
46A When I'm with You There's Only One Thing I Can Say...

47A I Wish We Were Married
48A You've Given Me Something to Live for
49A You're Like Sugar Candy
50A I Keep Your Picture in My Room...
51A Since I Met You I Can't Eat, I Can't Drink, I Can't Go Any Place.

52A I'm Yours Forever
53A You're Out of This World
54A With a Friend Like You...
55A When I Met You, I Went Overboard
56A Have You Ever Considered Acting?
57A Please Answer My Question!

58A Darling, You're My Whole World
59A We Have Something in Common
60A Everything I Have Is Yours
61A I Used to Think You Were a Conceited Fool
62A I Like You

63A I've Grown Accustomed to Your Face
64A If You Were the Only Girl in the World...
65A When I'm with You I Can't Catch My Breath
66A Who Says No One's Perfect?

"GOOFIES" (19K)   1 5/16" X 4 1/2"

Previously listed in the American Card Catalog as "Questions & Answers," the true name of this Fleer novelty is "Goofies." The cards came inside packages of "6 Big Chews," which has the statement "with Comic Card" printed on the front of the wrapper. They actually served two purposes: a prize for the purchaser and a gum tray/package stiffener to hold and protect the product. The cards are numbered (number 19 is the highest thus far reported), and the long edges of each have "nubs," indicating that each had detachable side walls. The front of each card is printed in green and orange and has the title "let's Play GOOFIES" and the set-up line of a joke. The back contains the punch line and an uncolored drawing (for use with crayons). About one inch of the card reverse is marked as a "fold back" area, allowing either side to be made into a stand-up toy. Despite the simplicity of design, very few "Goofies" are known to exist, and they are highly prized by specialists in Fleer issues, Dubble Bubble fans, and type collectors. The reference number is R764-3.

ITEM	EX	AVE
Card	10.00	3.00
Wrapper	20.00	––

GOOFY SERIES POST CARDS (60)   2 1/2" X 3 1/2"

You can imagine the consternation down at the post office when Topps issued its "Goofy Series" of post cards back in 1957! Sure, maybe there would have been substantial revenues from all the three-cent stamps needed to mail them, but sorting and handling would have been a major problem. Luckily, there was no tidal wave of mailings (we've never even seen a card with a stamp on it); kids probably just collected them for the pictures and gags.

The cards are standard size, and the fronts have cartoon-style drawings in a wide range of colors. Each picture depicts a humorous event and has one or two lines of dialogue. The reverse sides have the set title and card number in a mailbox design, with a humorous message printed below. The wrapper colors are black and yellow, and both 1-cent and 5-cent demoninations have been found. The reference number is R708-3.

ITEM	EX	AVE
Card	1.00	.20
Set	70.00	12.50
Wrappers		
1-cent	125.00	––
5-cent	25.00	––

1 The Drinks Are on Me!
2 Herbert, I Hope You Did Your Good Turn Today!
3 Heres Looking at You!
4 Butterfingers!
5 Hot Dog
6 Herman's Trying to Break into Television!
7 Rock N Roll
8 A Four Leaf Clover! This Is My Lucky Day!!!
9 Mr. Smith Is Tied Up at Da Moment!
10 Henry, I Told You Never to Go Out without Your Shoes!
11 When I Kiss You I Feel Warm All Over!
12 You're Cute!
13 Doc, Can't I Stop Taking These Reducing Pills Yet?
14 When Is the Next Train Coming Through?
15 (Goat Sticks Head Through Window of Bedroom)
16 Congratulate Me! I Got a Blind Date with a Circus Gal!
17 Herb's Sleeping Over Our House Tonight!
18 I'm Teaching Her to Lay Scrambled Eggs
19 Love at First Sight!
20 I'm Sure We Can See Eye to Eye
21 How to Get up in the World!
22 We're Going Around Together!
23 Hey, Fellows We Eat!
24 Hm-m Just as I Thought You Need Glasses!
25 Once There Were Three Men Riding in an Airplane—
26 All You Can Eat 50 Cents— Closed
27 Sir, I Want to Report a Leak!
28 Ha, Ha, You Never Touched Me!
29 Slow Down! Running Makes Him Mad!
30 My Specialty Is Indian Warfare!
31 This Is a Ripe One! Wrap It Up!
32 Whee, George, Isn't This Fun?
33 Sorry, I'm Wanted on the Phone!
34 I'm Fishing for Catfish!
35 How Did He Do That?
36 I'll Be Right Over!
37 Did You Find the Socket Yet?
38 I Kinda Feel Run Down Today!
39 Beware of Dog
40 Nice of the Chief to Have Us for Dinner!
41 Aim a Little Higher Next Time, Bud!
42 Now We Musn't Forget to Wipe Off Our Fingerprints Before We Leave!
43 Melvin, That Nice Man Won't Like That!
44 I'm Takin' the Local—I'm Going to Visit the Toy Department!
45 Don't Laugh When I Say I Love You!
46 If the Chute Doesn't Open, Fill Out Report 64321.
47 Use Grow-Well Dog Food to Make You Dog Grow!
48 G'Wan! Don't Believe Everything You Read!
49 I Told You Not to Get Junior That Chemistry Set!!!
50 Let's Get Together Real Soon Fellows!
51 It Saves a Lot of Money on Gas!
52 I Guess We Ought to Turn Off the Air Conditioner!
53 Hey, the Pump Is Broken— Nothing Comes Out
54 No, No, Miss De Vere You Don't Understand!
55 Boy, I'll Say It Works'
56 Sh, Herbert's Holding His Breath Under Water—1003— 1004—1005—1006
57 What's Hard Luck About Walking Under a Ladder?
58 Tip Your Hat To Mrs. Green Richard, It Never Cost Anything to Be Polite!
59 I Wag Mine Up and Down—I Live in a Small Apartment!
60 This Shopping Makes Me Tired!

GUESS WHAT? (?)

2 1/4" X 3 11/16"

The "Guess What?" series of candy boxes is listed in both the pre-war and post-war sections of this book because that's the way it appears in the early catalogs. However, many collectors feel that both groups of boxes were distributed AFTER the end of the war, in 1947-48 and in 1956. Because the boxes are not dated and there are few details, if any, to help differentiate between them, we can only suggest that they be regarded as a single issue and

priced as such. A number of intact "Guess What?" boxes have been coming out of Chicago, where the Williamson Company was located, and these are actually more common than "cut" (detached) cards. The "modern" reference number for this series is R776.

ITEM	EX	AVE
Card	2.00	.50
Box	20.00	5.00
Display Box	100.00	20.00

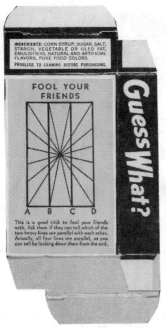

HIT STARS (88)

2 1/2" X 3 1/2"

The "Hit Stars" series issued by Topps was first reported in The Card Collectors Bulletin in February, 1958; this means that 1957 was the year it was released. The set is composed of 88 color photos of movie, television, and recording stars. Many of the pictures appear to be studio-issued portraits and "publicity stills." The cards have horizontal backs printed in red and blue on gray stock. They contain the card number and a short biography of the celebrity. The wrappers are red and yellow; the 1-cent wrapper is a "continuous" or "repeat" design type, while the 5-cent wrapper is much more artistically detailed. The 1-cent box illustrated comes from the collection of Robert Marks. The reference number for the set is R710-3. NOTE: Hit Stars cards are notorious for being off-center; take this fact into consideration when you grade and evaluate them. Cards in "excellent" grade must be reasonably well-centered. "Mint" cards must be perfectly centered.

ITEM	EX	AVE
Set	575.00	100.00
Wrappers		
1-cent	15.00	––
5-cent	15.00	––
Box	325.00	85.00

STAR	EX	AVE		STAR	EX	AVE
1 Clyde McPhatter	5.00	1.00		45 Janice Harper	3.50	.70
2 Mickey & Sylvia	3.50	.70		46 Rhonda Fleming	3.50	.70
3 Al Hibbler	3.50	.70		47 Paul Anka	3.50	.70
4 The Coasters	3.50	.70		48 The McGuire Sisters	3.50	.70
5 Jimmy Bowen	3.50	.70		49 Jim Lowe	3.50	.70
6 Johnny Mathis	5.00	1.00		50 Fats Domino	7.50	1.50
7 Joe Turner	3.50	.70		51 The Crickets	10.00	2.00
8 Clovers	3.50	.70		52 The Chordettes	3.50	.70
9 Frankie Laine	3.50	.70		53 Jerry Lee Lewis	7.50	1.50
10 Eydie Gorme	3.50	.70		54 Gene Vincent	3.50	.70
11 Guy Mitchell	3.50	.70		55 Andy Williams	3.50	.70
12 Steve Lawrence	3.50	.70		56 Charlie Gracie	3.50	.70
13 Chris Conner	3.50	.70		57 Roy Hamilton	3.50	.70
14 The Drifters	5.00	1.00		58 Del Vikings	3.50	.70
15 The Four Aces	3.50	.70		59 Elvis Presley	15.00	3.00
16 Tony Bennett	3.50	.70		60 Platters	7.50	1.50
17 Debbie Reynolds	5.00	1.00		61 Jimmie Rodgers	3.50	.70
18 Teenagers	3.50	.70		62 Alan Freed	3.50	.70
19 Screamin' Jay Hawkins	3.50	.70		63 James Dean	10.00	2.00
20 Ivory Joe Hunter	3.50	.70		64 John Saxon	3.50	.70
21 LaVern Baker	3.50	.70		65 James Dean	10.00	2.00
22 The Diamonds	3.50	.70		66 James Dean	10.00	2.00
23 The Bobbettes	3.50	.70		67 Anita Ekberg	3.50	.70
24 Nick Noble	3.50	.70		68 Burt Lancaster	3.50	.70
25 Bobby Darin	7.50	1.50		69 Tony Curtis	3.50	.70
26 Four Lads	3.50	.70		70 Taina Elg	3.50	.70
27 Jerry Lewis	6.00	1.25		71 James Dean	10.00	2.00
28 Sonny James	3.50	.70		72 Bob Hope	10.00	2.00
29 Don Rondo	3.50	.70		73 Anthony Perkins	3.50	.70
30 Ruth Brown	3.50	.70		74 Kirk Douglas	3.50	.70
31 George Shearing	3.50	.70		75 Betty Lou Keim	3.50	.70
32 Vaughn Monroe	3.50	.70		76 Warren Belinger	3.50	.70
33 Buddy Knox	3.50	.70		77 Gene Kelly	5.00	1.00
34 Nat King Cole	7.50	1.50		78 Sal Mineo	3.50	.70
35 Little Richard	10.00	2.00		79 Pier Angeli	3.50	.70
36 Teddy Randazzo	3.50	.70		80 Cyd Charisse	3.50	.70
37 Frankie Laine	3.50	.70		81 Steve Allen	5.00	1.00
38 Ferlin Husky	3.50	.70		82 Guy Mitchell	3.50	.70
39 Della Reese	3.50	.70		83 Sammy Davis, Jr.	7.50	1.50
40 Barbara Lang	3.50	.70		84 Tony Curtis	3.50	.70
41 Crew Cuts	3.50	.70		85 Elizabeth Taylor	10.00	2.00
42 The Cleftones	3.50	.70		86 Jerry Lewis	6.00	1.25
43 Jodie Sands	3.50	.70		87 Russ Tamblyn	3.50	.70
44 Sal Mineo	3.50	.70		88 Debbie Reynolds	5.00	1.00

HOCUS FOCUS (117K)   7/8'' X 1 7/16''

Topps issued two types of develop-with-water pictures: "Magic Photos" in 1949 and "Hocus Focus" in 1956. There has been much confusion about these sets since both employ the words "Magic Photos" and "Hocus Focus" on their wrappers and in their advertising copy. However, the cards of each set are easily identified: the words

"Hocus Focus" are printed on the back of every card of the 1956 set while there is no set title on the 1949 issue (it reads "see directions inside wrap" in the same spot). The wrappers of the two sets are dissimilar enough to be easily identified.

Although it was issued seven years after Magic Photos, the

Hocus Focus set has yet to be completely checklisted, and the set total is unknown (we have all this information for Magic Photos). We know that there were a number of titled sub-groups — the card illustrated is from a 20-card "Sports Thrills" category — but we haven't completely identified these either. In general terms, there are photos of aircraft, buildings, baseball players, world leaders, actors, miscellaneous sports, submarines, automobiles, and famous landmarks. Inevitably, most photos encountered are faint or underdeveloped, and clear pictures command a premium price. An excellent card with a clear photo of a "common" subject is worth $3.00; the most valuable photo in the set, Babe Ruth (No. 117) would bring at least $150.00. Normal underdeveloped cards are valued from 75 cents to one dollar. The 5-cent package, which has "Bubbles Inc." listed as the producer, held a sheet of four cards, a "Directions" card, and a slab of gum. The reference number for the set is R714-26.

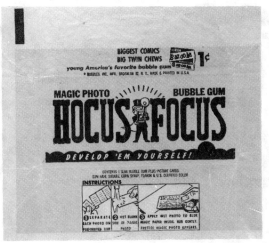

ITEM	EX	AVE
Wrapper	50.00	––

INSTRUCTION CARD FOUND
IN EVERY PACK

MOST CARDS
HAVE VERY
FAINT PICTURES

HOLIDAY GREETINGS (4K)

MANY SIZES

Over the years, the E. Rosen Company (Providence, RI) issued cardboard greeting cards with pre-punched slots on each card to hold a single lollipop. These were marketed for Valentine's Day and Halloween, and the cards come in a variety of colors and styles. All we have seen have one printed side (the backs are completely blank). Although they were first mentioned in The Card Collectors Bulletin of November, 1960, Holiday Greetings have been issued since 1948 ("Be Mah Valentine") and, in fact, are still being issued today. No one has attempted to make a precise listing of all the styles and designs, and these novelty items don't seem to attract much of a following among card collectors. Prices range from $3.00 to $5.00, depending upon the subject and attractiveness of the artwork, for a Greetings card in excellent condition. The reference number for the set is R811-1.

HOPALONG CASSIDY (238)   2 1/16" X 2 5/8"

William Boyd proved that success in Hollywood could come in the twilight of an actor's career. Formerly in silent films, Boyd made the transition into the "talkies" with relative ease, compared to some of his peers, but he never became a major star. The role of Hopalong Cassidy changed all that, at least for a few brief years. He was so magnificent, so utterly suited to the character, that we actually didn't notice that he was middle-aged.

Topps released the "Hopalong Cassidy" set in 1950, when "Hoppymania" was at its peak. The first 186 cards of the series are devoted to eight all-different adventure stories (corresponding to a series of movie matinee serials currently in the theatres). These cards are actual photographs "colored" in a monochrome tint, so the cards of one story are easily distinguished from those of the others. The so-called "multicolor" cards (187-230, two different adventures) are really black & white photographs "enhanced" with unnatural shades of red, blue and yellow. One "header" card, with a foil surface on the front, was printed for each of the eight monochrome subsets. Not only were these damaged in the packs (by gum sticking to the surface), but also they were mangled as kids carried them around as the top card on the stack. As a result, foil cards are the scarcest and most desirable cards in the Hoppy set.

One-cent Hoppy wrappers were made of durable wax paper and come in colors of white and green (the former is the most common). The 5-cent wrapper was made of layered color cellophane, and it is found with either yellow (most common) or green as the primary color. In addition, Hoppy cards were packed in loaves of Bond Bread in a simultaneous promotion, with two different wrappers associated with the bread. One has the standard "continuous design" of the gum wrapper, with the left side of the wrapper altered to advertise Bond Bread. The other bread wrapper has a completely new design with Hoppy in a horseshoe-shaped center. The box lid illustrated is from a 24-count box; it had a detached cardboard insert to stand up in one end. The reference number is R712-2. NOTE: the set price DOES NOT include foil cards.

ITEM	EX	AVE
Cards		
1-186	4.00	.80
187-230	6.00	1.25
Set	1200.00	225.00
Foils (each)	75.00	15.00
Wrappers		
1-cent white	35.00	---
1-cent green	40.00	---
5-cent yellow	125.00	---
5-cent green	175.00	---
Bond Bread regular	75.00	---
Bond Bread horseshoe	75.00	---
Box	350.00	90.00

DANGEROUS VENTURE

1	"Trouble Ahead"	13	"A Clever Trick"
2	"The Lying Rustlers"	14	"Vicious Partners"
3	"The Sheriff Talks"	15	"The Wounded Indian"
4	"Almost Knifed"	16	"Death Struggle"
5	"Hoppy Strikes Back"	17	"Hoppy's Warning"
6	"Solemn Promise"	18	"A Fatal Boast"
7	"Hoppy Falls"	19	"Human Sacrifice"
8	"Ready for Trouble"	20	"Two-Gun Man"
9	"Treachery"	21	"On Hoppy's Trail"
10	"The Bargain"	22	"Deadly Creed"
11	"Shooting Fury"	23	"What's Ahead?"
12	"False Evidence"		

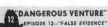

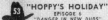
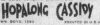

22 "DANGEROUS VENTURE"
EPISODE 22 – "DEADLY CREED"

Dr. Atwood, fighting with the rustlers against Hoppy, sees a golden urn standing on the sacrificial altar. His greed getting the best of him, he runs madly towards the urn, only to be stopped short by an Indian spear that pierces his chest. At that, the remaining rustler surrenders!

SEE EPISODE 23 – "WHAT'S AHEAD?"
23 Cards Complete DANGEROUS VENTURE

HOPALONG CASSIDY
© WM. BOYD, 1950   PRINTED IN U.S.A.

12 "DANGEROUS VENTURE"
EPISODE 12–"FALSE EVIDENCE"

Hoppy shows Dr. Atwood an Indian spear that's been left behind by the rustlers after their attack on the expedition. The treacherous doctor suggests that perhaps the expedition should be disbanded because of the hostile Indians. Hoppy and his partners saddle their horses and ride away.

SEE EPISODE 13 – "A CLEVER TRICK"
23 Cards Complete DANGEROUS VENTURE

HOPALONG CASSIDY
© WM. BOYD, 1950   PRINTED IN U.S.A.

33 "BORROWED TROUBLE"
EPISODE 10 – "SHOOT FAST"

Hoppy catches the glint of light on Mawson's gun barrel. In a flash, he whirls, draws his gun and fires. Steve Mawson's gun clatters to the floor as Hoppy hits him squarely on the right hand. "Pick up your gun," warns Hoppy, "and don't try any of that stuff on me."

SEE EPISODE 11 – "HOPPY TEACHES"
24 Cards Complete BORROWED TROUBLE

HOPALONG CASSIDY
© WM. BOYD, 1950   PRINTED IN U.S.A.

53 "HOPPY'S HOLIDAY"
EPISODE 6
"DANGER IN NEW DUDS"

Hoppy and Lucky get all dressed up for the dance at the Mesa City celebration. They take California across the street to the clothing store to get him a new outfit because he has no good clothes with him. Little do they realize the danger they're getting into with California's new duds.

SEE EPISODE 7 – "BATTLE WITH BANKROBBERS"
24 Cards Complete HOPPY'S HOLIDAY

HOPALONG CASSIDY
© WM. BOYD, 1950   PRINTED IN U.S.A.

BORROWED TROUBLE

24 "Pay Day"	36 "California's Troubles"
25 "Where's California"	37 "The Secret Cabin"
26 "Unseen Enemy"	38 "Silent Danger"
27 "Fighting School Teacher"	39 "Watch Out, Hoppy"
28 "Ready Guns"	40 "Flying Fists"
29 "Hoppy Arrives"	41 "Get Hoppy"
30 "The Threat"	42 "An Old Trick"
31 "Missing Teacher"	43 "Hard Words"
32 "Look Out, Hoppy"	44 "You Did It"
33 "Shoot Fast"	45 "Hoppy Faces Death"
34 "Hoppy Teaches"	46 "Lucky Apple"
35 "The Clue"	47 "What's Next"

HOPPY'S HOLIDAY

48 "Big Celebration"	60 "Protect California"
49 "Mess in Mesa City"	61 "California on the Spot"
50 "Suspicious Character"	62 "Caught Red Handed"
51 "Don't Trick Hoppy"	63 "A Sudden Shot"
52 "Hoppy's Surprise"	64 "Hoppy is Wounded"
53 "Danger in New Duds"	65 "Fighting Fury"
54 "Battle with Bankrobbers"	66 "The Gateaway"
55 "Blazing Guns"	67 "The Posse Rides"
56 "Unexpected Treasure"	68 "Fighting Back"
57 "California's Arrest"	69 "Desperate Change"
58 "The Trap"	70 "Duel of Death"
59 "Make California Talk"	71 "Found Money"

45 "BORROWED TROUBLE"
EPISODE 22
"HOPPY FACES DEATH"

When Hoppy accuses Davis of kidnapping the teacher, the saloonkeeper pulls a gun and backs toward the door. There's a deadly quiet as Davis snarls to Hoppy, "If you hadn't come along everything would have been all right. In one second, I'm putting a bullet in your head."

SEE EPISODE 23 – "LUCKY APPLE"
24 Cards Complete BORROWED TROUBLE

HOPALONG CASSIDY
© WM. BOYD, 1950   PRINTED IN U.S.A.

35 "BORROWED TROUBLE"
EPISODE 12 – "THE CLUE"

Right in the school, Hoppy gets a clue as to where he might find the missing school teacher. One of the pupils tells Hoppy how he once found a deserted cabin in the hills when he was bear hunting. The cabin belongs to Steve Mawson. Is the teacher there?

SEE EPISODE 13 – "CALIFORNIA'S TROUBLES"
24 Cards Complete BORROWED TROUBLE

HOPALONG CASSIDY
© WM. BOYD, 1950   PRINTED IN U.S.A.

71 "HOPPY'S HOLIDAY"
EPISODE 24 – "FOUND MONEY"

The Mayor congratulates Hopalong Cassidy and his two pals for their round-up of the bankrobbers and the return of the stolen money. "Guess we'll head back to the Bar-20," says Hoppy. "We'll find a little peace and quiet there for a while . . . maybe."

THE END

24 Cards Complete HOPPY'S HOLIDAY

HOPALONG CASSIDY
© WM. BOYD, 1950   PRINTED IN U.S.A.

70 "HOPPY'S HOLIDAY"
EPISODE 23–"DUEL OF DEATH"

Hoppy creeps close to the gang's hideout, pushes the door open, and fires at the same instant. Dunning's return fire is wild. His gun clatters to the floor as his lifeless body slumps over the suitcase containing the stolen $100,000. Hoppy's won again!

SEE EPISODE 24 – "FOUND MONEY"
24 Cards Complete HOPPY'S HOLIDAY

HOPALONG CASSIDY
© WM. BOYD, 1950   PRINTED IN U.S.A.

73 "FALSE PARADISE"
EPISODE 2
"STOP THOSE HORSES"

Hoppy touches his heels to his horse's flank and urges, "Get 'em, boy." The runaway team runs madly, kicking up dust and stones. Gradually, Hoppy shortens the gap between them, straining his horse to the limit. Hoppy reaches over and grasps the bridle of the lead horse.

SEE EPISODE 3 – "NEW NEIGHBORS"
24 Cards Complete FALSE PARADISE

HOPALONG CASSIDY
© WM. BOYD, 1950   PRINTED IN U.S.A.

114 "UNEXPECTED GUEST"
EPISODE 19
"FIGHT TO THE FINISH"

Hoppy follows the mysterious figure into the secret room behind the wall. A flash of steel catches his eye just in time to prevent a knife thrust in his back. Grasping the stranger's right arm, Hoppy slowly forces the knife from his grasp.

SEE EPISODE 20 – "WHO IS IT?"
23 Cards Complete UNEXPECTED GUEST

HOPALONG CASSIDY
© WM. BOYD, 1950   PRINTED IN U.S.A.

FALSE PARADISE

72 "Runaway"	84 "Death Strikes"
73 "Stop Those Horses"	85 "Dangerous Rescue"
74 "New Neighbors"	86 "Happy Hoppy"
75 "Bad News"	87 "Strange Alliance"
76 "Buried Riches"	88 "Hoppy Sees Treachery"
77 "Binding Sale"	89 "Ambush"
78 "A Secret Disclosed"	90 "Surprise Defense"
79 "Meeting of the Thieves"	91 "Trail That Gang!"
80 "The Knock Out"	92 "Bullets of Death"
81 "The Dangerous Loan"	93 "Cornered"
82 "A Bad Accident"	94 "Payment at Gun Point"
83 "Dynamite Roars"	95 "Pals Together"

UNEXPECTED GUEST

96 "California's Dead Relatives"	107 "Secret Drawer"
97 "Was It Murder!"	108 "Sounds in the Wall"
98 "The Strange Will"	109 "Friend in Trouble"
99 "Another Dead Relative"	110 "Hoppy's Danger"
100 "Hunting the Killer"	111 "Jump for Life"
101 "The Talking Dead"	112 "Talk or Die"
102 "Investigations Halted"	113 "Mystery Man"
103 "Attempted Murder"	114 "Fight to the Finish"
104 "Buried Wealth"	115 "Who Is It?"
105 "Smoking Guns"	116 "Pals Separate"
106 "Safety First"	117 "Sudden Decision"

Hopalong Cassidy

94 "FALSE PARADISE" EPISODE 23 "PAYMENT AT GUN POINT"
Hoppy forces the banker and his accomplice to ride back to the mill where the ore is ready. The Professor is able to pay his debt to the banker on time. Hoppy gives the banker and Bentley twenty-four hours to leave town. "You'd better not be here to-morrow at this time," he warns.
SEE EPISODE 24 — "PALS TOGETHER"
24 Cards Complete FALSE PARADISE
HOPALONG CASSIDY
© WM. BOYD, 1950   PRINTED IN U.S.A.

93 "FALSE PARADISE" EPISODE 22 "CORNERED"
Hoppy follows Bentley clear into town and corners him in the banker's office. "Get your hands up," he orders. "You're both coming with me." There is only a short time left before the loan payment is due, and Hoppy must get the banker to the mill on time. He keeps his guns ready.
SEE EPISODE 23 — "PAYMENT AT GUN POINT"
24 Cards Complete FALSE PARADISE
HOPALONG CASSIDY
© WM. BOYD, 1950   PRINTED IN U.S.A.

97 "UNEXPECTED GUEST" EPISODE 2 — "WAS IT MURDER?"
When Hoppy, Lucky and California arrive at the ranch belonging to California's recently deceased cousin, they are greeted by Miss Hackett, the housekeeper. She startles them with her positive assertion, "I don't think your cousin died a natural death."
SEE EPISODE 3 — "THE STRANGE WILL"
22 Cards Complete UNEXPECTED GUEST
HOPALONG CASSIDY
© WM. BOYD, 1950   PRINTED IN U.S.A.

96 "UNEXPECTED GUEST" EPISODE 1 — "CALIFORNIA'S DEAD RELATIVES"
California Carlson has received word that his cousin out in his cousin's ranch for the reading of the will. As California spruces up for the occasion, Hopalong Cassidy rereads the letter. "Maybe you'll be a rich man, when the will is read."
22 Cards Complete UNEXPECTED GUEST
HOPALONG CASSIDY
© WM. BOYD, 1950   PRINTED IN U.S.A.

126 "DEVIL'S PLAYGROUND" EPISODE 9 — "HANDS UP"
Hoppy chases one of the suspected murderers through the rocky paths of the "Devil's Playground" and finally corners him in an open spot. "Get your hands up," he calls, "and don't try any tricks." With the capture of the Judge, all the men are caught and are to be charged with murder.
SEE EPISODE 10 — "LOCKED UP"
24 Cards Complete DEVIL'S PLAYGROUND
HOPALONG CASSIDY
© WM. BOYD, 1950   PRINTED IN U.S.A.

160 "FOOL'S GOLD" EPISODE 19 "RACE AGAINST TIME"
Hoppy and his pals leave the Professor tied in his shack, grab his cart, and race madly down the road in a last minute attempt to prevent the Army payroll robbery. "I hope we're not too late," says California. "I'm aimin' to get a shot at those varmints."
SEE EPISODE 20 — "FALSE SIGNATURE"
24 Cards Complete "FOOL'S GOLD"
HOPALONG CASSIDY
© WM. BOYD, 1950   PRINTED IN U.S.A.

DEVIL'S PLAYGROUND
118 "Ghost Riders"
119 "Wounded"
120 "Heading for Danger"
121 "A Warning Ignored"
122 "Where's the Girl?"
123 "Hidden Gold"
124 "Map of Death"
125 "River Fight"
126 "Hands Up"
127 "Locked Up"
128 "Hoppy in Jail"
129 "Sudden Pains"
130 "Escape"
131 "Search for Gold"
132 "Stupid Sheriff"
133 "Hoppy in Trouble"
134 "Hoppy Defies the Law"
135 "Unexpected Danger"
136 "Robber's Loot"
137 "Kill Them All"
138 "Out of Ammunition"
139 "Hoppy's Surrender"
140 "Smoke Screen"
141 "Keep Smiling"

FOOL'S GOLD
142 "Action Wanted"
143 "Dangerous Mission"
144 "Followed"
145 "Ordered to Leave"
146 "Rough Treatment"
147 "Runaway Cart"
148 "Spider Collector"
149 "Problem for California"
150 "Plans Overheard"
151 "The Meeting"
152 "Forced Accomplice"
153 "Knocked Out"
154 "Mysterious Laboratory"
155 "Fake Gold Bricks"
156 "Hoppy Finds His Man"
157 "Bound Hands"
158 "Danger of Death"
159 "Tables are Turned"
160 "Race Against Time"
161 "False Signature"
162 "Flying Lasso"
163 "One Man Less"
164 "Victory Yell"
165 "Bar-20 Ahead"

130 "DEVIL'S PLAYGROUND" EPISODE 13 — "ESCAPE"
Hoppy pretends to be sick and tricks the Sheriff into sending him to the doctor for treatment. Once there, they grab the Deputy, throw him into a closet and get set to follow the trail of the missing girl. "We've got to find her before she gets killed."
SEE EPISODE 14 — "SEARCH FOR GOLD"
24 Cards Complete DEVIL'S PLAYGROUND
HOPALONG CASSIDY
© WM. BOYD, 1950   PRINTED IN U.S.A.

120 "DEVIL'S PLAYGROUND" EPISODE 3 "HEADING FOR DANGER"
The wounded girl slowly awakens and sees the friendly faces of Hoppy and his two partners. She refuses to say how or why she's been shot. When they try to question her, she faints. Hoppy says that he's going to investigate a little further ... in the "Devil's Playground."
SEE EPISODE 4 — "A WARNING IGNORED"
24 Cards Complete DEVIL'S PLAYGROUND
HOPALONG CASSIDY
© WM. BOYD, 1950   PRINTED IN U.S.A.

166 "THE DEAD DON'T DREAM" EPISODE 1 "LUCKY'S WEDDING"
Hopalong Cassidy and his two friends, Lucky and California, are dressed in their best clothes when they arrive at the "Last Chance Inn" for Lucky's wedding to Mary Benton. Hoppy is going to be best man for his pal. Does this mean the breaking up of their partnership?
SEE EPISODE 2 — "MARY'S MISSING UNCLE"
21 Cards Complete "THE DEAD DON'T DREAM"
HOPALONG CASSIDY
© WM. BOYD, 1950   PRINTED IN U.S.A.

205 "SILENT CONFLICT" EPISODE 19 "BACK TO NORMAL"
When Lucky recovers from Hoppy's knock out punch, he remembers nothing of what has happened to him for the past twenty-four hours. Hoppy concludes that Lucky has been hypnotized by Doc Richards. "Get your guns ready," he says. "Let's get Richards."
SEE EPISODE 20 — "HIDEOUT"
22 Cards Complete SILENT CONFLICT
HOPALONG CASSIDY
COPYRIGHT WILLIAM BOYD 1950   PRINTED IN U.S.A.

"THE DEAD DON'T DREAM"
166 "Lucky's Wedding"
167 "Mary's Missing Uncle"
168 "The Search Begins"
169 "A Dead Body"
170 "New Suspect"
171 "The Death Room"
172 "Another Disappearance"
173 "Evidence of Murder"
174 "The Missing Corpse"
175 "Suspicious Intruders"
176 "Where Is the Sheriff?"
177 "Dead Men Don't Talk"
178 "Prospect for Murder"
179 "The Killer Is Here"
180 "Death Descends"
181 "A Killer Trapped"
182 "Partners in Murder"
183 "Hoppy Breaks Away"
184 "The Shot"
185 "California to the Rescue"
186 "Together Again"

SILENT CONFLICT
187 "Too Much Money"
188 "Strange Friends"
189 "Lucky Won't Talk"
190 "Lucky Talks too Much"
191 "Unexpected News"
192 "Dangerous Tea"
193 "Stolen Gold"
194 "Secret Meeting"
195 "Hoppy Is Suspected"
196 "Orders to Kill"
197 "Quick on the Draw"
198 "Explanation not Wanted"
199 "One Gun for Four"
200 "Danger in the Hills"
201 "Instructions for Murder"
202 "Lucky Shoots at His Pals"
203 "Quick Action Needed"
204 "Fight for Life"
205 "Back to Normal"
206 "Hideout"
207 "Ready to Shot"
208 "A Crook Surrenders"

Hopalong Cassidy

FOIL CARD

SINISTER JOURNEY
209 "Runaway Horse"	217 "A Shot in the Night"	225 "The Killer Strikes"
210 "Urgent Request"	218 "False Accusation"	226 "Missing Suspect"
211 "Plot for Murder"	219 "A Warning"	227 "Hoppy Finds the Accused Man"
212 "Special Assignment"	220 "Quick Thinking"	228 "California Pulls a Switch
213 "A Threat"	221 "Unknown Enemy"	229 "Caught"
214 "Furious Fists"	222 "Name the Killer"	230 "Hoppy's Trick"
215 "Trouble Brewing"	223 "A Treacherous Shot"	
216 "California in Trouble"	224 "The Lie"	

GREEN 1-CENT WRAPPER

WHITE 1-CENT WRAPPER

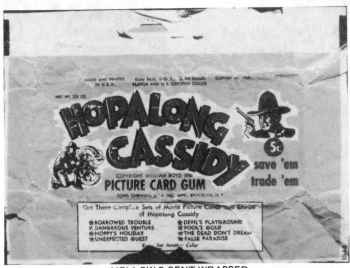

YELLOW 5-CENT WRAPPER

275

TWO STYLES OF WRAPPERS FOR HOPPY CARDS
DISTRIBUTED IN BOND BREAD

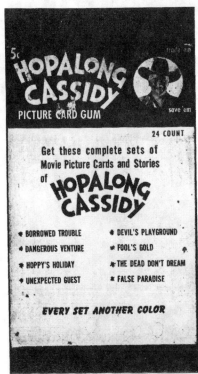

STORE ADVERTISING SIGN

DISPLAY CARD FOR
5-CENT HOPPY BOX

COMING SOON!
UPDATE TO THE 1960-PRESENT NON-SPORT PRICE GUIDE

HOPPY POPS PUZZLES (2K)

Here is another Hopalong Cassidy set distributed by Topps; few collectors know or care about it because it is not a standard card format. There are two components to the set: a 8 1/4" square box with slots to hold 15 lollipops, and the individual wrappers for those lollipops. The box illustrated has a connect-the-dots puzzle in the center and is "Puzzle 2" of the series (length unknown). The wrappers on the suckers were all the same: two main designs with "western" decorations (spurs, ropes, etc.) on the sides. Hoppy Pops were issued in 1950; no reference number

8 1/4" SQUARE

has been assigned. NOTE: wrappers were twisted around the lollipops, and this fact should be taken into consideration when evaluating them.

ITEM	EX	AVE
Box	60.00	20.00
Wrapper	50.00	20.00

INDIAN GUM (96)

Goudey Gum, attempting to re-enter the bubble gum market after World War II, re-printed 96 cards from one of the company's most successful sets — "Indian Gum." The fronts have the identical artwork of certain original cards, but the backs were printed with black ink and carried completely different advertising at the bottom. The series was released in 1947 and 1948 in the wrapper and box illustrated here. In the October, 1958 issue of The Card Collectors Bulletin, Howard Leheup reported that "Indian Gum is out again. Same cards." So, there is a possibility that the series was being "dumped" at that time. This recycling of Indian Gum was Goudey's last known

2 3/8" X 2 7/8"

card issue. The reference number is R773.

ITEM	EX	AVE
Card	5.00	1.00
Set	550.00	110.00
Wrapper	30.00	––
Box	125.00	30.00

Indian Gum

— No. 54 —

VICTORY CRY

Many of the hearty, loyal pioneers that established the Western frontiers of American civilization had cause to feel their blood run cold when the VICTORY CRY of the savage redskins rang near their homes on the prairie. After a good scalping or the massacre of a few innocent whites, the Indians would give vent to their murderous intentions with a VICTORY CRY which could be heard for miles.

INDIAN GUM
The original picture pack gum
This is one of a series of cards illustrating Indian and Pioneer romantic days
THE GOUDEY GUM CO. • BOSTON, MASS., U.S.A.
MAKERS OF CH BOY GUMS

5¢

INDIAN CHEWING GUM

INDIAN CHEWING GUM

Ingredients: Gum Base, Sugar, Dextrose, Corn Syrup, Artifical Flavor and U. S. Certified Colors.
THE GOUDEY GUM CO., BOSTON, MASS., U.S.A.

INDIAN CHEWING GUM

GET THIS INDIAN HEAD RING   SAVE INDIAN GUM BOX TOPS

THIS SNAPPY OXIDIZED SILVER FINISH INDIAN HEAD RING. YOURS FOR ONLY 5 INDIAN GUM BOX TOPS AND 15¢. EVERY RING ADJUSTABLE TO YOUR FINGER.
THE GOUDEY GUM CO., BOSTON 34, MASS.

SAVE THIS BOX TOP FOR VALUABLE PREMIUMS

1 Chief of the Shienne Tribe	13 Chief of the Pawnee Tribe	25 A Surprise Attack	47 Another Redskin Bites the Dust
2 Warrior of the Ioway Tribe	14 Chief of the Ottoes Tribe	26 Defense of the Stockade	48 Fight at the Army Post
3 Chief of the Konzas Tribe	15 Chief of the Ogallala Tribe	27 Fight on the Precipice	49 The Pony War Dance
4 Chief of the Pawnee Tribe	16 Chief of the Omaha Tribe	28 Primitive Fire Making	50 Acoma Tribe
5 Chief of the Delaware Tribe	17 Chief of the Osages Tribe	29 Struggle to Death	51 Painting
6 Warrior of the Sioux Tribe	18 Warrior of the Osages Tribe	30 Custer's Last Stand	52 Fishing
7 Warrior of the Ojibway Tribe	19 Warrior of the Camanche Tribe	31 Caught in the Attempt	53 Huichol Tribe
8 Chief of the Ute Tribe	20 Warrior of the Kioway Tribe	32 The Battering Ram	54 Victory Cry
9 Chief of the Flathead Tribe	21 Squaw and Child	33 Setting Fire to the Fort	55 Weaving
10 Chief of the Potowatomies Tribe	22 Chief of the Sioux Tribe	34 Marauders	56 Charge on the Sun Pole
11 Chief of the Pawnee Tribe	23 Chief of the Manden Tribe	35 Tracking Game	57 Eagle Dance
12 Chief of the Sioux Tribe	24 Chief of the Blackfoot Tribe	36 Making a Canoe	58 Zy-You-Wah
		37 Foiled	59 Fire Dance
		38 Puritan Days	60 Nascapee Tribe
		39 Trapped in their Ambush	61 Tshi-Zun-Hau-Kau
		40 Torturing their Victims	62 Toh-Ki-Ee-To
		41 Wampum	63 Stee-Cha-Co-Me-Co
		42 Chief Red Cloud	64 Genitoa
		43 Arrow Making	65 Kishkalwa
		44 Indian Naval Warfare	66 Luqaiot
		45 Vengeance	67 Hee-Ohks-Te-Kin
		46 Pipe of Peace	

68 Chief Bread
69 Shoo-De-Ga-Cha
70 Wat-Che-Mon-Ne
71 White Deer Skin Dancer
72 Yo-Ho-Lo-Micco
73 Steel
74 Little White Cloud
75 Many Shots
76 Sounding Sky
77 Medicine Man
78 Yellow Tepee
79 Nootka
80 Saving General Putnam
81 Osage Oil Wells
82 The Great King
83 Trailing a Prairie Schooner
84 Caught in the Circle
85 He Who Travels Everywhere
86 Wood
87 The Thinker
88 Running Fox
89 Perils of the Plains
90 Unhorsed
91 Throwing the Putch-Kohu
92 Chief White Cloud
93 Wolf Collar
94 Minnevana
95 White Cap
96 Sassacus

INDIAN TRADING CARDS (80)   2 1/2" X 3 1/2"

Although the artwork of this Fleer series of "Indian Trading Cards" is not as sophisticated as some collectors might like, the set is full of interesting information. There are several subsets of cards dealing with specific groups of Indians — Pacific Coast, Wood-land, Plains, etc. — and each of these subsets has a symbol which appears on the fronts of its cards. The backs have informative paragraphs dealing with Indian culture, plus an illustrated feature entitled "Indian Picture Writing." The beautifully-colored wrapper reads "Chief Halftown's Indian Trading Cards," and card No. 40 tells us something about this real-life Indian: "I am the direct descendant of the original Chief Halftown who signed a Peace Treaty with the United States in 1794. This is the oldest active peace treaty with the Indians, and I still receive a yearly grant of cloth and money from the government." The series was probably sold mostly in cello-packs as very few of the wax wrappers have found their way into the hands of collectors. Some reversed pictures have been reported. The reference number is R730-2.

Chief Halftown

INDIAN TRADING CARD
NO. 40
Collect All 80

I am a direct descendant of the Chief Halftown who signed a Peace Treaty with the United States in 1794. This is the oldest active peace treaty with the Indians and I still receive a yearly grant of cloth and money from the government.

INDIAN PICTURE WRITING
WISE MAN

ONE OF A SERIES OF 80 CARDS ON WOODLAND INDIANS

ITEM	EX	AVE
Card	.50	.10
Set	45.00	10.00
Wrapper	150.00	——

Indian Mother With Papoose Board

1	Sitting Bull	22	Indian Girl "Doing the Dishes"	39	Indian Smoking Carved Pipe
2	Indian Scout "Riding Trail"	23	Indian Making a Fire	40	Chief Halftown
3	Indian Boy with Dog Travois	24	Seneca Carving Mask from	41	Smoke Signals
4	Buffalo Dancer		Living Tree	42	Spear Fishing for Salmon
5	Indian Women and "Stove"	25	Indian Making a Birchbark	43	Carving a Totem Pole
6	Plains Indians' Teepees		Canoe	44	Northwest Indian Rain Hat
7	Indian Lauching Bullboat	26	Indian Woman Grinding Maize	45	Indian Dancer
8	Indian Mother Preparing	27	Indians Playing Lacrosse	46	Girl with Raven Head Spoon
	Pemmican	28	Indian in Winter Dress and	47	Warrior in Slatted Armor
9	Indian Musician with Turtle		Snowshoes	48	Sea-going Canoe
	Rattle	29	Indian Woman Preparing	49	Northwest Indian Splitting Logs
10	Rabbit-skin Leggings		Deerskin	50	Geronimo
11	Indians Speaking Sign Language	30	Indian Longhouse	51	Apache Masked Dancer
12	Dancing Sioux	31	Young Brave Coming Back	52	Mudhead Doll
13	Sacajawea		from Hunting Trip	53	Navaho Sandpainter
14	Chief Washakie	32	Indian Mother with Papoose	54	Hopi Snake Dancer
15	Medicine Man		Board	55	Navaho Warrior
16	Hunting a Buffalo	33	A Seminole Dugout Canoe	56	Pueblo Village
17	Chief Joseph	34	Iroquois Warrior	57	Butterfly Dancer
18	Assiniboin Warrior	35	Seminole Hunting Alligator	58	Hoop Dancer
19	Buffalo Horn Head Dress	36	Osceola	59	Cochise
20	Wampum Belt	37	Seminole Man in Costume	60	Indian Farmer Digging
21	Seminole "Chickee"	38	Making a Dugout Canoe		Irrigation Ditch

61	Navaho Rug Weaver
62	Apache Horseman
63	Navaho "Hogan"
64	Zuni Pottery Drum
65	Indian Dressed for the Toloache Ceremony
66	California Indian Woman with Burden Basket
67	Launching a "Balsa" Raft
68	Making Acorn Bread
69	California Indian Woman Gathering Berries
70	Eskimo on a Seal Hunt
71	Eskimo Comedy Mask
72	Eskimo in Kayak
73	Eskimo Wrestling
74	Eskimo Woman Mending Boots
75	Eskimo with Wounded Polar Bear
76	Eskimo with Snow Goggles
77	Eskimo Woman Fishing
78	Eskimo Returning to His Igloo
79	Eskimo Repairing Arrows
80	Eskimo Dog Sled

INVENTOR SERIES (10)   1 15/16" X 2 5/8"

This is another candy box set which is not much to look at but very difficult to find. Produced by the CeDe Company (Bloomfield, NJ), the series of ten "Inventor" cards was first reported in the August, 1955 issue of The Card Collectors Bulletin. The artwork of the cards is one-color and uninspiring, but ten of them returned to the company (with the correct answers to the questions on the cards) got the owner a prize. It is not known if mailed-in cards were returned, but that is one possible explanation for the short supply today. The reference number is R753-2.

ITEM	EX	AVE
Card	3.00	.60
Set	35.00	7.00
Box	20.00	5.00

ISOLATION BOOTH (88)

No doubt the public fascination with television quiz shows in the mid-1950's inspired the production team at Topps to launch the "Gee Whiz Quiz" series, better known to collectors as "Isolation Booth" (from the format on the backs of the cards). The set was first mentioned in the "new issues" section of the February, 1958 edition of The Card Collectors Bulletin, so it is likely that it appeared in the fall of 1957. The cards boast color artwork fronts with yellow "question" panels. The answers were available on the bizarre orange backs, provided you had the overlay to read the message hidden under the text ("Magic Red Paper Tells All"). This red cellophane sheet measures 2 1/8" by 3 1/8" and is often the one item which modern collectors overlook about this set. The cards were sold in two wrappers: a 1-cent "continuous design" type and a 5-cent type of equally uninspired format. One interesting detail on the latter is a panel advertisment for the scarce "Archie Comics" series. The reference number is R714-10.

ITEM	EX	AVE
Card	2.00	.45
Set	220.00	45.00
Wrappers		
1-cent	45.00	--
5-cent	30.00	--
Box	200.00	45.00
Magic red paper	5.00	1.50

1 How Tall Was the World's Tallest Man?
2 Who Was the World's Smallest Man?
3 Who Was the World's Thinnest Man?
4 How Old Was the World's Oldest Man?
5 Name the Tallest and Shortest U.S. Presidents.
6 Who Was the Heaviest U.S. President?
7 What Was the Greatest Naval Battle in History?
8 Where Is the World's Smallest Army?
9 What Is the Fastest Submarine in the World?
10 How Big Was the World's Largest Gun?
11 What Is the World's Largest Snake?
12 Who Was the Worst Murderer in History?
13 What Was the Biggest Robbery in History?
14 What Was the Largest Crowd in History?
15 Where Was the World's Worst Earthquake?
16 How Hot Is the Hottest Place on Earth?
17 Where Is the World's Coldest Place?
18 How High Was the World's Biggest Wave?
19 How Big Is the World's Largest Living Thing?
20 What Is the Brightest Star in the Sky?
21 How Large Is the World's Largest Land Animal?
22 How Tall Is the Tallest Land Animal?
23 What Is the Smallest Land Animal?
24 What Is the World's Most Precious Gem?

25 How Big Was the World's Largest Diamond?
26 How Big Is the World's Largest Telescope?
27 How Tall Is the World's Tallest Statue?
28 Where Is the World's Longest Suspension Bridge?
29 What Is the World's Most Expensive Car?
30 What Is the World's Fastest Car?
31 Which Ship Crossed the Atlantic the Fastest?
32 What Is the World's Largest Aircraft?
33 Where Is the World's Largest Clock?
34 How Accurate Is the World's Most Accurate Clock?
35 Name the World's Worst Catastrophe.
36 What Was the Greatest Flood in History?
37 What Was the Worst Tornado in History?
38 What Was the Worst Typhoon in History?
39 Where Was the World's Greatest Landslide?
40 Where Was the Worst Fire in History?
41 Where Was the World's Worst Forest Fire?
42 Name the Top Speed at Which a Pilot Bailed Out.
43 What Was the World's Worst Airship Disaster?
44 Who Was the Most Decorated Hero in U.S. History?
45 What Was the Highest Mountain Ever Climbed?
46 What Was the Deepest Penetration into the Ocean?
47 Who Was America's Greatest Air Ace?
48 What Was the Fastest Land Speed Ever Recorded?

49 What Is the Record for the Greatest Speed on Water?
50 What Is the Most Barrels an Ice Skater Ever Leaped?
51 How Many Balls Did the Greatest Juggler Juggle?
52 Who Was the World's Greatest Tightrope Walker?
53 Who Is the World's Richest Man?
54 What Is the World's Hamburger-Eating Record?
55 What Is the Record for Eating Boiled Eggs in One Day?
56 Who Was the World's Greatest Non-stop Runner?
57 What Is the Greatest Non-stop Distance Ever Walked?
58 Who Was Stranded on a Raft the Longest?
59 What Is the Greatest Distance a Man Ever Swam?
60 What Is the Record for Staying Underwater?
61 Who Was the World's Greatest Non-stop Talker?
62 Who Went the Longest without Eating?
63 Who Lived the Longest without Sleep?
64 Who Parachuted from the Greatest Altitude?
65 Who Parachuted from the Lowest Height?
66 Who Fought the World's Longest Title Fight?
67 Who Was the World's Tallest Boxer?
68 What Was the Most Knockdowns in a Fight?
69 What Was the Greatest Weight Lifted by a Man?
70 Where Is the World's Smallest Prison?
71 Which Language Is Spoken By The Most People?

72 What Is the Longest Name in the World?
73 What Is the World's Most Common Name?
74 What Is the World's Smallest Book?
75 How Big Is the World's Biggest Drum?
76 What Was the World's Greatest Explosion?
77 What Was the Greatest Single Day's Rainfall?
78 How Big Was the World's Largest Hailstone?
79 Which Plant Has the World's Largest Leaves?
80 What Was the Largest Litter of Puppies?
81 How Long Was the World's Longest Bicycle?
82 How Fast Is the World's Fastest Train?
83 What Was the World's Highest Flying Balloon?
84 How Small Was the Smallest Baby Ever Born?
85 Who Had the Longest Hair in History?
86 How Long Was the World's Longest Beard?
87 Who Was the World's Fattest Man?
88 Who Had the Most Fingers in History?

IT HAPPENED TO A PRESIDENT (20)   4 5/8" X 6 3/16"

The series entitled "It Happened To A President" is actually printed on thin tissue paper attached to the interior side of "Golden Coin Bubble Gum" wrappers. The

1 Andrew Jackson
2 George Washington
3 Ulysses S. Grant
4 Theodore Roosevelt
5 Abraham Lincoln
6 George Washington
7 Andrew Johnson
8 Grover Cleveland
9 Zachary Taylor
10 James Monroe

11 James A. Garfield
12 John Adams
13 John Quincy Adams
14 Abraham Lincoln
15 James Madison
16 Franklin Roosevelt
17 Thomas Jefferson
18 Calvin Coolidge
19 Woodrow Wilson
20 William H. Harrison

front (or outside) of the wrapper is gold foil with a green currency design in the center. It bears a copyright date of 1948 in small letters to the left, but the date of issue, 1949, is printed in the top right corner. The tissue paper story on the interior side is rust colored, and each relates a "true incident" in the life of a U.S. President. Card and wrapper collectors often ignore the fact that a plastic "President Coin" was also inserted into every package (listed in this book under the title "President Coins").

It Happened To A President was also issued in Canada in 1956. The Canadian wrapper has a "5" printed in the upper corners of the center design (rather than the dates "1789" and "1949" of the original American wrapper). A Topps advertising flyer dubbed the product "Golden Coin" to be "1949's Biggest Hit." It also stated that the coins were metal (they were plastic), and that there were

It Happened to a President

33 different wrapper-stories (only 20 were ever printed). The reference number for the set is R711-5. NOTE: prices listed are for wrappers with stories attached.

ITEM	EX	AVE
Wrapper/		
Story	30.00	10.00
Box	100.00	20.00

JETS (240)

2 1/16" X 2 15/16"

The Korean War involved the first full-scale use of jet-propelled aircraft, and Topps decided to cash in on the new public interest in jet planes with this 1956 series of 240 cards. The full title of the series is "Photo Album Jets," and this title appears on all the packaging. Actually, the black & white photos do not all show jets; there are a variety of propeller-driven planes pictured as well. The card backs are two-toned: about 35 percent of the background is eggshell white, while the rest is pastel green. The descriptive text is printed at the left with either a "Spotter Series" (the cards 1-120) or "Plane Facts" (cards 121-240) feature at the right. The set contains 240 cards, and the last 120 cards are twice as difficult to obtain as the first 120. There are three wrappers associated with the set: the standard 1-cent and 5-cent versions, plus a newly-discovered one called "Fighting Planes" in a 1-cent package that held two cards and a piece of gum. We have also illustrated parts of the 1-cent and 5-cent boxes, plus the photo album box, which contained eight albums (15 cents each) designed to hold the set. A full list of the 240 planes in the set, complete with checkoff boxes, was printed in the album. The reference number is R707-1.

ITEM	EX	AVE
Cards		
1-120	1.00	.25
121-240	2.00	.50
Set	415.00	100.00
Wrappers		
1-cent, Jets	20.00	––
5-cent, Jets	35.00	––
1-cent, Fighting Planes	50.00	––
Boxes		
1-cent	75.00	20.00
5-cent	60.00	15.00
Album (15 cent)	50.00	12.50
Album	20.00	7.50

Auster B-4

JETS 98
Auster B-4
British Ambulance-Freighter

Britain's Auster B-4 is a small ambulance-freighter that can be adapted to a single or double-tier stretcher carrier or seat three passengers and a pilot. Powered by a 180-hp Bombardier 70? piston engine, the B-4 can lift a payload of 550 lb. It also can be used for aerial photography.

© T.C.G. Printed in U.S.A.

SPEED	RANGE	CEILING	GROSS WT.	SPAN	LENGTH	ENGINES
105 mph.	330 mi.	No info	2,600 lbs.	37'	24' 8"	1

Handley Page T. MK. 11

JETS 223
Handley Page T. MK. 11
British Trainer

This triple-fin, four-engine aircraft is being used to train Britain's Royal Air Force as an advanced trainer for air navigators. Originally designed as a 32-passenger transport for feeder airlines, the high-wing plane now carries a pilot, signaler, navigation instructor and two student navigators.

SPEED	RANGE	CEILING	GROSS WT.	SPAN	LENGTH	ENGINES
202 mph	630 mi.	18,000	30,000 lbs.	65'	52' 1"	4

8 count

JETS PHOTO ALBUM

space for 120 pictures   check list of complete series

BIGGEST COMICS
TWO BIG CHEWS   1¢
young America's favorite bubble gum
© TOPPS CHEWING GUM, INC., MFR., BROOKLYN 32 N.Y. MADE & PRINTED IN U.S.A.

PHOTO ALBUM
JETS 5¢
BUBBLE GUM
FIGHTERS BOMBERS ROCKETS

official JETS photo album

space for 120 pictures plus check list of complete series. Ask your retailer or send 15c to: JETS, Box 100, Brooklyn 32, N.Y.

buy your official JETS PHOTO ALBUM here! see wrapper

PHOTO ALBUM
JETS 1¢
BUBBLE GUM

120 COUNT

PHOTO ALBUM
JETS 1¢
BUBBLE GUM

PHOTO ALBUM
JETS 5¢
BUBBLE GUM
FIGHTERS BOMBERS ROCKETS

CHECK LIST FOR OFFICIAL JETS CARDS

Use this list to check off your cards as you mount them into this album. At a glance you can always tell which cards you still need to complete your collection.

☐ 1. Cessna CH-1	☐ 31. McDonnell F3H-IN
☐ 2. SFECMAS Ars 1301	☐ 32. De Havilland Comet
☐ 3. Lanier Paraplane II	☐ 33. Convair B-36D Ficon
☐ 4. Short S.A. 4	☐ 34. Piasecki Workhorse
☐ 5. Fiat G.82 Grifo	☐ 35. Doman YH-31
☐ 6. F7U-3 Cutlass	☐ 36. Nardi FN333
☐ 7. Gyrodyne Model 33	☐ 37. Grumman Albatross
☐ 8. F-89D Scorpion	☐ 38. Bell X-1A
☐ 9. FD-25B De.....	☐ 39. De Havilland 110
☐ 10. Boeing 707	☐ 40. F-86D Sabre
☐ 11. Pilatus P-3	☐ 41. Sikorsky HR2S-1
☐ 12. Kaman HTK-1	☐ 42. Fairchild Avitruc
☐ 13. Handley Page Victor	☐ 43. Douglas Skyshark
☐ 14. Custer CCW-5	☐ 44. Colonial C-1 Skimmer
☐ 15. SAAB J-29C	☐ 45. Lockheed XFV-1
☐ 16. Douglas Skyhawk	☐ 46. Sud-Ouest Vautour
☐ 17. SAAB A-32 Lansen	☐ 47. De Havilland Otter
☐ 18. Canadair Sabre Mk. 5	☐ 48. British Canberra
☐ 19. Avro-Canada CF-100	☐ 49. Supermarine 525
☐ 20. Fokker S. 13	☐ 50. Douglas F4D Skyray
☐ 21. Gloster Javelin	☐ 51. Hiller YH-32
☐ 22. Northrop X-4	☐ 52. Aero 45
☐ 23. Avro B-1 Vulcan	☐ 53. Goodyear ZP2N-2
☐ 24. Short S.B. 5	☐ 54. M.K.E.K. Model 5A
☐ 25. Saro Princess	☐ 55. Convair Samaritan
☐ 26. Lockheed Neptune	☐ 56. Piasecki H-25A
☐ 27. Kaman HTK-1	☐ 57. Vickers Viscount
☐ 28. Rotor-Craft Pinwheel	☐ 58. Airspeed Ambassador
☐ 29. Grumman Tiger	☐ 59. Fairey Firefly
☐ 30. Supermarine Swift	☐ 60. Hurel-Dubois H.D. 32

☐ 61. Gyrodyne 2C	☐ 97. Karhu 48B
☐ 62. Avro Tudor	☐ 98. Auster B-4
☐ 63. Fokker S.11	☐ 99. Sud-Est Caravelle
☐ 64. SAAB 91B Safir	☐ 100. Fairey Gannet
☐ 65. Lockheed XFV-1	☐ 101. Convair R3Y-2
☐ 66. Percival Provost	☐ 102. Short Sealand
☐ 67. MiG-15	☐ 103. Vickers Varsity
☐ 68. Farnham Fly-Cycle	☐ 104. Sud-Est Armagnac
☐ 69. Short Seamew	☐ 105. Sud-Est Grognard II
☐ 70. Fairey VTO	☐ 106. Beecraft Honey Bee
☐ 71. SAAB 210 Draken	☐ 107. Lockheed ZF-80A
☐ 72. De Havilland Heron	☐ 108. Cessna XL-19B
☐ 73. Lockheed PO-1W	☐ 109. Ilyushin IL-12A
☐ 74. Bristol Britannia	☐ 110. Dassault Mystere IV
☐ 75. Bristol 173	☐ 111. No. Amer. T-28A
☐ 76. Swift F. Mk. 4	☐ 112. Breguet Deux-Points
☐ 77. Super Constellation	☐ 113. Sud-Est 3120
☐ 78. B & G Beverly	☐ 114. Sud-Ouest Bretagne
☐ 79. Armed Provost	☐ 115. Sikorsky XHSS-1
☐ 80. Douglas DC-7	☐ 116. Convair YF-102
☐ 81. Brantly B-2	☐ 117. De Havilland Beaver
☐ 82. Chance V. Regulus	☐ 118. Piaggio P. 136
☐ 83. Hughes XH17	☐ 119. Lockheed YC-130A
☐ 84. Auster Aiglet	☐ 120. De Havilland Drover
☐ 85. Douglas X3	☐ 121. Kaman HOK-1
☐ 86. Sud-Est Mistral	☐ 122. Sud-Ouest Farfadet
☐ 87. Bristol 171 Mk. 50	☐ 123. Short Sunderland
☐ 88. Goodyear ZP3K	☐ 124. SIPA 200 Minijet
☐ 89. Fouga Gemeaux	☐ 125. Short Shetland
☐ 90. Convair Pogostick	☐ 126. Potez 75
☐ 91. Fairchild Packet	☐ 127. Nord 2501 Noratlas
☐ 92. Ambrosini Grifo	☐ 128. Nord 1402 Noroit
☐ 93. Nelson N-4	☐ 129. M.S. 755 Fleuret
☐ 94. Convair YC-131C	☐ 130. M.C. 101
☐ 95. F9F-5 Panther	☐ 131. Breguet 960 Vultur
☐ 96. Boeing B-47E	☐ 132. Béarn Super Minicab

☐ 133. Béarn Minicab	☐ 169. F9F-8 Cougar
☐ 134. Commonw'lth Sabre	☐ 170. Martin P5M-2 Marlin
☐ 135. " Winjeel	☐ 171. Thunderflash
☐ 136. Supermarine 535	☐ 172. Stits Sky Baby
☐ 137. Gloster Meteor	☐ 173. Casmuniz 52
☐ 138. Fairey Rotodyne	☐ 174. Helio Courier
☐ 139. Balliol	☐ 175. McKinnie 165
☐ 140. Avro Shackleton	☐ 176. Sud-Ouest SO-30
☐ 141. F-100 Super Sabre	☐ 177. Short Sherpa SB-4
☐ 142. B-52 Stratofortress	☐ 178. A/W Rocket
☐ 143. B-50D Superfortress	☐ 179. Sikorsky XH-39
☐ 144. Stratofreighter	☐ 180. Bell X5
☐ 145. F-94C Starfire	☐ 181. Fouga CM170R
☐ 146. Thunderstreak	☐ 182. Dassault Ouragan
☐ 147. Fiat G. 46	☐ 183. Boeing Bomarc
☐ 148. Cessna 319	☐ 184. Glenview Flyride
☐ 149. Douglas Nike	☐ 185. Guided Missile
☐ 150. Douglas A3D-1	☐ 186. I. Ae. 34 Sun Ray
☐ 151. Beechcraft Mentor	☐ 187. Handley P. C. Mk. 3
☐ 152. SIPA 300R	☐ 188. Lear Learstar
☐ 153. M.S. 760 Fleuret II	☐ 189. Wideroe C.5 Polar
☐ 154. Sud-Ouest Djinn	☐ 190. Aerocar Model 2
☐ 155. SFECMAS Gerfaut	☐ 191. B'chcraft Super 18
☐ 156. Fairey Jet Gyrodyne	☐ 192. Bell 47G-1
☐ 157. Fairchild Packplane	☐ 193. Martin XB-51
☐ 158. Piasecki YH-16	☐ 194. Boeing Stratocruiser
☐ 159. Fulton Airphibian	☐ 195. Cessna 310
☐ 160. Emigh Trojan A-2	☐ 196. Cessna 195
☐ 161. Sud-Est Baroudeur	☐ 197. Chance-V. Corsair
☐ 162. Thalman T-4	☐ 198. Convair Sea Dart
☐ 163. Fairey F.D. 1	☐ 199. Globemaster
☐ 164. Riley Twin Navion	☐ 200. Douglas Skynight
☐ 165. Temco Buckeroo	☐ 201. Douglas A-26B
☐ 166. Temco Plebe	☐ 202. Douglas R4B-8
☐ 167. Aero Commander	☐ 203. Grumman S2F-1
☐ 168. Goodyear Balloon	☐ 204. Grumman Mallard

☐ 205. Grumman Avenger
☐ 206. Lockheed T-33A
☐ 207. Martin 404
☐ 208. Martin M-270
☐ 209. McDonnell XV-1
☐ 210. Mooney M-18L Mite
☐ 211. No. American F-86H
☐ 212. No. Amer. F-510
☐ 213. Piper Tri-Pacer
☐ 214. Piper Apache
☐ 215. Sikorsky HRS
☐ 216. Avro Ashton
☐ 217. Avro 707B
☐ 218. Bristol 170
☐ 219. De Havilland Dove
☐ 220. Chipmunk
☐ 221. Sea Hornet
☐ 222. Hermes
☐ 223. T.Mk.11
☐ 224. Sea Fury (Mk. 11)
☐ 225. Percival Prince
☐ 226. Pioneer II
☐ 227. Seagull
☐ 228. Folland Midge
☐ 229. Can-Car Harvard
☐ 230. Avro Lancaster
☐ 231. Arsenal VG-90
☐ 232. Breguet BR. 111E
☐ 233. Farman Monitor
☐ 234. H. D. 31
☐ 235. Payen P. A. 49
☐ 236. SNCASE Languedoc
☐ 237. Sud-Ouest Trident
☐ 238. Sud-Ouest-Corse II
☐ 239. Tachikawa RO 53
☐ 240. Nord S.V. 4A

Made and printed in the U.S.A.

JETS, ROCKETS, SPACEMEN (108)   2 1/16" X 3 1/8"

"Jets-Rockets-Spacemen," another treasure-trove of inovative color artwork and text, was released by Bowman in 1951. The series was like n0 other ever issued and caused a sensation among kids across the country. A total of 108 cards were actually printed, but 180 were planned. Unfortunately, the artwork for cards 109-144 was somehow "lost," and production of the set was halted. (The material for cards 145-180 was recovered by col-lectors and reprinted about ten years ago.) The 108 original cards depict the adventures of earthlings on far-flung worlds. Jets-Rockets-Spacemen were printed in three groups of 36 cards, with the middle run, strangely enough, being the most difficult to obtain. The wrappers are blue: two 1-cent types and one 5-cent variety are confirmed. The 5-cent display box illustrated is dull in design but is almost impossi-ble to find. Bowman dumped boxes of J-R-S onto the market in 1955 in a futile attempt to raise money for continued operations. The reference number is R701-13.

ITEM	EX	AVE
Cards		
1-36	6.00	1.50
37-72	12.00	3.00
73-108	8.00	2.00
Set	1250.00	300.00
Wrappers		
1-cent		
Planet	250.00	——
1-cent,		
Spaceman	300.00	——
5-cent	250.00	——
Box	400.00	100.00

91.   Videoscope
One day King Trunlon took us to the brain peo-ple's observatory, where we saw a videoscope with which Krotonian astronomers often probe the Milky Way. The instrument had powers of magnification that cannot be expressed in Earth-ian terms. The King focused it on rays of earth-light that had traveled through space for eight years. The next moment we were looking at a baseball game that the Indians and White Sox had played eight years before.
JETS ☆ ROCKETS ☆ SPACEMEN

284

1	Spacemen Inspect Rocket Center	27	Detained by Martians	54	Undersea Realm	82	Landing on Kroto
2	Seeing a Rocket Built	28	Martian City	55	Equipped with Gill Gears	83	Turned into Dwarfs
3	To The Launching Ring	29	Phobos—Moon of Mars	56	Underwater Hunting	84	Brought to King Trunion
4	Final Check Before Blastoff	30	Slaying Deimos Rock Dragon	57	In the Realm of Prince Frost	85	At Kroto's Radial Center
5	Blastoff	31	Observing Martian Dust Storm	58	Polar Cats Invade Runways	86	Menaced by Vegetable Men
6	Receding Earth	32	In Deadly Peril	59	Ice Capital	87	Assembling Ice Robots
7	Free of Gravity	33	Battling Space Cell	60	Thoughts of Planet Ex	88	Strange Battle
8	Looking at the Universe	34	"Cutlass"	61	Over Saturn's Rings	89	Duel Over Fierson Pit
9	Repairing Rocket in Flight	35	Futuristic Fighter	62	On Saturn	90	Capt. Argo Rescues Count Melchor
10	Space Station	36	"Matador"	63	Visiting Titan		
11	Dodging Meteor Showers	37	"Panther"	64	Fur Men of Ganymede	91	Videoscope
12	Attacked by Ray Fighters	38	"Scorpion"	65	Navigating in Planetoid Belt	92	Palace in the Sky
13	Approaching the Moon	39	Fighting Giant	66	End of a Spaceship	93	Attacked by Funnel Rockets
14	Circling Moon for Landing	40	Spacemen Examine Wreckage	67	Captured by Space Pirates	94	Prisoners of Iron Men
15	On the Moon	41	Battle of Rockets	68	Released by Asteroid Men	95	Sentenced by Krator the Cruel
16	Lunar Observatory	42	Landing in a Venusian Jungle	69	Saving an Asteroid World	96	Making Deno—Ray Adapter
17	Leaping Lepons	43	Riding a Dinosaur	70	Escape from Space Pirates	97	Magnetizing Iron Men
18	Mantis Men	44	Caught by Tentacle Vines	71	Defending Space Station	98	Ending Krator's Reign
19	Bound for Mercury	45	Octoplant Thwarts Jaguan Attack	72	Home to Manhattan	99	Thor Mogon's Ultimatum
20	Crash-Landing in Mercurian Bog			73	Set for New Adventure	100	Help Arrives
21	Hypnotized by Steam Frogs	46	Through Volcanic Caves	74	Invention of the Zaratron	101	In Wild West Fashion
22	Overcoming Steam Frogs	47	Seeing King Vulcor's Realm	75	Bigger and Better Rocket	102	Final Day on Kroto
23	Rocket Repair and Formula Q	48	Rescued from Icy Sub-Cavern	76	Test Flight	103	Visit to Pluto
24	Fighting Off Fire Beetles	49	Back to the Outer World	77	Spacemen Hold Convention	104	Close Call
25	Wrestling Saber-Toothed Tiger	50	Strange Burst	78	All Is Ready	105	Malpo the Mighty
26	Exploring in Heat Gliders	51	Seen on the Telescreen	79	On our Way	106	Avro 707
		52	Over Planet Ex	80	Trans-Solar World	107	Voodoo and Demon
		53	A Long Dive	81	Hypnotized by Brain Man	108	Thunderjet

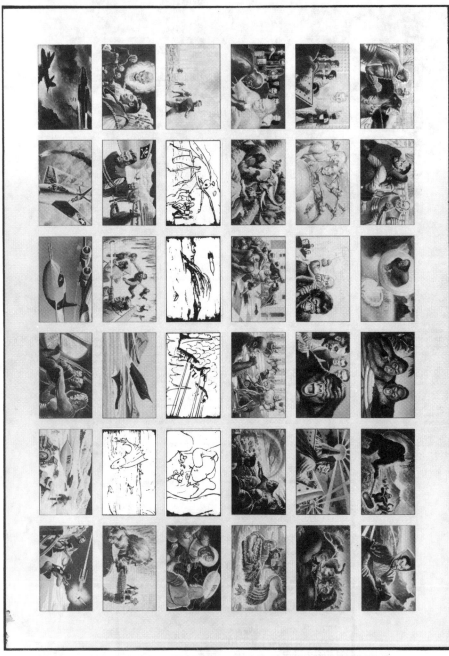

ARTWORK FOR A LAST SERIES OF NEVER-PRINTED CARDS WAS
REPRODUCED IN MODERN TIMES BY COLLECTORS PAUL KOCH
AND JIM TREVOR

JIGGLEYS (60)

The "Jiggleys" series, distributed in wrappers without gum, is composed of 60 titles: 30 in a mixed series of circus and western subjects (1-30), and 30 more with a military theme (31-60). The cards have multi-color artwork fronts, with die-cut firgures which can be "punched" and then detached. Unlike most other diecut cards, the two figures on each Jiggley card are held together by two horizontal (cardboard) "holding bars" which are stapled to them on the back. The de-

tached figures can be made to "move" by wiggling the holding bars and can be stored by replacing them back into the original frame. Experience has shown that the first thirty cards of the series are easier to obtain than the last thirty; in fact, a quanity of unopened boxes of the circus and western Jiggleys was discovered some years ago and is still supplying the market with cards and unopened packs. The cards bear a copyright date of 1950; the military wrapper is dated

1951. The series was manufactured by the Model Airplane Company (Brooklyn). The reference number for the set is R775.

ITEM	EX	AVE
Cards		
1-30	3.00	.75
31-60	3.50	.85
Set	235.00	55.00
Wrappers		
Circus/		
Western	10.00	——
Military	150.00	——
Box	100.00	25.00

1	The Rodeo	21	Indian Warfare	41	LST Landing
2	The Fighting Sheriff	22	Bronco-Bustin'	42	Revele
3	Panning for Gold	23	The Lion Tamer	43	M1 Rifle
4	The Monkeys	24	Klip and Klop	44	
5	Mopey the Gorilla	25	The Pugilists	45	Link Trainer
6	The Square Dance	26	Indian Ceremonial Dance	46	Jet Fighters
7	On the Open Range	27	Hunting Buffalo	47	Aircraft Carrier Landing
8	Stage-Coach Holdup	28	The Aerial Acrobats	48	Army Jeep
9	Buster and His Seal	29	The Big Race	49	Helicopter Rescue
10	The Bareback Rider	30	The Firefighter	50	
11	The Corner Tavern	31	Bazooka Team	51	Paratroop Invasion
12	Fighting on the Rapids	32	Bayonet Practice	52	
13	Capture of the Badman	33	Submarine	53	Hand Grenade Attack
14	Sleepy JoJo	34	KP Duty	54	
15	Animal Antics	35	105 mm. Howitzer	55	Jeep-Mounted Weapons
16	The Indian Scout	36	Submarine Gun Practice	56	Mine Detectors
17	Corralling the Herd	37	Armored Tank	57	Aerial Torpedo
18	The Sleeping Deamon	38	Military Band	58	Flame Throwers
19	Monkey Shines	39		59	BAR Rifle
20	Blind Driving	40	Communications	60	

287

JOE PALOOKA (11K)   2 1/4" X 3 1/4"

This series of multi-color artwork drawings of characters from the "Joe Palooka" comic strip has not yet been positively attributed to a specific company and product. The attachment "nubs" on all four edges of each card suggest a candy box format. It is also possible that retailers had

HUMPHREY PENNYWORTH

pre-scored sheets of these cards and pulled a card off to give away with the purchase of penny candy. The cards are printed on thick cardboard and are blank-backed. The number on each is printed in a red circle, and the highest number seen is No. 15. The character is named below the drawing, and the artist's name, "Ham Fisher," is found both in script (near artwork) and in type (lower left corner) on every card. The set was not listed in the early catalogs, and no reference number has been assigned.

ITEM	EX	AVE
Card	4.00	1.50

JOE PALOOKA BOXERS (6K)   2 7/16" X 3 3/4"

Here is an interesting set of candy box cards which is listed in the Non-Sports Guide because the sports card "experts" don't know that it exists. As far as we know, the six cards mentioned in the October, 1958 edition of The Card Collectors Bulletin are the only ones in the set. Each card was originally the back panel of a "Joe Palooka" candy & toy box. They are not numbered, and the panel below the drawing is found in either white or yellow. The artwork is rough but has just enough detail to be interesting. Some biographical data and fight results are given for each subject. Of considerable interest to researchers is the phrase on the front panel which reads "Candy, Toy and Traders Card In Each Package." Perhaps some cards of the preceding set were packed inside these boxes, making "Joe Palooka Candy & Toy" a doubly-good buy. However, we will have to wait for an unopened box to surface for this theory to be confirmed or disproved. The reference number is R437.

BOXER	EX	AVE
James J. Corbett	20.00	6.00
Jack Dempsey Nonpareil	20.00	6.00
Jake Kilrain	15.00	4.00
Benny Leonard	15.00	4.00
Battling Nelson	15.00	4.00
John L. Sullivan	25.00	8.00

JOE PALOOKA TRANSFER PICTURES (?)   2" X 3 1/2"

It is more than likely that the "Joe Palooka Transfer Pictures" booklet shown here was one of the insert prizes that

came in "Joe Palooka Candy & Toy" boxes. The orange color of the cover matches the orange background of the Joe Palooka boxer cards. The size is also right. The cover and transfer pages were stapled together at the top; each "page" had three different drawings which could be applied to the skin by wetting and applying the designs. A machine-made perforation line between individual transfers made detaching easy. The word "Japan" is printed on every sheet of transfers, and that is why this item is listed under the reference category R774 (Japanese-made novelties and inserts).

ITEM	EX	AVE
Transfer Booklet	7.00	3.00

LICENSE PLATES — 1949 (75)

7/8" X 1 7/16"

"Topps Gum of Brooklyn continues its series of odd novelty cards [with] pictures of autos on one side and license plates on the other. The small size and the two-sided feature may not be popular with collectors ..." Judging from the limited quantity of these small license plate cards which are in today's marketplace, the December, 1949 issue of The Card Collectors Bulletin made an accurate assessment about its popularity. The fronts of the cards depicted state license plates in artwork form; all the plates are marked 1949. The backs displayed a new type of novelty: approximately 70 percent of the space was covered by a gray coating, under which lay the "answer" to a question posed in the remaining uncoated area. The two themes of the questions are car identification and state landmarks.

With 48 states, plus the District of Columbia and Quebec, the set might have logically stopped at 50 cards, but Topps decided to confuse the issue by printing 25 of the plates with different questions on the back. [NOTE: this is a tentative figure based on the "75" set total listed in the early catalogs. If the 1950 License Plate checklist is a mirror of the 1949 set, then there are actually 100 cards in the set — two groups of fifty printed with both "car" and "landmark" questions. In that case, two different license plate fronts would share a single car identification question and picture, since only 25 of these exist, as compared to a landmark question for every plate.] The fact that these small cards are not numbered (like the 1950 set) makes research even more difficult.

The tiny wrapper for the 1949 series is basically yellow with black, red, and green accents. It carries a 1949 copyright date and has advertising for the "Scratch Off The AUTO—MAGIC Paint" feature on the back: "Guess The Cars! Guess The Landmarks! Find the hidden color picture to prove your answer." Modern collectors are not much interested in license plate sets; this is one that will require much more investigation before we can confirm the set total. The reference number is R714-11.

ITEM	EX	AVE
Cards		
Coating intact	2.00	.50
No coating	1.50	.35
Wrapper	50.00	——

LICENSE PLATES — 1950 (75)   1 3/4" X 2 7/8"

The 1950 "License Plates" set by Topps is basically a reprint of the 1949 series in a larger format. The company made one major improvement by numbering the cards, which has allowed us to research the 1950 set more accurately than was possible with the unnumbered 1949 series. There are 100 cards in the 1950 edition, 50 with landmark questions and 50 with "Guess The Car" questions. This means that there are two different backs for every plate, but only 75 different backs in all (there are only 25 cards questions, and each one is shared by two different plates). The sequence is this: cards 1-25...one plate only on front, landmark question on back; cards 26-50... two plates

have the same card number and share an identical car-question back; cards 51-75... one plate only on front, landmark question on back. As an example of the confusing second run, cards of "Michigan" and "Washington" are both found with number 26, and both have the same "Guess The Car" answer on back: "Frazer." The double-numbered cards are clearly indicated in our checklist.

The 1-cent wrapper is yellow with green/red stripes. It bears the title "Auto Magic," which refers to the new Topps gimmick of hiding part of the card under a colored coating. No price is indicated on the wrapper. The 5-cent version also has no price marked and

bears a 1950 copyright date. It carries the "Stop 'n Go" title used in the 1949 series, but the 1950 date is printed in the center design. The bottom panel is devoted to explaining the "Auto-Magic" scratch-off feature. The reference number is R714-12.

ITEM	EX	AVE
Cards		
Coating intact	1.50	.35
No coating	1.00	.25
Wrappers		
1-cent	60.00	––
5-cent	75.00	––
Box	100.00	20.00

TWO SIDE PANELS FROM THE
1950 LICENSE PLATE DISPLAY BOX

1 Washington	26 Michigan	38 Indiana	51 Michigan
2 West Virginia	Washington	Rhode Island	52 Minnesota
3 Wisconsin	27 Minnesota	39 Iowa	53 Mississippi
4 Wyoming	West Virginia	South Carolina	54 Missouri
5 Quebec	28 Mississippi	40 Kansas	55 Montana
6 Tennessee	Wisconsin	South Dakota	56 Kentucky
7 Texas	29 Missouri	41 Connecticut	57 Louisiana
8 Utah	Wyoming	New York	58 Maine
9 Vermont	30 Montana	42 Delaware	59 Maryland
10 Virginia	Quebec	North Carolina	60 Massachusetts
11 Oregon	31 Kentucky	43 District of Columbia	61 Idaho
12 Pennsylvania	Tennessee	North Dakota	62 Illinois
13 Rhode Island	32 Louisiana	44 Florida	63 Indiana
14 South Carolina	Texas	Ohio	64 Iowa
15 South Dakota	33 Maine	45 Georgia	65 Kansas
16 New York	Utah	Oklahoma	66 Connecticut
17 North Carolina	34 Maryland	46 Alabama	67 Delaware
18 North Dakota	Vermont	Nebraska	68 District of Columbia
19 Ohio	35 Massachusetts	47 Arizona	69 Florida
20 Oklahoma	Virginia	Nevada	70 Georgia
21 Nebraska	36 Idaho	48 Arkansas	71 Colorado
22 Nevada	Oregon	New Hampshire	72 California
23 New Hampshire	37 Illinois	49 California	73 Arkansas
24 New Jersey	Pennsylvania	New Jersey	74 Arizona
25 New Mexico		50 Colorado	75 Alabama
		New Mexico	

LICENSE PLATES – 1953 (75)   1 7/8" X 3 3/4"

Compared to the 1949 and 1950 License Plates sets issued by Topps, the 1953 version is a snap to describe. Included in the 75-card set are 48 states, the District of Columbia and Alaska, 9 Canadian provinces, 4 Australian states, 3 Swiss cantons, and 9 foreign countries. The backs are orange and blue (on off-white stock) and contain the card number, vital statistics, and a quiz (answer revealed by holding the card to a mirror). The 1-cent wrapper is the only denomination found as of this date. The reference number is R714-13.

ITEM	EX	AVE
Card	1.00	.20
Set	85.00	17.50
Wrapper	15.00	———

1	New York
2	Tennessee
3	Arizona
4	Arkansas
5	California
6	Colorado
7	Pennsylvania
8	Delaware
9	Florida
10	Georgia
11	Idaho
12	Illinois
13	Mississippi
14	Missouri
15	Nevada
16	Nebraska
17	Montana
18	New Mexico
19	New Hampshire
20	Indiana
21	Canada—Province of Alberta
22	Kansas
23	Iowa
24	Canada—Prov. of Prince Edward Isle
25	Kentucky
26	Louisiana
27	North Carolina
28	Maine
29	Texas
30	Maryland
31	Canada—Province of Saskatchewan
32	Virginia
33	Michigan
34	Dist. of Columbia
35	Wisconsin
36	Minnesota
37	Massachusetts
38	Alabama
39	Utah
40	Canada—Province of New Brunswick
41	Canada—Province of Ontario
42	Vermont
43	Rhode Island
44	Alaska
45	Wyoming
46	South Carolina
47	New South Wales, Australia
48	Ohio
49	South Dakota
50	South Australia, Australia
51	Oklahoma
52	Canada—Province of Nova Scotia
53	Canton of Berne, Switzerland
54	Oregon
55	Canada—Province of British Columbia
56	Canton of Baselland—Switzerland
57	Norway
58	Canton of Geneva, Switzerland
59	Queensland, Australia
60	Canada—Province of Manitoba
61	Tasmania, Australia
62	North Dakota
63	Connecticut
64	Argentina
65	New Jersey
66	Belgium
67	France
68	West Virginia
69	Israel
70	Italy
71	Washington
72	Netherlands
73	United Kingdom
74	Mexico
75	Canada—Province of Quebec

LICENSE PLATES — 1955 (60)

The Leader Candy Company took on an ambitious task when it produced its license plate series of 1955. Each "miniature auto license plate" was made out of heavy "tin." This construction must have presented some difficult manufacturing and packaging type problems. There are 60 plates in the set, but so few are seen today that we do not have a checklist available (although it is obvious that all then-current 48 states were represented). Unlike the metal "Wheaties" plates of the same era, the Leader license plates are flat, not embossed. The plates were inserted into small 5-cent candy boxes along with a few pieces of taffy. The reference number is PX103.

ITEM	EX	AVE
License Plate	4.00	1.00
Box	25.00	10.00

LONE RANGER (120)

2" X 2 5/8"

Until recently, the "Lone Ranger" series by Ed-U-Cards was one of the best bargains in the hobby, simply because no one really knew about it. Now collectors have realized that this is the ONLY post-war Lone Ranger series to actually picture two legendary western actors, Clayton Moore and Jay Silverheels, and interest in the set has increased dramatically. The 120 cards were divided into four 30-card adventures: "Outlaws Revenge," "Thieve's Money," "Danger Ahead," and "A Drink of Water." The pictures are black & white photos from television shows that were "painted" with color to make them more appealing. The card number is printed in a horseshoe design on the text back. The cards were printed in panels of three and sold in cardboard sleeves. The sleeves came in eight different colors — each the same except for the color and the series number it bore — red (series 1), blue (series 2), light orange (series 3), green (series 4), yellow (series 5), fuchsia (series 6), light brown (series 7), and dark orange (series 8). It seems logical to assume that each adventure was contained within two of the series (four adventures, eight series); however, this hypothesis has not been confirmed. The reference number is W536. NOTE: these cards are more commonly found in strips than as singles.

ITEM	EX	AVE
Card	4.00	1.00
Strip of 3	15.00	4.00
Set	600.00	140.00
Sleeves, each	12.00	4.00

Outlaw's Revenge
1 "Big Trouble"
2 "A Job for Tonto"
3 "Important Meeting"
4 "Pointed Guns"
5 "Suspicious Voices"
6 "Voice in the Dark"
7 "Crashing Gun"
8 "The Sheriff Faces a Gun"
9 "Trapped"
10 "Will There Be Trouble?"
11 "Steady Aim"
12 "Surrounded"
13 "Murder in the Dark"
14 "A Warning"
15 "An Inside Job"
16 "A Banker's Disguise"
17 "Sworn Vengeance"
18 "The Lone Ranger's Plan"
19 "Impersonation"
20 "Thrown Into Jail"
21 "Almost Helpless"
22 "Tonto's Secret Move"
23 "For Law and Order"
24 "Accused"
25 "Be Quiet"
26 "Dangerous Chance"
27 "Only A Hunch"
28 "Two Against One"
29 "Tonto Is In Trouble"
30 "Get the Lone Ranger"

Danger Ahead
31 "Hostage"
32 "A Treacherous Blow"
33 "Encouraging Words"
34 "The Dummy Won't Talk"
35 "For Law and Order"
36 "Bad News for Lone Ranger"
37 "Partners in Murder"
38 "Deadly Decision"
39 "Sudden Shots"
40 "Tables are Turned"
41 "Death in the Opera House"
42 "The Crooks are Fooled"
43 "Tell-Tale Tracks"
44 "Witness to Murder"
45 "New Sheriff"
46 "Finding a Clue"
47 "Through the Back Door"
48 "Trouble for Tonto"
49 "Possibility of Trouble"
50 "Not To Be Trusted"
51 "To The Rescue"
52 "Frightened Away"
53 "Steady Guns"
54 "Tricky Plan"
55 "Two-Gun Man"
56 "Looking at Death"
57 "Witness in Trouble"
58 "Dangerous Plan"
59 "Advice From the Lone Ranger"
60 "Fake Prisoner"

Lone Ranger

A Drink of Water

CARDBOARD SLEEVES WERE PRINTED IN
DIFFERENT COLORS ACCORDING TO SERIES

LOOK 'N SEE (135)

"Look 'n See," one of the classic sets of the post-war era, was marketed by Topps in 1952. The fronts depict 135 famous people in glorious color portraits, and every detail, including the captions, caption frames, and decorative accents, blend together in splendid harmony. Compared to the fronts, the backs are downright ugly. To make their "spy hidden pictures" gimmick work, Topps resorted to the orange colored cardboard previously used in "X-Ray Roundup" and "Isolation Booth," two other novelty sets. In effect, the descriptive text was made barely legible so that kids could use a thin piece of red cellophane to reveal an illustrated "answer" to a Look 'n See question about each subject. As the wrapper advertising said, "Only you can spy the hidden pictures on the back...by placing the magic red paper... on the red back of each card." Both the 1-cent and 5-cent wrappers are difficult to find compared to other wrappers of this era, possibly because

Topps also issued Look 'n See in clear cellophane packs and in overstock "bricks." The reference number is R714-16. NOTE: the cards are individually priced in the checklist printed below.

ITEM	EX	AVE
Set	950.00	225.00
Wrappers		
1-cent	75.00	––
5-cent	175.00	––
Magic		
Paper	6.00	1.50

294

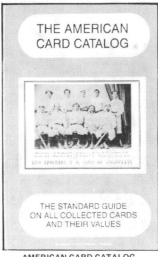

AMERICAN CARD CATALOG
$ 10.00 plus postage & handling

The American Card Catalog has finally been reissued. This 1960 edition is the last updated version put out by the late Jefferson Burdick, the Father of Card Collecting. This book is the grandaddy of all trading card collecting books, and has had more far reaching influence on card collecting than any publication other than the Sport Americana Baseball Card Price Guide. This is the book that gave cards their nomenclature and made an effort to price them (the prices in this volume are antiquated). This is a book that definitely belongs in the library of all card collectors.

THE ANDY GRIFFITH SHOW SET
$ 10.00 plus postage & handling

Pacific Trading Cards has produced this 110-card set of what is now America's most watched syndicated TV show. The cards, some in color and some in black and white, feature Andy, Barney, Opie, Aunt Bee, Gomer, and all the show favorites. Use Style 9 or 9T plastic sheets for display.

THE WIZARD OF OZ
$ 10.00 plus postage & handling

This brand new 110-card set features the antics of Dorothy, the Scarcrow, the Tin Man, and the Cowardly Lion in color (with a few Black & white) photos taken from the original 1939 movie. The cards are standard-sized, so use Style 9 or 9T plastic sheets for display.

TERRORIST ATTACK
$ 10.00 plus postage & handling

This full-color, 35-card set brings back the great non-sport card artwork of the 1930s and early 1940s. From the gore of a nuclear attack to the pomposity of a Hitler or a Mussolini; from the half-crazed stare of a Manson to the dignity of a Gandhi — the cards in this set examine a cross-section of the real and potential terrorism prevalent in 20th Century living. Use Style 9 or 9T plastic sheets for display.

Look 'n See

		EX	AVE
1.	Franklin D. Roosevelt — Pres.	10.00	2.00
2	Woodrow Wilson — Pres.	7.00	1.50
3	Thomas Jefferson — Pres.	7.00	1.50
4	Abraham Lincoln — Pres.	7.00	1.50
5	Harry Truman — Pres.	7.00	1.50
6	Theodore Roosevelt — Pres.	7.00	1.50
7	Ulysses S. Grant — Pres.	7.00	1.50
8	Andrew Jackson — Pres.	7.00	1.50
9	George Washington — Pres.	7.00	1.50
10	Gen. G. W. Goethals — Engineer	4.50	.90
11	Nathan Hale — Patriot	4.50	.90
12	Francis Scott Key — Composer	4.50	.90
13	Wilbur Wright — Inventor	4.50	.90
14	Jefferson Davis — Confederate Pres.	4.50	.90
15	Babe Ruth — Baseball Player	75.00	20.00
16	Paul Revere — Patriot	4.50	.90
17	Patrick Henry — Patriot	4.50	.90
18	Washington Irving — Author	4.50	.90
19	Alexander Hamilton — Patriot	4.50	.90
20	Albert Einstein — Scientist	4.50	.90
21	Benjamin Franklin — Patriot	4.50	.90
22	Daniel Webster — Orator	4.50	.90
23	James A. McNeill Whistler— Artist	4.50	.90
24	Phineas T. Barnum — Showman	4.50	.90
25	George Eastman — Manufacturer	4.50	.90
26	Geo. Washington Carver — Scientist	4.50	.90
27	Luther Burbank — Botanist	4.50	.90
28	Stephen Foster — Composer	4.50	.90
29	Mark Twain — Author	4.50	.90
30	Col. Charles A. Lindberg — Aviator	15.00	3.00
31	Henry Ford — Automobile Producer	4.50	.90
32	Gen. Douglas MacArthur — Soldier	7.00	1.50
33	Comm. Oliver H. Perry — Naval Hero	4.50	.90
34	Gen. Robert E. Lee — Soldier	7.00	1.50
35	Gen. Matthew Ridgeway — Soldier	4.50	.90
36	Gen. Claire Chennault — Soldier	4.50	.90
37	Gen. George A. Custer — Indian Fighter	7.00	1.50
38	Stephen Decatur — Naval Hero	4.50	.90
39	Gen. George S. Patton, Jr. — Soldier	7.00	1.50
40	Stonewall Jackson — Soldier	7.00	1.50
41	Gen. Dwight D. Eisenhower— Soldier	7.00	1.50
42	John Paul Jones — Naval Hero	4.50	.90
43	Eleanor Roosevelt — U. N. Delegate	4.50	.90
44	Cleopatra — Queen of Egypt	4.50	.90
45	Amelia Earhart — Aviatrix	20.00	4.00
46	Annie Oakley — Crack Shot	7.00	1.50
47	Admiral Peary — Explorer	4.50	.90
48	Ferdinand Magellan — Explorer	4.50	.90
49	Ponce De Leon — Explorer	4.50	.90
50	Admiral Byrd — Explorer	4.50	.90
51	Christopher Columbus — Explorer	4.50	.90
52	Balboa — Explorer	4.50	.90
53	Kit Carson — Scout	7.00	1.50
54	Buffalo Bill — Scout	7.00	1.50
55	Daniel Boone — Pioneer	7.00	1.50
56	Geronimo — Indian Chief	7.00	1.50
57	Jesse James — Outlaw	7.00	1.50
58	Sitting Bull — Indian Chief	7.00	1.50
59	Cochise — Indian Chief	7.00	1.50
60	Wild Bill Hickok — Sheriff	7.00	1.50
61	Sam Houston — Soldier	4.50	.90
62	Bat Matterson — Western Sheriff	7.00	1.50
63	Billy the Kid — Outlaw	7.00	1.50
64	Winston Churchill — English Leader	4.50	.90
65	Mahatma Ghandi — Leader	4.50	.90
66	William Shakespeare — English Playright	4.50	.90

		EX	AVE
67	Napoleon Bonaparte — French Leader	4.50	.90
68	Sir Isaac Newton — English Scientist	4.50	.90
69	Guglielmo Marconi — Inventor	4.50	.90
70	Samuel B. F. Morse — Inventor	4.50	.90
71	Thomas A. Edison — Inventor	4.50	.90
72	Cyrus H. McCormick — Inventor	4.50	.90
73	Robert Fulton — Inventor	4.50	.90
74	Alexander Graham Bell — Inventor	4.50	.90
75	Elias Howe — Inventor	4.50	.90
76	Louis Pasteur — Scientist	4.00	.80
77	William Penn — American Patriot	4.00	.80
78	Thomas Paine — Writer	4.00	.80
79	Edgar Allan Poe — Writer	4.00	.80
80	Will Rogers — Humorist	4.00	.80
81	Sir Walter Raleigh — Explorer	4.00	.80
82	Rembrandt — Artist	50.00	15.00
83	Clara Barton — Humanitarian	4.00	.80
84	Julius Caesar — Roman	4.00	.80
85	Chiang Kai-Shek — Chinese General	4.00	.80
86	Benvenuto Cellini — Artist	4.00	.80
87	Marie Curie — Scientist	4.00	.80
88	Roald Amundsen — Explorer	4.00	.80
89	Hans Christian Anderson — Writer	4.00	.80
90	Benedict Arnold — Traitor	4.00	.80
91	Enrico Caruso — Singer	4.00	.80
92	Louis Daguerre — Inventor	4.00	.80
93	Admiral George Dewey — Naval Hero	4.00	.80
94	Sir Francis Drake — Explorer	4.00	.80
95	Alfred E. Smith — Statesman	4.00	.80
96	Tecumseh — Indian Chief	4.00	.80
97	Jules Verne — Writer	4.00	.80
98	Adlai Stevenson — Statesman	4.00	.80
99	Lester B. Pearson — U.N. Delegate	4.00	.80
100	Lord William Beaverbrook — Statesman	4.00	.80
101	Daniel De Foe — Author	4.00	.80
102	Anne of Cleves — Queen of England	4.00	.80
103	Duke of Windsor — King of England	4.00	.80
104	Queen Elizabeth II — Queen of England	4.00	.80
105	Leonardo Da Vinci — Artist	4.00	.80
106	Machiavelli — Statesman	4.00	.80
107	George C. Marshall — General	4.00	.80
108	Michelangelo — Artist	4.00	.80
109	Admiral Horatio Nelson — Naval Hero	4.00	.80
110	Nero — Roman Emperor	4.00	.80
111	Florence Nightingale — Humanitarian	4.00	.80
112	John D. Rockefeller — Industrialist	7.00	1.50
113	Sir Walter Scott — Writer	4.00	.80
114	Percy Bysshe Shelley — Poet	4.00	.80
115	John Philip Sousa — Composer	4.00	.80
116	Robert Louis Stevenson — Writer	4.00	.80
117	Arturo Toscanini — Conductor	4.00	.80
118	Amerigo Vespucci — Explorer	4.00	.80
119	H. G. Wells — Writer	4.00	.80
120	Wendell Wilkie — Statesman	4.00	.80
121	Emile Zola — Writer	4.00	.80
122	Capt. William Kidd — Pirate	7.00	1.50
123	Sir Henry Morgan — Pirate	7.00	1.50
124	Charles Darwin — Scientist	4.00	.80
125	Charles Dickens — Writer	4.00	.80
126	Leif Ericson — Explorer	4.00	.80
127	Galileo — Scientist	4.00	.80
128	Genghis Khan — Conqueror	4.00	.80
129	Johannes Gutenberg — Inventor	4.00	.80
130	Victor Herbert — Composer	4.00	.80
131	Henry Hudson — Explorer	4.00	.80
132	Henry VIII — King of England	4.00	.80
133	Joan of Arc — French Heroine	4.00	.80
134	Lafayette — Military Hero	4.00	.80
135	Dolly Madison — President's Wife	7.00	1.50

UNCUT STRIP OF FOUR CARDS WITH WRONG BACKS

MAGIC CARD (?)

Some things never change! The "Magic Card" package illustrated here wes found in an unopened candy box dating from the mid 1950's. Yet just last year, in Houston, I walked into a toy & novelty shop and found a whole box of the same item sitting on the counter! Apparently, this is a standard design which some Japanese company has been producing for over 30 years. Each pack contains three cards, and the last, or bottom card, has two cellophane wings attached at the back in a way that allows the cellophane to wrap around the front of the card from the two sides. By laying the red cellophane wing on the card you get one picture; remove the red and place the blue cellophane wing on the card and you get another. Hence

1 3/4" X 2 1/2"

the title "Magic Card." Of the three cards in the old pack, two depict sports scenes.

The wrapper is red with white faces and a blue title. The reference number for this set, and all other Japanese-produced candy box insert novelties, is R774. The only way to tell the old version from the new is by comparing the color of the wrapper: the old pack is a darker red and blue, while the new packages are preceptibly lighter in coloration. As a collectible, this item isn't very important, but it does demonstrate that you have to be careful about what you buy.

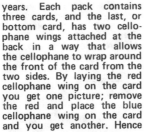

VALUES FOR "OLD" VERSIONS PICTURED HERE
ARE $3.00 FOR THE CARD AND $5.00 FOR THE WRAPPER

Topps offically copyrighted the "Magic Photos" product idea in 1948, but the series did not go on sale until the following year. It consists of 252, small, develop-with-water photographs in 19 different categories, with each subset having a letter designation and its own numbering system. Each card was actually blank until the image on it was "activated" by wetting the surface and applying a developing agent. In the case of the 1-cent wrapper, the developing chemical was saturated into a designated section on the interior side of the wrapper, and the picture was developed by rubbing this special area on the moistened surface of the blank card. Topps refined the process in the 5-cent pack by concentrating the developing chemical in a piece of "orange mystery paper," on which the wet blank was pressed for ten seconds. Needless to say, a considerable number of "Magic Photos" were poorly developed —

attributable to the combination of primitive technology and youthful impatience and carelessness. Collectors should have no difficulty distinguishing between the "Magic Photos" of this series and the similar "Hocus Focus" set issued by Topps in 1956. Hocus Focus cards have the set title written on back, while Magic Photos have the line "See Directions Inside Wrap" printed in the same spot. Most of the checklist and many of the photos in this presentation were privided by Tom Reid. It should be noted that the baseball photos appearing in this series were the first baseball cards ever printed by Topps. The 126-card album was available via the mail from the company for ten cents. The reference number is R714-27.

PRICE ADVISORY: prices listed below are for common-demand cards, and collectors should expect to pay premium prices for high-demand photos, such as Joe Louis, Babe Ruth, and other sports figures. Underdeveloped photos cannot be graded as "excellent."

CARDS	EX	AVE
A Boxing Champions	10.00	3.00
B All-American Basketball	8.00	2.50
C All-American Football	10.00	3.00
D Wrestling Champions	6.00	2.00
E Track & Field Champions	5.00	1.50
F Stars of Stage & Screen	4.00	1.25
G American Dogs	2.50	.75
H General Sports	5.00	1.75
I None issued		
J Movie Stars	4.00	1.25
K Baseball Hall of Fame	15.00	5.00
L Aviation Pioneers	3.00	.90
M Famous Landmarks	2.50	.75
N American Inventors	2.50	.75
O American Military Leaders	3.00	.90
P American Explorers	2.50	.75
Q Basketball Thrills	6.00	2.00
R Football Thrills	6.00	2.00
S Figures of the Wild West	6.00	2.00
T General Sports	4.00	1.25

SIX-CARD STRIP OF PHOTOS CAME IN 5-CENT PACK

ORANGE MYSTERY PAPER FROM 5-CENT PACK CONTAINED DEVELPING AGENT

"DEVELOPING " SIDE (INTERIOR) OF 1-CENT WRAPPER

Magic Photos

COVER OF MAGIC PHOTOS ALBUM

PROMOTION SHEET

SERIES A—BOXING CHAMPIONS

1	Tommy Burns	13	Max Baer
2	John L. Sullivan	14	James J. Braddock
3	James J. Corbett	15	Joe Louis
4	Bob Fitzsimmons	16	Gus Lesnevich
5	James J. Jeffries	17	Tony Zale
6	Jack Johnson	18	Ike Williams
7	Jess Williard	19	Ray Robinson
8	Jack Dempsey	20	Willie Pep
9	Gene Tunney	21	Rinty Monaghan
10	Max Schmelling	22	Manuel Ortiz
11	Jack Sharkey	23	Marlel Cerdan
12	Primo Carnera	24	Buddy Baer

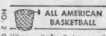

SERIES B—ALL AMERICAN
BASKETBALL

1	Ralph Beard	4	Kevin O'Shea
2	Murray Wier	5	Jim McIntyre
3	Ed Macauley	6	Manhattan Beats Dartmouth

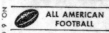

ALL AMERICAN FOOTBALL

Who is the Penn boy selected A. A. by 9 out of 10 coaches. Led Notre Dame to 26—0 victory over Army?

SEE DIRECTIONS INSIDE WRAP

SERIES C—ALL AMERICAN FOOTBALL

1 Barney Poole
2 Pete Elliott
3 Doak Walker
4 Bill Swiacki
5 Bill Fischer
6 Johnny Lujack
7 Chas. P. Bednerick
8 Joe Steffy
9 George Connor
10 Steve Suhey
11 Bob Chappins
12 Columbia 23—Navy 14
13 Army—Notre Dame

WRESTLING CHAMPIONS

Name a top flight wrestler whose claim to fame is his knockdown of Joe Louis in a championship title bout.

SEE DIRECTIONS INSIDE WRAP

SERIES D—WRESTLING CHAMPIONS

1 Frank Gotch
2 Hackenschmidt
3 Stanuslaus Zbyszko
4 Jim Browning
5 Jim Londos
6 Strangler Lewis
7 George Becker
8 Ernie Dusek
9 Rudy Dusek
10 Dean Detton
11 Masked Marvel
12 Maurice Tillet
13 Olaf Swenson
14 Tony Galento
15 Frank Sexton
16 George Calza
17 Arm Lock
18 Flying Dropkick
19 Primo Carnera
20 Gino Garabaldi
21 "Lord" Jan Blears
22 Joe Savoldi
23 Dick Shikat
24 Wadleslaw
25 Steinke

TRACK AND FIELD CHAMPIONS

Who was the anchor man on the California mile relay when the American record was made?

SEE DIRECTIONS INSIDE WRAP

SERIES E—TRACK AND FIELD CHAMPIONS

1 Jesse Owens
2 Leo Steers
3 Ben Eastman
4 Harrison Dillard
5 Greg Rice
6 Kolehmainen
7 Gunoer Hagg
8 Chas. Pores
9 Grover Kelmmer
10 Boyd Brown
11 Pat Ryan
12 Charlie Fonville
13 C. Warmerdam
14 Army—Navy Tie
15 Haaken Lidman (Sweden)
16 Morris—Army Wins
17 M. Jarvinen—Javelin

STARS OF STAGE AND SCREEN

Who created a stir in Hollywood with her portrayal of the sharp witted secretary in "Mr. Smith Goes To Washington"?

SEE DIRECTIONS INSIDE WRAP

SERIES F—STARS OF STAGE AND SCREEN

1 Clark Gable
2 Barbara Stanwyck
3 Lana Turner
4 Ingred Bergman
5 Betty Grable
6 Tyrone Power
7 Oliva DeHavilland
8 Joan Fontaine
9 June Allyson
10 Dorothy Lamour
11 William Powell
12 Sylvia Sidney
13 Van Johnson
14 Virginia Mayo
15 Claudette Colbert
16 Eve Arden
17 Lyn Bari
18 Maureen O'Hara
19 Jean Arthur
20 Hazel Brooks
21 Martha Vickers
22 Noreen Nash

AMERICAN DOGS

Originally English sheep herder. Favorite boys' dog. Golden brown, thick fur and white mane.

SEE DIRECTIONS INSIDE WRAP

SERIES G—AMERICAN DOGS

1 Terrier
2 Chow
3 Cairn Terrier
4 White Sealyham
5 St. Bernard
6 Boston Bull
7 Greyhound
8 Dalmation
9 Pointer
10 Cocker Spaniel
11 English Bulldog
12 Champion Pointer
13 Setter
14 Boxer
15 Russian Wolfhound
16 Doberman
17 Collie

SERIES H—GENERAL SPORTS

1 Mr. & Mrs. George Remington
2 Bernice Dossey

Magic Photos

EDDIE ALBERT

MOVIE STARS

What star of the smash hit "Brother Rat" is now starred in the thriller, "The Dude Goes West"?

SEE DIRECTIONS INSIDE WRAP

"BABE" RUTH 714

BASEBALL HALL OF FAME

This greatest of baseball personalities hit how many homers to earn the title, "King of Swat"?

SEE DIRECTIONS INSIDE WRAP

SERIES J—MOVIE STARS

1 Johnny Mack Brown
2 Andy Clyde
3 Roddy McDowall
4 Keye Luke
5 Jackie Coogan
6 Joe Kirkwood Jr.
7 Jackie Cooper
8 Arthur Lake
9 Sam Levine
10 Binnie Barnes
11 Gertrude Niesen
12 Rory Calhoun
13 June Lockhart
14 Hedy Lamarr
15 Robert Cummings
16 Brian Aherne
17 William Bendix
18 Roland Winters
19 Michael O'Shea
20 Lois Butler
21 Renie Riano
22 Jimmy Wakely
23 Audie Murphy
24 Leo Gorcey
25 Leon Errol
26 Lon Chaney
27 William Frawley
28 Billy Benedict
29 Rod Cameron
30 James Gleason
31 Gilbert Roland
32 Raymond Hatton
33 Joe Yule
34 Eddie Albert
35 Barry Sullivan
36 Richard Basehart
37 Claire Trevor
38 Constance Bennett
39 Gale Storm
40 Elyse Knox
41 Jane Wyatt
42 Whip Wilson
43 Charles Bickford
44 Guy Madison
45 Barton MacLane

SERIES K—BASEBALL HALL OF FAME

1 Lou Boureau
2 Cleveland Indians
3 Bob Elliott
4 Cleveland Indians 4—3
5 Cleveland Indians 4—1 (Boudreau Scoring)
6 Babe Ruth—714
7 Tris Speaker—793
8 Rogers Hornsby
9 Connie Mack
10 Christy Mathewson
11 Hans Wagner
12 Grover Alexander
13 Ty Cobb
14 Lou Gehrig
15 Walter Johnson
16 Cy Young
17 George Sisler—257
18 Tinkers and Evers
19 Third Base—Cleveland Indians

NIAGARA FALLS

FAMOUS LANDMARKS

This scenic landmark has become the world's most famous honeymoon spot. What is it?

SEE DIRECTIONS INSIDE WRAP

SERIES M—FAMOUS LANDMARKS

1 Niagra Falls
2 Empire State Building
3 Leaning Tower of Pisa
4 Eiffel Tower
5 Lincoln Memorial
6 Statue of Liberty
7 Geyser—Yellowstone
8 Sphinx
9 Washington Monument

JAMES DOOLITTLE

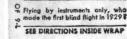

AVIATION PIONEERS

Flying by instruments only, who made the first blind flight in 1929?

SEE DIRECTIONS INSIDE WRAP

SERIES L—AVIATION PIONEERS

1 Colonial Airlines
2 James Doolittle
3 Wiley Post
4 Eddie Rickenbacker
5 Amelia Earhart
6 Charles Lindbergh
7 Doug Corrigan
8 Chas. A. Levine
9 Wright Brothers

General DWIGHT EISENHOWER

AMERICAN MILITARY LEADERS

What University President rose from Lt. Colonel to 5-Star General and head of the Combined Allied Command during World War II.

SEE DIRECTIONS INSIDE WRAP

SERIES O—AMERICAN MILITARY LEADERS

1 Joseph Stillwell
2 Admiral Chester Nimitz
3 George Patton
4 General John Pershing
5 Admiral David Farragut
6 Jonathan Wainright
7 Douglas MacArthur
8 General Omar Bradley
9 George Dewey
10 General Dwight Eisenhower

BENJAMIN FRANKLIN

AMERICAN INVENTORS

What historical statesman, philosopher and scientist invented the lightning rod in 1752?

SEE DIRECTIONS INSIDE WRAP

SERIES N—AMERICAN INVENTORS

1 Eli Whitney
2 Thomsa A. Edison
3 C. E. Duryea
4 Benjamin Franklin
5 V. K. Zworykin
6 Robert Fulton
7 Samuel Morse
8 Alexander Graham Bell

AMERICAN
EXPLORERS

NO. 1 OF 2-P

Name the explorer who first led an expedition to the North Pole in 1892, and whose buried records were found in 1948.

SEE DIRECTIONS INSIDE WRAP

BASKETBALL THRILLS

NO. 3 OF

What college basketball team in a surprise upset broke N.Y.U.'s string of 19 straight victories in 1948?

SEE DIRECTIONS INSIDE WRAP

SERIES Q—BASKETBALL
THRILLS
1 St. Louis University
2 Long Island University
3 Notre Dame
4 Kentucky 58—42
5 Depaul 75-64

SERIES P—AMERICAN
EXPLORERS
1 Admiral Robert Peary
2 Richard E. Byrd

SERIES S—FIGURES OF THE
WILD WEST
1 General Custer
2 Buffalo Bill Cody
3 Sitting Bull
4 Annie Oakley
5 Jessie James
6 Geronimo
7 Billy the Kid

FOOTBALL
THRILLS

NO. 5 OF 5-R

Frank Bradley was a brilliant ball carrier for what Eastern College team in 1948?

SEE DIRECTIONS INSIDE WRAP

GENERAL
SPORTS

NO. 6 OF 7-T

What punishing two-arm hold in professional wrestling is known as the "nut-crusher" or "egg-shaper"?

SEE DIRECTIONS INSIDE WRAP

SERIES R—FOOTBALL THRILLS
1 Wally Triplett
2 Gil Stephenson
3 Northwestern
4 Yale vs Columbia
5 Cornell

SERIES T—GENERAL SPORTS
1 Soccer
2 Motor Boat Racing
3 Ice Hockey
4 Water Skiing
5 Gallorette
6 Headlock
7 Tennis

MAGIC PICTURES (40)(120)

2 1/2" X 3 3/4"
1 1/4" X 2 1/2"

Now here is a story of "riches to rags." Around my neighborhood, Bowman's "Magic Pictures" was one of the most popular sets of the season, especially among the younger kids. For a brief period, the fad raged on with all the fury of a full-blown hurricane...and then dissipated overnight. I was lucky. Just looking at the blury yellow, green and blue patterns made me queasy, and I steered a clear path away from them and their wildly-enthusiastic juvenile advocates. Others kids were not so fortunate, for when the dust settled, many a Mays and Mantle had been traded away for a stack of these hallucinatory cards. Still today, the sight of them makes me uneasy.

Magic Pictures were sold concurrently in 1-cent and 5-cent gum packs. The 1-cent package contained a single 1 1/4" X 2 1/2" card with two pictures on it, a plastic lens, and a piece of gum. The 5-cent package held three 2 1/2" X 3 3/4" cards (each was really an uncut strip of three of the smaller cards), a plastic lens (same size), and a bigger piece of gum. The pictures on the fronts could be made to "Spin - Jump - Change" using the

instructions printed on the backs of the cards. The set total of 240 refers to the number of different pictures, which means that 120 small cards and 40 large cards were issued (each design in the tandem has its own number). Very often, kids cut the bigger cards down into smaller cards for easier handling. This scissorial work accounts for the incidence of small cards with uneven borders. Packs of both denominations are commonly found in the hobby and are not highly valued. The reference number is R701-8.

ITEM	EX	AVE
Cards		
2-picture card	.35	.10
6-picture card	1.00	.25
Wrappers		
1-cent	4.00	——
5-cent	10.00	——
Boxes		
1-cent	75.00	20.00
5-cent	95.00	25.00

MAGIC PICTURES (8K)

2 7/8" X 3 7/8"

This is one of the mystery sets of the 1950's. No one knows how many cards there are in the set (No. 8 is the highest seen), how it was sold, or who produced it. The only thing we know for certain is the 1958 copyright date which is printed on each card. The cards are larger than standard size and have black, gray, and red details set against yellow backgrounds. The people and objects drawn on the cards are indistinct until the rigid plastic overlay is placed on top. When moved from side to side, the overlay causes the designs to "move," hence the title of the set. The subjects were some of the most popular of the period; for example, the card we have illustrated, "Rock and Roll Riley," is a take-off on Elvis Presley (card No. 5 is entitled "Mars attacks the earth"). Given the nature of the process involved in producing these novelty cards, it is no coincidence that the "Spin - Jump - Change" directions on the backs are nearly identical (word for word) to the instructions printed on the backs of Bowman's Magic Pictures. No reference number has been assigned. NOTE: prices given are for the card complete with plastic overlay.

ITEM	EX	AVE
Card	20.00	7.50

MANDRAKE (?)

MANDRAKE

Collector Gordon Burns provided the illustration of the "Mandrake" card presented here. It formed part of a candy box because it carries a tiny "net wt 3/8 oz" line in the upper right corner, and it probably belongs to the R756 category listed in The American Card Catalog. If this is so, the card shown here was the front panel of the candy box, and a four-cell comic strip was printed on the back. The card has rouletted edges, which means that the perimeter was machine-perforated to allow for easy removal. The back is blank and there is no card number. The words "King Features Syndicate" appear in tiny print at the left near the bottom.

ITEM	EX	AVE
Card	10.00	4.00

MICKEY MOUSE CANDY & TOY (?)

"Mickey Mouse Candy and Toy" was a successful candy box series produced by the Super Novelty Candy Company of Newark, NJ. Both the front and back panels of every box pictured a Walt Disney character. Although it is clear that the panels containing these multi-color artwork characters were designed to be used as trading cards, some had perforations for easy removal and some did not. Where the card designs were machine-scored, the perforation line divides the character from the section which reads "Candy and Toy," and the thus-detached card measures 2 7/16" X 3 5/8". None of the cards is numbered and all are blank-backed. In addition to the nine characters confirmed so far, at least one box was printed with a detachable cardboard "official" Mousketeers emblem (Mickey Mouse Club). The date of issue is thought to be the late 1950's. No reference number has been assigned.

ITEM	EX	AVE
Card	3.00	.75
Box	20.00	6.00
Mousketeer emblem	6.00	2.00
Box with emblem	25.00	7.50

PARTIAL CHECKLIST

Bashful
Daisy Duck
Doc
Donald Duck
Fiddler Pig
Huey
Louie
Mickey Mouse
Mousketeers Emblem
Pluto

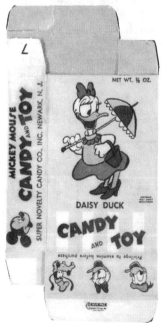

MINIATURE COMIC BOOKS (12K)   1 13/16" X 3 3/8"

"This is one of a series of 24 different miniature comic books published exclusively for SCHMOO hard candy packages!" That's how the advertising copy on the back cover of each comic begins, and it continues with a list of premiums available via the mail from Delmonico Foods for two "L'il Abner" side panels and change. The Hobby Card Index has no record of what the "Schmoo Hard Candy" box looked like, but it is certain that such an item would command a premium price in today's marketplace. Each of the miniature color-artwork comics is numbered on the front cover. Some of the characters appear in more than one comic. There are credit lines printed for several different publishers, indicating that Delmonico went to non-mainstream producers for their "strips." Although the set total was advertised as 24, the highest numbered comic seen to date is No. 12. The series was not reported in the early catalogs and has not been assigned a reference number as of this time.

ITEM	EX	AVE
Comic	8.00	2.00

1 The Duke and the Dope
2 The Girl Friend
3 Cindy
4 Doc Bark
5
6 Giles
7 Texas Tim, Ranger
8 Pickles
9 Gus the Ghost
10 Izzy and Dizzy
11 The Girl Friend
12 The Duke and the Dope

MOVIE & SPORTS STARS (77?)   1 3/8" X 2 1/4"

This series of cards was produced in Milan, Italy by the Zaini Chocolate Co. for import into the Untied States. Each card came packed with a piece of chocolate in a small red- and white-accented cello-

phane wrapper (see illustration of card in wrapper). The card pictured in this book and the one in the 1983 Benjamin Guide (Gia Scala) are the only two reported to The Hobby Card Index since 1979. Undoubtedly, the "foreign" look and content of these cards might not appeal to many collectors, but there still is

great curiosity about the identities of the "sports stars" referred to in the early catalogs. Until more are discovered, prices for Zaini cards and wrappers will have to remain at levels higher that their apparent instrinsic value, simply because the demand for them by "subject-specific" and "type" collectors is great. The reference number for the set is R808.

ITEM	EX	AVE
Card	5.00	1.50
Wrapper	25.00	——

MOVIE PREVIEW FLIPBOOKS (24) 2" X 2 1/2"

Why Bowman tried to immortalize this group of atrocious matinee movies by showcasing them in a bubble gum set is beyond understanding. But try they did, and had they not, modern collectors would have lost the opportunity to see acting stalwarts such as Allan "Rocky" Lane and Alfonso Bedoya in action scenes from "Real Movies" like "Renegades of Sonora" and "Angel on the Amazon." Each flipbook is numbered and is printed with a "Series No. 1" line (mercifully, no second series was printed).

Only four movies are mentioned in the titles so far reported to The Hobby Card Index, and perhaps these were the only four features in the series. The set was probably issued in 1949 (it is listed for the first time in the 1953 edition of the ACC). The wax wrapper is red and blue on white. The reference number is R701-4.

ITEM	EX	AVE
Flipbook	15.00	4.00
Set	475.00	110.00
Wrapper	200.00	—

MOVIE STAR PLAYING CARDS (56) 2 1/4" X 3 7/16"

Although Maple Leaf Gum did most of its business in Canada, some of its gum products found their way into northern U.S. towns. This series of 56 "Movie Star Playing Cards" was one of the sets that "crossed the border." The cards which are marked "Printed in Holland" on the blue and green playing card style backs, were first reported in the June, 1959 issue of The Card Collectors Bulletin. The fronts have "technicolor" photos of movie stars in the center, with the name and studio of the subject printed below. Front surfaces are glossy, but card backs are flat-finished. We have a complete checklist of the playing card suits, but the identity of only one of the four "jokers" in the deck is know at this time. No packaging has been discovered for the series. The reference number is R778-1. NOTE: cards of this series are often found miscut. Monroe ($25.00) is the most valuable card in the set, and collectors can expect to pay more than the "common" price listed below for other "demand" cards. No set price is listed because the checklist is not complete.

ITEM	EX	AVE
Card	3.00	.75

Hearts		Spades		Diamonds		Clubs		Jokers (4)
Ace	Judy Holliday	Ace	Randolph Scott	Ace	Mary Murphy	Ace	Anthony Steele	Eddie Constantine
Deuce	Lilli Palmer	Deuce	Ingrid Bergman	Deuce	Mara Lane	Deuce	Joanne Dru	Remaining three are unknown
Tray	Zsa Zsa Gabor	Tray	Paulette Goddard	Tray	Mar. Lockwood	Tray	Natalie Wood	
Four	Jean Peters	Four	Doris Day	Four	Pier Angeli	Four	Rita Hayworth	
Five	Marilyn Monroe	Five	Ann Sheridan	Five	Jane Powell	Five	Jan Wyman	
Six	Coleen Gray	Six	Linda Christian	Six	June Haver	Six	Jennifer Jones	
Seven	Martine Carol	Seven	Denise Darcel	Seven	Trevor Howard	Seven	Joan Rice	
Eight	Teresa Wright	Eight	Deborah Kerr	Eight	Sofia Loren	Eight	Romy Schneider	
Nine	Tyronne Power	Nine	Robert Mitchum	Nine	Clifton Webb	Nine	Rex Harrison	
Ten	M. Schell	Ten	Anita Ekberg	Ten	Linda Darnell	Ten	Gloria de Haven	
Jack	Orson Wells	Jack	G. Peck	Jack	Jeff Chandler	Jack	Red Skelton	
Queen	Diana Dors	Queen	Kim Novack	Queen	Donna Reed	Queen	Vivien Leigh	
King	Laurence Olivier	King	Gary Grant	King	Victor Mature	King	Errol Flynn	

"NEW - BIG PROFIT ITEM... BUBBLE GUM CARD SER— IES FOR GIRLS!" That's the way Bowman Gum advertised its 1948 set of "Movie Stars" in the confectionary trade papers. It might have helped if the company had gone after some big name film personalities, rather than the "B" movie actors and actresses pictured in the set, but that would have cost more money than J. Warren Bowman was willing to spend. The photographs on the fronts of the cards are uncaptioned and they have a dull gray appearance. The backs contain the card number, the star's name, his or her vital statis-

tics, and a paragraph of biographical and promotional text. More than 20 percent of the reverse on each card carries advertising (in red ink) for a series of mail premiums; these involved sending in varying amounts of "Movie Star Bubble Gum" wrappers (plus money), which explains why modern collectors have a difficult time finding this wrapper. The backs of every card in the set can be found

printed in either black or blue ink (the reason for this is unknown). According to a statement on the cards, the "stars" in the set were selected by "Photoplay" magazine. Wholesalers were required to purchase a minimum of sixty 24-count boxes from Bowman at 72 cents per box. These cards are often found with backs from other Bowman sets, but these variations are not any more valuable than normal cards. The reference number is R701-9.

ITEM	EX	AVE
Card	6.00	1.50
Set	275.00	65.00
Wrapper	125.00	——

1	Diana Lynn	10	Laura Elliot	19	Helena Carter	28	Eve Arden
2	Adele Mara	11	Carolyn Butler	20	Marta Toren	29	Jane Greer
3	Paul Lees	12	William Demarest	21	Donald O'Connor	30	Robert Preston
4	Adrian Booth	13	Colleen Townsend	22	Mona Freeman	31	Bonita Granville
5	Margaret Field	14	Roberta Jonay	23	Barbara Lawrence	32	Frances Gifford
6	Monte Hale	15	Cesar Romero	24	Dan Duryea	33	Nancy Guild
7	Mary Hatcher	16	Carole Mathews	25	Gail Russell	34	Lloyd Nolan
8	Jean Ruth	17	Yvonne De Carlo	26	Shelley Winters	35	Sonja Henie
9	Sterling Hayden	18	Dan Dailey	27	Sonny Tufts	36	Ann Blyth

ADVERTISING POSTER FOR BOWMAN "MOVIE STARS"

NON-SPORT UPDATE
P.O. BOX 5858, HARRISBURG, PA 17110

MOVIE STARS (70)   1 9/16" X 2 3/4"

Another Maple Leaf Gum "invader" from Canada, the 70 cards in this series would

Humphrey Bogart ⓒ W.B.

Susan Hayward ⓒ Un. Int.

be difficult to identify except for the "number in circle" description printed in the early card catalogs. The fronts have interesting color photographs of some of Hollywood's biggest stars, and their names and studios are printed below each picture (along with the famous "number in circle"). The cards backs are blank. The series fascinates collectors not only for the superstars it contains, but also because it includes some stars

rarely seen on cards (Humphrey Bogart, for example). At $20.00, John Wayne is the most expensive card in the set, but there are many others that command a higher value than the "common" price listed below. No packaging has been found for the series. The reference number for this set is R778-2.

ITEM	EX	AVE
Card	2.00	.50

1 Patricia Wymore (W.B.P.)	19 Bing Crosby (Paramount)	37 Doris Day (W.B.)	54 Wanda Hendrix (20th Cent.)
2 Pier Angelie (M.G.M.)	20 Greer Garson (M.G.M.)	38 Gene Nelson (W.B.)	55 Brenda Marshall (M.P.)
3 Nancy Olson (W.B.P.)	21 Esther Williams (M.G.M.)	39 Dana Clark (W.B.)	56 Patricia Roc (E. Lion)
4 June Allyson (M.G.M.)	22 Gregory Peck (20th Cent.)	40 Betsy Drake (W.B.)	57 Mickey Rooney (M.G.M.)
5 Barbara Hale (Eur. Columbia)	23 June Haver (20th Cent.)	41 Maureen O'Hara (20th Cen.)	58 Rhonda Fleming (Paramount)
6 Kerima (Art. Rank)	24 Jane Russell (United Artists)	42 Marlene Dietrich (W.B.)	59 Bob Hope (Paramount)
7 Ginger Rogers (M.G.M.)	25 Diana Lynn (20th Cent. Fox)	43 Janet Leigh (M.G.M.)	60 Loretta Young (Paramount
8 John Wayne (W.B.P.)	26 Burt Lancaster (Hall Wallis)	44 Claudette Colbert (U.I.)	61 Doris Day (W.B.)
9 Joan Crawford (W.B.P.)	27 Lana Turner (M.G.M.)	45 Gene Kelly (M.G.M.)	62 Linda Darnell (20th C.F.)
10 Viveca Lindfors (20th C.F.)	28 Lauren Becall (W.B.P.)	46 Humphrey Bogart (W.B.)	63 Gloria de Haven (M.G.M.)
11 Yvonne de Carlo (Universal)	29 Virginia Mayo (W.B.P.)	47 Eleanor Parker (W.B.)	64 Alexis Smith (U.I.)
12 Lizabeth Scott (Paramount)	30 Gary Cooper (W.B.P.)	48 Joan Fontaine (Paramount)	65 O'Sullivan (M.G.M.)
13 Corinne Calvet (20th Cent.)	31 Ray Milland (W.B.P.)	49 Shelley Winters (Un. Int.)	66 Stewart Granger (Ar. O.)
14 Polly Bergen (Hall Wallis)	32 Olivia de Havilland (Paramount)	50 Joan Caulfield (Paramount)	67 Priscilla Lane (M.G.M.)
15 Mona Freeman (Paramount)	33 Roy Rogers (Centhra)	51 Peggy Daw (Un. Int.)	68 Doris Day (W.B.)
16 Howard Keel (M.G.M.)	34 Leslie Caron (M.G.M.)	52 Danny Kaye (W.B.)	69 Susan Hayward (Un. Int.)
17 Walter Pidgeon (M.G.M.)	35 Clark Gable (M.G.M.)	53 John Lund (Paramount)	70 Ava Gardner (M.G.M.)
18 William Holden (W.B.P.)	36 Montgomery Clift (Paramount)		

MOVIE STARS (?)   19/32" X 13/16"

The cards on this strip of movie stars produced by American Chewing Products might be small in size, but many of the celebrities were "big" in Hollywood. The quadragenarians

AVA GARDNER

among you may remember that the strips of film personalities and baseball players (listed separately in the old catalogs at R423) were sold in gumball machines. There was even a plastic ring with a frame designed to hold an individual picture. The photos are black & white and the celebrity is named below. The backs have a white "camera-man" design set on a colored background (green,

purple, and orange have been reported so far). Each strip contained 13 photos, so the one illustrated is missing a single picture. The value of a single "common" card is 75 cents; naturally, the more famous film stars will cost more (up to $5.00). Intact strips are not uncommon and can generally be purchased in the $15.00 to $20.00 range. The set total is not known . The reference number for the set is R783.

FRONT & BACK OF MOVIE STAR STRIP (R783)

BASEBALL PLAYERS WERE LISTED SEPARATELY
(R423) IN THE EARLY CATALOGS

MOVIE STAR SERIES (?)   1 3/4" X 2 3/4"

You are looking at one of the longest running series of cards ever issued. The cards were printed in Holland by Dandy Gum and were sold in Canada and the northern U.S. by Maple Leaf Gum. First mentioned in the February, 1958 edition of The Card Collectors Bulletin, they are still in production today. Over the years, the cards have displayed slight detail differences and have been printed on both thick and thin cardboard, as well as on paper. The one constant identifying mark is the "serie" designation which appears on all cards EXCEPT for the first group (see Burt Lancaster card in illustration). The "serie" ("series" in French) was marked on all subsequent series along with a letter. In our presentation, Tony Curtis is a "serie A" card, Ricky Nelson, a "serie B," and Martin & Lewis are "serie S." The photographs in all series are in color (many have painted backdrops). In recent years recording artists have been added to the sets. The cards have a distinctly foreign "look" and are not widely collected in the United States. Values depend exclusively on the celebrity: the age of the series is not a factor (after all, the cards are not dated, and they are all very similar in appearance). The reference number is R778-3. NOTE: price range is 50 cents (common) to $10.00 (John Wayne, Brigitte Bardot, etc.).

39   Burt Lancaster
United Artists

Tony Curtis   Universal
Serie A   165

Ricky Nelson
Serie B · Printed in Holland · No. 45

Dean Martin Jerry Lewis,
Serie S   Paramount   No. 61

NOVEL CANDY BOXES

Bubble gum trading cards were big business in the 1950's, but they did not go unchallenged in the battle for young America's hearts (and allowances). Bowman, Topps, Fleer, and Philly Gum were met head on in the marketplace by a host of confectionary companies who produced and distributed an amazing variety of small, self-contained candy boxes. These boxes competed directly with the gum companies not only in terms of the confection — inedible gum versus edible candy — but also on the basic issue of price. For the gum companies of the post-war era, the 5-cent pack was the top-of-the-line-profit maker (the pre-war standard was 1-cent), and any item that might divert a single nickel from their product was a serious threat.

The "ultimate weapon" of the candy companies was the package. Most candy boxes were far bigger than gum packs, and children equate "bigger" with "better." There was more surface to decorate and more interior space to hold candy (several pieces, rather than one slab of gum) and prizes (novelties, small toys, etc.). Making part of the box (usually the back panel) double as a trading card was an old trick which the candy companies had invented before World War I and had used extensively in the 1920's and 1930's. In the 1950's, they dramatically improved production technology, design, and marketing strategies, and the public was treated to a barrage of fascinating candy boxes manufactured by a growing number of firms.

Arroe, CeDe, Super Novelty, Leader, Phoenix, Williamson — all produced candy box cards and novelties which the kids of yesteryear loved and the collectors of today covet. But one company stood head and shoulders above all the rest— The Novel Package Corporation of Brooklyn, NY. Novel may not have had the best-tasting candy or the most interesting toys, but their art department and development team was the best in the business, and they had ALL the best themes and characters of the period. From the stirring adventures of King Arthur's Court to the modern exploits of Dick Tracy and the comic antics of Casper and Winnie Winnkle, Novel had a box to suit every taste. The best part was the price...all you had to do was find five empty soda bottles and one of Novel's little treasure chests was yours!

The Hobby Card Index has 21 different Novel Candy Corp. boxes on record as of this date. The details of each type of box are summarized in the following displays. The price listed for "card" refers to a single card which is totally detached from the box. The box price applies ONLY to intact boxes with no pieces missing or detached (a flattened box with one seam carefully cut is permissible). Boxes with pieces missing and cards with panels or flaps attached fall between the two price levels.

ADVENTURES OF DICK TRACY (12)   2 7/16" X 2 7/8"

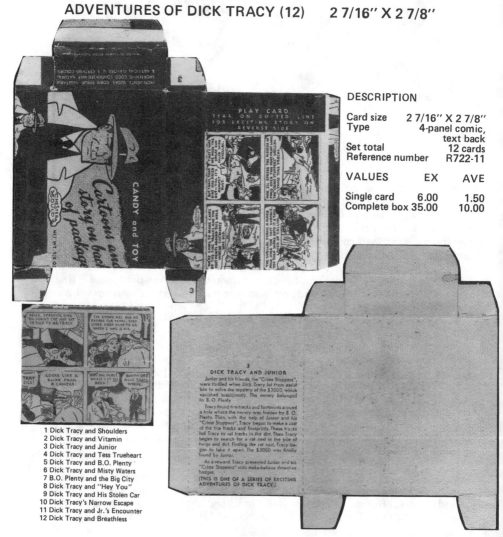

DESCRIPTION

Card size	2 7/16" X 2 7/8"
Type	4-panel comic, text back
Set total	12 cards
Reference number	R722-11

VALUES	EX	AVE
Single card	6.00	1.50
Complete box	35.00	10.00

1 Dick Tracy and Shoulders
2 Dick Tracy and Vitamin
3 Dick Tracy and Junior
4 Dick Tracy and Tess Trueheart
5 Dick Tracy and B.O. Plenty
6 Dick Tracy and Misty Waters
7 B.O. Plenty and the Big City
8 Dick Tracy and "Hey You"
9 Dick Tracy and His Stolen Car
10 Dick Tracy's Narrow Escape
11 Dick Tracy and Jr.'s Encounter
12 Dick Tracy and Breathless

BARREL OF FUN (?)

2 3/8" X 3 3/4"

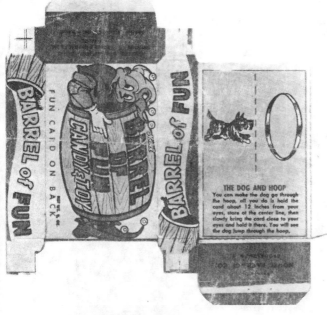

THE DOG AND HOOP

You can make the dog go through the hoop, all you do is hold the card about 12 inches from your eyes, stare at the center line, then slowly bring the card close to your eyes and hold it there. You will see the dog jump through the hoop.

DESCRIPTION

Card size	2 3/8" X 3 3/4"
Type	single picture front, blank back
Set total	unknown
Reference number	R722-13

VALUES	EX	AVE
Single card	2.00	.50
Complete box	20.00	5.00

COMBAT SOLDIERS (?)

2 7/16" X 3 3/4"

DESCRIPTION

Card size	2 7/16" X 3 3/4"
Type	single picture front, blank back
Set total	unknown
Reference number	R722-14

VALUES	EX	AVE
Single card	3.50	1.00
Complete box	none seen	

CRIME BUSTER STORIES (4K)

2 7/16" X 2 3/4"

DESCRIPTION

Card size	2 7/16" X 2 3/4"
Type	single picture front, text back
Set total	unknown, No. 4 seen
Reference number	R722-2

VALUES	EX	AVE
Single card	3.00	.75
Complete box	25.00	6.50

4
EMERGENCY SQUAD

The Emergency Squad is a specially trained unit within the Police Department. They work with special equipment and are called on, as their name indicates, when extreme emergencies arise.

The Emergency Squad is called upon when there are serious accidents, fires, riots, public disorders, drownings and when it is necessary to administer oxygen in the attempt to save a human life.

All members of the Emergency Squad must be specially trained in rescue work, first aid, and use of emergency equipment. They operate on land, air and sea, and are highly respected because of their proven bravery and courage.

[THIS IS ONE OF A SERIES OF EXCITING CRIME BUSTER STORIES.]

DANIEL BOONE (?)

2 7/16" X 3 3/4"

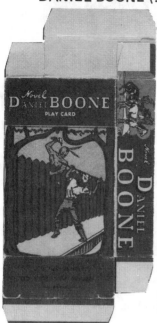

DESCRIPTION

Card size   2 7/16" X 3 3/4"
Type   single picture front,
                  blank back
Set total   unknown
Reference number   R722-15

VALUES	EX	AVE
Single card	4.00	1.50
Complete box	50.00	15.00

DAVY CROCKETT (?)

2 7/16" X 3 3/4"

DESCRIPTION

Card size   2 7/16" X 3 3/4"
Type   single picture front,
                  blank back
Set total   unknown
Reference number   R722-16

VALUES	EX	AVE
Single card	3.50	1.25
Complete box	60.00	15.00

FIRE FIGHTER STORIES (3K) 2 7/16" X 2 7/8"

DESCRIPTION

Card size	2 7/16" X 2 7/8"
Type	single picture front, text back
Set total	unknown No. 3 seen
Reference number	R722-17

VALUES	EX	AVE
Single card	4.00	1.50
Complete box	none seen	

FOREIGN LEGION (?) 2 7/16" X 2 3/4"

DESCRIPTION

Card size	2 7/16" X 2 3/4"
Type	single picture front, blank back
Set total	unknown
Reference number	R722-18

VALUES	EX	AVE
Single card	3.00	1.00
Complete box	35.00	10.00

HARVEY FAMOUS CARTOONS (?) 2 3/8" X 3 3/4"

DESCRIPTION

Card size	2 3/8" X 3 3/4"
Type	single picture front, blank back
Set total	unknown
Reference number	R722-9

VALUES	EX	AVE
Single card	3.00	1.00
Complete box	25.00	6.50

313

INDIAN CHIEF STORIES (9K)   2 7/16" X 2 3/4"

DESCRIPTION

Card size	2 7/16" X 2 3/4"
Type	single picture front, text back
Set total	unknown No. 9 seen
Reference number	R722-3

VALUES	EX	AVE
Single card	3.00	.75
Complete box		none seen

JOE PALOOKA BOXING LESSONS (8K)   2 7/16" X 2 3/4"

DESCRIPTION

Card size	2 7/16" X 2 3/4"
Type	single picture front, blank back
Set total	unknown No. 8 seen
Reference number	R722-19 old number was R444

VALUES	EX	AVE
Single card	7.00	2.00
Complete box		none seen

JUNGLE KING STORIES (12)   2 7/16" X 2 7/8"

1 Tiger
2 Zebra
3 Elephant
4 Giraffe
5 Gnu
6 Hippopotamus
7 Rhinoceros
8 Lion
9 Chimpanzee
10 Crocodile
11 Leopard
12 Hyena

DESCRIPTION

Card size	2 7/16" X 2 7/8"
Type	single picture front, text back
Set total	12
Reference number	R722-1

VALUES	EX	AVE
Single card	2.50	.50
Complete box		none seen

KING ARTHUR STORIES (5K)

2 7/16" X 2 3/4"

DESCRIPTION

Card size	2 7/16" X 2 3/4"
Type	single picture front, text back
Set total	unknown No. 5 seen
Reference number	R722-10

VALUES	EX	AVE
Single card	3.50	1.00
Complete box	25.00	6.50

MR. MAGIC TRICKS (12)

2 1/2" X 2 7/8"

DESCRIPTION

Card size	2 1/2" X 2 7/8"
Type	single picture front, text back
Set total	12
Reference number	R722-4

VALUES	EX	AVE
Single card	3.00	.75
Complete box	25.00	6.50

THE TOUGH NAPKIN

You can tell your friends that you can prove you're stronger than all of them. Twist a napkin like a rope and ask everyone to see if they can tear it in half by pulling on the ends. They'll find they can't do it. While they're trying to tear it, you dip your fingers in a glass of water. When your friends give up you tell them you can do it easily. Twist the napkin very tightly, wetting the center of the napkin while you're doing it. Your friends will stare in amazement when they see the napkin break after you pull the ends.

(THIS IS ONE OF A SERIES OF EXCITING MR. MAGIC TRICKS)

PIRATE ADVENTURES (12)

2 7/16" X 2 7/8"

DESCRIPTION

Card size	2 7/16" X 2 7/8"
Type	single picture front, text back
Set total	12
Reference number	R722-5

VALUES	EX	AVE
Single card	3.00	.75
Complete box	50.00	15.00

BART PORTUGESE

Bart Portugese was among the pirate buccaneers who infested the Spanish Main. In a boat manned with thirty fellow pirates he assaulted a great ship off Cape Corrientes. He was beaten off many times, but he kept the fight goin' until he won the ... st. However, in a s... ...attack by the ... panish, Portugese was ...ceated and ... barely escaped with his life. He got another band of pirates together and set sail again only to encounter the same Spanish boat. This time he got away with the Spanish boat but soon afterward he went down with it in a hurricane just off the Isle of Pines.

(THIS IS ONE OF A SERIES OF EXCITING PIRATE ADVENTURES.)

316

ROCKET RANGER STORIES (6K)   **2 7/16" X 2 3/4"**

DESCRIPTION

Card size	2 7/16" X 2 3/4"
Type	single picture front, blank back
Set total	unknown No. 6 seen
Reference number	R722-6

VALUES	EX	AVE
Single card	5.00	2.00
Complete box	60.00	15.00

6
JUPITER

Jupiter is 483 million miles away from the sun, which is about five times further away than the Earth. It is the largest of all the planets, and is about 1,300 times the size of the Earth.

One day on Jupiter is less than half as long as a day on Earth, and its temperature is about 220° below zero. Another interesting feature about Jupiter is its eleven moons.

A trip to Jupiter is long and dangerous, and the Rocket Rangers do not like to go there because of the very cold climate. However, when trouble arises the Rangers make the trip, and stay there until their mission is accomplished.

(THIS IS ONE OF A SERIES OF EXCITING ROCKET RANGER STORIES.)

1946 EDITION OF
THE AMERICAN CARD CATALOG

317

SAD SACK (2K)   2 7/16" X 3 3/4"

DESCRIPTION

Card size	2 7/16" X 3 3/4"
Type	currency style front, blank back
Set total	unknown
	two denominations seen
Reference number	R722-20

VALUES	EX	AVE
Single card	4.00	1.50
Complete box	50.00	15.00

SUPER CIRCUS STORIES (12)   2 7/16" X 2 3/4"

3
TRAPEZE ARTIST

The Trapeze Artist requires a lot of skill and timing and strength. These people swing on the trapezes and make beautiful patterns in the air in time to music.

Usually, two or more people perform on the trapeze. One of them is called the catcher and the other is called the flyer.

The catcher grasps the flyer as he comes through the air, and holds him. Then he throws the flyer back in the direction of his trapeze. The flyer looks very graceful as he goes sailing through the air away up at the top of the big tent.

This is how we got the expression "flying through the air with the greatest of ease."

(THIS IS ONE OF A SERIES OF EXCITING NOVEL SUPER CIRCUS STORIES.)

DESCRIPTION

Card size	2 7/16" X 2 3/4"
Type	single picture front, text back
Set total	12
Reference number	R722-7

VALUES	EX	AVE
Single card	3.00	.75
Complete box	none seen	

Look for us in the 1961-1991 SPORT AMERICANA PRICE GUIDE TO THE NON—SPORTS CARDS

SUPERMAN (?)

2 7/16" X 3 3/4"

DESCRIPTION

Card size   2 7/16" X 3 3/4"
Type   single picture front,
     blank back
Set total   unknown
Reference number   R722-21

VALUES	EX	AVE
Single card	10.00	3.00
Complete box	90.00	25.00

WILD WEST ADVENTURES (24)

2 7/16" X 2 7/8"

DESCRIPTION

Card size   2 7/16" X 2 7/8"
Type   single picture front,
     blank back
Set total   24
Reference number   R722-8

VALUES	EX	AVE
Single card	3.00	.75
Complete box	35.00	10.00

THE CARD COLLECTORS BULLETIN. . . .
. . . .SERVING THE HOBBY SINCE 1938.

319

WINNIE WINKLE
RINKYDINK STORIES (8K)

2 7/16" X 2 7/8"

DESCRIPTION

Card size	2 7/16" X 2 7/8"
Type	single picture front; blank back
Set total	unknown No. 8 seen
Reference number	R722-12

VALUES	EX	AVE
Single card	2.50	.60
Complete box	25.00	6.50
Display box	125.00	25.00

BOX LID

PIN–UP PLAYING CARDS (53)   1 7/16" X 2 3/4"

It's hard to imagine that this set of pin-up style playing cards of Hollywood celebrities was issued in gum packs, but the early catalogs identify the maker as Maple Leaf Gum. If that is the case, then the series was probably sold only in the states bordering Canada (which was Maple Leaf's primary market). The "cheesecake" style of the cards was undoubtedly considered risque at the time, and this may explain why few cards of the series have been found by modern collectors. The color photographs are quite striking, and the set includes some very famous female stars and starlets. The only men featured in the set are the "kings" representing the four suits. Only a single "joker" has been found. The backs of the cards have a standard Maple Leaf playing card design, except that the "Made in Holland" line is missing. The fronts have glossy surfaces but the backs are flat-finished. The reference number is R778-4. NOTE: the more famous stars are worth a premium over the "common" listed below.

ITEM	EX	AVE
Card	3.00	1.00
Set	225.00	60.00

Hearts		Spades		Diamonds		Clubs	
Ace	Marie Branchard	Ace	Leigh Snowden	Ace	Joan Caufield	Ace	Abbe Lane
Deuce	Esther Williams	Deuce	Katryn Grandstaff	Deuce	Abbe Lane	Deuce	Linda Sterling
Tray	Cyd Charisse	Tray	Unnamed	Tray	Debbie Reynolds	Tray	Jane Harker
Four	Piper Laurie	Four	Mamie V. Doren	Four	Julia Adams	Four	Allison Hayes
Five	Sally Forrest	Five	Unnamed	Five	Barbara Ruick	Five	Joyce Holden
Six	Mamie V. Doren	Six	Mamie V. Doren	Six	Mara Corday	Six	Rita Hayworth
Seven	Vera Ellen	Seven	Yvonne De Carlo	Seven	Gloria De Haven	Seven	Martha Hyer
Eight	Kathleen Hughes	Eight	Kathleen Hughes	Eight	Linda Christian	Eight	Peggy Castle
Nine	Mamie V. Doren	Nine	Mara Corday	Nine	Hazel Brooks	Nine	Corinne Calvet
Ten	Colleen Miller	Ten	Hil Rombin	Ten	June Haver	Ten	Joan Taylor
Jack	Corine Calvet	Jack	Mara Corday	Jack	Mary Wilson	Jack	Barbara Lawrence
Queen	Patricia Medina	Queen	Paula Drew	Queen	Ronda Fleming	Queen	Anne Baxter
King	Fernando Lamas	King	Judo Champion	King	Jiu-Jitsu Champion	King	Body Building Champion

The Jolly
Joker   Colleen Miller

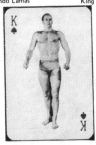  

PIRATE CARDS (49)   2 3/8" X 2 7/8"

There was a little bit of the old "Jolly Roger" at Leaf Gum when they issued the "Pirates Cards" series in 1948. For one thing, the artwork on the front of the cards, plus the process used to reproduce it, were so primitive that the cards are downright ugly. Secondly, Leaf skip-numbered the cards to make kids buy more and more of them to get the missing numbers. If these two things were not bad enough, the company was arrogant enough to print the following on the back of some of the cards: "You'll be proud to show your gorgeous collection of Pirate cards in [a] beautiful, specially-designed 32-pg. Album. Get it for only 5 Wrapers and 25 cents. Striking color cover. Large (11" X 8 1/2") heavy black pages. Can display 168 different cards." This type of advertising can only be characterized as "The Big Lie."

Some collectors find this set repelling; others think it has a strange and fascinating air about it. Collecting it, in any case, can be a challenge. Many of the cards are found out of focus which, considering the dot pattern of the artwork, makes them uncollectable (regardless of the condition of the rest of the card). Furthermore, many dealers have attemped to convince the public that Leaf Pirate Cards are on an equal plane of rarity with the Leaf baseball and boxing issues of the same period. This is merely an effort to drum up demand for an unattractive set. Considering that a horde of Leaf Pirate Cards recently turned up in Chicago, the traditional supply-moderate/demand-poor ratio has become even more disproportionate on the supply side. If you like this set, the new influx of cards should enable you to pick and choose for condition at moderate prices.

The wrapper for the series

came in a 1-cent denomination only, and it is red and blue on white with crimped edges. Two slightly different display boxes are known: one merely advertises the cards on front, while the other speaks of "A Swell Tattoo on Back of Each Wrapper and a Pirate's Picture Too!" The latter has some collectors scrambling to find the tattoos, but no one has come up with any confirmed samples to date. In

addition to out-of-focus cards, Leaf Pirates have also been found with blank backs and printed without numbers. A variety of different premiums (besides the album) were offered on the backs of the cards in exchange for wrappers and coin. The set is considered to be complete at 49 cards, yet we know that Leaf actually printed a mysterious 50th card in its boxing series, and some collectors wonder if there isn't a parallel "extra" card in the Pirates set. The reference number is R790. NOTE: cards in "excellent" grade must be in reasonable focus and well-centered.

WALKING THE PLANK

One of the commonest of the Pirates' methods of getting rid of captives was by forcing a prisoner to walk the plank. The pirates bound the prisoner's arms and tied a blindfold around his eyes. They placed him on a narrow plank reaching out over the water. Then, with shouts and jeers and abuse, they forced the luckless prisoner to walk to the end of the plank from where he fell into the sea and was drowned.

PIRATE BUBBLE GUM

You'll be proud to show your gorgeous collection of Pirate cards in beautiful, specially-designed, 32-pg. Album. Get it for only 5 wrappers and 10c. striking color cover. Large (11" x 8½") heavy black pages. Can display 168 different cards.

Send Wrappers and Coin to
LEAF GUM CO., Box 1867 CHICAGO 90, ILL.
Copyright 1948

ITEM	EX	AVE
Card	6.00	1.50
Set	375.00	90.00
Wrapper	100.00	––
Boxes		
2, each	250.00	100.00

1	Captain Edwards	24	Edward Lowe	50	William Lewis	100	Capt. John Criss
2	Capt. Robert Deal	28	Barbarossa	51	Joto and Cisco	101	John Derbrake
5	Hirain Breaker	30	Capt. Jackman	58	Edward Teach	112	Ringrose, Basil
7	Slave Trading	31	Bartholomew Roberts	62	Major Bonnet	116	Jean La Fitte
8	Dead Men Tell No Tales	35	Charles Gibbs	65	Capt. Bannister	124	Capt. John Augur
9	Capt. Robert Kidd	38	Walking the Plank	73	Capt. Crackers	125	Grillo Diego
11	"Black Taylor"	40	Marooning	78	Peter M'Kinlie	133	William Dampier
13	Ali Basha	41	Pierre Le Grand	79	Capt. Dansker	136	Dr. Thomas Dover
16	Sieur De Grammot	42	Anne Bonney	80	Sir Henry Morgan	158	Joseph Bradley
21	Capt. Condent	45	Charles Bellamy	88	Edward Davis	164	John Avery
22	Buccaneer	46	Capt. Johnson	92	Edward England	165	Francis L'Olonis
23	Sacking of Panama	49	Thomas Anstis	96	Captain Greaves	168	Angria
				99	George Cumberland		

PIRATE CARDS (?)

In the 1950's, the firm of McLean & Son produced a line of small candy-and-toy boxes under the copyrighted name "Treasure Chest." Most of these boxes were smaller than the box illustrated, and they were plainer in design and did not incorporate a trading card into the design. This particular box has a distinctive striped pattern on the front along with the pirate figure and the treasure chest brimming with coins and jewelry. The card on back is simply drawn and occupies 70 percent of the panel. All the text is on the front (the back is blank), and there is no card number. The borders have dotted lines making cutting and removal easier. This box has been assigned the reference number R762 by The Hobby Card Index.

ITEM	EX	AVE
Card	3.00	.75
Box	20.00	7.00

PLANES (120)

The first series (1-60) of Topps "Planes" was issued in the spring of 1957 (see listing in the August, 1957 edition of The Card Collectors Bulletin), and the second series (61-120) followed in the early summer. The colored artwork card fronts depict planes, dirigibles, and helicopters, with the name of the aircraft and one line of description located in a small yellow panel inside the picture area. The card number, data chart, text, and a "Jr. Skywatcher Quiz" are printed on the back. A Public service ad - "Earn Your Wings... Join The Ground Observer Corps" — sits at the very bottom of each card.

There has been much discussion about the detail differences found in this set. The most important of these is the color of the accents on the gray stock backs: blue and red. Every card in the series is found in both colors, prompting collectors to ask "Topps, why did you do this?" Well, Topps doesn't plan to answer this question, but hobby veterans have a theory which goes beyond the usual "we-ran-out-of-that-color-ink" explanation. It goes like this: Topps had recently bought Bowman Gum, so they decided to test out their newly acquired equipment by printing the Planes set in one color with their old presses, and in another color with Bowman's presses (using Bowman's cardboard, ink, and gum. This speculation is made more plausable by the fact that the Planes checklist comes with advertising lines for both "Bazooka" and "Blony" gum (the latter was Bowman's brand).

At any rate, blue back cards are twice as numerous as their red back counterparts, and the second series of both types is harder to find than the first. In addition, card No. 9 appears on many want lists and it is considered the "key" to completing the set.

The 1-cent wrapper is made of wax paper and has red, white, & blue planes repeated on alternating red and yellow bands. The 5-cent wax wrapper is yellow and green with a single red, white & blue plane in the center. The Bazooka and Blony checklists are identical except for the brands. Robert Marks furnished the illustration of the 5-cent display box (a 1-cent box has yet to be found). The reference number is R707-2.

ITEM	EX	AVE
Cards		
1-60		
Red	3.00	.75
Blue	1.50	.35
61-120		
Red	5.00	1.25
Blue	3.00	.75
Sets		
Red	575.00	140.00
Blue	310.00	77.50
Wrappers		
1-cent	100.00	––
5-cent	125.00	––
Box	200.00	45.00

Planes

1 F4D Skyray	31 Convertiplane	61 Cessna YH-41
2 Lockheed T2V-1	32 MIG I5	62 Leduc O-21
3 F7U-3 Cutlass	33 Hare Russian Helicopter	63 Douglas C-133A
4 YC-130 A Hercules	34 Lansen	64 FB-30 Vampire
5 Convair B-36H	35 M-4 Horse	65 Bell X-2
6 Thunderstreak	36 TU-104	66 Boeing Drone
7 Stratofortress	37 Caravelle	67 Aerocar
8 AD-6 Skyraider	38 Rubber Plane	68 Boeing 707
9 Propeloplane	39 Avro Shackleton	69 DC-7C Seven Seas
10 Lockheed WV-2	40 Fairey Delta 2	70 Sikorsky H-34 A
11 XP6M-1 Seamaster	41 Convair 880	71 Flying Platform
12 Douglas DC-8	42 Aerocycle	72 Rotor Craft
13 UF-1 Albatross	43 Colonial Skimmer	73 Hughes Falcon
14 Bell XH-40	44 YH-16 Transporter	74 Lockheed X7
15 F9F-8 Cougar	45 SG-4 Blimp	75 Martin Matador
16 F89-D Scorpion	46 F-84 Thunderjet	76 AVRO 707B
17 Trident	47 F3D-2 Skynight	77 DHC-3 Otter
18 T-33A Shooting Star	48 F3H-2N Demon	78 MK-6 Sabre
19 Bristol 173	49 Grumman Avenger	79 Follan Gnat
20 MS 760 Paris	50 Martin B-57	80 MK-7 Swift
21 Hurel-Dubois	51 F-104A "Starfighter"	81 DH-106 Comet
22 Djinn	52 KC-97G Stratofreighter	82 Victor B1
23 F84-K Ficon	53 Fairchild C-123	83 170R Magister
24 Avro CF-100	54 Convair XC–99	84 Dassault Mirage
25 Vautour	55 1049-G Super Constellation	85 Coleopter
26 Britannia	56 A3D-1 Skywarrior	86 XF2Y-1 Sea Dart
27 F-100 Super Sabre	57 Douglass RB-66	87 Convair F-102A
28 B-47E Stratojet	58 F11F-1 Tiger	88 F5D-1 Skylancer
29 F-86H Sabre	59 A4D-1 Skyhawk	89 F-86D Sabre
30 Percival Provost	60 FJ-3 Fury	90 F-101A Voodoo

91 F8U-1 Crusader	106 YC-123 E
92 F-94C Starfire	107 P4M-1 Mercator
93 Douglas AD-5	108 Cessna OE-2
94 Yak - 9P	109 Cessna T-37A
95 Grumman S2F-1	110 Temco TT-1
96 P2V-7 Neptune	111 Yak-17
97 B-26C Invader	112 T-37 Bison
98 B-45C Tornado	113 LA-9
99 Superfortress	114 IL-28 Beagle
100 AJ-1 Savage	115 Jet Mentor
101 Pulqui II	116 Yak-12
102 Boeing KC135A	117 Vickers Valiant
103 Convair R4Y-1	118 TU-31 Barge
104 R3Y-2 Tradewind	119 TU-35 Bosun
105 Globemaster II	120 MIG-9

PLAY COINS OF THE WORLD (120)   7/8" DIAMETER

"Foreign Coins have Magic for Youngsters and Parents too!" They must have been "magic" for Topps' bank account also, because the company marketed the series in two distinct ways. Single coins were packed in 1-cent packs of gum with the title "WORLD Play Money COINS" (wrapper is blue and red, with white and blue printing, and bears a copyright date of 1949). Coins were also distributed in boxes of "Play Money Pops," where they were enclosed in a strip of cellophane in the center of the box (see illustration). According to the advertising on the back of the lollipop box, "There are 72 coins to the complete set, made up of 24 different countries. Each country's play coin has three denominations, 25, 50 and 100. Each denomination is in a different color." Supposedly, the coins had a plastic core coated with metal: brass, copper, or nickel. The set total stated in all of Topps' advertising is at odds with the "120 in set" listing in the American Card Catalog, and we have opted to believe the catalog figure until it is disproved. The reference number is PX4.

ITEM	EX	AVE
Coin	1.00	.25
Wrapper	35.00	––
Gum Box	75.00	20.00
Lollipop Box	35.00	10.00

PARTIAL CHECKLIST

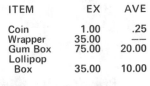

Argentina	Peso	25, 50 & 100
Belgium	Franc	25, 50 & 100
Brazil	Reis	25, 50 & 100
Canada	Cent	25, 50 & 100
China	Yuan	25, 50 & 100
Cuba	Peso	25, 50 & 100
England	Shilling	25, 50 & 100
Finland	Markka	25, 50 & 100
France	Franc	25, 50 & 100
Holland	Gulden	25, 50 & 100
India	Rupee	25, 50 & 100
Iran	Rial	25, 50 & 100
Italy	Lire	25, 50 & 100
Mexico	Pesos	25, 50 & 100
Norway	Krone	25, 50 & 100
Peru	Centavo	25, 50 & 100
Sweden	Krona	25, 50 & 100
Turkey	Kurus	25, 50 & 100

Foreign Coins have Magic for Youngsters and Parents too!

Plated Coins of the World!

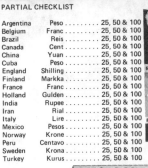

ADVERTISING PAGE FROM A CONFECTIONARY TRADE MAGAZINE

POPEYE (?)

2 3/8" X 3 11/16"

This nicely-colored "Popeye" card was cut from a 5-cent candy box, but we have been unable to determine whether it was printed on the front or back panel. The "King Features Syndicate" line inside the picture area at the lower left indicates that the series was part of the R756 category in the American Card Catalog. The back is blank and there is no card number. The "Candies and Toy" panel at the bottom was obviously meant to be cut away from the card. Until a partial or complete box is found, we shall be unable to confirm the name of the manufacturer.

ITEM	EX	AVE
Card	4.00	1.00

POPEYE (?)

1 7/16" X 3 3/4"

The Phoenix Candy Company (Brooklyn, NY) produced this "POPEYE And His Pals" box for the crayon-toting crowd. The sample in our illustration has a blue front and side pan-

els with red, yellow, and black accents. Popeye "hisself" is flesh-colored, and he is wearing his white sailor's attire and smoking a yellow "balloon pipe." The back panel contains a black-outline drawing marked with small numbers; these correspond to a coloring "key" printed at bottom. There are several different cartoon characters pictured in the color-by-the-numbers format issued by Phoenix, but we have to deal with them character by character because the cards are often found with this phrase and the color key removed. The reference number is R821. NOTE: cards that have been colored cannot be graded excellent.

ITEM	EX	AVE
Card	2.50	.50
Box	25.00	6.00

POPEYE TATOOS (3 SETS)

1 9/16" X 3 1/2"

This category contains three different wrapper/tattoo issues with the same theme: Popeye, The Sailor Man. The blue and white wrapper (Popeye has the American flag on chest) was the first to appear; it is mentioned in the August, 1958 edition of The Card Collectors Bulletin. The yellow "New Series" wrapper probably appeared later that same year. The "Mystery Color Tattoo" is generally believed to have been sold in late 1959 or early 1960, since it was not mentioned in the 1960 edition of the American Card Catalog, as are the first two wrappers.

The wrapper side of this item is far more appealing to most collectors than the tattoo on the interior side. The original and "new" series transfers are drawn in the same colors and none are numbered. The mystery color tattoos were printed under a black coating, through which the design would appear on the skin after being "activated," All three series of transfers were applied with water. Given the appeal of the wrappers, the tattoos are too expensive to collect as a set (even if the total for each series was known), although the prices listed are very reasonable for the age of the products. The reference number is R711-6.

ITEM	EX	AVE
Wrapper/ Tattoos, each	10.00	––

POPEYE (66) & POPEYE ACTION (?) TRADING CARDS 2 1/2" X 3 1/2"

The Ad-Trix Company of New York did not produce bubble gum or candy: it specialized in manufacturing trading card sets to be sold in variety stores and arcades. Their two sets "Popeye Trading Cards" and "Popeye Action Picture Cards" are examples of two different card formats used by the firm.

The set entitled Popeye Trading Cards is a standard card issue in terms of both mea-surements and format. The fronts have artwork drawings rendered in unimaginative shades of green, blue, and brown. There are no captions as such, merely dialogue spoken by the characters depicted. The backs are done in blue ink on gray stock and each carries an advertisement for a specious product rather than text. The card number is printed in a circle at bottom. Many of the scenes on the cards are violent: humans and animals being clobbered, vacuum cleaners sucking in babies, police being humiliated or attacked, etc.

As far as can be determined, the set named "Popeye Action Picture Trading Cards" duplicates all the cards of the first set, but with "action" created by moving a plastic screen across the surface of the cards. A card from this set is easily identified by the blurry features, an alteration of the original printing which allows the pictures to "move." These are not true 3-D cards, like "Tarzan's Savage Fury," but a "motion" or "action" enhancement employed from time to time by various companies. The reference number is R738-1.

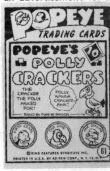

ITEM	EX	AVE
Cards		
"Trading Cards"	2.00	.50
"Action Picture"	2.50	.60
Sets		
"Trading Cards"	150.00	35.00
"Action Picture"	Set total unknown	

EXAMPLE OF HOW THE SAME
CARD FRONTS WERE USED
FOR BOTH THE "2-D" (TOP)
AND THE "3-D" (BOTTOM)
POPEYE SETS CREATED
BY AD-TRIX

POWER FOR PEACE (96)

2 1/2" X 3 3/4"

The 96-card "Power For Peace" series contains excellent color photographs of the most modern weaponry available to America's Armed Forces in 1954. Each "Official Navy Photo" is surrounded by a black frame line and white borders. The card number is printed on the back only, in a red "eagle" panel which also carries the set title. The card caption and descriptive text (blue ink on gray stock) occupy the rest of the back. The beautiful red, white & blue wrapper has the word "POWER" printed in yellow with a red outline. The 5-cent denomination box (furnished courtesy of Robert Marks) is the only type of packaging found as of this date. The reference number is R701-10.

ITEM	EX	AVE
Card	1.50	.25
Set	160.00	25.00
Wrapper	225.00	—
Box	250.00	50.00

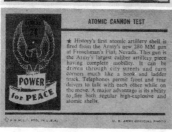

Power Peace

PREMIERE TRADING CARDS

"Premiere trading cards are made for use in vending machines manufactured exclusively by the Oak Manufacturing Company, Inc., Culver City, California." This statement, printed on the back of all Premiere Trading Cards, has led some collectors to suggest that they were strictly a regional issue. It is more likely, however, that they were sold wherever Oak Vending Machines were in use — and that means all across the country. The five sets of cards presented here share a number of characteristics: dull color photographs and uninspired style and format are their biggest liabilities. They were very poor competition for the more colorful and interesting gum cards of the period, and modern day collectors rarely ask for them. All five sets of Premiere Trading Cards were cited in the February, 1958 issue of The Card Collectors Bulletin, which makes it likely that they were originally marketed in 1957.

AIRPLANES (?)   2 5/8" X 3 3/4"

DESCRIPTION

Reference number		R724-1
Set total		unknown

VALUES	EX	AVE
Card	.50	.10

ANIMALS (21)   2 5/8" X 3 3/4"

DESCRIPTION

Reference number		R724-6
Set total		21 cards

VALUES	EX	AVE
Card	.50	.10
Set	12.00	2.25

African Lion and Lioness
American Black and Cinnamon Bears
Australian Dingo Puppy
Bactrian Camel and Young
Burchell's Zebra, Africa
California Grey Fox
Cheetah, Africa
Colobus-Monkey, Africa
Common Eland and Baby, Africa
European Fallow Deer
Hamadryas Baboon
Hippopotamus
Indian Elephant
Kodiak Bear, Alaska
Llama and Young, So. America
Northern Fur Seal Cow and Pup
Ocelot Kittens, American Tropics
Orang-utan
Polar Bear
Reticulated Giraffe, Africa
Sumatran Tiger

**WHEN YOU BUY CARDS. . .
MAKE SURE THE CONDITION MATCHES THE PRICE.**

ANTIQUE AUTOS (72)

2 5/8" X 3 3/4"

1902 FRANKLIN

This is a 1902 Franklin

H. H. Franklin Company, Syracuse, N.Y. John Wilkinson built an experimental four-cylinder, overhead valve, air-cooled car in Syracuse. It took two months to build, cost $1100, and sold for $1200. The bore and stroke was 3¼ x 3¾, peaking at 750 RPM and driving the car at the dizzy speed of 15 miles per hour. Franklin, a decorating company, undertook to manufacture these cars in quantity with immediate success.

"Premiere trading cards are made for use in vending machines manufactured exclusively by the Oak Manufacturing Company, Inc., Culver City, California."

DESCRIPTION

Reference number   R724-3
Set total   72 cards

VALUES	EX	AVE
Card	.50	.10
Set	40.00	8.00

PARTIAL CHECKLIST

A.B.C. (1908)
Achille Philion (1892)
Adams-Porwell (1898)
Alfa Romeo
Allord Cadillac
American Traveler (1908)
Arnolt Bristol
Auburn (1931)
Autocar (1906)
Beardsley Electric (1917)
Buick (1903)
Buick (1910)
Case (1911)
Chevrolet (1914)
Chrysler (1924)
Crane Simplex (1919)
Croxton Keeton (1910)
Cunnigham (1923)
Dajmar (1922)
Detroit Electric (1909)

Doble (1925)
Duesenberg (1921)
Duryea (1893)
Duryea (1894)
Etnyr (1909)
Fageol (1918)
Firestone-Columbus (1908)
Ford (1896)
F.W.D. (1910)
Haynes (1895)
Hupmobile (1911)
Interstate (1912)
LaSalle (1928)
Lincoln (1933)
Locomobile (1909)
Lozier (1913)
Marmon 34 (1916)
Maxwell (1910)
McFarlon (1911)
Mercer Raceabout (1920)

Miller (1930)
Mitchell (1907)
Moretti
National (1906)
National (1917)
Packard (1899)
Peerless (1900)
Rambler (1905)
Rouch & Long Electric (1914)
Regal Underslung (1913)
Reo (1904)
Rolls Royce (1926)
Ruxton (1929)
Scripps Booth (1915)
Studebaker (1915)
Stutz Bearcat (1915)
Thomas (1911)
Tourist (1908)
White Steamer (1903)
Winton (1897)

1908 TOURIST

This is a 1908 Tourist

Auto Vehicle Company, Los Angeles, Calif. This Company was organized in Los Angeles in 1902. Engine double opposed 5 x 5 30 H.P. water-cooled mounted under front seat. 90" wheelbase, 30 x 3½ tires, 1750 pounds. Planetary two-speed gear controlled by two side levers. Single chain drive. Company prospered for nine years and was put out of business by the Selden Patent suit.

THIS PARKHURST CARD SET ISSUED IN CANADA (V339-16) USED THE SAME FORMAT AS THE PREMIERE ANTIQUE AUTOS SERIES

BIRDS (42)

2 5/8" X 3 3/4"

BELTED KINGFISHER (F)

1 • The bird who uses his long, stout bill as a fishing tackle and as a pick axe when building his deep, dirt-tunnel nest.

2 • Larger than a Robin—13".

3 • Female has an additional chestnut band across the belly and chestnut shaded sides.

4 • Perches on a limb overhanging a stream or on a railing of a harbor boathouse with his tousled, crested head pitched forward and his tail jerking. When hovering over water, he "changes gear" in flight, alternating between rapid and slow wing beats before diving head-first and full speed after his prey.

5 • Call note is a rasping rattle or harsh staccato sound.

"Premiere trading cards are made for use in vending machines manufactured exclusively by the Oak Manufacturing Company, Inc., Culver City, California."

DESCRIPTION

Reference number   R724-2
Set total   42 cards

VALUES	EX	AVE
Card	.35	.05
Set	16.00	2.25

Acorn Woodpecker (M & F)
Allen's Hummingbird (young)
Avocet
Barn Owl
Belted Kingfisher (F)
Black-Tailed Gnatcatcher
Bluebird
Bobolink
California Jay (young)
California Thrasher
Cinnamon Teal (M & F)
Cliff Swallow
Cooper's Hawk
Costa Hummingbird (F on nest)

Golden-Crowned Kinglet (M)
Golden Eagle (young)
Great Blue Heron
Green-backed Goldfinch
Greenheaded Mallard Duck (M & F)
Hooded Oriole (M)
House Wren
Killdeer
Lark Sparrow
Meadowlark
Mockingbird
Mountain Chickadee
Oregon Junco (M)
Phainopepla (F)

Pied-Billed Grebe (young)
Pigmy Nuthatch
Pileolated Warbler (M)
Robin
Rose-Breasted Grosbeak (M)
Say's Phoebe
Scarlet Tanager (M)
Screech Owl
Shrike
Sierra Red Crossbill (M)
Steller's Jay
Western Gull (young)
White Pelican
Yellow Warbler

DOGS (48)

DESCRIPTION

Reference number	R724-4
Set total	48 cards

VALUES	EX	AVE
Card	.50	.10
Set	27.50	5.50

LABRADOR RETRIEVER

Not really a native of Labrador but of Newfoundland, this relative newcomer to the U.S. is proving himself an expert small-game retriever. His qualifications include a good nose, amazing endurance, and resistance to extremely cold water.

A favorite in duck hunting and field trials, he first gained popularity among English sportsmen in the last century. This good-looking animal is rapidly gaining favor in indoor bench-show competition.

He is strongly built, of medium-size, and has a short-haired coat that is usually black.

Premiere trading cards are made for use in vending machines manufactured exclusively by the Oak Manufacturing Company, Inc., Culver City, California.

PARTIAL CHECKLIST

Bedlington Terrier
Boston Terrier
Chow-chow
Dachshund (Smooth)
Doberman Pinscher
English Setter
Fox Terrier (Wirehaired)
Golden Retriever
Gordon Setter
Greyhound
Irish Setter
Irish Terrier
Labrador Retriever
Miniature Pinscher
Old English Sheepdog
Pekingese
Pointer
Pomeranian
Poodle
Pug
St. Bernard
Weimaraner
Welsh Terrier
Wolfhound (Irish)

PRESIDENT COINS (34)

The "President Coins" set by Topps demonstrates that perfection is an elusive thing. The cardboard package clearly states "Collect The Complete Set Of 33 Coins," and then has 34 numbered coins listed on the back flap! The "coins" are made of "golden" plastic and measure 1 1/8" in diameter. Each is numbered according to the subject's place in the sequence of First Executives, meaning that Grover Cleveland has two different coins (numbered "22" and "24"). The fronts bear bust portraits (in relief) of the Presidents, with their specific times in office printed at the sides. The reverses have an eagle atop a shield, in which the set title and coin number are printed (also in relief). The "Golden Coin" cardboard package does not have a price indicated on it. The reference number is PX15.

ITEM	EX	AVE
Coin	1.50	.30
Set, 34 coins	60.00	12.00
Package	30.00	8.00

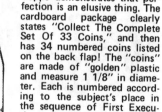

GOLDEN COIN

PRESIDENTS OF THE UNITED STATES

COLLECT THE COMPLETE SET OF 33 COINS

THE PRESIDENTS OF THE UNITED STATES

1. GEORGE WASHINGTON	11. JAMES K. POLK	18. ULYSSES S. GRANT	25. WILLIAM McKINLEY
2. JOHN ADAMS	12. ZACHARY TAYLOR	19. RUTHERFORD B. HAYES	26. THEODORE ROOSEVELT
3. THOMAS JEFFERSON	13. MILLARD FILLMORE	20. JAMES A. GARFIELD	27. WILLIAM H. TAFT
4. JAMES MADISON	14. FRANKLIN PIERCE	21. CHESTER A. ARTHUR	28. WOODROW WILSON
5. JAMES MONROE	15. JAMES BUCHANAN	22. GROVER CLEVELAND	29. WARREN G. HARDING
6. JOHN QUINCY ADAMS	16. ABRAHAM LINCOLN	23. BENJAMIN HARRISON	30. CALVIN COOLIDGE
7. ANDREW JACKSON	17. ANDREW JOHNSON	24. GROVER CLEVELAND	31. HERBERT C. HOOVER
8. MARTIN VAN BUREN			32. FRANKLIN D. ROOSEVELT
9. WM. HENRY HARRISON			33. HARRY S. TRUMAN
10. JOHN TYLER			34. DWIGHT D. EISENHOWER

ANOTHER COIN IN EVERY PACKAGE

UNFOLDED CARDBOARD
PACK HAD THE PRESIDENT
COINS CHECKLIST PRINTED
ON THE BACK

PRESIDENTS (32)

1 7/16" X 2 3/16"

The value of the early card catalogs is evident in the identification of this "Presidents" set issued by Cracker Jack. The card itself is devoid of any copyright or credit lines. Were it not for the "leaf borders" reference in the 1960 American Card Catalog section on Cracker Jack issues, cards of this series would probably have been assigned to the "anonymous" group (which is the "Twilight Zone" of card collecting). The presidential portraits are brown in tone, and the ornate borders are a wavy leaf design. On the backs, biographical details are given for each subject. The cards are not numbered per se, but they do list each First Executive's place in the presidential sequence (see the card back illustrated for Cleveland).

It is assumed that these Presidents cards were packed in boxes of Cracker Jack, and the year of issue, according to The Card Collectors Bulletin, was 1957. The reference number is R720-7.

ITEM	EX	AVE
Card	2.00	.35
Set	75.00	12.50

George Washington (1)
John Adams (2)
Thomas Jefferson (3)
James Madison (4)
James Monroe (5)
John Quincy Adams (6)
Andrew Jackson (7)
Martin Van Buren (8)
William Henry Harrison (9)
John Tyler (10)
James Polk (11)
Zachary Taylor (12)
Millard Fillmore (13)
Franklin Pierce (14)
James Buchanan (15)
Abraham Lincoln (16)

Andrew Johnson (17)
Ulysses S. Grant (18)
Rutherford B. Hayes (19)
James Garfield (20)
Chester A. Arthur (21)
Grover Cleveland (22) (24)
William McKinley (23)
Theodore Roosevelt (25)
William H. Taft (26)
Woodrow Wilson (27)
Warren Harding (28)
Calvin Coolidge (29)
Herbert Hoover (30)
Franklin Roosevelt (31)
Harry S. Truman (32)
Dwight D. Eisenhower (33)

PRESIDENTS OF THE UNITED STATES (33)

2 11/16" X 2 3/4"

Issued in 1960, "Presidents of the United States" cards were printed in panels of three on the backs of 20-count Bazooka Gum Boxes. The portraits are black, gray, and white, and contrast is added by means of horizontal lines drawn across the subjects. The starry frames are blue in the top half and red in the bottom half. The cards are numbered, so to speak, by the sequence of presidential terms. There are 33 in the set. The reference number is R714-28.

ITEM	EX	AVE
Card	1.00	.20
Set	40.00	8.00
Panel	5.00	1.50
Box	25.00	6.00

George Washington — 1st President
John Adams — 2nd President
Thomas Jefferson — 3rd President
James Madison — 4th President
James Monroe — 5th President
John Quincy Adams — 6th President
Andrew Jackson — 7th President
Martin Van Buren — 8th President
William H. Harrison — 9th President
John Tyler — 10th President
James Polk — 11th President

Zachary Taylor — 12th President
Millard Fillmore — 13th President
Franklin Pierce — 14th President
James Buchanan — 15th President
Abraham Lincoln — 16th President
Andrew Johnson — 17th President
Ulysses S. Grant — 18th President
Rutherford B. Hayes — 19th President
James A. Garfield — 20th President
Chester Arthur — 21st President
Grover Cleveland — 22nd & 24th President

Benjamin Harrison — 23rd President
William McKinley — 25th President
Theodore Roosevelt — 26th President
William H. Taft — 27th President
Woodrow Wilson — 28th President
Warren Harding — 29th President
Calvin Coolidge — 30th President
Herbert Hoover — 31st President
Franklin D. Roosevelt — 32nd President
Harry Truman — 33rd President
Dwight Eisenhower — 34th President

RAILROAD TRADING CARDS (?)   2 1/4" X 3 1/2"

Hey Kids!
You'll get railroad trading cards in every box of Brach's Choo Choo Mix, made in America's biggest candy factory.

Brach's FINE CANDIES

Brach's modern plant with 20 acres of floor space and staffed by skilled candy craftsmen produces over 100 different kinds of candy. They're made to taste better — try some soon!

Locomotive Illustration courtesy Electro Motive Division — General Motors.

BURLINGTON LINES' Zephyrs streak over 11,000 miles in 14 states from Chicago to serve the Corn Belt, the wheat region, the cattle country, and many scenic wonderlands in the heart of the Rockies.

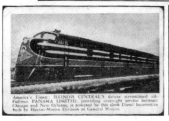

America's Finest: ILLINOIS CENTRAL'S deluxe streamlined all-Pullman PANAMA LIMITED, providing overnight service between Chicago and New Orleans, is powered by this sleek Diesel locomotive built by Electro-Motive Division of General Motors.

A Winner For Dinner

SCHMIDT'S **Blue Ribbon** BREAD

The multi-color drawings of streamlined diesel locomotives which appear in Brach's "Railroad Trading Cards" were created from artwork provided by the Electro-Motive Division of General Motors. The backs contain the statement, "HEY KIDS! You'll get railroad trading cards in every box of Brach's Choo Choo Mix, made in America's biggest candy factory." These Brach cards have a flat finish and are rectangular in shape; the same pictures — printed on glossy stock with rounded corners — have been found with bread company advertising and with blank backs. The length of the Brach set is not known (11 titles have been registered with the Hobby Card Index). It was issued in 1955. No "Choo Choo Mix" packaging has been seen to date. The reference number is R797.

ITEM	EX	AVE
Card	2.00	.50

RAILS AND SAILS (200)   2 5/8" X 3 3/4"

If you like trains and ships, Topps' "Rails and Sails" is the set for you! This 1955 series of 200 cards depicts 130 railroad locomotives and cars and 70 types of sailing vessels. The gorgeous color and excellent detail work on each artwork picture have made this series famous among collectors. The train designs have

white borders on front, and the card number is located in a semaphore accent on the back. The ship cards are borderless, and the card number for them is printed next to an anchor in the bottom left corner on the reverse. For reasons yet to be determined, 100 cards of this series are easy to find (1-80 &131--150),

while 100 others (81-130 & 151-200) are twice as hard to get. Some of the cards were distributed in a promotion with Doeskin Tissues; these have wide side borders and the Doeskin name is printed on the back. Both the "repeating design" 1-cent wrapper and the single-design 5-cent wrapper are red, white & blue in color. The reference number is R714-17. NOTE: printing defects are common in this set and they should be taken into consideration when grading.

ITEM	EX	AVE
Cards		
1-80 & 131-150	2.00	.35
81-130 & 151-200	4.00	.75
Set	700.00	125.00
Wrappers		
1-cent	35.00	––
5-cent	15.00	––
Boxes		
1-cent	300.00	70.00
5-cent	200.00	45.00

"Mississippi" Natchez & Hamburg Railroad

Refrigerator Car Railway Express Agency

24 'The Mississippi' Natchez & Hamburg

WHAT DID THE CRY 'DOWN BRAKES' MEAN?

This little locomotive was the first to appear along the river of that name, running on the Natchez & Hamburg R.R. on the east bank. There was no railroad west of the Mississippi River until 1857. The "Mississippi" is noteworthy for its unusual cab, a large, open structure covering almost the entire locomotive, with a long pipe leading to the whistle extending out of the roof. The locomotive was probably originally built without any cab, and it is not known when the cab shown may have been added.

To set the locomotive and car brakes as quickly as possible.

37 Refrigerator Car Railway Express Agy.

HOW MUCH DOES A LOCOMOTIVE COST?

Express refrigerator cars are used for the rapid transportation of milk, eggs, and other fresh dairy products and are often owned by the American Railway Express, or by groups of dairymen. Usually longer than regular refrigerator cars, they are designed to be operated either as part of a passenger train, or as solid trains of express refrigerator cars. For this reason they are usually fitted with passenger car type trucks, couplers and draft gear equipment.

A modern three- or four-unit diesel locomotive costs more than $500,000.

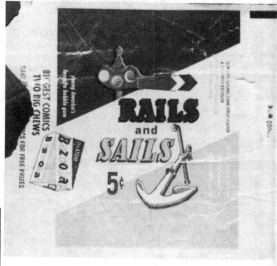

RED ARROW EXPRESS *Swiss Railways*

LEFT: DOESKIN TISSUE VARIETY
HAS WIDE BORDERS ON THE SIDES

87 Early Switcher, 0-4-0 Type, 1866
88 Electric Type, Great Northern Railways
89 Passenger Car, Lackawanna Railroad, c.1870
90 Incline, Mauch Chunk, c.1830
91 Theatrical Car, Private Owner, c.1900
92 Demonstration Locomotive, Stevens Design, 1826
93 "John Bull" Camden & Amboy Railroad
94 Experimental Locomotive, Fontaine Design, c.1885
95 0-6-0 Switcher, Missouri Pacific Railroad
96 Dining Car, Pennsylvania Railroad
97 Sugar Cane Car, Plantation Use
98 Ore Car, Great Northern Railway
99 Automobile Boxcar, N.Y. Central Railroad
100 Private Car, Delaware & Hudson Railroad
101 "Joshua Rhodes" First Porter Locomotive
102 Steam Streamliner, New York Central Railroad
103 Refrigerator Car, Railway Express
104 The "Hiawatha" C.M.St. P.&P. Railroad
105 Narrow Gauge, Sandy River Railroad, c.1910
106 "Best Friend" South Carolina Railroad
107 The "Pioneer First" Chicago Locomotive
108 Subway Train, New York City
109 Electric Type, Italian State Railways
110 Electric Type, New York Central Railroad
111 Streamlines Steam Locomotive, B&O Railroad
112 0-8-0 Switcher, Missouri Pacific Railroad
113 Camel Type, Baltimore & Ohio Railroad, c.1855
114 "Old Ironsides" First Baldwin Locomotive, 1832
115 Grasshopper Type, Baltimore & Ohio Railroad
116 Multiple-unit Train, New York Central Railroad
117 Open-end Day Coach, D.I. & W. Railroad, c.1890
118 Electric Type, Virginian Railway
119 High-pressure Locomotive, D&H Railroad
120 Cab Forward Locomotive, Southern Pacific Railroad
121 ACF Talgo, Lightweight Streamliner, 1954
122 Steam Locomotive, B&O Railroad
123 Red Arrow Express, Swiss Railways
124 Monster, Camden & Amboy Railroad
125 Steam Streamliner, North & West Railroad
126 Steam Locomotive, Union Pacific Railroad
127 Single Wheeler, Reading Rcilroad, c.1880
128 Steel Boxcar, Private Owner
129 Baldwin Locomotive, 4-2-0 Type
130 First "Zephyr" Burlington Route
SHIPS
131 War Galley, 12th Century Venetian Craft
132 Whale Back, Great Lakes Cargo Steamer
133 Destroyer, United States Warship
134 Caravel, 16th Century Light Vessel
135 Express Cruiser, Chris Craft Pleasure Boat
136 Norwegian Long Ship, Viking Raider
137 Santa Maria, 15th Century Carrack

138 Fishing Vessel, Java Sea Inter-island
139 Skaffie, Scottish Fishing Boat
140 U.S.C.G.C. Comanche, Coast Guard Cutter
141 Canal Boat, Erie River Vessel
142 Charles H. West, Mississippi Stern Wheeler
143 Indian Canoe, Birch Bark, American
144 Flat Boat, Early Western Cargo Carrier
145 Anne Morgan, New York Harbor Tug Boat
146 East Indiaman, English Merchant Ship
147 Show Boat, Mississippi River Steamer
148 Herring Drifter, English Fishing Boat
149 Fishing Junk, Modern Chinese Fishing Vessel
150 Outrigger Canoe, Malay Trading Boat
151 Ferryboat Double-ended, New York Harbor
152 Queen Elizabeth, Luxury Liner
153 Fishing Cruiser, Pleasure Power Boat
154 Submarine, U.S. Navy
155 Oyster Boat, Chesapeake Bay Fishing Boat
156 Greek War Ship, Ancient Fighting Galley
157 New Tender, U.S. Navy
158 Dutch Botter Zuiderzee, Sailing Craft
159 Ore Carrier, Great Lakes Freighter
160 Trawler, British Steam Power Fisherman
161 Freighter, General Cargo Carrier
162 Egyptian Ship, Oared Merchantman
163 English Hoy, 18th Century Workboat
164 Catamaran, American Design
165 Tramp Steamer, Steam Merchantman
166 Sub-chaser, U.S. Navy
167 Light Ship, Danish Coast Guard
168 Surf Boat, U.S. Coast Guard
169 Oil Tanker, Sea-going Gas Station
170 Steam Packet, Early Steamship
171 Brigantine, Early Sailing Vessel
172 S.S. United States, Passenger Liner
173 Hawaiian Liner, Luxury Cruise Ship
174 Torpedo Boat, U.S. Navy Patrol Ship
175 Miss Liberty, Sightseeing Boat
176 Gloucesterman, Fishing Schooner
177 Racing Boat, Slo-mo-shon IV
178 Cruiser, U.S. Navy
179 Crash Boat, Air Force Rescue Launch
180 U.S.S. Indiana, U.S. Navy, 1894
181 Tuna Clipper, American Fishing Boat
182 Harbor Dredge, Work Barge
183 Speed Boat, Blue Bird II, Custom Built
184 Constitution, Revolutionary Warship
185 Whale Ship, Floating Factory
186 Salvage Tug, Royal British Navy
187 Fire Boat, New York City
188 S.S. Caronia, Passenger Liner
189 Landing Ship, U.S. Navy
190 U.S.S. Missouri, U.S. Navy
191 Hastings Lugger, British Fisherman
192 Shrimp Boat, Fish Trawler
193 Minesweeper, U.S. Navy
194 Cable, English Offshore Workboat
195 Great Eastern, Cable Ship
196 Roman Trireme, War Vessel
197 English Warship, Medieval Fighting Craft
198 Tow Boat, Tennessee River Barge
199 Hospital Ship, U.S. Navy
200 Flattop, U.S. Navy Aircraft Carrier

1 "999" Locomotive, New York Central Railroad, c.1895
2 Covered Hopper Car, Private Owner
3 Electric Locomotive, Pennsylvania Railroad
4 First Electric Type, New York Central Railroad
5 "Daylight" Streamliner, Southern Pacific Railroad
6 Camelback Locomotive, Central Railroad of New Jersey
7 Electric Locomotive, French National Railways
8 Electric Locomotive, C.M.St.P.&P. Railroad
9 Steel Caboose, Clinchfield Railroad
10 Ballast Dump Car, Private Owner
11 Stock Car, Missouri Pacific Railroad
12 Steam Turbine Locomotive, Pennsylvania Railroad
13 Three-dome Tank Car, Private Owner
14 Wooden Tank Car, Private Owner, c.1900
15 Chlorine Container Car, Private Owner
16 Enclosed Cab Locomotive, Canadian Pacific Railroad
17 Depressed-center Flat Car
18 Steam Locomotive, New Zealand Government Railroad
19 Tank Locomotive, British Railways
20 Steel Box Car, Pennsylvania Railroad
21 Diesel Locomotive, Minneapolis & St. Louis Railway
22 Shark Nose Diesel Locomotive, Pennsylvania Railroad
23 PCC Trolley, Modern Streamliner, 1954
24 "Mississippi" Natchez & Hamburg Railroad, c.1838
25 "North Star" English Single Wheeler, c.1850
26 Diesel Switcher, National Railways of Mexico
27 Rack-rail Locomotive, Mt. Washington Railway, 1870
28 Electric Locomotive, Coal Mining, c.1920
29 Ballast Hopper Car, Western Pacific Railroad
30 "William Mason" Baltimore & Ohio Railroad, 1856
31 Wedge Snow Plow, New Haven Railroad
32 Diesel Streamliner, Union Pacific Railroad
33 First Consolidation, 2-8-0 Locomotive, c.1870
34 Rotary Snow Plow, Long Island Railroad
35 Inspection Engine, Lehigh Valley Railroad
36 Diesel Switcher, Missouri Pacific Railroad
37 Refrigerator Car, Railway Express Agency
38 Pacific Type Locomotive, Pennsylvania Railroad
39 Steam Locomotive, Climax-geared Type, c.1910
40 "Holman's Absurdity" Experimental Locomotive, c.1897
41 First Diesel, Central Railroad of New Jersey
42 Diesel Switcher, Southern Pacific Railroad

43 Wooden Caboose, Missouri Kansas Texas Lines
44 Muddigger" Baltimore & Ohio Railroad, 1844
45 Switching Engine Diesel—hydraulic
46 Birney Trolley Car, Safety Type, c.1925
47 Forney Locomotive, New York Elevated, c.1880
48 Bay-window Caboose, Baltimore & Ohio Railroad
49 "Fireless Cooker" Switching Locomotive, c.1912
50 "Rocket" Long Island Railroad
51 Gas-turbine Locomotive, Union Pacific Railroad
52 Diesel Locomotive, New Haven Railroad
53 Vista Dome Coach, Burlington Lines
54 Gas-electric Car, New Haven Railroad
55 "York" Baltimore & Ohio Railroad, 1831
56 "General" Civil War Locomotive
57 Steam Locomotive, Great Northern Railroad
58 "Lafayette" Baltimore & Ohio Railroad, 1837
59 Sailing Car, Baltimore & Ohio Railroad, 1830
60 Stephenson's "Rocket" English Locomotive, 1829
61 Street Car, Horse-drawn, c.1885
62 McKeen Motor Car, Union Pacific Railroad
63 "Eddy Clock" Boston & Albany Railroad, c.1855
64 One-dome Tank Car
65 Casey Jones' Locomotive, Illinois Central Railroad, c.1900
66 Cable Car, San Francisco
67 Live Poultry Car, Private Owner
68 Diesel Locomotive, New Haven Railroad
69 Crampton Locomotive, Camden & Amboy Railroad
70 Electric Locomotive, New Haven Railroad
71 Horse Treadmill Car, Baltimore & Ohio Railroad
72 8-wheel Trolley, New York & Queens Co. Railway Company
73 Wrecking Crane, Lehigh Valley Railroad
74 Wooten Camelback Locomotive, Reading Railroad, 1880
75 Rail Diesel Car, Budd Company
76 "Sandusky" Mad River & Lake Erie Railroad, 1837
77 Observation Car, Rock Island Railroad
78 First Mogul, New Jersey Railroad & Transport Co.
79 Stourbridge, Lion Steam Locomotive, 1829
80 Steam Locomotive, Shay-geared Type, c.1905
81 South Carolina, Double-ender Type
82 Diesel Locomotive, Egyptian States Railways
83 Commodore Vanderbilt, N.Y.C. Railroad
84 Pulpwood Car, Louisiana & Arkansas Railway
85 "20th Century" New York Central Railroad, 1902
86 Articulated Type, N.&W. Railroad

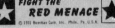

Bowman Gum's "Red Menace" is one of the most popular and colorful trading card sets of the post World War II era. The series was a product of the "scare years" which saw communist takeovers in Eastern Europe, the invasion of Korea, Russian A-bomb tests, and the emergence of leftist political movements in Latin America. The glorious artwork reminds collectors of "War Gum" and "Horrors of War," sets produced before World War II when Bowman operated under the name "Gum, Inc." Some of the cards, like No. 19, "Atomic Doom," and No. 23, "Ghost City," were positively frightening. There are 48 cards in the set, which was issued by Bowman in 1951. Each card has the subheading "Children's Crusade Against Communism" printed on the back at the top. The card number, card title, and text are found below. The cardboard stock on the reverse may be gray or tan: every card comes in both colors. The wrapper is blue (5-cent denomination only) with white and red stars and the words "Red Menace" printed in a blood-red color. The reference number is R701-12.

ITEM	EX	AVE
Card		
Gray Back	8.00	2.00
Tan Back	10.00	2.50
Sets		
Gray backs	500.00	110.00
Tan backs	600.00	135.00
Wrapper	200.00	—

1 Reds Invade South Korea
2 MacArthur Heads UN Forces
3 Slave Labor
4 "Mustangs" Rout Red Planes
5 Hill 303
6 Landing at Inchon
7 Trouble on the Docks
8 Bridging a Stream Under Fire
9 Police State
10 Lieutenant Russell Brown
11 Fleeing the Reds
12 Heroes of Turkey
13 Putting Out Atomic Fire
14 Sabres Win Air Battle
15 Red Battle Wagon
16 Negro GIs Hold Line

17 War in Malaya
18 General Walton H. Walker
19 Atomic Doom
20 "Big Mo" in Action
21 Mined Harbor
22 Alaska Lookout
23 Ghost City
24 General "Ike" in Command
25 Red Rule in Manchuria
26 Finns Defend Country
27 Red Guerrillas in Greece
28 Berlin Airlift
29 Red Riot in Bogota
30 Helicopters in Action
31 Case of Cardinal Mindzenty
32 UN Counterattack

33 Berlin Kidnaping
34 "Tiny Tim"
35 Visit by Red Police
36 Commander in Korea
37 Concentration Camp
38 "Lightning Joe" Collins
39 Soviet Rocket Fighter
40 Frontier Patrol
41 To the Mines
42 Naval Chief
43 Huk Raiders
44 One-man Stand
45 Ambush in Indo-China
46 Fighting Marine
47 War-maker
48 "Doughboy's General

HALT! Mousey Tung says, "Go back three pages."
"No, go forward three pages." "No, go back three pages."
"No, go forward three pages." . . .

RIDDLES & FORTUNES (?)

2 3/8" X 2 1/2"

You have to look closely at these "Swell Bubble Gum" wrappers to see the tiny "riddle" and "fortune" compartments printed on the left-hand edge. The nearly-square wrapper is red and white in the center with alternating blue and red strips on either side. The issue was first reported in the June, 1959 edition of The Card Collectors Bulletin. It is of far greater interest to wrapper and "type" collectors than to mainstream card enthusiasts. The reference number is R788-5.

ITEM	EX	AVE
Wrapper	10.00	——

ROBIN HOOD (60)

2 1/2" X 3 1/2"

The "Robin Hood" set of 60 cards was marketed by Topps in 1957. All the color photographs were taken from a 1950's rendition of the film starring Richard Greene. The cards are captioned on both front and back, with the front title printed in a red sword design. The story area on the back is gray with black print, surrounded by a pale green border. Robin Hood cards are so numerous, in proportion to the number of wrappers found, that we assume they were issued by Topps in cello packs and vending box "bricks" (500 cards). The "Lucky Penny" card was an advertising insert found in 5-cent packs (it was also inserted into other Topps sets), and it carries pictures of both Bazooka and Blony Gum on the back. The reference number is R714-18. NOTE: cards with printing streaks cannot be graded excellent.

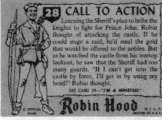

ITEM	EX	AVE
Card	2.50	.50
Set	180.00	35.00
Wrappers		
1-cent	55.00	——
5-cent	125.00	——
Lucky Penny		
Card	10.00	2.00

1 Strange Welcome	31 Taking the Treasure
2 "Pay or Else"	32 Striking by Surprise
3 Sheriff's Justice	33 "Duel, Villain!"
4 "Call the Guards"	34 Robin's Victory
5 "I Demand Justice"	35 Robin is Wounded
6 Sinister Plot	36 To the Rescue
7 Ready for Battle	37 Setting the Trap
8 Clashing Steel	38 The Friar's Decision
9 "Fight for Justice!"	39 Overhearing the News
10 Flashing Swords	40 "I'm Not Afraid"
11 The Holdup	41 Strange Champion
12 Joining the Outlaws	42 Choosing Weapons
13 Robin Hood, Outlaw	43 Ready for Combat
14 Evil Prince John	44 Watching the Battle
15 Superhuman Strength	45 Fight to the Death
16 Little John's Task	46 Robin in Armor
17 Forest Combat	47 Deadly Duel
18 Robin Makes a Friend	48 "Surrender or Die!"
19 A Fearful Sight	49 The Sheriff Dares Robin
20 The Message	50 "The Greatest Archer"
21 The Raid	51 John is Worried
22 "Surround the Camp"	52 Robin Takes Aim
23 Aiming at Robin	53 "I Can't Believe It!"
24 Ready and Waiting	54 Curious Visit
25 A Soldier Falls	55 "Hail King Richard"
26 Suspecting Trouble	56 Blocked Passage
27 Friar Hears the Plan	57 Surprise Visit
28 Call to Action	58 "Fight, Traitor!"
29 "I'm a Minstrel"	59 Blocking the Blow
30 Robin's Disguise	60 Justice Triumphs

ROUND—UP (80)

"Roundup" is a beautifully-designed set of 80 cards which deals with the lives and adventures of some of America's most famous frontiersmen and western characters (see the side panel illustrated below). Each person is featured in a series of ten multicolor-artwork cards. The card caption on front is printed in a red panel next to the yellow "longhorn" box containing

the subject's name. The text on back is limited to a few lines of print and then switches over to a four-cell illustrated strip. The title of the next card in the set is given at the bottom. The 1-cent wrapper is made of durable wax paper and is blue with yellow and red accents. The 5-cent wrapper is composed of more fragile layered cellophane and it is mostly red, with blue and white accents. A paper version of the 5-cent wrapper has also been found. The box is yellow and has a two-gun marshall picture on the left side of the lid. The set was issued by Topps in 1956. The reference number is R714-3.

ITEM	EX	AVE
Card	2.00	.35
Set	190.00	35.00
Wrappers		
1-cent	25.00	——
5-cent	100.00	——
Box	250.00	50.00

1	Wild Bill Hickok	11	Calamity Jane	
2	Charge!	12	"Daring Rescue"	
3	Slashing Claws	13	Indian Attack	
4	Wild Bill Strikes!	14	Sharpshooting	
5	Quick Shooting	15	Reach	
6	Ready to Draw	16	Hooray for Jane!	
7	Fighting Fury	17	Rough Riding	
8	Pounding Hoofs	18	Fighting Mad	
9	Deadly Mistake	19	Queen of the Wild West	
10	The Last Shot	20	The Last Ride	

21	Buffalo Bill	41	Daniel Boone	61	Geronimo
22	Bullseye!	42	Captured!	62	Massacre!
23	Race with Death	43	Wagon Trail	63	Wall of Flame
24	Buffalo Hunt	44	Beating 'em Off	64	Double Crossed!
25	Surprise Raid	45	Pow-wow	65	Escape
26	Daring Jump	46	Flashing Knives	66	Revenge
27	The Royal Hunt	47	Dangerous Mission	67	Night Riders
28	Taking Aim	48	Storming the Walls	68	Flaming Terror
29	Roaring Welcome	49	Landslide!	69	Peace Talk
30	Frontier Fun	50	Frontier Justice	70	Fast Action
31	Wyatt Earp	51	Jesse James	71	Kit Carson
32	Put Down that Gun!	52	Cruel Beating	72	Bucking Broncos
33	Flying Fists	53	The Raid	73	Ambush!
34	Shower of Lead	54	Crossfire	74	Gun Duel
35	Wyatt's Big Fight	55	The Holdup	75	Perfect Shot
36	Running Battle	56	Trapped	76	The Chase
37	Rustlers	57	Daring Robbery	77	Independence Day
38	Gunfight	58	The Blast	78	Surrounded!
39	The Showdown	59	Fight for Life	79	Kit's Gamble
40	Leaping Fury	60	Sneak Attack	80	Indian War

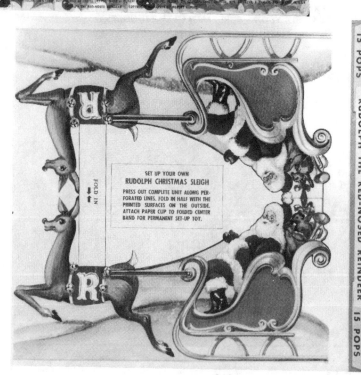

"RUDOLPH the red-nosed reindeer POPS" were issued by Topps during the Christmas holiday season of 1950. The 8 1/4" square box held 15 lollipops in the holly design which encircles Rudolph's head on the front of the box. The back of this box contains a punch-out-and-assemble "set-up toy" of Rudolph pulling Santa and his sleigh. As this format is exactly like the "Hoppy Pops" box described earlier in this book, it is likely that the lollipops had a decorative wax wrapper covering them, but none have been found to date. This item has not yet been assigned a reference number.

ITEM	EX	AVE
Box	20.00	6.00

SET UP YOUR OWN
RUDOLPH CHRISTMAS SLEIGH

PRESS OUT COMPLETE UNIT ALONG PERFORATED LINES. FOLD IN HALF WITH THE PRINTED SURFACES ON THE OUTSIDE. ATTACH PAPER CLIP TO FOLDED CENTER BAND FOR PERMANENT SET-UP TOY.

FOLD IN

15 POPS RUDOLPH THE RED-NOSED REINDEER 15 POPS

SCOOP (156)   2 1/16" X 2 15/16"

Once upon a time, "Scoop" was merely a classic non-sport set that was virtually unknown outside our sector of the hobby. Now that the "sports cards" in the series have been "discovered," demand for them specifically, and for the set in general, has risen dramatically. Scoop was issued in 1954 by Topps, whose advertising campaign called it "A prize collection of great American newspaper miniatures with full-color pictures of world headlines..." Portions of each card were covered with a black band ("Scratch It - Peel It - See It Now!") which had

to be removed before the entire card could be viewed. The fronts are multi-color artwork paintings of famous events, with a caption and date in a white box to one side. The horizontal backs are printed in newspaper format, with the story printed in column form plus a B&W picture of the subject. The card number is printed on the back only, and the next card in the series is named in a black panel at the bottom. The reference

number is R714-19. PRICE ADVISORY: the prices listed in the checklist below refer to cards WITHOUT the black scratch-off bands. We do not consider the set to be collectable with these bands intact. Our prices for the "sports" cards in this set will necessarily be lower than those found in the sport card marketplace.

ITEM	EX	AVE
Set	1500.00	325.00
Wrappers		
1-cent	40.00	––
5-cent	40.00	––
Boxes		
1-cent	250.00	60.00
5-cent	200.00	45.00

SCOOP CARDS CAME WITH TWO BLACK
SCRATCH-OFF BANDS ON THE FRONT

THE ORIGINAL ARTWORK FOR CARD NO. 42
"MASSACRE IN CHICAGO"

		EX	AVE			EX	AVE
1	San Francisco Earthquake — April 18, 1906	7.00	1.50	33	MacArthur Returns — October 20, 1944	4.00	.80
2	Fire Sweeps Chicago — October 8, 1871	4.00	.80	34	Doolittle Bombs Tokyo — April 18, 1942	7.00	1.50
3	Lindbergh Flies Atlantic — May 21, 1927	10.00	2.00	35	Gold Discovered — January 24, 1848	4.00	.80
4	Battleship Maine Blown Up — February 15, 1898	4.00	.80	36	Marines Land at Iwo Jima — February 19, 1945	4.00	.80
5	Lusitania Sinks — May 7, 1815	4.00	.80	37	John Brown's Raid — October 16, 1859	4.00	.80
6	Lincoln Shot — April 14, 1865	4.00	.80	38	Oklahoma Land Rush — April 22, 1889	4.00	.80
7	Monitor Battles Merrimac — March 9, 1862	4.00	80	39	Dempsey Defeats Williard — July 4, 1919	20.00	5.00
8	Alamo Falls — March 6, 1836	4.00	.80	40	Joe Louis New Champ — June 22, 1937	20.00	5.00
9	Garfield Shot — July 2, 1881	4.00	.80	41	Babe Ruth Sets Record — September 30, 1927	75.00	20.00
10	Panama Canal Opened — August 15, 1914	4.00	.80	42	Massacre in Chicago — February 14, 1929	4.00	.80
11	Statue of Liberty Unveiled — October 28, 1886	4.00	.80	43	Normandie Capsizes — February 9, 1942	4.00	.80
12	First Atom Bomb Dropped — August 6, 1945	4.00	.80	44	East Meets West — May 10, 1869	4.00	.80
13	Victory for Rough Riders — July 1, 1898	4.00	.80	45	Custer's Last Stand — June 25, 1876	7.00	1.50
14	President McKinley Shot — September 6, 1901	4.00	.80	46	Pony Express Starts — April 3, 1860	4.00	.80
15	First Airplane Flight — December 17, 1903	4.00	.80	47	Armistice Signed — November 11, 1918	4.00	.80
16	D—Day Landing on Normandy — June 6, 1944	4.00	.80	48	Blizzard Sweeps New York — March 11, 1888	4.00	.80
17	S.S. Titanic Sinks — April 15, 1912	4.00	.80	49	Black Tom Explodes — July 30, 1916	4.00	.80
18	World War I Declared — August 2, 1914	4.00	.80	50	Fulton's Steamboat — August 17, 1807	4.00	.80
19	Pearl Harbor Attacked — December 7, 1941	7.00	1.50	51	Washington Inaugurated — April 30, 1789	4.00	.80
20	Dirigible Hindenburg Burns — May 6, 1937	4.00	.80	52	Queen Elizabeth II Crowned — June 2, 1953	4.00	.80
21	U.S. Troops Reach France — June 26, 1917	4.00	.80	53	Gandhi Murdered — January 30, 1948	4.00	.80
22	United Nations Born — June 26, 1945	4.00	.80	54	Stock Market Crashes — October 29, 1929	4.00	.80
23	War in Korea — June 25, 1950	4.00	.80	55	Peary Discovers North Pole — April 6, 1909	4.00	.80
24	Retreat from Dunkirk — May 26, 1940	4.00	.80	56	Byrd Reaches South Pole — November 28, 1929	4.00	.80
25	King Edward Abdicates — December 11, 1936	4.00	.80	57	Victory in Europe — May 8, 1945	4.00	.80
26	Atlantic Charter Drafted — August 14, 1941	4.00	.80	58	Japanese Surrender — September 2, 1945	4.00	.80
27	Bob Feller Strikeout King — October 2, 1938	40.00	10.00	59	Big 3 Meet at Yalta — February 11, 1945	4.00	.80
28	Boston Tea Party — December 16, 1773	4.00	.80	60	Acrobat Crosses Niagara — September 14, 1860	4.00	.80
29	Battle of Britain — September 15, 1940	4.00	.80	61	Berlin Airlift Begins — April 1, 1948	4.00	.80
30	Landings on North Africa — November 8, 1942	4.00	.80	62	Bandits Rob Brink's — January 14, 1950	4.00	.80
31	Roosevelt Wins 4th Term — November 7, 1944	4.00	.80	63	Morro Castle Burns — September 8, 1934	4.00	.80
32	World War II Begins — September 1, 1939	4.00	.80				

		EX	AVE			EX	AVE
64	Quintuplets Born — May 28, 1934	4.00	.80	111	Declaration of Independence — July 4, 1776	7.00	1.50
65	Marciano K.O.'s Walcott — September 23, 1952	20.00	5.00	112	Gen Braddock Defeated — July 9, 1755	7.00	1.50
66	Jet Breaks Speed Record — October 29, 1953	4.00	.80	113	Spanish Armada Defeated — July 29, 1588	7.00	1.50
67	Korea Truce Signed — July 27, 1953	4.00	.80	114	Suez Canal Opened — November 17, 1869	7.00	1.50
68	Jet Passes Sound Barrier — October 14, 1947	4.00	.80	115	Napoleon Loses at Waterloo — June 18, 1815	7.00	1.50
69	Piccard Descends 2 Miles Under Sea — September 30, 1953	4.00	.80	116	Daimler Tests First Auto — November 10, 1886	7.00	1.50
70	Mt. Everest Climbed — May 28, 1953	4.00	.80	117	Flagpole-Sitting Record Set — July 20, 1930	7.00	1.50
71	John L. Sullivan Defeated — September 7, 1892	20.00	5.00	118	Julius Caesar Assassinated — March 15, 44 B.C.	7.00	1.50
72	Ederle Swims Channel — August 16, 1926	4.00	.80	119	Plague Sweeps London — May 8, 1665	7.00	1.50
73	Johnstown Flooded — May 31, 1889	4.00	.80	120	Mutiny on the Bounty — April 28, 1789	7.00	1.50
74	Mussolini Dead — April 27, 1945	4.00	.80	121	West Point Trains Cadets — April 29, 1812	7.00	1.50
75	Dillinger Shot — July 22, 1934	4.00	.80	122	"Wild Bill" Hickok Shot — August 5, 1876	7.00	1.50
76	Brooklyn Bridge Opened — May 24, 1883	4.00	.80	123	Boy Scouts Organized — February 8, 1910	7.00	1.50
77	Hurricane in Florida — September 19, 1947	4.00	.80	124	Top Nazis to Hang — September 30, 1946	7.00	1.50
78	War with Mexico — May 13, 1846	4.00	.80	125	New State of Israel — May 14, 1948	7.00	1.50
79	British Lose at New Orleans — January 8, 1815	7.00	1.50	126	Carlsen Quits Sinking Ship — January 10, 1952	7.00	1.50
80	Nathan Hale Hanged — September 22, 1776	7.00	1.50	127	Flying Saucers — July 29, 1952	7.00	1.50
81	John Paul Jones Wins Naval Battle — September 24, 1779	7.00	1.50	128	Jesse Owens Races Horse — December 26, 1936	12.50	2.50
82	Hamilton Shot in Duel — July 11, 1804	7.00	1.50	129	Ben Hogan New Golf King — July 10, 1953	12.50	2.50
83	Battle of Manila Bay — May 1, 1898	7.00	1.50	130	Braves Go to Milwaukee — March 18, 1953	35.00	8.00
84	Chief Red Cloud Defeated — August 2, 1867	7.00	1.50	131	Corrigan Flies Wrong Way — July 17, 1938	7.00	1.50
85	Jesse James Robs Train — July 21, 1873	7.00	1.50	132	Eisenhower Elected — November 4, 1952	7.00	1.50
86	Indians Defeat Gen. Crook — June 17, 1876	7.00	1.50	133	Erie Canal Opened — October 26, 1825	7.00	1.50
87	Joan of Arc Burned — May 30, 1431	7.00	1.50	134	First Balloon Flight — June 5, 1783	7.00	1.50
88	Troy Falls to Greeks — February 4, 1184 B.C.	7.00	1.50	135	Flood Kills Hundreds — May 18, 1927	7.00	1.50
89	Rome Burned — September 13, 64 A.D.	7.00	1.50	136	Franklin D. Roosevelt Dies — April 12, 1945	7.00	1.50
90	Columbus Discovers America — October 12, 1492	7.00	1.50	137	New York World's Fair — April 30, 1939	7.00	1.50
91	Pompeii Destroyed — June 28, 79 A.D.	7.00	1.50	138	Radar Beam Reaches Moon — January 10, 1946	7.00	1.50
92	U.S. Navy Battles Pirates — February 16, 1804	7.00	1.50	139	Air Speed Record Set — November 20, 1953	7.00	1.50
93	United States Gets Flag — June 14, 1777	7.00	1.50	140	British Burn White House — August 24, 1814	7.00	1.50
94	Lewis & Clark Reach Pacific — November 7, 1805	7.00	1.50	141	Cornwallis Surrenders — October 19, 1781	7.00	1.50
95	Chief Sitting Bull Killed — December 15, 1890	7.00	1.50	142	Gold Stored at Fort Knox — June 23, 1938	7.00	1.50
96	Geronimo Surrenders — September 3, 1886	7.00	1.50	143	Louis XVI Guillotined — January 21, 1793	7.00	1.50
97	Captain Kidd Hanged — May 24, 1701	7.00	1.50	144	Franklin's Famous Experiment — June 14, 1752	7.00	1.50
98	Witch-Hunts in Salem — September 22, 1692	7.00	1.50	145	Brodie Jumps Off Brooklyn Bridge — July 24, 1886	7.00	1.50
99	Fort Sumter Surrenders — April 13, 1861	7.00	1.50	146	"Liberty of Death" — March 23, 1775	7.00	1.50
100	Battle of Tippecanoe — November 7, 1811	7.00	1.50	147	Indians Sell Manhattan — April 1, 1623	7.00	1.50
101	Perry Opens Door to Japan — June 13, 1854	7.00	1.50	148	U.S. Buys Louisiana — October 19, 1803	7.00	1.50
102	Stanley Finds Livingston — November 10, 1871	7.00	1.50	149	Leif Ericsson Finds Finland — April 17, 1000 A.D.	7.00	1.50
103	Magellan's Ship Circles World — September 16, 1522	7.00	1.50	150	Pocahontas Saves Colonist — March 22, 1608	7.00	1.50
104	Pilgrims Land at Plymouth — December 26, 1620	7.00	1.50	151	United States Buys Alaska — March 30, 1867	7.00	1.50
105	U.S.S. Panay Sunk — December 12, 1937	7.00	1.50	152	Ship Sets Speed Record — July 15, 1952	7.00	1.50
106	Bridge Crashes — November 7, 1940	7.00	1.50	153	T.V.A. Completed — July 16, 1945	7.00	1.50
107	Circus Blaze — July 6, 1944	7.00	1.50	154	26-Inning Tie Game — May 1, 1920	50.00	15.00
108	Skyscraper Crash — July 28, 1945	7.00	1.50	155	Charge of the Light Brigade — October 25, 1854	7.00	1.50
109	Bikini A-Bomb Test — June 30, 1946	7.00	1.50	156	World's Largest Telescope Built — June 3, 1948	7.00	1.50
110	Notre Dame's 4 Horsemen — November 17, 1923	25.00	6.00				

SHIPS & PLANES (30)(30)

As you can see by our illustrations, Peco ship and plane cards were printed on the back panels of candy cigarette boxes. The artwork pictures — done in two shades of blue with red accents — were developed from actual photographs. The card number is printed in a red star on the

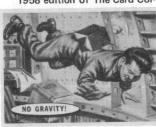

TWO SIZES

front. Each card can be found in two sizes (corresponding to the size of the candy box): 1 5/16" X 2 3/4" and 2 3/4" X 3 5/8". According to The Card Collectors Bulletin, these candy boxes were marketed in 1956. There are 30 cards in the series (each size has the same checklist). The reference number is R800.

ITEM	EX	AVE
Cards		
Small	1.50	.50
Large	2.00	.65
Sets		
Small	55.00	18.00
Large	75.00	22.50
Intact Boxes		
Small	10.00	3.00
Large	12.50	3.50

1 USS Constitution
2 Vultee Coronado
3 USS Chester — Cruiser
4 Vultee Liberator
5 USS Ranger — Aircraft Carrier
6 USS Saratoga — Aircraft Carrier
7 USS Missouri — Battleship
8 Grumman F6F Navy Fighter
9 Curtiss SB2C-3 Navy Bomber
10 USS Wasp — Aircraft Carrier
11 Landing Ship, Tanks — LST
12 USS Arkansas — Battleship
13 USS Constitution
14 USS Erie — Gunboat
15 USS Zane — Minesweeper

16 USS Bon Homme Richard
17 USS Texas — Battleship
18 USS Anderson — Destroyer
19 F-84G — Thunderjet Fighter
20 USS PT117 — Motor Torpedo Boat
21 F-86E — Sabre Jet
22 Lockheed F-94B ASAF
23 USS Minneapolis — Cruiser
24 Douglas XF4D-1 — Navy Fighter
25 USS Preble — Minelayer
26 USS Colorado — Battleship
27 USS PT 17 — Motor Torpedo Boat
28 USS 0-8 — Submarine
29 Goodyear L-1 Blimp
30 USS Hambleton — Destroyer

SPACE CARDS/TARGET: MOON (88)(88) 2 1/2" X 3 1/2"

To speculate as why Topps would issue identical sets of cards under different names is useless, because only the company knows, and they aren't telling. "Space Cards" and "Target: Moon" cards are identical front and back EXCEPT for the set title printed on the back. The former were first reported in the February, 1958 edition of The Card Collectors Bulletin, making it likely that the set was issued in 1957. Whether Target: Moon was issued at the same time, or later, is conjectural. The 88 cards of this category feature color drawings of futuristic scenes and events in man's conquest of space. The 1-cent and 5-cent wrappers for each series are similar in design but differ slightly in coloration and details. The reference number for "Space Cards" is R714-20a while the reference number for "Target: Moon" is R714-20b. NOTE: "Target: Moon" cards with salmon-colored backs were issued in a popsicle promotion in 1958.

ITEM	EX	AVE
Cards		
"Space"	3.00	.60
"Target"	5.00	1.00
Sets		
"Space"	315.00	60.00
"Target"	525.00	100.00
Wrappers		
"Space"		
1-cent	125.00	——
5-cent	100.00	——
"Target"		
1-cent	150.00	——
5-cent	125.00	——

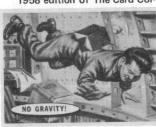

IDENTICAL EXCEPT FOR THE SET TITLE

THE ORIGINAL ARTWORK FOR CARD NO. 44, MOON MOUNTAIN CLIMBING (COURTESY OF BOB MARKS)

TWO DIFFERENT REVERSES FOR CARD NO. 44 (BOTTOM CARD IS THE POPSICLE TYPE)

OUTER SPACE STATION

68 OUTER SPACE STATION

As the first step to interplanetary travel, an outer space station is sent aloft from the moon. This listening post will record various phenomena of outer space and also act as a jumping off site for a trip to Mars and Venus. Soon a squad of interplanetary ships are anchored by the space station refueling while the space pilots are briefed for their Martian and Venus trips.

See Card No. 69—TAKEOFF FOR OTHER PLANETS

TARGET: MOON

1 Sputnik I
2 Dog in Sputnik II
3 Launching U.S. Satellites
4 Recovering the Rocket
5 Sputnik Descending
6 Three Stage Rocket
7 Target: Moon
8 Robot Nears Moon
9 Radio Telescope
10 Space Flight Headquarters

11 Testing a Space Pilot
12 Briefing for Space Flight
13 Space Suit
14 Preparing for Flight
15 Zero Hour
16 Strapped Down for Takeoff
17 Rocket Blastoff
18 Heading for Outer Space
19 Diagram of Spaceship
20 No Gravity!

A PARTIAL LID FROM THE DISPLAY BOX

21 Space Checker Game
22 Space's Practical Jokes
23 Meteor Peril
24 If Meteor Hit New York
25 Space Acrobat
26 Flying Practice
27 Fixing Meteor Damage
28 Sunset on the Earth
29 50 Miles to the Moon
30 Preparing to Land
31 Moon Landing
32 Rocket Jet Heat
33 First Men on the Moon
34 Moon Explorers
35 Lunar Scouting Patrol
36 Conquest of the Moon
37 High Jumping on the Moon
38 It's Easy—On the Moon!
39 Trapped in Meteor Shower
40 Lunar Crater

41 Famed Copernicus Crater
42 Moon Huts
43 Moon Surveying Squad
44 Moon Mountain Climbing
45 Photographing Moon Craters
46 Collecting Minerals on the Moon
47 Lunar Mists
48 Lunar Explosions
49 Palomar Observatory
50 Enjoying Earthshine
51 Eclipse of the Earth
52 Working in Space
53 Space Supply Depot
54 Assembling Supply Ship
55 Supplies for Moon Pioneers
56 Solar Generators
57 Lunar Airplant
58 Lunar City
59 Gymnastics on the Moon
60 Lunar Lookout Post
61 Farming on the Moon
62 Moon Trains
63 Space Message Center
64 Lunar Spaceport

65 Chasing Comets
66 Heading Home
67 Return to Earth
68 Outer Space Station
69 Takeoff for Other Planets
70 Refueling Interplanet Ship
71 Venus Dust Storms
72 Mysterious Mars
73 Martian Landscape
74 Martian Dust Storm
75 Martian Air Base
76 Visit to Mercury
77 Mercury's Amazing Climate
78 Studying the Sun's Surface
79 Melting in the Sun's Heat
80 Exploring Jupiter
81 Jupiter's Terrain
82 Hurricane on Jupiter
83 View of Saturn
84 Spectacular Saturn
85 Saturn's Rings
86 Pluto—The Coldest Planet
87 Discovering a New Sun
88 Life on Other Planets?

SPALDING SPORTS SHOW (?)   2" X 2 3/4"

Here's an interesting set that doesn't get any recognition from sports card collectors and researchers (they probably don't know it exists). It is a series of rust-colored cartoons "from the Spalding Sports Show as drawn by Willard Mullin." The cartoons are printed directly on the interior side of 1-cent Bazooka foil wrappers. The subject matter deals with all types of sports. The set was issued in 1949 (see illustration of page from Topps' September, 1949 price list). The number of cartoons in the set is unknown. The reference number is R414-1.

ITEM	EX	AVE
Cartoon/Wrapper	10.00	3.00

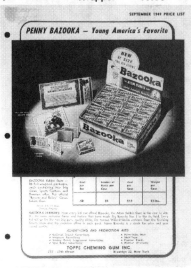

"SPORTS SHOW" WAS PACKED IN PENNY BAZOOKA PACKS

SPINS AND NEEDLES (80)   2 1/2" X 3 1/2"

The 80-card "Spins and Needles" set, marketed by Fleer in 1960, captured in cardboard some of the greats and not-so-greats of the early days of rock 'n roll. Each color picture is nicely decorated with a golden frame. The backs are printed in red and blue on shell-white stock, and they contain a biography of the personality. The card number is located on the reverse in a crown design (the crown is Fleer's logo). Cards are individually priced in the checklist below. The reference number is R730-4.

ITEM	EX	AVE
Set	300.00	60.00
Wrapper	75.00	——
Box	250.00	50.00

RECORDING STAR	EX	AVE
1 Della Reese	5.00	1.00
2 Jill Corey	2.50	.50
3 Jodie Sands	2.50	.50
4 Dick Roman	2.50	.50
5 Jimmy Clanton	2.50	.50
6 Julius La Rosa	2.50	.50
7 Paul Anka	6.00	1.20
8 Dorothy Collins	2.50	.50
9 Steve Lawrence	6.00	1.20
10 Betty Johnson	2.50	.50
11 Guy Mitchell	2.50	.50
12 Dale Hawkins	2.50	.50
13 Pat Boone	8.00	1.50
14 The Goofers	2.50	.50
15 Andy Williams	4.00	.80
16 Lu Ann Simms	2.50	.50
17 Don Cornell	2.50	.50
18 Tina Robin	2.50	.50
19 Nick Todd	2.50	.50
20 Leslie Uggams	2.50	.50
21 Lillian Briggs	2.50	.50
22 Rod Lauren	2.50	.50
23 Eydie Gorme	6.00	1.20
24 Sheb Wooley	2.50	.50
25 The Poni Tails	2.50	.50
26 Four Naturals	2.50	.50
27 Lloyd Arnold	2.50	.50

	EX	AVE
28 LaVerne Baker	2.50	.50
29 Lee Andrews	2.50	.50
30 Dee Clark	2.50	.50
31 The Drifters	10.00	2.00
32 Joe Medlin	2.50	.50
33 Mary Swan	2.50	.50
34 Danny & The Juniors	4.00	.80
35 The Brigidi Sisters	2.50	.50
36 Jerry Lee Lewis	8.00	1.50
37 Ersel Hickey	2.50	.50
38 Ruth Brown	2.50	.50
39 Roy Hamilton	2.50	.50
40 Bill Haley	15.00	3.00
41 Jimmy Dean	2.50	.50
42 George Hamilton IV	2.50	.50
43 The Gaylords	2.50	.50
44 Dion & The Belmonts	6.00	1.20
45 Les Paul & Mary Ford	2.50	.50
46 Budd & Travis	2.50	.50
47 Lloyd Price	2.50	.50
48 Clyde McPhatter	2.50	.50
49 The Kalin Twins	2.50	.50
50 Bobby Pedrick, Jr.	2.50	.50
51 Dick Caruso	2.50	.50
52 Jack Scott	2.50	.50
53 Somethin' Smith	2.50	.50
54 Carl Perkins	2.50	.50
55 The Four Coins	2.50	.50
56 The Four Freshmen	2.50	.50
57 The Crescendos	2.50	.50
58 The Casuals	2.50	.50
59 Duane Eddy	5.00	1.00
60 Bobby Rydell	6.00	1.20
61 Dave Castle	2.50	.50
62 Dave Apple	2.50	.50
63 The Impalas	2.50	.50
64 Bobby D'Fano	2.50	.50
65 Dicky Doo & The Don'ts	2.50	.50
66 Dolores Hawkins	2.50	.50
67 Bernie Early	2.50	.50
68 Sarah McLawler	2.50	.50
69 Sam Hawkins	2.50	.50
70 The Virtues	2.50	.50
71 Shirley & Lee	2.50	.50
72 The Skyliners	2.50	.50
73 Quintones	2.50	.50
74 Jan & Dean	5.00	1.00
75 Shirelles	10.00	2.00
76 Richard Otto	2.50	.50
77 Cappy Bianco	2.50	.50
78 Charlie Gracie	2.50	.50
79 Big Al Sears	2.50	.50
80 The Champs	2.50	.50

STATE & TERRITORIAL FLAGS (?)   1 5/8" X 2 3/8"

Cards of this series have no marks or printing to identify the issuing company, but the format and size clearly signal that they came from Cracker Jack. The multi-color flags pictured on the fronts are set on a large, cream-colored background, and the state or territory is named below. The backs contain a simple listing of the most important facts about each subject. The card corners are rounded and the front and back surfaces have a semi-gloss finish. The set was first mentioned in the June, 1956 edition of The Card Collectors Bulletin. There are 54 cards in the series. The reference number is R720-4.

First Settlers	Amer. Pioneers
Admitted to Union	1889
Population	619,636
Capital	Bismarck
Largest City	Fargo
Prin. Agri. Prod.	Wheat, Potatoes
Prin. Industry	Livestock raising
Scenic Feature	N. Dak. Bad Lands
State Flower	Wild Rose
Nickname	Flickertail State

ITEM	EX	AVE
Card	1.00	.25
Set	60.00	15.00

SUPER CIRCUS (19K)

1 5/16" X 3"

Super Circus tight-rope walker balances dangerously high above the arena!
© 1952. Mars Inc., makers of fine Candy bars.

The cards entitled "Super Circus" were printed on Mars candy bar trays. Each card was machine-scored around the edges for easy removal, and single cards have tiny attachment "nubs" on the perimeter. The artwork is very simple: red and blue drawings, with a line of text printed underneath. A copyright date of 1952 appears on every card. The set total has not been determined and card No. 19 is the highest number seen. The reference number is R801.

ITEM	EX	AVE
Card	5.00	1.50

SUPER DUPER KNOWS (?)

3 5/8" X 4 5/16"

"Super Duper Knows" is a humorous series of one-cell comics printed on the exterior (or "advertising") side of 1-cent Shelby "Super Duper Blo Bubble" gum. The latter was cut "chunk" style so the wrapper was twisted around each piece. The character named "Super Duper" is a talking gum bubble used to illustrate riddles and jokes. The wrappers are found in various color combinations of red, blue, and green, and there is at least one comic per wrapper (along with parts of two others). Occasionally, two complete comics are found on one wrapper. This item may not look like much, but it is highly sought after by wrapper and "type" collectors. The year of issue appears to be 1959. The reference number is R802.

ITEM	EX	AVE
Wrapper	25.00	——

TALES OF THE VIKINGS (66)

2 1/2" X 3 1/2"

63 – Scar Face
TALES OF THE
VIKINGS
UNITED ARTISTS TV PRESENTATION
© BRYNAFROD SA 1960   PRINTED IN U.S.A. BY AD-TRIX, CORP., NEW YORK 13

Here's a sure formula for success: take a lousy motion picture and make a lousy card set about it! Ad-Trix did just that in 1960 with this 66-card salute to the utterly forgetable United Artists production called "Tales of the Vikings." The card fronts contain photographs from the film, and each can be found in three monochrome shades (or "casts") of color: green, gray, and rust. Regardless of the color of the picture on front, the humorous caption, set title (with illustrations), and other print on the card backs is all navy blue (on gray stock). The cards are numbered. The tiny attachment "nubs" on the edges indicate that they were issued in sheets or strips. The reference number is R738-5.

1 This Is Murder
2 Two Heads Are Thicker Than One
3 Home from the Hill
4 Try and Get Me
5 This Is Legal?!
6 Having a Ball
7 Opp's I'm Sorry
8 I'll Take Half
9 Think Fast
10 Down You Go
11 Please Don't
12 These "Compacts" Are Easy to Pack
13 I Wonder Where the Yellow Went
14 I Missed
15 Say Your Prayers
16 Catch Me
17 Put It Down and I'll Hit You
18 I've Got the Potatoes...Where's the Meat
19 You're Next!
20 Crew Cut
21 Where's the White Charger?
22 Let's Re-arrange the Furniture
23 Your Move John
24 Where's the Target? On the Wall. Where's the Wall?
25 All Tied Up in Knots
26 Would You Mind Moving that Sword Off My Foot
27 Ouch!
28 Killer
29 Practice Makes Perfect
30 Devil May Care
31 You Win!
32 Batter-Up!
33 I'm Just Getting the Hang of This
34 Patty Cake...Patty Cake...!
35 Rock'n Roll Waltz
36 I've Got Something in My Eye
37 The Dude
38 The Firing Squade
39 You Meany
40 Look Who's Coming!
41 They're Mine
42 All Dressed Up
43 Perfect Target
44 I'm Meeting My Mother-in-Law
45 Convince Me!
46 Where's the Mouse?
47 Ready—Aim—Back Fire
48 Who's Up First
49 Interferance
50 Give It to Me
51 Shave, Sir?
52 Have Sword—Will Cut
53 Like an Invisable Shield—Protecting You
54 Toothpick—Anyone?
55 Guess Who
56 You're Peeking
57 Was It a Bird?
58 The Cheering Squad
59 Three Squares
60 Stop Rocking the Boat
61 Viking Ship
62 Just Try It
63 Scar Face
64 Be Sociable
65 I'm Not Father Time!
66 Look Ma—No Cavities!

ITEM	EX	AVE
Card (all colors)	.60	.10
Set	40.00	8.00

TARZAN & THE SHE DEVIL (60)   2 5/8" X 3 3/4"

No sooner had we seen the 1953 movie "Tarzan & the She Devil" in the theater than we found these cards in the neighborhood candy stores. Three-dimensional items were one of the biggest fads of the "Fifties" so Topps jumped on the bandwagon by producing two separate sets based on the Tarzan movies currently playing around the country. Cards of the "She Devil" set are green on both front and back and are numbered from 1 to 60. The following directions were printed on the 5-cent wrapper: "Tilt card back and forth and see Tarzan in action. Hold card at arm's length and the effect will be even more startling." (Many of us found out just how startling when we tried to look at these cards while riding bikes!) The 1-cent wrapper is made of durable wax paper (the 5-cent is layered cellophane), and it has a repeating design. This 1-cent wrapper was once considered to be scarce, but a quantity or them has since entered the marketplace. The 3-D glasses may have been inserted directly into gum packs or given away by the retail merchant. The reference number is R714-21.

ITEM	EX	AVE
Card	4.00	.80
Set	300.00	55.00
Wrappers		
1-cent	40.00	––
5-cent	25.00	––
Box	250.00	60.00

1 Lord of the Jungle	21 Practice for Battle	41 The Stockade is Built
2 Leaping Death	22 The Safari Approaches	42 The Faithful Friend
3 Arrival at Dagar	23 Rolling Death	43 After Fresh Food
4 A Plan is Made	24 A Warning from Tarzan	44 Bullets Against Tusks
5 Tarzan and his Mate	25 The Elephants Approach	45 Treachery is Overheard
6 Underwater Fun	26 Treachery is Planned	46 Jane is Trapped
7 Cheeta Steals an Egg	27 The Laikopos are Trapped	47 Tarzan is Helpless
8 Help is Needed	28 Struggle Against Capture	48 A Shot in Time
9 Running in Danger	29 Escape from Flames	49 Tarzan Sees Jane
10 The Lion Leaps	30 Through the Trees	50 Tarzan Submits
11 Captured Slaves	31 Tarzan Falls	51 The Gun is Ready
12 Waiting to Strike	32 The Ropes are Broken	52 Tarzan's Yell
13 Tarzan Attacks	33 Can Jane be Dead?	53 An Answer from the Jungle
14 Freeing the Slaves	34 Captured	54 The Elephants Charge
15 Cheeta Joins the Fun	35 Threat from a Snake	55 "Into the Stockade"
16 Race for Safety	36 Carried to Safety	56 Jane Must be Rescued
17 Tarzan Surrounded	37 Tarzan is Whipped	57 Not a Minute to Lose
18 Fight wih a Giant	38 Moving Through the Jungle	58 Rocky Protection
19 Tarzan Wins	39 Slashing Jaws	59 The Laikopos are Free
20 Over the Wall	40 Cheeta Tries to Help	60 Free Once More

TARZAN'S SAVAGE FURY (60)   2 5/8" X 3 3/4"

This is the second of two Tarzan movies made into a card set by Topps. The company used the very same wrappers, boxes, and 3-D glasses in marketing both series. The fronts of "Savage Fury" cards are the same shade of green as those of "She Devil," but the backs of this series are orange. Once again, there are 60 cards in the set, numbered from 1 to 60. The Savage Fury cards are more difficult to find than those of "She Devil." The reference number is R714-22.

ITEM	EX	AVE
Card	6.00	1.20
Set	450.00	80.00

—desert torture

1 Jungle Master	21 Facing a Rhino	41 Temple of Diamonds	
2 Treachery	22 Building a Raft	42 Tarzan's Mission	
3 A Strange Plan	23 Crossing the River	43 Cheeta's Discovery	
4 Living Bait	24 The Hippo Charges	44 Rokoff's Magic	
5 Gaping Jaws	25 Rescue	45 Thieves at Work	
6 Tarzan Fights	26 Mountain Terrors	46 Murder!	
7 Tarzan Meets Joe	27 Desert Torture	47 A Message for Tarzan	
8 Jungle Friends	28 The Water-Hole	48 Tarzan's Old Home	
9 Food Needed	29 Deserted Village	49 Inside the Hut	
10 Terror-Filled Eyes	30 The Cannibals	50 Thieves' Escape	
11 Jungle Travel	31 Cannibal Attack	51 Over the Cliff	
12 Tarzan and Jane	32 A Direct Hit	52 Tarzan in Danger	
13 In the Water	33 Tarzan's Fight	53 Threat to Jane	
14 Danger Approaches	34 The Wazuri	54 Joe and the Lions	
15 The Meeting	35 Surrounded	55 Help from a Pal	
16 Magic Tricks	36 The Wazuri Village	56 Tarzan's Fury	
17 Memory of the Past	37 The Witchdoctor	57 Death for a Killer	
18 Jane's Plea	38 The Prisoners	58 Race Against Time	
19 On the Trail	39 The Torture Machine	59 Jane Is Saved	
20 Black Death	40 Wazuri Chief	60 Homeward Bound	

TATOO BUBBLE GUM (30K)   THREE SIZES

From the different sizes of wrappers and the variety of boxes and bins seen under this set title, we must assume that "Tatoo Bubble Gum" was distributed by Topps more than once. The wrappers can be divided into two basic styles: (1) without and (2) with illustrated directions on how to apply the transfers. The "without directions" variety appears to be the oldest. These were marketed in cardboard "tourist" pouch, the round container, or bin, and the "Carnival" box. "Directionless" wrappers all bear a copyright date of 1948 and list the manufacture as "Bubble Inc."

Wrappers with application directions on the exterior side are not dated but appear to have been sold in 1953. This style wrapper comes in two sizes: 1 3/8" X 2 5/8" and 1 9/16" X 3 1/2". The manufacturer is listed as "Topps." We have seen only a single box for this variety and it also has the directions sequence printed on it.

Because the tatoos, or "tranfers," of both the 1948 and 1953 varieties seem to be identical, we have listed them together in the descriptive checklist printed below. Although the 1960 edition of the American Card Catalog says there are 150 designs in the series, a lack of collector interest has resulted in only 30 confirmed pictures as of this time. The reference number is R711-7.

DIRECTIONS Remove this wrapper carefully. Apply lightning TATOO inside, to moistened surface. Pat gently and lift. HARMLESS CERTIFIED COLORS

1948 WRAPPER & TATOO

ITEM	EX	AVE
Tatoo/Wrapper		
1948	7.50	––
Not dated	10.00	––
Boxes		
Tourist pouch	35.00	10.00
Bin	95.00	25.00
"Carnival"	50.00	15.00
"Directions"	45.00	12.50

Tatoo Bubble Gum

1953 WRAPPER

1953 TATOO

1953 WRAPPER & TATOO

1949 "BIN"

BOX OF 1949
"TOURIST" POUCHES

1949 1-CENT
DISPLAY BOX

1953 1-CENT
DISPLAY BOX

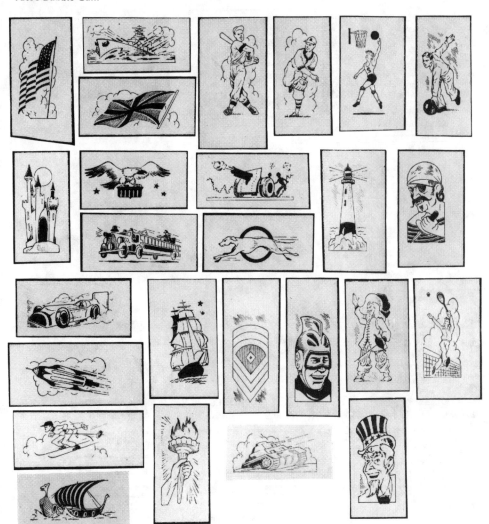

TEE—VEE SKYFLYERS (60)   2 7/8" X 2 3/4"

Here is an unusual set of cards which escaped the attention of collectors for many years. It is called "Tee-Vee Skyflyers," and it was marketed by the Feature-Pak Candies Company of Chicago. The cards are black and white artwork scenes of mankind's journey into space, and there are two numbered pictures on every card (our illustrations show the two sides of a six-card strip). We believe that six

scenes (on three actual cards) were packaged in every "television" style candy box. The back panel of the box gives the set total, 60 cards, and advises that the box can be used to store a complete set. A series of space badges and insignia were also packed with the cards, and we believe that 30 of these were produced. Tee-Vee Skyflyers was manufactured in 1952. The set has yet to be assigned a re-

ference number. NOTE: cards of this series are commonly found in strips, and the prices below refer to one double-sided card, regardless if it is a "single" or still attached.

ITEM	EX	AVE
Card	2.00	.50
Set, 30 cards/		
60 scenes	75.00	15.00
Badges	3.00	1.00
Box	15.00	4.00

13. Half-Way Stop-Stations "The Big Dipper"   14. Rocket Repair And Checkup   15. Another Station-Star For Refueling

16. At Weather Star To Check Flying Conditions   17. Suspended Refreshment Stand   18. Sky Journey

BADGES

1 One Night A Visitor Came To Our House
2 Aloon, A Little Man From Space Beyond
3 He Was Very Friendly And Made Us Laugh
4 Gift Of Space Suits
5 A Ride Over The Town
6 Goodbye To A Friend
7 Looking At Home From Planet-Viewer
8 Another Adventure
9 A Trip To Aloon's Planet
10 Friendly Welcomers
11 His Father, The King
12 Traveling Over City Streets
13 Half-Way Stop-Stations "The Big Dipper"
14 Rocket Repair And Checkup
15 Another Station-Star For Refueling
16 At Weather Star To Check Flying Conditions
17 Suspended Refreshment Stand
18 Sky Journey
19 Milky Way Highway
20 Searching The Space Underneath

21 There Are Still Undiscovered Planets
22 Space Deer
23 Planet Goat
24 Chicken And Duck On Mars
25 Moon Rabbits
26 Remote Controlled Space Farm
27 Jupiter Mule
28 Space Dog
29 Metal-Plated Bird
30 Fierce Planet Rhino-Bull
31 Gyroman Formation
32 Starman Driving Back Star Dragon
33 Sun Resistant Suit
34 Spiral Ship Preparing To Leave Rocketport
35 Looking Down From Floating Dome City
36 Space Pig
37 Exploding Planet
38 Dome City With Protective Covering
39 Radar Planet Station
40 Radar Patrol Finding Lost Man

41 Interplanetary Police
42 Moving Through Space Blizzard
43 Space Navigator
44 Revolving Into Universe
45 Viewing Moon Through Telemagnifier
46 Blizzard Scout Car
47 Suspended Space Patrol Station
48 Space Patrol Helmet
49 Fogman Throwing Radar Waves
50 All Star Man Baseball Game
51 Space Patrol Exploring Unknown Planet
52 Fog Man With Radar Weapon
53 Rocket Ship Zooming Into Space
54 Starmen Gazing Into Space From Ship
55 Self Breathing Creature From Unknown Planet
56 Self Breathers In Patrol Ship
57 Star Man Shooting Through Space
58 Flying Saucers Over Moon
59 Rocket Fleet Over City
60 Rocket Airport

TELEVISION & RADIO STARS OF N.B.C. (36)

2 1/2" X 3 3/4"

Bowman Gum released its 36-card set of "Television & Radio Personalities of N.B.C." in 1952. Each card is a lavish color photograph — virtually a studio portrait — surrounded by a black frame line and white borders. The star is identified on the back, and his or her career is described in a paragraph of biography. The cards of this series are easily distinguished from those of the following set by their horizontal backs and by the way the set title is written. The wrapper is white, with blue and red accents, and only a 5-cent type has been found. The reference number is R701-14.

ITEM	EX	AVE
Set	275.00	50.00
Wrapper	35.00	––

KATE SMITH

Star of "The Kate Smith Hour," NBC Television
BORN: GREENVILLE, VA., MAY 1, 1909

As Kathryn Elizabeth Smith, made first public appearance at four, singing in a church choir. Entered show business at 17, appearing in many Broadway musicals. Attracted attention of Ted Collins who became her manager and placed her in radio in 1931. In World War II, she traveled nearly 52,000 miles to service camps and training stations throughout the country. Carried her radio success into television in 1950. Now is one of TV's most popular personalities.

TELEVISION & RADIO STARS OF N.B.C.

B.G., H. L. I., Printed in U. S. A.   No. 29

STAR	EX	AVE
1 Gertrude Berg	7.50	1.50
2 Bob Elliot & Ray Goulding	7.50	1.50
3 Joan Davis	5.00	1.00
4 Eddie Cantor	5.00	1.00
5 Judy Canova	5.00	1.00
6 Bob Considine	5.00	1.00
7 Robert Cummings	5.00	1.00
8 Dennis Day	5.00	1.00
9 Jimmy Durante	10.00	2.00
10 Ralph Edwards	5.00	1.00
11 Dave Garroway	5.00	1.00
12 Dolores Gray	5.00	1.00
13 Phil Harris & Alice Faye	5.00	1.00
14 Bob Hope	15.00	3.00
15 George Jessel	7.50	1.50
16 Jim & Marian Jordan	5.00	1.00
17 Pinky Lee	7.50	1.50
18 Paul Winchell	5.00	1.00
19 Groucho Marx	15.00	3.00
20 Joel McCrea	5.00	1.00
21 Randy Merriman	5.00	1.00
22 Bess Myerson	6.00	1.25
23 Jan Murray	5.00	1.00
24 Walter O'Keefe	5.00	1.00
25 Jane Pickens	5.00	1.00
26 Marguerite Piazza	5.00	1.00
27 Martha Raye	6.00	1.25
28 Dinah Shore	7.50	1.50
29 Kate Smith	7.50	1.50
30 Olan Soule & Barbara Luddy	5.00	1.00
31 Bill Stern	5.00	1.00
32 Martha Stewart	5.00	1.00
33 John Cameron Swayze	6.00	1.25
34 Lee Tracy	5.00	1.00
35 Willard Waterman	5.00	1.00
36 Meredith Willson	5.00	1.00

TELEVISION AND RADIO STARS OF THE NATIONAL BROADCASTING COMPANY (96)

2 1/2" X 3 3/4"

In 1953, Bowman followed up the 1952 set with another set of NBC radio and TV personalities, this time with vertical backs and the set title expressed differently on the backs of the cards. The color photos are of the same style as the previous set, and comparison of the pictures of stars appearing in both sets indicates that most were "shot" in the same session. Wrappers of two denominations are known for this set, and both are similar except for the price and color accents. The 1-cent wrapper has the word "one cent" written in the "Stars of Today" panel, which is green. The 5-cent version has alternating red and blue "Stars of Today" bars and no price is written after those words. The colorful 5-cent box is illustrated courtesy of Robert Marks. The reference number is R701-15.

ITEM	EX	AVE
Card		
Odd numbers	3.50	.70
Even numbers	2.50	.50
Set	400.00	75.00
Wrappers		
1-cent	90.00	——
5-cent	10.00	——
Box	150.00	40.00
Specials:		
No.8	15.00	3.00
No.10	5.00	1.00
No.33	10.00	2.00
No.41	10.00	2.00
No.95	15.00	3.00

MacDONALD CAREY

Star of NBC Radio's "Jason and the Golden Fleece"
BORN: Sioux City, Iowa, March 15, 1913

Well-known for his radio, movie, stage work. Began acting in high and prep school productions. Graduate of University of Iowa. Sang bass-baritone roles in musical comedy and Gilbert and Sullivan operettas. Directed a Cedar Rapids community theatre. In 1937 helped found Radio Theatre Guild in Chicago. Big break came playing male lead opposite Gertrude Lawrence in "Lady in the Dark." Married to Betty Heckschar, former actress. Has four children.

QUESTION: What was his earliest film success?

ANSWER: Wake Island.

TELEVISION AND RADIO STARS OF THE NATIONAL BROADCASTING COMPANY

G & G, H.I.   No. 20   Printed in U.S.A.

1 Jack Lescoulie	25 Stan Kenton	49 Helen Strohm	73 Sammy Kaye
2 Bob Elliott & Ray Goulding	26 Les Brown	50 Loretta Young	74 Joseph Kearns
3 Florence Freeman	27 George Hicks	51 Richard Harkness	75 Fred Allen
4 Ralph Edwards	28 Jeri Lou James—Dennis Ray	52 Jeffrey Lynn	76 Florence Williams
5 Jim Backus	29 Kenneth Banghart	53 Lucille Wall	77 Bob Hamilton
6 Olan Soule & Barbara Luddy	30 Buzz Podewell	54 J. Fred Muggs	78 Eli Mintz
7 Carl Reiner	31 Bud Collyer	55 Betty & Jane Kean	79 Jack Barry
8 Groucho Marx	32 Jack McCoy	56 Susan Levin	80 Claire Niesen
9 Everett Mitchell	33 Sid Caesar	57 Helen Halpin	81 Walter Tetly
10 Dinah Shore	34 Anne Whitfield	58 Ronnie Walken	82 Rhoda Williams
11 Billy Williams Quartet	35 Ezio Pinza	59 Robert Harris	83 Marlin Perkins
12 Morgan Beatty	36 Lucille Norman	60 Virginia Dwyer	84 Imogene Coca
13 Hoagy Carmichael	37 Bambi Linn and Rod Alexander	61 Phil Harris	85 Merrill Mueller
14 Russell Arms	38 Bob Hastings	62 Estelle Parsons	86 Sallie Brophy
15 William Bendix	39 Donald Curtis	63 Paul Lavalle	87 Verna Felton
16 Audrey Meadows	40 Bill Conrad	64 Claudia Morgan	88 Harry Holcombe
17 Johnny Dugan	41 Eddie Fisher	65 Patti Page	89 Tom D'Andrea
18 Patricia Wheel	42 Mark Stevens	66 The Hamilton Trio	90 Marvin Miller
19 Tommy Bartlett	43 Ned Wever	67 Jeannine Roose	91 Dennis Day
20 MacDonald Carey	44 Cliff Arquette	68 Arlene McQuade	92 Phyllis Hill
21 Harry Babbitt	45 George Fenneman	69 Tony Martin	93 Wm. Waterman
22 Dorothy Warenskjold	46 Ted Mack	70 Don Herbert	94 Wesley Morgan
23 Ann Elstner	47 Carmen Dragon	71 Arnold Stang	95 Bob Hope
24 Vivian Smollen	48 Arthur Hughes	72 Kathi Norris	96 Dan Gibson

TELEVISION FLIP—IT—MOVIES (24)   1 1/2" X 2 9/16"

Gum Products, manufacturer of the "Adventure" series presented earlier in this book, marketed these flip books sometime before 1953. There are 24 books in the set, improbably numbered 100 to 123, and they depict epic events such as "Beanie Stalk Meets the Giant" and "Slugger Hits a Home Run." The character in each "movie" is ge- neric, although there are some similarities (intentional, no doubt) to real people and to licensed comic strip and cartoon figures. The cover of each flip book is sallow yellow and green, with the set and book title positioned inside a TV screen. There is no indication that the flip books were issued in a gum package. The reference number for the set is R770.

ITEM	EX	AVE
Flip Book	5.00	1.50
Set	140.00	40.00

THE KATZENJAMMER KIDS (?)

One of the nicest boxes produced by the Super Novelty Candy Co. (Newark, NJ), "The Katzenjammer Kids" is a "double-whammy" for collectors. The front panel of the box contained a 2 7/16" X 2 3/4" cut-off card of "The Captain." (Once it was removed from the box, this blank-backed card has no identifying marks except for the "King Features Syndicate" line.) The back panel held a four-cell comic strip which

TWO SIZES

measured 2 7/16" X 3 1/2". It is not known at this time whether there are different front-panel cards and back-panel cartoons than the one illustrated here. The reference number for this category of double-sided boxes is R756.

ITEM	EX	AVE
Character Card	4.00	1.50
Comic Strip	6.00	2.00
Box	25.00	8.00

THE STORY OF THE ATOM BOMB (18)

"The Story of the Atom Bomb" is one of a group of three "Bazooka" gum tray sets that frustrate collectors trying to get a "type" of every Topps card ("Famous American Heroes" and "Famous Stamps" are the others). The "Atom Bomb" card illustrated here is mostly red with white accents and print. It formed one-half of a gum tray/package stiffener in 5-cent rolls of Bazooka Gum. The other part of the panel was printed (red print on white) with a mail-in premium offer. A set total of 18 cards was listed in the early

7/8" X 2 1/4"

catalogs, but this number has yet to be confirmed. It is thought that the series was issued in 1949. The reference number is R709-3.

ITEM	EX	AVE
Card	15.00	5.00
Panel	25.00	10.00

THE U.S. ARMY IN ACTION (64)　　2 1/2" X 3 1/2"

Here is a set which has engendered some discussion among collectors. Some have taken the 1776-1953 dates printed on the card backs to mean that the series was issued in 1953. Others say that Rosan wasn't printing cards that early and that the cards look distinctly more modern. Our feeling at The Hobby Card Index is that the set was based upon a book dealing with this particular historical period, and

that the cards were probably issued in 1961. Until we can gather more precise information, the set will be listed here in the 1946-1960 section.

The fronts of the cards depict various events in U.S. Army history. The artwork is multi-colored and is derived from both classic paintings of military engagements and political cartoons. The caption only appears on the front under the

picture, which is surrounded by thick black borders. The back is headed by the set title, under which is printed a short description of the subject pictured on front. Two rough drawings are located at the left on the back — one is a strange-looking "eagle" which has the card number underneath; the other is the symbol of an army unit. The color of the cardboard stock is gray and the print is black. Judging from the number of Civil War battles depicted, it seems likely that the set was issued at the beginning of the Civil War Centennial. No reference number has been assigned as of this date.

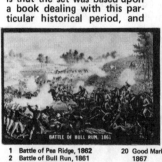

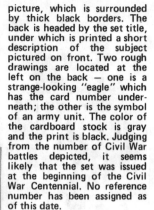

ITEM	EX	AVE
Card	1.00	.20
Set	75.00	15.00

1　Battle of Pea Ridge, 1862
2　Battle of Bull Run, 1861
3　Battle of Murfreesboro, 1862
4　Battle of Fredericksburg, 1862
5　Battle of Champion-Hills
6　The Fall of Petersburg
7　Battle of Lookout Mountain
8　Battle of Missionary Ridge
9　Bunker Hill, June 17, 1775
10　Battle of Franklin
11　"Follow Me!", 1944
12　Battle of Five Forks, Va.
13　American Patriots
14　The Stars and Stripes
15　The Battle of Vera Cruz, 1847
16　Knocking Out the Moros, 1913
17　"I'll Try, Sir!", 1900
18　The Battle of Ft. Sumter
19　The Battle of Tippecanoe, 1811

20　Good Marksmanship and Guts!, 1867
21　Inauguration of George Washington
22　Washington Crossing the Delaware
23　The Road to Fallen Timbers, 1794
24　4th of July 1776
25　Battle of Mill Spring, 1862
26　Battle of Kenesaw Mountain
27　Battle of Nashville
28　Breakthrough at Chipyong-Ni, 1951
29　Remember Your Regiment, 1846
30　Battle of Chancellorsville
31　Battle of Ft. Donelson, 1862
32　Battle of Cold Harbor

33　Theodore Roosevelt's Rough Riders
34　Gatlings to the Assault, 1898
35　Battle of Gettsburg
36　The Battle of Cerro Gordo
37　First at Vicksburg, 1863
38　The Start of the Revolution at Concord
39　Paul Revere's Ride
40　Lord Cornwallis' Surrender
41　The Battle of Spottsylvania
42　The Battle of Williamsburg, 1862
43　The Spanish American War
44　Merry Christmas, 1776
45　Battle of Antietam, 1862
46　Battle of Corinth, 1862
47　Capture of Ft. Fisher
48　Battle of Chattanooga

49　"Those Are Regulars, By God!", 1814
50　The Battle of Quingua, 1899
51　Death of Militarism
52　Battle of the Bighorn
53　General Washington at the Battle of Monmouth, June 28th, 1778
54　The Rock of the Marne, 1918
55　Gen. Grant and the Civil War
56　Battle of Bull Run July, 1861
57　Remagen Bridgehead, 1945
58　The Monitor and The Merrimac
59　Raid on Ploesti, 1944
60　Battle of Chickamauga
61　Battle of the Wilderness
62　Battle of Cedar Creek, 1864
63　Battle of Atlanta
64　Battle of Shiloh, 1862

THE 3 STOOGES (96)　　2 1/2" X 3 1/2"

Few non-sport sets have attracted as much attention as "The 3 Stooges" series produced by Fleer in 1959. The card fronts have color photgraphs of the three zanies in humorous poses and situations, with stooge-like captions printed underneath. The card stock on back can be found in gray or white for all card numbers; the back print and designs are the same colors (red, blue, and pink) for both. The famous Fleer crown

logo holds the card number.

According to Dan Lange, "The original 1959 box contained 24 packs of cards and each pack contained five cards and a slab of bubble gum. The checklist cards are very scarce. They appear only on the backs of cards 16, 63, and 64, and on no others. The checklists were available only in the gum packs and could not be purchased or ordered separately. I was told that they ap-

peared only on the final print run of the cards and only as a last minute decision due to a problem with original dies on the three cards."

In addition to the three very valuable checklist-back variations, the first three cards of the set — portraits of Curly, Moe, and Larry — are in very high demand. The wrapper for this set, seen in a 5-cent denomination only, is fairly common but is also subject to high demand. The reference number for this set is R730-1. NOTE: many cards are found off-center; take this into consideration when evaluating and grading.

Who's that goodlooking guy behind us?

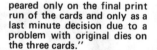

Larry: Do you think we ought to put him in the act.

Moe: No! Three Stooges is enough.

ITEM	EX	AVE
Card	6.00	1.50
Set	850.00	200.00
Wrapper	35.00	—
Box	500.00	120.00

THESE THREE NUMBERS WERE PRINTED IN BOTH THE REGULAR
VARIETY BACKS AND IN A CHECKLIST VARIETY BACK

Larry

Moe

Curly

1 Curly
2 Moe
3 Larry
4 You'll Sleep in the Room in the Basement and Like It.
5 They Went Thatta-Way!
6 Hey Moe, Don't You Think There's Room for Yours on Top?
7 Uh! Uh! I've Got Eyes in the Back of My Head.
8 I Told You Wise Guys You'd Never Get Away with It!
9 You Lied! You Told Me He Couldn't Punch His Way Out of a Paper Bag.
10 Come on, Give Back That Baseball! We Know You Swallowed It.
11 There's 4 Needles in My Pants and You Better Get Them Out!
12 Hold Still — I'm a Tailer!
13 C'mon Curly — The Horse Is the One in Front of Larry!
14 I Tell You — Humans Have 13 Ribs — You've Got 19 — You Ain't Human!
15 Don't Worry — You Can Breathe Through Your Mouth!
16 You Can't Keep Your Money in Your Shoes and Walk at the Same Time.
17 See No Evil, Hear No Evil, Speak No Evil.
18 One More Rehearsal and I Think We'll Be Good Enough to Play at the Met.
19 Hey Fellows, I Think I've Got a Bite.

20 How Do You Like This for a Fancy Finish.
21 Peek-a-Boo!
22 What Do You Think I Am, a Pair of Pants?
23 Not Even George Washington Would Sleep Here!
24 Look Out Below.
25 Next Time We'll Take the Elevator!
26 The "Tree" Stooges
27 Somehow I Have the Feeling We're Not Wanted.
28 What Happened to Our Reservations!
29 Your Nose Is too Big and Your Brain Is too Small.
30 This One's in the Bag.
31 Bargain Hunters
32 Cleaning Up the West!
33 Let Me Know When My Number Comes Up.
34 Birds of a Feather.
35 Who's That Goodlooking Guy Behind Us?
36 Get Your Nose Out of My Business!
37 I Told You to Turn Off the Fan!
38 Contact!
39 If You Don't Stop My Name Will be Whirley Instead of Curly!
40 I Never Miss — Except with the First Shot.
41 About Face!
42 A Hair Raising Experience.
43 No Down Payment.
44 No Use. That Hat Won't Fit!

45 Dig That Crazy Chicken!
46 Singing in the Shower.
47 Just Thought I'd Drop By!
48 Larry Plays By Ear!
49 Always on the Go.
50 Rome Wasn't Burned in a Day.
51 Be Careful, This Is My Only Suit.
52 It Must Have Been Something I Ate!
53 That's an Order — a Quart of Milk and 3 Doughnuts.
54 I Could Have Sworn I Just Shaved Him Yesterday.
55 When You Hear the Tone, the Time Will Be...
56 Just a Little Off the Top.
57 That Oughta Hold Him!
58 Curly Always Did Want to Be in Pictures!
59 Did You Have to Sneeze?
60 Betcha 8 to 5 You Miss Me Again.
61 We Never Took a Lesson in Our Lives!
62 Congratulations Curly, You've Just Been Elected Treasurer.
63 Curly, the First Thing a Fighter Must Learn Is How to Get into the Ring.
64 Checklist — You Won't Fool Anybody with That Haircut!
65 Dinner Music.
66 He Has 40 Teeth and 4 Cavities!
67 Curly, I Tell You It Is Not a Dog!
68 Quick — Call the S.P.C.A.!

69 What Are You Planting — Roses or Noses?
70 C'mon You Guys, Quit Horsin' Around!
71 Getting Even with Moe.
72 Give Me Back My Hula Hoop.
73 Bang!
74 Just Don't Break Anything!
75 Take Me to Your Leader!
76 Now You Know Where We Got All That Corn!
77 Where Has That Doggone Dog Gone?
78 Good Health Means Good Fun.
79 I Hate to Say This, But Somebody's Flat!
80 You Say It Was Right Here That You Lost Your Mind?
81 He Must Be Aound Here Somewhere.
82 This Looks Like a Bad Case of "Permiss of the Fatastan."
83 Is There a Doctor in the House!
84 Strong Backs — Weak Minds.
85 Give Me a Hand, I Can't Carry It All By Myself!
86 Round and Round She Goes.
87 Nobody Leave the Room.
88 At Least, Throw Us a Bone!
89 Why Are Fire Engines Red?
90 What's Wrong — No More Chairs in This Room?
91 That's Using Your Head, Curly!
92 He's Got a Good Head on Him — for Fishing!
93 We Didn't Do Anything and We'll Never Do It Again.
94 I Tell You Your Nose Is too Long!
95 Sorry, This Line Is Busy!
96 Trying the Squeeze Play.

TOMMY SWELL'S GANG (?)

Topps had "Bazooka Joe," Fleer had "Pud" (et al), but who was their counterpart over at Philadelphia Gum? "Tommy Swell's Gang," that's who! We have no specific record of when Tommy Swell appeared, and the comics do not have any dates indicated on them (at least, that we can decipher). Despite the absence of information, comic wrapper collectors will find these colorful strips both interesting and

SEVERAL SIZES

challenging to find. Suggested prices are $2.00 for older, larger comics, down to 10 cents for the modern day versions. The reference number for the set is R788-7.

TORRONE CANDY BOXES (14 SETS)

This series of Italian-manufactured candy boxes was first recorded in the 1958 edition of the American Card Catalog. Although the foreign look of the boxes does not appeal to

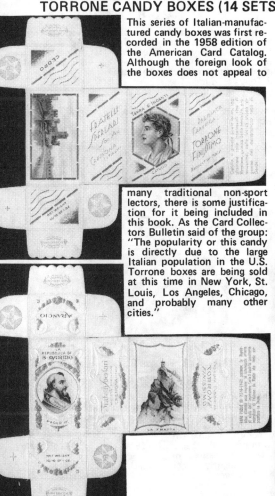

many traditional non-sport lectors, there is some justification for it being included in this book. As the Card Collectors Bulletin said of the group: "The popularity or this candy is directly due to the large Italian population in the U.S. Torrone boxes are being sold at this time in New York, St. Louis, Los Angeles, Chicago, and probably many other cities."

1 1/4" X 2"

There were no less than 14 different Torrone sets listed in the 1956 American Card Catalog, plus a fifteenth category for sets produced by other firms. We have illustrated three Torrone boxes showing the range of subjects covered: explorer Robert Peary, Pope Paul III and the Roman lyric poet Catullus on front; maps and Italian landmarks on back. The boxes are made of shell-white cardboard stock, and all the artwork is done in beautiful color. A complete box from this early period sells for $15.00 in excellent condition. The reference number for this category is R726. NOTE: we have also illustrated, for purposes of comparison, two candy boxes of a similar style purchased in 1987.

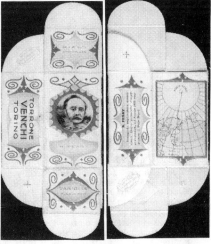

TRUE FACT SERIES (4K)

2 3/8" X 4 7/16"

Collector Mike Gallela reported this series of miniature comic books, produced by Topps, to the Hobby Card Index several years ago. Their appearance touched off a debate about the method of distribution, because no wrapper or box had been seen for the set. We have since found an ad from a confectionary trade magazine which illustrates the comic books and explains that they were a bonus insert packed exclusively for the retailers who sold Topps products. The comics are 16 pages long and were made for Topps by Custom Comics of New York City. They deal with both sports and non-sports topics. No. 4 is the highest number seen so far. No reference number has been assigned for this set.

ITEM	EX	AVE
Comic	10.00	3.00

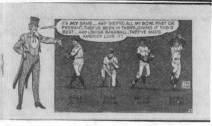

T.V. WESTERNS (71)

2 1/2" X 3 1/2"

Take a trip down the old Nostalgia Trail with the 1958 Topps set of "T.V. Westerns!" In it you'll meet Matt Dillon, Hoby Gilman, Josh Randall, Paladin, Yancy Derringer, Bart McCellan, Seth Adams, Vint Bonner, Jim Hardie, Shane Adams, and Matt Wayne. Each of these characters is pictured in a series of color photographs from the shows in which they appeared. The name of the show and the card caption can be found on both sides of the card; the card number is printed on the back only. A copyright date of 1958 is printed on the back. The set was also issued in England (in a slightly larger card size). The wrappers are red and yellow and come in 1-cent and 5-cent denominations. Printing defects are common in this set and they must be taken into consideration when grading. The reference number is R712-4.

ITEM	EX	AVE
Card	3.00	.60
Set	260.00	50.00
Wrappers		
1-cent	25.00	——
5-cent	200.00	——
Box	250.00	65.00

GUNSMOKE

SHOWDOWN!

10 **SHOWDOWN!**
NO. 10 OF 15 GUNSMOKE CARDS

Matt hated gun fighters—they were a menace to the town. Once when Matt approached a gunslinger and advised him to leave town, the trigger-happy desperado challenged him to a showdown. They met at night on the main street, while the citizens crowded behind the houses to watch. The gun fighter drew first but Matt's blazing pistol had the last word, and Dodge City was quiet again.

BE SURE TO WATCH JAMES ARNESS IN
GUNSMOKE
ON THE C B S TELEVISION NETWORK

T.V. WESTERNS
PICTURE CARD BUBBLE GUM
1¢

T.V. WESTERNS
PICTURE CARD BUBBLE GUM
1¢

bubble gum

BIGGEST COMICS
BIG TWIN CHEWS
IN EVERY PACK

YOUNG AMERICA'S FAVORITE

SAVE Bazooka COMICS FOR FREE PRIZES

5¢

T.V. WESTERNS

GUNSMOKE
WANTED - DEAD OR ALIVE
WAGON TRAIN
HAVE GUN, WILL TRAVEL
THE CALIFORNIANS
TALES OF WELLS FARGO

GUNSMOKE
1 James Arness As Matt Dillon
2 Dennis Weaver as Chester
3 Doc and Matt
4 Man of Justice
5 Chester and Kitty
6 Advice from Doc
7 Ready to Ride
8 Danger Ahead
9 Matt in Action
10 Showdown!
11 Quick on the Draw
12 Deadly Aim
13 Happy Prisoner
14 Dodge City Social
15 Tall and Tough
TRACKDOWN
16 Robert Culp as Hoby Gilman
17 Search for Clues
18 Surprise Visit
19 Fierce Battle
20 The Pursuit
WANTED: Dead or Alive
21 Steve McQueen as Josh Randall
22 Josh's Weapon
23 The Bounty Seeker
24 Difficult Task
25 Man Hunter
PALADIN
26 Richard Boone as Paladin
27 Dangerous Foe
28 Fighting the Mob
29 Running Battle
30 Paladin Takes Aim
31 The Gentlemen
32 Indian Trouble
YANCY DERRINGER
33 Jock Mahoney as Yancy Derringer
34 Yancy the Gambler
35 Tense Moments
36 Unexpected Guest
37 Pahoo Ka Ta Wah
38 The Signal
39 Yancy's Persuader
40 Yancy and Pahoo

UNION PACIFIC
41 Jeff Morrow as Bart McCellan
42 Bart Takes Over
43 On Patrol
44 Gail and Bart
45 Bart's Problem
WAGON TRAIN
46 Ward Bond as Major Seth Adams
47 Robert Horton as Flint McCullough
48 The Warning
49 Scouting Mission
50 Gun Fight
51 Looking Ahead
THE RESTLESS GUN
52 John Payne as Vint Bonner
53 On the Move
54 Vint the Gunman
55 The Fastest Gun
56 Street Battle
TALES OF WELLS FARGO
57 Dale Robertson as Jim Hardie
58 Trouble Shooter
59 Jim Senses Trouble
60 Rugged Rider
61 Protection Plan
62 Alert for Action
63 Guarding the Gold
BOOTS AND SADDLES
64 Jack Pickard as Shane Adams
65 Call to Action
66 Luke Cummings the Indian Scout
67 Apache Combat
68 Charge!
THE CALIFORNIANS
69 Dick Coogan as Matt Wayne
70 Fight for Justice
71 Ready for a Job

RICHARD BOONE
HAVE GUN, WILL TRAVEL
as PALADIN

RICHARD BOONE
HAVE GUN, WILL TRAVEL
as PALADIN

26 **RICHARD BOONE** as Paladin
NO. 1 OF 7 HAVE GUN, WILL TRAVEL CARDS

Richard Boone has had a varied career both on and off television. He was twice nominated for the prized "Emmy" award for his role in the TV series "Medic." Before World War II, the six-foot, two-inch Boone planned to be an artist, but when the war came along he became an aerial gunner in the Navy and was torpedoed on the Carrier Intrepid. Richard is a 7th generation nephew of Daniel Boone.

BE SURE TO WATCH RICHARD BOONE IN
HAVE GUN, WILL TRAVEL
ON THE C B S TELEVISION NETWORK

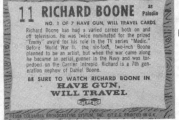

11 **RICHARD BOONE** as Paladin
NO. 1 OF 7 HAVE GUN, WILL TRAVEL CARDS

Richard Boone has had a varied career both on and off television. He was twice nominated for the prized "Emmy" award for his role in the TV series "Medic." Before World War II, the six-foot, two-inch Boone planned to be an artist, but when the war came along he became an aerial gunner in the Navy and was torpedoed on the Carrier Intrepid. Richard is a 7th generation nephew of Daniel Boone.

BE SURE TO WATCH RICHARD BOONE IN
HAVE GUN, WILL TRAVEL

PALADIN CARD ON RIGHT, SLIGHTLY LARGER THAN TOPPS VERSION, WAS ISSUED BY A & BC GUM IN ENGLAND (1959)

UNCLE MILTIE (?)

1 5/8" X 2 9/16"

The "Uncle Miltie" jokes and pictures series has proved to be one of the most elusive items ever manufactured by Bowman Gum. It was sold in 1952 to exploit the phenomenal success of television comedian Milton Berle, but judging from the number of wrappers and comics which have survived, the product had a very short run. The outer wrapper is green with black, white, and yellow accents. The comics, which were folded around the piece of gum, are red and black drawings with related jokes printed underneath. They are not numbered and we have no clue as to length of set. The reference number is R701-7.

ITEM	EX	AVE
Comic	20.00	8.00
Wrapper	125.00	––

THEY TOLD ME
I WOULD BE MAKING A
CLEAN SWEEP OF CITY HALL.

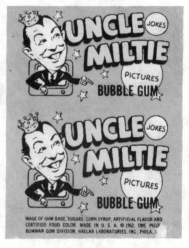

U.S. NAVY VICTORIES (48)

2 1/2" X 3 3/4"

The beautiful color pictures in Bowman Gum's set of "U.S. Navy Victories" are like miniature oil paintings. They depict famous naval engagements in American history, and there are no captions or other designs on the card fronts to detract from the scenes. The card number, caption, and text are all located on the reverse. The print on the backs of the cards can be found in either blue or black ink, a subtle detail difference which does not seem to matter to collectors. The information used in developing the set was provided by the Peabody Museum of Salem, Massachusetts. The 1-cent and 5-cent wrappers are mostly blue, with white smoke clouds (from the guns) and red-print titles and accents. The vertical "chain" lines on either side of the main designs are yellow. The set was issued in 1954. The reference number is R701-16.

ITEM	EX	AVE
Card	3.50	.70
Sets		
Mixed print color	200.00	37.50
One color	235.00	45.00
Wrappers		
1-cent	100.00	––
5-cent	125.00	––

1 The Bonhomme and Serapis	10 First Salute to Our Flag	20 "Long Live our Constellation"	29 "Don't Give Up the Ship"	39 Military Stores Blown Up
2 "To the Shores of Tripoli"	11 Vera Cruz Captured 1914	21 Los Angeles Captured	30 Naval Force Lands at Mulije	40 Hobson Sinks Ship
3 Niagara Fights Alone	12 Perry Transfers Flag	22 U.S.S. Congress Blown Up	31 Farragut Captures New Orleans	41 Saipan Victory
4 Bombardment of Vera Cruz	13 Naval Forces Take Monterey	23 "Fire When Ready, Gridley"	32 "Remember the Maine"	42 "Tin Fish" Victory
5 "Destroyed Albemarle by Torpedo"	14 "Full Speed Ahead"	24 German U-Boat-58 Surrenders	33 Mining the North Sea	43 United States vs Macedonian
6 Spanish Fleet Destroyed	15 Cuban Shore Landing	25 "Gung Ho"	34 11 Men Against 500	44 Naval Battle on Lake Champlain
7 Destroyers Convoy Troop Ships	16 Y Gun Helps Defeat Enemy	26 Korean Bridge Hit	35 Frogmen Cut Nets	45 Merrimac Rams the Cumberland
8 Victory over the Kamikaze	17 "D" Day Victory	27 "Glover's Amphibians" Ferry Washington Across Delaware	36 First American Submarine - 1776	46 Marine "Flame Throwers"
9 Landing at Inchon	18 Victory through the Air	28 Decatur Burns the Philadelphia	37 Algerian Pirates Repelled	47 Merrimac and Monitor Battle
	19 "I Have Not yet Begun to Fight"		38 Constitution Bests Guerriere	48 "Long May It Wave"

U.S. PRESIDENTS (36)

2 1/2" X 3 3/4"

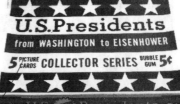

The popularity of this 1952 Bowman Gum set of "U.S. Presidents" has been hurt by the fact that the artwork was also used by Topps on two other occasions after they purchased the Bowman company in 1956. Each card has a color drawing of a president set against a background scene, with his name printed in a eagle-and-banner design. The gray-color backs list the term of office and give a long paragraph of biographical information about the subject. The wrapper is red, white & blue, and only the 5-cent denomination has been found. The reference number for the set is R701-17.

ITEM	EX	AVE
Card	2.00	.35
Set	85.00	15.00
Wrapper	30.00	—
Box	200.00	40.00

Washington Takes Command	13	John Tyler	25 Grover Cleveland
Declaration of Independence	14	James Polk	26 Benjamin Harrison
George Washington	15	Zachary Taylor	27 William McKinley
John Adams	16	Millard Fillmore	28 Theodore Roosevelt
Thomas Jefferson	17	Franklin Pierce	29 William H. Taft
James Madison	18	James Buchanan	30 Woodrow Wilson
Burning of White House	19	Abraham Lincoln	31 Warren G. Harding
James Monroe	20	Andrew Johnson	32 Calvin Coolidge
John Quincy Adams	21	Ulysses S. Grant	33 Herbert C. Hoover
Andrew Jackson	22	Rutherford B. Hayes	34 Franklin D. Roosevelt
Martin Van Buren	23	James A. Garfield	35 Harry S. Truman
Wm. Henry Harrison	24	Chester A. Arthur	36 Dwight D. Eisenhower

U.S. PRESIDENTS (36)

Topps used the artwork newly acquired from its buyout of Bowman Gum to reissue the "U.S. Presidents" series in 1956. The color artwork fronts are identical to those of Bowman's 1952 set, but the back design is new. The cards were sold in both 1-cent and 5-cent gum packs; the latter had a Mt. Rushmore centerpiece. Naturally, the wrapper colors are red, white & blue. The 1-cent and 5-cent boxes used the same artwork but differ in size. The reference number is R714-23.

ITEM	EX	AVE
Card	1.50	.25
Set	65.00	12.50
Wrappers		
1-cent	10.00	——
5-cent	10.00	——
Boxes		
1-cent	200.00	45.00
5-cent	125.00	30.00

WACKY PLAKS (88)

Topps issued the original "Wacky Plaks" set of 88 faux postcards in 1959 (we say "faux" because it's difficult to imagine that they were actually sent through the mail). The card fronts contain a small color-artwork drawing accompanied by a one or two-line joke. The woodgrain background, with side notches, is the wall "plak," and it even has a fake tack hole at the top. The backs are drawn in a postcard format, and the card number is printed in the upper left corner. Topps scrambled the numbers around and reissued this set in 1965 as "Kookie Plaks" (We have marked our checklist with the corresponding number of the card as it appears in the later set). Topps also "farmed out" the series to Scanlens (Australia) and to A & BC (England); these cards have company identification lines which easily distinguish them from the original Topps set. The reference number is R708-4.

ITEM	EX	AVE
Card	2.00	.35
Set	210.00	35.00
Wrapper	65.00	——

1 If You Have Nothing To Do... (Don't Do It Here!) [6]
2 Money Can't Buy Poverty [59]
3 How To Get Good Marks (Cheat) [3]
4 In Case of Fire — (Please Yell "Fire") [23]
5. Keep Calm! [9]
6 We Aim For Accuracy [82]
7 Think (Before You Louse Things Up!) [19]
8 Your Visit Has Climaxed An Already Dull Day. [46]
9 Plan Ahead [22]
10 Work Fascinates Me (I Can Sit and Watch It for Hours.) [52]
11 Think You Got Troubles? [33]
12 I Spend 8 Hours A Day Here (Do You Expect Me To Work Too?) [31]
13 Absence Makes The Heart Grow Fonder (So Get Lost!) [43]
14 Be Neat [24]
15 Come In (Everything Else Has Gone Wrong Today.) [47]
16 Early To Bed/Early To Rise (Dull Isn't It!) [21]
17 Keep Your Eye On The Ball/Keep Your Shoulder To The Wheel/Keep Your Ear To The Ground (Now Try to Work in that Position.) [40]
18 Time Wounds All Heels [14]
19 Who's Excited [28]
20 With My Brains and Your Looks (We're In Real Trouble.) [41]
21 I Never Forget A Face But in Your Case I'll Make an Exception. [48]
22 Smile (Later Today You Won't Feel Like It.) [55]
23 If You're So Smart Why Ain't You Rich [34]
24 Looking for Someone With A Little Authority? (I Have as Little as Anyone.) [29]
25 Don't Let School Work Get You Down (Flunk Now and Get It Over With.) [62]
26 Whether You're Rich or Poor It's Good to Have Money. [26]
27 The Early Bird Catches The Worm! But Who Wants Worms? [79]
28 Think or Thwim [77]
29 Never Do Today What You Can Put Off Till Tomorrow [17]
30 I'd Like To Compliment You On Your Work (When Will You Start?) [87]
31 All People Are Created Equal (Only Some Are More Equal than Others...) [38]
32 Somebody Goofed [10]
33 I'd Rather Be Handsome Than Rich [73]
34 Cheer Up! You're Not Completely Worthless. (You Can Always Serve as a Bad Example.) [57]
35 Think (It May Be a New Experience.) [34]
36 The Marines Build Men (But Even They Couldn't Help You!) [65]
37 Join Me For Dinner... (At Your House.) [20]
38 I'm Not Hard of Hearing (I'M Just Ignoring You.) [32]
39 If At First You Don't Succeed (To Heck With It!) [15]
40 You're Head and Shoulders Above Everyone [85]

SCANLENS WRAPPER ISSUED IN AUSTRALIA IN 1963

369

41 Looks Aren't Everything (It's A Good Thing You're Rich!) [5]
42 Some People Can't Do Anything Right! [75]
43 Money Isn't Everything (But It's Way Ahead of Whatever's In Second Place!) [11]
44 How To Get Rid of Ten Pounds of Ugly Fat. (Cut Off Your Head.) [80]
45 Be Reasonable (Do It My Way!) [16]
46 Stop Talking When I'm Interrupting [88]
47 Tell Me All You Know (I've Got A Minute to Spare.) [1]
48 Don't Just Do Something (Stand There!) [81]
49 I'm The Brains Of This Outfit [53]
50 You're Certainly Trying (Very Trying) [2]
51 What's On Your Mind? (If You Will Forgive the Overstatement.) [83]
52 Mistakes Will Happen. [4]
53 Keep Your Temper! (Nobody Else Wants It.) [68]
54 We're Friends Till The End (This Is The End.) [12]
55 If You Ever Need A Friend (Buy a Dog.) [56]
56 Your Service Was Excellent (Sorry I Don't Believe in Tipping.) [72]

57 You Must've Been A Beautiful Baby. (But What Happened?) [78]
58 Barking Dogs Never Bite (Except When They Stop Barking.) [50]
59 Think (Maybe You Can Dodge This Work.) [84]
60 Why Be Difficult? (With A Little Effort You Can Be a Real Stinker.) [71]
61 I Am a Self-Made Man. [54]
62 I Was Born This Way (What's Your Excuse?) [70]
63 I May Look Busy (But I'm Only Confused!) [74]
64 Are You Looking For An Ambitious Man? (Keep Looking!) [76]
65 You Ought To Go To Hollywood (The Walk Would Do You Good.) [64]
66 Thanks (For Seeing Me Through!) [7]
67 I'd Like To See You Get Ahead (You Need One!) [64]
68 Concentrate [25]
69 I'd Give $1,000 Dollars To Be A Millionaire! [8]
70 I'd Like To Help You Out (Which Way Did You Come In?) [69]
71 No Experience/No Talent (But I'm Willing to Start at the Top.) [69]
72 Remember The Old Chinese Saying: [45]

73 Have You Forgotten Anything? [30]
74 You're Tops In My Book [60]
75 Silence [27]
76 Cleanliness Is Next To Godliness (And Next to Impossible, Too) [36]
77 To Be Seen — Stand Up/To Be Heard — Speak Up/To Be Appreciated — Shut Up [51]
78 Smile (Even If It Hurts) [18]
79 Not Everyone Has Your Brains (Some People Are Smart.) [42]
80 Quiet (Genius At Work) [35]
81 Use Your Head! (It's the Little Things That Count.) [13]
82 Nobody Tells Me What To Do! [81]
83 To Err Is Human (But Why Must You Be So Human?) [37]
84 Be An Optimist (So Far Not Bad At All!) [58]
85 This Is A Non-Profit Organization (We Didn't Plan It That Way.) [86]
86 Stop Worrying (You'll Never Get Out Of This World Alive.) [67]
87 Do It Tomorrow (You Made Enough Mistakes Today.) [49]
88 I'm A Genius (Do I Have to Prove It?) [63]

1963 WACKY PLAK BY
SCANLENS (AUSTRALIA)

1962 WACKY PLAK BY
A & BC GUM (ENGLAND)

WALT DISNEY CHARACTER TRANSFERS (?)

2" X 2 1/2"

This set of Leaf Gum tattoos was unknown until a quantity of them was recently discovered and found its way into the hobby. Each paper sheet has two named characters from a Walt Disney animated film or short. The designs could be used as water activated skin tattoos or applied to cloth with a hot iron.

The transfer sheets were packed in "Zip Color Bubble Gum" packs and were sold in 1948. The piece of gum in each pack was protected by a generic "Leaf Gum" wrapper of its own (which also kept the transfer sheet from being damaged). The set total is not

know (six different names have been confirmed so far), and no reference number has been assigned.

ITEM	EX	AVE
Transfer Sheet	3.00	1.00
Wrapper	20.00	––

IN DOUBT ABOUT MAKING A PURCHASE?
GET A SECOND OPINION.

WHO–Z–AT STAR (80)   2 5/8" X 3 3/4"

Mona Freeman
COURTESY REPUBLIC PICTURES

To Topps Gum goes the honor of producing the most important American movie star set of the post-World War II era: "Who-Z-At Star." The name of the set comes from the identification quiz printed on the back of every card (the answer was revealed on another card, of course). The fronts have color photographs framed nicely by gray borders. The backs (white and yellow print on blue stock) carry a short list of vital statistics and a long paragraph of biographical information. Both 1-cent and 5-cent wrappers were used to market the series, which was released to the public in 1953. The set reference number is R710-4. NOTE: many cards of this set have printing streaks or are mis-cut. To be graded "excellent," cards must be well-centered and be devoid of streaks.

ITEM	EX	AVE
Set	550.00	100.00
Wrappers		
1-cent	110.00	––
5-cent	125.00	––

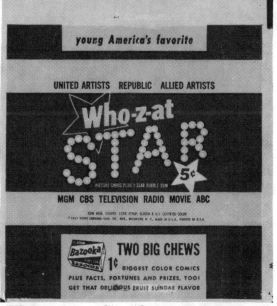

STAR	EX	AVE				
1 Brian Donlevy	6.00	1.25	26 Harry Cary, Jr.	5.00	1.00	
2 Rex Allen	5.00	1.00	27 Deborah Kerr	6.00	1.25	
3 Forrest Tucker	5.00	1.00	28 Polly Bergen	6.00	1.25	
4 Allen "Rocky" Lane	6.00	1.25	29 Pier Angeli	5.00	1.00	
5 Joan Leslie	5.00	1.00	30 William Powell	6.00	1.25	
6 Roy Barcroft	5.00	1.00	31 William Campbell	5.00	1.00	
7 Ella Raines	5.00	1.00	32 James Craig	5.00	1.00	
8 Rod Cameron	5.00	1.00	33 Gig Young	5.00	1.00	
9 Fred MacMurray	6.00	1.25	34 Ricardo Montaban	5.00	1.00	
10 Vera Ralston	5.00	1.00	35 Howard Keel	5.00	1.00	
11 Dennis O'Keefe	5.00	1.00	36 Eleanor Parker	5.00	1.00	
12 Ruth Hussey	5.00	1.00	37 Gene Kelly	7.50	1.50	
13 Eve Arden	5.00	1;00	38 Keenan Wynn	5.00	1.00	
14 William Demarest	5.00	1.00	39 Clark Gable	15.00	3.00	
15 Scott Brady	5.00	1.00	40 Cara Williams	5.00	1.00	
16 Buddy Baer	5.00	1.00	41 Marge & Gower Champion	5.00	1.00	
17 John Lund	5.00	1.00	42 Van Johnson	5.00	1.00	
18 Katy Jurado	5.00	1.00	43 June Allyson	5.00	1.00	
19 Audrey Totter	5.00	1.00	44 Janet Leigh	5.00	1.00	
20 Elaine Stewart	5.00	1.00	45 Ava Gardner	6.00	1.25	
21 Jane Powell	6.00	1.25	46 Red Skelton	10.00	2.00	
22 Vera–Ellen	5.00	1.00	47 Robert Taylor	6.00	1.25	
23 Lionel Barrymore	5.00	1.00	48 Carleton Carpenter	5.00	1.00	
24 Betta St. John	5.00	1.00	49 Ester Williams	7.50	1.50	
25 Marjorie Main	5.00	1.00	50 Walter Pidgeon	5.00	1.00	

51 Stewart Granger	5.00	1.00
52 Elizabeth Taylor	20.00	4.00
53 Cyd Charisse	6.00	1.25
54 Lana Turner	7.50	1.50
55 Greer Garson	5.00	1.00
56 Vic Damone	6.00	1.25
57 Ann Miller	5.00	1.00
58 Robert Horton	5.00	1.00
59 Vittorio Gassman	5.00	1.00
60 Rita Gam	5.00	1.00
61 Steve Forrest	5.00	1.00
62 Leslie Caron	5.00	1.00
63 Ann Blyth	5.00	1.00
64 Spencer Tracy	10.00	2.00
65 Red Buttons	6.00	1.25
66 Johnny Sheffield	5.00	1.00
67 Wayne Morris	5.00	1.00
68 Leo Gorcey	6.00	1.25
69 The Nelsons	15.00	3.00
70 Arleen Whelan	5.00	1.00
71 Richard Anderson	5.00	1.00
72 Barry Sullivan	5.00	1.00
73 Mona Freeman	5.00	1.00
74 Preston Foster	5.00	1.00
75 Robert Stack	5.00	1.00
76 Slim Pickens	5.00	1.00
77 Debbie Reynolds	7.50	1.50
78 Nanette Fabray	5.00	1.00
79 Errol Flynn	10.00	2.00
80 J. Carrol Naish	6.00	1.25

WILD MAN (72)

"MAN'S PAST is stained with BLOOD; His FUTURE can be bright with PROMISE — if in the PRESENT he will wage PEACE." Gee, now there's a light and entertaining theme for a children's bubble gum trading card series. Bowman Gum, naturally, was the company which produced it. The 72 cards chronicle the sum of mankind's violent past and his potential for a violent future. The color artwork is so incredibly beautiful and detailed that each card is a miniature masterpiece, but such quality also had its "down side." There is evidence that Bowman intended to produce as many as five series of "Wild Man" cards (180 in all), but artwork and production costs were beginning to undermine the Bowman empire. Wild Man, sadly, was the last of the Bowman post-war sets to be produced in the grand tradition that its flamboyant owner had established in the halcyon days of Gum, Inc.

The first series of 36 cards was issued in the summer of 1950, right on the heels of the wildly successful "Wild West" set. A second run of 36 cards followed, but the market for the series was much softer than Bowman had envisioned, and less of these were made. None of the Wild Man cards are easy to obtain, but the second series (37-72) is definitely harder to find. We have illustrated two 1-cent wrappers to point out that there are five different heads drawn on them, and that only three full heads fit on any one wrapper. Wrapper collectors might wish to look for a tandem which shows all five characters. The display box for this set has yet to be reported in any collection. The reference number is R701-18.

Hunting the Mammoth
Most people today think of hunting as a sport. But to the cave man it was work. Eating or going hungry depended upon the outcome of the chase. The mammoth, a shaggy ancestor of the elephant, was one of the huge beasts that cave men killed for meat—perhaps by stampeding it over a cliff and then attacking it with their stone weapons.
MAN'S PAST is stained with BLOOD; His FUTURE can be bright with PROMISE—If in the PRESENT he will wage PEACE.
© 1950 Bowman Gum, Inc., Phila., Pa., U.S.A.
12 in the First Series of 36 Wild Man Picture Cards.

Battle of Waterloo
One of the most terrible battles in the story of mankind was fought at Waterloo, Belgium, June 18, 1815. Amid scenes of frightful slaughter, the English and Prussians defeated the French army of Napoleon Bonaparte. This ended a series of bloody wars. Napoleon was exiled to the lonely island of St. Helena. There he spent the rest of his life.
MAN'S PAST is stained with BLOOD; His FUTURE can be bright with PROMISE—II in the PRESENT he will wage PEACE.
© 1950 Bowman Gum, Inc., Phila., Pa., U.S.A.
44 in the Second Series of 36 Wild Man Picture Cards

ITEM	EX	AVE
Cards		
1-36	8.00	2.00
37-72	12.00	3.00
Set	900.00	200.00
Wrapper	100.00	——

1 The First Murder
2 Fight for a Cave
3 In the Roman Arena
4 Hannibal Crosses the Alps
5 Attila and the Huns
6 Crusaders Storm Antioch
7 Poison Gas
8 Hiroshima
9 Seeing the World
10 Marco Polo in the East
11 Fire Aids Early Man
12 Hunting the Mammoth
13 Building the Pyramids
14 Falconry
15 Last Bare-Knuckle Bout
16 Piracy
17 Stretcher Bearers
18 Rescue at Sea
19 Civil War in China
20 Snorkel
21 Reign of Terror
22 Border Incident
23 Jungle Bombing
24 Saboteurs
25 Amazon Frontier
26 Skyliner
27 Riverjack
28 Daredevils
29 Concentration Camps
30 To Siberia
31 Quest for Peace
32 Land of Promise
33 War Rockets
34 Atomic Doom
35 Flying Suits
36 Trip to the Moon

37 That's Mine
38 Red Sea Death
39 Alexander Conquers Persia
40 Viking Fury
41 Joan of Arc
42 Private War
43 Fort William Henry Massacre
44 Battle of Waterloo
45 Pearl Harbor
46 Gallant Tanker
47 Death of Capt. Cook
48 Stanley Seeks Livingstone
49 Stone-Age Hunt
50 Winning a Home
51 Whaling Days
52 Chariot Race
53 Men Against Beast
54 Guillotine
55 Martyred Hermit
56 Dive Bomber
57 Flame Thrower
58 Land Mine
59 Guerrilla War
60 South American Revolution
61 Foreign Legion in Action
62 Danger Zone
63 Australian Bushman
64 Search for Uranium
65 Jet Pilot
66 Under the River
67 Salvaging Treasure
68 Communists Seize U.S. Consul
69 Cornered
70 City of the Dead
71 Raiding Germ Laboratory
72 Attack from Space

ON THIS PAGE: PROMOTION
MATERIAL FOR "WILD MAN"
NEXT 4 PAGES: ISSUE NO. 2
OF " THE COLLECTOR" MAGAZINE
DISTRIBUTED BY BOWMAN.

The COLLECTOR

Dedicated to:

**CHILD, CHURCH,
HOME, SCHOOL,
COMMUNITY**

through

Cartophily

PICTURE CARD · COLLECTORS CLUB · 5-STAR BOWMAN SERIES

Published by BOWMAN GUM, INC., PHILADELPHIA 44, PA., U.S.A. No. 2

Bowman Releases "WILD MAN"

Another New "5-Star" Series of Collectors Cards is packed with Bowman Picture Card Gum

WILDER THAN WILD WEST

How wild is man? How much has his nature changed from the earliest cave-man days up to the year 1950? See the new, terrific picture-story cards in WILD MAN Picture Card Gum. Save them as each new series of 36 cards is issued every few weeks.

A History of MAN

Your complete collections of these exciting, full color WILD MAN cards will record the story of MAN through thousands of years. His early days; his struggles for existence; his rise and fall; his work and play; his science and arts; his inventive skills; his explorations and discoveries; his wars and conquests; his sins and crimes; his power to love; his hopes and fears; his dreams of peace.

MAN Must Wage Peace

Is MAN yet WILD? What can TAME him? Get the answer in WILD MAN picture cards. "Man's past is stained with blood; his future can be bright with promise; if in the present he will wage peace."

You thought WILD WEST cards were wild? Wait until you see WILD MAN! And be sure to start right in saving and trading to complete your collection. Did

**Card No. 1 in the WILD MAN series.
Cain kills his brother Abel.**

you manage to collect all 180 of the Wild West cards issued so far? Many collectors did. Don't miss any of these WILD MAN cards! Your friend the Candy Store Man has WILD MAN Picture Card Gum. One thrilling card and a piece of delicious bubble gum for one cent.

Join the Collectors Club

If you have not yet joined the Picture Card Collectors Club, send five wrappers for a free membership card (see back page). Card collecting—cartophily—is a pleasant hobby.

HUNDREDS JOIN THE COLLECTORS CLUB

Free Membership Cards Offered

UPWARDS of a hundred million Wild West picture cards were issued last fall by Bowman Gum, Inc., of Philadelphia. Five sets of 36 subjects were released—180 different action stories in all. Saving and trading Wild West cards became the principal hobby of thousands of boys and girls across America in 1949.

Five hundred thousand copies of The COLLECTOR magazine were issued through storekeepers. Many hundreds of readers wrote in for the free membership card of the Picture Card Collectors Club, signed by Uncle Bob, the national president.

Mr. J. R. Burdick, of Syracuse, N. Y., the dean of American card collectors, called this effort of Bowman Gum, Inc., "the greatest single boost to juvenile card collecting."

Members to Get Magazine

Bowman will mail this issue of The COLLECTOR to every member of the Club. Later issues will also be available for all members who wish them. The magazine will contain valuable information and news for card collectors. Anyone can become a member of the Picture Card Collectors Club merely by sending five wrappers from any Bowman Picture Card Gum, together with name, address, postal zone number, and age to "Uncle Bob," Bowman Gum, Inc., Philadelphia 44, Pa. A membership card like that pictured on the back page will be sent free.

Organize Local Chapters

A few collectors in any city, town, or community may join together in a local chapter of the Picture Card Collectors Club. You may have regular meetings, swap sessions, exhibitions, and other activities to advance your hobby. When you have met and elected your officers— a president, secretary, and treasurer— send the information to Uncle Bob and a Local Chapter certificate will be sent to you. Further suggestions and a sample constitution will be mailed on request.

A reduced-size picture of the new WILD MAN Picture Card Gum, 1c.

New "Five-Star" Series

Even while the interest in Wild West cards is at its height in some parts of the country, Bowman is releasing another in its famous "5-Star" series of picture cards.

The new series is called WILD MAN and promises to be even more exciting than Wild West (see front page).

Like other Bowman "5-Star" Series, WILD MAN picture cards are beautifully printed in full color, from the finest original artwork, historically accurate in every detail. And as always, these Bowman cards are intensely appealing to children and yet morally constructive.

When you write to Uncle Bob . . .

DO NOT send him cards that you wish to trade for others. He cannot undertake to do this. He simply would not have enough to meet all special requests.

He wants you to trade cards with your friends. That is why he suggests that you get your friends together and form a local collectors club.

Uncle Bob does send you a membership card, of course. And he answers all questions possible, either directly or through the columns of The COLLECTOR magazine.

Thank you for the hundreds of letters to Uncle Bob.

Address Uncle Bob, c/o Bowman Gum, Inc., 4865 Stenton Ave., Phila. 44, Pa., U. S. A.

How many Wild West cards have been issued in the 1949 series?

Mary Freholtz
(and many other readers)

Five sets of 36—180 cards in all so far. They are best arranged in an album by groups: Division A, Winning the West, has 40 cards; the other seven groups, Divisions B to H, have 20 cards each. Later on, more Wild West cards will be issued. Just now we are releasing WILD MAN. ✱ ✱

In buying Wild West Picture Card Gum to complete my fifth set I sometimes get cards of earlier series. Why is this?

(Several readers)

As new cards are issued, a very few of the preceding series are packed with them to give new collectors a chance to complete their sets. Duplicate cards are desirable so that you can mount one card face up and one with the story side up, below it. Extras may be matched or traded. ✱ ✱

What do you mean by tossing or matching cards? How do you do it?

(Many readers)

These are games of skill at which two or more can play with great fun. In tossing, the players stand 10 or 12 feet from a wall and, by turns, each one tries to toss a card as close to the wall as possible. The one coming closest wins the other cards.

In matching, or flipping, hold a card by the long edges, thumb above and fingers below. Give the card a short upward fling to start it revolving as it falls to the ground. The second player does likewise; and wins if he matches the first player's card (head or tail), loses if he does not. Loser plays first. An experienced player develops skill. Ask Dad, he knows.

TIPS FOR COLLECTORS

■ Small cellophane envelopes are suggested as a means of filing individual cards and of mounting them in an album so that both sides of the card may be viewed. (Hinge at one end of envelope with scotch tape.)

■ A mail auction sale of earlier Bowman Gum cards and many other varieties of 19th and 20th Century trade and cigarette cards is a regular feature of the "Card Collector's Bulletin," published every two months by Charles R. Bray, a veteran cartophilist, of East Bangor, Penna. Subscription to the bulletin is 50c a year (sent to Mr. Bray, NOT to us).

■ The more serious card collectors will want a copy of the American Card Catalog, a 144-page book, size 6 x 9 inches, in which are listed several thousand different series of tobacco, candy and gum cards, and other souvenirs, of the 19th and the 20th centuries, together with their approximate values. Although published in 1946, the catalog is still a reliable reference; and a 1949 Supplement is included at the price, $1.00. The book may be ordered direct from the publisher, J. R. Burdick, 420 So. Crouse Ave., Syracuse 10, New York.

Mr. Burdick is a well known card collector and a patron of the hobby. He is presenting his exhaustive collection to the Metropolitan Museum of Art, New York City, where the items are being mounted in albums for permanent reference. More than 25,000 of Mr. Burdick's 19th Century tobacco inserts have already gone to the Museum.

■ Suggestions for games to play at one of the local club meetings, or a special "Collectors Party":
1. *Jig-Saw Scramble*—Cut some picture cards (extras that are soiled or cannot be traded) into odd-shaped pieces. Give each person an envelope containing all the pieces for five cards. Start on signal. The person putting his cards together first wins.
2. *Quiz Cards*—Divide the group into two equal teams. Appoint one person "Quizmaster" to ask questions of one person at a time, on alternate teams, about information on the backs of the picture cards which everyone has read. Those who miss must step out, until the one final winner is left.

LITTLE VISITS TO FAMOUS CARD COLLECTORS

**Visit to Robert B. Jones
1469 No. Redfield Street
Philadelphia 31, Pa.**

Collector Bob Jones with a few of his cards.

BOB JONES started to save picture cards more than 25 years ago as a young lad. His grandfather used to bring him the cards which then were packed with cigarettes.

As he completed first one set, and then another, the love of collecting grew with him, and he has been an ardent cartophilist ever since.

He has many sets of early 20th Century tobacco cards and silks (and even some 19th Century cards). He has one of the finest collections of candy and gum cards we have ever seen, and of course most of the Bowman Gum card series are represented by complete, or nearly complete sets.

A Genial Host

Bob soon invites an interested guest past his living room and into another room of his house where, on a leather covered table, he opens up album after album of his prized collection. All his cards are well preserved, some protected by cellophane; and all are neatly indexed. He has a careful record of the cards he needs to complete sets, and he carries on an extensive correspondence with collectors across the land. He says he has never counted them, but he must have more than 25,000 cards.

When Bob accumulates more of any series of cards than he needs, he sells or trades them to other collectors direct by mail, or offers them through the mail auction conducted by Charles Bray.

A Recognized Authority

Although Mr. Jones collects cards entirely as a hobby, and not as a means of livelihood, he is well known as an authority on candy and gum cards. He is a good judge of subject matter and has admired Bowman cards through the years. He advises children to save picture cards because "Card collecting is interesting, educational and character-building."

JOIN THE CLUB. SEND FOR YOUR MEMBERSHIP CARD

Just mail us five wrappers from Wild Man (or Wild West) Picture Card Gum together with your name, address, and age and we will send your membership card in the Picture Card Collectors Club. Address "Uncle Bob" at Bowman Gum, Inc., 4865 Stenton Ave., Philadelphia 44, Pa. Get some friends together and start a local chapter.

This is to certify that

----

is a member of the

PICTURE CARD COLLECTORS CLUB

which is dedicated to the advancement of CHILD, CHURCH, HOME, SCHOOL, & COMMUNITY through the fellowship & interest of Cartophily.

-------------------   -------------------
DATE   NATIONAL PRESIDENT
ADDRESS "UNCLE BOB," BOWMAN GUM, INC., PHILA. 44, PA.

WILD WEST (180)

2 1/16" X 2 1/2"

Although a copyright date of 1949 appears on every card, Bowman Gum's "Wild West" series was not released to the public until 1950. By all accounts, it was a smash hit; the company's New York representative alone sold more than 250,000 boxes in three months. The series was issued in 36-card groups, and each group contained eight cards from sub-series "A" and four cards each from subseries "B" through "H" (see checklist below for subseries' titles). In this way, Bowman made sure that collectors would have to keep on buying packs to complete their favorite subgroups.

The color artwork of Wild West cards is detailed and beautiful, and the card designers were smart enough not to clutter up the fronts with captions and other types of print. The backs contain all the printed information: subseries number and title, card title, and text. The famous Bowman "Picture Card Collectors Club" logo with the "5-Star Bowman Series" center is printed on every card. The 1-cent and 5-cent wrappers are white, with two shades of brown used for the "bucking bronco" drawing and the print lines. Only the 1-cent wrapper has the price marked on it. The display box has a center section on the lid which was marked to be cut away and used as a display card. The reference number is R701-19.

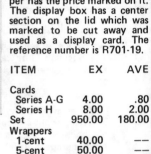

ITEM	EX	AVE
Cards		
Series A-G	4.00	.80
Series H	8.00	2.00
Set	950.00	180.00
Wrappers		
1-cent	40.00	—
5-cent	50.00	—
Box	350.00	85.00

WINNING THE WEST
A–1 Capturing British Fort
A–2 Louisiana Is Ours
A–3 Exploring the Wilds
A–4 Mountain Men
A–5 Trap-Line Troubles
A–6 Horseback Duel
A–7 Shooting the Rapids
A–8 At War with Britain
A–9 Battle of New Orleans
A–10 Death at the Water Hole
A–11 "Lonestar" Settlers
A–12 The Alamo
A–13 Fremont in the Rockies
A–14 Indians Attack Wagon Train
A–15 Buffalo Stampede
A–16 Prairie Fire
A–17 Battling a Tempest
A–18 Gun Runners
A–19 Mormons Settle Utah
A–20 James Marshall Strikes Gold
A–21 The Gold Rush Is On
A–22 Out to Stake a Claim
A–23 Dealing with Claim-Jumpers
A–24 Virginia City Boom
A–25 Panning Gold
A–26 Stage Coach Robbery
A–27 Saddling Pony Express
A–28 Ambush
A–29 Indians Attack Iron Horse
A–30 Buffaloes Stop Train
A–31 Train Robbery
A–32 Down Goes the Telegraph
A–33 Peril at the Pass
A–34 Hazards of Track Laying
A–35 Bridge Disaster
A–36 Snowbound Train
A–37 Relay
A–38 "Pike's Peak or Bust"
A–39 Montana Gold
A–40 Chicago Fire

INDIAN CUSTOMS
B–1 Scalp Dance
B–2 Running the Gauntlet
B–3 Race
B–4 Bow and Arrow Hunting
B–5 Sign Language
B–6 Smoke Signals
B–7 The War Whoop
B–8 An Indian Never Forgets
B–9 Stalking Game
B–10 Peace Pipe
B–11 Young Indian Learns
B–12 Building Birch Bark Canoe
B–13 Woman's Work
B–14 Cliff Dwellers
B–15 Torture Stake
B–16 The Medicine Man
B–17 Indian Lacrosse
B–18 Fishing for Salmon
B–19 Buffalo Trap
B–20 False Face Society

FAMOUS CHARACTERS
C–1 Tecumseh
C–2 Kit Carson
C–3 Col. James Bowie
C–4 "Pawnee Bill"
C–5 "Calamity Jane"
C–6 "Buffalo Bill"
C–7 Captain Jack
C–8 Daniel Boone
C–9 Davy Crockett
C–10 Annie Oakley
C–11 Chief Joseph
C–12 Sam Houston
C–13 Blackhawk
C–14 Marcus Whitman
C–15 Geronimo
C–16 Sitting Bull
C–17 Andrew Jackson
C–18 Simon Kenton
C–19 Red Cloud
C–20 White Bear

INDIAN WARFARE
D–1 Defeat of General Harmer
D–2 Defending Their Home
D–3 Captives' March
D–4 Indian Mercy
D–5 Boy Captives
D–6 Burnt-Arrow Punishment
D–7 Ransom
D–8 Battle of Tippecanoe
D–9 Battle of Horseshoe Bend
D–10 Escaping the Comanches
D–11 Rushing a Stockade
D–12 Saving the Wounded
D–13 Battle of Bad Axe
D–14 In the Nick of Time
D–15 Angry Squaw
D–16 Fort Kearny Massacre
D–17 Wagon Box Fight
D–18 Death by Moonlight
D–19 Hayfield Fight
D–20 Perilous Work

COWBOY LIFE
E–1 Trail Drive
E–2 Roping Wild Horses
E–3 Roundup
E–4 Bulldozing a Longhorn
E–5 Cowboys Go to Town
E–6 Pony in the Parlor
E–7 Branding a Calf
E–8 Bronco Buster
E–9 Stampede
E–10 Fighting a Blizzard
E–11 Range War
E–12 Battle of Wild Stallions
E–13 An Easterner Learns
E–14 Cowgirl Race
E–15 Chuck Wagon
E–16 Sheep and Cattle War
E–17 Night Visitors
E–18 Cowboy Capers
E–19 Look! The Stage Coach!
E–20 Killer Bear

LAW AND ORDER
F–1 Sheriff Gets His Man
F–2 Vigilantes Ride
F–3 Horse Thieves
F–4 Surprising Cattle Rustlers
F–5 The Daltons
F–6 Deputy Sheriff
F–7 Bill Hickock at Hays City
F–8 Jail Break
F–9 Sheriff Defies Mob
F–10 Outlaws at Bay
F–11 Two-Gun Marshall
F–12 Run Out of Town
F–13 "Stick 'Em Up"
F–14 Rangers Ride
F–15 Rangers Battle Outlaws
F–16 Rangers Chase Apaches
F–17 Jesse James Holdup
F–18 Whip Beats Pistol
F–19 Citizens Rout Bandits
F–20 Wells Fargo Holdup

RIVER DAYS
G–1 Mighty Paul Bunyan
G–2 Flatboatmen on Rampage
G–3 King Cotton
G–4 Lone Traveler, Beware!
G–5 Villains' Cave
G–6 River Pirates
G–7 Strategem
G–8 Wreck of the "Tennessee"
G–9 Cub Pilot
G–10 Steamboat Burns Bridge
G–11 Hark! The Calliope
G–12 Seeing the Show
G–13 New Orleans Bullfight
G–14 Rifles at 30 Yards
G–15 The River Rises
G–16 The Steamboat Race
G–17 The "Moselle" Blows Up
G–18 Tornado
G–19 Heroic Captain
G–20 Riding Out an Earthquake

WESTERN STARS
H–1 "Lash" LaRue
H–2 Al "Fuzzy" St. John
H–3 James Ellison
H–4 "Cannonball" Taylor
H–5 Chris-Pin Martin
H–6 James Millican
H–7 Andy Clyde
H–8 Max "Alibi" Terhune
H–9 Monte Hale
H–10 Raymond Hatton
H–11 Allan "Rocky" Lane
H–12 Pat Brady
H–13 Rex Allen
H–14 Don "Red" Barry
H–15 Holly Bane
H–16 Robert Lowery
H–17 Ray Bennett
H–18 Marshall Reed
H–19 John Cason
H–20 Tom Neal

ORIGINAL ARTWORK FOR CARD NO. A-32, "DOWN GOES THE TELEGRAPH"
(NOTE HAND-WRITTEN NUMBER IN LOWER RIGHT CORNER)

The COLLECTOR

Dedicated to:

CHILD, CHURCH, HOME, SCHOOL, COMMUNITY

through *Cartophily*

Published by BOWMAN GUM, INC., PHILADELPHIA 44, PA., U.S.A. No. 1

YOUR FRIEND ... THE STOREKEEPER

Your candy-store man is your friend. He is always ready to serve you with good things for a penny. He sells Bowman Quality Bubble Gum. One is called BLONY. It is a big piece; and it blows the biggest bubbles.

Another is called WILD WEST. It contains a piece of good, sweet bubble gum and a very beautiful picture card printed in full color.

Save these picture cards. They tell about the early West. Pioneers. Cowboys. Indians. Sheriffs. Outlaws. Steamboat Days. Famous Characters. And Modern Western Movie Stars.

Join the Picture Card Collectors Club. Make an album and try to get a complete set of cards. They are valuable.

Your storekeeper can get more of these magazines from his supplier. Tell your friends to save WILD WEST cards, too.

Collecting Picture Cards Is a Thrilling Hobby

CALLED "CARTOPHILY" ABROAD

In England thousands of boys and girls save the picture cards that came in packages of cigarettes. Grown-ups save them also. They call this hobby "cartophily." And they have clubs, and dealers, and exhibitions, just as they do in stamp collecting, which is called "philately."

In America it is better. The picture cards come in Bowman Bubble Gum. And parents don't mind if children chew bubble gum—at the right time, of course. (Never chew it in the schoolroom, nor just before meals. After meals or while at play is the best time.)

Saving Cards Is Fun

Every Bowman 5-Star Series of Picture Cards is a clean, interesting, instructive set. WILD WEST is one of them. Try to save all the different cards. Get your friends to save, and trade duplicates to increase your collection. Arrange them neatly in an album.

Join the Club. (Free membership card for five wrappers mailed to headquarters.) Organize a local chapter. Put on an exhibit of your collections.

Write to "Uncle Bob" at any time and he will answer your questions about cartophily.

VOLUME 1 OF "THE COLLECTOR," PUBLISHED BY BOWMAN GUM IN 1950.

380

Bowman Releases "WILD WEST"

First 36 of a new "Five-Star" Series of full-color picture cards dealing with the Early West are offered with WILD WEST penny gum.

Cards are this size, in full color

Here is a list of titles of the first 36 WILD WEST picture cards:

Division A—Winning the West
1. Capturing British Fort
2. Louisiana Is Ours
3. Exploring the Wilds
4. Mountain Men
5. Trap-Line Trouble
6. Horseback Duel
7. Shooting the Rapids
8. At War With Britain

Division B—Indian Customs
1. Scalp Dance
2. Running the Gauntlet
3. Race
4. Bow-and-Arrow Hunting

Division C—Famous Characters
1. Tecumseh
2. Kit Carson
3. Col. James Bowie
4. Pawnee Bill

Division D—Indian Warfare
1. Defeat of General Harmer
2. Defending Their Home
3. Captives' March
4. Indian Mercy

Division E—Cowboy Life
1. Trail Drive
2. Roping Wild Horses
3. Roundup
4. Bulldozing a Longhorn

Division F—Law and Order
1. Sheriff Gets His Man
2. Vigilantes Ride
3. Horse Thieves
4. Surprising Cattle Rustlers

Division G—River Days
1. Mighty Paul Bunyan
2. Flatboatmen on Rampage
3. King Cotton
4. Lone Traveler, Beware

Division H—Western Stars
1. "Lash" LaRue
2. Al "Fuzzy" St. John
3. James Ellison
4. "Cannonball" Taylor

C-3 FAMOUS CHARACTERS
Col. James Bowie
While Col. James Bowie was fighting with some Mexicans, during the troubles between Texas and Mexico, his sword was broken down to within a few inches of the hilt, but he did so well with the shortened weapon that he won the fight. It gave him the idea of inventing the bowie knife. Later he was killed at the Alamo.

WILD WEST
PICTURE CARD GUM
© 1949 Bowman Gum, Inc., Phila., Pa., U. S. A.

Specimen of text on reverse side

NEW SERIES ISSUED REGULARLY

To become an expert at card collecting you must learn to judge quality of printing. WILD WEST picture cards are reproduced from original full-color paintings by the four-color process. They are printed by offset lithography on good cardboard.

Ask your Dad about these terms. He probably knows this is high quality work. He will also know about card collecting. Maybe he was a collector himself, as a boy.

Show WILD WEST cards to your teachers, too. They will tie in with her lessons on early American history. They make a good class project—or a personal project for you.

Prepare to save a lot of WILD WEST cards, because there will be a new series every month —for a long time if you like them.

ASK *Uncle Bob*

Editor: *The* **COLLECTOR**

Address Uncle Bob, c/o Bowman Gum, Inc., 4865 Stenton Ave., Phila. 44, Pa., U.S.A.

What is the best kind of album to use for mounting my cards?   *James Fenway*

A scrap book or photograph album bought in the "5-and-10" will do. Some collectors glue the cards in the album, but this requires two cards of a kind, so that you can mount one face up and another, below it, with the reverse side, or story, showing. Most collectors use art corners, bought in a stationery store, for mounting. This way the card can be removed for reading the back. Some people cut an opening in the leaf, the size of the card, and hold the card in this opening by scotch tape along the edges, on both sides.

* *

I notice that the Wild West cards are not numbered in order from 1 up. Why is this?   *George Young*

Each *division* is numbered from 1 up. There are eight divisions. Eventually the cards in each division, grouped together, will make a historical story. It is well to wait until you have all the early numbers in each division before starting to mount them.   * *

If I save all the Wild West cards will they be worth money?   *Eugene Fisher*

Complete sets, in perfect condition, will become more and more valuable as the years go by. Sets of 240 Horrors of War cards issued by Bowman 10 years ago are bringing a fancy price. Ask around among grown-ups and see whether you can locate complete sets of picture cards issued years ago. Write me about them and I will judge their value.

TIPS FOR COLLECTORS

An old shoe box makes a good file cabinet for preserving your cards. It may be trimmed down in height. A cardboard divider placed lengthwise will permit you to store two rows. Small index dividers placed between divisions or series may be labeled with the name. Keep the lid; and have clean hands, because only clean cards are worth keeping.

———

A ruled composition book is good for keeping a list or index of all your cards. Also keep the names and addresses of other children who are saving cards. You may want to exchange your duplicate cards for others you do not have.

———

Do you have a projector of the reflector type? Your cards will look well when projected large upon a screen or white cardboard. Invite members of your club to a showing.

Some Other Bowman Series

The first Wild West cards were issued in 1933. Since then there have been Pirates; Mickey Mouse; G-Men; Horrors of War; War News; Uncle Sam; Home Defense; Lone Ranger; The World In Arms; Movie Stars; Football; Basketball; and many series of Baseball players.

We shall be glad to hear from collectors who have complete sets of any of these series, and we shall be glad to offer them in our classified column without charge.

CLASSIFIED ADVERTISEMENTS

WANTED: A complete set of 240 Horrors of War cards in perfect condition, unmounted. State price. BOX 100.

———

EXCHANGE: Will trade duplicates of Wild West cards. What numbers do you have, and what do you need? BOX 101.

This Large Collection of Very Old Picture Cards
Belongs to a Colonel of the U. S. Marine Corps

Colonel J. J. Carter, U.S.M.C.R., who lives in Lansdale, Pennsylvania, still has the collection of picture cards which he gathered as a boy.

The cards are some of those which came packed in cigarettes many years ago. They bear pictures of many interesting subjects, including birds, animals, famous places and people, sportsmen, ball players, etc. All the cards are neatly arranged in a large photograph album, shown below.

Going through this album is like turning back the pages of history and looking in on the manners and customs of the early 20th Century in America.

Says Colonel Carter: "I have never regretted spending so much time as a boy in the collection of these picture cards. It was interesting and educational. And it still delights me to look over the old album.

"I think every boy and girl should have a hobby, and the collecting of picture cards is a good one. Especially today, when the cards come in Bowman chewing gum, instead of in cigarettes."

The COLLECTOR is grateful to the Colonel for his permission to print this photograph. It would be happy to learn of other similar collections.

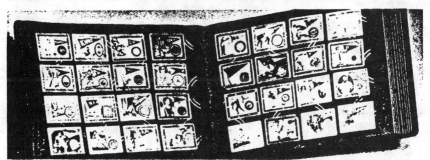

Do You Want to Join the CARD COLLECTORS CLUB?
HERE'S HOW TO GET YOUR MEMBERSHIP CARD

Send five wrappers from WILD WEST Picture Card Gum, together with your name, address, and age to Bowman Gum, Inc., Philadelphia 44, Pa., and we will send you your membership card in the Picture Card Collectors Club.

Try to be first in your neighborhood to flash this impressive card. It shows that you are a member of the Picture Card Collectors Club.

This is to certify that

----

is a member of the

PICTURE CARD COLLECTORS CLUB

which is dedicated to the advancement of
CHILD, CHURCH, HOME, SCHOOL, & COMMUNITY
through the fellowship & interest of Cartophily.

-------------------------   -------------------------
DATE   NATIONAL PRESIDENT
ADDRESS "UNCLE BOB," BOWMAN GUM, INC., PHILA. 44, PA.

500 M—8-49—Printed in U. S. A.

WINGS (200)
2 5/8" X 3 3/4"

The "Wings" series of 200 artwork pictures of airplanes is one of the most commonly-encountered of Topps early non-sport issues. It has been erroneously reported that the set was marketed in 1954-55, which is impossible as it was listed in the 1953 edition of the American Card Catalog, and the box bears a 1952 copyright date. The color paintings of planes, created from actual photographs provided by the Herald Tribune, are captioned on the front in large white letters. The card number is found on the back in a red panel, along with a written description of the aircraft and a "Friend or Foe" quiz (answer given on next card in sequence). A number of Wings cards were reissued, with larger side borders, by Doeskin Tissues in the fall of 1955 (they have "Doeskin" printed on the back). Wings gums packs were issued in 1-cent and 5-cent denominations and both are hard to find as Topps issued a larger quantity of these cards in cello packs and vendor's boxes than in wax packages. The reference number is R707-4.

ITEM	EX	AVE
Card	2.00	.40
Wrappers		
1-cent	125.00	—
5-cent	125.00	—
Box	225.00	55.00

"WINGS" ISSUE BY DOESKIN TISSUES WAS MARKETED IN 1955

1 T-33	26 F-80 Shooting Star
2 MIG-15	27 Sea Attacker
3 XC-120 Pack Plane	28 F6F Hellcap
4 Lincoln	29 P2V Neptune
5 F-51 Mustang	30 Avro Jetliner
6 AT-7 Navigator	31 C-121 Constellation
7 PBY Catalina	32 C-74 Globemaster—1
8 B-26 Invader	33 F-84F
9 XF-91	34 F4U Corsair
10 F7U Cutlass	35 Firefly
11 Vampire	36 C—125 Raider
12 B-57 Canberra	37 C-46 Commando
13 Sunderland	38 PE-2
14 PB4Y-2 Privateer	39 AF Guardian
15 T-28	40 C-82 Packet
16 Wyverne Mk. 2	41 R60 Constitution
17 Balliol T. Mk. 2	42 IL-12
18 F-47 Thunderbolt	43 Hastings
19 HUP-1	44 AJ Savage
20 Hermes	45 F-82 Twin-Mustang
21 L-17 Navion	46 XF4D Skyray
22 F3D Skyknight	47 T-6 Texas
23 AM Mauler	48 C-123 Avitruk
24 B-36	49 JRM Mars
25 F8F Bearcat	50 Meteor

51 B—29 Superfortress	96 P4M Mercator
52 IL-10	97 C-124 Globemaster II
53 B-45 Tornado	98 TU-4
54 LA-5	99 YAK-15
55 Comet	100 F9F Panther
56 H—13D	101 AE-27 Pulqui
57 PE-8	102 AE-33 Pulqui
58 C-97 Stratofreighter	103 O-10 Leduc
59 H-2I	104 MD-450 Ouragan
60 FH-1 Phantom	105 SO-6021 Espadan
61 B-47 Stratojet	106 SO-M2
62 L-20 Beaver	107 SO-6000 Triton
63 FJ Fury	108 V6-90
64 F-94	109 Nord 1601
65 Shackleton	110 Nord 2200
66 S-51 Helicopter	111 707A Delta Wing
67 A-20 Havoc	112 Avro Aston
68 IL-2 Stromovik	113 Supermarine 535
69 C-119 Packet	114 Vickers 660
70 DC-4 Skymaster	115 Hawker P-1081
71 F-86 Saber	116 Short SB-3
72 Venom	117 Handley Page 88
73 H-19	118 Target Plane
74 TBM Avenger	119 Fokker S14
75 C-F 100 Canuck	120 MIG-19
76 F-84 Thunderjet	121 Saab 29-A
77 F-86D	122 F9F6 Cougar
78 Sea Hawk	123 YB 60 Heavy Bomber
79 SA-16 Albatross	124 XF 88A Voodoo
80 202	125 F-84-G Thunderjet
81 B-50 Superbomber	126 XC-99 Cargo Transport
82 Convair 240	127 XC-123A Jet Avitruc
83 Ambassador	128 X-4 Northrop
84 IL-4	129 PO-1W Lockheed
85 Viscount	130 S.E. 24l5 Gronard II
86 B-25 Mitchell	131 Swift Supermarine 541
87 YAK-3	132 Gloster GA5
88 C-47 Skytrain	133 SR A-1
89 A2D Skyshark	134 Short SA 4
90 F-89 Scorpion	135 Unknown Russian Jet Plane
91 IL-18	136 XA 2 J1 Savage
92 P5M-Marlin	137 FJ 2 North American
93 H-12	138 AD-5 Skyraider
94 F7F Tigercat	139 PBM-5 Mariner
95 F-24 Banshee	140 XP5Y-1 Vultee

141 TO-2 Lockheed
142 XF-92A Vultee
143 XF 3H-1 Demon
144 DC 6A Douglas
145 YRB-49A
146 Target Aircraft
147 D.H. Sea Hornet
148 DH 112 Venom
149 XH-26
150 G-80
151 YB1 Blackburn
152 XF 90 Lockheed
153 Bristol 171 MK-3
154 Saro-Cierva Airhorse
155 Sikorsky H.C. MK-2
156 S.O. 1120 Ariel III
157 Breguet Type III
158 LZ IA
159 G.C.A. Model-2
160 Hiller 360
161 MC-4
162 M-14
163 YH-18
164 HO 4S-1
165 Boulton Paul P-III
166 Avro Athena T. MK-2
167 T. MK-20 Avro Anson
168 Blackburn Firebrand
169 Bristol 170 MK-31
170 D.H. 104 Dove Light Transport
171 Meteor N.F. MK-11
172 Handley Page Marathon
173 Sea Fury MK-11
174 Percival P-50 Prince Transport
175 Short Sealand
176 Sea Gull
177 Varsity Aircrew
178 Canadair Four
179 DHC-1 Chipmunk
180 Aero 45
181 Hiller Hornet
182 C.M. 88-R Gemeaux
183 Breguet 76-1
184 C.A.S.A. 201 Alcotan
185 Douglas Skyrocket
186 Fouga C.M. 8-R.I3 Sylphe
187 Morane-Saulnier M.S. 703
188 S.O. 30—P Bretagne
189 Saab-90 A-2 Scandia
190 Beechcraft D18S
191 "Vautour"
192 C-1 Skimmer
193 Saab-210 Draken
194 CF-100 "Canuck"
195 Mooney M-18L Mite
196 TE-1 Buckaroo
197 Saunders-Roe
198 Kaman HTK-1
199 T.H.K. 2
200 Fairey "Gyrodene"

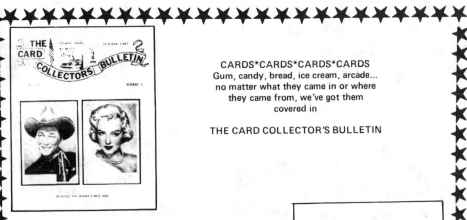

WOODY WOODPECKER TATTOOS (?)   1 9/16" X 3 1/2"

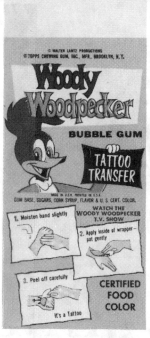

Woody Woodpecker was one of the most popular cartoon characters of the day when Topps decided to produce this set of "tattoo transfers" in 1959. The outer, or "exterior," side of the wrapper is primarily yellow, with red, blue and black as the secondary colors. Directions for applying the water-activated transfers are illustrated in three steps, and a line advises "Watch the Woody Woodpecker T.V. Show." The tattoo designs, printed on the interior side of the wrapper, are neither numbered nor captioned. They are finished in dull shades of red, blue and yellow. The number of transfers in the set has yet to be determined. Most collectors are interested in the outer wrapper rather than the tattoos, so the price for this item has remained moderate. The reference number for the set is R711-8.

ITEM	EX	AVE
Wrapper	15.00	— —

WORLD FAMOUS STAMPS (12)   1" X 4 5/8"

The "World Famous Stamps" set, printed on the interior trays used to hold the gum and reinforce the packages, is the last of three "Bazooka Gum" tray sets which have tormented "type" collectors and card researchers for years ("Famous American Heroes" and "The Story of the Atom Bomb" are the other two). According to the early catalogs, there are 12 panels in the set. Each depicts a "famous" stamp from a foreign nation and explains why it is so popular. In terms of scarcity, World Famous Stamps panels are one of the most difficult to find of all post-World War II issues, but the undistinguished one-color make-up and size have kept demand and value low. The reference number is R714-4.

ITEM	EX	AVE
Panel	25.00	10.00

WORLD FAMOUS STAMPS

THE LOVE STAMP OF SWEDEN. This stamp was issued in 1918. The number "12" was overprinted upside down by mistake. A youth living in Guliksberg used a number of these stamps in writing to his sweetheart. She kept the letters and later discovered the error. A stamp dealer bought the entire lot, which provided the young couple with enough money to get married.

IT'S BAZOOKA FOR BIGGER BUBBLES

WORLD MAP/YOUR FORTUNE/ RIDDLE (?)

The title of this set is simply derived from the sequence of items on a three-section cellophane insert which was packed into "Missile Gum." To the left on the sheet is an advertisement for "Hammond's International World Map," which could be obtained by sending in three "Missile" wrappers and 25 cents. The center section is an unnumbered feature entitled "Your Fortune," and the right-hand section is simply labeled "Riddle." All the drawings and print on the cellophane sheet are done in combinations of red and blue ink. At this time, we have no idea of how many fortunes and riddles were put on these sheets by Philadelphia Gum, or whether there were any premium offers other than the world map. The reference number is R788-6. NOTE: the "Missile Gum" wrapper is priced in the "Fact or Fantasy" set listing presented earlier in the post-World War II section of this book.

ITEM	EX	AVE
Insert Sheet	6.00	2.00

WORLD ON WHEELS (180)

This series is commonly known as "World on Wheels," rather than the simple "Wheels" which appears on the wrappers, because of the "World on Wheels" feature printed on the back of most cards (on some cards it says "See The World on Wheels"). The highly-detailed artwork pictures depict many different types of automobiles, from the earliest types to the up-to-date models of 1955. The make, model, and year of the car are stated on the front, and the card number and descriptive text are found on the back.

There are two mysteries associated with this set, the first of which involves the date of issue. Both wrappers clearly indicate the scope of the set to be 1896-1954, yet collector Jim Kroeger has an insert from a 5-cent pack which gives a contest expiration date of December 20, 1953. Given the way new car models are introduced in the fall of the preceding year, it is quite possible that "Wheels" first became available in late 1953 (there are certainly enough 1954 autos featured in the set!). On the other hand, we have the run of 1955 wrappers which appear at the very end of the series, evidence that "Wheels" was also around in the fall of 1954. To make matters worse, The Card Collectors Bulletin of August, 1956 states that "Topps added 20 cards to Wheels in 1956." Surely, this last reference is mistaken and the writer meant to say "1955."

The second "mystery" — the case of the different color backs — has a definite but as yet unexplained association with the first. It now appears that Wheels was originally a set of 160 cards, and that 20 more cards were added later on. These last 20 cards are as difficult to find as the first 160 are easy. To confuse the situation, cards 161-170 are found with red backs and cards 171-180 with both red and blue backs! No reasonable explanation has surfaced for why cards 161-170 are so hard, or why 171-180 are so hard AND come with either red or blue backs. Collectors can only pray that they come across any cards numbered 161 or above, because those numbers keep most people from ever completing the set. The reference number for the set is R714-24.

ITEM	EX	AVE
Cards		
1-160, red back	1.50	.30
161-180, red back	20.00	5.00
171-180 red or blue back	20.00	5.00
Set	725.00	160.00
Wrappers		
1-cent	35.00	––
5-cent	25.00	––
Box	200.00	45.00

THIS INSERT FROM A 5-CENT "WHEELS" PACK BEARS A 1953 DATE

1 Diamond T Concrete Mixer	16 Pierce Arrow Station Wagon 1911	29 Simplex Speed Car 1910	44 Panhard Racer 1902
2 Cummins Diesel/American Racer	17 White Opera Coupe 1910	30 Alfa Romeo Racing Car	45 Franklin 1904
3 Connaught Sports Car	18 Cemo Turbo — French Experimental Car	31 Hose Truck	46 Belly Tank 3-Wheeler
4 1910 Buick Toy Tonneau	19 Pegaso Sports Car	32 Renault Victoria Runabout 1909	47 U.S. Army Anti-Aircraft Half-Truck
5 Mercer Raceabout 1911	20 Pierce Motorette 1903	33 Willys Jeep	48 Packard Landaulet 1912
6 Excalibur J Sports Car	21 Brush — Panel Delivery 1911	34 Borgward Hansa Sports Car	49 The Long Island Automotive Museum
7 Norton English Motorcycle	22 Lago Talbot/French Sports Car	35 EEFYH Racer	50 Dream Car
8 Lumber Truck Straddle Type	23 Lakester, American Hot Rod	36 Locomobile 1907	51 Vertias Sports Car
9 Buick Runabout 1911	24 Pierce Great Arrow Touring Car 1905	37 Ford Model T Roadster 1910	52 Locomobile Stanhope 1899
10 Lancia Sports Car	25 Airport Fire Truck	38 Kenz Twin Ford Hot Rod	53 Studebaker Touring Car 1906
11 Masterati Racing Car	26 Cooper — Bristol Racing Car	39 BRM — British Racing Car	54 Cunningham Sports Car
12 Mack Diesel Tractor	27 Mercedes Benz 300 SL	40 Columbia Surrey 1900	55 U.S. Army 2½ Ton Truck
13 Maxwell 1911	28 Ford Runabout 1903	41 Stanley Steamer Touring Car 1911	56 Cadillac Touring Car 1906
14 Gatso "Cyclops"		42 M24 Light Tank	57 Vim Stage 1916
15 Osca Maserati — Italian Sports Car		43 Twin Tanker American Hot Rod	58 Dream Car
			59 Alfa Romeo "Flying Disc"

60 Success Auto Buggy 1906	90 Ford Fire Chief's Runabout 1915	123 Frazer-Nash Roadster	153 Pope Toledo Touring Car 1904
61 White Steamer 1906	91 Chrysler New Yorker 1953	124 Packard Tonneau 1904	154 Pope Hartford 1902
62 U.S. Army Self-Propelled Guns 40 mm Dual	92 Mercury Custom 1953	125 Stevens-Duryea Roadster 1910	155 Columbia Royal Victoria 1905
63 Ferrari	93 Studebaker Champion 1953	126 Triumph Streamlined Roadster	156 Royal Touring Car 1906
64 Pierce Arrow Raceabout 1916	94 Ford Coutry Squire 1953	127 Riley Roadster	157 General Motors Electric Taxicab 1912
65 Thomas Flyer Raceabout 1910	95 Buick XP300	128 Hudson Roadster 1912	158 Columbia Landaulet 1905
66 Jaguar XK Super Sports	96 Healey Silverstone	129 Hoffmann-Vespa Motor Scooter	159 Thomas Flyer Limousine 1904
67 Delahaye Custom	97 Packard Patrician 1953	130 Volkswagon Convertible	160 Haynes Apperson Light Touring Car 1905
68 Oakland-Roadster 1911	98 Kaiser Frazer DKF-161	131 M.G. Mighty Midget	161 Chevrolet 1954
69 Knox Surrey 1904	99 Buick Roadmaster 1953	132 Ford Cargo King	162 Mercury Monterey 1954
70 1500 Gallon Pumper, Fire Engine	100 Pontiac La Parisienne	133 Packard Racing Car 1904	163 Packard 1954
71 Lincoln Mercury XL500	101 Elgin Sweeper Truck	134 Lucciola Miniature Car	164 Cadillac Series 62 1954
72 Hudson Touring Car 1911	102 Cisitalia Sports Car	135 Reeves Octoauto 1911	165 German Miniature Car 1954
73 Ford Runabout 1906	103 Ford School Bus	136 Glasspar	166 Hudson Italia 1954
74 Cadillac El Dorado 1953	104 Napier Touring Car 1904	137 Land Rover	167 Microbo Miniature Car 1954
75 Willys Aero-Falcon 1953	105 Adams Farwell 1906	138 Siata Sports Car	168 Bristol Convertible 1954
76 Peerless Roadster 1913	106 Allard Sports Car	139 Checker Taxicab	169 Ford Thunderbird 1954
77 Northern Touring Car 1904	107 Williams Dream Car	140 Kaiser De Luxe 1953	170 Buick Skylark 1954
78 Hudson Wasp 1953	108 Moon Raceabout 1912	141 Cartercar Three Passenger Coupe 1913	171 Pontiac Strato-Star
79 Plymouth Cranbrook 1953	109 Leon Bollee Tricycle 1898	142 Thomas Limousine 1905	172 Chevrolet Biscayne Dream Car
80 Pierce Stanhope 1905	110 Apache — American Hot Rod	143 NSU-Lambretta	173 Buick Wildcat III
81 Dodge Coronet 1953	111 Nardi Grand Prix Racer	144 Greyhound Bus Scenicruiser	174 Messerschmitt
82 Henry J. Corsair Deluxe	112 De Dion Bouton Tricycle 1896	145 American La France 1911	175 De Soto Fireflite 1955
83 Pontiac Chieftan 1953	113 Oldsmobile 1905	146 Columbia Double Victoria 1906	176 Chrysler The "300" 1955
84 Lincoln Capri 1953	114 Dream Car (Sakhnoffsky)	147 Knox Surrey 1905	177 Cadillac Eldorado Brougham 1955
85 U.S. Army 48 Medium Gun Tank	115 Reliant Three-Wheeled Bantam	148 Apperson Toy Tonneau	178 Nash Rambler "Cross Country" 1955
86 Chrysler "Special" Sport Model	116 Knox Runabout 1905	149 Oldsmobile 1904	179 Dodge Custom Royal Lancer 1955
87 General Motors Le Sabre	117 Ford La France 1920	150 Columbia Limousine 1904	180 Ford Crown Victoria 1955
88 Nash Ambassador 1953	118 Kurtis Two-Seater Speedster	151 Knox Touring Car 1904	
89 Chevrolet Bel Air 1953	119 Hudson Super Jet	152 Oldsmobile Defender Coupe 1912	
	120 Ohio Roadster 1908		
	121 Brewster Town Car		
	122 Fiat Runabout		

X—RAY ROUND UP (200)

It is ironic that Topps, which by 1952 had begun a media blitz boasting of its "Giant Size" cards, actually produced some of the smallest trading cards in history when it first started making insert cards in 1949. Consider this "X-Ray Round Up" series, for example. It was issued in aptly-named "Pixie Bubble Gum" packs. The individual cards in the set measure a scant 7/8" X 1 7/16". To their credit, however, these small cards pack an artistic wallop because of their flamboyant coloration and interesting details. The set is divided into four categories: Figures of the Wild West, Indian Chiefs, Pirates of the Spanish Main, and Savage Tribesmen (50 cards per group). It should be noted that the "Western" subgroup contains pictures of movie stars (such as Mae West) who portrayed westerners in film, and that most, but not all, of

the Indians were copied directly from a classic 19th century tobacco card set issued by Allen & Ginter.

The set title, "X-Ray Round Up," refers to the "gimmick" backs of the cards, which are far more interesting that most collectors imagine. When you flip the card over, you see a drawing created by printing wavy orange lines onto the white cardboard stock. The cards of each subgroup have a number of different scenes (pirate themes for Pirate cards, etc.), but the actual number of different orange-colored pictures for each category has never been recorded (different fronts have identical backs). Underneath the orange picture there are visible to the naked eye a series of fine blue-green lines which, when an enclosed slip of red "X-Ray" is placed on top, reveal another totally-different picture! Each of these hidden pictures is captioned, and from the cards studied, it appears that none is repeated and that there are 200 different hidden pictures.

7/8" X 1 7/16"

Topps employed several methods to distribute the X-Ray Round Up set to the public. We have already mentioned the 1-cent "Pixie" gum package. The interior side of this wrapper carries instructions for revealing the hidden back pictures, plus a mail-in offer for a "combination Pixie card holder and personal viewer" (15 cents). Illustrated below are two different comic book ads showing that "double-feature Wild West Cards" were offered in 10-card lots (with plastic viewer) directly from the company (5 cents plus Bazooka Gum wrappers). The discovery of some 100-picture sheets of the artwork fronts with stamp backs (to moisten for placing in an album) is evidence that Topps, or a licensee, also sold the set in this unusual manner (the stamp sheets are machine perforated and are much thinner than the uncut card sheets illustrated in our presentation). A "Pixie Picture Album" and permanent plastic viewer could also be ordered from Topps for 15 cents (see pictures of the cover, the checklist pages, and the page with cards). The reference number is R714-25.

ITEM	EX	AVE
Card	2.50	.50
Set	550.00	110.00
Wrapper	40.00	——
Album	50.00	15.00

389

X-Ray Round Up

A "FIGURES OF THE WILD WEST" CARD

A "PIRATES OF THE SPANISH MAIN" CARD

TINY "PIXIE GUM" WRAPPER HAD INSTRUCTIONS FOR REVEALING THE HIDDEN PICTURES ON THE INTERIOR FACE

COMIC BOOK ADS OFFERING 10-CARD
LOTS OF X-RAY ROUND UP "WILD WEST CARDS"

1 Geronimo/Apache Tribe
2 Sitting Bull/Chief of the Dakota Sioux
3 Black Beard/Cruelest of all Pirates
4 Chief Gall/Hunkpapa Sioux Tribe
5 Portuguese Barthelemy/West Indies Pirate
6 Red Shirt /Dakota Sioux Tribe
7 Black Hawk/Sac & Fox Tribe
8 Captain Kidd/Most Bloodthirsty of Pirates
9 Pierre Picard/Attacked City of Maracaybo
10 Sir Henry Morgan/Commander 37 Pirate Ships
11 Captain Bradley/Raided Panama City
12 Striker/Apache Tribe
13 Captain Edward Low/ Bloodthirsty Pirate Chief
14 Iron Bull/Crow Tribe
15 Wetcunie/Otoes Tribe
16 Anne Bonney/Woman Pirate
17 Always Riding/Yampah Ute Tribe
18 Big Elk/Ponca Tribe
19 Spotted Tail/Blackfeet Sioux Tribe
20 Big Snake/Winnebagoes Tribe
21 Chief Joseph/Nez Perces Tribe
22 Captain Bart Roberts/Hanged on the Gallows
23 King of the Crows/Crow Tribe
24 Deer Ham/Ioway Tribe
25 Black Hawk/Dakota Sioux Tribe
26 Clam Fish/Warm Springs Tribe

27 White Swan/Lower Yanktonas Sioux
28 Arkikita/Otoes Tribe
29 Big Bear/Missouria Tribe
30 Big Chief/Ponca Tribe
31 Bartholomew Sharp/Buccaneer of the Spanish Main
32 Bull Head/Pawnee Tribe
33 Red Thunder/Blackfeet Sioux Tribe
34 Captain Francis Spriggs/Master of the Ship "Delight"
35 Sam Bellamy/Terrorized New England Coast
36 Hairy Bear/Winnebagoes Tribe
37 Captain Charles Vane/Hanged at Jamaica
38 Agate Arrow Point/Warm Springs Tribe
39 Mary Read/Fought Duel to Save Her Lover
40 General George A. Custer/Indian Fighter
41 Calamity Jane/Famous Figure of the Old West
42 Ned England/was Marooned at Mauritius
43 Col. William F. Cody (Buffalo Bill)/Scout and Marksman
44 Captain Jack Rackam/Hanged at Gallows Point 1720
45 Yellowstone Kelly/Indian Fighter
46 Kit Carson/Indian Fighter
47 Mansvelt/Sacked the Kingdom of Granada
48 California Joe/Western Scout
49 Billy the Kid/Western Outlaw
50 Moses Vauclin/Ship Deserter and Mutineer

51 Captain Martel – Daring Sea Raider
52 Jesse James – Famed Outlaw
53 Andy Clyde – Featured in "Chrashing Thru"
54 Raymond Hatton – In the motion picture "Gunning for Justice"
55 John Gow – Pirate of Barbary Coast
56 Gilbert Roland – Starring in "The Dude Goes West"
57 James Gleason in the motion picture "The Dude goes West"
58 Peter the Great – Pirate of Tortuga
59 Cathy Downs – Featured in "When a Man's a Man"
60 Howel Davis – Pirate Chief Killed in Action
61 Robert Preston – Featured in "Tulsa"
62 Sieur De Montauban Became Pirate at Age of 16
63 Barton MacLane in "The Dude Goes West"
64 Thomas Anstis – Murdered by His crew
65 Johnny Mack Brown – "Gunning For Justice"
66 Jimmy Wakely Starring in "Gun Law Justice"
67 Barry Sullivan in "Badman of Tombstone"
68 Montbar – Brutal Pirate Leader
69 Cannibal Chief Zumperi Tribe
70 Cannonball Taylor in "The Rangers Ride"

71 Guy Madison – Starring in "When a Man's a Man"
72 A Bowman – Fali Tribe
73 Scott Brady in "Montana Belle"
74 A "Fuzzie-Wuzzie" Hadendowah Tribe
75 Max Terhune in "Hidden Danger"
76 Whip Wilson Starring in "Crashing Thru"
77 Johnny Mack Brown in "Hidden Danger"
78 Rod Cameron Starring in "Stampede"
79 A Bassari Tribesman – French West Africa
80 Chief Black Kettle – Cheyenne Leader
81 British – Ioway Tribe
82 Sudanese Warrior
83 Man and Chief – Pawnee Tribe
84 Cayatanita – Navajo Tribe
85 A Bell Ringer – KonKombo Tribe
86 Keokuk – Sac and Fox Tribe
87 White Bear – Kiowas
88 Red Bird – Chippeway
89 Noon Day – Chippeway Tribe
90 Great Bear – Delaware Tribe
91 Many Horns – Blackfeet Sioux
92 Sitting Bull Sioux Warrior and Medicine Man
93 Little Wolf – Cheyenne Tribe
94 Crow's Breast – Gros Ventres Tribe
95 A Guardesman – Ashanti Tribe

UNCUT SHEET OF 100 X-RAY ROUND UP CARDS

96 True Eagle — Missouria Tribe
97 A Senegal Tribesman
98 Big Razor — Blackfeet Sioux Tribe
99 Two Moons — Cheyenne Tribe
100 A Congo Bushman
101 Chief Little Crow — Sioux Tribe
102 A Karamojo Tribesman
103 Trailing · The · Enemy Kiowa Tribe
104 Old Bull — Sioux Tribe
105 Lean Wolf — Gross Ventres Tribe
106 Little Chief — Cheyenne Tribe
107 A Kikuyu Tribesman
108 Red Cloud — Sioux Tribe
109 Lone Wolf — Kowa Tribe
110 Black Eye — Blackfeet Sioux Tribe
111 A Lion Hunter — Masai Tribe
112 Rushing Bear — Pawnee Tribe
113 A Lumbwa Warrior
114 Daniel Boone — Famous Frontiersman
115 A Kavirondo Chieftain
116 A Chief of the Azande Tribe
117 Captain Merriweather Lewis Explorer of the West
118 A Spearman — Nyam-Nyam Tribe
119 Old Warrior — A Didinga Tribe
120 Annie Oakley — Crack Shot
121 A Boatman — from the Niger Delta

122 A Guardsman — Kitumbene Tribe
123 Wild Bill Hickok — Frontiersman
124 A Pygmy Chief — M'Buti Tribe
125 Bat Masterson Deputy Sheriff of Dodge City
126 Lee Neuman — Western Badman
127 Pat Garrett Sheriff who shot Billy the Kid
128 Fighting Man — Rei-Bouba Tribe
129 Congo Warrior — Shilluck Tribe
130 Congo Fighter
131 Bob Dalton — Western Outlaw
132 Frank Dalton — Sheriff
133 John King Fisher — Deputy Sheriff
134 Elephant Hunter — Central Africa
135 John Selman Western Gambler and Badman
136 Horseman — from the Niger Valley
137 J.H. (Doc) Holliday — Western Badman
138 Tom Smith — Marshall of Abilene
139 John Phillips — Killed in Mutiny
140 Ben Cravens — Western Outlaw
141 Rose of The Cimarron — Oklahoma Outlaw

142 Sebe Barnes — Outlaw and Gunman
143 Sam Bass — Western Badman
144 Cattle Annie — Woman Outlaw
145 Little Breeches — Woman Outlaw
146 Mickey Free — Government Scout
147 Stede Bonnet — Hanged at Charleston
148 Bill Dalton — Outlaw
149 Captain Halsey — American Pirate
150 Captain Worley — Killed in Action
151 Grat Dalton — Western Outlaw
152 Jack Avery — Captured Rich Arabian Ship
153 William Fly Captured by his own Prisoners
154 Arkansas Tom Outlaw and Badman
155 Roc, The Brazilian Cruel Pirate Leader
156 Sieur De Grammont sacked the City of Vera Cruz
157 Michael Le Basque Burned The City of Gibraltar
158 Captain Jack Crawford Poet and Scout
159 Captain Condent Pardoned by the King
160 Captain Wm. J. Fetterman Indian Fighter
161 John Davis Sacked the Town of Granada
162 George Lowther Captain of the Vessel "Happy Delivery"
163 Captain Lewis started Pirate Career at age of 15
164 Pierre Francois Daring Pirate of Tortuga
165 Alexander Bras-De-Fer Pirate of Tortuga
166 Lewis Scot Sacked the City of Campeche
167 Bradish — Executed in England
168 Captain Tew Killed by Cannon Fire
169 Captain Sawkins Raided Panama with 300 Pirates
170 Lawrence DeGraff Led 1200 Pirates Against Vera Cruz
171 John Ireland Starred in "I Shot Jesse James"
172 Mae West As Diamond Lil
173 Fuzzy St. John Famous Western Star
174 Ginny Jackson — Screen Star
175 Henry Hull Famous Stage and Screen Star
176 Sudanese Rain Dancer
177 Bago Yangi — Snake Dancer
178 Zulu Bodyguard
179 King of the Bakubas
180 Mongo Trailer
181 Wanderobo — Plainsman
182 Lala Jungle King
183 Watosi Warrior
184 Native Nagaoundere
185 Court Guard of Dahome Yan
186 Nubian Fighter
187 Kalahai Desert Man
188 Timbucton Musician
189 South Highland Warrior
190 New Guinea Headsman
191 Native of Timbuctu
192 Rhodesian Axeman
193 Native of Nigeria
194 Kaffir Spearman
195 Bakwese Fighter
196 Richard Basehart in Reign of Terror
197 Reed Hadley in "I Shot Jesse James"
198 Fuzzy Knight Popular Western Star
199 Douglas Dumbrille Favorite Screen Villian
200 Mary Beth Hughes Featured in "Rimfire"

ALBUM MAILING ENVELOPE

CARD COPIED FROM
ALLEN & GINTER SET

KING OF THE CROWS,
CROW.

CARD NOT COPIED FROM
ALLEN & GINTER SET

SITTING BULL,
DAKOTA SIOUX.

COVER OF X-RAY ROUND UP ALBUM

INTERIOR PAGE WITH
CARDS IN PLACE

(continued from inside front cover)

PIRATES OF SPANISH MAIN	SAVAGE TRIBESMEN
3. Black Beard	64. Thomas Anstis	74. Fuzzie-Wuzzie	85. Bull Ringer
5. Portuguese Bartholomew	68. Montbar	82. Sudanese Warrior	95. Guardsman Ashanti
8. Captain Kidd	129. John Phillips	79. Bassari Tribesman	176. Sudanese Rain Dancer
9. Pierre Picard	147. Stede Bonnet	73. Bowman	177. Bega Tung!
10. Sir Henry Morgan	149. Capt. Halsey	69. Cannibal Chief	178. Zulu Bodyguard
11. Captain Bradley	150. Capt. Worley	97. Senegal Tribesman	179. King of Bakuba
13. Captain Edward Low	152. Jack Avery	100. Congo Bushman	180. Mango Trailer
16. Anne Bonney	153. William Fly	102. Kuranega Tribesman	181. Wanderobo
22. Captain Bart Roberts	155. Roc The Brazilian	107. Kikuyu Tribesman	182. Lulo Jungle King
35. Sam Bellamy	156. Sieur de Grammont	113. Lumbwa Warrior	183. Matusi Warrior
37. Capt. Charles Vane	157. Michael le Basque	111. Lion Hunter	184. Nubian Hippopotamus
39. Bartholomew Sharp	159. Capt. Condent	115. Rooriando Chieftain	185. Bahama Tun
41. Capt. Francis Spriggs	161. Jake Davis	116. Chief Aconda Tribe	186. Mottan
59. Mary Read	162. George Lowther	118. Spearman	187. Rolathai
42. Ned England	163. Capt. Lewis	122. Gwandanan Kitamboro	188. Timbouton
44. Capt. Jack Rackham	164. Pierre Francois	119. Old Warrior	189. South Highland Warrior
47. Mansvelt	165. Alexander Bras-de-Fer	121. Boatman	190. Henderson
50. Moses Vauclin	166. Lewis Scot	128. Fighting Man	191. Native Timbucto
51. Capt. Martel	167. Smollith	134. Pygmy Chief	192. Rhodesian Axeman
53. John Gow	168. Captain Tew	129. Congo Warrior	193. Native Nigeria
58. Peter the Great	169. Sawkins	136. Elephant Hunter	194. Kaffir Spearman
60. Howell Davis	170. De Graff	135. Horseman	195. Bahama Fighter
62. Sieur De Montauban		130. Congo Fighter	

IF YOU OR YOUR FRIENDS WANT AN ADDITIONAL
PIXIE ALBUM AND PERMANENT MAGNIFYING VIEWER, SEND 15c TO:

TOPPS, BOX 20
MADISON SQ. STATION, NEW YORK 10, N. Y.

INSIDE FRONT COVER
(SEE PRECEDING PAGE)
& INSIDE BACK COVER
OF ALBUM CONTAINED
COMPLETE CHECKLIST
OF X-RAY ROUND UP CARDS

YOU'LL DIE LAUGHING (66)   2 1/2" X 3 1/2"

Controversial card sets have been good business for Topps. The moral crusade against Garbage Pail Kids, and its sensationalistic coverage by the print and electronic media, made GPK into the company's all-time best seller (including baseball cards). Ugly Stickers, Wacky Packages, and a host of other "insult" and "horror" sets — including the classic "Mars Attacks" — have been a constant element in Topps' rise to the pinnacle of the trading card arena. The basic premise that "shock value" can result in big profits was a lesson that Topps learned from its arch-rival, J. Warren Bowman, the head of Bowman Gum and Gum, Inc.

The first Topps set to cause a public commotion was "Funny Monsters," which was released to coincide with the Halloween season in 1959. (Note: collectors call this set "You'll Die Laughing" from the joke heading on the reverse, because the title "Funny Monsters" is not printed on the cards.) Media reaction was predictably mixed: one headline declared "Bubble Gum Heroes Now Monsters...Gone Are the Days of Baseball Players and Sports Heroes; Small Fry Now Collect Horrors" and went on to describe the set in a tone of bemusement. Other writers were less appreciative: Tex Reynolds observed "Nice way to promote the happy dreams of childhood..," while Ernest Tucker called them "nauseating" and wondered "who knows what terrors they might inspire in a 7-year old? I wish they'd let the little fellows alone." A group of mothers in Racine (WI) even formed a protest group and sent petitions to Topps and some of its advertising clients. However, the "little fellows" obviously found the monster cards more funny than frightening, because stores across the country sold out of the item and it was not interdicted in any way. "Negative publicity," observed a staffer at Burelle's Press Clipping Bureau (which gathered these newspaper articles for Topps) is better than no publicity." Topps has certainly adopted this as a motto by which to do business.

The obverses of the cards contain multi-color artwork pictures with comical themes and captions. Many, if not all, of them were drawn by noted illustrator Jack Davis. The backs bear the heading from which the set takes its name and have a line of ghoulish monsters surrounding a casket, on which is printed a joke. The card number and joke are printed in red ink, while the monster design is violet in color. Only gray-stock backs have been reported. The manufacturer is listed as "Bubbles Inc."

The packaging for Funny Monsters/You'll Die Laughing has been very difficult to track down. The 5-cent wrapper normally associated with this set is mostly green, with a red monster head, and is marked "Bubbles Inc." Another 5-cent wrapper, showing a haunted house, is illustrated on a "Funny Monsters" promotion sheet; some collectors believe this to be a prototype design which was never actually printed. To complicate matters, Topps records indicate that 1-cent, 10-cent, and 29-cent (rak pak) versions were also offered for sale, but no wrappers or boxes in these denominations have turned up as of this date. The reference number for Funny Monsters/You'll Die Laughing is R708-5.

"BUT DADDY, YOU ALWAYS SAID
TWO HEADS ARE BETTER THAN ONE."

ITEM	EX	AVE
Card	1.00	.20
Set	75.00	15.00
Wrapper	45.00	—
Box (5-cent)	350.00	90.00

LEFT: 1-CENT
WRAPPER &
BOX FROM
TOPPS' ARCHIVE.
NO SAMPLES
HAVE BEEN FOUND
BY COLLECTORS
TO DATE.

1 "I Just Came Back from the Beauty Parlor, Can't You Tell?"
2 "I'd Like a Pair of Eye Glasses Please!"
3 "I'd Like to Buy a Monster Mask!"
4 "Boy When I Get a Headache It's a Beaut!"
5 "Ma, Did You Call for a Baby Sitter?"
6 "Doc, Can I Stop Taking These Reducing Pills?"
7 "Doc, Those Hair Growing Pills Sure Worked!"
8 "What D'Ya Mean, There Are No Man-Eating Plants in Bongo Land?"
9 "Boy They Sure Got Ugly Girls in This Neighborhood!"
10 "So You Really Think You've Rediscovered the Jekyll and Hyde Formula, Eh, Twombley?
11 "Earth Monsters! Full Speed Back to Mars."
12 "What Happened? You're White as a Sheet?"
13 "Our Next Speaker Is an Expert on Plant Life!"

14 "What Do You Mean, Shirley, I'm Not Your Type?"
15 "Just One Drink and I Start Seeing the Strangest Things."
16 "Wait Till I Try This On the Next Customer!"
17 "I Told You Time and Again, Smoking Will Stunt Your Growth."
18 "I've Got Just the Gift for the Man Who Has Everything."
19 "Let's Tell Scary Stories."
20 No Caption—Fang Dentures in Glass
21 "Gulp! I Don't Know If I Have Blue Suede Shoes in Your Size."
22 "That's Right. Open Nice and Wide."
23 "Your Whole Family Will Enjoy This Picture."
24 "Trick or Treat Lady?"
25 "...And the Earth People Are Strange Creatures with Only One Head!"
26 "Start with the Ankles"
27 "What Have You Got in a Red Perfume That Smells Like Blood?"

28 "...And No Hitting Below the Belt"
29 "But Daddy, You Always Said Two Heads Are Better Than One."
30 "Doc, I Have Terrible Nightmares, I Dream About Human Beings—"
31 "I've Got Power Steering, Too."
32 "Two Pairs, Please!"
33 "Dear, I Have a Surprise for You."
34 "I Said You Could Beat Up His Dad!"
35 "Watch the Birdie!"
36 "Look, Ma, No Cavities."
37 "So There's a Fly in Your Room, So What?"
38 "Lovely Night, Isn't It?"
39 "What Did You Find in Your Prize Package?"
40 "Mr. Durstrum Is in Charge of Weird Stories."
41 "Did You Say There Was Somebody on the Phone, Dear?"
42 "Sure Makes You Look Ugly!"

43 "That Department Store— They're Always Sending Me the Wrong Thing."
44 "I Took 6 Lessons. How Come I Ain't Popular Yet?"
45 "Those Missionaries Did a Good Job Here."
46 "So I Said to the Witch Doctor, 'I Dare You to Shrink My Head'—"
47 "And Wait Till You See the View Around the Bend, Dear."
48 "Waddaya Mean, It's Bad Luck to Walk Under a Ladder?"
49 "Doc, You Got to Do Something, Everytime I Smile I Bite My Nose!"
50 "Pay No Attention to Him, Dear."
51 "If You Want Anything— Scream."
52 "Can I Borrow a Cup of Poison?"
53 "Who Put Pepper in My Bubble Gum?"
54 "Darn Few Arguments when Smedley Umpires a Game."

55 "How Are Your Silly 'Invisible Man' Experiments Going, Henshaw?"
56 "Do You Believe in Humans?"
57 "Would You Wrap It as a Gift, Please!!"
58 "I Told You We Dug too Deep!"
59 "You Will Soon Meet a Tall, Dark Man."
60 "It's Going to Rain. I Can Feel It in My Bones."
61 "There Will Be a Slight Additional Charge, Sir!"
62 "Tsk, Tsk! How Silly Can TV Get?"
63 "I Can't Understand Why Girls Don't Like Me!!"
64 "C'mon Charlie, You Can't Fool Me with That Silly Disguise."
65 "Heh! Heh! Wait Till They Find Out I'm the New Baby Sitter."
66 "This Photographer Does Beautiful Work."

"TRICK OR TREAT LADY?"

AND THE EARTH PEOPLE ARE STRANGE
CREATURES WITH ONLY ONE HEAD!"

TOPPS RE-USED SOME "YOU'LL DIE LAUGHING"
CARDS IN "PAK O' FUN" ISSUE OF 1969

YULE LAFF (66)   2 1/2" X 3 1/2"

The name of this 1960 Fleer set comes from the title printed on the wrapper, because the cards themselves have no identification other than a set of tiny "F.H.F." initials printed on the back. There are 66 cards in the set, each depicting a humorous Yuletide scene and a "set-up" greeting which is completed by a written or illustrated punch line on the reverse. Although they are standard card size, the backs were designed in post-card format, and it may be that some of these were actually sent through the mail. The card number is located in a snowman device at the top left corner on the reverse. While not unattractive, Yule Laff cards are too simple detail-wise and too general in characterization to appeal to most collectors. Most of the interest in this set centers on the colorful wrapper and box. The reference number is R730-5.

ITEM	EX	AVE
Card	.75	.15
Set	55.00	12.00
Wrapper	15.00	––
Box	150.00	45.00

35 Holiday Greetings (and Remember...)
36 Greetings [Santa hanging on the eaves]
37 Season's Greetings (Time to Mail Your Letter to Santa!)
38 Season's Greetings (I Hope Your Stocking Gets Filled...)
39 Season's Greetings [three carolers]
40 Season,s Greetings (Watch Out for Mistletoe...)
41 Season's Greetings [hat in snow, man in window]
42 Season's Greetings (Time for Santa to Be Coming...)
43 Holiday Greetings (You Should Feel at Home with Your Tree...)
44 Warm Holiday Greetings [Santa stuck in fireplace]
45 Season's Greetings To You
46 Season's Greetings [Santa with sack, petting dog]
47 Holiday Greetings (Wish You Were Here...)
48 Holiday Greetings (Will You Help Me Decorate My Tree?)
49 Holiday Greetings (To the Belle of the Town...)
50 Season's Greetings (If You're Near Our Place...)
51 Holiday Greetings (Hurry, Look at This Greeting...)
52 Holiday Greetings (I Hope I Can Get to Your House...)
53 Holiday Greetings (You Seem to Be Part of the Tree...)
54 Season's Greetings [man rolling snowball uphill]
55 Holiday Greetings (With You Doing the Decorating...)
56 Holiday Greetings (If You Make a Snowman...)
57 Season's Greetings (Don't Stand Under the Misletoe...)
58 Holiday Greetings (I Hope This Greeting...)
59 Holiday Greetings (I Hope You Get What You Want...)
60 Holiday Greetings [boy with shopping bag at bus stop]
61 Holiday Greetings [boy with horn in hand approaching sleeping man]
62 Greetings (To a Big Brain!)
63 Holiday Greetings (May Your Holiday Be...)
64 Season's Greetings (Look at All the Cards!)
65 Season's Greetings [unhappy boy walks past boy with candy cane]
66 Season's Greetings (A Big Bag of Gifts...)

1 Season's Greetings (To the Most Beautiful Girl in the World...)
2 Holiday Greetings (Boy, Are You Impatient!)
3 Greetings (I'm Late, So I'm Delivering This Card...)
4 Holiday Greetings (I Think You Can Use...)
5 Season's Greetings To...(...A Very Popular Guy!)
6 Season's Greetings (I Hope You Used Your Head Last Summer...)
7 Season's Greetings (Junior, Clean Off the Snow!)
8 Season's Greetings (If Your TV Set Doesn't Work Properly...
9 Holiday Greetings [dog licking candy cane on which man is leaning]
10 Season's Greetings (From Someone Who Is Stuck...)
11 Holiday Greetings (Hope You'll Be Close to the Top of the World in 1961...)
12 Fat Holiday Greetings
13 Holiday Greetings (To a Guy Who Saves...)
14 Holiday Greetings (To a Good Egg...)
15 Holiday Greetings [tramp with snowman]
16 Holiday Greetings (I Hope Your Trains Are Up...)

17 Season's Greetings (Give Santa a Warm Reception...)
18 Season's Greetings [sled hitting tree]
19 Holiday Greetings (I'm on My Way to Buy Your Gift.)
20 Sincere Holiday Greetings (No Fooling!)
21 Season's Greetings [policeman chasing carolers]
22 Season's Greetings (Where's My Bumper Jack?)
23 Season's Greetings (Most People Have Only Good Points and Bad Points...)
24 Season's Greetings (I Hope Santa Visits Your House...)
25 Holiday Greetings (Here's Hoping You Get Many...)
26 Season's Greetings (Xmas Trees—Sold Out)
27 Wishing You a White Xmas
28 Holiday Greetings (To a Real Doll!)
29 Holiday Greetings (Please Dress Your Tree...)
30 Holiday Greetings (I Know Your Dog Will Like Santa...)
31 Season's Greetings (I Hope You Get...)
32 Season's Greetings (Your Stocking for Santa...)
33 Season's Greetings (To "Speedy"!)
34 Season's Greetings (If You Don't Have a Fireplace...)

ZORRO (88)

Topps carved a "P" (for "pro-fit") with their blade when they issued this Zorro series in 1958. Each of the 88 cards in the set is a color photograph from the Walt Disney movie. The card caption and a Z-emblazoned Spanish hat are printed at the bottom of the picture area. The backs are orange and gray. The text explains the adventure on the

2 1/2" X 3 1/2"

front, and there is a portrait of Zorro to one side. Each card has a "preview" line on the back which reveals the caption of the next card in the series. The attractive wrappers are especially appealing to collectors: they come in a 1-cent "repeating design" wax wrapper and a 5-cent layered-cellophane version with a half-figure centerpeice. Zorro cards were also sold in 10-cent clear cello packs, but these have little value above that of the cards inside because there is no printing of any kind on the cellophane wrapper. Only the 5-cent box has been recovered so far. The reference number is R712-5.

Zorro

ITEM	EX	AVE
Card	2.50	.50
Set	250.00	50.00
Wrappers		
1-cent	65.00	——
5-cent	100.00	——
Box	300.00	85.00

1 Zorro!	23 Diego's Defeat	45 "I'll Get Torres"	67 The Clue
2 Diego the Swordsman	24 Diego Meets "Zorro"	46 Ruthless Plan	68 Sgt. Garcia's Lancers
3 Flashing Blades	25 The Capitan's Triumph	47 The Search	69 Fight for Life
4 Friendly Enemies	26 The Hostages	48 Cruel Tyrant	70 Cruel Sport
5 Bad News	27 "Help Us, Diego"	49 The Threat	71 Zorro's Rage
6 The Evil Scheme	28 The Execution	50 Work Slave	72 "Mercy, Zorro"
7 Soldier and Scholar	29 Full Gallop	51 Merciless Beating	73 Alejandro and Zorro
8 Garcia's Warning	30 The Rescue	52 Fearful Sight	74 Race Against Time
9 Diego's Homecoming	31 Locked Swords	53 A Ghost Story	75 The Chase
10 Faithful Bernardo	32 "After Him"	54 The Avenger	76 The Fox
11 Reign of Terror	33 Fierce Battle	55 Enter Zorro	77 Quick Change
12 Diego's Decision	34 Three Against Zorro	56 Wierd Noises	78 Diego the Troubador
13 Fighter for Justice	35 Bombarding Soldiers	57 The Ghost Strikes	79 The Captain's Vow
14 Ready to Strike	36 Trapping Zorro	58 Forced Rest	80 Relaxing with Garcia
15 Garcia's Choice	37 Zorro's Victim	59 Storm of Arrows	81 Careful Sergeant
16 Garcia Gets a Bath	38 Unleashed Fury	60 A Father's Shame	82 Diego's Guests
17 "You Shall Be Free..	39 Stop Zorro	61 The Argument	83 Rude Awakening
18 Surprise Meeting	40 Flight to Freedom	62 Trouble Ahead	84 Zorro and Tornado
19 Zorro's Prisoner	41 Daring Leap	63 Talk, Coward!	85 Rawhide Duel
20 Diego the Weakling	42 Surrounded!	64 Dangerous Mission	86 The Blade of Zorro
21 The Question	43 "You Fat Fool!"	65 Saving Alejandro	87 Strange Discovery
22 Challenge for Diego	44 The Capitan's Demand	66 Alejandro's Escape	88 Man of Mystery

ZORRO ADVENTURES (?)

2 1/2" X 3 11/16"

These comic-strip adventure cards printed on the back panels of "Zorro Candy and Toy" boxes were first reported in the June, 1959 edition of The Card Collectors Bulletin. The box and candy were products of the Super Novelty Candy Co. of Newark, N.J. The front panel, sides, and end flaps of the box are red, with the mounted Zorro and "Z" at the center in black and white. The adventure strip on the back is drawn in black & white only, and the "Secret Passage" episode in our illustration is the only one listed so far with the Hobby Card Index. The card back is blank. The number printed on the small end flap presumably is a box code rather than a card number. The reference number is R805.

ITEM	EX	AVE
Card	5.00	1.50
Box	35.00	10.00

ZORRO SUN PICTURES (10K)

1 9/16" X 2"

One veteran collector suggests a production date of 1962 for this series of "Zorro Sun Pictures," but we are including it here in the 1930-1960 book because it relates to the other Zorro sets in this section. Each foil package contained two "negatives," some pieces of contact paper, and a cardboard developing frame. The picture was produced by joining the negative and contact paper together in the frame and exposing it to the sun or some other source of intense light. When the white paper turned purple, the picture was considered developed. Each negative is numbered, but not captioned, and it is not known if any of the negatives match the color photographs which appeared in the 1958 Topps set. Neither the foil bag (yellow & black) nor any of the paper items bear a manufacturer's name. The box held 48 foil packages, and there is no price listed on ei- ther the bags or the box. A considerable amount of these surfaced in the hobby several years ago, and they are not as scarce or desirable as some people have tried to make them out to be. No reference number has been assigned.

ITEM	EX	AVE
Bag (with two negatives, developing paper, & cardboard frame)	15.00	3.00
Box	60.00	20.00

Zorro Sun Pictures

BAG AND CARDBOARD FRAME
FOR ZORRO SUN PICTURES

MANUFACTURERS INDEX

Manufacturers Index

AMERICAN CARD CATALOG REFERENCE NUMBER INDEX

GLOSSARY

This glossary defines many common terms frequently used in the collecting hobby of trading cards and closely associated material. There are exceptions to some of the definitions presented; however, to list all of the exceptions would only tend to confuse the reader and detract from the usefulness of the glossary.

ALBUM— A paper book of varying size issued by a card manufacturer to house the cards of a specific series. Generally available as a mail-in, premium offer only, but sometimes sold in retail stores.

BACKLIST or BACKLISTED— Refers to the practice of listing the cards of a set on the back of each card in that set, in effect, providing a checklist on each one. Backlisting is generally found in 19th century tobacco issues.

BREAD END LABEL— The paper label found on the end of a loaf of bread. Since the 1930's, many baking companies have issued bread with sets of cowboy, comic, etc. labels as a promotional device.

CABINETS— Very popular and highly valuable large cards on thick card stock produced in the 19th and early 20th century.

CAPTION— The title of a card as it appears under the illustration and/or on the back. It generally describes or identifies the subject(s) pictured but may also be a line of dialogue.

CHECKLIST— a) A list of the cards contained in a particular set. The list is always in numerical order if the cards are numbered or in alphabetical order if the particular set is unnumbered.
　　　　　b) A book containing a number of set checklists.

COLLECTOR— A person who engaged in the hobby of collecting non-sport card for his own enjoyment, without a profit motive.

COLLECTOR ISSUE— A set produced for the sake of the card itself, with no product or service sponsor. It derives its name from the fact that most of these sets are produced by collector - dealers.

CONVENTION— A large weekend gathering at one location of dealers and collectors for the purpose of buying, selling, and sometimes trading of non-sport cards. Conventions are open to the public and sometimes feature celebrities, door prizes, films, contests, etc.

CORNER CLIP— The design in the corner(s) of a wrapper which is specifically designed to be cut off and sent in as proof of purchase in a premium offer.

COUPON— A printed advertisement or form, found on older gum and candy wrappers and boxes, which could be cut out as proof of purchase and redeemed for prizes, premiums, etc.

CREASE— A wrinkle on the card, usually caused by bending the card.

DEALER— A person who engages in the buying, selling and trading of non-sport cards who anticipates a profit, direct or indirect, from each transaction. A dealer may also be a collector, but as a dealer, he anticipates a profit.

DIE-CUT— A card which by design has its stock partially cut through for removal or folding of one or more parts to the card. After removal of these parts and appropriate folding, the remaining part of the card can be made to stand-up.

EMBOSSED— Refers to a card on which the design has been stamped into the cardboard surface of the card from the rear, thereby giving the obverse surface a raised, or "relief" effect.

EXHIBIT— The generic name given to thick stock, postcard sized cards with single color obverse pictures. The name is derived from the Exhibit Supply Co. of Chicago, the princiapl manufacturer of this type of card.

FRAME LINE— A line of varying thickness and color which is printed around the picture area of a card to accentuate the main design and to separate it from the borders, or margins.

GRAVURE or PHOTOGRAVURE— A card printed by a specific process in which the ink on the card itself is actually raised slightly above the surface on which it is printed, thereby accentuating the design.

HIGH NUMBER— The cards in the last series of numbers in a year in which the higher numbered cards were printed or distributed in significantly fewer amounts than the lower numbered cards. The high number designation refers to a scarcity of the high numbered cards. Not all years have high numbers in terms of this definition.

INSERT— A card of a different type, a poster, or any other collectible contained and sold in the same package along with a card or cards of a major set.

ISSUE— Synonomous with set, but usually used in conjunction with a manufacturer, e.g. a Topps issue.

LATIN BINOMIAL— The two Latin words which comprise the scientific name (genus and species) for a plant or animal.

LAYERING— The separation or peeling of one or more layers of the card stock, usually at the corner of the card.

LEGITIMATE ISSUE— A set produced to promote or boost sales of a product or service, e.g. bubble gum, cereal, cigarettes, etc. Most collector issues are not legitimate issues in this sense.

MATTE or MATT— Refers to the dull or flat finish on the surface of a card, as opposed to a glossy or shiny surface.

MISCUT— A card that has been cut unevenly at the manufacturer's cutting stage.

NOTCHING— The grooving of the edge of a card, usually caused by the fingernail, rubber bands, or bumping the edge against another object.

OBVERSE— The front, face or pictured side of the card.

PANEL— An extended card that is composed of two or more individual cards. Often the panel forms the back part of the container for the product being promoted.

PLASTIC SHEET— A clear vinyl page (normally using 6—8 mil plastic and punched for insertion into a binder with standard 3—ring spacing) containing pockets for insertion of cards. Many different styles of sheets exist with pockets of varying sizes to hold different sizes of cards.

PICTURE— The main design or illustration on a card, whether it be a drawing, a painting, or a photograph.

POSTER PIECE or PUZZLE PIECE— The back of a card containing a partial design which, when joined properly with similarly designed pieces, forms a large picture or poster.

PREMIUMS— Cards, ictures, gifts or any other items offered as a promotional device in conjunction with a card set.

PUZZLE PIECE— See POSTER PIECE.

PUZZLE PREVIEW CARD or PUZZLE PROMOTION CARD— The side of a card — generally the back — which shows the completed puzzle or poster which can be made by properly assembling the various puzzle-backed cards in the set.

RARE— A card or series of cards of very limited availability. Unfortunately "rare" is a subjective and rather nebulous term sometimes used indiscriminately. "Rare" cards are harder to obtain than "scarce" cards.

REVERSE— The back or narrative side of the card.

SCARCE— A card or series of cards of limited availability. A subjective and nebulous term sometimes used indiscriminately to promote value. Scarce cards are not as difficult to obtain as rare cards.

SEPIA— A dark reddish-brown coloration used in some card sets instead of traditional black-and-white.

SERIES— a) The entire set of cards issued by a particular producer in a particular year e.g., the 1933 Indian Gum series.

b) Within a particular set, a group of consecutively numbered cards printed at the same time, e.g., the first series of Charlie's Angels.

SET— One each of the entire run of cards of the same type produced by a particular manufacturer during a single year. A complete set does not include error or variation cards unless specified.

SKIP-NUMBERED— A set that has many card numbers not issued between the lowest number in the set and the highest number in the set. A major set in which a few numbers were not printed is not considered to be skip-numbered.

STICKER— A card with a removable layer that can be adhered to (stuck onto) another surface.

STIPPLE— Refers to the process by which a painting or drawing is created by using dots rather than lines.

STOCK— The cardboard or paper on which the card is printed.

STRIP CARDS— A sheet or strip of cards, particularly popular in the 1920's and 1930's, with the individual cards separated by a broken or dotted line.

TAB— a) A part of a card set off from the rest of the card, usually with perforations, that may be removed without damaging the central character or event depicted by the card.

b) The grasping nib of a lid.

TEST SET— A set, usually containing a small number of cards, issued by a national card producer and distributed in a limited section or sections of the country. Presumably, the purpose of a test set is to "test" market appeal for this particular type of card.

TEXT— The principal written material on a card as distinguished from card titles, set titles, headings, numbers, advertisements, etc. It may be a narrative, a small scientific treatise, or simple dialogue.

TRIMMED— A card cut down from its original size.

UNCUT SHEET— (Also called full sheet) A complete sheet of cards that has not been cut up into individual cards by the manufacturer.

VARIATION— One of two or more cards from the same series with the same number (or player with identical pose if the series is unnumbered) differing from one other by some aspect, the different feature stemming from the printing or stock of the card, not from an alteration.

ABBREVIATIONS

ACC	— The American Card Catalog
ATC	— American Tobacco Company
BGHLI	— Bowman Gum
E(card)	— The ACC reference letter for pre-1930 candy and gum cards
ITC	— Imperial Tobacco Company
LBI	— Leaf Brands Inc.
IWC	— The Illustrated Wrapper Checklist
N(card)	— The reference letter denoting 19th Century tobacco cards
T(card)	— The ACC reference letter for 20th Century tobacco cards
TCG	— Topps Chewing Gum
V(card)	— The ACC reference letter for Canadian candy and gum cards
3-D	— Three-dimensional

CONDITION GUIDE

MINT (M OR MT)
A card with no defects. A card that has sharp corners, even borders, original gloss or shine on the surface, sharp focus of the picture, smooth edges, no signs of wear, and white borders. There is no allowance made for the age of the card.

EXCELLENT (EX OR E)
A card with very minor defects. Any of the following qualities would be sufficient to lower the grade of a card from mint to the excellent category: very slight rounding or layering at some of the corners, a very small amount of the original gloss lost, minor wear on the edges, slight unevenness of the borders, slight wear visible only on close inspection; slight off-whiteness of the borders.

VERY GOOD (VG)
A card that has been handled but not abused. Some rounding at all corners, slight layering or scuffing at one or two corners, slight notching on edges, gloss lost from the surface but not scuffed, borders might be somewhat uneven but some white is visible on all borders, noticeable yellowing or browning of borders, pictures may be slightly off focus.

AVERAGE (AVE)
A well handled card, rounding and some layering at the corners, scuffing at the corners and minor scuffing on the face, borders noticeably uneven and browning, loss of gloss on the face, notching on the edges.

FAIR (F)
Round and layering corners, brown and dirty borders, frayed edges, noticeable scuffing on the face, white not visible on one or more borders, cloudy focus.

POOR (P)
An abused card, the lowest grade of card, frequently some major physical alteration has been performed on the card, collectible only as a fill-in until a better condition replacement can be obtained.

Categories between these major condition grades are frequently used; such as, very good to excellent (VG—EX), excellent to mint (EX—MT), etc. The grades indicate a card with all the qualities at least in the lower of the two categories, but with several qualities in the higher of the two categories.

THE CREASE
The most common physical defect in a trading card is the crease or wrinkle. The crease may vary from a slight crease barely noticeable at one corner of the card to a major crease across the entire card; therefor, the degree that a crease lowers the value of the card depends on the type and number of creases. On giving the condition of a card, creases should be noted separately. If the crease is noticeable only upon close inspection under bright light, an otherwise mint card could be called excellent; whereas noticeable but light creases would lower most otherwise mint cards into the VG catagory. A heavily creased card could be classified fair at best.

BECKETT
BASEBALL

⚾ Beckett Baseball Card Monthly

Check the appropriate box:

		Reg. Price	Your Price
	1 year (12 issues)	$35.40	**$19.95**
	2 years (24 issues)	$70.80	**$35.95**
	3 years (36 issues)	$106.20	**$47.95**
	4 years (48 issues)	$141.60	**$59.95**

Do not send cash.
Please allow 6-8 weeks for
delivery of first issue.

Sub Total:	
Foreign postage ($1.00 per issue, payable in U.S. funds):	
Total enclosed: (Payment must accompany order)	

Please Print Clearly

Name _____ Age_____

Address _____

City _____ State _____ Zip _____

Daytime Phone Number: _____

☐ New Subscription ☐ Renewal

Payment enclosed via: ☐ Check or Money Order ☐ VISA/MasterCard

Card # ☐☐☐☐ – ☐☐☐☐ – ☐☐☐☐ – ☐☐☐☐

Signature _____ Exp. _____

Mail to:
Beckett Subscriptions, P.O. Box 1915, Marion, OH 43305-1915   DNS91